PETER STEYN

Birds of prey
of Southern Africa

This book deals with 68 diurnal raptors (inclusive of vultures) and 12 owls which occur in the South African sub-region south of the Cunene, Okavango and Zambezi river systems. As this region is technologically more advanced than the rest of Africa, its birds of prey are more threatened, and the serious decline of a number of species is cause for considerable concern.

Each species is dealt with under these headings: derivation (in which the meaning of the scientific name is explained), identification, habitat, status and distribution, general habits and breeding. There are 24 colour plates by Graeme Arnott which illustrate each species perched and in flight, as well as a number of line drawings to show aspects of identification or behaviour. Distribution maps are also included, and there are 238 black-and-white photographs, mostly by the author, which deal mainly with breeding biology.

The book ends with an extensive list of references and an index (which incorporates scientific names).

THE AUTHOR

Peter Steyn has had a lifelong interest in birds and took up bird photography at the age of 14. Born and educated in Cape Town, he obtained a B.A. at the University of Cape Town and then moved to Rhodesia in 1961 to teach at Falcon College near Bulawayo. After seventeen years in Rhodesia, during which time he made an intensive study of birds of prey, he returned to settle in Cape Town. He has contributed over a hundred articles and scientific papers on birds to various journals, his photographs have been published widely overseas and he has participated regularly in wildlife radio programmes both in Rhodesia and in South Africa. He wrote *Eagle Days* and *Wankie Birds*, and contributed two chapters and numerous photographs to *Birdlife in Southern Africa* edited by Kenneth Newman.

THE ILLUSTRATOR

Graeme Arnott was born and brought up on a farm bordering Wankie National Park in Rhodesia. He began to draw birds and animals from life at an early age and later received instruction from the famous bird artist David Reid Henry. He has illustrated several bird books in the Longmans Bundu Series published in Rhodesia. After giving up teaching to become a full-time artist, he settled at Kenton-on-Sea in the eastern Cape. His sensitive portrayals of birds and animals are much in demand and he has held successful exhibitions of his work in Cape Town and Grahamstown.

Paddy Swart.
August 1988.

PETER STEYN

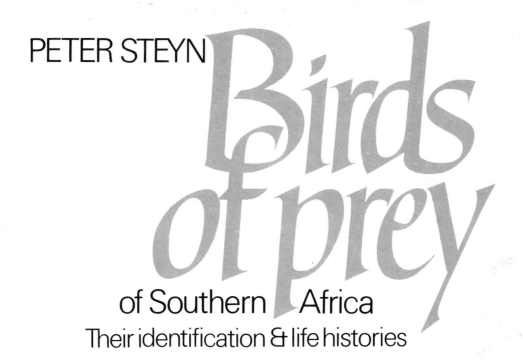

Birds of prey
of Southern Africa
Their identification & life histories

Illustrated by Graeme Arnott

TANAGER BOOKS
DOVER, NEW HAMPSHIRE

DAVID PHILIP
Cape Town & Johannesburg

CROOM HELM
Beckenham, Kent

First published 1982 in Southern Africa by
David Philip, Publisher (Pty) Ltd, 217 Werd-
muller Centre, Claremont, Cape, 7700 South
Africa

Published 1983 in the United States by
Tanager Books, Inc., Washington Street,
Dover, New Hampshire 03820

Published 1983 in the United Kingdom by
Croom Helm Ltd Publishers, Provident House,
Burrell Row, Beckenham, Kent

ISBN 0 908396 64 3 (David Philip)
ISBN 0 88072 025 5 (Tanager Books)
ISBN 0 7099 2382 1 (Croom Helm)

© text Peter Steyn 1982
© colour plates Graeme Arnott 1982

SECOND IMPRESSION 1985

Library of Congress Cataloging in Publication Data

Steyn, Peter.
   Birds of prey of southern Africa

   Bibliography: p.
   Includes index.
   1. Birds of prey — Africa, Southern. 2. Birds —
Africa, Southern. I. Title.
QL696.F3S73   1983   598'.91'0968   82-19685
ISBN 0 88072 025 5

Printed and bound by Creda Press (Pty) Ltd,
Solan Road, Cape Town, South Africa

Contents

Contents   *vii*

                                                          Plate   *Page*

DEDICATED TO THE MEMORY OF
DOUGLAS NCUBE
Waye yindoda emadodeni

Foreword

It is many years now since a young schoolmaster, then recently arrived to teach at Falcon College, Essexvale, near Bulawayo, first made his appearance in the Bird Room of the National Museum. I was then keeper of that department and, while I cannot recall our first meeting, no doubt it was to sort out a query about identification or to determine some feather or fragment of prey from a raptor's nest. It was during these earlier years when at Essexvale that Peter Steyn was to lay the foundations for his meticulous studies on the breeding biology and life histories of so many of our African birds of prey, and the high degree of excellence of the photographic record that accompanied them. He could not have been better situated than in that semi-arid savanna woodland, which supported his chosen subjects in undisturbed abundance and variety. Although in later years his studies were extended throughout the subcontinent, this earlier period was to set the pattern for the future. I often marvelled at how he managed to do so much and to sustain a teaching career before taking up the study of birds on a full-time basis and as a professional photographer of wild life.

Over these years we grew to know each other well, having many common interests — in the wilderness, in birds and their lives, and in their relationship to man. We also shared an enthusiasm for the great bird books of a bygone era, and for their illustrators.

When Peter asked me to write the foreword for this book I felt honoured, especially because as a professional ornithologist I was perhaps least knowledgeable about birds of prey. Rhodesia, as it was then called, was a breeding ground for many ornithologists and naturalists. Among these Peter Steyn has made an outstanding contribution as a dedicated, meticulous and enthusiastic field observer whose studies of the biology of southern African birds of prey have appeared in ornithological journals for over two decades. In my opinion he now clearly leads the field in southern Africa.

This book not only combines the knowledge and experience of the author, but brings together a mass of published and other information from many sources. It comes at a time when the knowledge that has been gained over the years can be looked at in a clearer perspective and with a truer understanding of the relationship between birds and their environment. It also coincides with events in the history of evolution which by their nature have not happened before. Terrestrial, indeed all, environments, and the animals that inhabit them, are now threatened as never in the past. Animal communities are in decline everywhere as man exerts greater and greater pressures and demands on the earth's resources for his own needs. Birds of prey often head the list of those species which as a result are endangered. The studies made now on some species could well be the last in a century more critical for life everywhere than any that has preceded it. There is thus an even greater need for mankind to understand and accept his place in nature if the wilderness of the future is not to be of another kind altogether.

A book such as this has many functions, not all of which may be obvious to the reader. It needs a special kind of dedication in the author and his artist to convey an appreciation and understanding of an often misunderstood group of birds. The book gives in easily understood terms the life-styles of birds who kill for the most part other warm-blooded vertebrates — as we ourselves do in vast numbers without question, yet we tend to condemn birds of prey whose very existence depends on hunting. Graeme Arnott's illustrations, so painstakingly and sensitively executed, are a fitting complement to the text.

Not only do I welcome this book but I wish it a successful and assured future, which I pray will be shared by its subjects, the diurnal and nocturnal birds of prey of southern Africa.

Michael P. Stuart Irwin
Director, National Museum
Bulawayo, Zimbabwe

Acknowledgements

The generous help that I have received from so many people over the years has been a constant spring of encouragement. Numbered among these are several to whom I owe an especial debt of gratitude. Michael Irwin, Director of the National Museum in Bulawayo, Zimbabwe, assisted with reference specimens for the plates and put the museum's library and ornithological card reference system at my disposal. He also provided much stimulating discussion and advice while we munched our lunchtime sandwiches in the 'Bird Room', surrounded by a priceless collection of magnificently bound books. I miss those times. He agreed then to write a foreword, a promise he has now generously fulfilled.

Richard Brooke was always ready to help, despite his own heavy schedule of work. He went to much trouble to provide the derivations of the scientific names and to track down the more elusive ones. His advice on taxonomic matters was invaluable. He also read most of the species accounts and made many suggestions for their improvement. Francois van der Merwe drew up a list of Afrikaans names and I have followed his suggestions without exception. Peter Mundy provided an advance copy of his thesis on southern African vultures just in time for me to prepare texts before my deadline, and he meticulously checked through them for me. Warwick Tarboton was a constant source of invaluable information. His census of the birds of prey of the Transvaal is an outstanding example of thorough and dedicated research. Alan Kemp of the Transvaal Museum was always ready to offer advice or practical assistance and he provided an outline of his detailed unpublished work on the Greater Kestrel. Mrs Mariette Broekhuysen, widow of Professor Gerry Broekhuysen, generously allowed me to use information on the Spotted Eagle Owl from his unpublished book *It's an Owl's Life*. Dr Harry Biggs, Dr André Boshoff, Rob Jeffery, John Colebrook-Robjent, Alec Daneel, Colin Saunders and Alex Masterson went out of their way to provide information, much of it on rarer species. To Professor Roy Siegfried, Director of the Percy FitzPatrick Institute of African Ornithology, I am grateful for research facilities, as well as for help in his personal capacity.

The late Dr Leslie Brown, the doyen of raptorphiles, was a friend for twenty years. He encouraged my first post-nestling raptor studies and, as I advanced to adult plumage, stimulated my progress through lively correspondence. He found out more about the lives of raptors through sheer hard work and superb powers of observation than any man I know.

Without the support of Jenny, my wife, this book may have fallen by the wayside. Having put my hand to the plough, on many occasions I had second thoughts about the heaviness of the soil and the length of the furrows. She accepted with equanimity a husband who spent long unsociable hours writing in his study or who was often absent in the field studying raptors. She also typed most of the text.

Douglas Ncube was my field assistant for eleven years in Rhodesia. During our time together in the Matabeleland bushveld finding out about birds of prey we established a bond for which words were unnecessary. Douglas became an innocent victim of the Rhodesian bush war. I shall never forget him and have dedicated this book to his memory.

The following contributors assisted with information, reference material for the plates, and in various other ways. To them all, whatever the extent of their contribution, I am deeply grateful. Although I have kept a careful record, it is possible that over a period of fifteen years some contributors may have gone unrecorded. I offer my apologies to any who may have been overlooked and hope that they will understand. In the case of the Falcon College Natural History Society it has been impossible to list the generations of members who assisted me while I was teaching there.

The generous contributors to this book are: D. Allan, A. J. Anthony, N. Arkell, Mrs A. M. Aspinwall, the late C. T. Astley Maberly, R. I. G. Attwell, D. Y. Barbour, B. Barnes, A. Batchelor, G. Bennett, C. W. Benson, Dr R. C. Bigalke, Mrs R. Biggs, Mrs B. Bomford, the late R. Borrett, P. Bowen, Dr D. G. Broadley, Mrs B. Brown, K. E. Cackett, Prof. T. J. Cade, R. Chenaux-Repond, R. Chennells, P. A. Clancey, C. H. Clinning, Dr J. B. Condy, J. Cooper, Dr T. Crowe, J. Culverwell, D. Cyrus,

B. Danckwerts, P. Danckwerts, R. Daugherty, W. R. Dean, B. G. Donnelly, R. J. Dowsett, Durban Museum, T. P. Dutton, East London Museum, R. Erasmus, B. Every, Falcon College Natural History Society, A. Fannin, J. Fincham, J. Fletcher, P. G. H. Frost, Mrs V. Gargett, I. Garland, P. Ginn, Dr J. H. Grobler, Mrs P. Guhrs, Dr J. Guy, C. Haagner, Mrs D. Hall, C. J. Hallamore, J. C. Harrison, R. Hartley, Dr R. M. Harwin, J. Harwood, the late D. M. Henry, G. M. Henry, E. T. Holder, P. F. E. Horncastle, J. Hosken, E. Hosking, J. Hough, W. W. Howells, J. Huntley, L. Hurry, K. Hustler, M. Impey, G. Jackson, H. D. Jackson, Mrs M. Jacobsen, Dr M. J. Jankowitz, Dr M. Jarvis, Dr R. A. C. Jensen, J. Jilbert, R. A. Jubb, Dr M. E. Keep, W. J. Kymdell, T. Lane, K. Langham, H. Langley, Dr J. Ledger, S. G. Lees, A. Lendrum, J. Lendrum, T. N. Liversedge, Dr R. Liversidge, P. S. Lockart, S. Lund, I. A. W. Macdonald, J. N. MacGregor, M. MacGregor, Prof. G. L. Maclean, the late J. Macleod, W. Mangold, Mrs E. Martin, J. Martin, R. Martin, W. Massyn, H. McArthur, D. McCulloch, Dr G. R. McLachlan, J. Mendelsohn, D. Metcalfe, Dr B.-U. Meyburg, F. Meyer, Dr H. Mikkola, W. T. Miller, P. Milstein, J. Morphew, W. Morsbach, N. J. Myburgh, M. R. Mylne, Natal Parks Board, National Museum (Bulawayo), Mrs M. Neatherway, P. Neatherway, C. Nel, K. B. Newman, Dr I. Newton, H. Nicolle, B. P. Nielsen, T. B. Oatley, C. Olwagen, D. Onderstall, G. W. Parnell, J. R. Peek, R. Phillips, D. Plowes, A. Pooley, V. Pringle, D. Prout-Jones, G. A. Ranger, A. Read, Mrs P. A. Richardson, E. L. Roberts, D. L. Robinson, S. Robinson, N. Robson, Dr J. Rourke, Mrs M. K. Rowan, D. Rushworth, J. Savory, R. K. Schmidt, G. Schütte, Mrs J. Scott, Mrs M. Shattock, J. C. Sinclair, C. J. Skead, R. G. Slaughter, Dr C. Smeenk, the late R. Smith, Dr R. H. N. Smithers, J. C. Snelling, South African Museum, Dr S. Spofford, Dr W. S. Spofford, W. P. Stanford, D. Steyn, G. Symons, J. M. Thiollay, R. Thompson, G. R. Thomson, W. R. Thomson, C. Thorpe, R. C. Tomlinson, Transvaal Museum, A. J. Tree, D. A. C. Tredgold, M. Tredgold, the late F. V. Tuer, Mrs J. Tuer, Prof. C. J. Uys, D. van Rensburg, C. J. Vernon, Prof. K. H. Voous, Vulture Study Group, H. Waller, M. Walters, A. Weaving, Mrs D. Webb, Miss J. Webber, Mrs D. Wheeler, Dr C. M. White, T. Whiting, V. J. Wilson, Prof. J. M. Winterbottom, I. Woolley, Dr A. W. Wragg.

Introduction

This book has three aims: to provide the bird-watcher with a guide to identification, to outline the present distribution and status of southern African raptors, and to give an account of their life histories. This is not a handbook along the lines of that commendable series *The Birds of the Western Palearctic* and no details of measurements, weights, moults, etc., have been included. No attempt has been made, except occasionally in the species accounts, to provide particulars of how various raptors are adapted to catching their prey. There is a plethora of popular books available dealing with eye-sight, talons, flight, hearing and all the other aspects which characterise a bird of prey.

I have written this book for ordinary bird-watchers, amongst whom I include myself as I am not a trained scientist. My main qualification is that I have been an enthusiastic 'raptorphile', if I may coin a word for this book, ever since I made observations on a Red-breasted Sparrowhawk's nest as a boy thirty years ago. Since then I have seen all but three (Egyptian Vulture, Sooty Falcon and Grey Kestrel) of the 80 raptors (inclusive of owls) dealt with in this book, and the nests of 56 of the 66 species breeding in southern Africa. Some of these, particularly eagles, I have been able to study intensively, while in the case of others such as the Taita Falcon I have had only a distant and tantalising view of a nest.

In compiling *Birds of Prey of Southern Africa* I have written the sort of book that I would have wanted when I began studying raptors, so that I could readily find out what was known about their life histories and avoid duplication of what was published in often inaccessible scientific journals. The standard textbook 'Roberts' provided an excellent guide to identification, even more so as successive editions were revised, but the text was of necessity brief and gave little more than basic information. When the monumental *Eagles, Hawks and Falcons of the World* by Leslie Brown and Dean Amadon was published in 1968, raptorphiles had something that they could use as a real basis for further research. Sadly, this book was never revised or reprinted, and became outdated and something of a collector's item. The burgeoning interest in raptor research in south-ern Africa during the 1970s resulted in a great deal of new information which I have incorporated in this book. However, as I write, I am aware that new material is constantly being gathered. In the circumstances the best one can do is to provide a platform at a particular point in time for others to build upon.

One of the functions of this book is to provide a bridge between the amateur and professional. The latter often resorts to obscure modes of expression and jargon, a fault by no means restricted to ornithologists, but it is perhaps significant that the word jargon is derived from French and means the chattering of birds. Wherever possible I have chosen to use simple terms and refer to eyes and legs rather than irides and tarsi, even if the last two are strictly speaking more precise. Very occasionally unfamiliar words (to the amateur) have been used for reasons of economy; an example of this is 'remiges', which refers to the primaries and secondaries together. The various names used are clearly indicated on the drawings in this introductory section. Scientific names have been included in the index and are only used in the text where meaningful common names are not available.

It has often been difficult to avoid a rather snippety presentation in the species accounts. Frequently only parts of the breeding cycle of a species are known, or observations are based on a single nest. Sometimes the only observations available come from elsewhere in Africa. At the risk of a lack of fluency in places, I have preferred to indicate the basis for statements rather than to make generalisations. Thus phrases such as 'at one nest' or 'from observations in Kenya' tend to crop up frequently.

There is little doubt that detailed and sustained raptor research in southern Africa is in advance of anything being done elsewhere in Africa. One has only to mention the long-term research on Black Eagles and other raptors in the Matopos in Zimbabwe, the survey of the raptors of the Transvaal by Warwick Tarboton, or the research and conservation activities of the Vulture Study Group, as examples of investigation of the highest order, comparing favourably with work done anywhere in the world. (Indeed the Matopos Black Eagle survey is probably unique.) However, for an enthusiastic raptorphile, the field is still wide open. On many occasions I have ended a species account with a statement that further observations are required, and in most cases a few sustained watches at a nest would greatly advance our knowledge. Examples of common species about which we know very little are Jackal Buzzard, Lizard Buzzard, Pale Chanting Goshawk, Dark Chanting Goshawk, Yellow-billed Kite, Rock Kestrel and African Scops Owl. There are still intriguing problems to solve such as the migratory movements of Ayres' Eagle, Wahlberg's Eagle, Black-breasted Snake Eagle and possibly the Bateleur. Does the Crowned Eagle adhere to a biennial breeding pattern in southern Africa as it does in Kenya? Does Cainism occur when a Wahlberg's Eagle hatches two chicks? What becomes of the second chick of the Giant Eagle Owl and Pel's Fishing Owl?

More detailed comments on the style, layout, nomenclature, conventions, etc. used in the text are given under their appropriate headings in the subsequent sections of this introduction. In concluding these general introductory remarks I am aware of the immense debt I owe to others since I began to gather material for this

project in 1965. The number of people mentioned in the acknowledgements indicates the extent of the generous help and co-operation I have received. Many have become justifiably impatient with the passage of years, but so much new and exciting information has become available in the last decade that I do not regret the' delay in publication. It has been a long road, in the last three years an arduous one, and I now know what my friend Peter Mundy meant when he described his thesis on southern African vultures as 'this burning chunk of my soul'.

GEOGRAPHICAL LIMITS

This book covers southern Africa, also known as the South African sub-region, and is the area south of the Cunene, Okavango and Zambezi rivers. I have often been asked why I have confined myself to this region rather than Africa as a whole. The answer is twofold. Firstly, southern Africa is the region of which I have personal experience; and, secondly, it is technologically the most advanced area of Africa with problems of conservation differing markedly from the rest of the continent. A brief

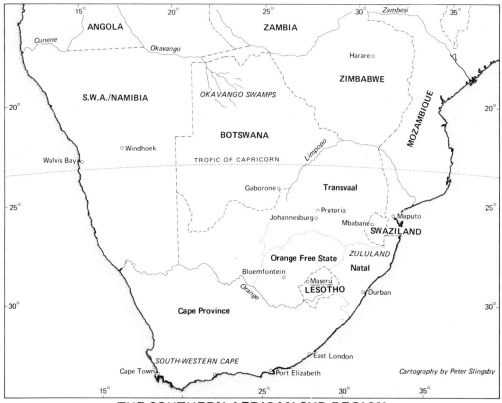

THE SOUTHERN AFRICAN SUB-REGION

outline of these problems is given in the section on conservation.

For the purposes of this book any mention of 'our area' means southern Africa, and 'South Africa' embraces traditional political South Africa but excludes Namibia or South West Africa. It seemed both convenient and logical to treat Namibia as though it were a separate country in the same way as Botswana, Swaziland and Lesotho. However, the various new homelands springing up like mushrooms have not been differentiated, so that any reference to the Cape Province, the Transvaal or the other provinces should be taken as referring to the whole province inclusive of the homelands. An exception is Natal, where it is convenient to refer to Zululand (the area north and east of the Tugela and Buffalo rivers) as a distinct area containing several major game reserves of particular importance to the survival of raptors in the province.

AUTHENTICITY AND SOURCES OF MATERIAL

Every effort has been made to check the authenticity of all information. Standard textbooks have been used with the utmost circumspection because records are difficult to trace to source and, usually, the same information is repeated from one book to the next without critical reappraisal. The criterion I have adopted is to reject records where any doubt of their validity exists. While this approach may be considered 'holier than thou', I prefer to think of it as pragmatic.

A few examples will illustrate my point. In *Eagles, Hawks and Falcons of the World* the authors recorded that on desert islands off the Arabian coast Black-shouldered Kites nested on rock ledges. They based this on an article appearing in *Ibis* in 1949, in which a nest-site in a small cave high up on a rocky outcrop is illustrated, together with a picture of a chick that does not resemble a kite. In fairness to the authors this record was not officially rejected until 1974, also in *Ibis*, when the 'Black-shouldered Kites' were revealed to be Egyptian Vultures! This example shows how important it is to examine unusual records with extreme caution. In various reference books the Southern Banded Snake Eagle is said to lay one or two eggs, and egg sizes are given. Despite exhaustive searching I have been unable to trace a single authentic record of an egg measurement for this species; also, snake eagles lay a single egg. I have rejected published records which attribute a clutch of four eggs to Pel's Fishing Owl, as this species normally lays two

eggs, and the observers did not substantiate their observations sufficiently. Many other similar examples could be given. It should be mentioned that only in a few exceptional cases, where no other source was available, have egg measurements been taken from textbooks, and then only after critical assessment. Wherever possible, measurements were taken from original sources such as nest cards or from egg collections, but always with great care to check their authenticity.

Originally January 1980 had been set as a cut-off date for the inclusion of information. However, so much new material came to hand during the year that a more realistic cut-off date was December 1980, although by that advanced stage of preparation only minor inserts were still feasible.

Information was obtained from the following sources:

Literature

This was the most important source of material, derived from a wide variety of bird club news sheets, popular publications, scientific journals and books. The search through the relevant literature has been as thorough as possible, but I do not claim that it is exhaustive. Inevitably, material in obscure publications tends to be overlooked, but the important material on southern African birds of prey was located and forms the core of this book.

In keeping with the simple presentation of the text, references are listed at the back of the book for those who wish to delve into the sources of information derived from the literature. References are of two types: general publications such as *Eagles, Hawks and Falcons of the World* or volume two of *The Birds of the Western Palearctic*, which were consulted extensively for many species; and specific references applicable to a particular bird of prey. The general references are listed first, followed by the references relevant to each raptor and listed by species. The species references should be used on a 'snowball' basis; an example is the paper by Gargett in *Ostrich* 46:1–44 on the spacing of Black Eagles in the Matopos. By reference to this paper the researcher will find a figure in brackets after the citation, indicating that the paper contains 80 references. By this method the reader is able to consult the material relevant to the territorial spacing of Black Eagles, and it obviates the need to give each of the 80 citations, which would result in an excessively long list of references on the Black Eagle. To illustrate the economy of the 'snowball' system the 31 references listed under the Black

Eagle may be expanded into 258 citations, although inevitably the total number of different references would be somewhat fewer because some of the same references would occur in two or more papers. Where a single reference to a raptor is contained in a long paper, only the relevant page is listed so that it may be quickly located. An example under Martial Eagle is Maclean's paper on the Sociable Weaver in *Ostrich* 44:241–253, where only page 250 is cited because here a mention is made of a Martial Eagle breeding on top of a Sociable Weaver's nest.

Contributors

Over a period of some fifteen years numerous contributors have generously supplied me with unpublished observations, or drafts of their work in preparation for publication. Their names are recorded under acknowledgements, and where major unpublished observations have been made available they are acknowledged at the end of the species accounts too. Several egg-collectors provided invaluable information and I have respected their wish not to be identified. I have been accused of condoning their activities by using their records, a somewhat extraordinary line of thought. Since the eggs had already been collected it seemed illogical to reject the material merely because it emanated from collectors. Dr Ian Newton has set a sensible precedent in Britain where by consulting egg-collectors (and respecting their anonymity) he was able to show conclusively that the thinning of the shells of raptors' eggs was linked to the introduction of DDT into the environment.

Nest Cards

The nest record card collection of the Southern African Ornithological Society is housed by the Percy FitzPatrick Institute of African Ornithology at the University of Cape Town. The available cards on raptors were all examined. The nest record cards were a rich source of information on nests and nest sites, breeding seasons, clutch sizes, egg measurements, incubation and nestling periods and also sometimes prey. Each record was examined critically, as experience had shown that there was a great deal of unreliable information. During the preparation of a paper on the Brown Snake Eagle in 1971 I consulted sixteen nest cards, using several criteria to check their authenticity. In the end only two were found to be reliable. It is because of the uncritical incorporation of material such as this that textbooks have perpetuated many inaccurate statements on aspects of raptor breeding biology. Some records housed in the collection were patently ludicrous, as for example a card describing the nest of an African Scops Owl on the floor of a barn with egg measurements far too large for this species.

Own Observations

While I have published a number of contributions on birds of prey, particularly eagles, since 1960, many less extensive observations have remained in notebooks, although what was available in about 1965 was supplied to Leslie Brown for incorporation into the species accounts in *Eagles, Hawks and Falcons of the World*. Since then much additional information has been gathered in the field and is included in my book. Perhaps the most exciting unpublished information comes from observations at a Black Harrier's nest within an hour's drive of my home in Cape Town. This was when the 'final' text on this species had been written, but after several long watches the text was redrafted in time for submission to the publisher.

TAXONOMY AND SCIENTIFIC NAMES

The *S.A.O.S. Checklist of Southern African Birds* published by the Southern African Ornithological Society in 1980 has been closely followed both for the order of species and the scientific names. However, consideration of races (or subspecies) has been avoided wherever possible because they are not relevant to the nature of this book. In two cases trinomials have been used in the species headings to achieve clarity. It was necessary to distinguish the Yellow-billed Kite *Milvus migrans parasitus* from the nominate race (the race first named and described) the Black Kite *Milvus migrans migrans*. Both have been treated in separate texts as though they were different species, and it is not improbable that in time they will be given specific status. In the case of the African Peregrine *Falco peregrinus minor* it was necessary to use a trinomial to distinguish it from the migrant Peregrine *Falco peregrinus calidus*, which reaches southern Africa. The only change to the order of the S.A.O.S. Checklist was to remove the Lizard Buzzard from its illogical and uncomfortable position between the Crowned Eagle and the Brown Snake Eagle and place it between the buzzards and the sparrowhawks.

The S.A.O.S. Checklist agrees with my instinctive inclination to 'split' rather than 'lump' species and the Tawny Eagle and Steppe Eagle are treated as separate species, as are the Jackal Buzzard and Augur Buzzard. This approach makes for clarity. I recall my confusion when reading *Eagles, Hawks and Falcons of the World*, where the Tawny Eagle of Africa and the Palearctic Steppe Eagle were treated as conspecific and discussed in a single text. There were other examples too, and these have emboldened me to take the advice of Richard Brooke and treat the African Hawk Eagle *Hieraaetus spilogaster* and the Black-breasted Snake Eagle *Circaetus pectoralis* as distinct species rather than as races of Bonelli's Eagle *Hieraaetus fasciatus* and the Short-toed Eagle *Circaetus gallicus* respectively. While this approach may be condemned as parochial, it has very real advantages for a book confined to southern Africa which does not claim to be a definitive handbook.

Scientific names of birds other than birds of prey are also taken from the S.A.O.S. Checklist and are given beside the English names in the index. Scientific names for other animals and plants are taken from the following sources:

SWANEPOEL, P., SMITHERS, R. H. N. and RAUTENBACH, I. L. 1980. A checklist and numbering system of the extant mammals of the Southern African Subregion. *Annals of the Transvaal Museum* 32(7): 155–196.

FITZSIMONS, V. F. M. 1962. *Snakes of Southern Africa*. London: Purnell.

PIENAAR, U. de V. 1966. *The Reptiles of the Kruger National Park*. Pretoria: National Parks Board of Trustees.

PALGRAVE, K. P. 1977. *Trees of Southern Africa*. Cape Town: Struik.

ENGLISH NAMES

As with the scientific names, the S.A.O.S. Checklist has been closely followed. However, for aesthetic reasons, I have preferred not to compound names so that Black-shouldered Kite is used in preference to Blackshouldered Kite and hyphens have been retained throughout. I have prefixed African or European in a few cases to remove all possible confusion between species with similar names occurring in southern Africa (e.g. European Hobby) or outside Africa (e.g. African Fish Eagle and African Hawk Eagle). The Checklist follows the convention of usage in southern Africa, so that Black Eagle is used instead of Verreaux's Eagle, and Little Banded Goshawk instead of Shikra. Although alternative names are not given in the species headings, mention is made in the section on derivations if other names are used outside southern Africa. In keeping with the principle of usage (which the Checklist departs from in this case) I have used Rock

Kestrel in preference to Common Kestrel. Another minor departure from the Checklist is the use of falcon in preference to kestrel for the Eastern and Western Red-footed Falcons. I could not bring myself to use Fasciated Snake Eagle for Southern Banded Snake Eagle, even though this species thus differs little in name from the Banded Snake Eagle. However, fasciated and banded mean the same thing, so that the attempt to distinguish them is artificial. Various other attempts to differentiate the names of the two species have been made without success; perhaps one day the Southern Banded Snake Eagle may be called the Forest Snake Eagle, but I lack the courage to cause further confusion at this stage. Likewise, despite convincing pressure, I have not changed Mountain Buzzard to Forest Buzzard, especially as elsewhere in Africa it does inhabit mountains.

AFRIKAANS NAMES

In Afrikaans the convention is to compound names, and hyphens are used where confusion of sense could arise or two vowels are brought next to each other (e.g. Steppe-arend). Afrikaans names for birds of prey, except the more characteristic ones, do not have a tradition of individual identification of species and 'lammervanger' or 'kuikendief' were indiscriminately applied to eagles and hawks respectively. Where names were given in textbooks they tended to be literal translations of the English names and were often cumbersome and colourless. The situation with regard to Afrikaans names is less than satisfactory.

In an attempt to achieve some clarity I asked Francois van der Merwe, a law student at the University of Stellenbosch, to come to my aid. He is a keen ornithologist with a good knowledge of birds of prey and is an authority on the Black Harrier. The result was a list of names that was both meaningful and practical, containing a number of innovations. It is his intention to have these names accepted by the Suid-Afrikaanse Akademie vir Wetenskap en Kuns.

Certain guidelines were followed. Wherever possible a name with derogatory connotations was replaced by a more meaningful one, thus the Peregrine has been called the Wandelvalk in preference to Slegvalk. In keeping with the trend towards descriptive names those of people attached to bird names have been avoided where possible, thus Bruinarend in preference to Wahlbergse Arend, although in the case of Dickinson's Kestrel a suitable alternative could not be found. Certain improvements in the sense of names were introduced, for example Jakkalsvalk instead of Jakkalsvoël, and singvalk in preference to witvalk to avoid the contradictory name Donkerwitvalk which becomes Donker-singvalk. The Tawny Eagle was changed from Kouvoël (why 'chewing bird'?) to Roofarend. The Bateleur has traditionally been given the name Berghaan in bird books, but is not a cock and does not live in mountains. This name is also confusing because it is applied to the Black Eagle in many areas. Thus the descriptive alternative name Stompstertarend has been used.

The names used are vigorous and meaningful and it is to be hoped that they will achieve general acceptance.

MARGINAL OR DOUBTFUL SPECIES

A number of species in the 1980 S.A.O.S. Checklist are inserted in square brackets to indicate that no specimen evidence has been obtained or that the record is equivocal for some reason. For purposes of this book these species have not been dealt with in the main text and are listed below.

Red Kite *Milvus milvus*: Visually recorded and photographed in the northern Cape in January 1972. Opinions differ on the acceptability of the photographic evidence.

Long-legged Buzzard *Buteo rufinus*: Said to have been recorded in Namibia and Botswana but confirmation is required.

European Sparrowhawk *Accipiter nisus*: A single equivocal record is based on a specimen from Swellendam in the south-west Cape collected at an unknown date, but probably during the second half of the last century. This specimen is in the South African Museum in Cape Town where I have examined it and consider it to be a Red-breasted Sparrowhawk in transitional plumage between juvenile and adult. A colour photograph of an immature Redbreasted Sparrowhawk breeding in the southwest Cape illustrates plumage very similar to that of the Swellendam specimen.

Barbary Falcon *Falco pelegrinoides*: In the S.A.O.S. Checklist this species is treated as a race of the Peregrine *Falco peregrinus*. It is stated to have been identified among birds photographed in the Kalahari Gemsbok National Park in January 1972. However, the evidence is tenuous and controversial; confirmation is required.

Merlin *Falco columbarius*: A single specimen in the South African Museum was obtained in Natal in February 1891. It was probably lost by a falconer or escaped from an aviary. This Palearctic species normally winters in southern Europe and northern Africa.

In addition to these records in the S.A.O.S. Checklist, Ian Sinclair informs me that Alan Vittery (who has wide experience of European raptors) saw Eleonora's Falcon *Falco eleonorae* on Inhaca Island off Maputo in Mozambique during the summer of 1977. Sinclair also saw a photograph of a dark form of this falcon taken by an unknown American in Ndumu Game Reserve, Zululand, also in the summer of 1977. However, no account of these records has yet been published.

All the above species are described and illustrated in volume two of *The Birds of the Western Palearctic*, which should be carefully consulted as a guide to authentication should any of them be seen in southern Africa.

THE ILLUSTRATIONS

All the colour plates and line drawings are by Graeme Arnott, without whose contribution this book would not exist. It has been our aim to design plates that are both accurate and aesthetically pleasing, and early in the planning stage we rejected the idea of serried ranks of raptors, all in the same posture. For obvious reasons the flight plates allowed less latitude for variety, but different styles have been used so that they are not stereotyped. In keeping with the aesthetic approach the plates have not been numbered, the individual species being identified by means of a reduced numbered halftone on the facing page. Wherever feasible species that may be confused are illustrated on the same plate, and most of the brown eagles are grouped together for this reason, even at the risk of driving off some bird-watchers to study an easy group like robins instead!

Adults and juveniles are illustrated throughout, one exception being an immature Lammergeyer with characteristic dark head and neck shown on the perched plate and a juvenile on the flight plate. We decided to avoid illustration of immature plumages on the plates as they are extremely variable and confusing and it would have been both difficult and costly to attempt to depict them. We felt that if the juvenile plumage was clearly illustrated the observer would have a reasonable chance of deducing the intermediate plumage. It is far more confusing, as has been the case in some books, to illustrate an immature stage and no juvenile. For the Southern Banded Snake Eagle and the Banded Snake Eagle no juvenile plumages have been illustrated; we had no specimens or other visual reference material and preferred not to guess or attempt illustrations from written descriptions.

The plates were prepared over a period of six

years, the initial stages much disrupted by the Rhodesian bush war. Eventually we both settled in South Africa, but in different places, so that most of the plates were planned by correspondence. Despite these difficulties, author and artist have achieved a result to their mutual satisfaction. In some instances we were overtaken by events, as for example by the discovery of sexual dimorphism in the White-headed Vulture long after the plate was complete; the difference has here been illustrated by a line drawing.

All black-and-white photographs are by the author unless otherwise acknowledged in brackets after the caption. Wherever possible a nest is illustrated, as well as stages of nestling growth, but treatment varies considerably owing to lack of material for many species. As a rule eagles are comprehensively illustrated and tend to outnumber photographs of other species. Where photographs are available and relevant, other aspects are illustrated, for example an immature plumage or a nestling snake eagle pulling a snake from its parent's mouth.

CONSERVATION

Birds of prey in southern Africa are most threatened by the technological advancement of the region. Habitats are dwindling through farming activities or urban sprawl, and the land available for reserves and National Parks has mostly been taken up. An alarming aspect is that even where National Parks have been established they are not necessarily inviolate. It appears that if they are found to have valuable minerals mining activity can take place 'in the national interest', a disturbing concept because to oppose this 'interest' is construed as unpatriotic. The problem here is no different from elsewhere in the world where conservationists have to fight every inch of the way against vested interests. However, the tide may be turning, and politicians have taken note of the conservationists, even if only for votes rather than altruistic motives on occasions.

Of all the vicissitudes faced by raptors, loss of habitat is often the most serious. A pertinent example falls within my own experience, concerning the African Marsh Harrier. While at school in Cape Town in the 1950s my friends and I regularly found several nests in the Zeekoe Vlei area every season, sometimes two or three nesting pairs during a weekend. The species has almost entirely disappeared from this locality, indeed it is now rare in the extreme south-western Cape. Urban sprawl and other development on the Cape Flats and elsewhere have destroyed its habitat.

It appears that vultures are the most threatened group of raptors in southern Africa. Details of the various problems facing the endemic Cape Vulture are discussed in the text on that species. Poisoning is a major threat to vultures; the third issue of *Vulture News* cites incidents in which at least 322 vultures were known to have died during the period September 1979 to January 1980. The impact of this figure is best gauged against the fact that this represents ten times the world's total population of California Condors, numbering about 30 birds. Most of the vultures were killed in the eastern Caprivi Strip by an agricultural insecticide. It was placed on carcasses, probably to kill lions, but the vultures were the main victims. When confronted, the chemical company concerned disclaimed responsibility on the grounds that the substance had not been used according to the instructions. They also threatened legal action if they were named. A more bizarre fate overtook vultures during the Rhodesian war in the fenced minefields of the border areas. When approaching to feed on animals killed by mines they were themselves blown up.

As a rule large birds of prey such as vultures and eagles are most seriously threatened. It is often difficult to know how to direct conservation activities, but perhaps the only approach is a practical one. There is little point in trying to do anything for the Egyptian Vulture, which has all but disappeared from southern Africa, but what about the Palm-nut Vulture, which has such a restricted breeding range and numbers a few pairs in Zululand? As long as its habitat survives, so will the Palm-nut Vulture, but there is little of practical value, short of planting large groves of palm trees, that can be done to help it. The Lammergeyer's survival hinges on primitive pastoral conditions, and while these are available in Lesotho it will continue to occur in fair numbers. The well-being of the Martial Eagle outside National Parks depends to a large extent on the farming community, whose attitude is traditionally hostile. The farmer must come to realise through conservation propaganda that this magnificent species is not a threat to domestic stock. The Crowned Eagle and the Southern Banded Snake Eagle depend on their respective forest habitats for survival; the latter occurs mainly in the Zululand game reserves in South Africa (its status in Mozambique being little known). Except for that of the Cape Vulture, the decline of the Bateleur is the most alarming of all our birds of prey. The situation has only recently been noticed and the reasons are unclear, but like several of the vultures it seems destined to become a raptor that is rarely seen outside game reserves over most of southern Africa.

It is difficult to generalise about the various threats faced by our birds of prey, although poisoning, habitat destruction and direct persecution all play their part. Too little is known at present to assess the pesticide menace, which has had such catastrophic effects in other regions, but it should not be underestimated. A species like the African Fish Eagle could well be faced with a serious decline in some areas as a result of pesticides washed into waterways and contaminating fish. Lesser dangers are unscrupulous falconers and egg-collectors, whose relative impact is not great at present. In Europe they have had a serious effect on raptors, but only because the numbers of many species have become dangerously low. Many of our falconers are playing an important part in preserving birds of prey, and it is only fair to add that some of our foremost ornithologists began as egg-collectors, and sometimes are still active. Unfortunately the unscrupulous falconers and egg-collectors forfeit all public sympathy for their activities. I learnt only recently that three Transvaal egg-collectors stole eight Lappet-faced Vultures' eggs from the Namib Desert National Park, where too in another incident a falconer was foiled in his attempt to capture Red-necked Falcons. Such behaviour can only reinforce one's belief that *Homo sapiens* is a misnomer and that *Homo horrendus* would often be more appropriate.

SPECIES ACCOUNTS

Each species is described under headings, requiring some clarification.

Derivation

The Latin and Greek components of the scientific names are given, as well as any relevant information on the names of people linked to a species, for example Wahlberg's Eagle. Where alternative English names are used outside southern Africa, these are remarked on too. The only book in which I have seen derivations given is Cayley's guide to Australian birds, *What Bird Is That?* Latin is no longer widely studied in schools and it is unusual to encounter anyone who included Greek in his curriculum. However, the components of scientific names are extremely interesting, and most become much easier to remember once understood. I have relied almost entirely on Richard Brooke's classical knowledge for the derivations, some of which proved extremely elusive and open to several interpretations. In the case of *alcinus*, the specific name for the Bat Hawk,

the source eluded us completely. We do not claim omniscience and have little doubt that improvements on some of the interpretations will be forthcoming.

Identification

This is dealt with under two headings, *Adult* and *Juvenile and immature*, or only *Juvenile* if there is no intermediate immature stage. The term *juvenile* is taken to mean the first plumage in which the young bird of prey leaves the nest; *immature* refers to all subsequent plumages until full adult plumage is acquired. Very occasionally the term *sub-adult* may be used in the text, of a bird that appears to be adult except for some minor vestiges of immature plumage.

The flight outline of a raptor is the most useful single guide to identification — even if someone sprayed a Black Eagle or a Bateleur bright yellow they could still be distinguished by their characteristic shapes. Thus the flight plates are probably the most important part of the book and should be studied carefully to familiarise oneself with the various groups such as eagles, buzzards, falcons, sparrowhawks, etc. Some of these groups have a diagnostic outline, for example the sparrowhawks or falcons, but there is much variation between species in a group like the eagles; one has only to study the illustrations of Tawny, Black and Wahlberg's Eagles to see the variety of shapes. However, once the characteristic features have been learnt, the observer will be able to identify raptors even at a considerable height.

In the accounts the salient features of the perched and then the flying bird are described, as well as any confusion that may arise with other species. The detailed plates make feather-by-feather descriptions superfluous, but the colours of the soft parts are always given. The 'soft' parts are the eyes, bill, cere, legs and feet, most of which are rather hard, so the term is something of a misnomer. Unless separate mention is made, males and females must be assumed to be alike in colour, although in many birds of prey females are larger, sometimes strikingly so. The term 'form' has been used where dark and pale forms of a species occur, in preference to 'phase' or 'morph'.

Finally, for those thrown into despair by the variety of species and plumage, I quote from a leaflet which preceded the publication of *Flight Identification of European Raptors*: 'Often, too, the birds are seen at long range, and the authors believe that when travelling extensively in Europe even the expert cannot hope to identify more than seventy per cent of the raptors seen.' In lighter vein Ogden Nash sums up the predi-

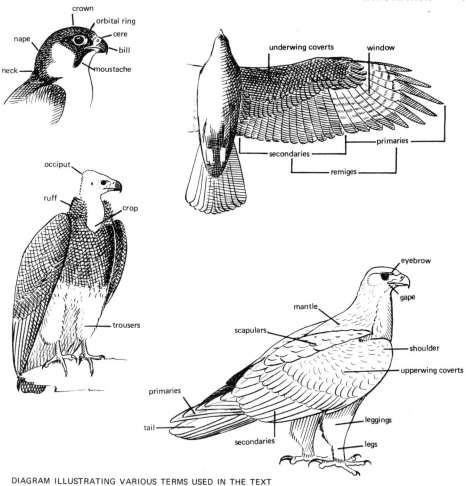

DIAGRAM ILLUSTRATING VARIOUS TERMS USED IN THE TEXT

cament of many an embryonic raptorphile:

'You rush to consult your Nature guide
And inspect the gallery inside,
But a bird in the open never looks
Like its picture in the birdie books —
Or if it once did, it has changed its
    plumage,
And plunges you back into ignorant
    gloomage.'

Habitat

As many birds of prey, especially the larger ones, are highly mobile, it is often difficult to define their habitat with any precision. Thus habitat descriptions are sometimes necessarily vague, and 'woodland', 'savanna' or 'bushveld' are some of the rather loose terms used for the environment of many raptors. However, two terms used required definition, especially for readers outside Africa. 'Miombo' is used to describe what was formerly known as Brachystegia woodland, or in more popular terms Msasa trees. In southern Africa this woodland is found mainly in Zimbabwe, where it is fast disappearing as land is cleared for agriculture. The term 'fynbos', originally called 'macchia', is the sclerophyllous vegetation characteristic of the south-western Cape, composed mainly of plants with fine, hard, heath-like leaves or reedy stems.

Status and distribution

Under this heading comments are made on whether a species is resident, nomadic or migratory, and also on abundance or rarity. Where a species is declining, reasons are considered and aspects of conservation discussed. Migratory raptors are of two main types, intra-African migrants such as the Yellow-billed Kite or Wahlberg's Eagle which migrate within Africa, and Palearctic migrants like the Steppe Buzzard, Pallid Harrier or European Hobby. The Palearctic region embraces Africa north of the Sahara, Europe, and Asia north of the Himalaya range. 'Nomadic movements', as the name suggests, refers to movements with no fixed pattern, for example to an area of temporary prey abundance.

The southern African distribution of each raptor is outlined, and briefly its extralimital range. The accompanying maps show the main distribution in fine spotting, occasional records being indicated by single bold dots. Where species such as the Secretary Bird or Black-shouldered Kite occur throughout southern Africa, no map is given. The past and present distributions of the Lammergeyer and the Egyptian Vulture are of particular interest and are indicated by the use of different symbols. Where the distribution of a species is doubtful in some regions, a query (?) indicates that more information is needed.

The distribution of raptors in some areas is little known. As a rule Zimbabwe, southern Mozambique, the Transvaal, Natal and the Cape are regions well documented because meaningful checklists or atlases have been, or are being, prepared. However, Botswana, especially the vast central Kalahari region, Namibia and the Orange Free State are areas where comprehensive distributional work has been lacking, mainly because there are too few active ornithologists there. The commendable publication *An Atlas of Speciation in African Non-passerine Birds* was consulted with caution for southern Africa. No distinction between old and recent records is made, so that the picture of present distribution is misleading. However, this atlas was an invaluable source of reference for the extralimital range of our raptors.

General habits

This section is an outline of the habits of a species with the emphasis on how it hunts and what it eats. This is followed by a description of its voice, an aspect notoriously difficult to express because each observer interprets sounds differently. I hope that my renderings will be generally recognisable and meaningful (my wife's irreverent mirth when typing some of them gives me cause for disquiet).

Breeding

This aspect of raptor biology has been one of my main interests for thirty years, during which I have spent countless hours observing at nests. This interest is reflected in the black-and-white photographs accompanying many of the texts.

The breeding account has not been divided into subheadings, but the following outline has been used throughout.

(a) Nuptial behaviour and displays.

(b) Nest site, nest, building activity, duration of sites, breeding density/territory. Although some information on breeding density was available for many species, detailed studies of territory were available for very few. The Black Eagle and Augur Buzzard have been closely studied; for the latter it was found that the size of territory differed in the breeding and non-breeding seasons.

(c) Breeding season, clutch, egg descriptions and size. The egg measurements are expressed in millimetres in the traditional way, with range and average. The breeding season of many raptors in southern Africa is constant throughout the region. Thus a Black Eagle breeding from about May to September in the winter rainfall region of the south-west Cape will experience wet, inclement conditions, while its counterpart in the summer rainfall area of the Matopos breeding at the same time will hatch its eggs and raise its eaglet during the cool, dry winter months. However, there are a number of exceptions; Black-shouldered Kites for example breed mainly in spring in the south-west Cape but during all months in the Transvaal, with two peaks, one in spring and the other in autumn.

(d) The incubation period deals with the intervals at which eggs are laid, parental behaviour, especially whether the sexes share incubation, and the duration of the incubation period.

(e) The nestling period deals with sibling aggression where applicable (this behaviour is also referred to as Cainism or the Cain and Abel struggle, in which the smaller chick is killed by its older sibling). This is followed by an account of growth and the emergence of feathers, the development of co-ordination (usually poorly known), parental care and the duration of the nestling period.

(f) The post-nestling period is concerned with the time taken for the young raptor to become independent of its parents. This aspect is often poorly known, and in the case of many smaller raptors is difficult to study because the young soon disperse from the vicinity of the nest.

(g) Breeding productivity is expressed as the number of young raised per pair per year, where known. This information should be used with caution because so many variables and imponderables are involved, but where there are many pair-years the productivity figure becomes more meaningful.

The Plates

PLATE 1

Black Eagle

A pair of Black Eagles in typical
mountainous habitat

PLATE 2

Bateleur and Secretary Bird

1 Bateleur: adult female
2 Bateleur: juvenile
3 Bateleur: adult male with creamy-
   coloured back
4 Bateleur: adult male
5 Secretary Bird: adult
6 Secretary Bird: juvenile

PLATE 3

Lammergeyer and small vultures

1 Palm-nut Vulture: adult
2 Palm-nut Vulture: juvenile
3 Hooded Vulture: adult
4 Hooded Vulture: juvenile
5 Lammergeyer: immature
6 Lammergeyer: adult
7 Egyptian Vulture: adult
8 Egyptian Vulture: juvenile

PLATE 4

Large vultures

1 White-backed Vulture: adult
2 White-backed Vulture: juvenile
3 White-headed Vulture: juvenile
4 White-headed Vulture: adult
   female
5 Lappet-faced Vulture: juvenile
6 Lappet-faced Vulture: adult
7 Cape Vulture: juvenile
8 Cape Vulture: adult

G G Arnott

PLATE 5

Secretary Bird, Lammergeyer and vultures

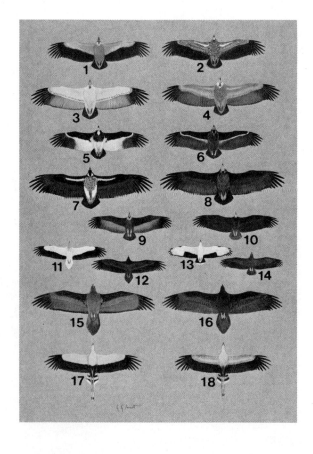

1 White-backed Vulture: adult
2 White-backed Vulture: juvenile
3 Cape Vulture: adult
4 Cape Vulture: juvenile
5 White-headed Vulture: adult
   female
6 White-headed Vulture: juvenile
7 Lappet-faced Vulture: adult
8 Lappet-faced Vulture: juvenile
9 Hooded Vulture: adult
10 Hooded Vulture: juvenile
11 Egyptian Vulture: adult
12 Egyptian Vulture: juvenile
13 Palm-nut Vulture: adult
14 Palm-nut Vulture: juvenile
15 Lammergeyer: adult
16 Lammergeyer: juvenile
17 Secretary Bird: adult
18 Secretary Bird: juvenile

G G Arnott

PLATE 6

Kites, Cuckoo Hawk, Bat Hawk and Honey Buzzard

1   Cuckoo Hawk: adult
2   Cuckoo Hawk: juvenile
3   Black-shouldered Kite: adult
4   Black-shouldered Kite: juvenile
5   Bat Hawk: adult
6   Bat Hawk: juvenile
7   Honey Buzzard: pale form
8   Honey Buzzard: dark form
9   Honey Buzzard: barred form
10   Black Kite: adult
11   Black Kite: juvenile
12   Yellow-billed Kite: adult
13   Yellow-billed Kite: juvenile

G G Arnott

PLATE 7

Tawny, Steppe, Lesser Spotted, Wahlberg's and Booted Eagles

1 Wahlberg's Eagle: dark brown plumage
2 Wahlberg's Eagle: light brown plumage
3 Wahlberg's Eagle: pale form
4 Booted Eagle: dark form
5 Booted Eagle: pale form
6 Booted Eagle: pale form juvenile
7 Lesser Spotted Eagle: juvenile
8 Lesser Spotted Eagle: adult
9 Tawny Eagle: blond plumage
10 Tawny Eagle: uniform tawny plumage
11 Tawny Eagle: juvenile
12 Tawny Eagle: streaky plumaged female
13 Steppe Eagle: adult
14 Steppe Eagle: juvenile

PLATE 8

Tawny, Steppe, Lesser Spotted, Wahlberg's, Booted and snake eagles

1 Wahlberg's Eagle: pale form
2 Wahlberg's Eagle: brown plumage
3 Lesser Spotted Eagle: adult
4 Tawny Eagle: juvenile
5 Tawny Eagle: blond plumage
6 Tawny Eagle: streaky female
7 Brown Snake Eagle: adult
8 Banded Snake Eagle: adult
9 Booted Eagle: juvenile pale form
10 Booted Eagle: pale form
11 Booted Eagle: dark form
12 Steppe Eagle: juvenile
13 Steppe Eagle: adult
14 Black-breasted Snake Eagle: juvenile
15 Black-breasted Snake Eagle: adult
16 Southern Banded Snake Eagle: adult

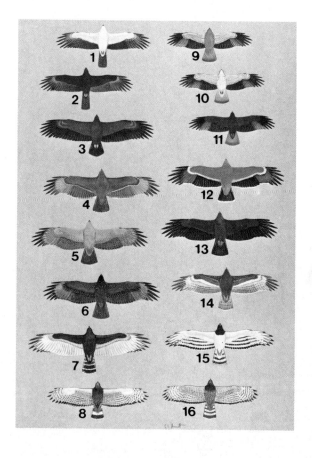

PLATE 9

Black, African Hawk, Ayres', Long-crested, Martial and Crowned Eagles

1   African Hawk Eagle: adult
2   African Hawk Eagle: juvenile
3   Ayres' Eagle: juvenile
4   Ayres' Eagle: adult
5   Long-crested Eagle: adult
6   Martial Eagle: adult
7   Martial Eagle: juvenile
8   Crowned Eagle: juvenile
9   Crowned Eagle: adult
10 Black Eagle: juvenile
11 Black Eagle: adult

PLATE 10

Black, African Hawk, Ayres', Long-crested, Martial, Crowned and African Fish Eagles; Bateleur and Osprey

1 Long-crested Eagle
2 Bateleur: juvenile
3 Bateleur: adult female
4 Bateleur: adult male
5 Black Eagle: juvenile
6 Black Eagle: adult
7 Martial Eagle: juvenile
8 Martial Eagle: adult
9 Ayres' Eagle: juvenile
10 Ayres' Eagle: adult
11 African Hawk Eagle: juvenile
12 African Hawk Eagle: adult
13 Osprey
14 African Fish Eagle: juvenile
15 African Fish Eagle: adult
16 Crowned Eagle: juvenile
17 Crowned Eagle: adult

G.G.Arnott

PLATE 11

Snake eagles, African Fish Eagle and Osprey

1   Brown Snake Eagle: adult
2   Banded Snake Eagle: adult WESTERN
3   Southern Banded Snake Eagle:
    adult
4   Black-breasted Snake Eagle: adult
5   Black-breasted Snake Eagle:
    juvenile
6   African Fish Eagle: adult
7   African Fish Eagle: juvenile
8   Osprey

G G Arnott

PLATE 12

Buzzards

FOREST

1 Mountain Buzzard: juvenile
2 Mountain Buzzard: adult
3 Steppe Buzzard: juvenile
4 Steppe Buzzard: adult with distinct
   gorget
5 Steppe Buzzard: adult in dark
   plumage
6 Steppe Buzzard: adult with
   reddish blotched plumage
7 Augur Buzzard: juvenile
8 Augur Buzzard: adult male
9 Jackal Buzzard: juvenile
10 Jackal Buzzard: adult

G G Arnott

PLATE 13

Kites, Bat Hawk, buzzards and Gymnogene

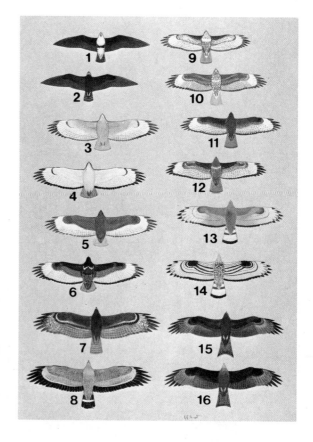

1 Bat Hawk: juvenile
2 Bat Hawk: adult
3 Augur Buzzard: juvenile
4 Augur Buzzard: adult
5 Jackal Buzzard: juvenile
6 Jackal Buzzard: adult
7 Gymnogene: juvenile
8 Gymnogene: adult
9 Mountain Buzzard: adult
10 Steppe Buzzard: juvenile
11 Steppe Buzzard: adult in dark
   plumage
12 Steppe Buzzard: adult with distinct
   gorget
13 Honey Buzzard: dark form
14 Honey Buzzard: barred plumage
15 Yellow-billed Kite: adult
16 Black Kite: adult

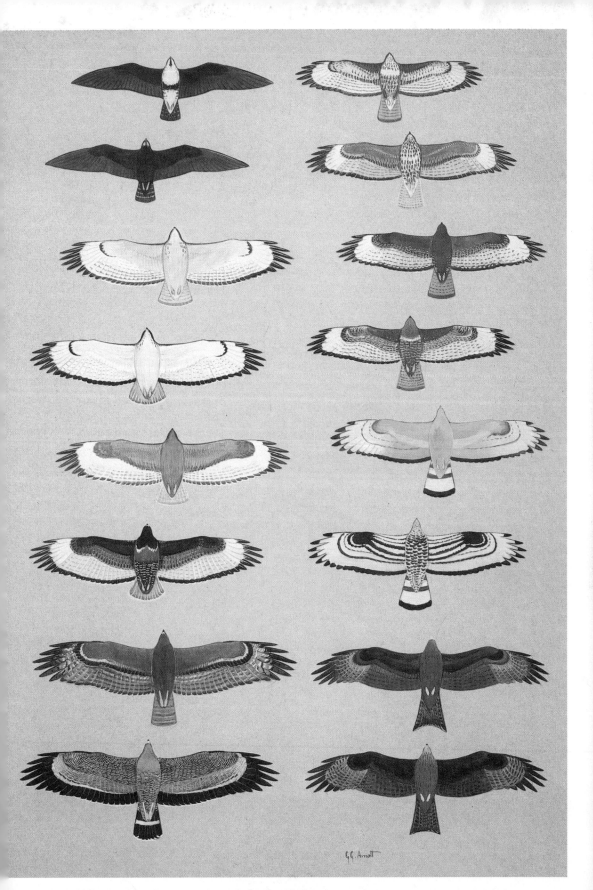

G.C.Arnott

PLATE 14

Sparrowhawks, small goshawks and Lizard Buzzard

1 Little Sparrowhawk: juvenile
2 Little Sparrowhawk: adult
3 Little Banded Goshawk: juvenile
4 Little Banded Goshawk: adult
5 Red-breasted Sparrowhawk: juvenile
6 Red-breasted Sparrowhawk: adult
7 Gabar Goshawk: juvenile
8 Gabar Goshawk: adult
9 Gabar Goshawk: adult melanistic form
10 Ovambo Sparrowhawk: adult
11 Ovambo Sparrowhawk: juvenile red-breasted form
12 Ovambo Sparrowhawk: juvenile pale-breasted form
13 Ovambo Sparrowhawk: adult melanistic form
14 Lizard Buzzard

G G Arnott

PLATE 15

Black Sparrowhawk, African Goshawk, chanting goshawks and Gymnogene

1 Black Sparrowhawk: juvenile
  white-breasted form
2 Black Sparrowhawk: juvenile red-
  breasted form
3 Black Sparrowhawk: adult
4 Black Sparrowhawk: melanistic
  form
5 African Goshawk: adult female
6 African Goshawk: juvenile
7 African Goshawk: adult male
8 Dark Chanting Goshawk: juvenile
9 Dark Chanting Goshawk: adult
10 Pale Chanting Goshawk: juvenile
11 Pale Chanting Goshawk: adult
12 Gymnogene: adult
13 Gymnogene: juvenile

G G Arnott

PLATE 16

Sparrowhawks, goshawks, Cuckoo Hawk and Lizard Buzzard

1 Little Sparrowhawk: juvenile
2 Little Sparrowhawk: adult
3 Little Banded Goshawk: juvenile
4 Little Banded Goshawk: adult
5 Gabar Goshawk: adult melanistic form
6 Gabar Goshawk: adult
7 Gabar Goshawk: juvenile
8 Lizard Buzzard
9 Red-breasted Sparrowhawk: adult
10 Ovambo Sparrowhawk: juvenile pale-breasted form
11 Ovambo Sparrowhawk: adult
12 Ovambo Sparrowhawk: adult melanistic form
13 Black Sparrowhawk: adult
14 Black Sparrowhawk: adult melanistic form
15 Black Sparrowhawk: juvenile red-breasted form
16 Black Sparrowhawk: juvenile white-breasted form
17 African Goshawk: adult female
18 African Goshawk: juvenile
19 Cuckoo Hawk: adult
20 Cuckoo Hawk: juvenile

PLATE 17

Harriers

1 Montagu's Harrier: adult female
2 Montagu's Harrier: adult male
3 Pallid Harrier: adult male
4 European Marsh Harrier: adult female
5 European Marsh Harrier: adult male
6 Black Harrier: juvenile
7 Black Harrier: adult
8 African Marsh Harrier: juvenile
9 African Marsh Harrier: adult

G G Arnott

PLATE 18

Chanting goshawks and harriers

1   Pale Chanting Goshawk: juvenile
2   Pale Chanting Goshawk: adult
3   Dark Chanting Goshawk: juvenile
4   Dark Chanting Goshawk: adult
5   Montagu's Harrier: adult male
6   Montagu's Harrier: adult female
7   Pallid Harrier: adult male
8   Black Harrier: juvenile
9   Black Harrier: adult
10 African Marsh Harrier: juvenile
11 African Marsh Harrier: adult
12 European Marsh Harrier: adult
    female
13 European Marsh Harrier: adult
    male

PLATE 19

Falcons

1 African Hobby: juvenile
2 African Hobby: adult
3 Pygmy Falcon: adult male
4 Pygmy Falcon: adult female
5 Red-necked Falcon: adult
6 Red-necked Falcon: juvenile
7 Taita Falcon: adult
8 European Hobby: adult
9 Lanner: juvenile
10 Lanner: adult
11 Peregrine: juvenile
12 Peregrine: adult

G G Arnott

PLATE 20

Falcons and Grey Kestrel

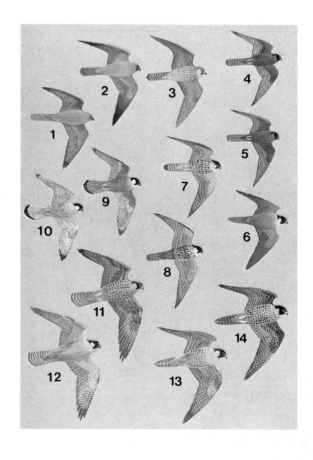

1   Grey Kestrel
2   Sooty Falcon: adult
3   Sooty Falcon: juvenile
4   African Hobby: juvenile
5   African Hobby: adult
6   Taita Falcon: adult
7   European Hobby: juvenile
8   European Hobby: adult
9   Red-necked Falcon: juvenile
10 Red-necked Falcon: adult
11 Lanner: juvenile
12 Lanner: adult
13 Peregrine: adult
14 Peregrine: juvenile

PLATE 21

Kestrels and falcons

1 Dickinson's Kestrel: adult
2 Western Red-footed Falcon: adult male
3 Western Red-footed Falcon: adult female
4 Sooty Falcon: adult
5 Sooty Falcon: juvenile
6 Eastern Red-footed Falcon: adult male
7 Eastern Red-footed Falcon: adult female
8 Greater Kestrel: adult
9 Grey Kestrel
10 Lesser Kestrel: adult female
11 Lesser Kestrel: adult male
12 Rock Kestrel: adult male
13 Rock Kestrel: juvenile

G G Arnott

PLATE 22

Kestrels, falcons and Black-shouldered Kite

1 Western Red-footed Falcon: adult male
2 Western Red-footed Falcon: adult female
3 Eastern Red-footed Falcon: adult male
4 Eastern Red-footed Falcon: adult female
5 Pygmy Falcon: adult male
6 Pygmy Falcon: adult female
7 Dickinson's Kestrel
8 Lesser Kestrel: adult male
9 Lesser Kestrel: adult female
10 Black-shouldered Kite: adult
11 Rock Kestrel: juvenile
12 Rock Kestrel: adult
13 Greater Kestrel: adult
14 Greater Kestrel: juvenile

PLATE 23

Barred, Pearl-spotted, African Scops, White-faced, Wood and Marsh Owls

1 Barred Owl
2 African Scops Owl
3 White-faced Owl
4 Pearl-spotted Owl
5 Wood Owl
6 Marsh Owl

G G Arnott

PLATE 24

Barn and Grass Owls, eagle owls, Pel's Fishing Owl

1 Spotted Eagle Owl
2 Barn Owl
3 Pel's Fishing Owl
4 Grass Owl
5 Cape Eagle Owl
6 Giant Eagle Owl

G.E. Arnott

1 Secretary Bird *118*

Sekretarisvoël

Sagittarius serpentarius

DERIVATION
bowman : interested in snakes — *sagittarius* (L) : *serpentarius* (L)

The popular belief that the English name originates from the resemblance of the bird to a secretary with a quill pen stuck behind his ear has recently been convincingly challenged. It has been suggested instead that the name derives from the Arabic *saqr et-tair* (*saqr* = hunter or hawk; *tair* = flight or is a collective term for bird). This argument is even more plausible if, as seems probable, the name was first corrupted into French as *secrétaire*.

IDENTIFICATION
Adult: This species is so characteristic in its shape, colour and behaviour that it cannot be mistaken for any other raptor, but at a distance it may possibly be misidentified as a Blue Crane. In flight the grey underwing coverts and body contrast with the black remiges, and the two central tail feathers project well beyond the long legs to give it an unmistakable outline. The sexes are alike.

Juvenile: Although closely resembling the adult, it may be distinguished by bare yellow (not red) skin on the face, a greyish instead of a brown eye and by shorter central tail feathers. On the underwing the coverts are tinged brownish and there is a white bar running across them.

HABITAT
It is found in a variety of habitats ranging from quite high altitudes in the Drakensberg to the semi-desert of the Kalahari, but not in forest (although in open country nearby) and true desert (coastal Namib). Open grasslands are its ideal environment, but it avoids areas where the grass cover is too rank.

STATUS AND DISTRIBUTION
Generally resident, but nomadic at times; large aggregations at water-holes in the Kalahari must come from a wide area. Although still common, its numbers have inevitably been reduced by urban sprawl into the countryside, or by certain types of agriculture inimical to its way of life (sugarcane, orchards). However, in the Transvaal, extensive bush clearing has probably increased its numbers in some localities.

It occurs in suitable environment throughout southern Africa, and extralimitally extends as far north as the Sahara.

GENERAL HABITS
This 'long-legged marching eagle' is usually seen in pairs walking over the veld with a steady gait of about 40 cm a stride at approximately 3 km/h. At irregular intervals the pace quickens, probably to surprise prey. Smaller items of food such as insects are captured by bending down and seizing them with the bill, but more agile quarry is killed by downward stamping blows with the blunt feet. At times prey is chased rapidly, the bird holding out its wings as it dashes about. Snakes are dispatched with accurate stamping blows to the head. In such encounters the wings are held outspread, but probably more for balance than with the deliberate intention of luring the snake to strike at them. Great care is taken to see that the snake is dead before it is swallowed, and reports that snakes are deliberately dropped from a height to kill them require authentication. When thick grass tufts are encountered, the bird stamps on them to flush anything that may be hiding there. A method used to obtain insects or their grubs is to break open dung heaps by stamping on them. Recently burnt areas attract the Secretary Bird, which will eat animals killed in the fire, but otherwise it does not normally eat carrion. Sometimes, larger prey may be cached under a bush, the bird returning for it later.

Secretary Birds do not rise at dawn, and when the grass is wet they may stay on their roosts until the sun has been up about two hours. In an average day they probably walk about 20–30 km before returning to roost in the late afternoon. They often use the nest as a roost throughout the year, or when farther afield a flat-topped tree such as a thorn tree. Up to five birds have been recorded roosting together, probably adults and young birds from previous broods in a family group.

One bird was seen to dust-bath, but it is not known if this is normal behaviour. In arid areas they drink regularly, and in the Kalahari up to 40 birds have been seen together at a water-hole.

When hurried, it prefers to run, but once airborne flies well. Quite often birds soar round on thermals, sometimes at a great height, and they have been recorded by pilots between 2 000 and 3 800 m above ground level. There is a case on record where a pilot was killed after his light aircraft collided with one of these birds.

The diet of the Secretary Bird is made up of virtually anything it can find and kill; to make a quantitative analysis of its prey is therefore difficult. Its cavernous gape enables it to swallow quite large items whole, so that no time is lost in tearing up prey, which it might easily lose to piratical species such as Tawny Eagles or Bateleurs. However, if a kill is too large, it tears it up in the same way as an eagle, holding it down with its feet. Mammals ranging in size from mice to hares, including hedgehogs, are taken. Avian prey is mostly the nestlings of ground-nesting species, particularly gamebirds, but it is also known to kill domestic chickens round African villages. A Yellow-billed Hornbill was found on a nest, but it was not known how the Secretary Bird obtained this unusual item of food. It also swallows the eggs of ground-nesting birds ranging in size from a lark to a guineafowl; in one case a whole clutch of francolin's eggs was regurgitated onto a nest. In a remarkable instance of mistaken identity one bird swallowed a driven golf-ball (leaving the nonplussed golfers debating whether to mark it down as a 'birdie'). Reptilian prey includes snakes, lizards, chameleons and small tortoises (swallowed whole), but it does not subsist to a great extent on snakes as is generally believed, merely including them in its varied diet when it encounters them. Quite large specimens are killed, including venomous species like Puffadders and cobras. A few amphibians are eaten, and freshwater crabs have been brought to a nest. A wide range of arthropods such as grasshoppers, beetles, termites, wasps, scorpions, millipedes, spiders and solifuges are eaten; it appears that these small prey items form an important part of the diet.

The pellets of the Secretary Bird, measuring about 40–45 mm in diameter and 30–100 mm in length, are usually made up of mammalian fur with a few small bones and the exoskeletons of arthropods. However, some may contain a considerable amount of grass, more than would be ingested in the swallowing of prey. Either grass constitutes part of the diet, or it is swallowed to assist pellet formation when mammals are scarce. Small stones have also been found in grass pellets; it has been suggested that they may assist in the digestion of grass in a mainly flesh-eating gizzard, but it is also possible that they help to break up the exoskeletons of larger invertebrates. Considerable numbers of pellets may be found on the nest, especially if it is used as a roost, and they give a good indication of the diet of a pair in a particular locality.

The normal call is a deep croaking *grok — grok — grok*, made at the nest or in display, and a soft version is emitted while feeding the nestlings; occasional whistling cries are also made, but generally this species rarely calls. Small young make a soft squealing, but later they solicit with a *chok-a-chok-a-chok-a-chok* call and also adopt the croaking call of the adult, which may be uttered with the head thrown back like an African Fish Eagle.

BREEDING

Courtship displays consist of soaring round uttering the croaking call. Undulating flights are also performed during which the bird slows up and stalls at the top of the upward loop before collapsing as if shot in the next downward plunge; these are either performed singly (by the male?) or by a pair, when the male dives down towards the female, who turns and briefly extends her feet towards him. Another display is rather like that of cranes; the two birds run round with raised wings, and sometimes several birds may join in a type of communal performance. Mating takes place on the ground or in trees.

Nests are situated on flat-topped trees, especially thorn trees, and whatever their height they are difficult to reach from below. In the south-west Cape they have adapted to nesting on lone pine trees in agricultural lands, and one such nest was 16,5 m above ground. In Natal they have been recorded nesting on Yellowwood trees. Nests are usually 2–12 m above ground and average about 5 m. They are large saucer-shaped platforms of sticks 1,5–2,5 m across, the central area lined with a thick pad of dry grass and other materials such as wool or dung.

Both sexes build the nest and they add lining, sometimes bringing prodigious beakfuls of straw, throughout the incubation period and during the first half of the nestling period. Occasionally sticks are also brought, even when there are young in the nest. All material is carried in the bill, and sometimes during nest building the birds perform a bowing ceremony before placing it in position.

Some pairs use the same nest for many years, others move frequently to new sites in the same general area. The main reason for the abandon-

Nuptial display flight of a Secretary Bird.

ment of an established nest is that it has become too heavy for the tree's canopy and begins to tilt or collapse in the middle.

Information on population density is limited; in the Kruger National Park a pair occupies 20 km^2, while elsewhere in the Transvaal in various localities pairs occupy areas varying in size from 100 km^2 to 230 km^2. One observer in the Kalahari Gemsbok National Park travelled in a direct line over a distance of 280 km and found pairs spaced approximately 12 km apart, giving a density of a pair every 140 km^2. A pair occupying a territory will defend it against intruding Secretary Birds by chasing them vigorously.

In many areas of southern Africa there is no fixed breeding season. In summer rainfall regions they may breed in most months, but in some localities breeding may not take place at all in some years. These variations are probably linked to food supply (and rainfall?). Conversely, in optimum conditions, two broods may be raised within ten months. In the south-west Cape eggs are laid in spring in August and September; in Zimbabwe eggs are recorded in all months, but with a definite peak in October and November. Further records are required for other areas to establish whether there are peak laying times there too. Eggs have been recorded in all months in the Transvaal.

The clutch is two or three eggs, chalky-white, rough in texture and pointed at the small end. Some eggs have blood smears or a few red speckles, and by the end of the incubation period they have brown nest stains. Measurements are: 78,1 × 57,5 (79), 69,0–87,0 × 53,0–62,6.

The female may sit on the nest during daytime as if incubating for a week or two before laying. Eggs are laid two to three days apart, and incubation commences with the laying of the first egg. So far as is known, the bulk of incubation is done by the female, but the male

occasionally incubates too. While incubating (or brooding small young) the bird sits extremely tight, lying flat until an intruder actually reaches the nest; occasionally it may stand up and threaten a human intruder with raised wings before flying off. During incubation the male brings food to the nest for the female. The eggs take at least 42 days to hatch; the incubation period has yet to be precisely recorded.

The newly hatched chick is covered in off-white down; its head is very large and appears almost too heavy for its body. The bare skin on its face and cere are pale yellow, the gape is bright orange and the legs are pale orange. By two weeks a thicker coat of greyish down has been acquired and at three weeks the crest feathers are the first to appear through the down. After four weeks the feathers on the anterior half of the dorsal surface begin to sprout rapidly in a similar way to the open-nesting snake eagles and the Tawny Eagle, and by seven weeks the nestling is fully feathered except for further development of the wings and tail.

Although young hatch two or three days apart, no evidence of sibling aggression has been recorded. However, in a brood of three, the smallest chick usually dies from starvation in the early stages and there is only one record of three young reaching flying stage together. Even in a brood of two it is not infrequent for only one young to be reared. The chicks develop slowly, and they can stand for the first time when about six weeks old, at which stage they can also feed themselves on larger food items regurgitated onto the nest. After about 60 days wing exercises commence, and when they are nearly ready to leave they flap vigorously and rise into the air before dropping back onto the nest. They may glide to the ground before they can fly properly, which may be as much as a week later.

(1) View of nest site of a Secretary Bird and surrounding habitat.

(2) This typical nest is placed on top of a low thorny tree.

(3) A close-up of the eggs showing their rather pointed shape at the small end.

(4) Chicks aged six and four days.

(5) A chick at two weeks old.

(6) A six-week-old nestling.

In the first ten days the young are almost constantly attended by the adults, mostly the female; the male also broods the chicks and feeds them by regurgitation, but his main task is to bring food. On arrival at the nest he brings up a mass of prey which the female then swallows and feeds later to the young by regurgitation. Some large meals may be brought, a young hare, a mouse and ten lizards on one occasion. Sometimes a bird will feed by regurgitation initially, then bring up a large item like a snake, continue feeding by regurgitation, then swallow the snake again. The process may be repeated several times; larger food items in the crop probably restrict the flow of liquid matter.

During the second ten-day period parental time on the nest drops to about 47 per cent during daytime, the female still roosting on the nest at night. Between 20 and 30 days adult time on the nest drops to about 13 per cent, but an adult is usually foraging within sight of the nest, and the young may still be brooded when a month old. After this the parents are on the nest only when delivering food; the young may still be fed by regurgitation when six weeks old, but thereafter meals are brought up onto the nest and they feed themselves.

The nestling period is very variable, ranging from 65 to 106 days, but usually about 80 to 90 days. Even in the same nest, the young may leave well apart, at about 90 and 106 days in one case. They normally fly when the parents are not in the vicinity, gliding down to the ground. Initially they remain near the nest tree, where they are fed by the adults. During this time they make mock kills by stamping on grass

A Secretary Bird feeding a nestling by regurgitation.

tussocks or sticks, and they can probably catch food for themselves about a week or two after leaving the nest. They use the nest as a roost, but often not for the first few days, probably being unable to fly up until stronger on the wing. Gradually they wander farther afield, having remained within a few hundred metres of the nest during the first month or so. No details are available on their subsequent period to independence, and observations are required.

Information on breeding success is scanty. The exposed nest renders nestlings vulnerable to predation by crows, ravens, Giant Eagle Owls and Ground Hornbills; no doubt other predators are also responsible.

2 Palm-nut Vulture /47.

Witaasvoël

Gypohierax angolensis   PLATES 3 AND 5

DERIVATION
vulture : hawk : Angolan — *gups* (G) : *hierax* (G) : *angolensis* (L)

IDENTIFICATION
Adult: The black-and-white plumage and bare red skin on the face serve to identify this species. The bill is pale yellowish, the cere pale blue, the eye yellow and the bare legs dull orange. At a distance from behind it could be mistaken for an African Fish Eagle, but the wing coverts are white, not red and black as in

that species. It also superficially resembles the Egyptian Vulture, but this has a long, thin bill, bare yellow skin on the face, and lanceolate feathers at the back of the head. In flight the Palm-nut Vulture has a distinctive black-and-white pattern, appearing mostly white below, with black on the secondaries and short, rounded tail with a diagnostic white tip. It can only be confused with the Egyptian Vulture, but this species has black not white primaries, and the long diamond-shaped tail is white.

Juvenile and immature: The juvenile is uniform drab brown with dull yellow on face and cere. The eye is brown and the legs dull white. It could be mistaken for juveniles of the Hooded Vulture and Egyptian Vulture, but both these have long, thin bills, the former with bare face and throat and dark brown down on the head, the latter with brown lanceolate feathers on the head. In flight it is brown with darker remiges and tail; it could most easily be confused with the juvenile Hooded Vulture but the bare throat and long bill distinguish this species. The juvenile Egyptian Vulture differs by having a long diamond-shaped tail. The juvenile Gymnogene is also superficially similar, but is much more slightly built, with longer legs and tail and a different flight outline.

Development to adulthood takes three to four years, the brown juvenile plumage gradually being replaced by black and white feathers, but no details of this development are known.

HABITAT

In southern Africa its occurrence is closely linked to that of the Raffia Palm *Raphia australis* growing in small areas of coastal forest in Zululand near rivers or lakes, also sporadically in other localities away from this type of habitat. Elsewhere in Africa it is found in forests, mangroves and wetter savannas wherever the Oil Palm *Elaeis guineensis* and Raffia Palm are found, usually near water. It is particularly common in some areas where these palms are cultivated commercially.

STATUS AND DISTRIBUTION

Although the southern African breeding population appears to be sedentary, juveniles and immatures wander widely and may turn up far from their normal range. Some of these stragglers undoubtedly come from outside our area (e.g. Angola). The Palm-nut Vulture has the distinction of being our rarest and most localised breeding raptor. So far as is known three pairs breed in Zululand, two near Kosi Bay and the other at Mtunzini, all in association with Raffia Palms. Our breeding population is peripheral and dependent on these palms. There is no evidence that the species has declined, indeed the palms at Mtunzini were planted at the turn of the century and a pair was first recorded there in about 1948, although they may have been there slightly earlier (Raffia Palms take 35–40 years to mature and bear fruit, after which they die). The establishment of a pair at Mtunzini has parallels elsewhere in Africa where isolated palm groves have been found and adopted by this species,

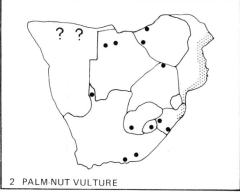

2 PALM-NUT VULTURE

probably discovered by wandering immatures. In Angola the species has expanded its range wherever palm plantations have been established and may be extremely common locally (at least 75 birds were recorded per 1,6 km on the Central Cubal River).

The main distribution of this species in southern Africa is along a thin coastal strip from Mtunzini northwards through Mozambique to the Zambezi. Stragglers have been recorded in Natal, eastern Cape, Lesotho, Orange Free State, Transvaal, Zimbabwe, northern Botswana, northern Namibia and the Kalahari.

Extralimitally it extends northwards to a line from Kenya through southern Sudan to Gambia in west Africa; locally it is very common in suitable habitat, e.g. Pemba Island, western Angola and west Africa.

GENERAL HABITS

The life of this curious species centres on its favourite diet of palm nuts, and it may spend the whole year in the general vicinity of its nest, near which it roosts at night. However, in areas with high populations, it has been recorded to roost communally in groups of about a dozen birds, sometimes with Hooded Vultures.

Its method of feeding is to pluck off a nut, often from the softer inside of the bunch, and hold it down with the feet while the husk is torn off with the bill and eaten; it does not feed on the kernel. For a long time it was thought that the rich source of vitamin A in the Oil Palm nuts was essential to its diet, but this is not so, and Raffia Palm nuts on which some populations subsist contain very little of this vitamin. Birds survive in captivity on a diet mainly of meat, but when one was given palm nuts after deprivation lasting eleven years it fed on them in preference to its usual meat diet. The stomach contents of many collected specimens have contained a mass of palm nut husks, often to the exclusion of all other food. Despite the large numbers found in commercially grown palm groves, the species is not persecuted in any way as it is not considered a threat to the prolific crop, on which other species such as hornbills also feed. Other vegetable matter recorded in the diet includes grain and the seeds of the Australian Wattle-tree *Acacia cyclops*.

Although most often seen perched, it flies with rapid wing-beats and can soar well. When fishing, either in the sea or in rivers, it usually planes down from a perch and snatches a fish from the surface of the water, and one was seen to submerge like an Osprey to catch one. It may also hunt by making short flights over the surface of the water. The strong claws suggest that it takes other live prey, but eye-witness accounts are rare. It has been reported to kill chickens and a domestic cat and to swoop down on a tethered goat kid, but such incidents are most unusual. An observer saw one catch and eat a lizard. A plucked dove and a Giant Rat have been found on nests, and mammalian fur in stomach contents.

Other food recorded has been mainly invertebrates, mostly found on the seashore or beside inland waters. Crabs are most often eaten, in addition to other crustaceans and molluscs, including giant *Achatina* land snails, which are extracted by bashing in the side of the shell. One bird in Zululand was seen to plane down from a high dune to take small crustaceans on the shore, returning to its perch between sorties. Large insects such as locusts are also eaten.

Occasionally it may rob other species; a White-necked Raven was relieved of a titbit it was eating, and an unsuccessful attempt was made to steal a fish from a Yellow-billed Kite. It is also a scavenger, feeding on offal and road kills, as well as the victims of veld fires. At times it gathers with other vultures at a carcass, usually out of curiosity, but it has also been seen to feed on large carrion such as a dead buck. Another form of scavenging is to follow fishing canoes for scraps thrown overboard.

The calls, although not often heard, are strange, consisting of various barking, cawing and growling notes, as well as a contented duck-like quacking at its roost. A guttural *pruk-kurrr* is made during display flights and in threat to other large birds near the nest; it is also said to emit a monotonous hissing whistle during courtship. A cawing *kwuk-kwuk-kwuk* is used by the pair as a contact call. A series of barks and long, deep growls — *karrr* — may be made when someone climbs to the nest. The nestling makes a plaintive begging cry.

BREEDING

Courtship consists of soaring at a great height and making mock dives, during which the birds may somersault. Mating takes place at the nest, the male making the *kwuk-kwuk-kwuk* call during coition.

In southern Africa the only nest site recorded in any detail was in a Raffia Palm, situated amongst the fronds near the top, about 18 m above ground; it was constructed of medium-sized sticks. The palm grew on the edge of a strip of coastal forest. The nest itself could not be reached, but was presumably not much different from those described elsewhere in Africa. They are substantial stick structures 60–90 cm across and 30–60 cm deep, lined with a thick mat of dry grass and other dry fibrous material, as well as dung. In west Africa nests have been recorded in forest trees as high as 60 m, but in Angola they were 6–27 m above ground.

The Angolan nests were situated mainly in Baobabs on lateral forks beneath the canopy, although a few were on top of the canopy. One nest was in the crown of a euphorbia, a site like that of a snake eagle. No nests were found in the nearby Oil Palm plantations, probably because of disturbance during harvesting. The use of Raffia Palms in Zululand (and elsewhere) shows that palms are not necessarily unsuitable sites. In west Africa it was noticed that weavers deliberately chose to establish a large nesting colony near a Palm-nut Vulture's nest, moving with the birds when they built in a

Nest and egg of a Palm-nut Vulture photographed in Angola (Photograph: Rob Jeffery).

new site.

Both birds build a new nest or repair an old one, the process taking four to six weeks in either case. Material is carried in the bill or in the feet, and most building is done in the early morning or late evening. Nests may be used year after year.

At Kosi Bay in Zululand only two nests are known, situated in Raffia Palms, in an area of palms 50 ha in extent. In the dense population on the Central Cubal River in Angola, nests were about 250 m apart, often in full view of each other.

In Zululand limited evidence indicates that laying takes place in August or September, and in Mozambique the bird is said to breed in September. Angolan eggs are laid mainly from May to July. A single egg is laid, white in ground colour, often obscured by a pale buff or rust wash; eggs are variably marked with rust-red freckles and blotches often concentrated in a cap at the large end. Most eggs are handsomely marked. There are no measurements of eggs in southern Africa. Measurements of eggs from elsewhere in Africa are: 71,2 × 53,6 (19); 66,1–78,3 × 50,2–56,8.

The incubation period is said to be between six and seven weeks, but there is no accurate record. Nothing is known about whether the sexes share incubation. When the sitting bird is flushed it may perch in a nearby tree 'growling disapproval' while the nest tree is climbed. The newly hatched nestling is covered in brown down, but nothing is recorded about its subsequent development of plumage and co-ordination. The young are fed on the husks of palm nuts, as well as on animal food; a fish, a bird, a large rat and snails have been found on nests.

The nestling period is not precisely known, but is stated to be about 90 days. The juvenile is fed near the nest for at least a month after fledging and it is able to feed itself on palm nuts quite soon after leaving the nest. At a nest in Zululand where an adult was incubating, an immature bird was seen feeding in an adjacent palm. Nothing is known about breeding success, but they may lay again if they are unsuccessful after a first attempt.

For a bird that is locally very common, the breeding biology is very little known, and it would be a rewarding species for further study, especially as this might throw some light on its vulturine or aquiline affinities.

---

3 Lammergeyer 119.

Lammergeier

Gypaetus barbatus

DERIVATION
vulture : eagle : bearded — *gups* (G) : *aetos* (G) : *barbatus* (L)

IDENTIFICATION
Adult: This large, imposing raptor is easily identified by its rufous underparts and neck, contrasting with white on the head. A bandit's mask of black hair-like feathers surrounding the eye extends onto the bill and forms a tuft under the chin, from which the alternative name Bearded Vulture is derived. The purpose of this tuft is not known, but it has been suggested that it may have a tactile function connected with feeding on marrow bones. The rest of the upperparts are slate-black, with the shafts of the wing coverts and scapulars white. The feathers at the back of the head are loose and lanceolate, giving the effect of a mane. The leggings are also very loose and baggy in appearance, with feathering to within 2,5 cm of the blackish toes. A red sclerotic ring surrounds the pale yellow eye and it inflames to a deeper red when the bird is excited. The bill is horn coloured. An interesting feature of the rufous coloration is that it is obtained 'cosmetically' (an aspect discussed more fully under General Habits) so that the amount of white on the head is rather variable and, usually, the deepest rufous is on the breast.

In flight the Lammergeyer is magnificent and resembles a giant falcon, particularly a Lanner, except for the long wedge-shaped tail. The dark brown underwing coverts have white shaft streaks and are darker than the rest of the underwing and tail which contrast with the rufous body. It is a huge bird with a wingspan of 2,5 m that cannot be confused with any other species.

Juvenile and immature: The juvenile is dark brown but almost blackish on head and breast. The eye is coloured like that of the adult and the 'beard' is diagnostic if a good view is obtained. On the upperparts it shows a mottling of white feathers. In flight it is identified by its characteristic outline and can be confused only with the juvenile Egyptian Vulture, which is very much smaller and has a long, thin bill. After the brown juvenile plumage it becomes much paler, almost buffy, on the underparts, and more mottled with white above, but the head remains dark brown in sharp contrast to the rest of the plumage. This characteristic 'black-headed' stage is possibly maintained for about two years or more, as birds like this are quite frequently seen. Little is known of subsequent development to adult plumage, but it appears that the head becomes white at the next moult. The progress to full adult plumage is protracted; a captive bird acquired it only between five and a half and six and a half years old.

HABITAT

In southern Africa, as elsewhere in its range, the Lammergeyer is almost entirely confined to mountainous terrain, and its present distribution is confined to the Drakensberg massif.

STATUS AND DISTRIBUTION

It is resident, although individual birds may occasionally stray beyond the Drakensberg. Adults remain in the vicinity of their nesting area as a rule, but juveniles and immatures tend to wander, and outnumber adults where there are garbage dumps etc. to attract them.

This species was formerly found in the south-western Cape within 100 km of Cape Town eastwards to the Drakensberg, but it has now disappeared from its former range beyond the Drakensberg. Probably never common except in the Drakensberg and environs, it shows a

Open circles indicate records of the distribution of the Lammergeyer prior to 1940 and the small spotting its present range.

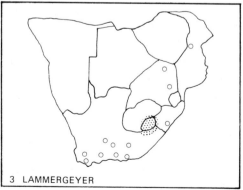

3 LAMMERGEYER

decline in the late 19th century closely parallel to that of the Egyptian Vulture (q.v.) except that conditions in Lesotho and adjacent areas have enabled it to maintain a viable local population.

Various subjective estimates of the size of the remaining population have been made, ranging from '20 pairs' to 'fewer than 100 birds', normally accompanied by the comment that the bird is threatened with extinction. Without minimising the need for the conservation of this species, it is necessary to examine its status more objectively to assess the truth of the situation. Several observers have made counts, some of them basing an estimate of total population on these, and, although admittedly imperfect, they clearly reveal that the present status of the Lammergeyer is not as serious as has been suggested. At the Giant's Castle Lammergeyer hide in 1968, where offal was put out specially for the birds, a minimum of two adults and seven immatures was seen in two days in May (when the adults would have been concerned with breeding). A recent account by experienced observers states that thirteen breeding pairs are known in the Natal Drakensberg between Sani Pass in the south and the Royal Natal National Park in the north, as well as at least 30 breeding pairs in Lesotho. If it may be assumed that immatures make up about a quarter of the population, as is the case in Ethiopia, then the *known* population is just over 100 birds. During visits to Lesotho two different observers recorded an average of one bird a day, another observer two birds a day. One of these observers was Leslie Brown, with much experience of Lammergeyers in Ethiopia, who estimated that the mountainous areas of Lesotho could have a population of 100 pairs. The best recent estimate is that of two observers who travelled 152 km and 228 km in 1978 and 1979 respectively in suitable Lammergeyer habitat in Lesotho. On the first journey of 12 days they saw 1,42 Lammergeyers per day (0,112 birds per km) and on the second trip of 17 days 1,82 birds a day (0,136 per km). In both years half of the birds seen were immatures, but counts were made during the early part of the breeding season when one adult is always on the nest, so that a bias would exist. However, extrapolating from their results, they arrived at an estimate of about 300 birds in 10 000 km^2 of suitable mountainous terrain in Lesotho.

From the foregoing it is clear that the present population of the Lammergeyer in southern Africa is much larger than was previously thought. The species undoubtedly suffers direct persecution; in Lesotho there are several known instances when young recently out of the nest have been killed and eaten by local people. Additional hazards are shooting, trapping and disturbance at the nest, but the main threat comes, ironically, from progress. Improved sanitation removes garbage dumps. Improved stock-keeping methods and veterinary services reduce the carrion food supply. The bird's optimum requirements are met by primitive pastoral conditions, where it is largely commensal with man. The facts speak for themselves: it has disappeared from most of its former range in the Cape Province; it is very common in Ethiopia. For as long as present pastoral conditions continue in Lesotho, it will survive there.

The Lammergeyer occurs in East Griqualand, in the Orange Free State where it borders northern Lesotho, in Lesotho and in western Natal. Extralimitally the African race *meridionalis* next occurs in northern Tanzania, thence northwards through east Africa and Ethiopia into Yemen. Another race of the Lammergeyer is found in north-west Africa, and from Spain to central Asia.

GENERAL HABITS

The Lammergeyer is well adapted to its cold mountainous environment. The broad, stiff, overlapping contour feathers prevent strong winds from penetrating to the downy insulating layer beneath; when the bird ruffles, the clatter of these stiff feathers is audible 30 m away. In flight the bare feet are covered by the undertail coverts and the baggy feathers of the leggings. At night it roosts in caves or on the wool-lined nest, and sleeps in a prone position with the feet tucked into the feathers as they are when flying. In captivity a bird will creep into a corner or a container large enough to hold it, behaviour unique amongst large African raptors. It has been shown experimentally in captivity that the body temperature does not drop overnight, so that it does not need to expend energy in rewarming itself next day.

The Lammergeyer often sunbathes with spread wings, an impressive posture, warming either its front or back, and it has been known to position itself in anticipation of sunrise. A number of nest sites in South Africa are known to face eastwards. However, in winter when the birds breed, the sun is often obscured by inclement weather, so that this source of heat would be unpredictable.

The rufous coloration of this species has been shown to be derived from contact with iron oxide. Some is probably picked up when sleeping in a prone position in caves, but they dust-bath too. They also have a regular drinking and bathing pool, and it is probable that some of the coloration is acquired where there is iron oxide in the water.

The Lammergeyer is on the wing at first light, often in cold, overcast conditions, but the almost constant air currents round the mountains make it independent of thermals. It glides and soars with a consummate grace matched by few other birds of prey. In a gentle downward glide one was estimated to be travelling at 130 km/h, and it is capable of tremendous bursts of speed. One was seen to pursue a White-necked Raven in a steep downward chase of 250 m, twisting and turning skilfully every time the raven attempted to elude it. A case is on record of a Lammergeyer dropping a bone from a great height and catching it in its bill before it reached the ground. Wing flaps are slow and buoyant like those of a Yellow-billed Kite, but it seldom flaps except to regain lost height.

The main diet is carrion, particularly bones. It has a huge gape (67 mm wide) and can swallow large bones with much swelling and contorting of its neck in the process. At carrion it is subordinate to large vultures and waits until they have finished feeding. Scavenging scraps round the primitive dwellings of man is a regular habit and it also follows the plough for grubs unearthed. Numbers of birds will gather at a grassfire to feed on the victims burnt in it. It is reliably reported to catch dassies in South Africa, in one case dropping the animal to the ground from about 100 m and then retrieving it. Reports that it knocks animals over cliffs have been doubted, but a reliable observer saw one swoop down at an Oribi grazing on the edge of a krans in Natal; the attack failed. One bird has been seen carrying a 45 cm monitor lizard which it had probably killed itself.

Another aspect of the behaviour of this remarkable raptor is its habit of dropping bones to break them, a process that has been seen by a number of observers in South Africa and elsewhere. The technique is for the bird to fly downwind, the bone pointing forwards to reduce air resistance in the same way that an Osprey carries a fish with the head pointing forwards. As it nears the dropping zone it dips sharply to increase velocity and releases the bone, which falls on a flat slab below, usually within an area of four square metres — very accurate estimating when one considers that the bone is dropped from a height of 30–40 m. The bird descends rapidly, turns into the wind, spreads its tail and flaps its wings rapidly to brake and alight beside the bone, in order to forestall ravens attempting to steal from the Lammergeyer. If the bird fails to break the bone, it will repeat the process, although sometimes it has to make an approach involving several kilometres to line up on its ossuary. One persistent bird in South Africa was seen to drop a bone fifteen times in ten minutes. Some ossuaries are used for long periods, and at one site fragments of bones that would have filled several buckets lay around in crevices like drift snow. The tongue is shaped like a marrow scoop to facilitate the extraction of marrow. Finally, it only remains to record that according to Pliny the Greek poet Aeschylus was killed when a tortoise was dropped on his bald pate by a Lammergeyer!

This species rarely calls, but it is said to make a whistling note in display. At a nest in Lesotho adults made a kestrel-like *keek-keek-keek* but much deeper. Juveniles were heard to make a drawn-out whistling *pee-wee-oo* at the Giant's Castle Lammergeyer hide, possibly a begging call, as a similar call was recorded at a nest where a nestling was being fed.

BREEDING

Courtship consists of undulating dives and upward swoops like those of many eagles, the birds calling as they display. They also roll and twist in flight, and one bird will turn and present its claws to its mate. Once a juvenile and an adult were seen to lock claws and cartwheel for a while, but this was probably aggression. A pair in Lesotho preened each other, and they mated on several occasions during the month prior to laying.

Nests in southern Africa are normally situated on sheer sandstone cliffs 120–180 m in height overlooking a river valley. There is some evidence that cliffs at lower altitudes are preferred, probably to avoid the extreme cold of the highest cliffs. Two nests in Lesotho were between 1 800 and 2 000 m above sea level. A pothole cave under an overhang is selected in an inaccessible position (without ropes) in the middle of the cliff, and nest sites are invariably well sheltered from the elements.

Nests are substantial structures of sticks thickly lined with sheep's wool, including large pieces of fleece, and a miscellaneous assortment of soft rubbish such as rags, sacking, skin, fur, and rope. Green leaves are not used as lining. The nest most closely resembles that of an Egyptian Vulture but is much larger. The size of nests is deceptive from a distance as they extend to the back of a pothole cave and do not appear particularly large. However, they are normally 150–200 cm across and about 60 cm deep; one exceptional nest was nearly 2 m deep, the configuration of the cave requiring it

to be built up.

Nest building or repair commences in late April and both birds work on the nest and gather material, carrying it in either the bill or the feet. A pair in Lesotho was watched for one and a half hours as they collected sticks, dry tussocks and small dead bushes, some of which were pulled out of crevices with the bill. Some material was collected from an alternate nest site. Most pairs have an alternate nest site nearby, sometimes several nests, and a Lesotho pair had five sites in a series of adjacent potholes on their regular nest cliff. Although there are no published long-term observations, it appears that a pair will use a nest for a while, then move to an alternate site, and later return to the previous nest. An explanation for their leaving a perfectly suitable site may be that it has become fouled and infested with parasites.

Little is known of the size of territory occupied by Lammergeyers, but it does not appear to be particularly large. In Lesotho three nests were within 20 km of each other, and in Ethiopia, where the species is about three times as common as in Lesotho, two nests were 3,5 km apart.

In southern Africa eggs have been recorded from May to August, but there are too few records to indicate a laying peak. Again, according to a limited number of records, two eggs are laid as often as one, although it had been hitherto believed that a single egg was the normal clutch. Eggs are oval, rough in texture, white in ground colour and entirely overlaid with a wash of pale red with some rusty speckles. They resemble Lanner's eggs but are much paler. Measurements are: 85,5 × 64,8 (7); 82,8–90,4 × 62,3–67,8.

In a clutch of two the eggs are laid several days apart, at least six days in one case, and incubation commences with the first egg. Both sexes incubate, the female at night, while the males roosts nearby on the nest cliff. During five daylong watches at a nest in Lesotho (where the sexes could not be distinguished) the eggs were brooded continuously with a maximum of three change-overs during any one day. The longest continuous spell of incubation lasted eight and a half hours, presumably by the female. Shorter periods when a bird sat for up to three hours were presumably when the male was relieving the female. As no food was brought to the nest when the sitting bird was relieved, it was assumed that the female scavenged for herself during her periods off the nest. On four days the presumed female was relieved between 08h00 and 09h00 after being on the nest overnight, and she flew off to search

(1) View of a Lammergeyer's nest cliff; the nest position is arrowed.

(2) A closer view of the same site.

(3) The eggs lie on a thick pad of sheep's wool and other debris (Photograph: Rob Jeffery).

for food. On several occasions when the sitting bird was relieved it would fly to a favourite pool across the valley to drink and bathe. The only activity of the incubating bird was to stand up, either to excrete or to tuck the eggs beneath itself before settling again, the latter process taking place twice within an hour on many occasions. Although the sun fell on the nest in the early morning on clear days, the sitting bird was not seen to sunbathe. It appears from these observations that because incubation takes place in the middle of a severe winter the eggs need to be constantly covered, and the male's substantial share of duty enables the female to leave the nest to drink, bathe and feed.

No aggression is shown at the nest towards humans, even when in a potentially vulnerable position at the end of a rope; the birds merely glide around in the vicinity. However, large raptors such as Black Eagles may be chased away when near a nest, and White-necked Ravens are not tolerated. At three nests out of five in Lesotho observers noted three fully adult Lammergeyers flying round amicably together.

The incubation period has not been accurately assessed in the wild, although it was estimated to be approximately 56 days at a nest in the Drakensberg. In captivity the period was between 55 and 58 days.

Where two chicks hatch, invariably only one survives. It is not known whether there is any sibling aggression, but the smaller chick disappears within a few days. In captivity the parents killed their second nestling within a day after it hatched. Such behaviour is not necessarily normal, although it should be watched for in the wild.

The chick is covered in dark grey down which is darker on the head and neck. At the age of five weeks it is still entirely downy, but nothing is recorded of its subsequent feather development, growth and behaviour.

Observations throughout the nestling period at a nest in Lesotho established a clear picture of parental behaviour. Both male and female brood, feed and shelter the nestling, the male doing a considerable share of these duties. Initially the chick is almost constantly brooded, mostly by the female, and the male brings in food carried in the feet or the bill. Although no food was regurgitated onto the nest, this method has been recorded elsewhere. By the third week both parents take turns at foraging, but an adult is on the nest all the time, and until at least seven weeks old the chick is never left alone. During this time the adults change over at the nest four to six times a day, food is brought two to six times daily, and the nestling is fed three to nine times per day. At some stage between its seventh and ninth week the chick is left alone for the first time for periods of up to three hours. By this time it is probably able to feed itself. Before this the adults pull pieces off carrion for it in the manner of an eagle, or feed it large chunks of offal, including bones up to 20 cm long, which it swallows. It is also large enough to defend itself against White-necked Ravens, which attempt to filch scraps from the nest and could easily kill a small unprotected nestling. However, even when not on the nest, the adults are often soaring within sight of it. By the twelfth week the longest time spent on the nest by an adult is about two hours, and by the thirteenth week the parents only visit the nest to bring food. Thus the pattern of behaviour is similar to that of an eagle except for regular brooding and feeding of the nestling by the male.

In captivity a nestling first flew at about 110 days. On two occasions at a nest in Lesotho the young flew in less than 120 days, but they did not fly strongly, and settled in accessible positions where they were injured by local people, one young bird eventually dying of its injuries. Limited observations indicate that the juvenile remains in the nest area for some months and is fed by its parents. It is not known at what stage it becomes independent, but apparently before the commencement of the following breeding season.

There are no details on breeding success in southern Africa. On present evidence this species breeds annually, despite the long breeding cycle.

Note: Details of the breeding cycle of the Lammergeyer in Lesotho are based on the unpublished observations of Dr Jeff Guy and Rex Tomlinson.

4 Egyptian Vulture /2o

Egiptiese Aasvoël

Neophron percnopterus

PLATES 3 AND 5

DERIVATION
Neophron : dusky : wing — *Neophron* (G) : *perknos* (G) : *pteros* (G)

Neophron was a character in the pseudo-mythological *Metamorphoses* of the second century writer Antoninus Liberalis. He was changed into a vulture by Zeus for a base trick he had played.

IDENTIFICATION
Adult: The predominantly white coloration, bare yellow face and forehead, long, thin bill and lanceolate feathers at the back of the head serve to identify this small vulture. The tip of the yellow bill is black, the eye deep red and the bare legs yellow. The face is often orange, possibly flushing this colour in excitement. It can most easily be confused with the Palm-nut Vulture, under which species their differences are discussed. At a distance the pale form of the Tawny Eagle has a superficial resemblance to this species, but the aquiline bill and feathered head and legs would distinguish it. In flight the Egyptian Vulture is white except for black remiges; the white diamond-shaped tail is a diagnostic field character distinguishing it from a pale Tawny Eagle, pale Booted Eagle and the Palm-nut Vulture (which has white primaries).

Juvenile and immature: The juvenile is brown with the bare skin of the face and legs dull greyish; the eye is brown. The most likely confusion is with the Hooded Vulture, particularly the juvenile, but the back of the head and neck of the Egyptian Vulture is well-feathered, not downy. The superficially similar Palm-nut Vulture juvenile has an aquiline bill and the top of the head is feathered; the very much larger juvenile Lammergeyer may be distinguished for these reasons too and it has no bare skin on the face. It may possibly be mistaken for a juvenile Gymnogene, but this species has a hawk's bill, much longer legs, more slender build and quite different habits.

In flight the juvenile appears uniformly dark brown from below, but the long diamond-shaped tail distinguishes it from juveniles of the Palm-nut Vulture and Hooded Vulture. The most likely confusion would be with the juvenile Lammergeyer, which has a similar shaped tail, but it is almost twice as large as the Egyptian Vulture, whose long, thin bill also distinguishes it.

The transition from juvenile to adult plumage takes about five years, the immature gradually acquiring white feathers, which prevent confusion with juvenile or immature Hooded Vulture, Lammergeyer and Gymnogene, although the Palm-nut Vulture immature would show a similar progression from brown to white and should be identified by characteristics already discussed.

HABITAT
This species is normally found in open country, either short grassland or more arid areas, even desert, not usually in areas of dense woodland with a high rainfall. As they require cliffs for breeding, resident birds are seldom far from rocky outcrops or mountains. In southern Africa the short grassland of the Transkei is where most birds have been sighted in recent times.

STATUS AND DISTRIBUTION
This species is now extremely rare in southern Africa, with fewer than 25 properly authenticated records between 1945 and 1980. In view of its rarity, observers must make detailed

Open circles indicate the range of the Egyptian Vulture prior to 1945 and black dots show sightings since 1945. In some cases, particularly in the eastern Cape Province, a single symbol may cover several records in the same locality.

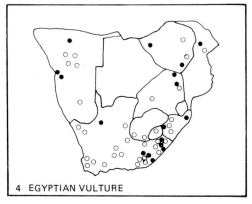

4 EGYPTIAN VULTURE

descriptions of any birds seen, particularly juveniles; such features as the feathering on the head as well as the bill and tail shape are essential to any record. In the 19th century it was mentioned by farmers, travellers and naturalists, was widely distributed, although nowhere common, and was recorded breeding in a number of localities. There is no evidence that the population was of recent origin; the Hottentots had their own name for it and it was mentioned by travellers as early as 1680.

Several reasons have been advanced for its decline, one being the collapse of the ungulate ecosystem as a result of intensive hunting between 1840 and 1880, when the vast herds of game were shot out. Soon after, the catastrophic rinderpest epidemic of 1896 virtually wiped out the domestic stock that had replaced the game herds. This sequence of events must undoubtedly have had an effect on the Egyptian Vulture population as it did on other carrion feeders. It also suffered from the indiscriminate poisoning of carcasses by farmers to eradicate predators, and it is known that it was shot by Ostrich farmers because of its habit of breaking and eating their eggs.

Another possible reason, which does not appear to have been considered, is that it is often commensal with man living in primitive conditions. According to the 19th century accounts one or two birds frequented most farm homesteads, no doubt for offal and other refuse thrown out. They would also have been attracted to African villages. With the disappearance of undeveloped rural conditions over vast areas, part of its livelihood disappeared; significantly, in recent times most sightings have been made in Transkei, where these conditions still prevail.

In view of the paucity of records, the current status of this species in southern Africa is difficult to establish, but it is probable that some birds in southern Africa are stragglers from other areas. However, these would not be Palearctic birds, which although migratory are not known to come farther south than the southern Sahara. It is possible that Transkei birds are resident and still breed there, despite the lack of any recent breeding evidence. As the species is so rare, nothing practical can be done for its conservation, although it could possibly benefit from measures being taken to conserve the Cape Vulture (e.g. 'vulture restaurants').

The distribution map shows records before and after 1945 and clearly indicates the paucity of recent sightings. Extralimitally the species is widely distributed and locally common, espe-cially where primitive living conditions are to be found. Its distribution extends from the Canary and Cape Verde Islands across north Africa and southern Europe east to Turkestan, Afghanistan and India. In Africa it is uncommon south of Tanzania but is found in Angola.

GENERAL HABITS

Although it has powerful feet for a vulture, it is primarily a scavenger and rarely kills prey for itself. It has been recorded to kill small flamingo chicks and an Ostrich chick. In a remarkable account from Israel one dropped a small monitor lizard from 100 m and then finished it off by throwing a stone onto it. In many areas it lives in association with man, feeding on offal, refuse and human excrement. Under such conditions it is common, even roosting gregariously. Away from the haunts of man it occurs singly, in pairs or in small groups. It arrives at carcasses with other vultures, but comes lowest in the peck order, being subservient to the similar-sized Hooded Vulture, which also feeds on small scraps that escape the attentions of the larger vultures. The two species are similar in their feeding habits at carcasses; the only difference observed is that the Hooded Vulture tends to pick up scraps from the ground whereas the Egyptian Vulture pecks off bones. It also forages around hyaena dens for offal. Other food records are of small items including termites, grasshoppers, dung-beetles, small crustaceans and snails.

At flamingo and White Pelican colonies it breaks eggs by picking them up and throwing them downwards onto rocks, then feeds on the contents. It also breaks open eggs with downward pecks, possibly eggs already cracked. The most remarkable behaviour, however, is its method of breaking Ostrich eggs. A stone, normally weighing 55–285 g but occasionally as heavy as 900 g and sometimes fetched from a considerable distance, is thrown by the standing bird downwards onto an egg until it breaks. Some birds are more adept than others, but as a rule about half of the throws score hits. When the eggs break, the birds feed on the contents but are often dispossessed by other larger vultures that have been watching nearby. Recent observations in Tanzania had been thought to be the first, but the behaviour was described as long ago as 1836 in South Africa, although in an obscure newspaper report. The breaking of Ostrich eggs by this method has been recorded also in Ethiopia and the Sudan. There has been considerable inconclusive discussion on the origin of this behaviour, which is generally considered as learnt rather than innate; whatever the arguments, it constitutes one of the few instances of tool-using by animals other than man. It has also been claimed that stones are dropped from a height or that the bird uses one as a hammer by holding it in the bill, but modern confirmation of these accounts is lacking.

The only call recorded is a mewing note; low grunts and hisses are made in excitement, but as a rule this species is largely silent.

BREEDING

The Egyptian Vulture was recorded breeding last century at various places in South Africa, at Colesberg, East London, Hopefield, Swellendam, Willowmore, Transkei and Natal. The last-known nest of this species was found on 8 December 1923 in the Transkei by W. W. Roberts, who published his account in *The Blythswood Review* in 1924. As the account is typical of the nesting of this species, it seems fitting to repeat it, especially as copies of this journal are virtually unobtainable. He writes:

'I found a beautiful pair of eggs in a nest situated high up on a ledge in a kranz in the Mqanduli District. These were richly covered all over with reddish-brown, and splashed with darker markings of the same colour. The nest was a large structure of sticks placed on a ledge in a natural depression, and was lined with pieces of sheep-skins, with the wool part facing the inside, which gave it the appearance of a kaross.

'Surrounding the nest was a very odd collection of rubbish, the bulk of which consisted chiefly of old bones, pieces of leather, cow-dung, bits of wood, and skulls of small rodents. Was this for the purpose of decoration or camouflage?

'The natives inform me that a pair of these vultures have nested on the same ledge for the past five or six years; and from my own observations I know that they have tenanted the same nest for the last three years.'

Whether breeding in December was typical is not known; other southern African vultures breed in the winter months. Two eggs comprise the normal clutch and they are handsomely marked. The measurements of eggs in Europe are: $66{,}0 \times 50{,}4$ (200); $58{,}2–76{,}4 \times 43{,}0–56{,}1$. The incubation period is about 42 days, and both sexes are said to incubate. The newly hatched chick is stated to be covered in white down, although one observer in Kenya describes it as being grey-brown on the head and paler and greyer over the rest of the body. No details are available on nestling development, but both parents tend the young. The nestling period is about three months. The breeding biology is poorly known, even though the bird is common in some localities.

---

5 Hooded Vulture /21.

Monnikaasvoël

Necrosyrtes monachus

PLATES 3 AND 5

DERIVATION

corpse : pulling at : monk — *nekros* (G) : *surtes* (G) : *monachus* (L)

The Greek word *surtes* means a cord for pulling, but in this context means pulling at corpses.

IDENTIFICATION

Adult: The sexes are alike in size and colour. This small vulture is mainly dark brown with some white feathers round the crop and on the 'trousers'. The crop patch and back of the head and neck are covered in creamy down. There is a small ruff at the base of the neck. The base of the bill, the bare throat and the face are pink, and the face flushes red in excitement. The tip of the long, thin bill is black, the eyes are black and the legs and feet pale blue. In flight it appears almost wholly brown except for a silvery 'lining' on the remiges, and white round the crop and on the 'trousers'.

Juvenile and immature: The juvenile is also mainly dark brown but the feathers of the upperparts are edged with buff, giving them a scaly appearance. The ruff consists of long, lanceolate feathers, and the top of the head and the back of the neck are covered in blackish down. The crop and surrounding feathers are blackish and there is no white on the 'trousers'. The bare face and throat are whitish, the face heavily covered with black whiskers. Its face can flush red but rarely does so (see under General Habits). The tip of the bill is black, whitish at its base, the eyes are black and the legs and feet brownish. In flight it appears wholly dark brown. Possible confusion with juveniles of the Palm-nut Vulture, Egyptian Vulture, Lappet-faced Vulture and White-headed Vulture are discussed under those species.

The time taken to assume full adult plumage is not known. The down on the head, neck and crop changes gradually to creamy and the black whiskers on the face disappear. The feathers of the ruff reduce and white feathers appear round the crop and on the 'trousers'. The legs begin to change to pale blue by the end of the first year. The white 'lining' appears on the wings at the first moult of the remiges.

HABITAT

This species occurs in bushveld savanna and on adjacent open plains. It prefers well-wooded country with perennial water for nesting and is not found in arid habitats.

STATUS AND DISTRIBUTION

Although regularly encountered in some areas, this species is nowhere plentiful in southern Africa. In South Africa it is another 'game reserve' vulture, rarely seen outside these areas.

Adults tend to be sedentary but one had moved a distance of 210 km five days after being ringed. A ringed immature was seen 150 km away eight days after being ringed and another was recorded 155 km away fifteen and a half months after ringing, but it had previously been sighted three times near its place of original ringing.

Distribution extends from southern Mozambique and the eastern Transvaal northwards to Zimbabwe and thence westwards across northern Botswana to northern Namibia. There are sporadic records (vagrants?) from various other localities in southern Africa.

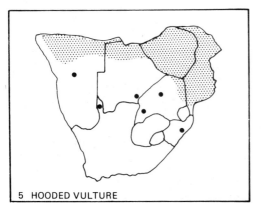

5 HOODED VULTURE

GENERAL HABITS

As one observer with experience of this species in Nigeria and in southern Africa points out, it really has 'two faces'. In west Africa and some other areas to our north it is locally abundant, and in the town of Sokoto in north-west Nigeria some 300 birds gathered round an abattoir and 100 at the marketplace. In Sokoto 279 nests were located in 40 km^2. It has been able to increase its numbers in such areas through lack of competition from other vultures and its symbiotic relationship with Man. On occasions it has even been recorded to perch on domestic animals such as goats. In southern Africa its other 'face' is quite different. Here it is shy, nowhere plentiful and rarely associates with humans except occasionally in the Okavango Swamps in Botswana.

The Hooded Vulture is usually seen in pairs or small groups and unlike the larger vultures will often perch within the canopy of a tree. In a study in north-west Zimbabwe, although it usually arrived after other species such as Bateleurs and White-headed Vultures, it was frequently the first species to land and feed. This is of necessity a hurried process as once the larger vultures come down it has to retreat to the outskirts where it pecks about for scraps like a chicken. It is able to hold down a chunk of food with its feet and pull off pieces with its bill. Sometimes it flies off carrying a piece of food in its bill. Once the carcass has been reduced to skin and bones it pecks in crevices with its thin bill for pieces the other vultures have been unable to remove. It is a clean feeder and does not become soiled.

Between one and nine (average 4,7) Hooded Vultures were recorded at carcasses and usually immatures came down first. They were easily dispossessed by adults, which blushed their faces deep red to establish dominance over them as well as over other adults. Sometimes, when only immatures were present, one would blush red and establish dominance over the others.

Apart from scavenging carcasses, including those of small animals, this species also eats both human and animal faeces. It feeds on dead and stranded fish as well as caterpillars, grubs, locusts and termites. Insects, when available, appear to be an important supplement to its diet. Elsewhere in Africa it follows the plough for grubs and other insects which are unearthed.

Little is known of its voice and it appears to be mainly silent. Shrill, sibilant whistling calls are emitted during copulation, and squealing and chittering calls in excitement. The feath-

(1) A Hooded Vulture's nest situated typically in a fork beneath the canopy.

(2) A nest and egg (Photograph: Peter Mundy).

(3) A nestling aged 51 days (Photograph: Peter Mundy).

ered nestling is said to make a *chiu-chiu* soliciting call.

BREEDING

No nuptial displays have been described. The pair bond appears to be strong and the two birds preen each other, nibbling in the down of the head and neck. Mating takes place on the nest or nearby or in trees near carcasses.

Few nests have been found in southern Africa, most of them in Zimbabwe. They are situated in large forks within the canopy of a leafy tree, often in thick riparian woodland, and are difficult to see. Most of the nests have been found in the ebony tree *Diospyros mespiliformis*, and the range of this tree closely overlaps that of the Hooded Vulture in southern Africa. Cliff sites, as occasionally reported elsewhere in Africa, have not been recorded in our area. Sometimes the nest is built on top of the old nest of some other bird of prey. The average height of seventeen nests was 18,1 m. Seven nests averaged 62 cm across (range 50–76 cm), 40 cm deep (range 25–61 cm) and with a cup 29 cm in diameter (range 23–32 cm). The cup is lined with some grass and a thick carpet of green leaves. This lining is replenished throughout the incubation period and for most of the nestling period.

Nest repair lasts about a month and both birds build. In Kenya a pair used the same nest for seven consecutive years. Alternate sites are used, usually after disturbance, and are never very far away. In one case a pair moved when a Giant Eagle Owl took over their nest.

Nesting densities such as found in Nigeria are found nowhere in southern Africa, and this species is usually a solitary breeder. In suitable riparian woodland, sites may be fairly close together on occasions; two occupied nests were only 50 m apart in one exceptional case. It appears that the vicinity of the nest is defended and intruding Hooded Vultures and other raptors such as Yellow-billed Kites are chased away, particularly at the beginning of the breeding season.

Eggs are laid from June to August and occasional later records are attributable to replacement clutches. A single egg is laid, but experiments in Nigeria established that two chicks can be raised together by a pair. Occasional eggs are plain white, but usually they are well marked with red-brown blotches which often form a cap at the broad end. Measurements are: 74,7 × 55,9 (10); 68,7–78,1 × 54,0–57,8.

Little is known about the incubation period except that both birds incubate and the brooding bird sits very tight. The incubation period in Nigeria was 51 days.

The newly hatched chick is sparsely covered in brown down which is replaced by a thick second coat of brown down by the age of three weeks. At a month old the first quills appear on the upperparts and wings. The feet are brownish and there is a blue eyelid ring round the eye. The chick is able to blush its face red at this stage. At five weeks the feathers begin to break from their quills and by eight weeks of age the nestling is well covered with feathers. From the age of ten weeks the black facial whiskers appear and shortly afterwards the feathers emerge on the underwing coverts. By thirteen weeks the nestling appears completely feathered although at this stage the down on the neck is chestnut-brown and cream-coloured on the crown. This down only changes to blackish at a later stage. There are no observations on the development of co-ordination of the nestling.

Observations on parental care are scant. Both parents tend the chick, and one or other of the adults is on the nest until it is seven weeks old, after which it is left alone except for feeds. The adults feed it by mouth-to-mouth regurgitation. A nest containing a five-week-old chick was watched for 25 hours on three days in Zimbabwe. It was fed each of the three days between 09h40 and 16h30 and one adult was constantly on guard at the nest.

The nestling period has not been accurately defined but is estimated to be about 100 days. In Nigeria the post-nestling period of dependence lasts for up to four months.

In 19 pair-years in Zimbabwe 0,32 young per pair per year were reared. Eggs are replaced if lost and one female relaid twice. The Giant Eagle Owl takes over nests and in one case was seen eating a Hooded Vulture nestling.

6 Cape Vulture *122*

Kransaasvoël

Gyps coprotheres

DERIVATION
vulture : dung : hunting — *gups* (G) : *kopros* (G) : *theres* (G)

IDENTIFICATION
Adult: This large vulture is predominantly white in appearance, the sexes being alike in size and coloration. There is a row of black spots along the bottom edge of the upperwing coverts. The bill is black, the eyes are yellow and the legs and feet black. The head is covered in white down but the thick blue neck is mainly naked. On either side of the crop are two bare blue 'eye' spots which are sometimes concealed by the downy chest feathers surrounding the base of the neck. In flight from below, the white body and underwing coverts contrast with the black remiges and tail. There is usually a row of black spots on the underwing coverts at their junction with the remiges. The secondaries have pale inner vanes that show up whitish in contrast to the black primaries and there is a narrow black line along the hind edge of the wing. The adult Cape Vulture can only be confused with the adult White-backed Vulture, which differs in being smaller with a thinner neck when the two species are seen together. It is usually, although not invariably, more buffy in colour than the Cape Vulture and has a white back; that of the Cape Vulture has a mottled brown and white pattern, although it may become white in some very old birds. The White-backed Vulture usually lacks the row of spots along the edge of the upperwing coverts, its eyes are black, not yellow, and its black neck is more downy and less naked at its base. In flight from below it resembles the Cape Vulture except that the secondaries are uniformly black.
Juvenile and immature: The juvenile is pale brownish with white streaks on the underparts and on the upperwing coverts. The bill, eyes, legs and feet are blackish. The head and neck are more downy than that of the adult, and the bare base of the neck and the 'eye' spots either side of the crop are red. The ruff consists of long lanceolate feathers and is more prominent than that of the adult. In flight it appears mainly pale brownish with streaking on the body and paler brownish-white underwing coverts. The secondaries do not show up paler than the

primaries at this stage. It can only be confused with the juvenile White-backed Vulture, which is altogether darker brown with narrow white streaks and no bare patch at the base of the neck. In flight the White-backed Vulture is much darker in appearance and shows a white bar near the leading edge of the wing.

Progress to adult plumage is gradual, but by the end of the first year the streaking on the underparts has disappeared, the upperparts become paler and the underwing coverts are whitish with the row of spots along their hind edge now clearly visible. The upperwing coverts moult during the second year and the streaking disappears as whitish feathers of adult plumage grow out. At this stage the eyes pale to brown. From the third year on, the adult underwing pattern develops and the secondaries become paler. By the end of the fourth year the long ruff feathers have been replaced by the downy 'powder-puff' feathers of the adult. The bare parts of the neck and the 'eye' spots are still dull reddish at this stage. From the fifth year the neck and 'eye' spots become blue and the eyes progress from orange to yellow by the sixth year, at which stage it may breed for the first time.

HABITAT
The Cape Vulture requires cliffs for breeding but may be encountered in almost any habitat including desert. It avoids continuous tracts of woodland and forest as a rule as these are unsuitable foraging areas.

STATUS AND DISTRIBUTION
This magnificent vulture is endemic to southern Africa. Formerly common and widespread, even occurring on Table Mountain above Cape Town, it is now considered threatened and vunerable and is the subject of urgent conservation attention. Breeding colonies have disappeared within living memory, particularly in the Cape Province and Orange Free State, and there is widespread evidence that the population is declining in most areas. At present there are only six colonies left where there are more than 100 pairs. The total population in southern Africa is estimated to be about 10 000 birds. At the only known colony in Zimbabwe no breed-

ing has been recorded since 1971 although birds still roost there.

What are the factors responsible for the situation and what are the remedies? Vultures are much misunderstood birds and one adverse report enjoys more credence than a hundred to the contrary. Accordingly, accounts of attacks on live sheep are rife, whereas careful field observations indicate that vultures are extremely wary about approaching even a dead animal. Prejudice is difficult to dispel and 'the hand of many farmers is turned against vultures as a clenched fist'. They are shot or poisoned, in the latter case sometimes unintentionally when bait is put out for some other animal. A single poisoned carcass can wipe out dozens of vultures. The remedy lies in favourable publicity and enlightenment, and this is in the forefront of the activities of the Vulture Study Group amongst its many other tasks and research projects. Other hazards compound direct human persecution, which includes disturbance at colonies as well as the killing of vultures by witchdoctors for 'medicines' and bones. Cape Vultures are regularly electrocuted on high-voltage electricity pylons; in one account 148 were reported killed in the south-western Transvaal in just over two years. Deaths are also caused by collision with wires, mainly by inexperienced juveniles. Solutions are being found and implemented as a result of co-operation between the Electricity Supply Commission (Escom) and representatives of the Vulture Study Group, to the mutual satisfaction of both parties — costly power failures are reduced and valuable vulture lives are saved. Vultures sometimes drown in circular reservoirs, possibly when poisoned and needing water.

Food shortage resulting from the extermination of the large migratory game herds was to a certain extent counterbalanced by the great increase in livestock. However, stock losses since 1950 have shown a considerable decline and carcasses are also often buried. This undoubtedly resulted in less carrion being available, but it is difficult to assess to what extent vultures are affected by this. However, a more insidious problem has been discovered. Previously hyaenas and other carnivores would break up the long bones of a dead animal, and vultures returning to the scene of the previous meal would swallow bone flakes which they found. These would be transported back to the nest in the breeding season and fed to the chicks as a vital source of calcium. The disappearance of hyaenas and other carnivores from most of the breeding range of the Cape Vulture has re-

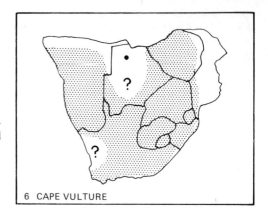

6 CAPE VULTURE

moved this source of calcium and instead the birds swallow pieces of china, glass, metal, plastic and other artefacts, all useless as a source of calcium. The lack of calcium causes a condition of metabolic bone disease (not strictly rickets) in which the paper-thin bones break, fold or bend with resultant malformation. Many a Cape Vulture chick's first flight from a cliff is also its last. The situation is being remedied by the establishment of 'vulture restaurants' where carcasses and crushed-up bones are put out. This also results in a bonus for the vulture researchers, who are able to record colour-ringed birds from colonies in the area.

It appears from present knowledge that adults are resident and usually return to their breeding or roosting cliffs nightly. However, especially outside the breeding season, it is possible that they wander to other areas and roost near a good supply of food. Juveniles and immatures have been shown to wander widely from their breeding colonies, usually in a southerly direction, and on average ringed juveniles have been recovered 390 km from their nest sites, and immatures 450 km away. It has been discovered that ranches near Kimberley serve as 'nursery' areas for young birds from colonies in the Transvaal. However, immatures have also been recorded at distances of 1 226 km and 1 192 km from their natal colonies.

The Cape Vulture occurs over most of southern Africa but is more common in the south and east of the region than in the arid west. In southern Mozambique it is an uncommon non-breeding visitor. Extralimitally it is occasionally recorded as a straggler in southern Zambia.

GENERAL HABITS

The Cape Vulture roosts colonially on cliffs and is usually on the wing by 08h00 (sometimes as early as 06h30) even on cold overcast days. The air currents round their cliff roosts make them independent of thermals to become air-borne. From a considerable height, where they are often invisible to the human eye, they scan the ground below for indications of a carcass. There is no evidence to indicate that smell is used to find carrion. More often than not food is located by observing other avian scavengers such as Pied Crows or White-necked Ravens, whose black-and-white plumage pattern makes them easily visible from the air. Mammals such as jackals or hyaenas (where they still occur) also guide them to carcasses. The vultures are spread out over several hundred kilometres and when one drops down it acts as a signal to other patrolling vultures which converge in a chain reaction towards the other descending birds. On arrival at the carcass they perch nearby, often in the company of other vulture species, and assess the situation before approaching. If anything arouses their suspicions they will not feed. Usually scavengers such as kites, crows, ravens, Tawny Eagles, Bateleurs or other vultures act as the 'all-clear' and then it becomes a case of no holds barred as the scrimmage begins. Birds bound in from the periphery with spread wings and extended necks and barge into the mêlée. Occasional dominance is achieved by a single bird spreading its wings in threat while standing on the carcass, but not for long. Quite often fights break out between two birds on the edge of the main mass and can be extremely vicious. Where the two species occur together the Cape Vulture is dominant over the White-backed Vulture, and because of their different feeding habits confrontations with Lappet-faced, White-headed and Hooded Vultures rarely occur. The scrimmage is accompanied by much noisy calling (see below).

The Cape Vulture is designed as an 'inside' feeder, hence its bare neck. Another adaptation is its tongue, which is scoop-shaped like a gardener's trowel and has projections along its side. The powerful bill rips into the muscle meat beneath the skin and into the intestines, often via the anus if the carcass has not already been opened in some way. The weak feet are not used to assist feeding. Within the short space of two or three minutes the vulture is capable of eating its fill of 1 kg of meat, and a group of about fifty Cape Vultures could probably demolish the carcass of a sheep except for the skin and bones in less than ten minutes.

The food of this species consists of muscle meat, intestines and, later, small bones if they are available. There are many accounts of attacks on sick or lambing sheep but these are rarely authenticated. Occasional cases that do occur should be weighed against the value of this vulture as an undertaker of incredible efficiency; it clears the veld of carcasses that would otherwise breed flies such as blowflies harmful to the farmer's stock. During feeding the vultures become covered in dust and their heads and necks are encrusted with dried blood. They bathe regularly and it is rare to see an unclean vulture except immediately after feeding. Even birds returning to the nests with food are clean and must presumably have bathed first. They also drink regularly, usually when they bathe.

The voice of this species, like that of other southern African vultures, is not notable for its euphony. At carcasses hoarse cackling and hissing noises are used in threat. Cackling calls are used when changing over at the nest or when bickering with neighbours. Initially nestlings emit soft cheeping notes and later loud shrieking calls in solicitation. The sounds made by this species and other southern African vultures still require more accurate description and interpretation of their functions.

BREEDING

As far as is known, no notable nuptial displays are performed. Fast flying of two or three birds making a 'jetting' noise as they hurtle through the air is probably a form of aggression rather than courtship. During such flights the top bird extends its neck and lowers its feet and may actually strike a lower bird. Flights during which birds alight on the nest ledge after a long 'spiral staircase' approach with legs lowered may have a display function. Copulation takes place on nest ledges; the male mounts the female and grips her ruff with his bill to maintain balance. The male utters a distinctive hoarse call during the process. In one observation birds were heard copulating at midnight under a full moon. Copulation may occur several months after the egg-laying period, even as late as December.

The Cape Vulture breeds colonially on cliffs, the only vulture to do so in southern Africa. As a rule cliffs face in a southerly direction so that they are in shade in the winter months when the birds breed. Nests are situated on ledges which are 15–150 m above the base of the cliff. Small colonies may number as few as six breeding pairs, while larger ones may contain over 300 pairs. However, colonies in excess of 100 pairs are now rare. In a large colony where ledges are plentiful there is evidence of groups of birds forming small 'colonies' within the main one. On suitable ledges nests may be very close to each other, sometimes almost touching. At large colonies in the Transvaal the average

(1) View of a Cape Vulture nest cliff in the Magaliesberg, Transvaal (Photograph: Peter Mundy).

(2) A nest ledge showing eggs and small chicks (Photograph: Warwick Tarboton).

(3) A nestling two weeks old.

(4) A 51-day-old nestling with skeletal deformity caused by metabolic bone disease (Photograph: Peter Mundy).

(5) A fully feathered nestling aged 75 days (Photograph: Peter Mundy).

(6) The head of a Cape Vulture to show the scoop-shaped tongue (Photograph: Peter Mundy).

distance between nests was 2,3 m with a range of 0,8 to 7,5 m.

Nests are very variable in the amount of material used and in some cases hardly any nest at all is built. Usually nests are flattened structures for which some sticks and much grass are used. The average of 46 nests was 70 cm across, 11 cm deep and with a cup 35 cm across. Nests vary from 45–100 cm across, 2–30 cm deep and with a cup 25–50 cm in diameter. Green leaves and plants may be used for nest lining and are added during the incubation period and nestling period. Nest material is gathered from the vicinity of the ledges, which may become denuded of grass, which is killed also by the excreta of the birds. In one case a fire that swept past a colony did not burn along the bare ledges, although the acrid smoke was thought to be the cause of mortality of a few chicks which fell from their nests when they panicked. Nest material is collected and carried in the bill and then trodden into shape. It is not known whether both male and female collect material, but as they share in other duties at the nest they may be presumed to do so. There are no observations on the duration of nest building.

The same nest-sites are used in successive years as a rule. In studies at several colonies an overall nest-site occupancy of 81 per cent was observed.

Although individual squabbles may break out when birds alight at the wrong nest, the vultures are generally tolerant of each other. Pied Crows and White-necked Ravens which frequent the colony for scraps are only occasionally threatened. Black Eagles elicit a vigorous threat response from birds on their nests. These eagles have been seen to prey on nestlings and to strike and kill a Cape Vulture in mid-air. Baboons are probably potential predators on nestlings, but are ignored when feeding above or below the cliffs. Humans are not attacked when at the nest and very occasionally a vulture will crouch protectively over its nestling with an observer right beside it.

Eggs are laid from April to July with a peak in May. Amongst groups of birds in the same colony a high degree of synchronous laying has been observed. The normal clutch is a single egg but very occasionally two eggs are found in a nest. At present it is not known if these are laid by a single female or whether two birds have laid in the same nest. The eggs are elongated chalky-white ovals. Occasionally eggs have some red freckles and blotches. By the end of the incubation period they become heavily nest-stained. Measurements are 91,7 × 68,3 (239); 83,2–103,0 × 62,5–73,8.

Both sexes incubate. Observations reveal that change-overs occur between 09h55 and 16h22 (average 13h44). The longest unrelieved stint by a single bird was almost 94 hours. The sitting bird occasionally stands up and changes position and rolls the egg about its axis before settling again. Sometimes it leaves the nest for short periods of one to seven minutes to shake and preen, to gather nest material or filch it from a neighbour's nest, or to chase a stranger away from near the nest. When the birds change over they are usually together on the nest for less than two minutes and no greeting ceremony takes place. Eggs are never left uncovered for more than about seven minutes, usually about three minutes. The incubation period has been obtained as approximately 56 days on a number of occasions; in one case it was between 57 and 59 days.

The newly hatched chick is covered in white down over its pink skin. There is a bare patch at the rear of the neck at its base. Its eyes are black and weakly open. At four weeks old it is clad in a thick second coat of white down. By six weeks old the main dorsal feather tracts emerge through the down and a week later the ventral tracts appear. The dorsal surface is well covered by nine weeks old and between ten and eleven weeks the nestling appears almost fully feathered with the characteristic pattern of white streaks on the upperwing coverts. This pattern causes it to blend in with the droppings on the rocks surrounding the nest so that it is not easily detected from a distance. The last area to be covered with feathers is on the underwing coverts, which are fully feathered by the age of fifteen weeks. By the age of eighteen weeks the bare skin at the base of the neck which was previously greenish has changed to red.

Very little is recorded on the development of the co-ordination of the nestling. By the age of nine days it shuffles backwards to defecate over the edge of the nest. It is not known when it first stands or begins wing exercises. From the age of about twelve weeks it reacts to human intruders by erecting its feathers, particularly those of the ruff. Another reaction to danger is to hang the head and shake it violently from side to side until it vomits.

Both parents take turns in tending and feeding the chick throughout the nestling period. Small young are closely brooded and are fed by mouth-to-mouth regurgitation, a method used even when the young are fully grown. Very rarely food may be regurgitated onto the nest and then picked up by the nestling. Small nestlings are fed several times during the day but large young practically empty the parent's crop in one feeding session. The incoming bird regurgitates almost immediately and sometimes the adult that has been on the nest also takes food from its partner's bill. The chick solicits for another feed by cheeping and trying to tap the adult's bill with its own. An adult is on the nest guarding the chick until it is at least 90 days old and even after this age a parent is often on the nest. One nestling 125 days old had an adult in attendance for half the time that it was watched. The bird on the nest recognises its mate seconds before it arrives by glancing around or standing up. When young are small the pair may remain on the nest for quite long periods up to 180 minutes but usually for about twelve minutes. Once the chicks are about eight to twelve weeks old the parents are not on the nest together for more than ten minutes, usually about three. Change-overs at this stage of the nesting cycle occur between 11h00 and 16h00 (average 13h20). The chick may still nestle its head and neck beneath the parent when ten weeks old. Bones (or substituted artefacts) are brought to the nest throughout the nestling period, but after the chick is six weeks old the numbers found on nests decrease as most of them are swallowed.

The nestling period is approximately 140 days, but more observations are required. Initially the young vulture flies clumsily and has difficulty in alighting. When an adult arrives with food it flies back to the nest ledge and begs vigorously, crouches, shakes its wings up and down and shrieks loudly. Even at this stage it is still fed by mouth-to-mouth regurgitation. Young up to three weeks out of the nest are fed daily and spend about 80 per cent of their time near the nest. The adults visit them for brief periods which are mainly concerned with feeding. Once the young are ten weeks out of the nest they are rarely seen at the nest ledges and are only occasionally fed by the adults. Young about five months out of the nest have been seen at nest ledges but they no longer beg. Precise details on when young become independent are lacking and are understandably difficult to obtain.

A total of 171 pair-years at colonies in the Transvaal gave an overall breeding success figure of 0,44 young per pair per year, with a range of 0,39–0,53. Further observations are needed, especially at threatened colonies where rapid decline is taking place. In one conservation article the Cape Vulture was called 'Twentieth Century Vulture'; all those who have had an opportunity to watch this magnificent soaring scavenger would want to wish it well into the twenty-first century and beyond, even though the odds are so heavily against it.

7 White-backed Vulture /23

Witrugaasvoël

Gyps africanus   PLATES 4 AND 5

DERIVATION
vulture : African— *gups* (G) : *africanus* (L)

IDENTIFICATION
Adult: The sexes are alike in size and coloration. The plumage is mainly buffy-white with a white back which is only visible if the wings are opened or when it is in flight. The colour of very old birds is almost white. The bill, eyes, legs and feet are blackish, as is the skin on the face and on the neck which is sparsely covered in whitish down. There is a downy 'powderpuff' ruff at the base of the neck. The crop, only visible when distended, is brown and the bare 'eye' spots on either side of it are usually hidden by the downy chest feathers. In flight from below it appears mainly whitish with white underwing coverts and black remiges and tail. It can be confused only with the adult Cape Vulture; differences are discussed in the text on that species.

Juvenile and immature: The juvenile is dark brown with narrow white streaking on the wing coverts and underparts. The lanceolate feathers of the ruff also have white central streaks. The skin of the neck is greenish, but is almost entirely obscured by thick woolly white down which also covers the head except for the bare blackish or greenish face. The bill, eyes, legs and feet are blackish. The back is dark brown with white streaks and the change in the colour of the back is the most useful feature for establishing the age of immatures. In flight it appears mainly dark brown from below with white streaks on the underwing coverts and body. There is a narrow white bar near the leading edge of the wing, and the remiges and tail are black. The only possible confusion is with the juvenile Cape Vulture and differences are given in the text on that species.

Progress to adult plumage is gradual and is basically similar to that of the Cape Vulture. First moulting starts when it is a year old and the paler brown contour feathers still have white streaks. The back pattern remains unchanged. During the second year the thick 'cotton wool' down on the head and neck begins to disappear slowly and patches of black skin appear. Little change occurs until the end of the third year except that the plumage becomes paler and the white streaks disappear. During the fourth year the long ruff feathers disintegrate to be replaced by the 'powder-puff'. The back feathers have white edges at this stage, and in the fifth year the back is half brown and half white. Finally, in the sixth year, the back is white except for a few brown feathers, which disappear in the seventh year. Immatures may breed when four years old, the only typical southern African vulture species to do so.

HABITAT

This species is typical of bushveld savanna and open plains in Africa. It avoids forest or continuous tracts of thick woodland as these areas are unsuitable for foraging.

STATUS AND DISTRIBUTION

This is the commonest vulture in southern Africa. Its breeding range has inevitably shrunk in more settled areas but it still occurs on large ranches. It is the common vulture in game reserves in southern Africa and is thus not in any danger, unlike the Cape Vulture which breeds almost entirely outside these safe areas. Its occurrence largely overlaps that of carnivores such as hyaenas which break up bones, so there is no evidence yet of metabolic bone disease affecting nestlings as with the Cape Vulture.

The pattern of movements is similar to that of the Cape Vulture; juveniles and immatures wandering more widely than adults. Information from ringing established that three adults moved between 67 and 362 km from their place of ringing. One fifth or sixth year sub-adult ringed in north-west Zimbabwe was recovered in Swaziland six months later, a distance of 980 km to the south. Five immature birds moved an average of 275 km (range 117–395 km) and two juveniles were recorded 647 km and 815 km from their place of ringing.

Distribution extends from the vicinity of the Orange River northwards, but this vulture is

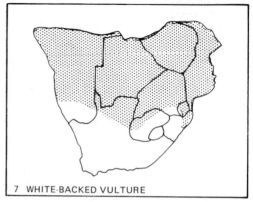

7 WHITE-BACKED VULTURE

largely absent from eastern Orange Free State, south-eastern Transvaal, Lesotho and Natal, although common in Zululand game reserves. Extralimitally it occurs northwards to the Sahara but not in the forested areas of the Congo basin.

GENERAL HABITS

The habits of this species are basically similar to those of the Cape Vulture except that it roosts in trees, often gregariously. Despite statements to the contrary, it is also an early riser and may arrive at a carcass before 08h00. It feeds in a similar way and has the same shape of tongue as the Cape Vulture. Observations in north-west Zimbabwe showed that immature Bateleurs and White-headed Vultures were the species which arrived first and acted as 'indicators' to foraging White-backed Vultures. However, the Bateleurs rarely fed first. White-headed and Hooded Vultures were usually the first to eat, both being displaced as soon as the White-backed Vultures came down to the carcass. For observation purposes an impala was put out with one hind leg removed (for the observer) and was opened up along the abdomen. The birds filled their crops between two and eight minutes, the average time 4,7 minutes. An impala was often consumed within ten minutes and in one case 23 kg of meat was eaten by approximately 50 White-backed Vultures in three minutes, an awesome spectacle. All that remained was skin, bones and a bare patch of dusty earth where the scrimmage had taken place. The birds are covered in dust and caked blood which they wash off at their nearest bathing place.

The vocalisations of this species are similar to those of the Cape Vulture.

BREEDING

No particular nuptial displays appear to be performed. However, a group of thirteen birds was seen circling slowly over a nesting area, some with lowered legs and outstretched necks — perhaps some form of communal breeding display. Frequently a pair of birds will 'jet' in noisily towards the nesting tree; this fast flight may have a display function. Copulation occurs in or near the nest tree but also in trees near carcasses. It is a clumsy affair, the male taking about a minute to get his balance as he clutches onto the female's ruff with his bill. The actual mating takes a few seconds to the accompaniment of hoarse calls and the female then throws him off or he jumps off. Both birds invariably preen afterwards and very rarely may preen each other. Occasionally incidents of 'rape' occur and there are also triangle relationships. In one case a female mated and then in the next twenty minutes she mated five times with a second male.

This species nests in loose colonies, often along river valleys where the tallest trees are. The average inter-nest distance of 141 nests in Zimbabwe was 0,37 km and at Kimberley the average distance was 0,41 km, although in the latter area some nests may not have been found. Rarely, two occupied nests may be found in the same tree or in adjacent trees. Occasionally nests are solitary; one was 7,6 km from the nearest pair. Various species of acacias are favoured, 91 per cent of 143 nest trees in Zimbabwe. At Kimberley all 80 nest trees were acacias, 78 of them camel thorns. In the Kruger National Park 65 per cent of 106 nests were in acacias. The average height of 86 nests in Zimbabwe was 18,6 m (range 12,2–24,4 m) and at Kimberley, where the trees were more stunted, the average height of 18 nests was 7,0 m (range 4,9–8,6 m). In the Kruger National Park the heights of nests ranged from 10–25 m. Nests are situated mostly on the canopy of trees, although occasional nests are built in forks beneath the canopy. These latter sites are always fairly open so that there are no problems of access for the vultures. In the Kruger National Park nests are often surrounded by Buffalo Weaver nests and may be built on top of these. The measurements of nests in Zimbabwe, Kruger National Park and at Kimberley varied from 34–100 cm in width, 10–90 cm deep and with cups 18–50 cm across. In Zimbabwe 86 nests averaged 64 cm in width, 27 cm deep and with a cup 29 cm across. The corresponding averages for 27 nests at Kimberley were 83 cm, 21 cm, and 40 cm. These latter nests were wider and flatter than those in Zimbabwe and were adapted to the dense flat-topped canopies of the camel thorn trees on which they were built. Nests are built mainly with non-thorny sticks up

to a maximum diameter of 3 cm and are lined with dry grass and quite often with green leaves. Sprays are plucked from leafy trees and carried in the bill. Leaves may be found in the nest prior to laying, throughout the incubation period and during most of the nestling period.

Nests repair or building may begin several weeks, sometimes up to seven weeks, before laying. It is not known if both birds build, but it is likely that they share this activity along with other duties at the nest.

Sites may be occupied for a number of years in succession, for nine consecutive years in one case in Kenya. In Zimbabwe in 208 possible site-years there was an 82 per cent occupancy of nests. Sometimes nests are taken over by other species such as Saddlebills or Tawny Eagles. Nests also blow down in high winds, or trees are pushed over by elephants or die and fall down after being debarked by elephants. The White-backed Vultures may themselves take over the nest of another eagle or vulture.

This species does not appear to be territorial and White-backed Vultures and other species are only threatened or chased away from the immediate vicinity of the nest. However, on occasions, strangers are tolerated at the nest, but they have not been seen to feed young and are even threatened by nestlings. Thus there is no evidence of co-operative breeding as has been suggested.

Nest sites may be occupied, albeit sporadically, during the rainy season when the birds are not breeding. Eggs are laid from the first half of April to July in southern Africa. In Zimbabwe laying occurs mainly from April to June whereas south of the Limpopo the season is mainly May and June. In Zimbabwe the start of laying was found to vary from year to year, but there was no obvious correlation between early or late laying and the amount of rainfall the preceding wet season. A single egg is laid but there is one record of two eggs in a nest in Zululand. Eggs are chalky-white, often with some rusty and lilac speckles near the broad end. Occasional eggs are handsomely spotted with red. Two-thirds of 33 eggs examined in the Kruger National Park had some markings. As incubation progresses eggs become heavily nest-stained. Measurements are: 88,2 × 66,4 (110); 79,5–96,5 × 59,2–71,5.

Both sexes share incubation and the relieving bird arrives with a full or nearly full crop. One bird incubated without a break for 63 hours. The sitting bird stands from time to time for several minutes and shuffles about, preens, pokes in the nest sticks and turns the egg before resettling. The egg is rarely left exposed to the sun and never for more than about twenty minutes. The incubation period obtained to the nearest day on two occasions in the Kruger National Park was 56 and 58 days.

The newly hatched chick is covered in pale grey down beneath which the skin is greenish. The eyes are open. At two weeks old the down is paler on the head but darker grey on the rest of the body. The three-week-old chick is covered with a thicker second coat of dark brownish-grey down, although this is not invariable and some nestlings remain pale grey. In the fourth week first quills emerge through the down on the wings and on the dorsal surface. A week later these tracts are fully out and the tail quills are emerging. At six weeks the ventral tracts emerge. By seven weeks the feathers are covering the dorsal surface and by ten weeks the nestling is well feathered with its head and neck covered in thick white down. The feathers of the underwing coverts emerge at eleven weeks and they are fully out by fourteen weeks.

Miscellaneous observations on the development of co-ordination of the chick indicate that it defecates over the nest edge at an early age. It preens itself when about a month old. At the age of eight weeks it threatens intruders at the nest by sitting erect, spreading its wings, stretching its neck and hissing. It cannot stand and balance at this age but can stand and walk well by the age of twelve weeks. Vigorous wing exercises begin from about the age of sixteen weeks.

The nestling is constantly brooded, shaded or guarded until it is 50 days old. Thereafter during daylight it is alone 6,5 per cent of the time from 51 to 70 days, 15 per cent from 71 to 90 days, 44 per cent from 91 to 110 days and 53 per cent from 111 to 120 days. These results were obtained from 315 hours of observation on 38 days at nests in Zimbabwe. Both sexes take turns at the nest and the incoming bird feeds the chick by mouth-to-mouth regurgitation, a method used throughout the nestling period. Bones are swallowed last by the adult and therefore regurgitated first, so that the hungry chick swallows them first. Bones are found lying on the nest until the chick is about six weeks old but not thereafter, indicating that it can cope

with all sizes of bones brought at this age. Although a number of bones too large to swallow and some artefacts were found in Kimberley nests, there is as yet no evidence there of the metabolic bone disease which affects Cape Vulture nestlings (see account under that species). During the 38 days of observations in Zimbabwe change-overs averaged one every 1,5 days until the chick was 90 days old and once every 1,7 days thereafter. No greeting ceremonies take place and the incoming bird starts to feed the chick immediately. When it is larger the chick solicits vigorously by crouching low, flapping its wings, which are partly open, and shrieking noisily. Most change-overs occur during the middle part of the day from 10h00 to 14h00 and the range is from 08h30 to 15h30. Even when the nestling is alone on the nest its parent may be in the area. In one case an immature Bateleur alighted at a nest containing a 94-day-old chick, which called out loudly; an adult suddenly appeared and chased off the eagle.

The nestling may jump from the nest before it can fly at 95 days old, if the tree is climbed. One accurate nestling period in the Kruger National Park was 126 plus or minus 2 days. A captive nestling made its first flight at the age of 125 days. Young birds crouch in the nest even after they can fly so that it is easy to estimate the period incorrectly as too long. Observations on the post-nestling period are scant but juveniles return to their nests for several months after their first flight. One was seen begging vigorously from a parent on its nest five and a half months after it had left the nest. Juveniles apparently become independent about six months after leaving the nest.

In 199 pair-years in Zimbabwe 0,52 young per pair per year were raised, the highest figure for any species of southern African vulture. Causes of breeding failure include human interference, predation on nestlings by small carnivores such as the Serval, chicks falling from nests, infertile eggs, eggs eaten by Pied Crows in one case, nests blowing down and trees being pushed over by elephants. Eggs may be replaced if lost for some reason. As far as is known this species breeds annually.

(1) View of a typical White-backed Vulture's nest situated at the top of a tree.

(2) A nestling four weeks old. (Photograph: Peter Mundy).

(3) A nestling approximately eight weeks old.

8 Lappet-faced Vulture

Swartaasvoël

Torgos tracheliotus

PLATES 4 AND 5

DERIVATION
vulture : throat : ear — *torgos* (G) : *trachelos* (G) : *otos* (G)

The compound Greek word *tracheliotus* draws attention to the naked throat and head of this species, the only bald vulture in Africa.

IDENTIFICATION
Adult: This impressive species is the largest southern African vulture in size although the Cape Vulture weighs more (about 6,5 kg and 7,5 kg respectively). The sexes are not distinguishable. Its predominantly black coloration is relieved by the distinctive white tibial down or 'trousers'. The chest is also covered in thick white down overlaid with long, lanceolate black feathers. The back of the neck is surrounded by an 'Elizabethan frill' of black feathers and white down. The massive bill is pale yellowish, the eyes are black, the cere, legs and feet are pale blue. The bare red skin of the throat and head has folds or lappets, and flushes deeper red in excitement. In flight from below the almost wholly black coloration is relieved by the prominent white 'trousers' and a narrow white bar near the leading edge of the wing.

Juvenile and immature: The juvenile appears almost wholly black. The 'trousers' are blackish-brown and the down on the chest is greyish. The bill is dark horn-coloured, the eyes are black and the legs and feet are dull greyish-pink. The bare skin of the throat and head is dull pinkish and has lappets like the adult. In flight it appears completely blackish and at a height would be difficult to distinguish from the juvenile Hooded Vulture; only a view of the longer bill of this species would separate them. The juvenile White-headed Vulture also appears mainly dark from below but has a narrow white bar separating the underwing coverts and remiges.

The age of immatures may be approximately assessed by the amount of white down on the 'trousers' which takes between five and six years to become fully white. A little white begins to appear at the end of the second year, and the 'trousers' are half brown and half white during the fourth year. At the end of the first year the young vulture has acquired a dappling of white feathers on its mantle and upperwing coverts which gradually disappear, except for occasional white feathers, by the time it is adult. The amount of dappling of immatures varies individually. The bill begins to turn yellow before it is a year old. The down on the chest becomes whitish during the second year, much more rapidly than that on the 'trousers', and the overlying lanceolate feathers become fewer so that the down shows through more clearly. The white underwing bar begins to appear between the first and second year. At this stage the legs and feet are turning bluish and the skin on the head is becoming more reddish.

HABITAT
This species occurs in bushveld savanna and especially in areas of low rainfall. In the arid western regions of Namibia it is the commonest resident vulture.

STATUS AND DISTRIBUTION
The range of this species has decreased, especially in the Cape Province where it is now only rarely recorded. In South Africa generally it is uncommon outside game reserves. It is most common in the Namib Desert in Namibia, but even there it is threatened by prospecting and proposed mining activities, some of which

A juvenile Lappet-faced Vulture to show white dappling on its mantle (Photograph: Peter Mundy).

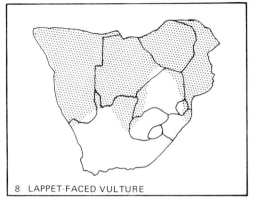

8 LAPPET-FACED VULTURE

intrude into the Namib Desert National Park. It is extremely sensitive to disturbance at the nest, and desertions have been caused by prospectors camping or resting under nests.

It appears that adults are resident although they may wander widely, particularly outside the breeding season. Juveniles and immatures disperse from their natal areas and colour-ringed birds from the Namib Desert have been resighted at distances of 120, 264, 480, and 700 km from their nests. The last record was of an immature seen in the Kalahari Gemsbok National Park.

Its distribution is now mainly north of the Orange River and it is largely absent from the Orange Free State, Lesotho and Natal, although it still occurs in Zululand, mainly in game reserves. Extralimitally it extends north-wards into the Sahara but is not found in the heavily forested regions of west Africa and the Congo basin. A small population occurs in the Arava Valley between the Dead Sea and the Red Sea in Israel.

GENERAL HABITS

This vulture is normally seen flying singly or in pairs. It is unusual to see more than a dozen Lappet-faced Vultures at a mixed gathering of vultures at a carcass and often only a few are present. In areas such as the Namib Desert, where it is the commonest vulture, it is sociable and gathers in groups at water-holes during the middle part of the day to bathe, drink and sunbathe with spread wings. They may loaf around these assembly points, sometimes in the company of a few Cape Vultures, for hours on end with only occasional signs of aggression between individual birds. As many as 26 Lappet-faced Vultures have gathered at the carcass of an Ostrich in the Namib.

Contrary to popular belief, it is not one of the first vultures to arrive at a carcass, and usually arrives last. Frequently Lappet-faced Vultures

show no inclination to feed and merely hang about on the outskirts of the mêlée. However, if an adult wishes to, it moves in to dominate the carcass and all other vultures give way. Immatures appear to be unable to establish dominance like the adults. This species is capable of pulling off and swallowing large pieces of skin with its powerful bill. Sometimes it moves away with a chunk of meat which it holds down with its feet like an eagle while tearing off pieces. It also pulls shreds and ligaments off bones that are too tough for any of the other vultures to manage. Unlike the Cape and White-backed Vultures it is a clean 'outside' feeder and does not soil its plumage. Its rate of feeding is much slower than these species and it rarely fills its crop. Occasionally it flies off with a piece of food in its bill.

The 'gripping' toes are strong and the claws well curved. This feature, combined with its frequent lack of interest in large carcasses, suggests that it feeds mainly on smaller carrion and probably kills small animals. The circum-stantial evidence from food remains found on nests supports this view. The only direct evi-dence of killing live animals comes from Kenya where it has been seen to prey on helpless young flamingoes as well as to eat the eggs. Food remains on nests in Zimbabwe, although they included large ungulates and carnivores, were mainly smaller items: duiker, steenbok, grysbok, goat, warthog, jackal, hare, mon-goose, civet, polecat, pangolin, porcupine, small rodents, monitor (leguaan), birds (five species) and fish. Many bones, including numer-ous hooves, have been recorded at nests. It has also been seen feeding on terrapin eggs and on insects such as termites and locusts. It also scavenges road kills, in one case a Secretary Bird.

The voice of this species is little known and it is largely silent. Shrill, sibilant whistling calls are emitted during copulation. Large young solicit with a shrill whistle.

BREEDING

No aerial nuptial displays have been des-cribed. Copulation takes place mostly on the nest but also in trees near carcasses. The male crouches on the female's back with bent legs and grips her ruff with his bill while flapping his wings to maintain his balance. Mating lasts 10–25 seconds. Sometimes, both before and after copulation, the birds display to each other by simultaneously hanging their heads and necks and then raising them again to full stretch, at the same time tilting their heads sideways.

(1) View of a Lappet-faced Vulture's nest in the Namib Desert.

(2) Close-up of an egg.

(3) A day-old chick (Photograph: Angus Anthony).

(4) A nestling about five or six weeks old.

(5) A 90-day-old nestling (Photograph: Angus Anthony).

(6) A Lappet-faced Vulture moves in with spread wings to dominate a carcass (Photograph: Peter Mundy).

Nests are built in the trees on top of the canopy and although cliffs are very occasionally used as sites elsewhere in Africa there are no such records in southern Africa. Usually the tallest trees in the area are selected and in the Namib Desert nests are most often situated in acacias along wadis. In the Gonarezhou National Park in the lowveld of Zimbabwe the preferred habitat was scrub mopane, where the tallest trees were Purple-pod Terminalias, used in 93 per cent of cases. From these high vantage points the vultures had a good view of the surrounding country. Quite often they use trees growing on anthills, usually covered by spiny scramblers such as *Capparis tomentosa* which make a nest difficult to see from below. The average height of 62 nests in the Gonarezhou National Park was 7,1 m (range 4,3–11,0 m) and in another study area in north-west Zimbabwe the average height of twelve nests was 8,8 m (range 6,1–15,2 m). Nests in the Namib Desert would average much lower than this but no figures are available.

The nest is an enormous flat structure of sturdy sticks, very similar in appearance to that of a Secretary Bird. In one case a Secretary Bird took over the old nest of a Lappet-faced Vulture. The average of 30 nests in Zimbabwe was 178 cm across the long axis (range 120–220 cm) and 50 cm deep (range 30–70 cm). The shallow lined central depression was 71 cm across (range 50–100 cm) and 18 cm (range 10–30 cm) below the outer rim of sticks at its centre. The nest is lined with short clumps of grass and grass stalks but as the nestling period progresses it becomes covered with a thick mat of hair from decomposed pellets. Green lining is very rarely added.

Repair of an old nest may start some two months before the egg is laid but there is no information on how long it takes to build a new nest. The birds may spend long periods perched on the nest at this stage. Observations on nest building in Zimbabwe established that the male left the nest for periods of about two minutes and returned each time with a stick in his bill. He attempted to place the sticks but the female would wrest them from him and place them herself. On the Serengeti plains in east Africa both birds have been seen to bring sticks to the nest.

This species regularly builds alternate nests which are clumped within the territory and are never much more than a kilometre apart, usually much less. It appears that moves to new sites are frequent; a pair may have up to four alternate sites. In the Gonarezhou National Park 25 pairs had 64 nests, an average of 2,6 nests per pair. Breeding pairs were spaced an average of 2,9 km apart (range 0,7–10,5 km) and there is evidence of regular spacing to support a degree of territoriality. Further evidence for this is that non-breeding birds occupy their nests during the breeding season, presumably to prevent a new pair moving into their area. It appears also that closely adjacent pairs adopt a 'flight path' when leaving or returning to their nests to avoid flying too close to their neighbours. Early in the breeding season two birds may perform 'tumbling' flights during which the upper bird extends its legs and drops towards the other. Both twist and turn as the lower bird takes evasive action to avoid attack. Apart from these occasions most territorial defence seems to be confined to the immediate vicinity of the nest. Little is recorded on relationships with other species except for a remarkable case in east Africa of a Greater Kestrel sitting on eggs on the vulture's nest only 65 cm from the incubating vulture. The two birds were in full view of each other.

Eggs are laid from May to July. In Zimbabwe it was found that July records were mostly replacement clutches after the failure of the first. The laying peak was found to vary from year to year in one study in Zimbabwe. Normally a single egg is laid but in rare instances there appear to be genuine records of two eggs laid by the same female. In captivity there is a case of a female laying two eggs. Eggs are pure white or are covered with rusty spots and blotches mainly in a cap at the broad end. Markings are very variable and some eggs are heavily blotched. As incubation progresses they become nest-stained. Measurements are: 92,7 × 71,1 (56); 85,6–102,0 × 66,9–78,6.

During a four-day watch at a nest in Zimbabwe it was established that both birds incubate. One bird sat continuously, including overnight, for at least 75 hours. During daylight one day the bird stood up sixteen times for an average of four minutes. It preened, looked about and prodded in the nest lining. The brooding bird sits very tight and because of the large nest cannot be seen from below. It is very wary about returning to the nest once it has been flushed and observers should keep disturbance at a minimum during this period. The incubation period is close on 56 days and may be slightly longer.

The newly hatched chick is covered in white down on its crown and body but the back of its head and neck are naked with lappets already forming. The skin of the body beneath the down is pink and on the face and legs it is greenish-grey. The black eyes are open. By the age of three weeks the down is thicker and has changed to a smoky-grey, but on the head the down is disappearing. At four weeks old the down covering is more dense and the quills of the feather tracts begin to emerge on the dorsal surface. The feathers start to emerge in the fifth week, by which time the skin of the head is whitish and the cere and legs are grey. The lappets are well formed by this stage. By the seventh week the upperparts are covered by feathers and they are beginning to emerge on the ventral surface. At nine weeks old the 'trousers' are covered in grey down and the chick appears fully feathered when lying down. The underwing coverts are still downy at this stage and only by the age of thirteen weeks have all the feather tracts on the underparts emerged fully. The ruff is well formed as a full 'Elizabethan frill' at this stage. The 'trousers' only turn brown about a month after leaving the nest.

Observations on the development of co-ordination of the nestling are scanty. It is not known when it first stands but it can do so by seven weeks old. It is docile and can be handled until about fourteen weeks old, when it becomes aggressive and pecks at an observer. In excitement it is able to blush its face red. At this stage it adopts a prone intruder position if it sees anyone approaching. Wing exercises start at this time and the nestling jumps up and down in the nest. It may also pounce on items such as a piece of skin in the nest, in the manner of a young eagle. Sometimes it stands with its back to the sun and hangs its head down in its own shadow; presumably a method of keeping cool.

Both parents share in the care of the nestling and until it is 30 days old an adult is constantly on the nest brooding or shading it. The adults may leave the chick alone at times after this, but until it is 60 days old a parent is usually on the nest. From this time on it is left alone on the nest except for feeds. The drop in parental attention coincides with the stage at which the chick is fully feathered dorsally. The nestling is fed by mouth-to-mouth regurgitation and during the process the adult's face flushes red while that of the chick remains pale. Once it is well grown it begs by crouching low and flat while flapping its partly open wings. It taps the parent's bill with its own and calls excitedly. Observations at two nests with young nearly ready to leave established that food was brought between 09h40 and 13h50 and that both parents may feed the nestling during the course of a day. Visits were brief and lasted between two and ten minutes. During the nest-ling period the adults are never on the nest together, except briefly when they change over, but they may perch together in the vicinity. In the Gonarezhou National Park in Zimbabwe the adults foraged up to 42 km from their nests, to areas where goat flocks occurred and carrion was available, but apart from this nothing is known of their foraging ranges.

Although young may fly prematurely before 120 days, the natural nestling period appears to be about 125 days. One flew for the first time in 128 days. In one observation the nestling made its first flight of 300 m without any effort or warning. It returned to the nest three and half hours later when it saw its parent approaching. The juvenile continues to be fed at the nest, but in one case an adult regurgitated food onto an alternate nest nearby and the juvenile flew over to feed on it. Juveniles may be fed until at least four and a half months after they leave their nests and may use them as perches for about another month. They are probably independent of adult care after they have been out of the nest for about five months.

In 42 pair-years in Zimbabwe 0,41 young per pair per year were reared. However, it appears that this species may not breed annually because of the long breeding cycle. In one study area in Zimbabwe a third of the chicks died, some possibly as the result of desertion caused by the observer's visits to the nests. If an egg is lost early in the incubation period it may be replaced. In view of the sensitivity of this species at the nest great caution needs to be exercised when making observations.

9 White-headed Vulture

Witkopaasvoël

Trigonoceps occipitalis

PLATES 4 AND 5

DERIVATION

triangle : head : occipital — *trigon* (G) : *ceps* (L) : *occipitalis* (L)

The name derives from the rather pointed occiput of this species.

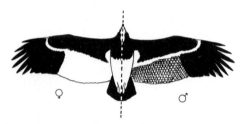

White-headed Vulture to show difference between male and female.

IDENTIFICATION

Adult: This species is sexually dimorphic, a distinction only very recently discovered (and too late to include in the coloured plates, where a female is shown). The female has white inner secondaries, the male dark grey, a difference that is easily seen both perched and in flight. The White-headed Vulture is a striking and beautiful bird more like an eagle than a vulture in appearance. The upperparts are black with pale buff edges to the wing coverts. Its 'Elizabethan frill' ruff and breast are black, contrasting with the white head, crop, abdomen and 'trousers'. The bill is orange-red, the cere blue, the large eyes are amber, and the legs and feet are dull red. The bare skin of the face is pale pink but can flush red in excitement. In flight its pattern is distinctive, the white abdomen and white or grey inner secondaries contrasting with the rest of the black underparts. Its characteristic plumage, both perched and in flight, prevents confusion with any other species.

Juvenile and immature: The juvenile is almost wholly dark brown. Its bill and cere are coloured like the adult but the eyes are dark brown and the legs and feet pale pink. It is superficially similar to the juvenile Lappet-faced Vulture but may be distinguished by the colour of the bill and cere and the brown down on the head. In flight it appears entirely blackish-brown except for a narrow white bar dividing the underwing coverts and remiges. The white bar prevents

confusion with the juvenile Lappet-faced Vulture, the juvenile Hooded Vulture and to a lesser extent the adult Hooded Vulture.

Progress to adult plumage is not well known but probably takes several years. Once it is a year old, white down gradually appears on the head and crop as well as some white feathers on the abdomen. The secondaries grow out white or grey at the first moult so that immatures may be sexed from this stage onwards. Towards the end of the second year the pale buff edges to the wing coverts appear, giving them a variegated appearance.

HABITAT

This species occurs in bushveld savanna, including quite dry country, but is not found in desert in southern Africa like the Lappet-faced Vulture.

STATUS AND DISTRIBUTION

Although nowhere numerous, this vulture may be regularly encountered in suitable habitat. In South Africa it is now rarely seen outside game reserves.

Adults appear to remain in the same areas but immatures seem to wander about. However, they are tolerated in areas occupied by adults and are not driven away. One bird ringed as an immature was recorded 117 km from its place of capture.

The White-headed Vulture's distribution is mainly in the eastern half of southern Africa from Zululand northwards to Zimbabwe, but it also occurs westwards across northern Bots-

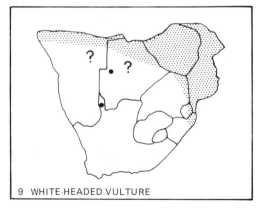

9 WHITE-HEADED VULTURE

wana to northern Namibia, as well as in the Kalahari Gemsbok National Park.

GENERAL HABITS

The White-headed Vulture, usually seen singly or in pairs soaring over the bushveld, is the most solitary of all southern African vultures. Observations in Zimbabwe established that after immature Bateleurs they were the next most frequent species to locate a carcass first. On many occasions it would arrive so soon after a Bateleur that it must undoubtedly have followed its movements. It was also observed that immature White-headed Vultures usually arrived before adults. Although this species landed at the carcass first in most cases, Hooded Vultures were most often the first to start feeding. Between three and eight White-headed Vultures (average six) were recorded at carcasses. Though adults, and to a lesser extent immatures, are dominant over individual White-backed Vultures, they are forced to retreat once the latter species comes down in numbers and the scramble for the carcass begins. Adult White-headed Vultures show no aggression towards Lappet-faced Vultures but immatures are able to dominate immature Lappet-faced Vultures on occasions. The White-headed Vulture is a clean 'outside' feeder and never becomes soiled or dusty. It cannot rip off skin although it sometimes tries to. On occasions it will rob White-backed Vultures of pieces of meat they have difficulty in swallowing. Like the Lappet-faced Vulture it can hold down chunks of meat with its eagle-like feet and tear off pieces. In common with other vultures it is often seen near water where it drinks and bathes.

As it has to give way to White-backed Vultures arriving in force at a carcass, the White-headed Vulture is frequently not able to fill its crop. It appears that it often feeds on smaller dead animals which it is able to locate first, or take over from other scavengers such as Yellow-billed Kites, Bateleurs and Tawny Eagles. It also feeds on road casualties, in one case a White-backed Vulture which had itself been killed as it fed on a small animal killed on the road. There is a record of one feeding in perfect amity with a Tawny Eagle on a hare killed by traffic. It also pirates food caught by other species and has been seen to rob Marabous of fish. In one incident an African Fish Eagle pirated a fish from a Marabou and was in turn robbed by a White-headed Vulture. Several other observations indicate that Bateleurs and Tawny Eagles are robbed of their kills, although in some cases it may be that the vulture had made the kill itself. There is much circumstantial and some direct evidence that the White-headed Vulture captures its own prey. It is known to kill helpless young flamingoes in Kenya and it captures catfish and Bullfrogs in drying pools. One was seen with a recently caught Puffadder, no other predator being in the vicinity. In other instances, although not conclusively, it appeared that an African Python, a Large Grey Mongoose and a Serval were probable victims of predation by this vulture. In north Africa the pastoral Somalis, who are astute observers, aver that this vulture kills dikdiks and guineafowl. However, there is no direct corroboration of these accounts by ornithologists. Remains on nests indicate that many small animals are included in the diet and it is probable that some may have been killed by the vulture. These records include small antelope, Pangolin, monkey, jackal, polecat, mongooses, civet, Caracal, Serval, genet, several guineafowl, a Red-crested Korhaan, monitors (leguaans) and a tortoise. The White-headed Vulture also feeds on termites and locusts.

This species is rarely heard to emit any call, and apart from chittering noises at a carcass nothing is described.

BREEDING

No nuptial displays or copulation behaviour have been described and the breeding biology of this species is not well known.

The nest is a large flat structure placed on the crown of a tree in open woodland, sometimes in a tree growing on a small koppie, and the site always commands a good view of the surrounding country. Although various trees may be used for nesting, Baobabs are preferred where available; 29 of 34 nests in Zimbabwe were in this tree. The average height of sixteen nests was 15,2 m (range 10,7–21,4 m). Six nests averaged 118 cm across (range 82–152 cm) and 36 cm deep (range 22–61 cm) with a cup 34 cm in diameter (range 30–47 cm). The cup is lined with dry grass tufts and occasional pieces of dung. No greenery is used. As the nestling period progresses the nest becomes carpeted with a thick mat of hair from regurgitated pellets. There is no information on nest building or repair.

This species may use the same nest for at least six years but also builds alternate nests; a new site is seldom more than 2 km away, usually less. It appears that it is territorial; the size of the territory has been estimated at approximately 50 km^2 in one study in north-west Zimbabwe. Aggressive interactions occur

(1) A typical White-headed Vulture's nest situated on top of a Baobab tree (Photograph: Peter Mundy).

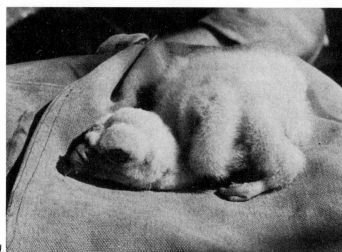

(2) A chick aged three days (Photograph: Angus Anthony).

(3) A 50-day-old nestling (Photograph: Peter Mundy).

in which other White-headed Vultures are chased away.

Eggs are laid in June and July. A single egg is laid and is chalky-white, sometimes with red spots which may form a cap at the broad end. Measurements are: 86,6 × 66,6 (20); 79,0–94,5 × 62,4–70,9.

Two nests in Zimbabwe were watched during the incubation period for a total of 53 hours on six days. It was established that both birds incubate. There were no obvious displays at change-overs and the pair remained on the nest together for between one and 52 minutes (average 16,5 minutes). During the 53 hours the incubating birds stood up on only nine occasions for periods of one to fifteen minutes (average 4,4 minutes). They turned around, shuffled about, preened or poked in the nest before settling again. The incubation period is estimated to be 56 days but has not been accurately obtained.

The newly hatched chick is covered in white down over its pink skin, and its eyes are open. At six weeks it is covered in thick white down, including the head. At this stage the soft parts have already acquired their juvenile coloration: orange-red bill, blue cere, black eyes and pale pinkish feet. The crop is black, although it is surrounded by white down. At this stage the main feather tracts are emerging through the down, mainly on the upperparts. When it is seven weeks old the occipital ridge is outlined in brownish down and the feathers are emerging rapidly. Its face blushes red in excitement. By the age of nine weeks it is well feathered dorsally. The downy underwing coverts begin

to feather from ten weeks on. By the time it leaves the nest the white down on the head is being replaced by brown so that it has a 'peppered' appearance. The head only becomes wholly brown when it has been out of the nest a month or two.

Nothing is recorded about the co-ordination of the nestling except that it indulges in much wing exercising as its time to leave the nest approaches.

There are few data on parental attention. Two nests, one with a medium-sized nestling and the other with one near to flying, were watched for 62 hours on seven days. The younger nestling was attended by a parent for one quarter of the 43 hours it was watched. In five days it was fed three times between 12h00 and 14h30. The older nestling was not guarded at all on the two days it was watched but was fed by both parents on both days between 09h50 and 15h00. The parents were not seen at the nest together and visits lasted between two and nine minutes. The nestling was fed by mouth-to-mouth regurgitation and it crouched low and flapped its wings. At neither nest did the chicks beg vigorously and no calls were heard.

The nestling period has not been obtained accurately but is estimated to be about 115 days. There are few observations on the post-nestling period, but juveniles have been seen on their nests and flying with adults up to five months after leaving the nest.

In Zimbabwe in seventeen pair-years 0,47 young per pair per year were raised. On present evidence it seems that this species usually breeds annually.

10 Black Kite /26

Swartwou

Milvus migrans migrans   PLATES 6 AND 13

DERIVATION
kite : migrating — *milvus* (L) : *migrare* (L)

IDENTIFICATION
Adult: The style of flight is the most characteristic feature of *Milvus* kites. The wings are held sharply bent at the carpal joint, the wing-beats are slow and buoyant and the tail is often twisted for steering. The plumage of this species appears mainly dull brown alleviated by greyish-white on the head. The bill is black, the

cere and legs are yellow and the eyes brown. In flight the closed tail is slightly forked but when spread has a straight tip. The underwing and tail are faintly barred below but from a distance the bird appears uniformly brown except for the whitish head. On the upperwing coverts are broad pale bands extending backwards from the carpal joints to form a shallow V pattern. Confusion with juvenile Yellow-billed Kites which have black bills can easily arise, but the latter have no white on the head. Possible

A Black Kite to show pale head and characteristic upperwing pattern.

confusion with Wahlberg's Eagle and dark-form Booted Eagle is discussed under those species.

Juvenile: It is paler and duller brown than the adult, with white edges to the feathers of the upperparts and whitish streaking on the head and underparts. The soft parts are coloured as in the adult. Its flight pattern is similar to that of the adult except for pale patches at the bases of the primaries. It is difficult to distinguish from the juvenile Yellow-billed Kite, which, however, is less streaky below and on the head. Also, because it only leaves the nest in November or December, it is in fresher plumage than the juvenile Black Kite which has been out of the nest since June or July.

HABITAT

It occurs in a wide variety of habitats but is found most commonly in open wooded country.

STATUS AND DISTRIBUTION

This race of the Black Kite is a Palearctic migrant to our area from October to late March. It appears that birds on the eastern side of southern Africa move westwards in late December to follow the main rain belts, but movements are very variable and depend on rainfall. The distribution of this species is mainly north of the Orange River, with occasional records from the eastern Cape Province.

The breeding distribution of this race of the Black Kite extends from north-west Africa throughout Europe to western Siberia (about 63° E), where it is replaced by the Asian race *lineatus* which is also said to reach our area occasionally. It is not easy to distinguish from *Milvus migrans migrans* and further clarification of its occurrence and status is required.

The Black Kite is one of the most numerous and widespread raptors in the Old World. It is found in Africa, Europe, the Middle East, India, Asia, Japan, Taiwan, Indonesia and Australia. Seven races are recognised.

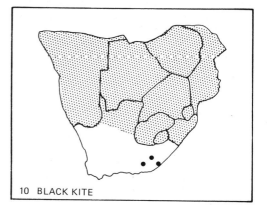

10 BLACK KITE

GENERAL HABITS

This gregarious migrant usually occurs in large flocks, sometimes numbering many hundreds of birds, and it roosts communally. It frequently mingles with other gregarious migrant raptors such as Steppe Eagles, falcons, kestrels and Yellow-billed Kites. Its feeding habits are the same as those described for the Yellow-billed Kite. In Africa, however, its food is mainly insects, particularly termites, to procure which it follows the rain belts. Thus it never stays in one area for long.

11 Yellow-billed Kite 126.

Geelbekwou

Milvus migrans parasitus

DERIVATION
kite : migrating : parasite — *milvus* (L) : *migrare* (L) : *parasitus* (L)

IDENTIFICATION
Adult: Similar to the Black Kite but with no white on the head and a yellow bill, the latter being the most important distinguishing feature. The tail is more deeply forked than that of the Black Kite but this distinction is not reliable when the tail is spread. It is most often seen singly or in pairs, although it may also occur in large flocks like the Black Kite, usually after the breeding season.
Juvenile: Rather similar to the adult but with light edges to the feathers above and some whitish streaking below. The bill is black. Distinctions between it and adult and juvenile Black Kites are discussed in the text on that race.

HABITAT
This species may be encountered in any habitat in southern Africa, even scavenging in coastal waters. It occurs regularly in built-up areas.

STATUS AND DISTRIBUTION
This intra-African migrant is a breeding visitor from August to March, although some birds arrive as early as July in Zimbabwe. Occasionally birds remain throughout the year. It is common, especially in the north of our area, but breeds as far south as the south-west Cape. As far as is known our birds migrate across the equator to eastern equatorial Africa but this requires clarification. It occurs throughout southern Africa. Extralimitally it extends northwards to the Sahara, apparently breeding throughout its range, but from the Kenya coast northwards to Egypt it is replaced by the race *Milvus migrans aegyptius*, which also has a yellow bill in the adult.

GENERAL HABITS
This ubiquitous raptor is usually seen flying slowly along at a height of 30–90 m with graceful buoyant wing-beats, the wings bent back sharply at the carpal joint, and the tail frequently twisted for steering. When it sees something, it drops suddenly as if shot, to scoop it up or, if it is too large to carry, to eat it on the ground. It is remarkably agile and will snatch food from a pot carried on an African woman's head or from a busy market stall or from amongst feeding vultures. On occasions it is capable of considerable bursts of speed and one was seen to catch a Hottentot Button-quail in flight. Insects, particularly termites, are caught dextrously with the feet and eaten in flight, although they are also taken on the ground as they emerge from their nests. It regularly attends grass fires to pick up insects that are disturbed. It will follow ships in coastal waters, snatching scraps from the surface of the water. It is also an accomplished fisher, taking fish from just below the surface of the water and immersing only its legs. Frogs are also taken from the water. In one observation a small swimming duckling was snatched. The nests of weavers are attacked and ripped open: in one instance the kite caught a nestling in mid-air as it fell out, and in another a nest was snatched from a branch and pulled apart as the bird flew along. Daring piratical attacks are made on other birds, either to snatch prey from them or make them disgorge, and the victims may be persistently harried. Piracy is opportunistic as the following few examples illustrate: an African Fish Eagle lost a piece of the fish it was eating when two kites attacked it, possibly a case of co-operative hunting; a Sacred Ibis was robbed of a 15 cm barbel it had caught; a frog was snatched from a Woolly-necked Stork as it was about to swallow it; a Giant Kingfisher had a fish taken from it. Finally, they are regular scavengers, often being first to arrive at large carrion, although sometimes they are unable to feed until vultures open the carcass. Their presence often acts as an indication of carrion to vultures. Roads are regularly patrolled for traffic casualties, and the kites are themselves sometimes killed by speeding cars. They regularly frequent primitive slaughter houses as well as fishing-camps for offal. In towns and villages they scavenge refuse and in more undeveloped areas they are often commensal with man.
Versatility in the feeding habits of the Yellow-billed Kite explains its abundance. It takes

any small live prey it can catch; birds, small mammals, reptiles, amphibians, fish and a wide variety of insects. It has also been recorded eating the husks of oil-palm fruits and feeding its young on them. Scavenging greatly increases the availability of food. Thus the varied diet, combined with opportunism and considerable dexterity on the wing, make for a highly successful raptor.

The call is a plaintive mewing whistle *kleeeeu-errrr* or a tremulous *kleeeeu-ki-ki-ki-ki-ki*. Both are used during courtship and as a contact call between the pair. The alarm call is a sharp *kleeeeu-yik-yik-yik-yik*. Nestlings solicit with *piu-piu* or *pee-peep pee-peep* calls.

BREEDING

Despite being widespread and common, the Yellow-billed Kite, with regard to its breeding biology, has not been properly studied in Africa. While the main details are similar to those of the Black Kite, there are variations, as for example in Ghana where two consecutive broods may be raised in one season.

Breeding territories are occupied as soon as the birds return from migration. Nuptial display, to the accompaniment of much calling, consists of slow, weaving, chasing flights, the male following the female. She may turn and present her claws to his and they interlock to cartwheel downwards before separating just above the ground. The male also calls excitedly to the female while perched and sways from side to side. Copulation takes place in trees near the nest, when the male makes a squealing call. Frequently copulation is associated with nest-building activity and he will fly directly to land on the crouching female's back after visiting the nest. The male also feeds the female regularly and she never moves far from the vicinity of the nest.

The nest is placed within the canopy of a tree, either in a main fork or on a lateral branch, and usually 6–15 m above ground but sometimes much higher. Sometimes the nest is placed in a euphorbia. It is a substantial structure of sticks 45–60 cm across and 30–45 cm deep. The shallow central depression is 20–25 cm across and lined with miscellaneous rubbish such as rags, paper, plastic bags, hair, sheep's wool, mud and dung. Green lining is not used. Shakespeare wrote, 'When the kite builds, look to lesser linen,' which perfectly sums up the nest-building habits of *Milvus* kites. One nest record from Zimbabwe succinctly states the contents of a nest as 'two eggs, two blue socks, a pair of pink panties, some dung — probably cow'. Sometimes a nest is built on top of the old nest

of another species, like the Hamerkop, Bateleur or Dark Chanting Goshawk.

Both birds build but the male is more active and, as well as adding to the nest himself, he will offer material to the female on her 'loafing' perch nearby and she will then take it to the nest. The same nests are normally used each year but sometimes an alternate site is built nearby. The size of territory is difficult to assess; the Yellow-billed Kite usually nests solitarily but also sometimes in loose colonies. In the south-west Cape several nests were spaced about 75–100 m apart in a clump of trees. In Ghana nests were 220–800 m apart with an average of 470 m. It will attack and drive off conspecifics and other birds of prey from near the nest. Humans climbing to nests are sometimes boldly attacked and the kite will strike and draw blood.

Eggs are laid in September and October throughout southern Africa. One to three eggs are laid, normally two, and there is a single record of four eggs from Zimbabwe. Eggs are white and very variably marked with spots, blotches and scrolls of dark red which are often massed in a cap at one end of the egg. Some eggs are very lightly marked, almost plain, while others are handsomely covered over the whole surface. As incubation progresses the white ground colour becomes stained yellowish. Measurements are: 53,5 × 40,1 (104); 49,8–58,5 × 38,0–45,0.

There is little information on the incubation period of the Yellow-billed Kite. In the Black Kite eggs are laid at intervals of two to three days and incubation commences with the first egg. As small young of the Yellow-billed Kite are different sizes, the same may be assumed to apply. The bulk of the incubation is said to be by the female, fed by the male. However, the male will probably be found to incubate, especially when the female leaves the nest to feed on prey he has brought, as does the Black Kite. The incubation period, on one observation in Kenya, is about 38 days. Further information is needed, especially as the incubation period of the Black Kite has been found to vary from 25–37 days. In India the average incubation period of 36 eggs was 31 days.

Although eggs hatch at intervals, there is no evidence of sibling aggression, and even in a three-egg clutch three young may be successfully reared. Newly hatched young are greyish-white above and white below. The eye is surrounded by a small black patch. On the head and back the down has fine hairlike plumes. The eyes are dark brown, the cere is very pale yellow and the legs are pinkish. There are few

(1) A Yellow-billed Kite's nest lined with wool and dung.

(2) A downy nestling about a week old and an infertile egg.

(3) A nestling approximately three weeks old.

detailed observations on subsequent development but contour feathers emerge through the down at about 20 days, and by 30 days the nestling is well feathered. It can feed itself at about five weeks old and moves out onto branches near the nest before its first flight.

Initially the female broods and tends the young, the male supplying prey. After the first week the female perches nearby and the young are left unbrooded much of the time. She continues to feed the nestlings on prey brought by the male, who does not feed them. Once they start feathering, both birds hunt actively and there is often an excess of prey on the nest. In one exceptional case a nest with one large

nestling in the south-west Cape contained 25 Cape Mole-rats, five field mice and a small snake. Much of the prey was decomposing.

The nestling period is about six weeks and the young remain near the nest or return to it during the first two weeks. They are fed by both parents, and the male will pass prey directly to them at this stage. Thereafter they wander farther afield and become independent about five to seven weeks after leaving the nest.

There is no information on breeding success in southern Africa. In Ghana a lost clutch was replaced and two consecutive broods were reared in a single breeding season. There is no evidence of double broods from our area.

12 Black-shouldered Kite /27

Blouvalk

Elanus caeruleus

DERIVATION
kite : blue — *elanos* (G) : *caeruleus* (L)

IDENTIFICATION
Adult: This graceful little hawk is blue-grey above with black 'shoulders' and white below. At rest the long, pointed wings project beyond the short, square tail. The head is broad with prominent orbital ridges beneath which are set the large ruby-red eyes. Its bill is black and the cere, legs and large feet are yellow. In flight it appears almost gull-like and is entirely white below except for the black wing tips. Above it is grey with the black 'shoulder' patches showing up prominently. The closed tail appears grey, but the white outer tail feathers are revealed when it is spread. The sexes are not distinguishable in the field.

Juvenile and immature: Both perched and in flight the juvenile has the same basic plumage pattern as the adult, but is washed with brown on the upperparts and the feathers have prominent white edges. The top of the head and the neck are brown. On the underparts there is a rufous wash. Except for the eyes, which are grey-brown, the soft parts are coloured like the adult. During the transition to adult plumage the brown wash and white edges to the feathers of the upperparts gradually disappear, as does the rufous on the underparts. The eyes undergo a slow change from grey-brown through deepening shades of yellow to orange and then orange-red. This process is variable but usually

takes approximately a year. The eyes then deepen further to ruby-red, although in some adults they remain orange-red. The time taken to moult into adult plumage varies according to the season in which the juvenile leaves the nest, because moulting only takes place in summer. Thus a young bird hatched from spring eggs undergoes an immediate body moult which extends over several months. However, it does not moult its wing and tail feathers until it is a year old, so is recognisable as an immature by the white edges to the wing feathers. Young hatched from autumn eggs leave the nest in winter and undergo a complete wing, tail and body moult in their first summer.

HABITAT
This species occurs in a wide variety of habitats including open savanna, semi-desert and agricultural lands. It is found in built-up areas if there are some open spaces available for hunting.

STATUS AND DISTRIBUTION
The Black-shouldered Kite is the most ubiquitous and probably the commonest bird of prey in southern Africa. It features prominently in roadside raptor counts, but accurate densities are difficult to assess because populations are unstable in many areas, with a continual turnover of individuals. In one locality which normally supported a single pair, at least seven pairs moved in to breed during a rodent plague.

There is no evidence that it is threatened by pesticides and it has probably increased in numbers where thick bush has been cleared for agricultural purposes.

Ringing and colour-marking projects in the Transvaal have established that a population in an area may appear resident and relatively stable while in reality individual turnover may be 25 per cent a month. Some birds are locally nomadic while others make long-distance movements. Both adults and young birds move about. One bird had moved 469 km in fourteen days. The longest movements recorded were of two birds from the Transvaal which were recovered in the eastern Cape Province and in northern Mozambique, distances of 645 km and 915 km respectively. Other recoveries were made at distances in excess of 300 km.

The Black-shouldered Kite occurs throughout southern Africa. Extralimitally it is found throughout the rest of Africa (except in the Sahara), in Madagascar and on the Iberian Peninsula. It also occurs in southern Asia eastwards to the islands of New Guinea.

GENERAL HABITS

This species is normally seen perched solitarily on a high vantage point such as a telegraph pole or in hovering flight. In direct flight its wing-beats are graceful and buoyant like those of a gull. The tail is often wagged up and down while perched, which appears to be a form of threat. Even when perched alone the kite is warning other Black-shouldered Kites that may pass that it is hunting in that area. This interpretation is supported by observations of excited tail-wagging during intraspecific territorial encounters.

A Black-shouldered Kite wagging its tail in threat.

Communal roosting is a regular aspect of behaviour throughout the year. When it is almost dark, birds arrive in ones and twos and gather for the night. Roost sites are often in reed-beds but trees are also used, the tops of pines in a 12 m high windbreak in one instance. When roosting in reeds the incoming birds either fly in directly or use nearby trees as a staging post on their way in. It appears that birds gather to roost from a wide area; assemblies of 50 and 70 birds have been recorded at some roosts. The kites leave the roost early and disperse to their individual hunting territories, where they may perch inactively or preen for about the first two hours before hunting. However, sometimes hunting starts before sunrise and quite often continues until after sunset.

The Black-shouldered Kite hunts from a perch or in hovering flight. Occasionally it may drop down onto prey from direct level flight, but this method has not been seen to be successful. Detailed observations on diurnal activity in the Transvaal established that during an average day a kite would spend 80 per cent of its time perched and 20 per cent flying. Hunting from perches occupied 71 per cent of the total hunting time, and hovering 29 per cent. When still-hunting from perches the kite changes to a new position frequently. While hovering, usually at heights of 20–60 m above ground, the bird maintains its position for about 10–20 seconds before moving to a new spot. In the Transvaal observations, periods of aerial hunting averaged 7,8 minutes with a range of one to 27 minutes. When prey is sighted from a hover, the kite parachutes down at 90 degrees, often checking on its way down, before a final rapid plunge with feet extended and wings raised high above the back. From a perch it merely drops down at an angle to grab its quarry. Once caught, the prey is taken to a perch to be eaten. Usually the head of the rodent is removed and eaten and then it is eviscerated, the small intestine frequently being discarded.

The daily food intake of a Black-shouldered Kite varies seasonally from about 37 g during the non-breeding season to about 52 g when there are young in the nest. This represents 15 and 21 per cent respectively of the average bodyweight of this species (243 g). The previous day's food is contained in a single pellet which is brought up next day in the early morning. In terms of energy expended, hovering costs almost seven times more than hunting from a perch, but results in 2,5 times more strike opportunities and a 2,2 times higher strike success rate than still-hunting. Expressed simply, hovering is more rewarding in terms of food caught in the time expended, but is more expensive and less efficient in terms of energy expended than hunting from a perch.

The Black-shouldered Kite has large, thick feet for its size and is a specialist in small rodents. However, it is capable of killing and carrying quite large prey; in one case a kite killed by a car was carrying a large rat weighing 164 g, or about 80 per cent of its own weight (210 g). An analysis of 3 408 prey items in the Transvaal gives a clear indication of its preference for small rodents, which comprised 98,2 per cent of the total, the balance being made up of birds (1,4 per cent) and lizards (0,4 per cent). Three rodents predominated: Angoni Vlei Rat (43,4 per cent), Striped Mouse (25,6 per cent) and Multimammate Mouse (23,3 per cent). In the south-west Cape a sample of 97 items comprised 84 per cent Striped Mice, 12 per cent reptiles (mainly lizards) and 4 per cent insects. Avian prey records are mainly of doves; Laughing Doves and Cape Turtle Doves are both recorded. Occasional small passerines are also caught, a male Pin-tailed Whydah in one instance. One kite seen rummaging amongst elephant droppings was presumably searching for insects. Once a Black-shouldered Kite dropped a small 10 cm tortoise onto a road to crack its shell and then flew up to a telephone pole to feed on it.

The two main calls of this species are a high-pitched whistling *peee-oo* and a wheezy whistle-scream *wee-ah*. The two calls are often intermingled. The *pee-oo*, which varies in length and tone, is a commonly used contact call between the sexes and may be emitted singly or in series. It is used during courtship and also in alarm or during intraspecific territorial encounters. The harsh *wee-ah* has also been described as the whistle and rasp call; the rasp may be sounded without the preceding whistle, to threaten intruding Black-shouldered Kites and other birds and animals, and also as a begging call by the female and young. Other less frequently heard calls are a chattering *kek-kek-kek* during territorial fights, an occasional chuckling call emitted by hunting birds and a rapid *tip-tip-tip* used in the breeding season and during territorial encounters. The calls of this species are complex and are difficult to interpret.

BREEDING

Nuptial display, to the accompaniment of much calling, consists of circling flights during which the male may dive down at the female, who sideslips out of his way or turns and presents her talons towards his. Very occa-

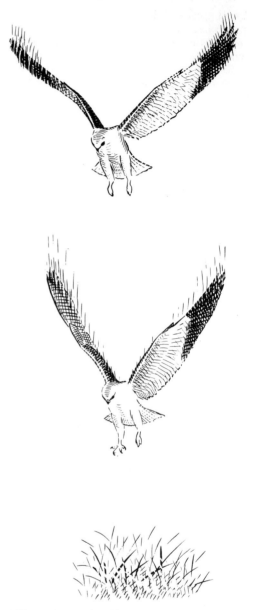

A Black-shouldered Kite dropping onto prey.

sionally the birds may lock claws and fall for a short way in cartwheeling flight. The male also flies round slowly with exaggerated, stiff wingbeats and dangling legs in a 'butterfly flight' courtship display. He brings prey for the female, three mice a day on occasions. Copulation takes place on perches near the nest with no preliminary display behaviour. The female crouches flat and spreads her tail, and the male mounts her while flapping his wings to maintain balance. Copulation is frequent in the nest-building stage, taking place most often in the early morning. One observer recorded an average of seven copulations a day during the nest-building stage. In one study the average time from first copulation to the laying of the eggs was 24 days. Mating has also been observed when there were large young in the nest, presumably prior to raising a second brood. The pair-bond is not strong in this species and studies of colour-marked birds have revealed that females tend to move around between males.

Nest sites are very variable but, where available, thorn trees are favoured. The nest is most often placed near the top of a tree below the level of the highest branches of the canopy. A shady situation is selected but the nest may become exposed when the tree loses its leaves. A feature of all sites is that they are easily accessible from the air. One nest site was on a telegraph pole and another on a power pylon. Occasionally the old nest of another species such as a crow may be taken over. Nests have been recorded as low as 0,75 m on a small bush and as high as 18 m on the top of a pine tree. Usually nests are not more than about 6 m above ground, but in the south-west Cape where pines are favourite sites they are often higher than 12 m. The nest is a flat platform of sticks 25–45 cm across and 4–10 cm deep. Most nests are about 30 cm across and 7 cm deep, but the dimensions vary according to the site. The central cup is lined with dry grass. Lining is added during the incubation period and early part of the nestling period. However, towards the end of the nestling period, the nest becomes thickly carpeted with fur from regurgitated pellets which break up.

Detailed observations on one nest-building pair established that both birds built in almost equal shares. An average of 38 trips per day was recorded and most activity was in the early morning from 09h00 to 11h00 (sunrise at 08h15). Sticks were collected 200–500 m from the nest and were broken off trees with the bill. Material was also collected from the ground, but only on 16 per cent of occasions. All sticks were carried in the bill. In most cases the male initiated the collection of material, this stimulating the female to collect as well, although the birds collected independently of each other. The female was not seen to hunt during the nest-building stage, and the male brought prey to her. Observations on the time taken to build a nest are scanty, but in one case the first egg was laid thirteen days after the nest was started. Sticks were added during the first ten days and lining during the remaining three days. Nor-

mally a new nest is built for each breeding attempt, but occasionally a nest may be used again. Owing to their flimsy structure they tend to fall down within a few months.

Males establish and maintain territories to which they attract females. They continue to occupy them once females have left. Females tend to wander about and select the best available territories occupied by males. The males are most active in territorial defence; one male defended an area extending to a radius of 800 to 1 000 m of his nest. Conspecifics, as well as other birds of prey, herons, crows, etc., are vigorously driven off. Breeding densities were studied in two areas in the Transvaal. On the Springbok Flats an area of 66 km^2 contained thirteen breeding pairs in 1977 and ten pairs in 1978. Near Nylsvley there were ten breeding pairs in 70 km^2.

Breeding occurs in all months of the year in southern Africa, but there are different peaks according to locality. In the south-west Cape eggs are laid mainly from August to November during spring and early summer (78 per cent of 50 records). In the eastern Cape and Natal the breeding season is not well known because of the lack of records and the poorly defined wet and dry seasons in this region. However, breeding occurs in all months, and there appears to be a peak in spring and early summer. In the Transvaal and Orange Free State there are two peaks, from August to November and from February to May. In Zimbabwe there is a peak from February to June (74 per cent of 61 records). Breeding is very variable, apparently in response to food supply. Nesting usually begins before prey abundance reaches a peak and it may be that the kites respond to rodent breeding activity in some way. One researcher has suggested that the presence of reproductive steroids in their rodent prey could trigger hormonal activity in kites. Individuals may breed several times in one year and not at all the following one. During a rodent plague consecutive broods may be raised. Three to six eggs may be laid, usually three or four. The eggs are white or creamy in ground colour and are usually heavily overlaid with red-brown and dark red blotches and streaks. In some eggs the ground colour is almost obscured while others may be mainly white with a cap of red at the broad end. Measurements are: 39,9 × 30,7 (75); 35,6–43,6 × 27,5–32,5.

Eggs are laid at intervals of one to two days and the commencement of incubation is variable. Sometimes it begins with the first egg, at other times when the clutch is nearing completion. Incubation appears to be almost entirely

(1) View of a Black-shouldered Kite's nest.

(2) Close-up of the eggs and a newly hatched chick.

(3) An adult with two-week-old nestlings.

by the female, although males may brood when females become inattentive during periods of food shortage. Further observations on the incubation period are needed. The male brings prey for the female and she leaves the nest to take it from him. Human intruders climbing to the nest may be attacked and occasionally struck, especially when the eggs are hatching. The incubation period is 30–32 days and averages 31 days.

There does not appear to be any sibling aggression when young hatch at intervals. Sometimes the smallest chick may die, possibly from starvation. In one brood three eggs hatched within a period of twelve hours, indicating that incubation started once the clutch was complete. The newly hatched chick is covered in buff down and its head appears too large for its body. The eyes are weakly open, the bill is black, the gape pink, the cere pale yellow and the legs are flesh-pink. At the age of a week the quills of the remiges appear and by ten days quills are breaking on the scapulars and tail. The down at this stage is thicker and has turned greyish. Feathers are emerging rapidly on the upperparts by the age of two weeks and the nestling is well feathered above and below by the age of three weeks. Thereafter the main growth is that of the wing and tail feathers.

The chicks do not defecate clear of the nest like most other young raptors; their mutes fall on the edge of the nest. By the age of two weeks they are active and shuffle about, preening a great deal and stretching their wings. They are able to swallow whole the rear half of a small mouse at this stage. At the age of three weeks they can swallow prey whole or tear it up if too large. Once a satiated 23-day-old nestling was seen to tear pieces off a mouse and feed its two younger siblings. The young lie flat if alarmed at this age and the white edges to the feathers of the upperparts act as an effective camouflage.

As the time of their departure approaches they perform vigorous wing exercises and move out to perch on branches near the nest.

The female broods the chicks closely during the first week. The male provides prey, and the female usually leaves the nest to take it from him, sometimes in flight. He has not been seen to brood or feed the young, but observations on parental care are scant. The female still feeds and shades the young when they are two weeks old, but she begins to leave them alone on the nest at this stage. Once they can feed themselves at three weeks they are left alone much of the time although she is usually in the area. The male continues to provide most of the prey but she may help with hunting if food is short. Prey is merely deposited on the nest, and the young cope with it themselves. Prey may be delivered frequently, four mice in less than an hour at one nest, and at another nine mice were brought in the morning and a further three in the afternoon.

The nestling period averages 35 days with a range of 30–38 days. The young return to the nest for the first few days after leaving to receive prey and to roost. After about ten days on the wing they roost in trees near the nest and collect their prey away from the nest. Once they are strong on the wing, prey may be taken from the adults in the air. The female deserts the young soon after they fly and the male cares for them. They may remain with him for up to three months; the average post-nestling period is 82 days.

Breeding productivity is difficult to establish and is highly variable from one year to the next and from locality to locality. In years of rodent plagues consecutive broods may be raised and a new clutch laid while the male is still feeding flying young from a previous brood.

Note: This account is based to a large extent on unpublished observations of John Mendelsohn.

13 Cuckoo Hawk /28.

Koekoevalk

Aviceda cuculoides

PLATES 6 AND 16

DERIVATION
bird : killing : cuckoo : like — *avis* (L) : *caedere* (L) : *cuculus* (L) : *eides* (G)

IDENTIFICATION
Adult: The breast, head and upperparts are dark grey and the rest of the underparts below the breast are broadly barred chestnut and white. There is a short crest at the back of the

head and a small patch of chestnut on the nape just beneath it. The long tail is dark grey above and silvery below with three broad black bars, the terminal one broadest. The large eyes, cere and short legs are yellow. In flight from below the underwing coverts are barred chestnut and white but appear mainly chestnut at a distance. The silvery remiges have three narrow black bars. The Cuckoo Hawk has a resemblance to the accipiters but differs in having short legs, a crest and long pointed wings like a falcon in flight. The chestnut underwing coverts eliminate confusion with any other accipiter except the male African Goshawk.

Juvenile and immature: The upperparts of the juvenile are dark brown with buff edges to the feathers. There is a promiment white eye-brow stripe. The white underparts are covered with brown tear-drop spots. The tail pattern is like that of the adult but is brownish rather than grey above. The eyes are grey and the cere and legs yellow. In flight the underwing coverts are pale buff with some dark brown speckling, and the remiges are barred like the adult. It resembles a juvenile African Gos-hawk, especially on the underparts; differences are discussed under that species.

The eye is greenish-yellow by the time it is six months out of the nest, and grey feathers are appearing on the upperparts as well as some barring on the abdomen. There appears to be a distinct intermediate stage between juvenile and adult plumage in which the imma-ture is white on the throat and breast with a heavy overlay of broad, spade-shaped, rufous-brown spots. The rest of the underparts are a mixture of brown barring and spotting. It is not known how long it takes to assume adult plumage.

HABITAT
This species occurs in thick woodland and forest. It is characteristic of *Miombo* woodland in Zimbabwe but is not confined to this habi-tat.

STATUS AND DISTRIBUTION
Although generally considered resident, it may make local movements in some areas in the winter months; five sightings in the central Transvaal were all in July and August. Its dis-tribution is mainly in the eastern part of south-ern Africa from the Knysna forest to Mozam-bique, and widely in Zimbabwe. Extralimitally it is found northwards to Kenya across to the forested areas of west Africa.

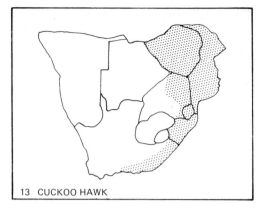

13 CUCKOO HAWK

GENERAL HABITS
This species is usually seen singly and is no-where common, although it can easily be over-looked. It hunts from a perch, sometimes in an exposed position in open ground, and is not particularly shy, although it does not sit in one place for long. It drops down to take prey on the ground and may pursue insects on foot with clumsy hops. Chameleons are sometimes snatched from leafy branches. In flight its wing-beats are rather slow and heavy.

Its diet is mainly insects; grasshoppers, beetles and caterpillars have been recorded. It also catches lizards, chameleons and occasion-ally small snakes. There are no records of mammals or birds in its diet in southern Afri-ca. Claims that it eats chickens have almost certainly resulted from misidentification. It has small, relatively weak feet not suited to this type of prey.

There are two main calls. One is a loud, plain-tive whistle *peee-ooo* and the other a treble-noted whistle *piti-ti-ooo*. Both calls appear to be used for contact between the pair and during display, although further investigation of the context in which they are used is needed. The young make a trilling *pi-pi-pi-pi* begging call.

BREEDING
Nuptial display consists of calling from a perch or aerobatics high above the trees when the birds perform undulations and tumble about to show the chestnut underwing coverts. Several birds may fly about together. The aerial displays are accompanied by much call-ing.

The nest is usually placed in the upper branches of a leafy tree, sometimes in euca-lypts, about 10–25 m above ground, and well concealed by surrounding foliage. It is a flimsy structure built with thin leafy branches, meas-uring about 25–30 cm across and 15–20 cm deep with a small leaf-lined cup 10–15 cm across. The leaves attached to the nest sticks dry out so that it looks like a pile of debris which can easily be mistaken for the nest of a galago. This, with the well-concealed site and unobtrusive behaviour of the adults, is the main reason for the paucity of breeding records.

Both birds build. Usually the female stays on the nest and the male brings her sticks; he may place material in position but she re-arranges it once he departs. Branches are collected from trees near the nest. The bird perches and peers about before flying upwards to grab the selected branch with its feet. Then it hangs flapping and snips off the branch with its notched bill-tip as though it were using secateurs. As it falls it rights itself dextrously, alights on a branch to transfer the stick to its bill, and then flies to the nest with it. Sometimes the bird may sidle along a branch like a parrot to snip off a stick. One male took eight sticks to the female on the nest in 36 minutes.

There is little information on how often nests are used. In one case a nest was used again but no young had been reared in it the previous season. Nothing is known about the size of territory but other raptors are driven away, a Long-crested Eagle in one instance.

Eggs have been recorded from October to February, mostly in October. The young are reared during the rainy season, when insects, lizards and chameleons are most plentiful. Two eggs are laid and are chalky-white in ground colour with a scattering of small spots and large irregular blotches of dark red. Measurements are: 42,7 × 34,9 (10); 41,5–43,8 × 34,0–37,0.

Both male and female incubate, with frequent change-overs. No prey is brought to the nest, so presumably each bird feeds itself when off the nest. Twigs with green leaves attached are brought throughout the incubation period. Either the sitting bird leaves to collect them or its mate delivers them, several in succession at times. The birds are unobtrusive and only call when changing over or delivering nest material. The incubating bird sits tight, its long tail protruding over the edge of the nest, and is difficult to flush. Once disturbed it flies off for some distance, but in one case the observer was dive-bombed when on the ground below the nest. The incubation period is unrecorded.

The downy nestling is undescribed and there are few details on the development of the young. At one high nest observed from the ground below, the nestling appeared well feathered on the wings at about two weeks old although still downy on the head. By three weeks old it was well feathered with no down on the head, and at 25 days it began perching on a branch beside the nest before its first flight at 28 days. Even allowing for slight inaccuracy in the estimated hatching date, the nestling period is clearly very short.

The nestlings are brooded and fed by both parents during the first ten days, whereafter they are capable of feeding themselves. Most of the prey brought to one nest consisted of lizards, chameleons and a few snakes, but insects would have been difficult to see from a distance.

There is no information on the post-nestling period or breeding success. The breeding biology of this species is poorly known and further observations are needed.

The small nest of a Cuckoo Hawk which is well concealed amongst surrounding foliage.

A Cuckoo Hawk alighting at its nest in a eucalypt; the exterior of the nest is covered with leafy spays (Photograph: Alan Weaving).

14 Bat Hawk

Vlermuisvalk

Macheiramphus alcinus

PLATES 6 AND 13

DERIVATION

fighting : hooked bill? — *mache* (G) : *ramphos* (G) : *alcinus* (G)

Macheiramphus may be freely translated as killing with a hooked bill. The meaning of *alcinus* could not be traced.

IDENTIFICATION

Adult: The plumage is variable and not fully understood. The main colour is blackish-brown but the bird appears black from a distance. Its dark coloration is presumably an adaptation for its crepuscular hunting habits. Usually the throat is white with a black line down the centre, and there may be some white on the abdomen. Some birds lack white on the throat. There is a short occipital crest. The large yellow owl-like eyes are a good feature for identification, and the 'eyelids' are white above and below them. The black bill is small and weak, the cere is grey, and the legs and long toes are bluish-grey. When the bird is sleeping during the day the lower white eyelids cover the eyes and there are two white nape spots. The effect is of two white 'eyes' both in front and behind, presumably to give the bird the appearance of being awake and thus to deter a possible predator.

In flight during daylight the bird appears mainly black with no noticeable barring on the wings or tail. It flies with the grace and speed of a falcon and has a similar outline. Confusion with falcons hunting at dusk is possible, but the habit of catching and swallowing prey whole in flight usually distinguishes it.

Juvenile: As in the case of the adult, the situation with regard to plumage is uncertain. It appears from young seen on the nest that the underparts are mainly white with a broad blackish-brown band across the abdomen. Otherwise they resemble adults. Descriptions of 'adults' with partially white breasts are probably immatures developing into adult plumage. Further investigation of plumages is required.

HABITAT

It is found in well-wooded areas, often in hilly country, especially where there are caves or old mine workings harbouring bat colonies.

Quite often it occurs near rivers but not necessarily. It is also found near human habitation, even in large towns in east Africa, probably because bats are attracted to buildings. Wherever it occurs, open spaces for hunting are needed.

STATUS AND DISTRIBUTION

As far as known it is resident. In South Africa it is rare but in Zimbabwe it is widespread although nowhere common. Its distribution is mainly in the east from Natal northwards. In the west it is found in northern Namibia. There is only one record from Botswana at Selebi-Pikwe but it is likely to occur more widely in the north-east. Extralimitally it extends northwards to the Sahara in suitable habitat. Other races occur in the Far East in Malaysia and Indonesia.

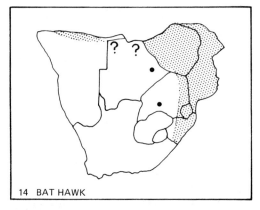

14 BAT HAWK

GENERAL HABITS

This species is crepuscular and roosts in trees during the day. It makes no particular attempt to conceal itself or seek shade and will perch quite openly in a leafless tree. It sits very upright and from a distance could be mistaken for a Wahlberg's Eagle. If disturbed during daylight it flies about quite normally. Its flight is graceful, its slow wing-beats belying its considerable speed. An interesting adaptation is its silent flight, enhanced, like an owl's, by the downy edges to its flight feathers.

It hunts mainly at dusk but also at dawn. Main activity centres on bats emerging in the evening although it can probably hunt perfectly well by moonlight too. It flies back and forth in a suitable area such as the mouth of a cave or over a river, alternatively flapping and gliding while selecting its victim. Then it accelerates after the quarry with rapid wing-beats, attacks from behind and usually from above, seizes the prey with its talons, swings it forward to its mouth, and swallows it whole. It is able to manoeuvre dextrously when hunting. Very occasionally it flies out from a perch to catch bats, which are always swallowed in flight.

Observations during six evening watches at a bat cave in Zambia are the most detailed available, giving a clear picture of the specialised hunting behaviour of this remarkable species. At dusk the hawk flew back and forth on a 70 m flight path past the mouth of the cave. Feeding bouts lasted for an average of 18 minutes per evening, during which time between four and eleven bats were caught and eaten, the average being seven. Half the bats caught were dropped, possibly because they were too large, or else were incorrectly grasped and may have bitten the hawk's legs or feet. The interval between each successful capture varied from one to four minutes, averaging just under three minutes. The same average time per kill was obtained by observers in Malawi and clearly indicates how important the short period when bats emerge at dusk is to the Bat Hawk's ecology. By means of its very large gape, bats are swallowed in periods of between three and eight seconds, averaging six seconds. The bird does not alight to tear up bats as this would be wasteful of vital hunting time. Selection of the correct size is therefore important and probably explains why bats are dropped.

There is a record from Nigeria of a Bat Hawk attacking a Straw-coloured Fruit Bat as large as itself but the attempt was unsuccessful. In Zululand a Bat Hawk was seen at 09h30 tearing at a large fruit bat clinging to some lianas. It was screaming loudly as the hawk tore its wing membranes to pieces. The bat eventually lost its grip and both dropped from view behind thick cover so that the outcome is not known. Such incidents are probably exceptional.

In the Zambian observations it was estimated that the hawk ate approximately 56 g in an evening, about 8,5 per cent of its body weight. Other observations indicate about 10 per cent of body weight consumed in an evening. At an average of seven bats an evening, a Bat Hawk would consume 2 555 bats a year. Where vast colonies of bats are involved this would be inconsequential, but it could have a serious impact on a small colony.

The diet does not consist exclusively of bats; birds are frequently taken and occasionally insects. Most prey is caught in flight and swallowed whole, but it must be assumed that the Bat Hawk alights to tear up larger birds or deposits them on the nest. The larger prey would compensate for the loss of hunting time. Birds are usually caught as they fly in to roost or when hawking insects over water at dusk. Avian prey records are: Cape Turtle Dove, Emerald-spotted Dove, Pennant-winged Nightjar, Mottled Spinetail, African Palm Swift, European Swallow, Brown-throated Sand Martin (five in one collected bird), Plum-coloured Starling, Yellow-eye Canary, bishop bird, waxbill and various unidentified passerines. A Bat Hawk has been known to pursue a White-collared Pratincole, which managed to evade capture.

A number of calls have been described but little is known of the context in which they are made. Its main call is a high-pitched but quiet *kwik-kwik-kwik-kwik*. Other calls, probably used for contact, are a soft musical *chuk-chuk-chuk* and a mellow *woot-woot-woot*. In alarm it utters a falcon-like *kek-kek-kek-kek*.

BREEDING
Nuptial displays, to the accompaniment of calling, consist of spectacular aerobatics, or chasing flights during which the birds may touch talons. They also dive from a height and zigzag through the branches of the nest tree before alighting.

The nest is almost always placed in a fork on a horizontal lateral branch of a tree, often on a hillside, at heights varying from about 10–25 m from the base of the tree. Various trees such as eucalypts, Baobabs, *Sterculia* sp. and Mountain Acacia are favoured, all smooth-barked and difficult to climb, and most leafless at the start of the breeding season so that the nest is initially unshaded and conspicuous. Sometimes it is situated near human habitation or beside a road, as the birds are not secretive in their breeding behaviour.

The nest is a characteristic structure made of sticks one centimetre thick with finer ones used for the cup. Smaller at the top than at its base, it has the shape of an inverted basin. The cup is fairly deep and sparingly lined with a few green leaves. One typical nest measured 56 cm across the top and 38 cm deep with a cup 14 cm across.

Both birds build, and collect dead branches from trees by 'colliding' with them and breaking them off with the feet. At one site the pair built until two hours after sunrise and ceased

(1) This Bat Hawk's nest is situated typically on a lateral branch (Photograph: Ron Thomson).

(2) A closer view of the basket-shaped nest (Photograph: Ron Thomson).

(3) The single egg lies on a sparse lining of leaves.

when the sun came over the hill and shone on the nest. Nests are re-used; there is little information on how often. Nothing is known about size of territory but pairs are not found near each other, probably because the specialised feeding habits preclude this.

Eggs are laid from September to November in Zimbabwe, where the majority of southern African nests have been found and the information recorded. Some instances of later laying have been as a result of the first clutch having failed. All recent reliable records indicate that only one egg is laid; any instances where two egg clutches are claimed require scrupulous authentication. The raising of a single chick is undoubtedly linked to the specialised feeding habits of the Bat Hawk. The egg is usually plain white with a rough texture and is a long oval uniformly rounded at both ends. Some eggs have red blotches and sepia speckles but it is rare for an egg to have any extensive markings. Measurements are: 61,6 × 46,2 (18); 57,7–67,2 × 43,0–49,3. The egg is very large for the size of the bird.

As far as is known, only the female incubates during the day and it would be difficult to establish whether the male takes a share at night. She sits very tight in the deep nest cup and is difficult to see from below. The male perches conspicuously in the nest tree or nearby. In the evening and early morning he may bring nest material. It is not known whether he feeds the female or if she feeds herself. In view of the short feeding period required she could easily catch enough prey before the egg cooled to any extent. There are several instances of humans' being attacked by the female when climbing to the nest, in one instance 'ferociously and repeatedly'. The incubation period is said to be about a month but there are no accurate observations.

There are no observations on nestling development, except that it is covered in white down when it hatches. Both parents bring prey to the nest at dusk and the female has been observed to hunt just before dawn. She feeds the chick by tearing up prey for it when it is small; the male apparently does not brood or feed it. In the early stages the female remains on the nest but at the end of the nestling period both birds perch in the nest tree or nearby.

Little is known of the post-nestling period, except that the young bird soon disappears from the vicinity of the nest. There are no observations on breeding success in southern Africa, except that a pair may attempt to breed again after a failure. In east Africa they breed regularly and raise a nestling each year.

15 Honey Buzzard /30

Wespevalk

Pernis apivorus

PLATES 6 AND 13

DERIVATION

hawk : bee : eat — *pternis* (G) : *apis* (L) : *vorare* (L)

The *t* in *pternis* was omitted by Baron Cuvier in error when the generic name was formed.

IDENTIFICATION

Adult: The plumage of this species is extremely variable but there are three basic types: a pale form that is mainly white below, either plain or with some streaking or spotting; a dark form varying from pale to dark brown below; and an intermediate form that is barred on the underparts. Examples of these three basic types are illustrated. Certain features distinguish Honey Buzzards whatever their colour. The head is small with a weak bill so that it has the appearance of a large pigeon. The eyes are relatively large and are yellow in females, orange in males. If a good view is obtained, the small scale-like feathers (usually greyish) between the eye and bill and on the forehead may be seen. They protect the bird from the stings of wasps. The cere is dark grey and the nostril is a narrow slit which keeps out sand when the bird is digging for wasp larvae. The yellow legs are heavily scaled for protection against stings; the claws are long, sharp and curved for digging. In flight there are usually two bars near the junction of the underwing coverts and remiges, and a broader bar along the hind edge of the wings. However, the pattern of barring on the tail, unique to this species, is the most important feature for identification. There are two bars close together near the base of the tail and a broader bar at the tip; this prevents any possible confusion with the Steppe Buzzard. Another distinction is that the small head and neck of the Honey Buzzard protrude well forward of the body at the shoulder, giving it a characteristic silhouette.

Juvenile and immature: Juveniles, as variable as adults, are recognisable as Honey Buzzards by the small head, which is characteristic both perched and in flight. They have brown eyes, a bright yellow cere and no grey on the face. Their legs are yellow like those of the adult. They have a different flight pattern, with a greater amount of black on the primaries, less distinct barring on the remiges, and four evenly distributed bars on the tail. Thus the diagnostic adult tail pattern falls away where juveniles are concerned. They resemble adults otherwise, but the juvenile of the pale form has the head and neck white with a dark patch near the eye. Juveniles moult gradually into adult plumage from the age of a year onwards, the eyes changing to yellow before the cere changes to grey.

HABITAT

The Honey Buzzard occurs in woodland.

STATUS AND DISTRIBUTION

This Palearctic migrant is a regular but scarce visitor to southern Africa from November to April. In view of the large numbers crossing into north Africa on southward migration, it is remarkable that only a small proportion of these reach southern Africa. Elsewhere in Africa they are nowhere common, so it remains a mystery where most of them go. They are most frequently recorded in west Africa, but in southern Africa distribution is mainly in the east from Natal northwards and including the Transvaal and Zimbabwe. There are occasional records from the Cape, and one was seen near Windhoek in Namibia. The breeding distribution, inclusive of various races, is very wide, extending from western Europe to Asia, India and Indonesia. The population breeding from Europe to western Siberia migrates to

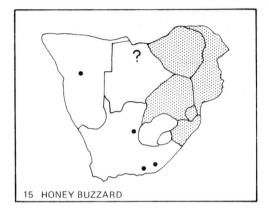

15   HONEY BUZZARD

Africa, and east Asian breeding birds go south to Burma and south-east Asia.

GENERAL HABITS

This species is solitary and unobtrusive in Africa and there are very few observations on its habits, although they are probably very similar to those recorded in the northern hemisphere. It flies with deep elastic wing-beats and may hunt in flight by catching insects such as termites or by following flying wasps back to their nests. It also watches from a perch or hunts on foot, walking about like a crow, sometimes for several hundred metres. Wasp nests are snatched from branches of trees or from under the eaves of buildings. They are also dug out of the ground with the feet, sometimes to a depth of 40 cm.

The diet consists mainly of the larvae and pupae of wasps. Indeed the Afrikaans name 'wasp hawk' is far more appropriate as there is little evidence that the Honey Buzzard feeds on the nests of honey bees. It feeds on a wide variety of insects as well as on spiders and worms. Other food includes small mammals, reptiles, amphibians, nestlings and eggs of birds, and vegetable matter such as berries and the fruits of oil palms. In southern Africa at least three birds have been shot while 'attacking fowls', although evidence is required that they actually kill them.

16 Black Eagle /31/

Witkruisarend

Aquila verreauxii

DERIVATION
eagle : of Verreaux — *aquila (L) : verreauxii* (L)

This magnificent eagle was named in honour of Jules Verreaux, the best known of three brothers (Alexis, Edouard and Jules), who all visited southern Africa in the first half of the last century to collect and mount birds and other animals before returning to Paris to run a taxidermy and natural history specimen business.

Although referred to as Verreaux's Eagle outside southern Africa, it is thought better to retain Black Eagle, by which name it is known throughout southern Africa.

IDENTIFICATION
Adult: The wholly black plumage, except for a narrow white V on its back, distinguishes the perched bird. The 'eyebrow', cere and feet are rich yellow. In flight it reveals a striking Y pattern of white on the back, and there are white 'windows' on the primaries visible above and below. The flight outline is also diagnostic: the secondaries are shorter nearer the body so that the wing has a leaf shape. The tail is long and is usually held partially spread, more so in females, although this is a subtle distinction requiring experience to discern.

Juvenile and immature: The juvenile has a handsome plumage, the most striking feature being the chestnut on crown and mantle. On the face, neck and breast it is black, merging to buffish on abdomen and legs, although the feathers have black edges. The blackish feathers of the wing coverts are broadly tipped with buff, giving a scaled appearance. The cere and feet are rich yellow. In flight it lacks the white back pattern of the adult, although the rump feathers are white, edged black. There are windows on the primaries, and the remiges and tail are barred below. The characteristic wing shape, as in the adult, prevents confusion with any other large raptor.

Adult plumage is acquired between three and four years of age, and black feathers gradually replace the coloured areas from the time it is about a year old. Birds may breed while there are still traces of brown immature plumage.

HABITAT
Throughout its range it occurs in rocky or mountainous terrain, but the environment may vary from semi-arid to areas of high rainfall. Its presence almost invariably coincides with that of its principal prey, the dassie.

STATUS AND DISTRIBUTION
Adults are resident, but juveniles and immatures wander away from the areas in which they were reared. Its generally inaccessible habitat has ensured that this eagle, though often persecuted by farmers, has shown no serious sign of an overall decline; it may even nest near populous areas (the Cape Peninsula supports at least three breeding pairs). Its existence depends on a plentiful supply of dassies, and a study in the Matopos hills of Zimbabwe revealed a marked decline in the Black Eagle population in formerly 'Tribal Trust' land where dassies were extensively snared or hunted with dogs by peasant farmers for food and their pelts, from which karosses are made. In the adjoining National Park, where the habitat was protected, the eagle population had increased slightly.

The Black Eagle is locally distributed throughout southern Africa in suitable habitats; it is absent from most of Botswana and Mozambique, where there is little suitable terrain. Extralimitally it occurs widely in the right environment as far north as the Sahara, extending through north-east Africa into Egypt, Arabia and Israel, but rarely outside Africa.

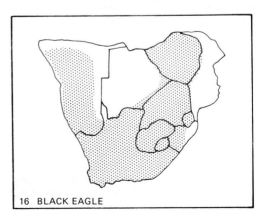

16 BLACK EAGLE

GENERAL HABITS

Paired birds may be seen in their territories all year round, and they fly, display, perch and roost together. The pair bond is very strong, the birds being presumed to remain together for their lifetimes. However, should a bird lose a mate, it soon replaces it with another one from the reserve population of unpaired adults (in one instance within a week).

This eagle is on the wing at first light and may go to roost when it is almost dark. The day is spent hunting, soaring, displaying or perching for long periods on a conspicuous outcrop, where it may sun-bathe with spread wings and tail. Its soaring flight is buoyant and extremely graceful. At other times it skims along a cliff face with one wing almost brushing the rock before swooping round a corner at unsuspecting prey.

It has several hunting techniques. Sometimes it attacks from a perch or with a tremendous stoop from a soaring position, but usually a planned sneak approach is used. Once prey has been seen from a soaring position, it drops out of view of the quarry behind an outcrop or ridge, suddenly appearing in a surprise swoop to make its kill. At times it may knock its victim off a cliff and then retrieve it below, but further observations are needed to establish whether this is a deliberate technique or merely that prey was not grasped firmly in the first place. Observations suggest that a pair will hunt co-operatively, one bird flying past sunbathing dassies which take cover initially before emerging to scold it; at this point the second bird attacks them from behind. It is known that a pair will share prey, so it is likely that this method is used, even though an actual kill has yet to be seen. Animals are also caught in treetops; a young baboon and a dassie have been taken in this way. Occasional instances of piracy are on record: a Martial Eagle was robbed of its prey; and a Lammergeyer was attacked for the carrion it was carrying — when it dropped the carrion the Black Eagle caught it in the air. This eagle's agility in flight is further borne out by an observation where a Black Eagle twice dropped prey it was carrying and caught it before it reached the ground. Once one was seen to catch a Redwing Francolin in flight as it took off.

The Black Eagle is extremely prey specific, dassies being the principal food throughout its range. In an intensive study in the Matopos extending over many years dassies made up 98 per cent of 1 892 prey items recorded. Despite variations in some localities, it is probably true to say that dassies very rarely constitute less than 90 per cent of the prey of this specialist hunter. Adult dassies weigh about 4 kg, more than a male Black Eagle (about 3 kg), and can seriously compete with sheep for grazing. A pair of eagles and their eaglet account for approximately 400 dassies in a year. Though they cannot keep a population explosion in check, their presence prevents the animals from emerging from the koppies to feed on the open veld, which they readily do where there are no eagles.

Other mammalian prey includes small antelopes, adult Klipspringers or half-grown Grey Rhebuck, as well as the lambs of larger species such as Bushbuck or Springbok. Undoubtedly it preys at times on the lambs of sheep or on goat kids, but eye-witness accounts are rare and, in view of the fact that it readily feeds on carrion, remains found on nests cannot be assumed to have been gathered from animals killed rather than scavenged. In observed instances of carrion feeding the Black Eagle has been seen at the carcass of a dog, on a bloated sheep and at the carcass of a zebra with vultures perched nearby. Additional mammals recorded as prey are: young baboons, Vervet Monkeys, mongooses, Suricates, cane rats, Bushbabies, red rock hares, Tree Squirrels and Ground Squirrels.

The extent to which avian prey is recorded is very variable; in the Matopos it was rarely noted, but in a study in Kenya it made up about 40 per cent of food seen brought to a nest. This is probably exceptional, and in southern Africa birds are infrequently reported as prey. In an unusual incident a Black Eagle was seen repeatedly to dive-bomb a perched Cape Vulture and, when it flew off, struck it down in flight and killed it. As no subsequent attempt was made to feed on it, this incident is difficult to interpret, but it may have been an attempt at piracy. Predation on the small chicks of Cape Vultures has also been recorded. Once an eagle attempted to attack the month-old chicks of a pair of Blue Cranes, but it was successfully driven off by the parents. Gamebirds such as guineafowl and francolins are most often recorded, and domestic chickens are also sometimes taken. Other avian prey includes Egyptian Geese, a Cattle Egret, a Black Sparrowhawk, a Speckled Pigeon nestling and racing pigeons.

Reptiles are occasionally preyed on: snakes, a Tree Monitor, a Plated Rock Lizard and tortoises have been recorded.

This eagle rarely calls, probably because its constant visible presence in its territory makes vocal advertisement unnecessary. One call is a ringing, melodious *keee-ooo keee-ooo*; a probable variant is a loud *whaee-whaee* used when chasing off intruders near the nest. A *yieup-yieup-yieup* call, as well as a soft *chirrup-chirrup*, is used in greeting or solicitation at the nest, and the *yieup* call is made by the nestling from the age of about two months when begging for food, often monotonously for long periods. Chittering notes are emitted by both female and feathered eaglets when mantling prey. Occasionally flying birds make a single clucking *kyuk*.

At one nest the eagles made the *whaee* call and raised their wings in threat when baboons came too close. Baboons are recognised as enemies and are dive-bombed when near nests, as also are leopards. It is relevant to mention here, in contradiction of sensational articles and a film, that Black Eagles do not normally attack humans unless the situation is abnormal or staged. At one nest in the Matopos, frequently visited by an observer during the course of research, the eagles became progressively bolder over the years and began to attack. However, this behaviour was unnatural, and was assessed accordingly. After hundreds of visits made to nests by reliable observers it can be said that this eagle never attacks humans under normal circumstances.

BREEDING

Courtship displays are similar to the territorial displays performed throughout the year and are done singly or by the pair. Spectacular, steep, undulating dives are executed. At the top of the upward swoop the bird turns sideways or somersaults and rolls into the next dive with wings held against the body. On the upward swoop, and during the turn at the top, the white back shows conspicuously as the wings are opened. In a different display performed exclusively for courtship the male flies behind the female with his wings curved up above his back in a more exaggerated position than during normal soaring; as he draws near her she may half roll and present her claws. Tumbling flights with interlocked claws are probably not a part of courtship and may be instances of occasional aggressive interactions with intruders; one encounter where both birds fell into the sea was almost certainly the result of a fight. Mating usually takes place on a favourite rock perch near the nest, to the accompaniment of calling.

Nests are usually built on cliffs or sheer boulder outcrops in a variety of situations; some may be on exposed ledges with little shade, others are placed in small caves or alcoves where they are sheltered. In the southwestern Cape Province nests are frequently situated on cliffs where the rock is reddish, presumably because these are sheltered areas with least weathering. At the coast nests may be built on sea cliffs. The height of nest cliffs is variable but the nest is usually in an inaccessible position. Occasionally the Black Eagle nests in trees (always in a rocky habitat), for example Mountain Acacias, a euphorbia and a Baobab.

New nests are flattish structures about 1 m across, but those in long use may grow to large proportions, especially if situated in an alcove or niche where they are protected from weathering; some are 1,5 m across and 2 m or more in height. One huge Transvaal nest was 4,1 m in height. The central leafy bowl is about

Displaying Black Eagles showing the characteristic pattern of white on the upperparts.

View of a nest site and habitat of a Black
Eagle in the Matopos, Zimbabwe.

This Black Eagle broods on top of its nest
which is 4,1 m in height (Photograph:
Warwick Tarboton).

30–40 cm across. Large sticks are used in nest construction and one measured 1 m long and 6 cm in diameter.

Both birds take part in the nest building, and sticks are carried with the feet, and leafy sprays in the bill. Sticks are collected on the ground or broken off dead trees with the feet during flight, and leafy branches are usually obtained by alighting in the crown of a tree, where a spray is broken off, often after much flapping about. Repair of an established nest takes about a month to six weeks, but building activity may be sporadic with bursts of activity when considerable progress is made in a short period. Sometimes two sites may be built up in one season. In some years a nest may be lined for 7–10 weeks without any breeding taking place. New nests take longer to build, probably about two months.

Normally one site is used year after year, but alternate sites are not infrequent, and birds may use them for no apparent reason and then return to a previous nest. Some pairs have been known to use four sites, but this is exceptional. A move to a new site may involve a few metres or as much as 2,5 km, but distant moves are not often made. Abandoned nests are used by other species such as Black Stork, Lanner and White-necked Raven. Nests are used by generations of Black Eagles for long periods, and the two longest known records are of sites occupied for 52 and 67 years.

In a population census area of 620 km^2 in the Matopos 60 pairs occur at a density of a pair to 10,3 km^2, probably the greatest for any large eagle species anywhere in the world. Actual territory sizes established from direct observation vary from 5,8 km^2 to 14 km^2, depending on the terrain, and nests vary from 1,3 to 4,5 km apart. Territories are various shapes, some roughly circular and others elongate and irregular. No comparable density occurs elsewhere in southern Africa; in the Magaliesberg range in the Transvaal 13 pairs are known along a distance of 120 km, with the two closest nests 3 km apart. Elsewhere in South Africa pairs are usually far more widely spaced, but no study comparable to that in the Matopos exists, so that direct comparisons cannot be made. In the Matopos an abundance of dassies and nest sites suggests that the main factor limiting population growth in this optimum environment is a minimum territory size.

In addition to territorial boundaries at ground level, an airspace territory in the shape of an inverted irregular truncated cone is also maintained, although at its higher levels intruders are more readily tolerated and soaring birds often fly into a neighbour's upper airspace and *vice versa* without hostile interactions. As already described, territories are maintained by undulating display flights; the birds also perch prominently within their territories, which serves to advertise their occupation. Actual physical contact is rare as the intruder usually flees when chased. Other raptors are generally tolerated, and more often it is they who molest the Black Eagles. White-necked Ravens, however, are chased away when near nests.

Eggs are laid from late April to June with a May peak throughout southern Africa; there are occasional records for July, possibly where birds have relaid after a failure. This consistent breeding season is remarkable because birds in the northern summer rainfall area raise their young in the cool, dry winter months while their southern counterparts are experiencing heavy rainfall and even snow. It has been suggested that a stable habitat supporting an abundant dassie population enables breeding to take place at the same time over a wide range, but the factors governing the actual timing of the breeding season are not yet fully understood. However, throughout its southern African distribution, young first fly in August to October (i.e. in spring).

Two eggs are normally laid; in 25 per cent of cases in the Matopos single egg clutches were recorded. In the south-western Cape Province clutches of three are laid very occasionally. There is some evidence to suggest that single egg clutches are laid by females breeding for the first time. Eggs are rough chalky-white, variably marked with rust-red blotches and occasional underlying mauve markings. Some eggs are almost unmarked, others very handsomely blotched, and clutches where both are unmarked, or both well blotched, as well as plain and blotched eggs together, have all been recorded. In clutches with a plain and a marked egg either may be laid first, although first eggs are always larger, and in some clutches there is a considerable difference in the size of the eggs. Measurements are: 75,0 × 58,3 (82); 66,7–86,0 × 52,0–62,0.

Eggs are laid three to four days apart, usually four; in one observation a second egg was laid in the evening at 17h00. First-laid eggs may not be incubated continuously on the day they are laid, but by the second day the egg is covered most of the time. During incubation the eggs are brooded about 92 per cent of the time during daylight, both male and female doing a share, his normally when he brings prey for the female and she leaves the nest to feed on it. However, she also leaves to kill for herself on occasions. The female sits overnight, and the male's share during daylight varies from pair to pair; in observed cases it has amounted to 6, 15 and 49 per cent. The last figure would seem to be exceptional, the birds not normally doing an equal share. Green sprays are brought by both sexes, frequently when relieving the partner at the nest. In the Matopos sitting birds are often pestered by stingless bees (*Trigona* species), which swarm round their eyes to obtain moisture. On being disturbed from the nest the eagle soars round nearby or high overhead, returning as soon as observers have departed. The incubation period is normally 44 days, but 45–46 days has once been recorded.

An egg takes about two days to hatch from the time first cracks in the shell appear, but before this the chick can be heard cheeping inside the shell. Eggshells are not removed, breaking into fragments which disappear under nest lining. When the second egg hatches three to four days later, the first chick has already developed its co-ordination, and a period of relentless sibling aggression (or Cainism) occurs during which the first-hatched chick (Cain) pecks its sibling (Abel) until it dies from a combination of its injuries and starvation. Both Cain and Abel are of course not necessarily male in the account which follows.

As soon as Abel hatches and moves about, it is attacked by Cain, who adopts a truculent posture with chest forward and downy wing stubs held out. Twisting downward pecks are delivered, mainly to the head and back, stimulated by any movement from Abel. Thus, when it tries to come forward to feed, Cain breaks off its own meal to attack it. The female makes no attempt to intervene in any way; the attacks may even continue beneath her breast feathers while she is brooding. Gradually Abel becomes weaker and weaker, loses weight, and no longer has the strength to try to feed. By this stage Cain, twice Abel's weight, shakes it about or even lifts it bodily. In the 72-hour life of one Abel it was pecked 1 569 times during 38 attack sessions. The intensity of the attacks increases from the second day when it moves about more. At the time of its death it is emaciated, with severe bruising around the eyes and abrasions on its back. Available observations indicate that the body is not eaten deliberately, although it may be confused with prey. Sometimes it is removed, but usually it becomes buried under nest lining.

Experiments in the Matopos have shown that sibling aggression may persist for at least six weeks, but if a hand-reared eaglet is replaced at eight weeks old two young can be raised successfully, although one is always dominant and feeds first. There is only one case known (in Kenya) where two young have been reared together under natural conditions. Various explanations for Cainism have been advanced, for example it has been suggested that food supply is the limiting factor. However, the evidence refutes this, for in the first two weeks of the nestling period there may be up to five or six dassies on the nest at one

(1) The nest of a Black Eagle.

(2) A six-day-old chick tears at the wound it has opened on the back of its day-old sibling.

(3) A four-week-old nestling; the remains of four dassies lie on the nest behind it.

(4) At five weeks the first feathers appear through the down.

(5) By six weeks feather growth is rapid.

(6) The nestling is fully feathered at eight weeks old.

time, enough food to rear several young at that stage. Another suggestion advanced is that a second egg acts as a 'reserve', conferring a greater chance of reproductive success. Again the facts do not support this: there is no difference in the breeding success of one-egg and two-egg eagle species. Thus the apparent biological waste of Abel is an intriguing phenomenon that remains to be convincingly explained.

The newly hatched eaglet is covered in fine white down; the cere and feet are flesh pink, the eyes black and the bill is horn coloured. During its first four weeks the nestling grows rapidly, acquiring a much thicker coat of white down through which first feathers are just appearing along the hind edge of the wings; the cere and feet are yellow at this age. At five weeks feathers are breaking on the scapulars and wing coverts, and first tail feathers appear. From six weeks on, it develops very rapidly until feathers cover the down at the age of eight weeks.

The feeble newly hatched eaglet may receive its first meal when only three hours old. During its first few days its co-ordination develops rapidly until at the age of four days it can direct accurate pecks at its sibling, as already described. It first stands when about a month old, and tries unsuccessfully to feed itself, which it can only achieve at the age of six weeks. However, because of the tough nature of its staple diet, the female continues to tear open dassie carcasses, as well as to feed it, until the end of the nestling period. Although it attempts some wing flaps as early as two weeks, proper wing exercises only take place once it is feathered, increasing in frequency at the end of the nestling period.

Parental attention in the nestling period is linked to the three main stages of the eaglet's development, which may be divided into its downy first month, the second month during which it becomes fully feathered, and the third period up to the time of its first flight. Variations obviously occur from one locality to another depending on the climatic conditions, but even in the same area chicks in exposed or sheltered nests would require different amounts of care. However, the overall picture is clear. In the first few days a parent is on the nest about 98 per cent of the time, and the chick is brooded a great deal; the male assists in this, but his share is small, and his main function is to bring prey, which he provides well in excess of the immediate requirements of the female and the chick. Once a male was seen to feed an eaglet. From about three weeks on, the eaglet is no longer brooded by day unless the weather is inclement, but the female continues to roost on the nest until the tenth week. During the first month a parent is at the nest 80–90 per cent of the time, but in the second stage the female leaves the eaglet alone for progressively longer periods. Even in an exposed site it no longer needs shading, once it is about six weeks old. The female now also hunts actively, and she continues to tear up prey for her offspring. The adults bring in birds plucked and dassies partially plucked. The nest is kept clean by the removal of bones and dry pieces of skin, and both sexes bring fresh lining, although not after two months. In the final stage parental time on the nest is mainly spent in delivering prey; one observer concluded that an eaglet was deliberately starved near the end of its time in the nest to induce it to fly, but this is not confirmed by observations in the Matopos.

The eaglet first flies when between 90 and 98 days old, although it can leave the nest as early as 80 days if disturbed. Its first flight is made independent of the adults' presence; one flew 200 m to an outcrop where it remained perched for five hours. In its first month the juvenile is not adept at flying, indeed it flies very little, spending much of its time on the nest (where it roosts) or on nearby perches. In its second month it becomes simultaneously more accomplished on the wing and more adventurous, exploring and expanding its range, as well as occasionally accompanying its parents for short distances. At night it continues to roost on the nest. During its third month out of the nest the juvenile wanders farther afield, often well out of sight of the nest. It begins to snatch up items such as a spray of leaves and to fly with it in its talons; this behaviour is linked to its increasing dexterity on the wing and serves as mock killing practice. It rarely visits the nest in daytime, although roosting on the nest or on perches in the area. Towards the end of the post-nestling period the parents begin to chase it away.

Throughout the post-nestling period the juvenile is fed regularly by the adults, and can always be located by its noisy cries of solicitation whenever it sees them. During the first month prey is brought to the nest, after which it is normally delivered at various other perches, although the juvenile may still carry the prey to the nest and feed on it there. If it does not finish a meal, the female will feed on what is left, but the young bird is always fed preferentially. It flies about very little with its parents, never accompanies them on hunting flights, and by the time it leaves the territory has yet to kill for itself. In one study it was estimated that the adults and their eaglet accounted for about 236 dassies from hatching until the independence of the juvenile after a thirteen-week post-nestling period.

In the Matopos the post-nestling period varies from 13 to 19 weeks. In Kenya a juvenile was still seen with the adults five months after leaving the nest; it also used the nest for four months as a feeding and roosting place. Once driven out of the territory, the juveniles wander, or are harried by neighbouring pairs, until they reach a peripheral neutral zone or 'empty quarter'. Ringed juveniles have been recovered at distances of 40, 72 and 176 km from their nest sites in their first year.

In a detailed thirteen-year breeding success study in the Matopos there were 652 pair-years with 442 breeding attempts from which 339 young were reared, a replacement rate of 0,52 young per pair per year. On average 68 per cent of the population bred each year (with variation from 46 to 89 per cent), pairs bred in two years out of three, and one in four attempts was unsuccessful. Some factors adversely affecting breeding success were above-average rainfall in the three months prior to breeding, proximity and intervisibility of nests, other species taking over nests, non-completion of a new nest before peak laying time, and the establishing or re-establishing of new territories.

Some of the predators on Black Eagle nestlings are baboons, White-necked Ravens and possibly pythons, leopards and small predatory mammals such as genets. Tropical Nest Flies *Passeromyia heterochaeta* enter hatching eggs and lay their eggs in the nostrils or on the body of the chick. The larvae hatch and cause discomfort, or even occasionally death from myiasis, an inflammatory condition. There are other hazards. One nest fell down with a six-week-old chick in it, whereupon the birds built a new nest and successfully hatched a chick at a time when their previous nestling would have been flying.

The Black Eagle has been intensively studied in the Matopos. Comparative observations from other localities in southern Africa would prove interesting and valuable.

17 Tawny Eagle *132*

Roofarend

Aquila rapax

PLATES 7 AND 8

DERIVATION
eagle : rapacious — *aquila* (L) : *rapax* (L)

IDENTIFICATION

Adult: The variable plumages of this species give rise to much confusion with other brown eagles, but observers should first concentrate on the basic features of its appearance before concerning themselves with problems of coloration. Of all southern African eagles, the Tawny probably has the most 'classic' aquiline build: a bold rounded head, strong bill, baggy 'trousers', powerful feet and a well-proportioned body. In flight the balanced proportions of wings and tail are also characteristic. These aspects alone help to distinguish it from Wahlberg's Eagle, Lesser Spotted Eagle, juvenile Bateleur, Brown Snake Eagle and juvenile Black-breasted Snake Eagle (the last three all having bare legs). The most likely confusion is with the migrant Steppe Eagle, whose distinguishing features are discussed fully in the text on that species.

Except on very pale individual birds, the various plumages all have tawny in them. Darkest birds have heavy dark brown streaking on neck, breast, scapulars and wing coverts, and show most tawny on the head, abdomen, leggings, lower back and tail coverts. It appears from field studies that the most heavily marked birds are females but some males with dark brown streaking also occur. Another plumage is a uniform tawny colour; from observations at nests it seems that this is usually found in males which do not develop dark streaking over the years. The situation with regard to almost white birds is still not fully understood, but it may be that some adults have this plumage. However, pale birds are discussed more fully below. The eyes are dull yellow and the cere and feet are yellow.

In flight the trailing edge of the wing is slightly curved outwards, indenting at the junction of primaries and secondaries, and the rounded medium-length tail is usually held spread. In uniform tawny birds the blackish remiges and tail contrast with the rest of the plumage above and below. However, in dark streaky birds, the upper and underwing coverts are also dark, so that they do not contrast as noticeably. If a good view is obtained, faint narrow barring on wings and tail may be seen, but this is not a good field character.

Juvenile and immature: In fresh plumage juveniles are identifiable by their uniform warm rufous-tawny colour, and the eyes are brown, not dull yellow as in the adult; they change gradually to yellow after approximately two years. In flight there is a narrow white trailing edge to the wing, and a less distinct narrow bar at the junction of the wing coverts and remiges, both above and below, but these bars are not usually as pronounced as in the juvenile Steppe Eagle.

Problems arise with immature plumages. It appears that juveniles fade almost to blond as their plumage wears. These pale birds frequently have some ginger feathers on the head, probably fresh feathers growing in. Through a succession of moults, thought to extend over a period of three to four years, adult plumage is acquired. Tawny coloration appears gradually and in streaky birds the first dark markings appear on the sides of the breast. However, to confuse the situation, blond individuals whose plumage appears in fresh condition are often seen, and there is an influx of these birds into the Kalahari with the rains in March. While they may all be immature birds, further research is required before the situation can be clarified.

HABITAT

The Tawny Eagle occurs in savanna, especially in acacia thornveld, and also in semi-desert regions. It is not found in areas of high rainfall or on mountains.

STATUS AND DISTRIBUTION

Adults are resident but sometimes make local movements to areas of prey abundance such as a Red-billed Quelea colony. Juveniles and immatures appear to wander widely, and

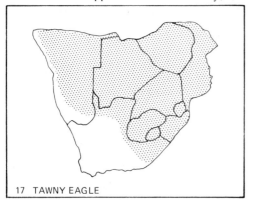

17   TAWNY EAGLE

aggregations which appear in localities of temporary food abundance (e.g. in the Kalahari during the rains) have probably been drawn from a very wide area.

The Tawny Eagle is common in suitable habitat but there is evidence of a decline in its former range. It has disappeared from areas in the central Transvaal and is no longer found in southern and central Cape Province. Its present distribution is now mainly north of the Orange River but it still occurs in the eastern and north-eastern Cape Province. Extralimitally it occurs widely northwards to the Sahara outside the forested Congo basin.

GENERAL HABITS

The Tawny Eagle owes its success as a species to its versatility. Opinions in various textbooks that it is 'sluggish', 'not very distinguished' and 'unimpressive' are wide of the mark. It is a rapacious eagle, as its specific name *rapax* correctly indicates. There are three facets to its feeding habits: it is a scavenger, a pirate and a rapacious killer.

Carrion, ranging in size from large ungulates to small road kills, is an important source of food, so that it is difficult to know whether food found on nests has been scavenged or killed, although it may be assumed that remains of larger items are found as carrion. In observed interactions between the Tawny Eagle and other carrion eaters, a varied picture emerges. At times it may feed in amity with other scavengers, for example with a White-headed Vulture on a dead hare; on other occasions it may be aggressive and dominant, as when one kept twenty vultures off a carcass. In southern Africa it now rarely associates with man for offal, although historically it did so when conditions were more primitive. In some parts of Africa it still frequents villages for whatever scraps it can glean. In another association with man, which may be considered opportunistic scavenging of a sort, it used to accompany shoots and carry off wounded birds. Again, this behaviour seems to be no longer recorded in southern Africa.

Dashing piratical attacks are made on other birds of prey ranging in size from a Black-shouldered Kite to a Martial Eagle; even Marabou Storks and Ground Hornbills do not escape its attention. Usually the victim is harried until it drops its food, but the Tawny Eagle also makes surprise attacks, as when it robbed a Secretary Bird of a Puffadder it had just caught. Although the Bateleur is itself a pirate, it may be robbed of prey by the Tawny Eagle. At a Red-billed Quelea colony smaller birds of prey were robbed by Tawny Eagles waiting nearby. In another incident, not strictly an instance of piracy, they retrieved wounded queleas from a shallow pan when the queleas had been struck but not held by Lanners preying on them. In this case they had to compete with Black-backed Jackals also feeding on the crippled queleas.

The Tawny Eagle hunts either from a perch or on the wing. It kills prey on the ground after a fast stoop, but it is also capable of killing flying birds. In Kenya it has struck down flamingoes, and has been recorded to kill a Speckled Pigeon in flight. Mammals up to 4 kg, twice the eagle's weight, have been killed. Studies at nests in eleven different localities recorded mammals, birds and reptiles in all prey samples except from one locality (the Karoo), where no reptiles were recorded. While there were basic similarities in most of the localities, there were also some striking differences. For example, mammals comprised 37–39 per cent of the totals in most areas, but 85 per cent in the Karoo. This indicates that prey choice is governed by local availability, or in some cases specialisation on a particular prey species, as at one nest in Zimbabwe where Tree Monitors (Leguaans) made up 29 per cent of the total of 83 items, but only 8 per cent of 107 items at three other nests in the same National Park. In all the studies mammals supplied the greatest bulk of food, even though more birds than mammals were recorded in some samples.

Mammals killed in southern Africa by the Tawny Eagle range in size from mice to the young of small antelopes or a baby Warthog and include squirrels, dassies, hares, mongooses and Suricates. Additionally, nocturnal animals such as genets and Springhares have been recorded in areas where there was no possibility that they may have been killed by traffic at night. One observer has recorded this eagle drinking and bathing at night at full moon, and suggested that it may even hunt on such occasions. While no evidence of night hunting exists, it is a possibility that should not be excluded. The extent to which it preys on small domestic stock is not known. The remains of domestic lambs and goat kids have been found in nests but there is no way of knowing whether they were killed or obtained as carrion.

Birds ranging in size from doves to guineafowl, korhaans and young Ostriches are killed in southern Africa, but predation on flamingoes has not been recorded. Gamebirds are often taken, and at times domestic chickens when they occur in free-range conditions. Other avian prey records include Cattle Egrets, a Hamerkop, Yellow-billed Duck, Red-knobbed Coot, Spotted Dikkop, plovers, Namaqua Sandgrouse, Grey Loeries, hornbills, rollers and starlings. There is also one record of a Secretary Bird, but there was no way of knowing if it was killed or found dead.

Various snakes are caught or found as carrion, including venomous ones such as the Boomslang, Puffadder, Black Mamba and cobras. As well as the Tree Monitors (Leguaans) already mentioned, smaller lizards and a chameleon have been recorded.

Termites and grasshoppers are eaten, as well as the occasional amphibian or fish. In one instance a Tawny Eagle waded into shallow water to catch a catfish large enough to give it a full meal. According to one unusual record it was seen eating the fruit of a Baobab on the ground.

Studies of the food of this eagle and the Bateleur show close similarities so that they would be directly in competition. However, they are probably ecologically separated by their different hunting methods, although the Tawny Eagle is dominant when they meet at carrion.

In a number of cases two birds, presumably a pair, have been seen to share a kill, so it is probable that they remain together throughout the year, perhaps hunting on a co-operative basis.

This eagle is not particularly vocal and is usually only heard to call during display in the breeding season when it utters a barking *kyow* and a guttural *kwork*, probably by male and female respectively. At the nest the female makes a sibilant *shreep-shreep* call of solicitation. The chick cheeps initially but once its feathers emerge it begs with a loud *we-yik, wee-yik* call.

BREEDING

Courtship consists of the pair flying round together, sometimes with exaggerated shallow wing-beats. Gentle undulations are performed, and occasionally they interlock claws in a tumbling flight, but courtship displays are not particularly spectacular compared with those of some other eagles.

The nest, probably the most characteristic of all African eagles, is almost always situated on the crown of a tree open to the sky; only very rarely is it placed beneath the canopy or on a lateral branch. Nests are situated at heights of 4,5–30 m, but usually between 6 and 15 m. In bare trees they are very conspicuous, but on top of a thorn tree in leaf a nest is difficult to detect. A variety of trees is used, but thorny acacias are preferred where available, and nests are generally inaccessible. Sometimes the nest may be built on top of another nest such as that of a Buffalo Weaver, or on an abandoned vulture's

(1) This Tawny Eagle's nest is placed typically on the crown of a tree.

(2) A close-up of the usual clutch of two eggs.

(3) A day-old chick.

(4) First feathers are just appearing through the down at the age of three weeks.

(5) By five weeks the upperparts are well feathered.

(6) The nestling is fully feathered by eight weeks old.

nest. Sites may be in flat, open country or on hills, but the eagle always has a good view of the surrounding country. In the south-western Transvaal they have taken increasingly to nesting on electricity pylons.

Nests are flat structures of fairly small sticks and measure about a metre across. If used for a number of years they are larger and assume the shape of an inverted cone as the nest gains in height. The central cup is 20–45 cm across, and is lined with various materials. Green leaves are used, but also dry materials such as grass, seed-pods and leaves, as well as oddments such as newspaper, paper packets and even a large polythene bag. The use of fresh green lining is not a regular habit as in most other eagles. Repair of the nest in two instances took a month and seven weeks; in the former most of the construction was completed in the first week. Once an eagle was seen to pull sticks off an old nest and take them to the new site. The share of the sexes in nest-building is not known.

While it may breed in the same area for at least 50–60 years in recorded cases, this eagle makes frequent moves to new nest sites. It is probable that it moves because the tree's crown can no longer support the nest, or growing branches inhibit easy access. As a rule nests are used for one to three years, but sometimes for much longer, and on occasions an abandoned site may be reoccupied again. The distance to a new nest site is not usually more than two kilometres.

There are various observations on nest spacing in southern Africa. In Zimbabwe three nests were 7–10 km apart in one study area. On the border of the Kruger National Park six or seven pairs were located in 460 km², but away from this conserved area, where birds were breeding regularly spaced on pylons in the south-western Transvaal, nests were 19–20 km apart.

Eggs are laid from April to June, and in Zimbabwe there is a distinct May peak. Occasional eggs have been recorded in July, August and September, possibly replacement clutches after the failure of earlier ones. The normal clutch is two eggs. They are chalky-white in ground colour and vary from being almost unmarked to being handsomely blotched with rust-red and a few underlying lilac spots. Eggs in the same clutch may vary from almost plain to well marked. Measurements are: 69,6 × 54,8 (67); 64,0–75,7 × 49,9–59,5.

Eggs are laid about two days apart and incubation commences with the laying of the first egg. The bulk of the incubation is by the female, with very occasional spells by the male. She sits very tight if the tree is climbed, not flying off until the last moment, and then she flies out of sight or high overhead. The male has not been seen to bring prey for her but further observations are required. Lining is added to the nest; whether brought by both sexes is not known. Two incubation periods have been obtained, 42–44 days and 39–40 days, the second being short for an eagle of this size.

When the second chick hatches it is vigorously attacked by its stronger sibling; in one instance the weights of the chicks at this stage were 85 g and 143 g respectively. Normally it does not survive these attacks and dies within a few days of hatching. In one case the remains of the smaller chick were found partly eaten on the nest and may have been eaten by the female or fed to the surviving chick. However, Cainism does not invariably have fatal results: there are three known cases in southern Africa where two young have been reared successfully together, although the older nestling always remains dominant.

On hatching, the chick is covered in white down. The bill is black, its cere and feet are yellow and the eyes brown. A thicker coat of white down is acquired by two weeks, and a week later first feathers appear on the scapulars and wing coverts. Wing and tail quills are emerging rapidly at this stage with first feathers just breaking from the wing quills. At four weeks old, feathers are emerging rapidly above and are appearing down the sides of the breast. By five weeks it has a good covering of feathers above, except on the head, but the underparts are still mainly downy. The wing and tail feathers are growing fast. The rapid development of this dorsal covering of feathers is to some extent comparable to that of other raptors with exposed nests, such as the snake eagles and the Secretary Bird. At this stage the female is released from the nest so that she can also hunt. At the age of seven weeks the eaglet is fully feathered except for some down on the neck and underwing coverts, but these areas are soon covered, whereafter the only feather growth is on the wings and tail until they attain their full length.

Initially the small chick is inactive and sleeps a great deal, brooded or shaded by the female and fed at intervals. By the age of two weeks it may be left alone on the nest for two and a half hours without any apparent discomfort. It first stands weakly at 22 days, but by 28 days can walk round the nest and may even attempt some wing flapping. From the age of five weeks it lies prone in the nest on seeing anyone below, but if the nest tree is climbed it adopts a truculent threat posture with gape wide open and neck feathers raised. It slaps at the intruder with its wings and uses its claws to defend itself. One 39-day-old eaglet could tear up prey for itself, but it was also fed by the female. From seven weeks on it performs vigorous wing exercises. At this stage it is left alone on the nest and spends its time sleeping, preening, nibbling sticks or bones in the nest, walking about and peering intently at events below such as the passing of a flock of guineafowl. Its *wee-yik, wee-yik* calls of solicitation become almost a squeal when a parent is nearby with food, a major event in its solitary day.

Parental behaviour is linked to the eaglet's growth. For the first ten days it is closely attended by the female, but from two weeks may be left alone on the nest for quite long periods, although the female is usually perched in the vicinity. It is not known at what stage her time on the nest drops markedly—she may still shade a three-week-old eaglet—but probably when the eaglet is about a month old, which is very early for an eagle this size. Up to this stage the male provides the prey, and once he was seen to feed a three-week-old eaglet. At one nest the female roosted in a tree 150 m from the nest when the eaglet was ten weeks old. Lining is added but is neglected at an early stage. During the later nestling period the nest becomes foul with bones, pieces of skin and various bits of decomposing carrion, but the adults make no attempt to remove these. This enables an observer to gather substantial prey samples if a nest is found after the eaglet has flown. The eagles may also have a favourite plucking perch in the area below which additional prey remains may be found.

In seven observations in Zimbabwe the eaglet made its first flight between eleven and twelve weeks. In one instance the juvenile was fed at the nest for about six weeks after it first flew, and it roosted there too. Thereafter it became independent of the nest area and ranged farther afield. One immature ringed as a nestling was shot 48 km from its nest two years after it first flew, and two marked juveniles were seen five and seven months later 50 km and 34 km from their nests respectively. On the evidence it appears that the juveniles disperse beyond the territory of the adults once they become independent.

In a study of breeding success in Zimbabwe 19 young were reared in 26 pair-years, a replacement rate of 0,73 young per pair per year.

18 Steppe Eagle /33.

Steppe-arend
Aquila nipalensis

PLATES 7 AND 8

DERIVATION
eagle : of Nepal — *aquila* (L) : *nipalensis* (L)

IDENTIFICATION
Adult: It is uniform dark brown with a small ginger patch on the nape. The cere and feet are yellow, as are the prominent fleshy edges to the gape, which is large and extends back in line with the back of the dark brown eye. In flight there is no pattern to aid identification, but the typical 'Tawny Eagle' shape with long rounded tail and shallow S-curve of the hind edge of the wing are characteristic.

The total absence of any tawny (except on nape) distinguishes it from resident Tawny Eagles, even dark streaky birds. Additionally, the eye of the adult Tawny Eagle is yellow, and the gape extends back only as far as a line through the middle of the eye. The difference is particularly noticeable if the birds are panting, when the gape of the Steppe Eagle appears huge. Other possible confusions are with Wahlberg's Eagle and the adult Lesser Spotted Eagle, but the Steppe Eagle is altogether a

A juvenile Steppe Eagle to show the characteristic pattern of the upperparts.

much bulkier species with a different flight outline. When it is perched, the baggy leggings distinguish it from the Lesser Spotted Eagle, which has tightly feathered 'stovepipe' legs.

Juvenile and immature: The juvenile is clay-brown and when perched shows a prominent double bar on the wing, one at the junction of wing coverts and secondaries and the other along the hind edge of the wing. The uniform clay-brown colour distinguishes it from all plumages of the Tawny Eagle, especially the rufous juvenile which has a similar pattern of bars on the wing in fresh plumage. The gape distinction also applies. In flight it is boldly patterned above and below with a white bar at the junction of remiges and wing coverts and another along the hind edge of the wing; there is also a white 'window' at the junction of primaries and secondaries. The tip of the tail is white, and there is a broad white U-shaped band on the upper tail coverts. From above, confusion with the juvenile Lesser Spotted Eagle is possible, but the Steppe is altogether more boldly marked, although the white on its rump is not as clearly U-shaped.

Adult plumage is gradually acquired in three moults over a period of about six years. During the transitional immature stage the contour feathers darken, the white hind edge to the wings and tail disappears, and the 'windows' on the wings and the white rump are much reduced. Thus an intermediate stage is reached in about the third year when there is a white band separating remiges and wing coverts below, although much reduced and faint above, and a narrow band on the rump.

HABITAT

It occurs in any open lightly wooded country, as well as in arid areas, but not in forested or mountainous terrain.

STATUS AND DISTRIBUTION

This Palearctic migrant is a common although somewhat unpredictable visitor to southern Africa (see General Habits) arriving in late October or November and departing in March. In its breeding range there is evidence of a decline in the population, mainly through contact with Man, and in some localities electrocution on power pylons causes the death of many birds.

The breeding range extends from the Balkans through southern Russia to south-western Siberia and Kazakhstan. They winter in Iran, Iraq and Africa, reaching southern Africa through east Africa where many birds remain. In southern Africa they occur south to the cen-

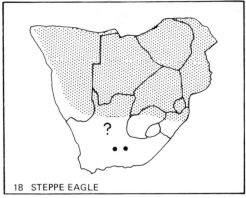

18 STEPPE EAGLE

tral Cape Province but are rare south of the Orange River.

GENERAL HABITS

These large eagles almost always occur in southern Africa in association with rain fronts and the accompanying humidity which causes the emergence of their main food, termite alates. They frequently travel in company with other termite-eating migrants such as Black Kites and Lesser Spotted Eagles, and aggregations of over a hundred Steppe Eagles in an area are not uncommon. They move with the rain, seldom staying for long in any locality, and in drought years are not seen at all. In Zimbabwe they occur mainly from November to mid-December, probably moving westwards through Botswana into Namibia to take advantage of the later rains there and in the Kalahari (January and February).

In Russia they prey on a wide range of small mammals, reptiles, amphibians, gamebirds and some insects; in east Africa they prey on mole-rats and feed on carrion as well as termites. However, in southern Africa, they feed to a large extent on termites, the only other important prey recorded being nestling queleas, which they obtain by scrambling amongst the branches of the nesting colonies. When a termite emergence is located they gather with other termitivores in large flocks, and they pick up the alates as they emerge from their nests or chase them on foot, lumbering after their minuscule quarry in ludicrous fashion. They have once been seen to take termites in the air with their feet and to feed on them in flight, not an easy task for such a large eagle. At any feast numbers of gorged eagles can be seen sitting on trees in the vicinity, where they may roost, before leaving next day if the rain belt has moved on.

Although tiny, their termite prey is highly nutritious, with a calorific value of 560 per

A flock of Steppe Eagles feeding on emerging termites.

100 g. It has been estimated that a Steppe Eagle would require approximately 1 600 to 2 200 termites a day, which it could obtain in three hours' feeding. As they lay down sub-

stantial fat deposits before their northward migration, the nutritional value of their diet is evident; the stomachs of two dissected birds contained 630 and 930 termite heads.

This eagle very rarely calls in Africa. All that is usually heard are a few throaty croaks when birds squabble over food or a perch.

The majority of birds seen in southern Africa are juveniles and immatures although a sprinkling of adults will be found in any large gathering. Until recently, despite the large numbers occuring, very little was known about the distribution of this species, probably because it could not be identified. Birds on northward migration do not appear to return through Zimbabwe, and much research is still required on the movements, distribution and behaviour of this eagle.

19 Lesser Spotted Eagle /34

Gevlekte Arend
Aquila pomarina

PLATES 7 AND 8

DERIVATION
eagle : Pomeranian — *aquila* (L) : *pomarina* (L)

Pomerania was a province of the former Kingdom of Prussia. A possible alternative derivation may be 'capped nostril', presumably a reference to the cere, from the Greek *poma*: cap or lid of a well and *rhinos*: nose or nostril

IDENTIFICATION
Adult: This uniformly brown eagle is not easy to identify when perched except by its long, tightly feathered legs. The cere and feet are yellow, and the yellowish eye helps to distinguish it from the brown-eyed Wahlberg's Eagle with which it is most easily confused. In flight it is long-winged with a short rounded tail, usually held spread, and its silhouette is different from Wahlberg's Eagle, which has a long square tail. It also has small white patches on the upper wing at the base of the primaries, and a faint narrow white band on the upper tail coverts. Some birds are pale yellowish instead of brown, but they are rare and comprise less than five per cent of the population.

Juvenile and immature: Juveniles are warm brown with bold spotting on the wing coverts, mainly in two rows, giving the effect of a double band on the wing. The underparts are variably streaked with yellowish and there is a distinctive ginger patch on the nape; the only

other eagle with this feature is the adult Steppe Eagle, but that species is uniform dark brown and much larger. The cere and feet are yellow and the eyes brown. In flight from below it appears mainly brown with a faint white line at the junction of the coverts and the remiges, and the undertail coverts are whitish. Above,

A juvenile Lesser Spotted Eagle to show the pattern of the upperparts; it is not as boldly marked as a juvenile Steppe Eagle.

the white line between wing coverts and remiges is distinct, and there are white 'windows' at the base of the primaries. On the tail coverts there is a U-shaped white band, and some birds also have a white patch in the centre of the back. Superficially, the dorsal pattern resembles that of the juvenile Steppe Eagle, but that species is altogether more boldly patterned.

Progression to adult plumage takes four to five years after two moults. After the first moult in the second year the characteristic juvenile plumage is lost; a darker brown plumage is acquired and the white markings above are gradually reduced.

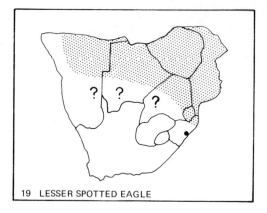

19 LESSER SPOTTED EAGLE

HABITAT

Like the Steppe Eagle, this species occurs in open woodland, but may be found in more heavily wooded areas too, especially near water.

STATUS AND DISTRIBUTION

This Palearctic migrant visits southern Africa from the end of October until March. In its northern breeding range there is evidence of a decline in the population, particularly as a result of the clearing of woodland. Although the Lesser Spotted Eagle is not seriously threatened at present, experiments have shown that its numbers in peripheral declining populations can be artificially increased. Two eggs are laid, but only one chick survives under normal conditions. If the second chick is rescued before it dies, it can be placed in the nest of a Black Kite and reared with its chicks until well feathered. Then it is replaced in its own nest from which two young will then fly successfully.

In its breeding range it occurs in eastern Germany, Poland, eastern Czechoslovakia, Hungary, Yugoslavia, Romania, Bulgaria, north-east Greece, western Turkey and the Soviet Union north to Leningrad and east to about 35° E. One bird ringed in the Kruger National Park was recovered just under a year later near Kusary in Russia to the west of the Caspian Sea, and a bird ringed in Latvia in August was recovered in November two years later at Filabusi in Zimbabwe. Large numbers have been seen migrating south over the Bosphorus, and thence along the coast of the Levant; others fly across the Mediterranean via Cyprus. Thereafter they migrate through Suez into Africa. In southern Africa they have been recorded in Zimbabwe, Botswana, Namibia, Transvaal, Swaziland, southern Mozambique, Zululand and Natal (rarely).

GENERAL HABITS

The habits of this species are very like those of the Steppe Eagle, and the two are often found together in mixed flocks of migrant and local raptors when termites are emerging. However, unlike the Steppe Eagle, this species is more likely to be encountered solitarily. It moves about a great deal following the rain fronts, seldom remaining for long in one locality.

In its northern range it feeds on small mammals up to the size of a young rabbit, as well as on reptiles, birds, amphibians and some insects. It hunts on the wing or from a perch, but also on foot, for which its long legs are suited. In southern Africa, in addition to termites, its principal food, it preys on quelea nestlings, small rodents and amphibians.

The migratory habits of the Lesser Spotted Eagle, like those of the Steppe Eagle, in southern Africa are still little known, and to an even greater extent it has been either misidentified or not recognised. This has resulted in its occurrence being overlooked in many areas until recently, although it is a regular and not uncommon visitor. The majority of birds recorded in southern Africa have been juveniles, and their identification should not present too many problems.

20 Wahlberg's Eagle *135.*

Bruinarend
Aquila wahlbergi

DERIVATION
eagle : of Wahlberg — *aquila* (L) : *wahlbergi* (L)

This eagle is named in honour of Johan August Wahlberg, a Swedish explorer and naturalist, who was killed by an elephant near Lake Ngami in 1856. The name should be pronounced 'vaal' as in Transvaal, not as in the English 'wall'.

IDENTIFICATION
Adult: This small eagle is usually brown in colour, but a pale form occurs and there are also a number of confusing plumage variations. In all plumages the eyes are dark brown and the cere and feet are yellow. As in the case of the variable Tawny Eagle, the important thing is first to concentrate on the general appearance of the bird. The size and rather small pointed face aid identification, as does a slight occipital crest, although this is not always visible. The flight outline is characteristic, with the leading and trailing edges of the wings parallel and the long tail held closed, so that it has the appearance of two crossed planks.

Brown birds vary in colour from warm brown to dark chocolate, the only features relieving this uniformity being the bright yellow cere and feet. In flight the bird appears almost entirely brown from below, but the remiges are pale grey, so that they contrast to a certain extent with the underwing coverts, but not strikingly as in the Brown Snake Eagle. Various confusions with other brown eagles are possible, the adult Lesser Spotted Eagle being the most likely. When perched, the latter has tight 'stovepipe' leggings, while those of Wahlberg's Eagle are baggy. In flight the Lesser Spotted Eagle has a more curved shape to the wings, and the tail is shorter, rounded at the tip and usually held partially spread. The dark form of the Booted Eagle may also cause confusion, but again the shapes of the wings and tail distinguish it and, if seen, the white shoulder patches at the junction of wings and body are diagnostic. The perched Brown Snake Eagle, which is superficially similar at a distance, may be identified by the bare white legs, large yellow eyes and loose cowl of feathers at the back of the head. The brown *Milvus* kites are also sometimes confused with this eagle; perched they are longer bodied and have very small heads so that they do not appear aquiline; in the air the forked tail and characteristic flapping and gliding flight immediately identify them.

The pale form is not common, comprising an estimated 7–13 per cent of the population and occurring more often in some areas than others. The true pale form is white except for grey feathers edged with white on the wing coverts, scapulars and back. In flight the white body and underwing coverts contrast with the dark remiges and tail. The most likely confusion is with the pale form of the Booted Eagle, which has a dark head and neck when perched, and a different silhouette in flight with spots on the underwing coverts if a good view is obtained.

Other plumage variations that occur are very confusing, but again the shape of the bird is the feature to concentrate on. Some of the colour variations are: very pale honey-brown, either uniform or with a dark head and neck; dark brown with a pale honey-coloured crown; dark brown with breast and whole head white; a mixture of dark and pale form with dark brown on back, neck and upper breast, grey on wing coverts and honey-brown on crown, lower breast and abdomen. Some of the unusual patterns may be caused by moulting, but the evidence suggests that it is a polychromatic species without any rigid genetic control of pigmentation.

Juvenile: There is no readily identifiable juvenile plumage. Young birds out of the nest resemble adults except that they appear more immaculate because of their fresh plumage. Juveniles of the pale form assume this plumage from the start.

HABITAT
This eagle occurs in well-wooded savannas varying from miombo to thornbush, but not in arid or very mountainous terrain. It is found in areas where there is a mosaic of woodland and cultivation.

STATUS AND DISTRIBUTION
This migrant to southern Africa from farther north in Africa arrives in the latter part of Au-

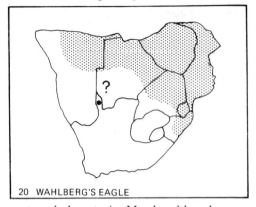

20   WAHLBERG'S EAGLE

gust and departs in March, although some birds may remain into early April. Its migratory movements are not properly understood, despite the fact that it is probably the commonest eagle in Africa. It is not known where it goes when it moves north, but perhaps to the southern Sudan. Concentrations have been seen moving south in east Africa from July to early September; if the birds on their way to southern Africa are drawn from these, which seems likely, then they 'leapfrog' those populations which also arrive and breed in east Africa from August to March. In west Africa a different situation exists; birds migrate north and south within west Africa, breed in the northern part of their range arriving in April/May, and leave in early December. However, as in the other populations, the birds breed during the rainy season. The migration pattern of Wahlberg's Eagle is still an intriguing problem requiring clarification, but on present circumstantial evidence our birds are trans-equatorial migrants. It is interesting to record that it was only in 1962 that attention was drawn to the fact that they were migrants to southern Africa.

The distribution of this species in southern Africa is confined to areas of summer rainfall in the northern part of the region. Extralimitally it extends northwards to the Sahara.

GENERAL HABITS

When perched within the canopy of a tree this eagle is unobtrusive and easily overlooked. However, it soars a great deal, often at a considerable height, and draws attention to itself when it calls. It hunts either by a quick dash from a perch or, more often, on the wing. In one incident a Long-crested Eagle was robbed of its prey in a piratical attack. It attacks from a soaring position with a spectacular stoop, or it may parachute initially before a final plunge with extended feet. The hunting techniques are

very similar to those of the Booted Eagle.

For its size it is a rapacious eagle, capable of killing large prey, and it is a versatile general predator. Various prey categories are mammals, birds, reptiles, amphibians and insects. Mammalian prey ranges in size from mice to hares (usually young ones) and includes mongooses, squirrels, a Night Ape, young dassies, various small rodents and the occasional bat captured when flushed during daylight. Birds up to the size of an adult Red-crested Korhaan, as well as Crowned Guineafowl and francolins are killed. Nestlings or young birds recently out of the nest are often preyed on, but the only eye-witness account of nest-robbing was an incident in which the eagle tore up the nest of a Bronze Mannikin and ate the chicks. Like many other raptors it also preys on Red-billed Quelea colonies. Some other avian prey records include Cattle Egrets, a kestrel, a Gabar Goshawk, button-quails, an African Crake, Crowned Plovers, a Wood Sandpiper, Spotted Dikkops, doves, a sandgrouse, a Grey Loerie, a Green Pigeon, a Barn Owl, a Pearl-spotted Owl, nightjars (scavenged off roads?), a Speckled Mousebird, a kingfisher, rollers, hornbills, barbets, larks, a Pied Crow nestling, an Arrow-marked Babbler, shrikes and starlings. Very occasionally domestic chickens are caught.

Birds brought to nests are well plucked and this often makes identification difficult. The examples given indicate the variety of avian prey. In one study in the Transvaal 33 species were listed and in another in Kenya at least 26 species. In the Transvaal study a total of 126 birds was recorded, gamebirds (30 per cent) and doves (13 per cent) comprising the two most important categories. Reptilian prey is made up largely of small lizards such as skinks and agamas, but snakes are also occasionally caught and a Boomslang, Herald Snake and Egyptian Cobra have been identified. The first two were small but the cobra was large and may have been scavenged. Amphibians recorded have been mainly Bullfrogs. Insect prey has included beetles, grasshoppers and termites, the last being eaten on the ground or hawked and eaten in flight in the manner of a Black Kite.

In four studies of prey found at nests in Kenya, Zimbabwe and the Transvaal there were variations in the various prey groups. Mammals made up 12–39 per cent, birds 31–64 per cent, reptiles 8–41 per cent and amphibians 0–8 per cent. In two of the studies where nest inspections were combined with long watches from hides, reptiles (mainly lizards) comprised 40 per cent of the total. Because few traces of reptiles can be found in random visits to nests, whereas bird and mammal remains are more easily recorded, it is clear that lizards are an important part of the diet of these eagles, at least while breeding. It is dificult to assess the extent to which insects are eaten, but this species, like other migrant raptors, readily feeds on swarming termite alates. In one instance a male was seen to regurgitate a mass of termites onto the nest for his chick. Insect remains are often found in pellets.

This eagle is extremely vocal and makes a loud fluting double-noted *kleeeee-ee*, usually while soaring, and a rapidly repeated *kyip-kyip-kyip-kyip*, which is mainly a contact call used by the pair at the nest. Excited squealing calls are also made, and a drawn-out yelping call, probably a variant of the *kleeeee-ee* call. The *kleeeee-ee* is characteristic, carries far and draws attention to a bird soaring at a great height. It is often heard during the post-breeding period February to March when the birds soar and call a great deal.

BREEDING

Soon after arrival in their breeding areas the eagles either perch near their nests or fly round a great deal making the *kleeeee-ee* call. Spectacular undulating display flights may be performed occasionally, but soaring flights appear to be the main form of courtship. At times the male dives down at the female, who rolls and presents her claws. Mating takes place in trees near the nest.

Nests are built in a wide variety of trees, including eucalypts, always below the canopy, where they are shaded for at least part of the day. River valleys are favoured nesting sites, probably because larger trees are to be found there, particularly in drier localities. Nests are usually between 8 and 12 m above ground; the average for 411 nests in the Transvaal was 10,8 m. The nest, a characteristically small but sturdy structure of small sticks, does not grow to particularly large porportions over the years like the nests of many other eagles. It is normally about 60–70 cm across and 30–40 cm deep with a leaf-lined cup 20–25 cm across.

There are no detailed observations on the share of the sexes in nest-building but both build and bring green lining during the breeding cycle. Branches may be broken off trees by hanging onto them and flapping. Nest construction or repair begins almost immediately the birds arrive, and usually takes about a month to six weeks. However, very rapid construction may occur: one new nest took no more than two weeks from the start of building to the laying of the egg. In established nests repair normally consists of building up the perimeter of the nest to form the cup, which is then lined with green leaves. The small size of the nest, and the speed at which it can be built or repaired, is probably related to the migratory pattern of this eagle, which has a limited time in which to complete its breeding. It has been noticed that a setback, such as a Giant Eagle Owl occupying a nest when the birds arrive, can cause a breeding failure. They are very attached to nest sites, using them year after year even when regularly raided by egg-collectors. When alternate sites are used they are generally very near a previous nest, and some pairs may use the same nest for many years, move to another site, and then back to the original nest. Occasionally pairs may have up to four sites over a period of years. Some territories have been occupied for at least 22 years.

Wahlberg's Eagles occur at a much higher density than other resident eagles, this being so because they are migrants arriving at a time of seasonal food abundance. In one detailed study in the Transvaal 15 pairs had an average territory size of 10 km^2; one recognisable male never went farther than 1,7 km from his nest and ranged over an area of about 900 hectares. In three localities in the Transvaal population densities varied from one pair per 8,5 km^2 to one pair per 26 km^2. Intruding Wahlberg's Eagles are chased out by territory holders, in one instance for a distance of a kilometre.

In keeping with the migratory pattern, the time at which eggs are laid is well defined. In Zimbabwe, where there are a great many nest records, eggs are normally laid in the last week of September or first week in October. The synchronised laying is borne out by one observation where chicks at four nests in the same locality hatched within five days of each other. Eggs are laid in September and October throughout southern Africa. Sometimes eggs are laid in the first half of September; there is even a single exceptionally early record for the end of August in Zimbabwe. Occasional records for November can usually be traced to a relaying when the first egg has failed, often because it has been taken by an egg-collector. The first rains fall when the egg is in the nest, and the nestling is reared during the rainy season.

The normal clutch is a single egg, occasionally two; only five per cent of 127 Transvaal clutches contained two eggs. Eggs are variably marked, ranging from almost plain dull white to others richly smeared and blotched with pale red and rust-red. Generally eggs are well marked and no two are alike. In descriptions of two-egg clutches, one egg was lightly marked and the

(1) View of a typical Wahlberg's Eagle nest in a tall tree beside a river.

(2) A nest with the normal clutch of one egg.

(3) A four-day-old chick which is covered with chocolate-coloured down.

(4) At four weeks old the down is smoky-grey.

(5) By six weeks feathers are emerging rapidly.

(6) The nine-week-old nestling is fully feathered.

other heavily. Measurements are: 61,5 × 49,0 (167); 57,0–66,0 × 44,0–52,9.

Incubation is mostly by the female, the male feeding her at the nest and taking over for short spells. At one nest, however, a male was seen to do a considerable share, and in 20 hours' observation on seven days the egg was covered 79 per cent of the time, 47 per cent by the female and 32 per cent by the male. Her longest continuous spell was just over six hours, and his just under two hours. An interesting feature observed at several nests was the mobbing of incubating birds by Fork-tailed Drongos. They make persistent dive-bombing attacks, and in several instances were noted to imitate the *kyip-kyip-kyip* call of the eagle while doing so. This mobbing behaviour continues into the nestling period. Incubating birds sit very tight and crouch flat on seeing someone approach, although often the long tail projecting over the edge of the small nest indicates that it is occupied. On being flushed, the bird flies out of sight or soars high overhead, but in one exceptional instance a bird dive-bombed an observer climbing to a nest, struck him, and drew blood. Greenery is added to the nest cup throughout the incubation period, but there are no observations on the share of the sexes in bringing this. One accurate incubation period was 44–45 days, another between 43 and 45 days, and 46 days has also been recorded.

There are no instances on record of two young being reared together; in one instance a weak smaller chick was found to have abrasions on its back suggesting that it had been pecked by its older sibling. Detailed observations at a nest where two young hatch would prove very interesting.

On hatching, the nestling is covered in dark chocolate down and has dark brown eyes and a pale yellow cere and feet. Chicks that develop into the pale form, it appears, have white down, but further observations are required. In the first two weeks the cere and feet darken to rich yellow, and the dark brown down pales to smoky-grey. At three weeks first feathers are just breaking from the wing quills and by four weeks brown feathers begin to sprout rapidly above and below. The six-week-old eaglet is well feathered with only a few areas of down remaining. A week later it is fully feathered, the only remaining feather growth being on the wings and tail.

Observations on the development of the co-ordination of the nestling are scanty, but it is able to stand up and flap its wings as early as 28 days old, by which stage it can swallow small prey items by itself. It may still be fed by the adults at seven weeks old, but is probably able to tear up prey for itself prior to this.

Although the eaglet is closely tended initially, the indications are that it is left alone for quite long periods fairly early in the nestling period. This may be because the nest site is usually shaded and the weather is warm, so that it needs to be sheltered only when it rains. Observations during the first two weeks indicate that a parent is on the nest about 60 per cent of the time during daylight. Both male and female have been seen to brood, and a male once fed a chick. The male is the main food-provider in the early stages of the nestling period, but after the first two weeks the female's time on the nest drops off steadily, and when the nestling is four weeks old both she and the male are actively hunting. In one observation spell of two hours and twenty minutes a month-old nestling was brought ten lizards, the male and female providing five each at an average rate of one every fourteen minutes, although the female once brought two lizards within five minutes of each other. By the time it is six weeks old the eaglet is left alone for most of the time and the female no longer roosts with it overnight. Green lining is brought during the first half of the period; at one nest it was added as late as the eighth week.

Young usually fly between 70 and 75 days, a fairly long nestling period for a species this size. Occasionally, young fly earlier, at about 60 days. Post-nestling observations are scanty, but the juvenile returns to the nest to be fed, and one was seen on a nest ten weeks after it flew. It is probable that the young eagle is independent some weeks prior to the northward migration, but further observations are required.

In one fifteen-year study of breeding success in Zimbabwe 37 young were reared in 66 pair-years, an average replacement rate of 0,56 young per pair per year. In 180 pair-years in the Transvaal there was an overall productivity of 0,42 young per pair per year with much variation from pair to pair. Two studies in Kenya based on small samples obtained productivity figures of 0,58 and 0,64. Wahlberg's Eagle usually breeds annually, although some pairs have non-breeding years. In one Transvaal locality during three years between 5 per cent and 24 per cent (average 17 per cent) of the pairs did not breed. Eight (12 per cent) of a possible 66 breeding years at seven nests in a Zimbabwe study were non-breeding years, but one pair accounted for 5 of these years.

21 Booted Eagle *136.*

Dwergarend

Hieraaetus pennatus

PLATES 7 AND 8

DERIVATION
hawk : eagle : feathered — *hierax* (G) : *aetos* (G) : *pennatus* (L)

IDENTIFICATION
Adult: This small, stocky eagle is about the size of a Steppe Buzzard. Two forms occur, a pale and a dark, the latter comprising about twenty per cent of the population in southern Africa. The pale form is brown above and white below with a variable amount of brown streaking on the sides of the breast. The brown on the head extends below the eye and there are blackish patches on the cheeks. A broad pale band of buff feathers extends across the wing coverts. The dark form is uniform dark brown except for a buff band on the wing coverts like the pale form. The heavily feathered legs, from which the name 'booted' is derived, are a useful feature for identifying perched birds. In both forms the eyes are light brown and the cere and legs yellow. Both forms could be confused with pale and dark forms respectively of Wahlberg's Eagle, under which species differences are discussed.

Both pale and dark Booted Eagles are more easily identified in flight, especially if the diagnostic 'landing-light' patch of white at the junc-

A Booted Eagle to show the diagnostic 'landing lights' — small white patches at the junction of the leading edges of the wings and body.

tion of leading edge of the wing and body is seen. The dorsal pattern of both forms is the same, with a broad V-shaped band of paler feathers extending diagonally across the wing coverts and a U-shaped white band on the tail coverts. Both forms have a small wedge of paler feathers on the hind edge of the wing at the junction of the primaries and secondaries. The dark form appears uniform dark brown from below except for the tail which is greyish. The pale form has black remiges which contrast strikingly with the white body and underwing coverts, the latter being spotted with black. The dark form could be confused with a Black Kite, especially from above, but the slightly rounded tail and soaring flight, in contrast to the constant flapping and gliding flight of the fork-tailed kite, serve to distinguish them; also, the Booted Eagle does not twist its tail about to steer, as the kite does.

Juvenile: Juveniles of the pale form are washed with rufous below and are rufous-brown on the head. In flight they match the adult pattern, except that the underwing coverts are pale rufous. The 'landing-light' patches, as well as the spots on the underwing coverts, serve to identify them. The most likely confusion would be with the juvenile African Hawk Eagle, and to a lesser extent the juvenile Ayres' Eagle, but these species are barred on the tail and have different underwing patterns. Pale birds resemble the adults after their first moult so that no immature stage can be distinguished. Juveniles of the dark form resemble the adult and cannot be recognised in the field.

HABITAT
In its breeding range in the Cape Province the Booted Eagle is typical of the dry transitional areas between fynbos and the semi-desert flora of the Karoo. Elsewhere it occurs in a wide variety of habitats ranging from true desert (Namib) to woodland and montane environments.

STATUS AND DISTRIBUTION
The status of this species in southern African is confused by the existence of two populations, an intra-African migrant one which breeds in the Cape Province, and a Palearctic

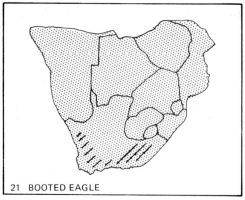

21 BOOTED EAGLE

*The oblique lines indicate the breeding range
of the Booted Eagle in the Cape Province.*

migrant one. Booted Eagles breeding in the
Cape Province arrive in early August and depart in March. Most sightings in the non-
breeding season from May to July have been in
the north-west Cape, Kalahari, Namibia and
southern Angola, which appear to be where
the bulk of the Cape population winters. However, there are also winter sightings, presumably of Cape birds, in Natal, the Transvaal,
Mozambique and Zimbabwe. Further investigation of the status of Booted Eagles in these
areas is needed, especially as they have been
seen near suitable breeding cliffs in northern
Transvaal in July. Palearctic Booted Eagles arrive in southern Africa in November and reach
the south-west Cape; they depart in March.
Althouth the breeding seasons of the two
populations are mutually exclusive, the fact
that they overlap in the Cape Province from
November to March makes it very difficult to
assess the extent to which they reach the Cape.
Booted Eagles seen outside the Cape Province
during November to March are presumed to
be Palearctic birds on present evidence. During the breeding season the Booted Eagle is
common in the Cape Province.

Booted Eagles are encountered throughout
southern Africa. The northern migratory limit
of the southern African breeding population is
not known at present, except that the birds
reach southern Angola. The breeding range of
the Palearctic population extends from north-
west Africa and the Iberian Peninsula to western Siberia and southern Asia.

GENERAL HABITS

The Booted Eagle is usually seen flying and
is inconspicuous when perched in a tree or on
a cliff face, where it may remain motionless for
long periods. Although it also attacks from a
perch, most of its hunting is done on the wing,
often from a height of 200–300 m. It stoops in
spectacular fashion with wings held against the
body and feet extended, although it may parachute initially and plunge rapidly as it nears
the ground. It will weave in and out of tree
branches in pursuit of quarry, and its speed
and agility on the wing match that of Ayres'
Eagle. In southern Africa it preys on birds up
to the size of a Speckled Pigeon or Namaqua
Sandgrouse, very rarely on poultry; and on lizards, rats and mice, as well as on insects such
as termites. In a sample of 55 prey items from
two nests in different localities the prey preferences were the same, with birds making up 54
per cent of the total, lizards 33 per cent and
small rodents 13 per cent. A variety of birds
was recorded, including doves, mousebirds,
larks, thrushes, starlings, buntings and a Namaqua Sandgrouse, the largest prey to be
brought. However, under conditions of falconry, a Booted Eagle caught Cape Francolins
and Cattle Egrets, and in Europe they prey on
rabbits and partridges in the wild.

The most commonly heard call is a high-
pitched *pi-pi-pi-pi-pi* . . . which is sometimes
uttered so fast as to have an almost trilled effect. A variant of this call is followed by more
drawn-out   notes: *pi-pi-pi-pi-peee-peee-peee*.
These calls are emitted during display and mating, by the male on visiting the nest, and when
chasing other birds from the vicinity of the
nest. Another call is a loud and rapidly repeated *kyip-kyip-kyip* . . . sometimes followed
by noisy squeaking and chittering notes in
cases of extreme excitement. This call is used
by the female in solicitation when the male is
near the nest with prey; also as a begging call
by the nestlings once they are about a month
old. It is almost identical to the call of a Wahlberg's Eagle. Though extremely vocal when
breeding, Booted Eagles are rarely heard to
call away from their nesting areas.

BREEDING

Courtship begins soon after arrival in their
breeding areas in early August and consists of
spectacular undulating display flights during
which the birds may perform a complete loop
or occasionally lock claws briefly. The displays
are accompanied by much calling. Mating
takes place on a cliff perch or branch of a tree
near the nest.

Nest-building commences soon after the arrival of the birds; in one instance the first egg was
laid 33 days after nest repair began. Both sexes
build, and may break small branches off trees
by hanging from them and flapping until they

break. All southern African nests have been on cliff faces; the nest is built on a small ledge, usually at the base of a tree or bush, and is difficult to find. One nest was situated on a bushy tree on a cliff on an old heron's nest.

The difficulty of finding their nests, combined with the remote areas these eagles generally inhabit, has undoubtedly caused them to have been overlooked as a breeding species before the first confirmed modern record in 1973. However, a breeding record of an Ayres' Eagle from Klaver in the Cape in 1917 has subsequently been shown to be attributable to a Booted Eagle. Thus the Cape-breeding Booted Eagles, far from being recent arrivals, have merely been overlooked, despite being one of the commonest breeding eagles in the Cape Province.

Nests are usually small structures of pencil-thick sticks measuring about 45–60 cm in diameter, although some nests are larger; the central leafy depression is about 30 cm across and 7 cm deep. The nests are normally rather flattened structures, probably because their site on a ledge at the base of a tree or bush does not require substantial base material. In the Palearctic region nests are built in trees and are much bulkier; but they are also recorded to breed on crags in Morocco.

Territories are not large: in one gorge there were four breeding pairs over a distance of 2,8 km, the closest nests only 0,5 km apart. This species is tolerant of other Booted Eagles in the area when breeding, rarely indulging in aggression towards other birds, including birds of prey. However, White-necked Ravens and Pied Crows are not tolerated near the nest and are attacked, and in one instance Egyptian Geese attempting to prospect a Booted Eagle's nest for their own use were driven off.

Eggs are laid during the second half of September; so far only two-egg clutches have been recorded, although in Europe one to three eggs may be laid. The eggs are white, although some may have a few faint reddish speckles. Only four clutches have been measured in South Africa: 54,3 × 44,2 (8); 51,5–58,0 × 42,2–45,8. These measurements fall within the range of egg sizes of Palearctic Booted Eagles.

Eggs are laid three to four days apart, incubation commencing with the laying of the first egg. Incubation is mostly by the female, who sits very tight, even when an observer is within a few metres of the nest. Once flushed, she flies out of sight or soars high overhead. During incubation she is fed by the male, who very occasionally incubates while she is off the nest feeding on the prey he has brought. A single accurate incubation period of 40 days has been recorded in South Africa.

On hatching, the young are covered in white or grey down, depending on whether they will develop into pale or dark adults. The eyes are grey, the bill is gun-metal blue at its base with a black tip, and the cere and feet are yellow. At two weeks old the first quills are just discernible along the hind edges of the wings, otherwise the chicks are still entirely downy. After three weeks wing and tail quills sprout rapidly, and by a month old the young are half feather and half down. Thereafter they feather rapidly and the last remaining down is on the forehead and front of the neck.

No Cain and Abel behaviour has been observed, even though there is at times a remarkable discrepancy in the size of the young, especially when a female hatches first, followed by a male. Although young hatch only three to four days apart, it sometimes appears as if they are at least ten days different in age; a half-feathered nestling and its almost entirely downy sibling may be found on the nest. At one nest the older nestling received most of the available food, so that a degree of starvation may retard the smaller nestling's development and may even occasionally cause its death. However, in South Africa, it appears that two young are normally reared.

The co-ordination of the nestling develops rapidly, and by ten days it stands weakly to defecate, preens itself and flaps its stubby wings. It may also attempt to peck at prey but is not very successful at pulling off pieces. By the time it is a month old it walks about the nest confidently, tears up prey for itself and performs wing exercises.

Parental attention is linked to the development of the young, dropping off rapidly once the young are about a month old. In observations totalling 71 hours 30 minutes at one nest the female was in attendance 94 per cent of the time during the first four weeks and only 11 per cent of the time thereafter until the young flew at seven weeks.

When the young are small they are brooded or shaded by the female much of the time and suffer discomfort if left exposed to the sun. She tends them carefully, preening their down gently and removing any food particles adhering to a chick's face. The young are fed from time to time, sometimes six times in a day, for periods up to 25 minutes until they are satiated or the available prey has been eaten. However, in the early nestling period, there is usually plenty of prey. The male alone brings prey at this stage; at one nest he was recorded to feed

(1) A view of Booted Eagle nesting habitat.

(2) This nest is situated at the base of a tree growing on a steep cliff.

(3) Chicks aged 1 and 4 days.

(4) Nestlings 15 and 12 days old.

(5) Nestlings 31 and 28 days old; the feathered female is well in advance of the smaller downy male.

(6) A fully feathered 50-day-old nestling at the stage at which it left the nest.

the chicks on several occasions and even brooded them for a short spell. Both male and female bring fresh greenery to the nest during the first three weeks of the nestling period but not thereafter, and the nest has a flattened and dilapidated appearance by the time the young leave. However, it is kept clean, the female removing pellets in her bill and flying off with them.

When the young are a month old they no longer require shading and the female's time on the nest is mainly concerned with feeding them, although they can feed themselves, and she may even feed an eaglet that has returned to the nest after its first flight. Although she spends little time on the nest, and no longer roosts there overnight, she is usually perched in the vicinity. She follows the male to the nest, calling excitedly when he delivers prey. The male still delivers all the prey and has been seen to feed almost fully grown nestlings. Only at the end of the nestling period at one nest was the female seen to deliver prey caught by herself, the male bringing in all 24 items recorded during watches

at the nest prior to this.

During the nestling period the number of prey deliveries at a nest varied from two to six in a day, although once the male actually delivered seven items because he brought a mouse and a lark together on one vist. The minimum time between prey captures was 23 minutes. There was no hunting peak, prey being brought at all times of the day. Prey was often brought decapitated and all birds were thoroughly plucked in the manner of a sparrowhawk before delivery.

Two nestling periods in South Africa were 50 and 54 days. After the first flight young may return to the nest to be fed and they remain in the vicinity for a week or two. Further observations are required on the post-nestling period, but young apparently range farther afield with their parents; one was seen with an adult 64 days after it first flew. Juveniles migrate soon after becoming independent but it is not known if they move off with their parents or separately. There are no observations on breeding success in southern Africa.

22 African Hawk Eagle *137.*

Grootjagarend

Hieraaetus spilogaster   PLATES 9 AND 10

DERIVATION
hawk : eagle : spotted : stomach — *hierax* (G) : *aetos* (G) : *spilos* (G) : *gaster* (G)

IDENTIFICATION
Adult: The blackish upperparts and head contrast with the white underparts which are covered with black streaks. The female is more heavily streaked below than the male. From a distance the streaking is not readily visible, so the eagle appears mainly black and white. The eyes are dark yellow, the feet and cere greeny-yellow. The perched bird shows a broad terminal band on the tail. In flight from below the underwing coverts are mottled black and white and the primaries and secondaries are white with a distinct black trailing edge to the wing. The band at the end of the tail is also a prominent feature. Seen from above, the wings have striking white windows at the bases of the primaries. For distinctions between this species and the adult Ayres' Eagle see the text on the latter species.

Juvenile and immature: The juvenile is dark brown above and rufous below with some nar-

row black shaft streaks on the sides of the breast. The colour of the cere and feet matches the adult, but the eyes are hazel-brown. Its

African Hawk Eagle to show characteristic white windows on the primaries; Ayres' Eagle has no windows.

coloration is basically similar to the red form of a juvenile Black Sparrowhawk, but the smaller size, bare yellow legs and habits of the sparrowhawk serve to distinguish it. The most likely confusion is with juveniles of Ayres' Eagle and Booted Eagle; differences are discussed under those species. In flight the underwing coverts are rufous and the remiges are silvery with several narrow black bars running across them. There is no dark trailing edge to the wing as in the adult, and the tail has no distinct terminal band.

The development through immature plumage to adulthood takes about three to four years. The upperparts darken, the rufous juvenile underparts give way to white, and the narrow shaft streaks on the breast are replaced by the bolder streaking of the adult. Adult plumage is only acquired after three moults, during which time the eye changes gradually to yellow, becoming fully yellow in the third year.

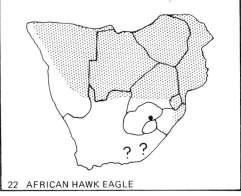

22 AFRICAN HAWK EAGLE

HABITAT

This eagle is found in well-wooded country, often in hilly terrain. It does not occur in very open country with only a few scattered trees, or in evergreen forest.

DISTRIBUTION AND STATUS

In suitable habitat this eagle is regularly encountered and is resident. It does not appear to have declined, although its former distribution apparently extended to the southern and eastern Cape Province. As there are no recent records south of the Orange River, these early records require careful authentication. It was probably never more than a vagrant to the Cape. Extralimitally it occurs northwards to the Sahara.

GENERAL HABITS

The African Hawk Eagle is rapacious and takes a wide variety of prey, including some heavier than itself. It has large feet for its size, and the span of the male's foot is only slightly smaller than that of the larger female, and both have a hind claw of the same length. The hunting techniques may be summarised into three main types: a quick dash from a perch like a sparrowhawk, often using cover to conceal its approach, which may be just above ground level; quartering low over the ground and seizing any prey it surprises; stooping from a soaring position. It is capable of taking birds in flight, but in the case of gamebirds usually prefers to 'throw up' above them and then kill them on the ground as they settle in panic. Also, if the quarry seeks shelter in cover, the

eagle will pursue it on foot. Its flight is silent, which enables it to make a stealthy surprise attack on prey. Quite often it hides in a tree near a water-hole and dashes out to capture doves and other birds that come to drink.

The main prey of the African Hawk Eagle is made up of gamebirds and mammals up to the size of a hare; reptiles are only occasionally taken. There is one case on record of a pair feeding on carrion, a dead Reedbuck, over a period of three days. A twelve-year study at two nests in Zimbabwe showed that birds (69 per cent of which were gamebirds) comprised 74 per cent by number of the prey recorded, mammals 25 per cent and reptiles one per cent. However, analysed by weight, the mammals made up 56 per cent of the food captured.

The gamebirds caught are mainly francolins but guineafowl are also killed. It also takes chickens but is not the poultry thief it is often made out to be. In the twelve-year study mentioned above, free-ranging chickens were available in the hunting range of a nesting pair, but not once was a chicken found on the nest. Birds commonly caught are doves, hornbills and Grey Loeries, but a variety of species ranging from Barn Owls to small birds such as a Three-streaked Tchagra and Three-banded Sandplover have been recorded. It is also reported to prey on Red-billed Quelea colonies. In east Africa it has been known to raid heronries and eat chicks in the nest.

Amongst its mammalian prey Scrub Hares, mongooses and Tree Squirrels are regularly taken, but any abundant small mammal will be caught, for instance in the Matopos hills in Zimbabwe dassies are the main prey. Other recorded items are rats, mice, gerbils, Suricates, a Ground Squirrel, a Springhare, a Greater Red Rock Hare, a genet, Night Apes and a young Vervet Monkey. An interesting record from west Africa is of two birds regularly perching in the same tree as a large roost of fruit bats, and preying on them.

Reptilian prey includes lizards, a chameleon and small snakes, although one eagle was seen eating a python which it was thought to have killed itself.

The account given must be considered to be a guide to the main prey of this eagle; there is little doubt that preferred species will vary from area to area. As mentioned, dassies are their main prey in the Matopos where they are particularly plentiful. In an overgrazed area of Namibia where there were few gamebirds a limited sample indicated that a pair fed mainly on mammals. In Botswana 28 Yellow-billed Hornbill and 5 Red-billed Hornbill beaks were found at a nest, while on the Zambezi escarpment in Zimbabwe a pair preyed mostly on Red-billed Hornbills.

The main call is a musical *klu-klu-klu-kluee* or *kluee-kluee* not unlike that of Wahlberg's Eagle but less drawn out and mellower. It is used during courtship, when driving other raptors away from its nest area, and as a contact call by the pair. Various other calls used during the breeding cycle include a loud broken-voiced *kwee-oo*, *kwee-oo* and *ko-ko-ko-kwee-oo*, *kwee-oo* emitted by a pair during nest repair; loud squealing *skwee-ya*, *skwee-ya*, *skwee-ya* and *shree-chok*, *shree-chok* calls of solicitation uttered by the female when the male is on or near the nest with food; a loud broken-voiced *kwaak* made by both male and female when excited near the nest; subdued 'conversational' calls made by the pair together at the nest, the female emitting clucking noises and *kwi-kwi-kwi* calls, the male responding with soft musical *kwip*, *kwip*, *kwip* and *ko-wee*, *ko-wee* notes. The feathered eaglet solicits for food with high-pitched insistent *wee-yik*, *wee-yik*, *wee-yik* cries.

BREEDING

The pair bond in this species is strong and the birds may be seen together throughout the year. It appears that they also sometimes hunt co-operatively. In nuptial display they call and soar near the nest and perform spectacular undulations. Sometimes the male dives at the female and she turns and presents her claws. The male brings prey for the female as part of courtship. One pair mated on branches near the nest, mainly during the nest-building stage. The female crouched low with her tail held to one side, and the male jumped onto her back and lowered his abdomen with his feathers fluffed out like a bathing bird.

Nests are normally placed within the canopy of a large tree, including eucalypts, in a major fork or on a substantial lateral branch at heights varying from 6–18 m or more, although usually between 9–15 m. One particularly low nest was only 4,2 m off the ground. Nests generally receive some shade during most of the day, but some sites are rather exposed, necessitating the shading of the eaglet by the female for longer into the nestling period. There are no records of breeding on cliffs in southern Africa, but this has been recorded in Kenya.

The nest, constructed with very substantial sticks and usually about one metre in width, is large for the size of the eagle. The nest cup, lined with green leaves, measures about 25–30 cm across. The depth of the nest varies considerably, depending on the site and the length of time it has been in use, but is usually about 0,8–1,0 m deep. Long established nests may be 1,25 m in depth.

Nest repair consists of building up the rim of the previous year's flattened structure by adding a new layer of sticks. This usually takes four to five weeks, mainly during May, but on some occasions repairs may take as long as eight weeks. The construction of a new nest may take several months. Limited observations at one site revealed that the male was most active in nest repair, adding dry sticks broken off from the nest tree. He also moulded loose sprays of green leaves into the nest cup with his breast. The female's only contribution was to bring green sprays to the nest but, as the observations were made in the later stages of nest repair, it may be found that she is more active in the initial stages or in the construction of a new nest.

The same nest or nest tree may be used for long periods, at least eighteen years in one study. One breeding site near Pretoria, still active in 1978, was in use in 1912 when the late Dr Austin Roberts collected a nestling there. When alternate nests are used they are never very far from a previous site. One pair with an unsuccessful breeding record used four different sites in nine years, behaviour not typical of this species.

In three localities in the Transvaal population densities varied from one pair per 77 km^2 to one pair per 110 km^2. The total Transvaal population is estimated at approximately 1 200 pairs. In bushveld in Zimbabwe two nests in a study area were 12 km apart while in the well-wooded Matopos nearby the closest nests were only 3 km from each other. In the Kruger National Park some nests were 5 km apart. African Hawk Eagles are strongly territorial and appear to remain in their territories throughout the year. In the Matopos, where they overlap with a large population of Black Eagles, they regularly attack them when they fly overhead. Sometimes they are aggressive towards human intruders at the nest and will attack and strike them.

Eggs are laid from late May to July with a peak in June. The normal clutch is two eggs, although a complete single egg clutch is not infrequently recorded, and there is one instance of a clutch of three eggs. They are chalky-white in ground colour and very variably marked. Some eggs are handsomely blotched and speckled with dull rust-red evenly distributed over the surface, while others have a cap of coalesced blotches at the broad or narrow end. Other eggs may be almost plain, and blotched and almost unmarked eggs may be found in the same clutch. Measurements are: $64,5 \times 51,3$ (123); $59,5-75,2 \times 46,0-55,7$. The above eggs include three large ones which measured $73,0 \times 53,2$, $73,5 \times 55,7$ and $75,2 \times 53,4$; these were the only eggs to exceed 70,0 mm on the long axis.

Eggs are laid three to four days apart and incubation begins when the first egg is laid. However, the female may leave the egg unattended for several hours on the first day. Most of the incubation is by the female, who sits for long periods and is not easily flushed from the nest. She is relieved for short spells by the male, usually when he brings prey for her on which he has already fed himself. She leaves the nest to receive this and feeds somewhere nearby before returning to resume incubation. The male may incubate for as long as an hour, but normally he is relieved by the female after a much shorter time when she has finished her feed. Twenty-eight hours of observation on nine days at two nests in Zimbabwe showed that the female incubated for 82,6 per cent of the time to the male's 7,1 per cent; these percentages are very similar to those at nests watched in Kenya. The female incubates overnight. During incubation the nest is lined from time to time with fresh green leaves brought by both the male and the female. The incubation period has been established fairly accurately in Zimbabwe as 42–44 days (43 ± 1 day).

In one case a chick took just under two days to hatch, from the time first cracking of the shell was observed. The female is aware that the egg is hatching and stands up to inspect it from time to time. At one nest she ate the mucous matter inside the shell of a recently hatched egg and then made two trips to drop the two halves of the egg some distance from the nest. The chick is given its first meal the day it hatches, but it is weak and sleeps a great deal. Only at the age of

three days can it co-ordinate properly and this usually coincides with the hatching of the second egg. The smaller chick stands little chance of survival. At one nest it weighed 62 g on hatching, when its older sibling was already 140 g. In another case the disparity was 64 g and 111 g. Not only is the smaller chick mercilessly pecked by the older, but it obtains little or no food. It eventually dies, beside an abundance of food, from a combination of its injuries and starvation after about two to three days. At one nest, during three days, the smaller chick lost 28 g of its 64 g at hatching, while the older chick gained 36 g on its original 111 g at the time the second chick hatched. Although there are no cases on record of two young being successfully reared together at nests in southern Africa, two young survived in about 20 per cent of nests observed in Kenya. It is difficult at this stage to advance any explanation for the difference in survival found in the two areas.

The newly hatched chick is covered in dark grey down with some whitish down on its abdomen and thighs. Its cere and feet are dull yellow. The first coat of grey down gives way to a thicker second coat of white down and by two weeks old only the head and back retain any grey down. By three weeks the down is predominantly white, except on the head, and on the remiges feathers are just breaking from their quills. Feathers develop rapidly once the eaglet is a month old, and by five weeks it is well feathered above although still mainly downy below. At six weeks the only remaining down is on the head, crop and abdomen, and a week later it is fully feathered except for further growth of its wing and tail feathers.

Parental attention may be loosely divided into three main stages: from hatching up to two weeks, from two until four weeks, and from four weeks to the time the eaglet flies.

During the first period the female remains on or near the nest most of the time, particularly in the eaglet's first week when she broods a great deal and feeds it when it indicates its hunger by cheeping. The male's role is to provide prey, but he has been known both to brood and feed a small eaglet. In the second week of its life the eaglet is not nearly as closely brooded by the female, although she still remains on the nest much of the time. In this first period the eaglet develops its co-ordination and begins to preen itself and shuffle round the nest, but much of its time is spent sleeping.

In the period between two and four weeks the female spends much less time on the nest, although she is usually perched in the nest tree. In an exposed site she would need to spend

(1) View of an African Hawk Eagle's nest site.

(2) The nest and eggs.

(3) A three-day-old chick.

(4) By three weeks old most of the dark grey down has disappeared and first feathers are appearing on the wings.

(5) At five weeks feathers are rapidly displacing the down.

(6) By seven weeks the nestling is fully feathered.

more time on the nest shading the eaglet. The male still provides most of the prey, and the female continues to feed the eaglet. When about 24 days old the eaglet is able to stand weakly for the first time and even attempts a few clumsy wing exercises.

During the third stage, after it is a month old, parental time on the nest drops markedly and the eaglet is mainly attended for feeds, but at an exposed site it may continue to be shaded by the female even when well feathered. The eaglet continues to be fed by the female and may have prey torn up for it until it is nearly ready to fly, even when it has been capable of feeding itself for some weeks. During this final period the eaglet develops rapidly, and by the time it is 32 days old it can stand well and exercises its wings. At this stage the female still remains on the nest overnight, but it is not known when she ceases to sleep on the nest with the eaglet. The growing eaglet preens a great deal and indulges in various activities such as nibbling at the nest sticks, stretching, and making mock kills of a bone in the nest, all of which are part of its developing co-ordination. Towards the end of its time in the nest its wing exercises increase and short flights across the nest are made. Although not often on the nest during this period, the adults spend more time perched in the nest tree or nearby than do other eagles at this late stage of the nestling period. It is only during this final period that the female catches prey to any significant extent for her eaglet. The nest continues to be lined with greenery from time to time, even when the eaglet is due to leave the nest, again for longer than is the case with other eagles. The nest is also kept very clean; the female will eat small pieces of meat that drop on the nest during a feed and will also pick up pellets in her bill and fly off with them. Birds are brought to the nest well plucked in the manner of a sparrowhawk, which makes the identification of avian prey difficult at times.

When the eaglet is ready to fly, it moves off the nest onto nearby branches. Its first flight is usually made between 60 and 70 days, and the smaller, lighter males tend to leave sooner than females. Four accurate nestling periods from Zimbabwe are 62 days ± 1 day, 66–67 days, 68–69 days and 70 days ± 1 day. Post-nestling attachment to the nest does not last long and the juvenile may continue to be fed at the nest for about three to four weeks. Thereafter it wanders farther afield with its parents and has been seen in their company up to two months after leaving the nest. One marked juvenile seen four months after its first flight had established itself 16 km from its nest site. Young birds probably mature and remain in the general area in which they are reared, and one bird ringed as an eaglet in the Matopos was recovered dead eight years later, 15 km from the nest in which it had hatched.

The African Hawk Eagle usually breeds annually. At a site observed for seventeen years in Zimbabwe there were only two non-breeding years. The productivity at this nest was 0,82 young per pair per year. In contrast no young were reared in nine years at a nest in the same locality, the infertility of eggs being one of the main reasons for failure. The combined productivity figure for these two pairs was 0,54. In Kenya 15 young were reared in 27 pair-years, a productivity of 0,56 young per pair per year.

23 Ayres' Eagle /38.

Kleinjagarend

Hieraaetus ayresii

PLATES 9 AND 10

DERIVATION

hawk : eagle : of Ayres — *hierax* (G) : *aetos* (G) : *ayresii* (L)

This species was named in honour of Thomas Ayres who lived in Natal and at Potchefstroom, where he did valuable ornithological work during the latter part of the last century. Two other species, Ayres' Cloud Cisticola *Cisticola ayresii* and White-winged Crake *Sarothrura ayresi* (so spelt), are also named after him.

IDENTIFICATION

Adult: This small, stockily-built eagle is handsomely but variably marked. The upperparts are slate-black and the white underparts are covered with black spade-shaped spots which coalesce in more heavily marked individuals. This spotting also extends onto the thighs. Usually there is a white patch on the throat. There is a small occipital crest, but as it is not often raised it is not a good field character. The black on the head extends to a line below the eye like an executioner's mask and there is often a small patch of white on the forehead. The 'shoulders' of the wings have a prominent white edge. As a rule the smaller males are less heavily marked than females and show more white on the head, often with a white eyebrow; some females have this too. The cere and feet are lime-yellow and the eyes are deep yellow, almost orange in some birds. A rare melanistic form occurs with the body entirely black or with some white on the breast, but the pattern of barring on the tail is present. The only record of a melanistic bird in southern Africa is a wholly black specimen in the Transvaal Museum, collected in Swaziland in July 1906.

In flight there are no white 'windows' on the primaries above, the underwing coverts are heavily spotted, and the remiges are traversed by several black bars, the broadest along the hind edge of the wing. The tail has a broad black terminal band and several narrower bars. White patches are often visible at the junction of the wings and body.

The only species with which the adult can be confused is the African Hawk Eagle. Ayres' Eagle has a stockier build and more rounded head and is much more heavily marked below with large spots, not streaks. The black on the head tends to form a more extensive dark cap and the spotting extends onto the legs whereas the African Hawk Eagle has white legs. A useful and completely reliable distinction, if a good view can be obtained, is that the shafts of the primaries are black in Ayres' Eagle and white in the African Hawk Eagle. However, perched birds can be confused, and an Ayres' Eagle should be flushed to confirm identification, for which the underwing pattern is diagnostic. The African Hawk Eagle has distinctive white windows on the primaries, more white on the underwing coverts, and no barring on the remiges. Thus it appears a much whiter bird from below than the heavily marked Ayres' Eagle. The tail patterns of the two species are very similar and do not serve to distinguish them. Any birds showing white on the head are Ayres' Eagles; African Hawk Eagles always have black heads.

Juvenile and immature: The juvenile is grey-brown above with rufous on crown, nape and mantle, the feathers of the scapulars and wing coverts tipped white which gives them a scaly appearance. There is usually a pale rufous eyebrow. The underparts are pale rufous with some dark streaks on the breast. Cere and feet are coloured as in the adult and the eyes are pale grey-brown or yellow; further investiga-

An Ayres' Eagle from above to show the absence of windows in the wings.

tion of the apparent variability of eye colour is needed. In flight the underwing coverts are pale rufous, the remiges and tail barred like the adult but not as boldly.

The most likely confusion is with a juvenile African Hawk Eagle, which is deeper rufous below and dark brown above with no light edges to the feathers, and it lacks the rufous nape and mantle. In flight it shows barring on the secondaries, but that of Ayres' Eagle is much bolder and extends onto the primaries. However, some juvenile Ayres' Eagles in the Transvaal have been almost identical to juvenile African Hawk Eagles, except for the heavy barring on the remiges and the pale yellow eye. Further investigation into juvenile plumages is required. The juvenile pale form Booted Eagle is also similar, but it lacks barring on the tail and light edges to the feathers of the upperparts; in flight the plain tail and unbarred remiges distinguish it.

No details are available on progression to adult plumage, but it will probably be found to be similar to that of an African Hawk Eagle.

HABITAT

This species occurs in well-wooded hilly country as a rule and not in dense forest or arid areas. In Zimbabwe a favoured habitat is *Miombo* woodland. Outside the breeding season it may be found in other habitats such as stands of eucalypts, even in or near large towns.

STATUS AND DISTRIBUTION

Although originally thought to be resident, this species has recently been found to be nomadic outside the breeding season, and the possibility of long-distance intra-African migration cannot be ruled out. In Bulawayo, Zimbabwe, it has been regularly recorded between September and early April; one female returned alone to the same stand of eucalypts in a suburban garden eight years running until she was shot. Regular moulting took place between November and February each year. In the Transvaal, where there are no authentic breeding records, 70 per cent of all records fall between January and April, many of them from the Witwatersrand. There are very few records for May, September and October, and none for June to August. This clearly indicates an influx of these eagles in their non-breeding season, but where they come from remains a mystery.

Throughout its range this eagle is nowhere common, and even allowing for the fact that it is probably overlooked or misidentified it is unaccountably rare. It has been suggested from observations on two pairs (and their successors) in Kenya that poor breeding success may be a reason, but it would be remarkable if this was a factor which applied to the whole population. It is an efficient predator feeding mainly on a superabundant supply of birds, so it would not suffer through competition with other raptors. Possibly its preference for climax woodland in hilly country may be a limiting factor, but even where this habitat is found it is not common. Like the Taita Falcon, the rarity of this dashing species remains an enigma.

A few juvenile specimens were collected before 1920 in the eastern Cape, where it was a scarce vagrant; the only recent sighting was from Kei Road in 1962. A few early specimens exist for Natal but it is very rarely recorded in recent times. It occurs in Zululand, Swaziland, Mozambique, Transvaal, Zimbabwe, northern Botswana and Caprivi, but it is only in the Transvaal and Zimbabwe that it is reported with any regularity. The only breeding records

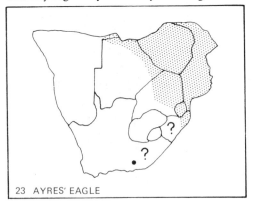

23 AYRES' EAGLE

in southern Africa are from Zimbabwe. Extralimitally its range extends northwards to the Sahara in suitable habitat.

GENERAL HABITS

This magnificent little eagle is not often seen. It soars at a great height or spends long periods perched inconspicuously in a leafy tree. It is the swiftest of all southern African eagles, combining the speed of a large falcon with the manoeuvrability of a sparrowhawk. From a soaring position it plummets at incredible speed, wing tips folded onto the tail, so that it has the shape of an inverted heart. At tree level it weaves in and out of the branches without any apparent slowing down, often emerging with a bird it has caught. Another frequent method of attack is a swift dash from a perch. Once this technique was used to capture a White-faced Duck, which the eagle caught in level flight, attacking from behind and below, and turning upside down with outstretched legs at the moment of impact. Other eye-witness accounts indicate that birds are regularly taken in flight. It also robs nests and has been seen to eat the nestlings of a Pied Crow, returning each day for three days until all the young were eaten. In another case the week-old young of a Black-eyed Bulbul were eaten.

The main prey is small birds usually ranging in size from bulbuls to pigeons, although it is capable of killing a guineafowl. Occasionally small mammals such as tree squirrels are caught. At a nest in Zimbabwe prey remains indicated that Grey Hornbills and glossy starlings were most frequently taken. The prey of a female that frequented a suburban garden in Bulawayo each year for eight years between September and April was carefully noted. The following birds were recorded: 76 Laughing Doves, 22 racing pigeons, 22 feral pigeons, 14 Black-eyed Bulbuls, 14 Kurrichane Thrushes, 9 Groundscraper Thrushes, 4 White Helmet Shrikes, 3 Crested Barbets, 2 Scimitarbills, a Black-collared Barbet, an African Hoopoe, a Black Flycatcher, a Gabar Goshawk, a Little Banded Goshawk and 8 unidentified birds. In all cases where kills were seen the birds were caught in flight after a sudden dash from a perch. The earliest prey capture seen was at 06h25 and the latest at 11h10, but kills were probably made at other times when the eagle left the garden for the day and returned to roost only in the evening. The bird showed no fear of humans, as is characteristic of this species, and the observer was able to train it to answer his whistle and come down for white mice put out for it. However, when bantams were offered, it would not respond. Other observations indicate that chickens are very infrequently taken. The predilection of this species for domestic pigeons is confirmed on the Witwatersrand, where one owner claimed that he had lost 40 birds to Ayres' Eagles in three years; at least one has been shot while chasing pigeons.

Although vocal in the breeding season, it rarely calls at other times. A high-pitched melodious whistling *hueeeep-hip-hip-hip-hueeep* is made, mainly in display. Another call is a rapidly repeated, piping *hip-hip-hip-hip*. A female emitted a loud falcon-like *kack-kack-kack* when someone climbed to her nest. The eaglet makes a high-pitched cheeping call.

BREEDING

Courtship displays consist of soaring round with much noisy calling during which spectacular weaving stoops are performed. The male also performs undulating flights near the soaring female. Sometimes when his mate is on the nest the male stoops from a great height and weaves through the branches above the female's head. Mating takes place on the branch of a tree near the nest to the accompaniment of loud calling.

Nests are placed in the fork of a large tree in thickly wooded terrain, usually on the side of a steep valley, and 8–20 m above ground. They are generally well hidden by surrounding trees, not conspicuous like those of the African Hawk Eagle which are generally situated in more open country. Nests measure 70–90 cm across and 45–90 cm deep with a cup 20–25 cm across. Small sticks up to 2 cm in diameter are used. In

The nest of an Ayres' Eagle showing a typical single-egg clutch (Photograph: Patrick Danckwerts).

This female Ayres' Eagle returned to the same stand of eucalypts in a suburban garden in Bulawayo for eight years until she was shot.

Kenya a pair built on top of a disused Gymnogene's nest.

Both sexes build or repair a nest, but activity tends to be intermittent until nearer laying time when many green branches are added. Normally only one nest is constructed, but a pair in Zimbabwe had an alternate nest. In Kenya nests were found to be insecurely built and tended to fall down, and in Zambia a nest containing an egg was disintegrating because an epiphyte partly supporting it had slipped off the branch.

Because of the rarity of this species the size of territory it requires is difficult to estimate. In Kenya it has been estimated that a pair probably occupies an area of about 25 km^2.

There are only six breeding records for southern Africa, all from Zimbabwe. One egg was laid in early April and the others in May, thus indicating an earlier laying time than the African Hawk Eagle which lays mainly in June. In Zambia two eggs were laid in May and another in July. As is invariably the case in Kenya, a single egg is laid, and several suspect records of two eggs for this eagle in southern Africa have not been included here. Such records have probably resulted from confusion with the African Hawk Eagle, which normally lays two eggs. Eggs are white in ground colour variably marked with spots and blotches of red-brown or dark brown, sometimes forming a cap at the large end, although two eggs had markings concentrated at both ends. Their markings cannot be distinguished from eggs of the African Hawk Eagle and are just as variable. Three eggs from

Zimbabwe measure $64,6 \times 52,0$, $62,5 \times 50,0$ and $61,8 \times 49,7$, which places them within the size range of the African Hawk Eagle. Three Zambian eggs are much smaller: $56,0 \times 44,5$, $55,7 \times 46,0$ and $52,3 \times 44,6$. Further authentic egg measurements are urgently required.

An incubating male has once been flushed off a nest in Zimbabwe, but in Kenya only the female incubated (for 95 per cent of the 153 and a half hours observed). She sat for long periods, once for seven hours without a break, and was fed at the nest by the male every two or three days, much calling taking place as he arrived. He stayed on the nest just long enough to deliver prey before flying off. The female then flew to a favourite tree to feed, returning within ten minutes to resume incubation. The male also brought green branches to the nest. When not away hunting he perched near the nest, but he did not roost nearby.

A number of observers have noted that this species readily attacks a person climbing to the nest, flying past close by at great speed but without actually striking. This behaviour also extends into the nestling period. In Kenya and Zimbabwe nests have been near those of a Peregrine and a Lanner respectively, and many aggressive interactions took place between the eagles and the falcons. In Kenya it was thought that the presence of the Peregrines inhibited the eagles from breeding in some years.

The incubation period has been recorded as 45 days on three occasions in Kenya.

When hatched the chick is covered in dull white down with a darker patch in front of the eye like a mask. The cere and feet are yellowish and the eyes pale grey-brown. It cannot be confused with a newly hatched African Hawk Eagle, which has dark grey down. At 24 days it is still entirely downy except for feathers just beginning to appear on the hind edge of the wing. Two days later first feathers appear on the back, and by 38 days its wing coverts and scapulars are well developed although the rest of the body is mainly downy; the tail is about 2,5 cm long. At this stage it appears to be wearing a dark cape on a downy body. By the time it is 53 days old it is almost entirely feathered except for a fair amount of down on the head and neck; a slight crest is visible.

The eaglet is first able to stand, weakly, at 26 days, and by 38 days it can stand confidently and walk about the nest. It attempts a few wing flaps and tries unsuccessfully to feed itself. At 53 days it is able to feed itself to a certain extent, but is still fed by the female. By 57 days it can feed by itself and mantles over any prey brought to the nest. Wing-flapping exercises become more frequent and by 64 days it walks out along branches near the nest. It is remarkably unafraid of humans, and the prone intruder position is not adopted when they are nearby.

In the first week of its life the chick is closely brooded by the female, who remains on the nest almost continuously. The male brings prey to the nest but does not brood or feed the chick. Thereafter her time on the nest gradually decreases, although she may still brood the chick when it is nearly four weeks old, but not thereafter. Between four and seven weeks she spends less time on the nest but perches nearby most of the day. When the male brings prey she comes to the nest to feed the eaglet. Occasionally she also hunts and brings prey. Green sprays are brought throughout the nestling period, mainly by the female. After the eaglet is seven weeks old she hunts actively and leaves it alone for long periods. The male continues to bring prey, providing more than the female. Birds are usually brought to the nest decapitated and well plucked, making them difficult to identify. Intruders are attacked at the nest, sometimes by both birds if the male is in the vicinity. The female roosts on the nest throughout the nestling period but, as during the incubation period, the male roosts elsewhere.

The eaglet leaves the nest after 75 days, a long period for a small eagle species; the Booted Eagle which is much the same size has a nestling period of about 50 days. The juvenile returns to the nest to be fed and to roost, together with the female in the first few days. It continues to roost alone on the nest until three weeks after its first flight. Thereafter it wanders farther afield, although it is seen with its parents up to three months after leaving the nest. It becomes independent soon after this.

Breeding success in Kenya is poor; in 40 pair-years 0,30 young per pair per year were raised. Factors influencing this result were: the frequent collapse of nests, sometimes with an egg or eaglet; interference from Peregrines nesting nearby; and predation by arboreal mammals, probably genets. Once a large bush shrike persistently attacked a 25-day-old nestling and would eventually have killed or seriously injured it, had the observer not shot the shrike.

No comparative study of the breeding biology of this species outside Kenya exists, so confirmation from another area of the details given here would prove both interesting and valuable.

24 Long-crested Eagle /39.

Langkuifarend
Lophaetus occipitalis

PLATES 9 AND 10

DERIVATION
crest : eagle : occipital feathers — *lophos* (G) : *aetos* (G) : *occipitalis* (L)

IDENTIFICATION
Adult: The black plumage and long floppy crest feathers make this eagle easy to identify. From the front the shoulder of the wing shows white, and in most birds the tight white leggings confirm identification. Some birds have brownish feathering on the leggings, but on present evidence this does not indicate a sexual difference. However, it is probable that males normally have slightly longer crests than females. The tail is barred black and white, the small bill is black, and the eyes, cere and feet are yellow. The yellow gape is large and extends almost in line with the back of the eye.

In flight this eagle is also easy to identify, with distinctive white windows on the primaries both above and below, and bold black and white barring on the tail. The underwing coverts are black, and the white remiges have several black bars, the broadest along the hind edge of the wing.

Juvenile: On leaving the nest it resembles the adult except for a short stubby crest and a

A fully grown juvenile which differs from the adult in having a grey eye and a shorter crest.

grey eye. Its leggings are white, so that brown leggings are not indicative of juvenile plumage as previously thought. If a good view is obtained, faint brownish edges to the feathers of the crown and nape may be seen. The crest reaches full adult length three months after leaving the nest, and then only the eyes, which have changed to hazel, distinguish it. After a further six months the eyes are dull yellow, by which time the juvenile is no longer distinguishable from the adult, although the eyes become deeper yellow in the next few months. A captive juvenile began its first moult when nine months old, first shedding contour feathers and then wing and tail feathers. Most of the crest feathers were also shed, but the new crest was no longer than the previous one. The moult was a gradual process and was not complete by the time it was seventeen months old.

HABITAT
This species is found in well-watered and well-wooded areas, often in cooler moist highlands above 1 500 m (e.g. eastern Zimbabwe). Favoured habitat is short grassland or marshy areas bordered by trees, but it also occurs on the edges of woodland along larger river systems. It has adapted to exotic plantations, particularly eucalypts, where it hunts and breeds.

STATUS AND DISTRIBUTION
Although normally sedentary, it appears to be nomadic at times, moving to an area of abundant food supply in suitable conditions. Thus it may be encountered unexpectedly in localities where it has been rarely, if ever, recorded before, usually after exceptional rains in areas of normally low rainfall. There appears to be no pattern to these movements, which are mainly opportunistic.

Although undoubtedly affected by the draining of marshy areas for agriculture, it is not a species that requires any conservation action at present; indeed this eagle benefits from the clearing of dense woodland and its replacement by paddocks and meadows. Exotic plantations, although much favoured, have not induced it to expand beyond its normal distribution like the Black Sparrowhawk in the Transvaal.

Its distribution, in keeping with its habitat

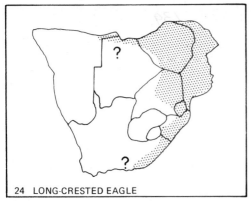

24 LONG-CRESTED EAGLE

requirements, is confined mainly to the eastern part of southern Africa. Formerly encountered from George eastwards, it is now rare in the eastern Cape and no longer occurs in the Knysna area. It is found in Natal, Zululand, Swaziland, eastern and northern Transvaal, Mozambique, Zimbabwe (mainly in the east), northern Botswana and north-eastern Namibia. Extralimitally it extends northwards to Ethiopia and west Africa in suitable habitat.

GENERAL HABITS

It is most often seen perched prominently on a tree, telegraph pole or fence post, where it remains for long periods intently surveying the ground below. Hunting may occur at any time of the day from early morning until it is almost dark. On seeing prey it glides down diagonally and grabs it, either swallowing it whole on the spot or returning to a perch with it. It has a series of perches in its territory which it uses regularly. When flying from one perch to another it has characteristic rapid, shallow wingbeats.

Prey is made up almost entirely of rodents, particularly Vlei Rats *Otomys* species. In a study in the eastern Transvaal 279 prey items were recorded: 98 per cent were rodents, of which 86 per cent were Vlei Rats. In Zimbabwe a similar result was obtained. The largest-known rodent kill on record in southern Africa was a half-grown Greater Cane Rat. Although a specialist rodent hunter, this eagle also feeds on other prey including birds up to the size of a Red-necked Francolin, crabs, insects, a small snake, lizards and trout at a hatchery. It has also been seen to eat mulberries and wild figs. Digestion of rodents is a thorough process, pellets comprising almost entirely hair and very few bones.

This eagle is noisy and calls while perched and during display flights; the most commonly heard call is a high-pitched scream *keeeee-eh* or

a series of sharp *kik-kik-kik-kik-kee-eh* notes, but there are also variations of these.

BREEDING

Courtship displays consist of undulating dives accompanied by calling. They have also been seen to half-close their wings during rapid level flight and to rock from side to side. These displays usually take place in the early part of the morning and at times neighbouring pairs may join in a type of communal flight without any aggressive interactions. The male feeds the female during courtship, and mating takes place in trees near the nest, accompanied by loud calling.

Nests are usually built in tall trees and are placed on a lateral branch or against the main trunk. Thorn trees and smooth-barked trees such as figs are used but, where available, eucalypts are preferred. Nests are situated within the leafy canopy, some well concealed on top of parasitic creepers. A tree on the edge of a clump or plantation is selected, often in a moist area, and nests are usually placed 8–20 m above ground, although one exceptionally high nest in a eucalypt was 45 m up.

Nests are small, similar in appearance to those of Wahlberg's Eagle. They usually measure about 60 cm across and 30 cm deep with a cup 25–30 cm in diameter, but some nests are larger. Occasionally they will take over the old nest of another raptor.

They are erratic breeders, often building new nests or repairing two sites in a season and then not laying. Such behaviour may be linked to cyclic population changes in their main prey species, but in one case harassment by Black Sparrowhawks trying to take over a nest prob-

View of a nest site.

(1) A 15-day-old nestling Long-crested Eagle.

(2) The nestling at 25 days old.

(3) By 40 days it is well feathered.

ably inhibited breeding. Nests may be used for one season only before a move to a new site, but usually remain within the same general area. Their unpredictable breeding behaviour and the inaccessibility of nests are the main reasons why they have only recently been studied at the nest. They may also be sensitive to disturbance, so observers should exercise caution.

Estimates of territory size vary, probably according to local conditions. In Zimbabwe adjacent pairs each occupied areas of about 4–6,5 km²; in the Transvaal a pair had a territory of approximately 25 km²; and six or seven pairs in the same locality occupied an overall area of 250 km². However, Long-crested Eagles are not aggressive towards their own species or other raptors and on several occasions have bred near an occupied Wahlberg's Eagle nest, once as close as 100 m. In an exceptional incident, a Long-crested Eagle incubated the deserted egg of a Wahlberg's Eagle for 44 days but it did not hatch. Such behaviour probably confirms observations of these eagles sitting as if incubating in an empty nest for several weeks without laying.

The breeding season is not as clearly defined as in most other eagles, probably because of their erratic breeding behaviour at times. Eggs are usually laid from July to November, with a peak in September, but they are also occasionally laid in other months.

The normal clutch is two eggs, but single egg clutches have also been recorded. The eggs are dull white in ground colour, variably marked with dark red blotches and smears, sometimes with underlying purple markings. Some eggs may be handsomely marked, others sparingly, and one egg in a clutch may be well marked, the other almost plain. Measurements are: 59,4 × 48,4 (37); 54,1–67,0 × 45,0–51,1.

A nest in Zimbabwe was watched each day during the 42-day incubation period for a total of 504 hours. The egg was covered 89 per cent of the time, 82 per cent by the female and 7 per cent by the male. The female takes breaks from the nest on an irregular basis, sometimes for only an hour during the day, but she may incubate the whole day without a break. During longer absences from the nest she may capture prey herself, but usually the male brings her prey and then takes over incubation when she leaves the nest to feed on it. He also comes to the nest to take over incubation without delivering prey; normally he sits for periods of half an hour to three hours, but sometimes longer. At the nest under observation he was seen to incubate on seventeen days. The female incu-

bates overnight and the male roosts in the nest tree or nearby. The nest is kept lined with green sprays which both male and female bring. An incubation period of 42 days is the only one so far obtained; further observations are required.

The laying gap between two eggs is not known, but instances where young are estimated to have hatched two weeks apart require confirmation. Where two young hatch, there is apparently no sibling aggression, although in one observed case the smaller nestling remained very weak and died from starvation. However, there are a number of records indicating that two young are regularly reared, even although the older eaglet is fed preferentially and develops more rapidly at the expense of its sibling. This difference in development has probably caused the misinterpretation of the hatching interval.

On hatching, the eaglet is covered in greyish-white down. The bill is black, the cere yellow, and the feet flesh pink soon turning yellow. At two weeks old the down is greyish above and white below, the crest is just discernible as a downy excrescence, and first quill stubs appear along the hind edge of the wing. By three weeks the down is much thicker and almost entirely white, a few quills are sprouting on the back and the wing quills are 2 cm long with first feathers just breaking from them. At 25 days blackish feathers are breaking rapidly on the dorsal surface and down the sides of the breast; tail feathers are just appearing and the crest is a distinct downy tuft. Thereafter feathers break rapidly until at 40 days the eaglet is covered by feathers except on the top of the head, neck and leggings. These areas are soon covered by feathers, and by the time it leaves the nest the crest is 6 cm long.

The eaglet's co-ordination develops gradually. At five days its eyesight is still weak although it preens itself. By two weeks it can sit up and shuffle about, and first attempts at wing flapping are made at 25 days. At five weeks old it can stand and walk about confidently, exercise its wings and feed itself.

Initially the male brings prey to the nest, and the female feeds the young, but the male has also been seen to feed them. The female assists with hunting after the young are about three weeks old (sometimes earlier) but the male is the main provider; of 52 items seen brought in during one study he supplied 38. Once he brought six rodents in thirteen hours. Although also carried in the bill or talons, prey is most often brought in the crop; the tail of larger rodents hangs out of the side of the mouth. Such food is regurgitated onto the nest and torn up for the young until they are able to feed themselves, but they may still be fed by an adult even when nearly ready to leave the nest. Green leaves are brought during the nestling period, and the nest is kept clean by the removal of pellets.

Before their first flight the eaglets make their way to surrounding branches, and they first fly between 53 and 58 days. Thereafter they return to the nest or its vicinity to be fed by the adults, and they may be dependent on them for three to four months. Further observations on the post-nestling period are needed. There are no details on breeding success.

25 Martial Eagle /40

Breëkoparend

Polemaetus bellicosus

PLATES 9 AND 10

DERIVATION
war : eagle : warlike — *polemos* (G) : *aetos* (G): *bellicosus* (L)

IDENTIFICATION
Adult: The dark brown head and upper breast, contrasting with lightly spotted white underparts, make this large eagle easy to identify. It can be confused only with the adult Black-breasted Snake Eagle; differences between the two are dealt with under that species. When the eagle is perched, its broad folded wings project at the 'shoulders', giving it a bold stance which is accentuated by the long legs. As the Afrikaans name indicates, it has a broad flat head, at the back of which is a short crest, not always raised. The eyes are rich yellow, the cere and large feet pale greenish. Females are altogether more heavily built than their mates and more spotted below; seen together, male and female are strikingly different in build, and experienced observers are able to sex single birds. In flight the underwing coverts are dark brown and the remiges and tail finely barred, so that it appears predominantly dark from below with a white lower breast and abdomen. In contrast the adult Black-breasted Snake Eagle appears white below with only the head and gorget dark. The long broad wings and short tail of the Martial Eagle give it a quite different shape from the Black-breasted Snake Eagle.

Juvenile and immature: The juvenile is grey above with white edges to the feathers, and immaculate white below, a striking and handsome plumage. The eyes are dark brown, the cere and feet pale greenish. In flight the underwing coverts are white and the remiges and tail finely barred, but when soaring at a height it appears mainly white below. The only species with which it may be confused is the juvenile Crowned Eagle; the distinctions are discussed under that species.

There is little information on the transition from juvenile to adult plumage, but it is a gradual process taking six or seven years, at least two years longer than in other large eagles such as the Black Eagle or Crowned Eagle. It appears that there is little change in the juvenile plumage during the first two years but thereafter dark brown feathers emerge on the upperparts, on the head and down the sides of the breast. At about five years old its breast feathers coalesce to form a gorget and spotting appears on the underparts. In one unusual instance a juvenile in its first or second year was paired with an adult female and assisted in normal duties at the nest. It was not known whether it mated with the female and it may merely have taken the place of the original male who disappeared early in the breeding cycle. The following year the immature eagle mated with the female and they reared an eaglet successfully.

HABITAT
This species may be found in a variety of habitats throughout southern Africa varying from the Drakensberg foothills to the arid Namib. It is probably most common in bushveld country such as that of the Kruger National Park.

STATUS AND DISTRIBUTION
Adults are resident, perhaps moving farther afield outside the breeding season, but not to any great distance. Juveniles and immatures tend to wander away from the area in which they are raised, but are sometimes seen near nests at the onset of the breeding season, and in this way are able to take the place of a lost mate. However, breeding in immature plum-

age is indicative of stress on the adult population.

With the exception of the Bateleur, this species is probably the most seriously threatened of all our eagles and in some areas its numbers have markedly declined. It is more directly persecuted than any other raptor. Inexperienced juveniles are most often trapped or shot: of 34 specimens examined in the National Museum in Bulawayo, 76 per cent were in their first plumage stage (i.e. wholly white below). In one year seven dead Martial Eagles were brought in to the Transvaal Museum. One observer keeping a record of 25 breeding pairs in the Transvaal found that three had disappeared between 1974 and 1978. The large territory it requires (an estimated 110 pairs in the whole Kruger National Park) and its rather erratic breeding behaviour at times further contribute to the decline of this also persecuted eagle. An additional hazard it faces is electrocution on power pylons. Attention to the conservation of this species is essential. It is widely distributed throughout southern Africa, although apparently absent from Lesotho, probably because of lack of breeding sites. In many areas it is now uncommon and in the south-west Cape it is only occasionally recorded as a vagrant. Extralimitally it extends northwards to the Sahara but is not found in large belts of forest.

GENERAL HABITS

The Martial Eagle soars to a great height, often beyond the range of human vision, and does most of its hunting on the wing. Very occasionally it may hover with spread tail and slowly winnowing wings in the manner of a Black-breasted Snake Eagle. It attacks in a long, shallow stoop; one was seen to start its descent on prey from a distance of 6 km. Where its quarry is seen in a more enclosed space it parachutes down at a steeper angle. At the point of kill it shoots its long legs forward and grabs its victim, often killing it on impact. An adult female Red Duiker weighing an estimated 7,65 kg was grasped round the neck and killed by strangulation. It also strikes down large birds in flight; there are records of Black-headed Heron, African Openbill, White-bellied Stork and Spurwing Goose being killed by this method. Occasionally it makes piratical attacks, as when a flying Lammergeyer was robbed of the dassie it was carrying. It hunts also while perched, dropping onto prey from a high vantage point.

This eagle is a versatile hunter and its preferred prey varies from locality to locality. Mammals preyed on include small antelopes and the young of larger ones. The species recorded in southern Africa are: Common Duiker, Red Duiker, Blue Duiker (rarely), Steenbok (frequently), Grysbok, Oribi, Impala and Springbok. Other mammals recorded are: young baboon, Vervet Monkey, Black-backed Jackal, dassies, hares, Springhare, young Warthog, Wild Cat, Serval, Caracal, Striped Polecat, genet, Suricate, Ground Squirrel, Tree Squirrel, Greater Cane Rat, mongooses and Pangolin. It also preys on domestic stock, as discussed later.

Avian prey is made up mainly of gamebirds, guineafowl, francolins and korhaans being most often taken. However, it also preys on larger birds; those recorded include young Ostriches, Egyptian Goose, Spurwing Goose, Sacred Ibis, Hadeda, Black Stork, White-bellied Stork, White Stork, Saddlebill, Black-headed Heron, African Spoonbill and Ludwig's Bustard. It has also been seen to prey on young herons in a heronry. As a rule smaller birds are infrequently preyed on, but a dikkop and a Yellow-billed Hornbill are on record. It has also been seen with other raptors near Red-billed Quelea concentrations and probably preys on them. Unfortunately, free-ranging chickens, especially round African villages, are often taken, leading to inevitable retaliation. The most unusual avian prey recorded was on a nest in Kenya where six Spotted Eagle Owls were found.

Snakes, including venomous ones such as puffadders, are occasionally caught by this eagle, whose main reptilian prey consists of monitor lizards or leguaans, favoured prey in many localities in southern Africa; at one Transvaal nest they made up just under half of the 52 prey items found.

Like other large eagles, it also eats carrion at times. Probably some domestic small-stock is acquired in this way, and there is no doubt that this eagle kills lambs, goat kids and even piglets. This has given it a bad reputation and some farmers shoot it on sight. However, the results of the only extensive quantitative study in southern Africa reveal that it is by no means a serious menace to farming interests. At nine nests distributed throughout the Cape Province 346 prey items were collected. Except for a few birds and monitor lizards, the bulk of the prey consisted of hares and other small mammals such as Suricates, mongooses, Ground Squirrels and dassies. Only eight per cent was found to be domestic small-stock, almost all of it from two of the nine nests. This is a very small amount, even if none of it was taken as carrion, and clearly indicates that the depredations of which this eagle is accused are usually grossly exaggerated. While individual 'rogue' birds undoubtedly occur, the overall damage to small-stock is minimal when compared with other hazards which they face.

Although not often heard, the calls are melodious and varied. The most frequent one is a musical *ko-wee-oh, ko-wee-oh*, used as a contact call by the pair, especially when prey is brought to the nest. As this call is also made by the feathered eaglet, it is undoubtedly a begging call too. Another call is a rapidly repeated trilling *kwi-kwi-kwi-klooee-klooee* made in display. A soft *quolp* is also uttered by the pair.

BREEDING

No spectacular courtship displays have been described. The pair fly round calling and the female may turn and present her claws to the following male. Sometimes a few undulating dives are performed.

This species normally nests in trees, but a pair frequenting a pothole in a cliff in Angola were almost certainly breeding. Near Kimberley and in the Transvaal nests have recently been found on high-tension power pylons, a habit that appears to be increasing. At times the nest may be built on top of that of a Sociable Weaver. Nests are often situated in the fork of a large tree in the neck of a valley where there are air currents but they are also found in flat country. They are usually at a height of 6–15 m. Sometimes nests are situated in a large tree in evergreen forest; one in a Yellowwood tree was 70 m above ground. Various large trees, including Baobabs and thorn trees are mainly used, but even small trees are often difficult to climb.

The nest is a large structure of sturdy sticks. Older nests reach massive proportions and may measure 2 m across and 2 m or more deep. New nests are much flatter, about 1,2–1,5 m across and 60 cm deep. The leaf-lined central depression measures 40–50 cm across. Repair takes two to six weeks and construction of a new nest much longer. In some years the birds repair their nest and then line it for two months or more without breeding. Both birds build; nothing is recorded on the share of the sexes in this activity. Most birds have one nest which they use for many years, at least 21 years in one case, although an alternate nest site is not infrequent. One exceptional pair in Zimbabwe built or repaired seven nests during seventeen years, although they bred in only five of these. One of their nests lasted at least thirteen years without being used. Old nests are sometimes used by other species for breeding.

In Kenya, in two different localities, territories were estimated to be 125 km² and 300 km².

In the Kruger National Park and adjoining nature reserves a pair occupies an area of 144 km², with an average distance of 11,2 km between nests. Near Naboomspruit in the Transvaal four pairs were spaced an average of 35 km apart in an area where previously six pairs occurred. In the Namib Desert Park the density was 250 km² per pair.

In southern Africa eggs are laid from March to August, mainly from April to July. The clutch is invariably a single egg which is chalky-white, rough in texture and variously marked with brown or pale red blotches or speckles and occasional mauve blotches. As a rule eggs are not well marked and some are almost entirely plain or very sparsely speckled. Eggs measure: 79,9 x 63,4 (57); 72,0–87,5 x 60,0–69,0.

There is little information on the incubation period except that the female does most of it, occasionally relieved by the male who may incubate for about three hours at times. It appears that the female leaves the nest to catch prey herself, although the male also brings prey for her. She flattens herself and sits very tight if anyone is below, relying on the nest to hide her from view, often flying off only when the nest is reached. The incubation period has only once been obtained with any accuracy and it was 47 to 49 days. In other cases it was established as not less than 47 days or more than 51 days.

The newly hatched chick has a two-tone down pattern which is dark grey above and white below. The eyes are dark brown, the cere is greyish and the feet are greyish-white. By four weeks the down has lightened to pale grey above, the feet are pale greeny-yellow and first feathers are breaking through the down above. At seven weeks feathers almost obscure the down and by ten weeks it is completely feathered except that the flight feathers are still growing.

Information on the development of co-ordination of the eaglet is scanty. It is not known when it first stands and it appears that it only learns to feed by itself at some time between nine and eleven weeks old. Vigorous wing exercises are performed from about ten weeks and prior to its first flight it may jump up onto branches surrounding the nest. Like the Crowned Eagle, males are more active than females and probably fly earlier too.

Observations on parental care of the nestling are very limited. Watches at a nest in Kenya where parental time on the nest dropped to about nine per cent in the eaglet's second week are certainly not typical, and observations in South Africa indicate that the female spends much of her time on the nest during the first

(1) View of a Martial Eagle's nest.

(2) A close-up of the nest cup and the egg.

(3) A day-old chick.

(4) A three-week-old nestling; a Coqui Francolin and two chickens lie on the nest.

(5) First feathers appear through the down at five weeks old; part of a Scrub Hare may be seen behind the nestling.

(6) At eight weeks the nest-ling is almost fully feathered.

three weeks, brooding the eaglet initially and then standing over it once it grows stronger. The male may also brood a small chick but his main task is to provide prey. He has never been seen to feed the eaglet. Avian prey brought to the nest is always thoroughly plucked. The time spent on the nest by the female drops markedly once the eaglet is seven weeks old and she begins to hunt herself. In one case monitor lizards were brought for the first time at this stage, which suggests that she could cope with stronger and larger prey than her mate. She takes over the role of main food provider but the male also continues to bring prey. Although the eaglet is left alone for most of the time at this stage, the female may continue to roost on or near the nest until the end of the nestling period.

Various estimated nestling periods have been between 90 and 109 days; two accurate ones were 96 and 99 days. One male eaglet flew prematurely at 75 days, when an attempt was made to ring it, so that natural nestling periods by males in less than 90 days are possible. One young eagle returned to the nest on the day it flew and was presumed to have roosted there. On the day after leaving the nest it was able to soar competently but it continued to return to the nest or its vicinity to receive food and roost.

Juveniles may be fed at the nest for at least three months after leaving, and are seen in the vicinity for up to eight months, sometimes even at the onset of the following breeding season. A juvenile in Zimbabwe was shot 65 km away ten months after it left the nest, and a marked juvenile in the Kruger National Park was seen 49 km away six months after it first flew. It appears that the post-nestling period is somewhat variable, some young eagles remaining with their parents for eight months while others disperse earlier.

Observations in Kenya established that various pairs reared between 0,25 and 1,00 young per pair per year, with an average of 0,55. In 63 pair-years in the Transvaal a productivity of 0,51 young per pair per year was obtained. In Zimbabwe a pair studied for eighteen years had a replacement rate of 0,44 but bred very erratically. They raised three young from four eggs initially, then in the next nine years they laid only twice and reared no young until they bred successfully again and raised five young in five consecutive years. The history at this nest illustrates the danger of drawing deductions with regard to breeding success when a nest is watched for only a few years. Erratic breeding behaviour has also been noted in Kenya and no explanation has been found for it.

26 Crowned Eagle *141.*

Kroonarend

Stephanoaetus coronatus

PLATES 9 AND 10

DERIVATION

crown : eagle : crowned — *stephanos* (G) : *aetos* (G) : *coronatus* (L)

IDENTIFICATION

Adult: The rufous underparts heavily overlaid with a mosaic of black feathers distinguish this imposing eagle from any other in southern Africa. There is an intermingling of white feathers as well and generally males show more white blotching on the breast than females. The long tail has three black bars, the terminal one broadest. The bird is uniform slate-black above, and there is an occipital crest, which is not a good field character unless it is raised by the wind or by the bird in excitement. The eyes are pale yellow and appear small in relation to the size of the head. The bill is black and the cere dark grey (erroneously illustrated yellow in most books). The flanges of the gape and the feet are yellow. In flight the rufous underwing coverts are diagnostic. There is a double row of black spots at their junction with the remiges, which are white with three black bars, the one along the hind edge of the wing being broadest. The tail is also white below with three bold bars. The impression after a glimpse in thick forest is of a very large barred eagle with rufous on the underwing.

In this species the male is about a third smaller than his mate and the difference is very striking when they are seen together. However, in one apparently unique pair in Kenya the female was smaller and the male dominant in his behaviour at the nest.

Juvenile and immature: The juvenile is quite different from the adult and is white below and on the head, with a faint wash of rufous on the breast when recently out of the nest. Above, it is grey with distinct white edges to the wing coverts. The eyes are grey, the cere is dark grey, the flanges of the gape are yellow and the feet yellow. In flight it has the basic adult pattern, but the underwing coverts are washed with pale rufous and there are four not three bars on the remiges and on the tail. The only species with which it might be confused is the juvenile Martial Eagle, but this is grey on the head and back of neck, with a shorter tail on which there are a number of closely spaced bars. In flight both the shape and underwing pattern of the two species are quite different.

Development from juvenile to adult plumage is estimated to take four years. Initial changes during the latter part of the first year are gradual. Black feathers first appear on the thighs and then on the crown of the head and crest. Later pale rufous feathers emerge on the breast, then on the rest of the underparts and on the head and nape to form a cap. No flight feathers are moulted at this stage. The eyes become progressively paler grey-brown. At the age of two years the immature has the appearance of a ragged version of the adult but it is still pale rufous on the head, and the upperparts are dark grey with pale edges to the wing coverts. New wing and tail feathers conform to the pattern of barring of the adult. The eyes are pale yellow at this stage. Thereafter it becomes progressively more heavily blotched below and darkens above and on the head until full adult coloration is acquired. The immature has been known to breed when three and a half years old.

HABITAT

Although essentially a forest eagle, this species also occurs in quite open woodland, and it is found in the thickly wooded rocky country of the Matopos hills in Zimbabwe. It may also inhabit thick riverine woodland and quite small relict forest patches.

STATUS AND DISTRIBUTION

It is resident throughout its range, and birds probably spend their adult lives within a relatively small area. It has suffered inevitable diminution of its range through the felling of forests, also through direct human persecution in the form of disturbance, shooting, trapping and destruction of nests. Its conservation depends to a large degree on the Department of Forestry in South Africa as it is in State forests that a major portion of the population occurs.

Its range extends from Knysna north-eastwards through the eastern Cape, Natal, Zulu-

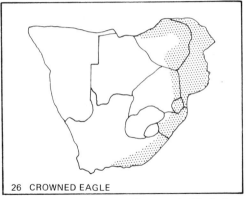

26 CROWNED EAGLE

land, Swaziland, eastern Transvaal, Zimbabwe and Mozambique. Extralimitally it is locally distributed in suitable habitats to west Africa and Ethiopia.

GENERAL HABITS

The dappled underparts provide excellent disruptive camouflage, so that this eagle is rarely seen when perched motionless within the forest canopy. This, combined with its sedentary habits, causes it to be overlooked during a short visit to an area. However, during the course of a day or two, the eagles will inevitably reveal their presence by undulating display flights over their territory, to the accompaniment of characteristic calling which carries over a great distance. These flights may be performed just above the forest canopy, or as high as 1 500 m above it, when they are invisible to the naked eye, although the call may be heard. The undu-

The blotched underparts of this female Crowned Eagle blend well with the surrounding leaves.

The undulating display flight of a Crowned Eagle above the forest.

lations, performed singly or by the pair, consist of flapping the wings in a vertical climb, at the top of which the bird stalls, falls backwards a short way, then dives down to commence the next vertical ascent.

The huge lethal talons of this eagle are more powerful than those of any other African eagle; the killing hind claw is as thick as a man's little finger. It is capable of killing a Bushbuck four to six times its own weight and has been seen to make an unsuccessful attack on one even heavier than this. Hunting is generally done in the early morning or late evening, either by waiting patiently on a perch and dropping onto prey on the forest floor or by killing on the wing. The flight is as silent as that of an owl, and prey is taken completely by surprise. When hunting in flight, the bird observes its victim from a perch initially and then uses its intimate knowledge of its terrain to plan a sneak approach. In one instance which is probably typical Vervet Monkeys were feeding in the canopy of a large tree. The eagle launched its attack from 150 m away, used cover to make an undetected approach, and was next seen bursting skywards through the canopy from below with a monkey grasped in its talons. As with the Black Eagle, there is evidence that a pair may hunt co-operatively, one flying above the canopy to draw the attention of monkeys in the tree-tops while the other attacks from behind. In two cases of attacks on Bushbuck a pair were observed close together, suggesting that they may combine to kill such large prey. As a pair often share prey, co-operative hunting may be regular behaviour.

When prey is killed on the ground, often in an enclosed space, the eagle is able to make a vertical take-off to a branch above. However, when the kill is too heavy to lift, it will be dragged into cover and dismembered and various parts cached in trees out of the reach of other predators such as leopards. Carcasses may be fed on for up to six days and provide food for both birds during that time. The amount of food eaten is variable, and it is estimated that at times (e.g. during the incubation period) a bird may survive for two weeks on only two to three per cent of its body weight daily, but it may gorge about fifteen per cent of its weight in one feed on other occasions.

A study of prey in Kenya by one observer established that about 98 per cent was mammalian, the balance being made up of a few reptiles and the occasional bird. The Suni was the most frequent prey by far, followed by dassies and some monkeys.

In southern Africa there are few quantitative analyses of prey but numerous random reports have been made by observers from many localities. While mammals predominate, as in Kenya, they include a much wider variety, as well as many more records of avian prey. Dassies are by far the most important mammalian prey and at nests in the Cape Province they comprised 42 per cent of 598 items. At one nest in Zimbabwe dassies made up 88 per cent of 51 prey items found. Apart from dassies, antelopes are next in importance, the Suni and the Blue Duiker, both small forest species, being most often killed. Other species recorded in southern Africa include Bushbuck, an Nyala calf, a Kudu calf (with deformed leg, so probably in a weakened condition), Grysbok, Common Duiker, Steenbok and Klipspringer. Of these, the Bushbuck is the heaviest prey regularly taken; from its horns one young ram was estimated to have weighed approximately 30 kg. In Kenya a Bushbuck of 18–20 kg was killed. Other mammal prey includes both Vervet and Samango Monkeys, Bushbabies, a young baboon, squirrels, cane rats, mongooses, a Small-spotted Genet, domestic cats and goat kids. However, domestic stock is rarely taken, and these eagles are not a serious threat to farming interests.

Avian prey records include guineafowl, francolins (eight at one nest), a Hamerkop, a Hadeda nestling, a Black-bellied Korhaan, chickens, turkeys and commercially reared Ostrich chicks. A Crowned Eagle was also seen raiding a Black-headed Heron colony to feed on nestlings. Reptilian prey is taken less often than avian, and lizards such as monitors (leguaans) and Plated Rock Lizards have been found on nests. In Kenya snakes, including venomous ones, have been recorded, but not in southern Africa.

One grisly item found on a nest in Zimbabwe by the famous wildlife artist D. M. Henry was part of the skull of a young African. That preying on young humans may very occasionally occur is borne out by a carefully authenticated incident in Zambia where an immature Crowned Eagle attacked a 20 kg seven-year-old schoolboy as he went to school. It savagely clawed him on head, arms and chest, but he grabbed it by the neck and was saved by a peasant woman with a hoe, who killed it, whereafter both eagle and boy were taken to a nearby mission hospital. The boy was nowhere near a nest, so the attack can only have been an attempt at predation. Although there are no recorded cases in southern Africa, this eagle may attack and claw humans climbing to its nest; in one case a man was knocked from a tree. Baboons in the vicinity of a nest are also attacked. Conversely, the eagles may themselves be molested. In a remarkable record of behaviour in Kenya a Sykes' Monkey was seen to bait a perched eagle, snatching at its feet. It also boldly jumped over an incubating female a number of times, despite being threatened by her.

With the possible exception of the African Fish Eagle, this species is the most vocal of all African eagles. In display flights the male emits a melodius *kewee-kewee-kewee* . . ., the female a deeper, mellower *koi-koi-koi* . . .; in all calls she is deeper voiced. They also utter *queee-queee-queee* cries at the nest, mainly the female in solicitation on seeing the male with prey; sometimes she also makes a begging chittering call. The birds also use soft *kew-kew-kew* contact calls at the nest. Once the eaglet starts feathering it adopts the *queee-queee-queee* soliciting call, but it is also capable of making the whole repertoire of adult calls at this stage.

BREEDING

As well as the undulating flights also used for territorial advertisement, the courting pair perform follow-my-leader chasing flights during which the female turns and presents her claws to the male. Sometimes they may interlock talons for a short spell of cartwheeling flight. Once a male was seen to glide after a female with winnowing wings held above his back while he called excitedly. Another occasional form of courtship takes place on the nest, during which the male runs round his mate with wings raised to display his chestnut underwing coverts. During the courtship period the male brings prey for the female. Mating takes place on the nest or on a branch nearby, two or three times on some days, and quite often after an aerial display or when nest material has been brought.

The nest is usually situated in a major fork of a large forest tree, often in a river valley, normally at a height of 12–30 m and frequently inaccessible without ropes or ladders. In the lowveld of Zimbabwe where the birds occur in more open woodland they nest in Baobab trees. Seven nests in the Transvaal were built in eucalypts. Nests are usually sited within the leafy canopy but some nests may be in exposed positions in a dead tree. Occasionally a nest is constructed on top of the old nest of a raptor such

This huge nest is almost two metres across; the female mantles over prey already in the nest when the male arrives for a visit.

as a Gymnogene or African Hawk Eagle. One unusual nest was situated on the lip of a disused quarry and was partly supported by a prickly pear bush, and another suspected site (a flying juvenile was seen nearby) was on a sheer 45 m cliff 18 m from the top.

The nest is usually very large and those used for a great many years may measure 2–2,5 m across and 2,5–3 m deep. Even newly constructed nests are substantial structures about 1,5 m across. Some of the larger sticks used may be 8 cm in diameter and 1,2 m in length. The central area is thickly lined with a pad of green sprays brought by both birds throughout the incubation and nestling periods, even sometimes during the post-nestling period, although this is probably preparation for the next nesting cycle once the juvenile becomes independent.

Both birds share in construction or repair. Sometimes the female stays on the nest while the male flies back and forth with material which she places in position. Sticks may be collected from the ground, but most material is broken off trees, green branches by bouncing up and down on them until they snap. Heavier branches are carried in the feet, and greenery in the bill. In Kenya a new nest takes four to five months to construct and an established site about one to three months to repair. No observations on nest repair or construction are on record in southern Africa. Nests are generally used for long periods, some larger ones being at least 50 years old. In Kenya the same nests are used for long periods but in southern Africa alternate sites appear to be used more often. In Natal a site was used for five consecutive years, another one nearby for three years, then the original nest was reoccupied.

Territories are maintained throughout the year by displaying above the forest canopy. In Kenya territories were estimated to be about 10–25 km^2. In the Transvaal in three areas breeding density estimates of one pair per 12, 16 and 68 km^2 were made. In localities of highest density active nests were only 2–3,5 km apart. In the Matopos pairs were approximately 13 km apart on average.

Eggs are laid from July to October in southern Africa, with two records in November and a single one in January. The bulk of records (75 per cent) are for September and October. The usual clutch is two eggs but single eggs are also recorded occasionally. The egg is a white oval, rough in texture and chalky-white when freshly laid, becoming stained with brown marks as incubation progresses. Very occasionally eggs may have a few reddish speckles; one exceptional egg was speckled all over with small spots

of brick-brown and larger underlying lilac spots. Eggs are rather small for such a large eagle and are very variable in size. Measurements are: 68,8 × 55,3 (49); 56,4–74,8 × 49,6–60,0.

As the egg is laid the female holds her tail in a raised position. Incubation commences with the laying of the first egg, and the second is laid about four days later. Most of the incubation is by the female, but assisted by the male. He usually brings prey for her every three or four days but she may go two weeks without food at times. On return to the nest when the male has been incubating she may bring prey for him, behaviour unique for an African eagle. The incubation period has been established as 49 days on several occasions, but it may last longer, at least 51 days according to one observer.

There is no known record of two young surviving from a clutch of two eggs. It has reasonably been assumed that the second chick is eliminated as a result of Cainism, but no account of this behaviour has been published, even in Kenya where the biology of this species has been intensively observed. On hatching, the chick is covered in white down. The bill is black, cere greyish, gape pink, eyes dark brown and legs flesh pink. By three weeks the chick has a thicker coat of white down and the feet are pale yellow. First feathers begin to appear on the hind edges of the wings at five weeks, and by seven weeks the eaglet is a mixture of feather and down. The crest is apparent by the time it is 60 days old and at eleven weeks it is fully covered by feathers, although the tail has not grown to its full length.

The eaglet is first able to stand at five weeks old, when it also attempts a few wing flaps, and by six weeks it is able to tear up prey for itself, when it is still mainly downy. Wing exercises are performed from seven weeks on, once feathers are emerging rapidly, and increase as the weeks go by. The eaglet's other main activities, apart from feeding, consist of preening and walking about the nest. When the time of the first flight approaches it may jump up onto branches surrounding the nest, but male eaglets are more adventurous than females in this.

During its first ten days the eaglet is brooded or sheltered almost continuously by the female. The male brings all prey and increases his killing rate to about twice that maintained in the incubation period. When he arrives the female snatches the food from him and mantles over it aggressively; he does not remain long on the nest and she ceases mantling once he departs. The male may brood and feed the eaglet but this behaviour varies from pair to pair. He only

(1) A juvenile Crowned Eagle perches above its nest in a tall yellowwood in thick forest.

(2) The five-week-old nestling is still entirely downy.

(3) At ten weeks old the nestling is well feathered.

feeds the chick in the female's absence, because of her aggressiveness towards him when there is prey on the nest. After the first ten days, and until the eaglet is six weeks old, the female's time on the nest gradually decreases. She shelters rather than broods it, although she still broods overnight. However, even when off the nest, she remains nearby, and the male still provides all the food. During this period the female fetches many green branches. The eaglet is able to feed itself at six weeks, although the female also continues to feed it until it is eight weeks old. During this time the male still provides all prey; she does not go far from the nest and continues to roost on it or nearby. After eight weeks the female is rarely near the nest during the day; she hunts actively and takes the male's place as main food provider. The eaglet feeds itself without assistance so that visits to the nest by the adults are purely concerned with bringing prey or the occasional green spray. The female may still roost in the nest tree, but irregularly. Towards the end of the nestling period fewer kills are brought to the nest but there is no evidence that the eaglet is intentionally starved.

The first flight is made between 103 and 116 days, males leaving sooner than females. The average nestling period of males is 106 days, that of females 114 days. The eaglet leaves in the absence of its parents and may go 50–100 m on its maiden flight.

The post-nestling period in Kenya has been extensively observed and there is no comparable study in southern Africa. In Kenya juveniles remain dependent on their parents for 270–352 days, which results in a breeding cycle of about 500 days, so that nesting can take place only every second year. The main explanation advanced for this protracted post-nestling period is that it enables the adults to produce a young eagle that is better able to fend for itself and survive to sexual maturity.

In southern Africa there is evidence that this biennial rhythm does not necessarily apply and there are many records from various localities of young being reared to the flying stage in two or three consecutive years, and possibly much longer at one nest. While it may be argued that none of these young survived to the following breeding season, this seems highly improbable.

In one case a juvenile from the previous year has been seen at a nest just prior to the female laying again. In the Matopos a juvenile was found dead 23 km from a nest three months after it first flew, when it must certainly have been independent if the Kenya pattern of the juvenile remaining near its nest is applicable. It would appear that the post-nestling period in southern Africa is different at times from that in Kenya. Further detailed observations from our area are essential in order to establish the extent of these differences.

In Kenya the juvenile remains within 800 m of its nest until it becomes independent and it is inactive much of the time. It calls a great deal when hungry and this is a good way of locating it, and the nest, in thick forest. In the vicinity of the nest it has a number of favourite perches and it roosts on the nest or nearby. Prey is brought every three to five days, mainly by the female, who maintains her dominant role as main provider established in the latter part of the nestling period. On arrival with prey, the adult calls to the young eagle, which flies to the nest to receive it, snatching it from its parent and mantling over it. The juvenile may make its first kill when two months out of the nest but it continues to be fed by the adults. It appears that its independence may be the result of irregular meals, sometimes two weeks apart. Eventually it kills regularly for itself and is not hungry when the parents bring food. Thus the break is made and there is no evidence that it is chased away.

In Kenya 21 young were reared in 54 pair-years, or 0,39 young per pair per year, an apparently low figure, but it must be taken into account that they breed biennially whenever an eaglet is successfully raised to independence. In 35 pair-years in the Transvaal 16 young were reared, a productivity of 0,46 young per pair per year. In the wild state Crowned Eagles have been estimated to have a life span of about 15 years, although they may live very much longer in captivity.

Note: Details on the breeding biology of this species have been drawn to a considerable extent from the long-term study of Dr Leslie Brown in Kenya. Extensive comparative work for southern Africa is not available and research would prove rewarding.

27 Brown Snake Eagle /42

Bruin-slangarend
Circaetus cinereus

PLATES 8 AND 11

DERIVATION
harrier : eagle : ashy — *kirkos* (G) : *aetos* (G) : *cinereus* (L)

IDENTIFICATION
Adult: One's impression of the perched bird is of a uniform brown eagle of very upright posture. If a clear view is obtained, the feathers of the dorsal surface show a slight purple gloss. The bare legs are dull white in colour, distinguishing this species from other brown eagles with feathered legs. The eyes are large and rich yellow, which, with the loose feathers at the back of the head, give the bird an owlish expression.

In flight the underwing coverts are brown, contrasting with the unmarked whitish remiges. The three evenly spaced narrow white bars on the tail also aid identification. Confusion is possible with juveniles of the Black-breasted Snake Eagle and the Bateleur. The former, however, are distinctly rufous-brown, especially below, and in flight show three narrow parallel bars on the remiges and no distinct barring on the tail. The juvenile Bateleur has a characteristic stumpy tail and the eyes are dark brown. In flight its outline is distinctive.

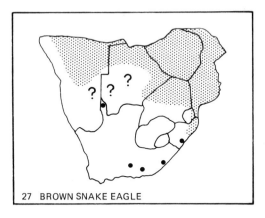

27 BROWN SNAKE EAGLE

A juvenile Brown Snake Eagle showing some white blotching on the underparts.

Juvenile and immature: Juveniles are rather variable, some being virtually indistinguishable from adults, while others have white flecks on lower breast and abdomen. Some individuals have white streaking on top of the head, others not. The limited available evidence indicates that juveniles moult into a confusing immature plumage with a variable amount of white on the feathers of the breast and abdomen, some individuals showing extensive patches of white. Whether this is applicable to all immatures or to certain individuals only is not as yet known. Further research is required on juvenile and immature plumages, especially on the time taken to pass through these stages, and to what extent individual variation occurs.

HABITAT
Found in a variety of drier bushveld habitats such as acacia or mopane, but not in forest or treeless plains. It is common in the wooded granite koppie country of the Matopos in Zimbabwe. Where the Brown Snake Eagle overlaps with the Black-breasted Snake Eagle, the former hunts in wooded country, the latter in more open habitat.

STATUS AND DISTRIBUTION
It is considered resident in most areas, although some movement may take place, as apparent 'stragglers' are reported from some areas (e.g. eastern Cape, Natal). Its distribution extends from the eastern Cape (rarely) northwards to Mozambique, eastern and

northern Transvaal and Zimbabwe, thence westwards through northern Botswana to Namibia as far south as Windhoek. As it occurs in the Kalahari Gemsbok National Park, it is probably more widely distributed in southeastern Namibia and southern Botswana than is known at present. Extralimitally it is found northwards to the Sahara in suitable habitat.

GENERAL HABITS

This eagle is usually seen singly on a prominent perch, often on a hilltop, from which it watches for long periods for prey. Still-hunting is undoubtedly the principal method of hunting, but on occasions it may hover on winnowing wings for short periods or, rarely, quarter the ground in the manner of a harrier. It soars well.

Prey is almost entirely reptilian, mostly snakes. These are grasped in the small, powerful feet and crushed while twisting pecks break the spine in various places. The legs are heavily scaled for protection against the bites of snakes, and the large gape enables the eagle to swallow all but the largest ones whole. One eagle was found enmeshed in the coils of a Mole Snake firmly grasped in its talons. They were separated by the observer, but the outcome may well have proved fatal for both. Both venomous and non-venomous snakes are killed; those recorded include various species of cobra, as well as Puffadder, Boomslang, Stripe-bellied Grass Snake, Blind Snake and Black Mamba. The largest known kill is of a Black Mamba in Zambia measuring 2,78 m, and one almost as large was killed in the Matopos. Other recorded reptiles include a Water Monitor (Leguaan) as well as smaller lizards and chameleons. In Kenya a toad, rats and birds, especially gamebirds, have been recorded, but these items have yet to be noted in their diet in southern Africa.

Unlike the Black-breasted Snake Eagle, this species is not known to swallow snakes in flight. However, it does bring a swallowed snake to the nest with the tail portion hanging from the bill in typical snake eagle fashion.

The call is a guttural *hok-hok-hok-hok-hok*, usually heard from soaring birds at the onset of the breeding season, and during the nesting period when adults call to each other. At the nest the adults may exchange soft *kwee-oo, kwee-oo* notes. Outside the breeding season it is rarely heard to call. The eaglet emits raucous *yak-yak-yak* and terrier-like *yip-yip-yip* begging calls once it abandons its infantile cheeping. From the age of 60 days it can utter the *hok-hok-hok* of the adults.

BREEDING

Courtship consists of soaring round making the *hok-hok-hok* call; often just a single bird is involved. During display flights birds may interlock claws briefly. A hovering 'butterfly' style of flight with one bird following the other has been noted. Dive-bombing behaviour at one nest where a bird swooped down at its perched mate is probably also an aspect of courtship display.

Most of the available breeding records come from Zimbabwe, where a definite breeding season is indicated, eggs normally being laid from December to February with a peak in January. Of seventeen records from Zimbabwe two were for eggs laid in December, ten in January and two in February. The remaining three were single records of eggs laid in March, July and August. In South Africa there is an instance of an egg laid in January in the Kruger National Park; a single Botswana record is also for January. Thus eggs are usually laid during the summer rains, and the young are reared during the cool, dry winter months. This breeding season is similar to that of the Bateleur.

The nest is a small, flat structure of pencil-thick sticks measuring 60–70 cm in width with a leaf-lined depression about 25 cm across. The depth of the nest is usually about 25 cm. Recorded sites have been between 3,5 m and 12 m above ground. Flat-topped trees, especially thorn trees, are favoured, and euphorbias are also used. The nest, placed on top of the tree's crown, is extremely difficult to detect. Very occasionally the birds may build their nest within the canopy of a tree. There are also a number of instances where the disused nest of another raptor has been utilised, the species concerned being Tawny Eagle, Wahlberg's Eagle, African Hawk Eagle and Gymnogene. The birds usually place fine sticks on top of the existing nest and add green lining. Descriptions of bulky Brown Snake Eagle nests have certainly originated from instances where another raptor's nest has been taken over. All nest sites are chosen so that they are easily accessible from the air. Construction may take about a month, but at other times it may be very protracted. At one nest both birds were observed to build. Frequent moves to new sites are made, and nests are rarely used more than twice in succession. These moves are probably due to the fact that the growing tree's crown no longer proves suitable to support the nest, or inhibits easy access. Accordingly, it is difficult to maintain continuous observation on a pair, even though the move to a new site is never much more than a kilometre. Nothing is known about territory size, but it is likely to be large, as these eagles are sparingly distributed, even in an optimum habitat such as the Matopos.

The clutch is invariably a single large egg, chalky-white when fresh, and either immaculate or with a few blood smears. As the incubation progresses, eggs may become fairly heavily nest-stained. Measurements are: 75,5 x 60,9 (12); 69,5–78,6 x 58,2–66,0.

On present evidence only the female has been known to incubate, sitting for long periods and fed by the male. More intensive observations during this period will probably reveal that the male relieves his mate for short spells, in common with other eagles. The female is a very tight sitter, crouching flat on the nest on the approach of an observer, even if in full view only a short distance away. At one nest the incubation period was 48–50 days (49 ± 1 day), at another at least 50 days. From first pipping, the chick may take two and a half days to break free from the shell. Throughout the period the nest is kept well lined with fresh green leaves, and this continues into the nestling period until the eaglet is about five weeks old, after which few leaves are brought.

The newly hatched chick has a large head and is covered in white down. The eyes are dark brown, the cere is grey, the bill is black and the legs are greyish-white. By the time it is a month old, feathers are sprouting rapidly on the anterior half of the dorsal surface and the eyes are pale yellow. At six weeks the feathers effectively cover the front half of the body and the eyes are fully yellow. Thereafter the eaglet develops steadily, although the tail grows slowly and it remains downy on its rump and flanks for some while in contrast to its feathered foreparts. By twelve weeks, however, it is fully feathered.

Parental attention is closely linked to the eaglet's feather development, and once it is about five weeks old the adults spend very little time on the nest except to bring it food. At one nest for example, parental time on the nest dropped from 70 per cent of the time observed to 1 per cent for the periods before and after five weeks respectively.

During its first three weeks the eaglet is closely tended by the female, with the male providing prey, although he has been observed to shade the eaglet during the female's absence. Her activities are mainly concerned with brooding, shading and feeding the eaglet. The male brings snakes to the nest half swallowed with the tail hanging from his bill. On arrival he hooks it out with his foot, or the female withdraws it from his throat with her bill. Initially the prey is torn up and small pieces are fed to the eaglet, but as early as its nineteenth day it is able to pull a snake from the adult's throat and swallow it whole. However, it is still necessary for the female to tear up larger snakes for it for some while after this. Between the third and fifth week the female begins to leave the eaglet unattended as its feather development accelerates.

From the fifth week the eaglet is left very much to its own devices. At this stage it is able to stand weakly, and by six weeks old the first wing-flaps while standing may be attempted, but it cannot walk about the nest with confidence until some weeks later. Except for preening, the eagle remains mostly inactive, even up to the time at which it is nearly ready to leave the nest. First serious wing exercises, and short flights across the nest, may be attempted as late as 104 days, when the eaglet is nearly due to make its first flight.

During this second stage of the nestling period both adults bring in snakes, the male more than the female. On seeing the adult approaching, the eaglet calls excitedly. Once the parent has alighted near the nest with food it adopts a submissive hunched posture and emits a soft squealing *yeeeeeee*. As soon as the parent is on the nest, the eaglet grasps the protruding snake in its bill, sometimes using its foot as well, while the parent strains back and the snake is disgorged. It then mantles over the prey, and the adult soon departs. It is able to swallow prodigious meals at this stage, such as a metre length of cobra, or a large Puffadder,

A 94-day-old nestling pulls a large Boomslang from the throat of the adult Brown Snake Eagle, which strains backwards to assist the process.

(1) A Brown Snake Eagle brings a small snake for the chick. The typical small, flat nest is situated on the crown of a thorn tree.

(2) The egg lies on a bed of green leaves; the small sticks used in the construction of the nest may be seen.

(3) A week-old chick showing the large head and brown eyes.

(4) The three-week-old nest-ling is still entirely downy but the eyes have changed to pale grey.

(5) The feathers break rapidly on the upperparts at four weeks old and the eyes are pale yellow.

(6) By six weeks old the upperparts are well feathered but the back and flanks are still mainly downy. The eyes are fully yellow.

gulping the meal down with many contortions of the neck at the rate of about 30 cm a minute. Snakes are always swallowed from the front end first. Although larger snakes are often brought with the head and neck already eaten by the adult, this is not regular, and the eaglet will swallow venomous snakes such as cobras and Boomslangs intact with no ill effects. There is evidence that towards the end of the nestling period the eaglet may be brought fewer meals by the adults.

The duration of the nestling period has been recorded on five occasions as follows: between 97 and 101 days, between 100 and 108 days, between 106 and 113 days, and in two instances it was accurately obtained as 109 days.

Post-nestling attachment to the nest is of short duration. The young eagle may still be fed on the nest for about a week after its first flight, and may be seen in the nest area for another week or so, but thereafter it wanders away. In one instance in Kenya a juvenile was seen with its parents two months after it had left the nest. Owing to the brief attachment to the nest site, observations during this period are difficult to obtain and little is known.

Breeding success is difficult to calculate because pairs move to new nest sites so often, but on seven occasions when one pair was known to have bred they reared four young. It appears from present evidence that this species usually breeds annually.

28 Black-breasted Snake Eagle *143.*

Swartbors-slangarend

Circaetus pectoralis

PLATES 8 AND 11

DERIVATION
harrier : eagle : breast — *kirkos* (G) : *aetos* (G) : *pectoralis* (L)

IDENTIFICATION
Adult: When this eagle is perched, the blackish upperparts, head and breast contrast with the rest of the unspotted white underparts. Some birds have a small patch of white on the throat. The large yellow owl-like eyes, rounded head with a loose cowl of feathers at the back, bare white legs and small feet, all serve to distinguish it from the Martial Eagle.

Seen in flight from below, the underparts appear almost entirely white except for a contrasting black head and gorget. There are three distinct black bands on the tail, and the white underwing has three parallel black bars across the remiges. In contrast, the Martial Eagle is predominantly dark on the underwing and tail from a distance, so that the impression is of a dark eagle with a contrasting white abdomen. The Martial Eagle also has a broader wing as compared with the long-winged Black-breasted Snake Eagle. Confusion with the flying Augur Buzzard may possibly arise, but the typical buzzard shape (broad wings, short tail) should be evident; there is no barring on the white underwing, and its tail is red. The perched Augur Buzzard has dark brown eyes and the short red tail is diagnostic.

Juvenile and immature: The juvenile is entirely rufous-brown, more richly coloured on its underparts, and the eyes are deep yellow as in the adult. The underwing has three faint black bars (narrower than the adult) and the tail is so indistinctly barred as to appear plain pale grey at a distance. For distinctions between the juvenile of this species and the Brown Snake Eagle see the text on that species.

The moult of a captive juvenile into imma-

An immature Black-breasted Snake Eagle 21 months old; it is a ragged version of the adult and still has brown spotting on its abdomen and flanks.

ture plumage has been recorded. At about six
months old blackish feathers appear in the region of the gorget, and by eight months the
rufous-brown coloration gives way to grey-
brown feathers, especially on the head, back
and wing coverts. From ten months old the
first white feathers slowly appear on the abdomen; these have brown centres which give the
underparts a spotted appearance.

During the second year moulting is heaviest,
blackish feathers increasing in the region of the
gorget, and the abdomen becoming progressively whiter although still spotted with brown.
Wing and tail feathers are gradually moulted
and the new feathers show the pattern of barring of the adult. At the age of two years the
immature has the appearance of a rather ragged and drab version of the adult, with some
brown spotting still present on the abdomen
and leggings; these are the last signs of immature plumage to disappear. Full adult plumage
is probably acquired in the third year.

HABITAT

Although living mainly in open plains or
lightly wooded country, it occurs in a wide variety of habitats from the Namib Desert to the
moist eastern highlands of Zimbabwe. It
avoids forested areas, although it may inhabit
open country adjoining forest. Where it coincides with the Brown Snake Eagle it inhabits
more open country.

STATUS AND DISTRIBUTION

The status of this species is intriguing in that
in some areas it is undoubtedly resident, while
elsewhere it is subject to nomadic movements
and possibly migration. Around Salisbury in
Zimbabwe there is an influx during the winter
months from May to September, and communal roosts have been noted. Communal roosting involving some 25 birds has also been seen
in May in the midlands of Zimbabwe and almost 200 birds were seen spread over a small
area in another observation there. In Matabeleland the species is apparently resident,
although small communal roosts have been
seen in June. What is interesting is that in
Matabeleland and elsewhere in Zimbabwe the
breeding season falls mainly during the winter
months, when influxes and communal roosts
have been recorded. It would seem at present
that two populations are involved, and the
question to be solved is where these 'migrant'
birds come from. Winter roosts have also been
recorded in Zambia; in one instance 43 birds
of various ages were spread over an area of approximately 20 hectares.

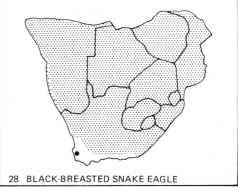

28 BLACK-BREASTED SNAKE EAGLE

Records from the central highveld of the
Transvaal indicate that there the species is
mainly a summer and autumn visitor from
November until May. In these sightings of
adult, juvenile and immature birds, communal
roosting and 'gregarious' hunting have been
noted. It is tempting to inter-relate the summer and winter pattern of occurrence in the
Transvaal and Zimbabwe respectively, but no
evidence exists to show whether these populations commute, and it remains an interesting
riddle to solve. Elsewhere aggregations may
occur, for example in the Kalahari after rains
have fallen. Interestingly, in the first decade of
this century, that astute observer Captain C. G.
Davies noted that this species was 'more or
less migratory' in eastern Pondoland (Port St
John's and environs) occurring there in spring
for a few days and moving on. Although it is
now very rare in these parts, Davies should be
accorded the distinction of having first observed the movements of this species in southern Africa.

The Black-breasted Snake Eagle is very
sparsely distributed and uncommon over most
of the Cape Province and Natal. North of the
Orange River it may be regularly encountered
in suitable habitat. Extralimitally it occurs
northwards to Zaire in the west and Ethiopia
in the east.

GENERAL HABITS

Although it may still-hunt from a perch in the
manner of a Brown Snake Eagle, this species is
most often seen hunting while soaring, or by
hovering on winnowing wings in the manner of
a giant Black-shouldered Kite but with slower
wing-beats. It usually hunts from heights of between 30 and 90 m but an attack may be made
from as high as 450 m. On seeing a snake it
drops down like a parachute, often in stages,
with claws extended, until it finally plunges to
grasp its prey. Small snakes are carried into the

(1) A Black-breasted Snake Eagle alights with a snake at its nest on the crown of a thorn tree.

(2) This nest in the crown of a euphorbia would be impossible to detect from below.

(3) A typical nest constructed with pencil-thick sticks.

(4) Feathers are breaking rapidly through the down of this three-week-old nestling; the nictitating membrane is drawn across the eye which is yellow by this stage.

(5) At five weeks old the nestling is well feathered except for its hindparts.

(6) By nine weeks old the nestling is fully feathered except for some growth on the wings and tail.

A hovering Black-breasted Snake Eagle.

air and swallowed whole after they have been crushed by being passed through the talons. On occasions the eagle may partially swallow the snake, then withdraw it and begin again, sometimes swallowing it and pulling it out with its feet several times in succession. Large snakes are killed on the ground where caught and are torn up and eaten on the spot.

Snakes form a major part of this eagle's diet, but as a rule it tends to take smaller ones than the Brown Snake Eagle, which has larger feet and a more powerful bill. However, it is capable of killing a cobra of 1,8 m as well as quite large Puffadders. Snakes killed by this eagle include cobras, adders, Boomslang, Tiger Snake, Stripe-bellied Grass Snake and Herald Snake, but it will undoubtedly prey on any snake it can catch and makes no distinction between venomous and non-venomous types. It also preys on various lizards, and is on record as having killed a metre-long Water Monitor (Leguaan). Chameleons also feature in its diet.

On present evidence this species takes a wider spectrum of prey than the Brown Snake Eagle. Rats and mice are regularly caught, as are toads and frogs, and it is recorded as having preyed on a guineafowl. Reports that it kills poultry should be carefully authenticated in view of its confusion with the Martial Eagle, but it is possible that it does prey on chickens very occasionally. In Kenya a hare was brought to a nest. At times it also eats insects, and beetles and termites have been recorded. It is attracted to grass fires, where it may be seen hovering above the smoke watching for prey disturbed by the flames. There is one record of this eagle catching small fish, by flying down from a perch and taking them from just under the surface of the water, only its legs being immersed.

Unlike the other snake eagles which are generally solitary, this species hunts gregariously on occasions, usually when communal roosts have also been observed. Six birds have been seen hovering over open country in sight of each other. Adult, juvenile and immature birds have occurred in these groups with no sign of friction. Communal roosts have already been mentioned: the eagles have been seen gathering at sunset on dead trees or power pylons, as many as seven birds perching on one tree or pylon with others nearby. One observer noted a gathering in a heavily overgrazed area in the very early morning. The eagles were roosting in dead trees, on low bushes and even on the ground.

Outside the breeding season calling is rarely heard. At the nest it may make a melodious *woo-dlay-oo, weeeu, weeeu, weeeu*, associated with a wing-raising display in which the wings are waved about slowly above the back. This behaviour is rare and has so far been recorded only in Kenya. Soaring birds, probably in display, may make a harsh *kaa-rrr, kaa-rrr, kaa-rrr* while dangling their legs, but as a rule calls are melodious. A *kwo-kwo-kwo . . . kweeu-kweeu-kweeu* call, very similar to that of the African Fish Eagle, is made by the pair near the nest or when driving other raptors from their territory. Fluting *piee-ou, piee-ou, piee-ou* as well as musical *yak, yak, yak* calls of solicitation are made by the female on seeing the male approaching the nest with prey. The *piee-ou* call is also used by the eaglet when begging for food, as well as a whistling *quee-quee-quee*, and both are accompanied by limp flapping of the wings. The eaglet is able to make the *kwo-kwo-kwo . . .* call when it is seven weeks old.

BREEDING

No spectacular display flights are performed; the birds merely soar round at a considerable height, calling and occasionally making undulating dives. During courtship the male feeds the female. A wing-raising display associated with calling has already been described.

The nest is indistinguishable from that of the Brown Snake Eagle and is generally placed at heights of 3,5 m to 7,5 m on top of a thorn tree or in the crown of a euphorbia or other trees. One nest in the eastern districts of Zimbabwe was situated in the crown of a pine tree at a height of 24 m. There is one record of an old African Hawk Eagle's nest being taken over. Details of nest-building are scanty; construction may extend over several months on occasions, and the nest may not necessarily be used in the end. Both sexes build.

In Zimbabwe two nests containing young of similar ages were situated only 1,6 km apart, but otherwise nothing is recorded on the spacing of breeding pairs. Other large raptors are driven off when they enter a pair's territory.

Like Brown Snake Eagles, they frequently move to new sites, so that regular observations on the breeding history of a pair are made very difficult. However, they continue to breed in the same general area.

The breeding season is not clearly defined; eggs are laid from March to October. In Zimbabwe, where most of the breeding records have been obtained, laying occurs mainly from June to September (82 per cent of 39 records). The few records from elsewhere in southern Africa indicate that eggs are laid in the winter months. A single large chalky-white egg is laid, becoming nest-stained as incubation progresses. Measurements are: 72,5 × 57,0 (32); 69,6–78,7 × 52,0–62,1.

Details of the breeding cycle are basically similar to those of the Brown Snake Eagle, except that the male has been known to do some of the incubation. The incubation period in one case was at least 51 to 52 days and was thought unlikely to have been very much longer. Tight sitting is characteristic also of this species. On return to the nest the parent may drop down like a parachute from a considerable height directly onto the nest. The major difference between the breeding cycles of the two species is the more rapid development of the eaglet, which shows its first feathers as early as two weeks, a week ahead of the Brown Snake Eagle. The change of the iris to yellow is also more rapid. In line with this, parental attention drops off markedly when the eaglet is a month old, a week in advance of the Brown Snake Eagle. Rather limited observations at one nest revealed the drop to be from 52 per cent to 3,5 per cent of the observed time before and after the eaglet was a month old. The fledging period is also shorter, 89–90 days in one case.

Little is recorded on the post-nestling period. At one nest the young eagle returned to roost two days after it had first flown. The juvenile may be fed on the nest by an adult six months after its first flight. Observations on breeding success are scanty. One pair bred in the same area in two nests during a five-year period. They raised an eaglet during each of the first two years, then apparently missed a year before moving to another site nearby where two more eaglets were reared. Further observation on the post-nestling period and breeding success are needed.

29 Southern Banded Snake Eagle /44.

Dubbelband-slangarend
Circaetus fasciolatus

PLATES 8 AND 11

DERIVATION
harrier : eagle : banded — *kirkos* (G) : *aetos* (G) : fasciolatus (L)

IDENTIFICATION
Adult: This greyish-brown snake eagle may be identified by the white and grey barring extending from the lower breast to its abdomen and thighs. When the eagle is perched, its long tail projects well beyond the wing tips. It has been likened to an outsize Cuckoo Hawk, and the comparison is apt except for its typical rounded snake eagle head with a loose cowl of feathers at the back. The bill is black, the cere yellow, the eyes are pale yellow and the bare legs dull yellow. There are three dark bars on the white-tipped tail, the terminal one being broadest, but only two would be visible on the perched bird seen from behind. In flight the underwing appears mainly whitish with a black band along the hind edge preceded by five narrow black bars. The underwing coverts are finely barred with sepia. The three dark bars on the tail and two prominent white bands between them serve to distinguish this species from the Banded Snake Eagle, the only species with which it is likely to be confused.

Juvenile and immature: The juvenile is dark brown above with distinct white tips to the feathers of the upperwing coverts. The crown is faintly streaked with white and the pale brown nape has white edges to the feathers. The chin and throat are white with some black streaking. The breast is buffy-white with narrow black streaks; the abdomen, flanks and thighs are white with brown barring. The overall impression is of a snake eagle that is dark brown above and pale below. The underside of the wings and tail is grey with a pattern of barring similar to that of the adult. The soft parts are the same colour as those of the adult. Nothing is known about the transition from juvenile to adult plumage.

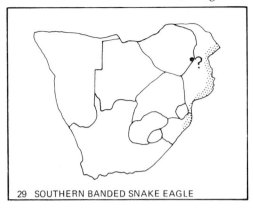

29   SOUTHERN BANDED SNAKE EAGLE

HABITAT

This snake eagle occurs in evergreen coastal and lowland forest or in thick woodland. It is often found near rivers, lakes or swamps.

STATUS AND DISTRIBUTION

The Southern Banded Snake Eagle is rare and localised in southern Africa. As far as is known it is resident. It appears that it was formerly more widely distributed in Natal but disappeared when its coastal habitat was reduced or destroyed. Its distribution extends from Zululand northwards to Mozambique; it occurs also in south-eastern Zimbabwe, though rarely. On present evidence its range in southern Africa does not overlap that of the Banded Snake Eagle. Extralimitally it extends up the east coast as far north as Kenya.

GENERAL HABITS

Very little is known about the habits of this species. It watches for prey by still-hunting from a perch, often on the edge of a clearing in forest. When it flies, the wing-beats are rapid and shallow like those of the Long-crested Eagle. Generally it flies a short distance to another perch where it resumes its watch for prey. Because of its sedentary habits it is easily overlooked, except when calling, and it soars above the forest canopy infrequently.

Its prey is mainly snakes, also lizards. Other items of food recorded include a mouse, a weaver, large beetles and termites. The label of a specimen collected in Zimbabwe comments, 'Eating chickens.'

The main call is a rapid, high-pitched *ko-ko-ko-ko-kaw*. It also utters a single sonorous *kowaaa* at intervals and a crowing *kurk-urr, kurk-urr* like a cockerel with a breaking voice. The feathered nestling begs with a loud squalling *kyaa-kyaa-kyaa-kyaa-kyaa* repeated at short intervals for long periods.

BREEDING

Soaring birds make the *ko-ko-ko-ko-kaw* call, presumed to be their nuptial display.

Authentic breeding records are extremely rare, and many of those published (see References) do not stand up to careful scrutiny. The *only* authentic southern African breeding record appears to be that of P.A. Sheppard (in Brooke 1971), who shot a male off a nest containing a single egg on 28 September 1909 near Beira in Mozambique. Unfortunately, no other details of this record exist.

The only detailed description of the nest of this species comes from Kenya, where a nest was situated well within the tree's canopy in a fork partly overgrown with creeper at a height of 7,6 m. Difficult to detect, it was a typical snake eagle nest made of pencil-thick sticks. The nest measured 60 cm across and 30 cm deep. Another Kenya nest was placed rather conspicuously in the fork of a thin creeper-festooned tree at a height of 10 m.

The September record of Sheppard is the only indication of breeding season in our area. The single egg he found agrees with the single-egg clutch of other snake eagles. There are no measurements or descriptions of the egg of this species but it will no doubt be plain white and large like those of other African snake eagles.

Nothing is known about the incubation and nestling periods except for Sheppard's evidence that the male incubates. At a nest in Kenya a juvenile was seen near its nest about two months after it first flew. Further information on all aspects of the biology of this species is urgently needed.

30 Banded Snake Eagle /4 5.

Enkelband-slangarend

Circaetus cinerascens

PLATES 8 AND 11

DERIVATION
harrier : eagle : becoming ashy — *kirkos* (G) : *aetos* (G) : *cinerascens* (L)

IDENTIFICATION
Adult: This species is mainly ashy-brown and when it is perched the wing tips nearly reach the end of the short tail so that it has a rather stocky appearance. There is some white barring on the abdomen and flanks, but this is often indistinct or absent altogether. The eyes are pale lemon-yellow, the cere and basal half of the black-tipped bill orange-yellow and the legs yellow. The most important field character, especially in flight, is the single broad white band across the middle of the black tail. The barred whitish underwing pattern is very similar to that of the Southern Banded Snake Eagle but the underwing coverts are plain white.

Juvenile and immature: The juvenile is brown above with prominent pale buff edges to the wing coverts, giving them a barred appearance. The top of the head is whitish. It is mainly pale buffy-white on the underparts, darker buff on the breast. The tail is paler brown than the rest of the upperparts and has a dark terminal band, but there is no diagnostic broad white central band as in the adult. More detailed information on juvenile plumage is needed. Little is known about immature plumages, but individuals that are completely brown in colour are probably immatures prior to assuming the ashy coloration of the adult.

HABITAT
In southern Africa the Banded Snake Eagle occurs in woodland near large rivers.

STATUS AND DISTRIBUTION
In southern Africa this resident snake eagle has a localised distribution although it is not uncommon in suitable habitat. Its distribution extends from northern Namibia across the north of Botswana into northern and north-eastern Zimbabwe as far as the Nyamkwarara River north-east of Umtali. It occurs mainly along the Okavango–Chobe–Zambezi river systems and its distribution is not known to

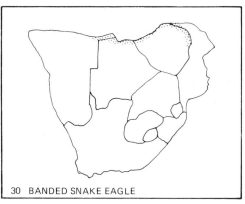

30 BANDED SNAKE EAGLE

overlap that of the Southern Banded Snake Eagle in southern Africa.

GENERAL HABITS
The Banded Snake Eagle, usually encountered while perched solitarily in riverine woodland, also hunts in open areas nearby. It is a still hunter, sitting for long periods surveying its surroundings. When prey is seen it swoops down to grab it, then flies up to eat it in a tree. Snakes may be caught in trees. Its flight is direct and rapid, with characteristic shallow wing-beats, but it seldom flies far.

It preys mainly on snakes; species identified include Boomslang, Eastern Green Snake and Puffadder. Other items of diet recorded are lizards, a newly hatched tortoise, small rodents, frogs, toads, fish and beetles.

The calls are very similar to those of the Southern Banded Snake Eagle, a high-pitched *kok-kok-kok-kok-kok-ko-ko* dropping in pitch at the end. It also makes a loud mournful *ko-waaa*. The feathered nestling begs with a drawn-out *k-yow* call repeated 10–20 times in succession.

BREEDING
Nuptial display is similar to that of the Southern Banded Snake Eagle, the pair calling loudly while soaring. The male feeds the female as part of courtship.

There are no definite breeding records, where the contents of nests have been inspected, for southern Africa. A nest on the Chobe River at Kasane, Botswana, stated to have

(1) View of Banded Snake Eagle habitat on the Chobe, Botswana.

(2) A nest site (circled) in thick foliage in trees on a river bank (Photograph: Steve Robinson).

(3) An empty nest well concealed in thick foliage; it is a typical small snake eagle structure (Photograph: Steve Robinson).

been used by this species, was a substantial structure about the size of a Wahlberg's Eagle nest and may have originally been that of another raptor. It was placed within the canopy of a creeper-covered tree at a height of 10 m. Two nests in the Okavango Swamps in Botswana were both situated on thick thorny creeper within the canopy and appeared to be typical small snake eagle nests. At one site an adult was sitting on the nest, apparently incubating, in December.

An authentic breeding record from Karonga, Malawi, is of a female shot off a nest on 15 March 1947. The nest was 9 m above ground near the top of an acacia growing in a banana plantation on the edge of a native village. It measured 60 cm across and 15 cm deep and was lined with green leaves. The single white egg was heavily nest-stained and was found to be close to hatching. It measured 70,6 × 54,9. A nest in Zambia in which an egg was apparently not laid was a typical snake eagle platform of pencil-thick sticks 50 cm across and 20 cm deep with a leafy depression 24 cm in diameter. It was built on thick creeper beneath the canopy near the top of an ebony tree *Diospyros mespiliformis* at a height of 15 m. From below it was very difficult to detect.

Nothing is known about the incubation and nestling periods. One juvenile that could be located by its persistent calling remained in the same area for several weeks, presumably near its nest. Further information on the breeding cycle of this species is urgently needed.

---

31 Bateleur *146*

Stompstertarend

Terathopius ecaudatus · PLATES 2 AND 10

DERIVATION
marvellous : face : without : tail — *teras* (G) : *ops* (G) : *e* (L) : *caudatus* (L)

While the Greek components of *Terathopius* are misinformed, and other interpretations are possible, the derivation given is the most logical. Bateleur is French for tumbler, juggler, acrobat or tightrope walker; the last seems most applicable, as the Bateleur rocks slowly from side to side in flight like the tightrope walker's long balancing pole. The bird was named by Francois Le Vaillant, the French naturalist and explorer.

IDENTIFICATION
Adult: This colourful species cannot be confused with any other raptor. Its stumpy appearance when perched, and apparent lack of tail, give it a characteristic silhouette even if seen in poor light. The mantle, back and tail are chestnut, contrasting with the mainly black plumage, and the wing coverts are grey. The feathers on the back of the head are loose, giving the effect of a cowl similar to that of the snake eagles but more pronounced. The eyes are deep honey-brown, and the skin on the face and cere is a vivid red, as are the bare, heavily scaled legs and feet. The bill is blue-grey at the tip merging to yellowish at its base. The perched female may be identified by the broad band of grey feathers on the secondaries, which are wholly black in the male.

A small proportion of the population is creamy or very pale reddish on the back. It is not known whether this is a genuine colour variant, or an indication of very old birds; further investigation is required. There is temporary variation in the colour of the face, legs and feet. At times these fade to pale pink or yellowish. This may occur when the bird is perched in shade or is bathing. Conversely, in captive birds, it was observed that they are reddest when angry or indulging in social and sexual interactions. It is not known whether these colour changes are vascular or caused by neural control of the pigment cells. Soon after death the red on face and legs fades to yellow.

The unique flight shape, with long wings and very short tail, rules out confusion with any other raptor except possibly the adult Jackal Buzzard. Reports of Bateleurs from areas where they no longer occur have probably resulted from Jackal Buzzards being misidentified as Bateleurs. On the silvery-white underwing females have a narrow black band along the hind edge of the wing, and males a broad black band; this is diagnostic and can be seen at a considerable distance through binoculars.

Juvenile and immature: Juveniles are light brown, slightly darker below, with buff edges to the feathers, especially on the head. The bill is black, the eyes are dark brown, the cere and face pale greenish-blue and the legs and feet whitish. In flight they appear uniformly brown from below, but the wing tips are rounder than those of the adult, and the tail projects 5 cm beyond the feet whereas in the adult the feet project this distance beyond the tail tip. The broader wings and longer tail probably give the inexperienced juvenile greater manoeuvrability at this stage of its life. The juvenile could possibly be mistaken for a Brown Snake Eagle and distinctions are discussed in the text on that species.

Progress from first juvenile plumage to adulthood takes about seven to eight years through a series of gradual moults, and it is possible to define several main stages. The juvenile does not moult during its first year, but by the time it is two years old it has replaced its tail, which is shorter and approximately equal in length to the backward-projecting feet in flight. Apart from the tail length, there are no other readily discernible differences. The next noticeable stage commences at about three years, when blackish feathers appear on the brown underparts so that the immature has a mottled appearance. Thereafter, between four and five years, the plumage becomes uniformly sooty-brown with some development of gloss above. The face is yellowish and the feet and legs are pinkish, darkening with age. It is probable that occasional reports of melanistic adults are birds at this stage of development. On the underwing, females begin to show the narrow trailing edge but males do not have a recognisable underwing pattern. However, in both, the underwing coverts are markedly darker than in previous plumages. The feet now project beyond the tail tip, and moulted tail feathers grow out progressively shorter until adult length is reached. Between the ages of five and seven years, during two moults, clearly recognisable adult plumage is gradually acquired. The best way of identifying birds at this stage is by the underwing coverts in flight, which are now mottled brown and white, and the pattern of both male and females is clearly defined. Thereafter adult plumage is acquired, the grey 'shoulder' patch on the wing coverts being the last area to obtain its full adult colour.

From records of sightings kept by observers, it appears that brown juveniles up to the age of two years make up about 30 per cent of the population, and those in subsequent immature plumages prior to adulthood comprise only 8 per cent, suggesting a high mortality rate.

HABITAT

This eagle occurs in open savannas and plains, including semi-desert thornbush. It is not found in forest and very mountainous terrain. However because of its wide daily range, it may overfly areas of unsuitable habitat at times.

STATUS AND DISTRIBUTION

In areas where they occur regularly Bateleurs are still relatively common. However, as it is the most aerial of all southern African eagles, a misleading picture of 'abundance' may be obtained. It appears that adults, as well as juveniles and immatures, are nomadic at times. Aggregations of Bateleurs encountered on occasions can only have been drawn from far afield. The extent of the movements of this species are little known and would prove difficult to investigate.

The Bateleur has disappeared from much of its former range in southern Africa, yet the decline has only recently been noticed. The total population in the Transvaal is roughly estimated to be 420–470 pairs, mostly in or near the Kruger National Park. It has disappeared from 80 per cent of its former range in the Transvaal, which must originally have supported some 2 500 pairs. The picture of widespread decline applies to most of southern Africa outside game reserves. Factors considered responsible are: habitat destruction, a lack of carrion for juveniles, and direct and indirect human persecution in the form of shooting, poisoned carcasses and disturbance at the nest. The extent to which pesticides have been responsible, if at all, is not known, but they could be an important factor.

The Bateleur originally occurred regularly in the eastern Cape Province, where it is now extremely rare, as in Natal (except in Zululand), Orange Free State and most of the Transvaal. Its present distribution is mainly north of the Orange River. Extralimitally it is found northwards to the Sahara and in Arabia and Iraq.

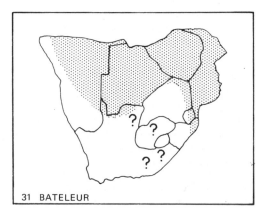

31 BATELEUR

GENERAL HABITS

A flying Bateleur is one of the majestic sights of Africa as it sweeps through the sky, the sun catching its silvery underwing when it cants from side to side. It flies directly across country or in wide circles, at a speed of about 50–80 kilometres per hour, usually at no great height, and seldom flaps its wings. However, on taking off from the ground or tree perch, it flaps very rapidly for a bird of its size. On the wing from about an hour after sunrise until late afternoon, it traverses several hundred kilometres daily, except when grounded in wet weather. However, it does not fly all of this time, and may be seen perched for long periods, often in the vicinity of carrion or a water-hole. It drinks and bathes readily, and while perched also sunbathes with wings spread open in a striking heraldic posture.

A juvenile Bateleur on the carcass of an impala; large carrion is an important source of food for young birds.

The Bateleur, a remarkably sociable species, may gather in quite large numbers made up of a variety of age classes of its own species, usually intermingled with other large raptors. In one gathering in the Kalahari made up of 60 eagles, 38 were Bateleurs and the rest Tawny Eagles.

Its prey and feeding habits are very similar to those of the Tawny Eagle, which is dominant in observed cases of interaction between them. Although it is traditionally described in the textbooks as primarily a scavenger, this picture has been refuted by recent prey studies. The Bateleur is in fact a rapacious killer of prey, including mammals up to 4 kg, and powerful reptiles such as monitor lizards (leguaans). It also kills a great variety of birds, being capable of taking them on the wing, although eye-witness accounts are rare. It normally kills prey on the ground after a steep stoop, but it may also descend gently like a parachute, wings held above its back and legs extended, and merely drop onto its quarry. Piratical attacks are also made, usually on large carrion-eaters like vultures; on one occasion a Martial Eagle was driven to the ground after repeated dives. Scavenging is undoubtedly also an important source of food, for example roads are patrolled for animals killed by traffic. Generally, brown juveniles are most often seen at large carrion, although adults feed on it too.

Four detailed studies of Bateleur prey have provided a good overall picture of food preferences, even allowing for local variations. Mammals (inclusive of carrion) provided the greatest weight of food, although in several of the studies greater numbers of birds were recorded. Mammals, species ranging in size from mice to small antelope the size of a Dikdik, included mongooses, hares, squirrels, dassies, large rats and galagos. In each study a single species was preyed on most; in Kenya it was Dikdiks and in the other studies Scrub Hares. The Scrub Hares and galagos, although nocturnal, were located and captured during daytime.

The most interesting aspect was the number and variety of birds recorded (27 species in one study). In most of the localities gamebirds up to the size of a korhaan, but particularly francolins and guineafowl, were killed. Other species often caught were doves, hornbills, rollers and glossy starlings. The Bateleur tends to prey on smaller birds more than the Tawny Eagle, otherwise their avian prey is very similar. Small birds recorded included kingfishers, wood hoopoes, barbets, a thrush, a bulbul, shrikes and buffalo weavers. Poultry is rarely taken, even where readily available in free-range conditions. The eggs of birds are also eaten; in one case a francolin's nest was found after a fire. Bateleurs are regularly attracted to burnt areas to scavenge.

Although it is said to prey to a great extent on reptiles, particularly snakes, this is not usually the case, and reptiles made up less than 11 per cent in all studies except one, in which 30 per cent of the total prey was reptiles, mainly snakes. Venomous species such as Puffadder and Boomslang were recorded, to the venom of which the Bateleur is not immune. Once an observer found one locked in death with a Puffadder that had managed to bite it during the struggle. Other reptilian prey recorded was mostly lizards, including monitors (leguaans). When snakes are carried to the nest they may be half swallowed in the manner of a snake eagle.

Carrion has been mentioned, but it should be

noted that it is sometimes difficult to establish whether certain items found in nests were killed or scavenged. It may reasonably be assumed that most, if not all, owls and nightjars are scavenged as road kills, and portions of large ungulates are undoubtedly obtained as carrion. Corpses left on the battlefield were a macabre source of carrion during the internecine wars in southern Africa.

Other recorded food includes some fish, probably obtained as carrion or caught when stranded in drying pools, a crab, and insects such as locusts and swarming termite alates, to which it is partial.

Although not a vocal species, its call is characteristic when heard, a loud, resonant bark *kow-aw* which carries a great distance. This call is made during courtship displays and when making piratical attacks. The male may perform a remarkable distraction display on a perch near his nest during which he adopts a crouching position, extends his wings limply and flaps them weakly. The behaviour appears to be injury feigning and is accompanied by a subdued and rapidly repeated (almost chattering) *ka-ka-ka-ka-ka* ... call. Small nestlings emit a melodious *twip*, but later an excited squeaking *kyup-kyup-kyup-keeaw-keeaw* when begging for food.

BREEDING

Spectacular chasing flights are performed during courtship, the male diving down at the female, who rolls to present her claws, and sometimes he flies on with legs dangling loosely. In addition to the *kow-aw* call, the wings may be flapped to produce a *whup-whup-whup* noise like a loose sail in the breeze. Very rarely a bird may execute several 360-degree lateral rolls, accompanied by loud *whup-whup* noises of the wings. At times the chasing display involves two males and a female, but during breeding only one male is active at the nest. The chasing flight is not necessarily nuptial and may be performed by birds of the same sex, or by an adult and an immature, and in such instances is probably linked to the sociability of the species. Sometimes it probably involves incidents of aggression.

Nests are situated in large trees, often beside a watercourse, either in hilly terrain or in open flat country. Usually 10–15 m above ground the nest is normally built within the canopy in a fork in the main trunk or on a lateral branch, so that it is shaded for most of the day. A variety of trees may be used, including Baobabs, but thorny acacias are favoured. One nest was placed amongst Buffalo Weaver nests and was

thus difficult to detect.

Although the old nest of another bird of prey such as a Wahlberg's Eagle may be taken over and added to, it normally builds its own nest. This is a solid structure of medium-sized sticks measuring about 60 cm across and 30 cm deep with a leafy cup 25 cm across. Both sexes are known to build, and nest repair takes about one to two months. Sometimes nest building may be protracted without any breeding that season. There are usually frequent moves to new nest sites, over distances of one to three kilometres, and at times an old nest site may be reoccupied. In one study nests were not used for more than three consecutive years, but in another locality a nest was used annually for five years. The nest of the Bateleur seems particularly favoured by the Lanner for breeding purposes, probably because the nestling has usually flown by July or August, when Lanners lay, but one nestling was persistently worried by Lanners during its last week in the nest, and they moved in as soon as it had flown.

In one study in ranching country in Zimbabwe nests were spaced 13–16 km apart, but information on the distribution of pairs is scanty and further observations are needed.

In Zimbabwe eggs are laid from December to June, with a single record each for August and October, and there is a laying peak in February and March. Quantitative breeding information from South Africa is not available, but in the Kruger National Park eggs are laid from January to April, and miscellaneous records from other areas indicate that the breeding season is similar to that in Zimbabwe. Nestling Bateleurs are therefore reared during the cool, dry winter months, and the earlier laying time (i.e. earlier than other winter breeding eagles) may be an adjustment related to the long incubation and nestling periods.

A single white egg is laid, sometimes with a few red marks, but by the end of the long incubation period it is usually nest-stained. It is very large for the size of the bird, similar in size to the much larger Black Eagle and Martial Eagle. Measurements are: 79,1 × 62,7 (50); 74,2–87,0 × 57,0–68,1.

Random evidence indicates that both male and female incubate, the male probably doing a greater share than most other eagles. He may bring food for the female, but she also leaves the nest for fairly long periods, probably to hunt for herself. During both the incubation and the nestling periods the male is more demonstrative than the female at the nest, sometimes performing the distraction display already described or, more often, making spectacular dive-bombing attacks if the nest tree is climbed. In contrast she does not usually come near the nest and flies round in the distance. Once a lone male baboon climbed a nest tree when the female was incubating and while she remained on the nest the male dive-bombed it. When this failed to drive it off, he settled on a branch between the baboon and the nest and threatened it with raised wings. However, the baboon could not be dislodged, and roosted in the tree. As an eaglet was eventually reared successfully, the baboon evidently did not molest the birds at the nest.

The Bateleur is extremely sensitive to disturbance when breeding. While it will permit regular inspection of the nest, it resents any attempt to erect a hide or conceal photographic equipment nearby and will readily desert, even when it has a small nestling. Thus attempts to photograph it at the nest should be rigorously avoided, especially in view of its serious decline in southern Africa. The incubation period is the longest of any African eagle, three records being: not less than 52 days; between 52 and 59 days; and, more accurately, 55 ± 1 day.

The newly hatched Bateleur chick is a delightful creature with a two-tone colour and a head that seems too large for its body. Its head is creamy with a chocolate-brown patch behind the eye that matches the rest of the down colour above. On its flanks it is also creamy. The legs and cere are pale greenish, the bill is black and the eyes are dark brown. At three weeks old it still has a downy white head, but the down colour above is paler brown. First brown feathers are just sprouting at the back of the head, on the scapulars and from the secondary quills. The legs are white at this stage. By four weeks it no longer has any white down on the head, where brown feathers are growing out, as are feathers on the scapulars, wing coverts and secondaries. At five weeks feathers are emerging steadily, and first primary feathers break from their quills, but their growth lags behind that of the secondaries. First feathers are also breaking from the tail quills and on the underparts. The six-week-old eaglet most closely resembles a snake eagle nestling with its anterior covering of feathers above, and the rump and flanks are still mainly downy. A pronounced crest has developed and, if just the head is seen from below, the nest appears to contain a fully grown eaglet. At seven weeks the nestling is feathered on the body, but wings and tail are still growing steadily. The last remaining down is on the underwing coverts, which disappears only when it is 12—13 weeks old, at which stage wing and tail feathers have almost reached their full length. An unusual feature of feather development, also found in the snake eagles, is the retarded growth of the primary feathers, which attain the same length as the secondaries at only 10–11 weeks; this is the probable reason for the long nestling period.

It is not known when the nestling first stands, but probably at about five weeks old when first wing-flapping is recorded. At the age of six weeks it is capable of feeding itself properly, although it can swallow small items earlier than this. At this age also it crouches prone in the nest on seeing anyone below. A nine-week-old eaglet gave an impressive threat display with wings and crest spread when an observer reached the nest.

Initially the chick is carefully tended by the female; she was on the nest 82 per cent of the time up to 10 days in one study in Kenya, her time dropping to 47 per cent from then until 20 days. After 30 days parental time on the nest dropped to 5 per cent, and from 60 days it was less than 1 per cent. The female roosted on the nest up to 30 days, but thereafter the chick was left alone at night.

The male also feeds and broods the chick in the early nestling period and appears to take a substantial share of nest duties, more than other eagles do. He was observed feeding a seven-week-old chick, but after this time visits to the nest by both sexes are concerned mainly with delivering prey. In one observation a male dropped a Crowned Plover to the female flying below him and she deftly caught it in flight and took it to the nest. Green lining may be added to the nest up to the seventh week of the nestling period, but at some nests this activity is neglected much earlier.

The duration of the nestling period needs to be assessed with care, as young may fly prematurely if the nest tree is climbed when they are nearly ready to leave. Also, because juveniles return to the nest after their first flight, the nestling period may be judged to be longer than it really is unless regular visits are made. Various nestling periods fall between 95 and 115 days, and one accurate period was 111–112 days.

Juveniles may leave the immediate nest area soon after their first flight, but normally they return to the nest or a regular perch tree nearby, where they are fed by the adults for about three months. One juvenile was still being fed in the nest area four months after it flew. Once a juvenile was observed to fly off after a female carrying a snake and take it from her in flight. In the early post-nestling period the young bird may perch in a prone position across a branch on seeing someone approach, even though it is

(1) A Bateleur's nest situated typically beneath the canopy of the tree.

(2) The small nest is sturdily constructed.

(3) A two-day-old chick.

(4) A nestling aged three weeks.

(5) Rapid feather growth is taking place by the age of six weeks. The pattern of feather development is similar to that of snake eagles.

(6) At eight weeks old the nestling appears fully feathered.

able to fly competently. After becoming independent juveniles range widely; one marked bird was sighted over an area of 1 347 km².

At four nests in Zimbabwe 22 young were reared in 27 pair-years, a replacement rate of 0,81 young per pair per annum, a figure that would have been higher but for direct human interference at nests. The only other causes of breeding failure were the infertility of two eggs and the unexplained disappearance of another. Elsewhere less breeding success has been recorded, and in the Kruger National Park Giant Eagle Owls were known to prey on Bateleur nestlings. It appears from one study that Bateleurs breed annually, even when young are reared successfully and regularly. If there are non-breeding years, they are infrequent on present evidence.

It is sad to record that this magnificent species may become another 'game reserve' raptor. Because it has so unobtrusively disappeared, it is difficult to know what practical conservation measures can be taken at this stage. The most useful approach is to monitor its status as widely as possible, towards which end several projects have already been implemented.

32 African Fish Eagle /48

Visarend

Haliaeetus vocifer

PLATES 10 AND 11

DERIVATION
salt water : eagle : voice : carrying (far) — *hals* (G) : *aetos* (G) : *vox* (L) : *ferre* (L)

IDENTIFICATION
Adult: This species is one of the most striking and easily identifiable of all African eagles. The white mantle, head and breast are set off against the chestnut abdomen and 'shoulders' and the rest of the black upperparts. The short white tail is often concealed by the folded wings. The cere and facial skin are yellow and the bare legs dull yellow. The eyes are hazel, and rather pale in some individuals. When perched together, male and female are usually distinguishable by their size, the female 10–15 per cent larger than the male. However, they may sometimes be much the same size. It appears also that the white 'bib' of the female is more square and less deep than that of the male. The difference has been established in a captive pair and by some field observations, but further confirmation is required to establish that the difference is consistent. In flight from below, the white head, breast and tail contrast with the chestnut abdomen and underwing coverts as well as the uniformly black remiges. The short tail and broad wings give this species a characteristic silhouette.

Juvenile and immature: The juvenile is drab brown above and whitish about the head with a brownish 'eyebrow'. The 'bib' is whitish, variably streaked with brown, and the rest of the underparts are heavily mottled with brown and white. The white tail, slightly longer than that of the adult, has a conspicuous black terminal band. In flight from below, the underwing coverts are white, contrasting with the black remiges which have white 'windows' on the secondaries and primaries. The short white tail and its black terminal band are diagnostic. Confusion with the Osprey may possibly arise; differences are discussed under that species.

The transition from juvenile to immature plumage begins when it is about a year old. The immature in its second year is altogether paler than the juvenile. Its upperparts are brown mottled with white and the underparts and head are whitish with some brown streak-

A pair of African Fish Eagles; the female is much larger than her mate.

ing. There is often a pronounced black 'eye-brow' at this stage. The tail is still tipped with black, although more narrowly, and the colours of the soft parts remain unchanged. As at the juvenile stage, plumage is variable, and it may be that females are paler than the males. In the next immature stage, beginning early in the third year, the young eagle assumes adult characteristics, and the mantle, head and breast are white with some black streaking. The abdomen is black and the 'shoulders' are brown. The cere and face are now pinkish, the legs pale yellow. In flight from below, the underwing coverts are black, so that, except for the white breast and tail (still tipped black) it appears wholly black. The final stages to adulthood, beginning at the end of the third year, are not as clear-cut as the preceding plumages. The mantle, head, breast and tail become pure white. Chestnut feathers grow in on the 'shoulders', underwing coverts and abdomen. The legs become yellower but the cere and face remain pinkish. Final adulthood is achieved when the 'shoulders' and abdomen are fully chestnut and the cere and face turn yellow. It is generally assumed that the adult plumage is attained in the fifth year, but carefully documented observations on a captive pair in the Transvaal (yet to be published) suggest that the period is longer than five years. Individuals may breed before they are in full adult plumage.

HABITAT

This eagle always occurs near water, usually large rivers, lakes and dams. It is also found in coastal waters where it frequents lagoons and estuaries.

STATUS AND DISTRIBUTION

Adults are sedentary but juveniles and immatures wander away from their natal areas. One Transvaal immature ringed as a nestling was recovered two and a half years later 200 km away.

The southern African population appears to be in no immediate danger, although pesticide-contaminated fish may pose a threat (this species would act as a good indicator of excessive contamination in waterways and dams). It appears that it is holding its own even near populous areas, and in some regions is increasing as a result of the widespread construction of dams, as for example in the Transvaal since the 1930s. Its effect on sporting or commercial fishing is negligible and it is rarely persecuted.

Although occurring throughout southern Africa, the African Fish Eagle, for obvious reasons of habitat, is more common in the east than in the arid central and western areas. Extralimitally it is found northwards to the Sahara.

GENERAL HABITS

This magnificent eagle is probably the most widely known of all African eagles. Its colourful appearance and ringing call at once command attention. Pairs are frequently seen together and spend much of their time perched in trees. Protracted watches in Kenya established that 90–95 per cent of the daylight time was spent perched. The rest of the day was spent soaring, displaying, making piratical attacks, chasing off intruders or fishing, the latter activity taking up little more than 1 per cent of the day. As a rule males were found to hunt more actively than females, who often pirated the male's prey. Prey may be caught at any time during the day; observations in Kenya established no particular pattern. However, at Lake St Lucia in Zululand, a definite midday peak was noted. These eagles are early risers and call at the first hint of dawn. Where they are plentiful, this sets off a carillon of echoing calls as neighbouring pairs join in the dawn chorus. At the end of the day they go to roost late and may even kill after sunset. The same regular roosts are used, the pair roosting together, often on the same branch.

The main prey of this species is fish and it has long claws with spicules on the pads of the feet for grasping them. The broad wings enable it to soar in even a light breeze and give maximum lift when rising off the water with a fish. It hunts from a perch or on the wing in short fishing sorties over the water, usually within about 50 m of the shore. Occasionally it hovers 10–20 m above the water, then drops down vertically with talons extended. Although it normally locates prey by sight, there is some evidence that it also uses the sound of a splashing fish to find it. Also, contrary to expectation, it often sees and captures fish in choppy, murky water. Fish are caught in a shallow dive, both feet being thrown forward just prior to the strike, and the eagle usually maintains its momentum and sweeps up gracefully clutching the fish. Fish are caught about 15 cm below the surface and not deeper than about 30 cm. Thus the eagle does not usually become immersed like the Osprey. Occasionally, when a fish too large to lift is caught, it rests with its wings on the water, gripping the prey to kill it before taking off and dragging it across the surface to the shore. Sometimes it paddles to the shore using its wings, but this method is hazardous and attempted robbery by a small crocodile has been observed.

In Kenya a long series of observations indicated that several attempts are usually necessary before a fish is caught. Adults averaged 7,5 attempts per kill made. The size of fish that this species can lift has often been the subject of exaggeration and conjecture. There are also reports of these eagles clinging on to huge fish and being drowned, but authentic evidence has never been produced. As a rule they do not catch particularly large fish. On Lake Naivasha in Kenya the average was about 217 g and in the Kazinga Channel in Uganda they weighed 400–500 g. On Lake Naivasha the daily food requirement of the eagles was estimated at about 5 per cent of their bodyweight. In Ndumu Game Reserve in Zululand twelve freshly killed fish from which eagles were chased off by the observer were much heavier, averaging 1,5 kg (range 810 g–2,9 kg). He also tested lifting capacity by placing a slightly stunned fish in the water where an eagle could see it. Fifty-five weighed fish were presented in this way and it was found that fish up to 2 kg were carried easily for an unlimited distance, usually into trees. Those weighing more than 2 kg and less than 3 kg were planed along the surface for not more than 50 m and were always eaten on the shore. Fish over 3 kg up to a maximum of 3,65 kg (about the weight of a female eagle) could not be transported more than 10 m and were paddled to the shore using the wings. Curiously, it was found that fish up to 1 kg were carried in both feet, while those from 1 to 3 kg were carried in one foot.

The fish caught by the African Fish Eagle are mainly species that swim near the surface, such as tilapia, catfish, lungfish, tigerfish and mullet. At Lake St Lucia mullet comprised 58 per cent of the fish caught, with catfish (13 per cent) and Spotted Grunter (8 per cent) being next in order of importance. Records of prey from various inland waters in Africa indicate that tilapia and catfish are most often caught. An observer in Uganda found 1 058 tilapia and 285 catfish in a sample of food remains.

The African Fish Eagle is an accomplished pirate and is capable of considerable speed and dexterity on the wing. In one incident a Great White Egret was chased until it dropped a frog, which the eagle caught in its talons before it reached the ground. Fish-eating birds are chased and harried until they disgorge or drop their food. Some of the birds robbed are pelicans, cormorants, Darters, egrets, herons (including the formidable Goliath Heron), Hamerkops and Ospreys. One male in Kenya specialised in robbing Pied Kingfishers of the fingerlings they

An African Fish Eagle taking off after catching a fish.

caught — scarcely a worthwhile return on the effort involved! African Fish Eagles also regularly rob each other of fish. Recorded incidents involving prey other than fish include an African Hawk Eagle robbed of a guineafowl, and an egret taken from a Tawny Eagle after a long chase. A Hooded Vulture was also harried but the eagle obtained nothing.

The diet of this eagle is far more varied than is generally known. It is a dashing predator and in east Africa has been recorded to kill adult flamingoes, although these may have been sick birds. It has been seen to catch a Red-knobbed Coot and a Cape Turtle Dove in flight and it chases species such as grebes and the African Jacana until they are exhausted and easily caught. Predation on the nestlings of colonial waterbirds such as cormorants, egrets, herons, ibises and spoonbills is regular and it appears that immatures most frequently raid heronries. The eggs of these colonial species are also sometimes eaten. The young of species such as the White-crowned Plover and African Skimmer, which nest on sandbanks, are also eaten. Both adult and young ducks are caught. Adult Red-knobbed Coot are regularly killed in some localities. Other avian prey records include a cormorant, adult Cattle Egret, Little Egret and Black-crowned Night Heron, a juvenile Egyptian Goose, a Pygmy Goose gosling, an adult Moorhen and young Black-winged Stilts. It has been seen at Red-billed Quelea colonies with other raptors. It also occasionally preys on domestic poultry. In one incident a guineafowl in a roosting flock was struck to the ground but not killed.

Mammalian prey is rarely taken but dassies have twice been recorded and an African Fish Eagle was seen feeding on a Vervet Monkey which it may have killed. Reptilian prey records are of crocodile hatchlings, terrapins and monitors (leguaans). In one incident an eagle was rescued while floating down a river with a monitor in its clutches. The tail of the lizard was wrapped round the eagle's wing and prevented it from taking off. Amphibians are only occasionally eaten. There is a record of this eagle feeding on termite alates. Other miscellaneous prey items are Louisiana Crayfish introduced experimentally into Lake Naivasha in Kenya and an octopus which the eagle had considerable difficulty in subduing in flight.

Carrion is also a source of food and African Fish Eagles have been seen at antelope carcasses, and in one instance at a rhinoceros, in the company of vultures. In the south-west Cape they have been seen at dead sheep. Dead fish are also eaten, sometimes in competition with gulls which are driven off. On the eastern Cape coast they have been seen feeding on dead gannets and penguins, apparently eviscerating them to obtain fish. One eagle fed on a tortoise run over by a lorry.

The ringing *weee kyow kow-kow* of the African Fish Eagle is one of the finest calls in Africa and is evocative of wild places. It is emitted with the head thrown well back, whether the eagle is perched or in flight, and the nape almost touches the back on the second syllable before being thrown forward again. The call carries over a great distance, even from a soaring bird almost invisible to the naked eye. The male's voice is a high-pitched treble, his mate's a mellower contralto. The female most often calls first, or alone. Duetting is frequent, one of the pair leading in with a *wee* followed by a syncopated series of high and low *kow-kow* notes. Although calling occurs throughout the year, the birds are most vocal at the beginning of the breeding season. Regular calling serves to maintain the close pair-bond and is important also for maintaining and advertising the territory throughout the year. Calling is used far more often than physical attack to warn off intruding African Fish Eagles. The pair frequently call to establish contact after being apart for a while; they also come together and call if one of the pair is disturbed off the nest. The immature is able, between its second and third year, to make a broken-voiced version of the adult's call. Other calls are a clucking noise during copulation and a *kwok* or *kwok-kwok* in anxiety if disturbed at the nest. Small nestlings beg by cheeping, but there is no information on the soliciting call that replaces this once they are older.

BREEDING

Although details of the breeding cycle of this common and widespread species are known in outline, no comprehensive account of the breeding biology has been published. Much of what is known derives from studies in east Africa.

Regular duetting not only strengthens the pair-bond but is also an integral part of nuptial display, so the birds are extremely vocal at the beginning of the breeding season. Often they are stimulated to call when neighbouring pairs begin calling. Much calling takes place aerially in combination with soaring displays. The birds may display and call either individually or as a pair. Undulating displays of dives and upward swoops are performed. In the most intense form of display the male rises high above his mate and dives towards her; as he reaches her she turns on her back and presents her talons to his. Sometimes several adjacent pairs may display together, a spectacular sight. Occasionally the pair may link claws and fall for several hundred metres in a whirling flight. In one incident two birds fell across a branch and hung down on either side with their claws interlocked; they parted when the observer approached. As fighting eagles also grapple claws, it may be that this incident did not involve courtship. Copulation takes place on the nest or on favourite perches in the vicinity. The male perches near the female, who crouches and slightly opens her wings. He then mounts her, flapping his wings to maintain balance. Sometimes he may fly from a distance and alight gently on the female's back. Mating is most frequent during nest-building and may occur several times during the day, six times in eight hours in one observation. Mating also takes place outside the breeding season or in years when they do not breed.

Nests are usually built in tall trees that are difficult to climb. Thorny acacias, smooth-barked trees and euphorbias are frequently used. The nests are situated within the canopy or in a dead tree or on top of a tree where there is not shelter from the elements. In southern Africa, especially near dams where there are often the tallest trees, eucalypts are commonly used. This eagle occasionally builds in pines and willows or, where tall trees are unavailable, in a low bushy tree on a steep slope. One nest was built on an old Crowned Eagle's nest. Nests are sometimes situated on an outcrop of rock or on a cliff face. One large nest on a sheer cliff appeared to have previously belonged to a Black Eagle. Frequently nests are within 100 m of water, but sometimes they are several kilometres away if there is no suitable site near water or too much disturbance there.

Nests vary in size and shape depending on their duration of use or on their site. Nests built on flat-topped trees are usually flat structures, whereas those in a major fork of a tree may become very large over the years, up to 180 cm across and 120 cm deep. Usually nests are about 120–150 cm across and 30–60 cm deep. The cup is lined with grass, green leaves and the occasional weaver's nest. Both sexes build and according to limited observations the male brings more material than the female. A new nest can be constructed in about two months whereas an established site is usually repaired within a few weeks. The pair may visit the nest outside the breeding season without adding material.

The number of nests used over the years varies from pair to pair. Sometimes a pair may have three nests, occasionally four, which are used with no particular pattern, irrespective of whether successful breeding took place the previous year. The duration of nest sites depends on the site and whether they are repaired each year. An exposed site which is unrepaired may last about three years; regularly used nests may last ten years or more. One nest in the Transvaal has been used annually for at least 21 years.

On lakes and waterways of east Africa the African Fish Eagle occurs in high densities, and the majority of territorial studies have been made there. In southern Africa there are few observations on population densities and only in the Okavango Swamps in Botswana is there any indication of density comparable to that found in east Africa. This eagle is probably the most territorial of all African birds of prey and where capacity populations occur they remain year-round in their territories, which would otherwise be taken over by a new pair. It was estimated that on Lake Naivasha a defended territory of on average 4 ha consisted of 300 m of shoreline, 30 m inland and 100 m across the lake, as well as an airspace of 150–200 m above ground. Low-flying intruders would elicit a calling response from the territory holders, while those passing high overhead were ignored. Some nests on Lake Naivasha were about 160 m apart and in one exceptional instance two breeding pairs were only 54 m from each other. On the Kazinga Channel in Uganda pairs were spaced about 600 m apart. On a section of the Boro River in the Okavango Swamps pairs were spaced 400–500 m apart. Along the Chobe River west of Kasane in Botswana 38 evenly spaced pairs were located over a distance of 55 km, a density of one pair every 1,4 km. On the shore of Lake Kariba in the Matusadona National Park in Zimbabwe approximately 50 pairs occur along a 200 km shoreline, an average of one pair per 4 km. However, nests were not evenly spaced over this distance. In the Transvaal three pairs on the Nyl River were spaced 10–12 km apart. Small dams in the province support only single breeding pairs whereas a large dam such as Loskop has three or four pairs. There are few observations on the population of this species elsewhere in southern Africa, but there appear to be few, if any, areas where there are densities such as found in Botswana.

Most of the available nest records are from Zimbabwe, where eggs are laid from April to June with a May peak (56 per cent of 68 records). South of the Limpopo records indicate that eggs are laid later, in late May, June and July. On the Chobe River several nests inspected contained small young of much the same age, which indicated synchronous laying. The situation is different in Kenya, where at the same time various nests may be under repair or contain small chicks or there may be young just out of the nest. One to three eggs are laid, usually two. They are normally plain white, sometimes with occasional red marks, but by the end of the incubation period they become heavily nest-stained. Measurements are: 70,3 × 53,7 (74); 63,5–76,8 × 48,2–57,9.

Eggs are laid at intervals of two or three days, and incubation begins with the laying of the first egg. Both sexes incubate and the male may sit for periods of up to 90 minutes. One male was thought to have brooded overnight; but confirmation is required. He brings prey for the female, but she also leaves the nest to make her own kills or pirate a fish off another African Fish Eagle. She sits tight and is reluctant to leave the nest. Humans are not attacked, but one female stood up with hackles raised and wings spread in threat when an observer looked over the rim of the nest. Baboons and monkeys near the nest are also threatened. Fresh lining is added during the incubation period. The incubation period is approximately 42–45 days but remains to be established accurately.

The chicks hatch at intervals of two or three days. In a brood of two, frequently only one chick survives. Sibling aggression has been observed, the older chick viciously pecking the smaller, which in one instance was found dead on the nest three days later. Observations on broods of three indicate that all three young may survive for two or three weeks before the third disappears. Detailed observations are needed, but it appears that smaller chicks may be killed or die from starvation. However, there are many cases of two young leaving the nest, though rarely three.

The newly hatched chick is covered in white down and its eyes are weakly open. The bill is horn-coloured, the cere is pale yellow and the legs are pink. At two weeks old it is still entirely downy although the white down is much thicker. By the age of three weeks the quills have emerged through the down on the wings and dorsal surface, and the feathers are just breaking from them. The bill is black, the cere dark grey and the legs are whitish. A week later feathers are emerging rapidly, particularly on the dorsal surface. From five weeks on, the feathers rapidly replace the down; by the age of seven weeks it is fully feathered except for further growth of the remiges and tail.

There are few observations on the development of co-ordination of the nestling. It can feed itself when it is seven to eight weeks old and performs vigorous wing exercises from the age of about nine weeks.

Small chicks are closely brooded during their first week for about 90 per cent of the time. This reduces to 25–30 per cent by the time they are 10–12 days old. During the first week the male may feed and brood for short periods but thereafter his visits are short and his role is confined to providing prey. The female's brooding time is sharply reduced once young are two weeks old and they are hardly brooded at all by the age of three weeks. The female is still on the nest much of the time at this stage, shading the young in exposed nest sites. After three weeks she may spend very little time on the nest, but this varies individually and to a certain extent according to whether a site is sheltered or exposed.

Once young are seven weeks old they are left alone on the nest except for feeds. One nest was watched continuously for three days when the nestling was 48–51 days old. The female was on the nest for 2 per cent of the time during daylight but was perched nearby for most of the day. She did not roost on the nest at night. One tilapia weighing 400–500 g was brought each day and only the male appeared to do the hunting. The female took the fish from him and fed the eaglet. She also fed on the prey brought, one fish a day being sufficient for herself and the eaglet. Once young are able to feed themselves by the age of eight weeks, they are left entirely alone except for brief prey deliveries by the adults. The female still spends much of the day perched near the nest while the male provides prey.

Young move out onto branches near the nest from the age of 65 days and will fly prematurely if disturbed at this stage. The nestling period has been obtained on several occasions and is 70–75 days. Juveniles are strong on the wing once they have been out of the nest for a week and they return to it to receive prey and roost for the first two weeks at least. In dense populations they are confined to the territory of their parents and are vigorously attacked by neighbouring pairs if they wander. They become independent of the adults about two months after leaving the nest, although some remain in the territory for several weeks after this. There is no evidence that they are harried by their parents and they move off of their own accord.

The available observations suggest that they then move to areas where there are no resident adults because there are no suitable breeding sites. On the Chobe River only two immatures were seen along a stretch of river where 38 pairs were breeding. The many young produced in this area simply disappear. At Lake Ngami in Botswana in July and August 1969 a large concentration of immatures ranging from first year to almost adult was seen near the delta, feeding on discarded catfish heads thrown away by local fishermen. On one day 52 immatures were seen in about 2 hectares; when fishing stopped in September they dispersed. The shoreline of the lake has no large trees for breeding, so this area provides an ideal 'empty quarter' for immatures. On the evidence of the single immature in the Transvaal found 200 km from its natal area the immatures at Lake Ngami could easily have come from the Okavango Swamps and even possibly from the Chobe River 380 km away. Only an intensive colour ringing operation would provide the answer. An influx of 17 immatures was noted at Lake McIlwaine in Zimbabwe during April and May one year and they dispersed by June. Thus it appears that immatures are nomadic, wandering to areas where food is available without competition from a large resident adult population.

Observations in east Africa, particularly on Lake Naivasha, suggest a high mortality of juveniles and immatures, particularly juveniles. Calculations based on sightings of various age classes indicate that 94–96 per cent of young die before adulthood. If this is so (observations of this nature involve a number of imponderables), then adults must live 16–24 years as breeding adults to replace themselves. There are no comparable observations for southern

(1) View of an African Fish Eagle's nest.

(2) This nest is placed on a huge granite boulder.

(3) A close-up of the eggs.

(4) A two-week-old nestling.

(5) By four weeks old feathers are emerging rapidly.

(6) At six weeks old the nestling is well feathered.

Africa and mobility of the young eagles makes a study of this nature difficult. Botswana would be an ideal place to attempt such a study.

The only long-term breeding success study in southern Africa was made at Zeekoei Vlei near Cape Town, where nine young were reared in nine pair-years, i.e. 1,0 young per pair per year. In three of these years twins were successfully reared, which made up for non-breeding in one year and failure in two others. In the south-west Cape it appears that pairs usually breed annually; and a Transvaal nest was used each year for 21 years, although breeding success at this nest was not recorded. In a single year's observation in Botswana eight young were reared in 20 pair-years, i.e. 0,4 young per pair per year. A year's productivity on Lake Kariba was estimated to be not less than 0,58 young per pair. It is very approximately estimated that in southern Africa twins are raised in about 10 per cent of nesting attempts; but further quantitative information is needed. There is one record from Zambia of three young being successfully reared.

In three areas in east Africa comprehensive observations established that overall breeding success figures for 233 pair-years varied from 0,42 to 0,57 young per pair per year. There was much individual variation and it was found that an average of 53 per cent of pairs bred in a year. One pair bred successfully twice in a year and another laid three times in eighteen months and reared four young. On Lake Victoria it was thought that pairs breeding on a group of islands were affected by intervisibility. It was found that three 'inside' pairs which could see each other and spent much time challenging each other vocally had an overall breeding success of only 0,11 young per pair. However, 'outside' pairs which could not see each other reared 0,92 young per pair per year. Observations are needed to establish whether breeding-success figures obtained in east Africa are applicable to southern Africa, especially in localities where the population is rather scattered.

33 Steppe Buzzard /49.

Steppevalk

Buteo buteo

PLATES 12 AND 13

DERIVATION
hawk — *buteo* (L)

IDENTIFICATION
Adult: This species could well be named the 'fingerprint' buzzard, as no two birds are alike. Three basic plumages are illustrated. A brown plumage with a distinct gorget and fine barring on the lower breast and abdomen is most commonly seen. Other birds are almost entirely dark brown with some indistinct barring on the abdomen. Yet others have reddish blotching and barring below with no distinct gorget. Between these three main plumages numerous variations occur, but the tail is almost always pale rufous above and has fine dark-brown barring with a broader band near the tip. This band distinguishes adults from juveniles. The eyes are dark brown and the cere and legs yellow.

In flight from below, the underwing coverts match the colour of the breast. There are small dark patches at the carpal joints, and the remiges are white with a narrow black border along the hind edge of the wings. The remiges are also narrowly and indistinctly barred, but at a height the main impression is of white remiges with a dark trailing edge.

The Steppe Buzzard is not easy to distinguish from the resident Mountain Buzzard, but over much of their mutual range they tend to be separated by their habitat preferences. Distinctions between the two species are discussed more fully under the Mountain Buzzard.

Juvenile and immature: The plumage of juveniles is also variable but they may be distinguished from adults by vertical streaking, not barring, on the underparts, biscuit or pale yellow eyes, and uniform narrow barring on the tail, which lacks a broader terminal band. The cere and legs are yellow. In flight they have the same basic underwing pattern as adults. Second-year immatures are not easily distinguishable in the field on plumage characters, but if a very good view is obtained the pale eyes may be seen to be tinged with darker brown. In the hand they may be seen to be undergoing an active moult whereas juveniles moult only slightly towards the end of their first summer in southern Africa.

HABITAT

It is found in open country, often where there are agricultural crops such as wheat, and is regularly seen perched on poles near roads. In some areas it occurs in light woodland.

STATUS AND DISTRIBUTION

This common Palearctic migrant arrives in October and departs by the end of March or early April. Juveniles apparently arrive later than adults in November, departing northwards also later than adults. Northward migration has been observed in the Transvaal during late February and the first three weeks of March, with an apparent peak in the second week in March. The buzzards follow the main mountain ranges such as the Drakensberg escarpment and the Lebombos. Linear population densities obtained from road counts are variable: in the south-west Cape there is one bird per 6 km; in the Transvaal 44 km per bird. Ringing recoveries have established that individuals return to the same locality each year.

The Steppe Buzzard occurs widely in southern Africa and is absent only from some of the more arid regions in the west. It breeds from eastern Europe to Siberia (96° E) as well as in northern India, and winters in India, Arabia and Africa. Ringing recoveries indicate that our birds come from Russia and Finland. The wintering areas in Africa are mainly in the east of the continent from the Sudan southwards; it appears that most birds enter via the Gulf of Suez.

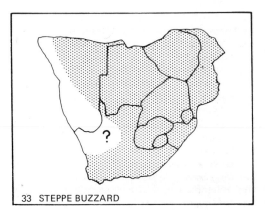

33 STEPPE BUZZARD

A Steppe Buzzard on a typical roadside perch.

GENERAL HABITS

This species is usually seen solitarily except on migration, when it occurs in quite large flocks. However, even birds which have established winter 'territories' may gather in small groups at an abundant food supply. It is most often seen on a prominent perch patiently surveying the ground. When prey is seen it drops down gently to catch it. It also hunts by hovering, but infrequently. Occasionally insects may be caught on foot.

Remarkably little is recorded of the prey of this species in southern Africa. It appears to prey mostly on small rodents but it also takes birds, lizards, small snakes, frogs and insects. Identified items of avian prey have been an adult Common Quail, the chick of a Harlequin Quail and a weaver. Insect prey includes beetles, locusts, termites and caterpillars.

Although largely silent and solitary, occasional pairs have been observed in circling and dive-bombing display flights, accompanied by calling, towards the end of their stay in southern Africa. However, most birds heard calling regularly from October to December are breeding Mountain Buzzards.

BREEDING

It has been suggested that buzzards breeding on the Cape Peninsula in the 1960s were Steppe Buzzards. However, it has now been established that Mountain Buzzards are found from Cape Town eastwards, and these breeding records should be attributed to this species.

34 Mountain Buzzard 150. (FOREST BUZZARD)

Bergvalk

Buteo tachardus

PLATES 12 AND 13

DERIVATION

hawk : Tachard — *buteo* (L) : *tachardus* (L)

As far as can be established this species was named in honour of Father Guy Tachard, a Jesuit astronomer, who made extensive observations at the Cape at the end of the seventeenth century.

IDENTIFICATION

Adult: Although plumage is rather variable, there is usually a broad band of white across the lower breast. The rest of the underparts are variably blotched with brown, more distinctly on the breast than on the abdomen. The tail and underwing pattern is similar to that described for the Steppe Buzzard. The eyes are dark brown and the cere and legs are yellow. The Mountain Buzzard is usually distinguishable from adult Steppe Buzzards by the greater amount of white on the underparts, with some individuals being mostly white below, but they can be confused with juvenile Steppe Buzzards, which often have a white band across the lower breast. The forest edge habitat of the Mountain Buzzard is an aid to identification in most cases, but in certain localities the two species overlap. Between April and September only the Mountain Buzzard will be seen, as it is non-migratory.

Juvenile and immature: The juvenile normally has a less distinct band of white below than the adult and is more streaked, especially on the abdomen. Like the Steppe Buzzard it may be distinguished from the adult by the pale biscuit or yellow coloured eye and the lack of a wider band at the tip of the tail. The underwing pattern is like that of the adult. No details are known of its progression to adult plumage, but the eye probably darkens to brownish in its second year like that of the immature Steppe Buzzard.

HABITAT

It has been suggested that a better name for this species would be Forest Buzzard because it is almost always found in association with indigenous forest or plantations, mainly pines. It normally occurs in clearings or on the edge of these habitats but it also hunts inside plantations. In southern Africa it is not a species of high mountains, which is the habitat of the Jackal Buzzard.

STATUS AND DISTRIBUTION

This species is resident and localised and a pair may occupy an area of about 10 hectares. Its distribution extends from Cape Town eastwards to the north-eastern Transvaal. Extralimitally another population inhabits much higher mountain regions from Tanzania northwards to Ethiopia.

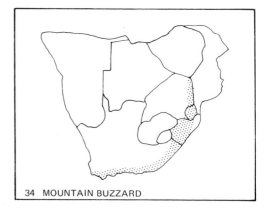

34 MOUNTAIN BUZZARD

GENERAL HABITS

Usually seen solitarily or in pairs it hunts mainly from a perch like the Steppe Buzzard. The blotched brown and white underparts blend well with the dappled light of the forest edge and undoubtedly assist in making it less conspicuous to its quarry. Its coloration and unobtrusive habits result in its being easily overlooked unless soaring above the forest. It catches prey by dropping onto it from a perch. Little is known of its prey but it appears to be mainly small rodents. Vlei rats and Striped Mice have been recorded. A lizard and a francolin chick were found in the crop of a collected bird. Frogs, chameleons and insects are also recorded.

The main call, a shrill *pee-ooo* repeated at intervals, is used in display and in alarm. A whistling *tzeee* is also described as a contact and soliciting call. Further observations on the calls of this species are required.

Nest and eggs of a Mountain Buzzard.

*A downy nestling of a Mountain Buzzard
(Photograph: Dave Barbour).*

BREEDING

Nuptial displays to the accompaniment of much calling consist of soaring above the forest and diving down, the male sometimes following the female with dangling legs to alight beside her. Undulating flights are also performed.

Very few nests have been found in southern Africa. All those so far recorded have been in indigenous yellowwood trees or in pines at heights of 9–30 m, usually about 18 m up. Nests measure about 60 cm across and 30 cm deep with a cup about 20 cm in width. The cup may be lined with green leaves, beard lichen or pine needles. One nest constructed with 5 mm thick pine sticks had only a few pine needles as lining.

From the few records available it appears that eggs are laid in October. Two eggs are normally laid, but one nest in the Cape Peninsula had a clutch of three. Eggs are white, variably marked with red-brown and dark brown, or some eggs are plain. One clutch of two measures 56,8 × 42,2 and 54,8 × 43,1. The three-egg clutch from the Cape Peninsula measures 58,2 × 44,6, 57,6 × 45,0 and 56,0 × 43,9.

Apart from the fact that the chick is clad in white down, there are no other details on the breeding biology of this species. Even a few regular visits and watches at a nest would extend our knowledge considerably.

---

35 Jackal Buzzard /52.

Jakkalsvalk

Buteo rufofuscus

PLATES 12 AND 13

DERIVATION

hawk : red : dark — *buteo* (L) : *rufus* (L) : *fuscus* (L)

IDENTIFICATION

Adult: The slate-grey upperparts, head and throat are separated from the dark rufous chest patch by a narrow, ragged white band. The lower breast and abdomen are barred black and dull white and the tail is plain rufous. The bill is black, the eyes are dark brown, and the cere and legs yellow. Very occasionally melanistic birds occur with the underparts entirely blackish. Conversely some individuals have dull whitish breasts merging into blackish colouring on the abdomen. They resemble Augur Buzzards but may be identified by their distinctive underwing pattern. White-breasted birds have been seen in the north-west Cape, giving rise to the belief that the range of the Augur Buzzard

(1) View of a Jackal Buzzard's nest on a cliff.

(2) This nest is situated in a pine tree.

(3) A two-week-old nestling.

(4) At three weeks old first feathers are emerging through the down.

(5) By six weeks old only a few areas of down are left.

(6) The seven-week-old nestling is fully feathered (Photographs 2–6 are by Nico Myburgh).

extends this far south.

The flight pattern from below is distinctive. The dark underwing coverts contrast with the white remiges, which have a narrow band along the hind edge of the wings. The short red tail is also diagnostic. Except for the dark underwing coverts, there is a superficial resemblance to the Bateleur, undoubtedly the explanation for most reports of Bateleurs in areas where they no longer occur.

Juvenile and immature: The upperparts of the juvenile are brown with buff edges to the wing coverts, and the underparts are uniform rufous. The soft parts are coloured as in the adult. In flight it has the basic underwing pattern of the adult except for rufous underwing coverts and some indistinct barring on the remiges. The tail is greyish with indistinct darker grey bars.

A captive juvenile had moulted by the time it was a year old. It was slate-grey above like the adult but still plain rufous below with no sign of a dark gorget. The tail was red with a narrow dark band near the tip, and the adult underwing coloration was developing. Like the Augur Buzzard full adult plumage is probably assumed when two to three years old.

HABITAT

This species occurs in hilly or mountainous terrain and is one of the few raptors regularly encountered in the highest mountain ranges. However, it is also found hunting in montane grassland or flat country some distance from mountains. In Namibia it occurs in arid regions near the coast.

STATUS AND DISTRIBUTION

Adults are resident but juveniles appear to wander widely. It occurs in suitable habitat in southern Africa south of the Limpopo in the east and is absent from most of Botswana. On the west it is found as far north as central Nami-

bia, where it overlaps with the Augur Buzzard; the exact extent of this overlap requires clarification.

GENERAL HABITS

It is seen either singly or in pairs, frequently on poles beside roads. It hunts from a perch or from a soaring position, where it hangs on an updraught of air above the crest of a hill. Sometimes it hovers on gently winnowing wings. Occasionally it makes spectacular stoops; one almost caught a Feral Pigeon in flight.

Prey consists of small mammals, birds, reptiles and occasionally termites. Carrion, including road kills, is also eaten. It is attracted to grass fires. Mammalian prey consists mainly of rats, mice and moles, but larger mammals such as a Greater Cane Rat, a young mongoose and a young dassie have been recorded. Avian prey up to the size of a francolin is caught and on one occasion two Marsh Owls, possibly young birds, were found on the nest. Lizards and snakes are eaten, the latter including venomous species such as the Puffadder. The only quantitative information on prey is from a nest at Grahamstown where 21 rats, 8 Striped Mice and 2 golden moles were recorded. These observations confirm that mammals are the main prey.

A high-pitched yelping *kyaah-ka-ka-ka* call is made, similar to that of the Black-backed Jackal, hence the name Jackal Buzzard. The female's voice is deeper than the male's.

BREEDING

Nuptial display consists of the male gently stooping at the soaring female with extended legs, to the accompaniment of much noisy calling. In one observation the male stooped down several times towards the perched female, alighted beside her and then mating took place.

Nests are most often on cliffs but they are also built in trees. Those on cliffs are placed on a ledge, often at the base of a small tree or bush. Pines are a favoured tree site, but other trees are also used and one nest was in a euphorbia. The nest is a bulky structure of sticks about 60–70 cm across, 35 cm deep with a cup about 20 cm across, lined with greenery. There are no records on the share of the sexes in the construction of the nest. Nests may be used at least three years in succession, alternate sites being never far from a previous nest, and a pair may be found in the same area year after year. Estimates of population density in three areas of the Transvaal are one pair per 16,5 km^2, 17,5 km^2 and 30 km^2. There are no details on the actual size of the territory.

Eggs are laid from May to October, mainly in

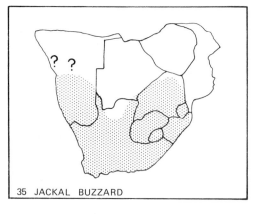

35 JACKAL BUZZARD

August and September with only isolated records in May, June and October. Two or three eggs are laid, usually two, and they are chalky-white with red-brown spots and blotches. Normally eggs are sparingly marked. Measurements are: 60,7 × 47,7 (26); 57,0–64,9 × 45,0–49,9.

At one nest the two young hatched three days apart so the laying interval was probably much the same. Little is known of the incubation period except that both birds incubate and the male feeds the female. Some females are aggressive and will attack an intruder climbing to the nest. The incubation period is about 40 days but accurate observations are required.

Chicks hatch several days apart and Cainism has been recorded by several observers. The smaller chick is not necessarily killed and two young may survive together to the flying stage. It seems, however, that it is unusual for two young to be reared. The newly hatched chick is covered in white down and has a yellowish cere and pale orange legs. By two weeks old the down is greyish-white and wing and tail quills are just sprouting through the down. At three weeks feathers are breaking on the wings, tail and scapulars, and a week later feathers emerge on the breast and on the head. The five-week-old chick is well feathered except for down on the breast, neck and head. At six weeks the last remaining down is on the head. Little is recorded on the development of co-ordination of the nestling except that it first stands at about three weeks old.

During the first two weeks the female is on the nest most of the time brooding or tending the young. The male provides prey. At one nest there were as many as seven rats on the nest at once. After two weeks the female's time on the nest is mainly given to feeding the nestling; it is not known when the nestling becomes able to feed itself.

Nestling periods have been between 50 and 53 days but further observations are required. Nothing is known about the post-nestling period or breeding success. The breeding biology is very poorly known and awaits further study.

36 Augur Buzzard *153*

Witborsvalk

Buteo augur

PAGE 12 AND 13

DERIVATION
hawk : augur — *buteo* (L) : *augur* (L)

An augur was a member of a group of religious officials in ancient Rome who interpreted omens provided by flying birds.

IDENTIFICATION
Adult: This handsome species is slate-black above and white below. The tail is red. Females have a black gorget but in males the throat is white. Sometimes there is a narrow black band near the tip of the tail, but this is probably a remnant of immature plumage. The eyes are dark brown and the cere and bare legs are yellow. Although melanistic birds are regular in east Africa, only partially melanistic individuals with some black blotching on the underwing coverts and abdomen have been recorded in southern Africa. They are very rare.

In flight the whole underwing is white except for a narrow black border along the hind edge of the wings and black 'comma' marks at the carpal joints. The short red tail is diagnostic and prevents confusion with the superficially similar Black-breasted Snake Eagle.

Juvenile and immature: The juvenile is brown above with buff edges to the wing coverts and buff below with some brown streaks on the sides of the throat and breast. The tail is brown above and greyish below with narrow darker barring and a broader blackish band near the tip. The soft parts are coloured as in the adult. In flight the underwing pattern is similar to that of the adult except for some indistinct transverse barring on the remiges.

The first moult of the contour feathers begins at about the age of a year and the streaking on the breast disappears as the white feathers emerge. Full adult plumage is acquired between the second and third year.

HABITAT
It occurs in mountainous country and areas of rocky koppies, being particularly common in the Matopos hills in Zimbabwe. Although normally found at higher altitudes, it also occurs at sea level in the most arid regions of the Namib Desert.

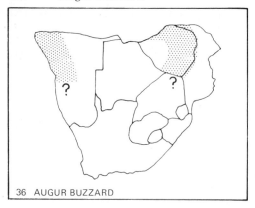

36 AUGUR BUZZARD

STATUS AND DISTRIBUTION

This resident species is restricted to the north of southern Africa and occurs in Namibia from about Windhoek northwards and in Zimbabwe and adjacent highland areas of Mozambique. The ranges of the Augur Buzzard and Jackal Buzzard overlap in central Namibia and possibly in the northern Transvaal, but further clarification of the situation is required. Extralimitally it is found in southern Angola and in the east it extends as far north as Ethiopia.

GENERAL HABITS

The Augur Buzzard hunts from a perch or a soaring position, often hanging motionless on an updraught of air or hovering with slowly winnowing wings. A total of 112 hours' observation of diurnal activity in the Matopos established that 58 per cent of its time was spent perched, 29 per cent flying or soaring and 13 per cent hovering. Prey is caught in a quick swoop from a perch, or in a rapid parachute drop with feet extended from a soaring or hovering position. Sometimes the bird drops down in controlled stages before the final plunge. The quarry may be followed with bounding hops if it is not caught in the initial stoop. Sometimes it may walk about for a short while when hunting insects.

The prey of this species, in order of importance, consists of reptiles, mammals, birds and insects. However, in east Africa, mammals are most often recorded and insects also feature prominently. The only quantitative prey studies are from Zimbabwe. At various nests in the Matopos 54 items were recorded: 59 per cent reptiles, 37 per cent rodents and 4 per cent birds. The identified reptiles comprised an almost equal number of lizards and snakes, the latter including highly venomous species such as Puffadder, Night Adder and Mozambique Spitting Cobra. The most commonly caught lizard was the Plated Rock Lizard but Water Monitors

(Leguaans) and Common Flat Lizards were also recorded. The Angoni Vlei Rat was the commonest item of mammalian prey but other small rodents as well as a Tree Squirrel, a young dassie and a young Scrub Hare were recorded. The avian prey consisted of two unidentified nestlings. At a single nest observed in another locality 23 prey items were identified: 83 per cent reptiles, 13 per cent rodents and 4 per cent nestling birds. Other random prey records indicate that birds up to the size of a francolin as well as unprotected chickens are caught. It has not been seen to feed on carrion but will probably be found to do so like the Jackal Buzzard.

The main call is a harsh *kow-kow-kow* sometimes preceded by a whistling note. These calls are used during display, as contact, for soliciting, and in alarm. Once the nestling has abandoned its infantile chittering it solicits with a penetrating *pi-pi-pi pee-ooo-pee-ooo*, which is repeated as long as it is hungry.

BREEDING

Various spectacular nuptial displays are performed. A bombing display consists of the male dive-bombing the perched female and pulling up just short of actual contact. Diving displays are commonly performed in which the pair gain height and dive down vertically. In another rarely performed display the male and female fly towards each other on a horizontal plane and veer off almost at the point of collision to bank into a spiral and twist sequence. Sometimes claws are locked at the end of a dive. These displays take place to the accompaniment of loud calling.

Mating takes place on prominent rocky outcrops or on the branches of trees. A case of polyandry where two males mated with the same female within twelve minutes is recorded, as well as an instance of polygyny where a male mated with two females. He assisted one of them in building a nest in which eggs were laid and the other female built a flimsy nest on her own but did not lay.

Nests are built on cliff ledges, at the base or in the branches of small trees growing from cliffs, and less often in trees on wooded hillsides. Nests in trees are usually placed within the canopy but they may also be on top of a tree with no shelter. Pines have been recorded as nest sites in eastern Zimbabwe. Cliff nests are often exposed to full sun for at least half of the day. Nests are built with sticks 2 cm thick and measure 45–65 cm across and 15–20 cm deep with a central cup lined with green leaves. Greenery is brought by both sexes during the incubation period and early part of the nestling

(1) View of the nest site (arrowed) and habitat of an Augur Buzzard.

(2) A close view of the same nest.

(3) This nest was situated in the crown of a thorn tree on a steep hillside. The female shades her 10-day-old nestling while the male looks on; note her dark gorget and his plain white throat.

period. Both birds share in the construction or repair of a nest, the main period of activity being in the early morning. Dead branches are snapped off trees or collected from the ground. The same nest may be used year after year, for twelve years in one instance, and if alternate sites are built they are usually nearby.

In a study area of 860 km^2 in the Matopos the population density was approximately one pair per 20 km^2. However, the actual territory size averaged about 3 km^2 in the breeding season and 6 km^2 in the non-breeding season. The reason for this difference was that pairs reduced their hunting range when breeding and tended to perch within sight of their nests. Adjacent pairs did not trespass into the territories of their neighbours. Other birds of prey and White-necked Ravens flying into a territory are vigorously attacked and driven away. Unlike the Jackal Buzzard, it has not been known to attack humans near the nest, although the birds may fly overhead and call.

Eggs are laid from July to October in Zimbabwe, with a peak in August and September. Two or three eggs are laid, rarely three, and they are chalky-white in ground colour with dark red and mauve spots. They are usually sparsely marked, sometimes with no spotting at all. In two-egg clutches first-laid eggs are larger. Measurements are: 57,1 × 46,3 (53); 55,1–59,3 × 43,5–47,2.

Just before laying, the female spends much of her time adding material to the nest, shaping the bowl or perching nearby. The male is not much in evidence at this time. Eggs are laid three to four days apart in a clutch of two and incubation commences with the laying of the first egg. Both sexes incubate. In the Matopos study the female incubated for 66 per cent of the observed time and the male 27 per cent. Two accurate incubation periods are 39 and 40 days.

Cainism has been regularly observed in this species; there appear to be no records of two young being reared together. As usual Cain pecks Abel viciously; in observed cases Abel survived for five to eight days before dying from a combination of injuries and starvation.

The newly hatched chick is covered in greyish-white down. The eyes are dark grey and the cere and legs are pale yellow. At the age of two weeks the first feathers appear along the hind edge of the wings and by three weeks feathers are also emerging on the scapulars and tail. Contour feathers emerge rapidly from this stage on and by five weeks old the nestling is almost fully feathered except for some down tufts. The forehead is the last area to be covered by feathers.

The nestling first stands at about eighteen days old and is able to pull off small pieces of prey for itself. However, it is still fed by the female until about a month old when it can feed itself competently. Small prey is swallowed whole. From the age of six weeks it exercises its wings vigorously and towards the end of the nestling period it wanders off the nest if the ledge is large enough.

The chick is brooded or shaded by the female in the early stages; in an exposed site it suffers heat stress up to the age of two weeks if left unprotected. The male provides prey, either bringing it to the nest or calling the female off to receive it nearby. At one nest the male fed a ten-day-old chick when the female was off the nest. After three weeks the female's time on the nest is mainly given to prey delivery.

The nestling period is between 48 and 55 days. A captive nestling made its first flight when 52 days old. Juveniles may remain in the nest area for about six or seven weeks after their first flight. One was still flying with its parents three months after leaving the nest and occasionally the juvenile may be seen near the nest the following breeding season, although it is completely independent at this stage.

In a twelve-year study in the Matopos 162 pair-years were recorded during which time the replacement rate was 0,42 young per pair per year. Predators that caused nest failure were White-necked Ravens, a python and baboons. Human persecution in the form of egg-collectors and local tribesmen who stoned nests also caused breeding failures. Larvae of the Tropical Nest Fly were found in the nostrils of small chicks, as many as 18 in one instance, and may have been responsible for the death of chicks where no other cause was apparent.

37 Lizard Buzzard /54

Akkedisvalk
Kaupifalco monogrammicus

PLATES 14 AND 16

DERIVATION
Kaup : falcon : one : lettered — *Kaupius* (L) : *falco* (L) : *monos* (G) : *grammikos* (G)

Kaup was a German zoologist who wrote extensively on birds, including a review of the diurnal raptors, during the 1830s and 1840s. The single 'letter' referred to by *monogrammicus* is the throat stripe of this species.

IDENTIFICATION
Adult: The upperparts, head and breast are grey and the white throat has a single dark streak down its centre. The rest of the underparts are white finely barred with grey. The bill is black, the cere and legs are red and the eyes dark brown. There is a conspicuous white bar on the blackish tail one third in from the tip; very occasionally there may be two bars on the tail. In flight this white bar and the broad band of white on the rump are diagnostic. The underwing coverts are white finely barred with grey, and the white remiges are traversed by narrow black bars, but the underwing appears mainly white from a distance.

The only species of similar size with which this species may be confused is the Gabar Goshawk but it lacks the white throat and black centre streak. In flight both have a white rump but the Lizard Buzzard has a single white bar on its tail while the Gabar Goshawk has several tail bars. The Lizard Buzzard is also more stockily built and plump in appearance.

Juvenile: Young resemble the adults when they leave the nest except for faint buff edges to the wing coverts and scapulars, a less distinct white tail bar and pale brown eyes. They are not easily distinguishable from adults unless a good view is obtained.

HABITAT
Found mainly in moister woodland it also occurs in drier habitat such as *Acacia*.

STATUS AND DISTRIBUTION
Although it is generally considered resident, there is some evidence of nomadic movements during the non-breeding season in some areas of the Transvaal. Further information is needed. One ringed bird was recovered in the same locality ten years later. The distribution of

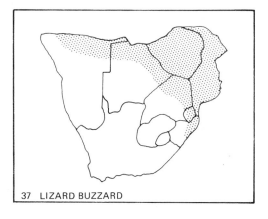

37 LIZARD BUZZARD

the Lizard Buzzard is mainly eastern from Natal northwards to Mozambique, the northern half of the Transvaal and Zimbabwe. On the west its range extends across northern Botswana into northern Namibia. Extralimitally it occurs northwards to the Sahara.

GENERAL HABITS
The Lizard Buzzard is usually seen perched in a tree, often in quite conspicuous positions. It is a still-hunter and prey is caught with a quick dash from a perch. Its flight from one perch to another is low and direct and it swoops upwards into a tree. Soaring flights are infrequent.

Lizards are its main prey and small snakes are also caught. In one incident the buzzard became enmeshed in the coils of a snake it had attempted to catch. Small mammals and birds are also occasionally eaten. Insects may be an important part of the diet but more detailed observations are needed. It has been recorded eating termites and grasshoppers.

There are two distinct calls, a loud sharp *pee-ooo, pee-ooo* and a musical 'laughing' *kli-oo-kluklukluklu*, the last part emitted with a quavering effect. Both calls may be made for long periods and probably both are used as part of courtship. However, little is known of the contexts in which the calls of this species are made. The *pee-ooo* is emitted by the female when she sees the male with prey, and feathered nestlings use it as a begging call. Calling is heard mainly in the breeding season.

(1) View of a Lizard Buzzard's nest site.

(2) A close-up of the nest and eggs; the cup is lined with Usnea *lichen.*

(3) An adult with a nestling about 10 days old.

BREEDING

Courtship apparently consists of long periods of calling by the perched birds. A pair seen flying about while emitting the *pee-ooo* call were probably courting.

Nests are placed in trees within the canopy either in a fork against the main trunk or on a lateral branch. One nest was situated in a euphorbia. Exotic trees such as eucalypts and pines may be used. Nests are usually 6–10 m above ground but sometimes much higher. They are small compact structures of sticks about 40 cm across with a cup of about 15 cm which is most often lined with *Usnea* 'beard' lichen where available, although dry grass and occasional green leaves are also used. One nest was built on top of the nest of a Gabar Goshawk used the previous year.

Both birds build but nothing is known of the share of the sexes in this activity. Sticks and lining may be added to the nest in the incubation period.

Eggs are laid from September to November, mainly October. Two or three eggs are laid but clutches of three are infrequent. Eggs are very variable in colour. Some are plain white or very faintly marked while others have red-brown blotching and speckling scattered over the surface. Plain and marked eggs may be found in the same clutch. Measurements are: 44,7 × 35,5 (108); 41,5–49,6 × 32,0–38,2.

At one nest the second egg was laid at least two and a half days after the first and incubation commenced with the laying of the first egg. There are few details on behaviour during the incubation period. Once a male brooded for six and a half hours shortly before the egg hatched. The pair may call to each other when the female is on the nest. The male is often in the vicinity and he drives other large birds away from near the nest. The incubation has twice been found to be between 33 and 34 days.

The newly hatched chick is covered in white down. Its bill is black, cere and legs are pale orange-yellow, and the eyes brown. By the age of two weeks quills are just appearing through the down, and the cere and legs are turning red. At three weeks old feathers emerge rapidly and by 33 days it appears fully feathered.

There are few details of parental care. A 12-day-old nestling was still brooded, shaded and fed by the female. She left the nest for about twenty minutes and returned with a lizard which she probably caught herself as the male was not seen in the vicinity at the time.

Prior to their first flight young may move out onto branches near the nest, usually a few days before they leave. One accurate nestling period was 40 days. For the first four days at one site the two young remained within 5 m of the nest, to which they returned to be fed and to roost. During their first three weeks out of the nest they never wandered more than 100 m from the nest and they could be located by their loud *pee-ooo* soliciting call. A first attempt at prey capture was seen when they had been out of the nest a month. Seven weeks after leaving the nest the young were no longer seen or heard in the nest area and had probably become independent.

38 Red-breasted Sparrowhawk /55

Rooiborssperwer

Accipiter rufiventris

PLATES 14 AND 16

DERIVATION

hawk : red : belly — *accipiter* (L) : *rufus* (L) : *venter* (L)

IDENTIFICATION

Adult: The plain rufous underparts and slate-coloured upperparts make this species easy to identify. In flight the wings and tail are boldly barred and there is no white on the rump. The bill is black and the cere, eyes and legs are yellow. The only confusion that may easily arise is with the rufous juvenile form of the Ovambo Sparrowhawk which differs in having a dark patch behind the eye (not a uniform cap like an executioner's mask), a white eyebrow, a brown eye, and pale edges to the wing coverts and scapulars. A more subtle difference is that the head is more pointed, that of the Red-breasted Sparrowhawk being rounded, rather like the difference between the heads of a cheetah and a leopard respectively. In the hand, or if a good view is obtained, the shafts of the tail quills of the juvenile Ovambo Sparrowhawk are white between the black bars on the tail; the tail shafts of the Red-breasted Sparrowhawk are dark throughout.

Juvenile: The juvenile plumage is rather variable and confusing. Some birds are mainly rufous below like the adults, others show more white. However, most juveniles would appear to have dark shaft streaks to the feathers of the underparts, which have rufous centres and a variable amount of white edging to give a faintly barred effect. The throat is usually white. The cere and legs are yellow as in the adult, but the eyes are pale greyish, changing to yellow by the time the juvenile is four months old. Nothing is recorded on the transition to adult plumage, and further investigation of the variability of juvenile plumage is needed.

HABITAT

This species is not often found in indigenous forest in southern Africa and prefers stands of exotic trees such as poplars, pines and eucalypts, especially for nesting. It occurs in quite small clumps of these trees in otherwise unsuitable open habitat, particularly in the Karoo and Orange Free State. In some regions (e.g. eastern Zimbabwe) it is found at higher altitudes, but it is by no means restricted to montane country. At times it may be encountered in areas with limited cover well away from the nearest trees.

STATUS AND DISTRIBUTION

The Red-breasted Sparrowhawk is unobtrusive outside the breeding season and may make local movements, but further investigation of its status is required. In suitable habitat this species is regularly encountered, and with the spread of exotic plantations it has undoubtedly increased its range.

Distribution extends from the south-western Cape eastwards to the Natal interior, eastern Orange Free State, Lesotho (rarely), western Zululand, Swaziland, eastern and northern Transvaal, eastern Zimbabwe and adjacent

highland areas of Mozambique. Extralimitally it occurs northwards to Ethiopia in montane habitat.

GENERAL HABITS

Except when soaring, this species is not often seen and it is especially unobtrusive inside plantations. It captures its prey with a quick dash from a perch, taking it on the ground or in flight. Another technique is to fly swiftly below the level of cover and then shoot over it in a surprise attack on anything that may be on the other side. Sometimes it will sit in an open place such as a road, possibly using this as a vantage point from which to watch for birds crossing the area. Birds have been seen to fly around until almost too dark to see, but it was not known whether they were hunting.

Prey is almost entirely birds ranging in size from small passerines to large doves. Some species recorded are larks, sparrows, canaries, a mousebird, a swift, European Starlings, a Red-winged Starling and a Bokmakierie. Occasionally mice are caught and in one instance a large bat, probably a fruit bat, was killed. They also eat some insects, particularly termites, which are caught in the talons in flight.

The main call is a staccato *kew-kew-kew-kew* . . . emitted by both birds, the male higher pitched than the female. This is made in display, as a contact call, and when attacking intruders at the nest. A plaintive, drawn out, mewing *kieee-u* is made by the female when soliciting the male for prey when he is near the nest, and it is adopted by feathered young as a begging call which they make repeatedly when they see the adults. The call is useful for locating a nest or young that have recently flown.

BREEDING

At one site a male was seen to take up residence in his nesting grove in May, having been absent since January. He called a great deal in the late afternoons. In August the female was first seen and nest construction began almost immediately. In the Orange Free State birds only returned to their nest groves in spring (early September) and they also disappeared in January after breeding.

Courtship consists of flying at a considerable height over the nest area and calling. The male brings food for the female, and mating often follows prey delivery.

Nests are placed in a fork against the main trunk 6–18 m above ground. Trees inside a plantation are chosen. The nest is a thick platform of small sticks about 40–45 cm across and

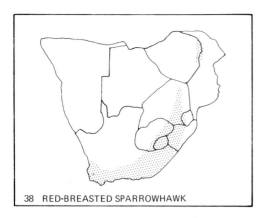

38   RED-BREASTED SPARROWHAWK

Close-up of the eggs of a Red-breasted Sparrowhawk (Photograph: Hans Grobler).

20–30 cm deep with a shallow cup in the centre. Usually the cup is unlined except for finer twigs, but some observers have recorded green lining. It is not known whether both birds build. Material may be collected on the ground, but most of the sticks are collected from trees by snapping them off with the feet in flight, or by alighting and using the bill to break them. Sticks are taken to the nest in the bill or the feet. One new nest was substantially complete after a month, but it was a further month before the eggs were laid. In most cases a new nest is built each year, never very far from a previous site. Little is known about size of territory. In eastern Zimbabwe seven nests were found 3–12 km apart, with an average of 6,4 km between nests. In a small plantation only one pair will be found.

Eggs are laid in September and October (mainly October) throughout southern Africa. Two to four eggs, normally three, are laid. They are white or pale greenish-white in ground colour with red-brown blotches which usually coalesce to form a cap at the large or small end. Markings are very variable, but most eggs are handsomely blotched. Egg measurements are: 41,1 × 32,1 (26); 38,3–43,3 × 30,8–34,5.

In a clutch of two the eggs were laid a day apart. Incubation begins with the laying of the first egg. The bulk of the incubation is by the female, and the male brings food for her at the nest. They both then leave the nest tree and he gives the food to her in a nearby tree. Usually the male makes no attempt to incubate, but once he was seen to return to the nest and incubate for ten minutes while the female fed. Intruders are boldly and vigorously attacked when climbing to the nest and even when on the ground below. The birds strike freely and in one instance a female flew through a small gap between the observer's body and the tree trunk. These attacks are continued into the nestling period. The incubation period, obtained only once, was 34 days.

The newly hatched chick is covered in white down. The eyes are brown, the bill is black, the cere and feet are yellow. At 10 days old the tips of the wing feathers are just visible through the down which is now greyish-white. By 18 days brown feathers appear through the down on the wing coverts and scapulars and the first rufous feathers break through on the sides of the breast. At 22 days the upperparts and underparts are covered by feathers except for a downy patch down the centre of the breast and on the forehead. The tail is growing rapidly and the barred pattern of the flight feathers is like that of the adult.

There is little information on the development of co-ordination in the young. The smaller chicks, especially in a brood of four, hatch 3–4 days after their siblings and their development lags behind that of the larger young. The chicks are able to stand at 18 days old and within a few days perform vigorous wing exercises.

Throughout the nestling period the female remains on or near the nest, fed by the male. All birds are brought thoroughly plucked, and the male has favourite plucking perches in the area. Once a female was seen to take prey from a male in flight. The larger young are fed first, which also accounts for their more rapid growth at the expense of their smaller siblings. The female hunts only when the young leave the nest.

If an observer climbs to the nest in the latter part of the nestling period, the young will fly prematurely, as early as 23 days in one instance. At one nest young first flew between 25 and 30 days; at another the larger chick left on its 31st day, its smaller sibling several days later. The young remain close to the nest for several days and return to it to be fed and to roost. By the time they have been on the wing for three weeks they attempt to catch prey for themselves but are still fed by the adults. At one nest the young were no longer seen in the area six weeks after they had first flown and were presumed to have become independent.

39 Ovambo Sparrowhawk 156.

Ovambosperwer

Accipiter ovampensis

PLATES 14 AND 16

DERIVATION
hawk : of Ovamboland — *accipiter* (L) : *ovampensis* (L)

IDENTIFICATION
Adult: The dull white underparts are entirely barred with grey, even on the throat. The upperparts are uniform grey. The grey tail has four broad blackish bars, and the shafts of the tail feathers are white between the dark bars, a useful aid to identification if a good view is obtained. The eyes are dark red, the bill and gape are black, and cere and legs orange-yellow. The head is smaller and more pointed than that of other sparrowhawks, but this is a subtle distinction. In flight four bars show on the tail, and the rump is grey. The white underwing coverts are finely barred with grey and there are about six black bars on the remiges.

A rare melanistic form occurs which appears entirely black when perched. The eyes, cere and legs are coloured as in grey birds. The dark grey tail has four black bars, and the white shaft streaks between these bars are useful in confirming identification. The underwing coverts are black and the silver-grey remiges are barred with black below. It can be confused with a melanistic Gabar Goshawk, but this species has red legs and cere, not orange-yellow, and the front surfaces of the legs have blackish blotching. In flight it has black and white barring on the primaries and tail. Another species which may cause confusion is the melanistic Black Sparrowhawk, but this is a much larger bird which has yellow legs and cere, no barring on the tail, and a white throat.

The grey-coloured Ovambo Sparrowhawk is most likely to be confused with the adult Little Banded Goshawk, but the latter is finely barred with russet, does not have the bold bars on the upper surface of the closed tail, and lacks white shaft streaks. The cere and legs are yellow and the eyes are cherry-red. The adult Little Sparrowhawk is also superficially similar, but has yellow legs, cere and eyes, a rufous wash on the sides of the underparts and an unbarred tail above with two small white 'eye' spots on it. In flight it has a white rump. The Gabar Goshawk should not cause confusion as it is grey on head and upper breast, has a red cere and legs, and a

broad white rump. The only other species with which confusion is possible is the African Goshawk, particularly the greyer female. However, this species has yellow eyes, cere and legs.

Juvenile: Two forms of juvenile plumage occur. A red-breasted form has been recorded, mainly in Zimbabwe. It is plain rufous below with a few thin dark shaft streaks, and brown above with buff edges to the wing coverts and scapulars. There is a dark patch behind the eye and a white eyebrow. Confusion with an adult Red-breasted Sparrowhawk can easily arise; distinctions between the two are discussed under that species. The other juvenile form is dull white below with dark brown streaking and some barring on the flanks. It also has a dark patch behind the eye and a white eyebrow, but the head and neck appear whitish. Otherwise the upperparts are like the rufous form. Both forms have brown eyes and yellow ceres and legs. Juveniles of the white-breasted form are somewhat variable in their markings.

Juvenile birds (at least in the case of the white-breasted form) apparently moult direct into adult plumage with no intermediate immature stage, but it is not known when this transition commences or how long it takes. Birds may breed while they still retain some of their juvenile plumage.

HABITAT
The Ovambo Sparrowhawk inhabits a variety of woodland habitats but is not found in thick forest or very dry areas. It shows a preference for exotic plantations where available, and in the Transvaal poplar groves are favoured, especially for nesting. In all wooded habitats it likes to have open areas nearby.

STATUS AND DISTRIBUTION
Although it is said to be migratory in southern Africa, this is not confirmed by the facts, at least in the Transvaal, where it was recorded in all months in two study areas. As with the Red-breasted Sparrowhawk, it is unobtrusive when not breeding and tends to be overlooked.

With the spread of exotic plantations this species has extended its range in the Transvaal and probably in other regions too.

In southern Africa it occurs in north-eastern

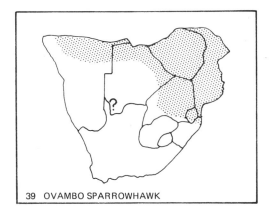

39 OVAMBO SPARROWHAWK

Zululand, Mozambique, Swaziland, Transvaal, Zimbabwe, northern Botswana and northern Namibia. Extralimitally it extends to Ghana on the west and Ethiopia and Somalia on the east; it is rare in some areas in the north (e.g. Kenya).

GENERAL HABITS

The flight of this agile species is quick, light and graceful and it can manoeuvre with great dexterity. It hunts in two ways, either making a sudden dash from a perch or stooping from a soaring position. Using the latter technique one made a kill from a height of 150 m. Most hunting is done in the early morning and late afternoon, and it seeks its prey both in woodland and in adjacent areas of open grassland.

Its diet is almost entirely made up of birds, with some insects at times. Species ranging in size from waxbills to Cape Turtle Doves are caught; other birds recorded include a Didric Cuckoo, bulbuls, larks, a Fork-tailed Drongo, pipits, queleas, weavers, a Cardinal Woodpecker, Paradise Flycatchers and a European Bee-eater. In one prey sample a total of 22 birds was recorded, of which half were doves. It has not been known to attack poultry, even where easily available near a nest.

Calling is rarely heard except just before and during the breeding season. A number of calls have been described and they are mellower than those of other small sparrowhawks. A frequent call is a sustained *kiep-kiep-kiep . . . kiep-kiep-kiep . . .* which appears to be the main contact call. A probable variant is a *kwee-kwee-kwee* by the female soliciting the male when he has prey. One female uttered a harsh *krrr-krrr-krrr* in threat towards a male. High-pitched *ki-ki-ki-ki* calls are made when driving off intruders from the nest. The calls of this species, and the contexts in which they are used, require more detailed description.

BREEDING

Courtship displays are apparently the same as for the Red-breasted Sparrowhawk, the male and female soaring round calling. An undulating flight performed by a male was probably part of a nuptial display.

Nests are placed in tall trees, often in exotics such as poplars, eucalypts and pines, and usually in a prominent fork against the main trunk. They are normally 10–20 m above the ground; the average height of 22 Transvaal nests was 15 m. Nests are constructed with small thin sticks 5–10 mm thick and measure 35–50 cm across and 15–20 cm deep with a cup 15 cm across and 5 cm deep. One large nest 60 cm across and 45 cm deep may originally have belonged to some other raptor such as a Black Sparrowhawk. Nests are normally unlined except for finer sticks, but occasionally small chips of bark, dry leaves or green leaves are used as lining.

The birds occupy their territory some months before laying, and sporadic building takes place. Activity increases in the month before laying. Both sexes build, usually in the early morning, and branches are snapped off trees with the bill and carried to the nest in the bill or feet, from a distance of 200–300 m away at one nest. At a nest site in a plantation of eucalypts the birds fetched sticks from indigenous trees outside the plantation. After both have brought a number of sticks the female stays on the nest to arrange them. One nest took 42 days from first repair until the laying of the eggs. Once when a nest fell down at the egg stage the birds built a new nest in two weeks and laid again.

Although birds occasionally use the same nest two or three times in succession, the usual pattern is to build a new nest each year which is within 30–100 m of a previous site. Birds nesting in a plantation will return to it year after year.

In one Transvaal locality pairs were found to be spaced according to the distance between plantations of suitable eucalypts. No plantation contained more than one pair, and no Ovambo Sparrowhawks were found breeding in the same clump as a pair of Black Sparrowhawks. Intruding conspecifics are driven away from the nest vicinity, although hunting areas outside the plantations may overlap. Breeding densities are very variable and in two study areas in the Transvaal there were one or two pairs in an area of 350 km² and in another locality there were 19 pairs in 600 km².

Eggs are laid in September and October in southern Africa; in one study area in the Transvaal the laying time was between the last week

(1) View of the nest site of an Ovambo Sparrowhawk.

(2) A close-up of a nest with a small downy nestling.

(3) A week-old nestling.

(4) At two weeks feathers are breaking through the down.

(5) The nestling at three weeks old.

(6) By four weeks it is fully feathered.

in September and the first week in October. One to five eggs are laid, but the normal clutch is three. Eggs are dull white in ground colour and very variably marked (even in the same nest) with blotches or marbling of dark red-brown, sometimes with some lilac or purple markings, and often forming a cap or zone at the large or small end. In one clutch of three, two eggs were well marked and the third was white. Measurements are: 41,0 × 32,8 (63); 38,5–43,8 × 30,0–34,4.

Incubation starts with the laying of the first egg and there is an interval of at least a day between the laying of each egg. The bulk of the incubation is by the female although the male may also occasionally brood. The female sits tightly, standing up every hour or so for a stretch and a preen. She is fed by the male and she often leaves the nest before he arrives and takes the prey from him in flight. Once a male pursued a Grey-hooded Kingfisher and drove it down to ground level within sight of the incubating female; she immediately left the nest and caught it in front of him. The male often perches in the vicinity of the nest tree when not hunting. Other birds up to the size of a Hadeda or Long-crested Eagle are driven away if they come too close and the female may leave the nest and join the attack. A Vervet Monkey in a tree near a nest was vigorously attacked and one bird settled nearby and threatened it with spread wings. Human intruders are also attacked, even when on the ground below. Both male and female may add sticks to the nest during the incubation period. One accurate incubation period was 35 days ± 1 day.

The newly hatched chick is covered in white down and has a dark brown eye and orange-yellow cere and legs. At the age of one week there is little change, but by two weeks old the down is greyish-white, the wing and tail feathers are just sprouting, and brown feathers are

emerging through the down on the scapulars. At three weeks the down has largely been replaced by feathers, although the head is still downy. By four weeks old the last traces of down have disappeared.

Newly hatched young are scarcely able to lift their heads and make a weak cheeping call. By 18 days old they are able to stand, and spend much time preening and scratching. They can make the contact call of the adults at this stage. As the end of the nestling period approaches, vigorous wing exercises are performed.

The female remains on or near the nest during most of the nestling period and the male brings prey, increasing his kill rate from three birds a day prior to the eggs hatching to seven a day by the time the nestlings are 18 days old. Birds are brought well plucked, from a favoured plucking perch in the area. Initially the female tends and broods the chicks closely and is very reluctant to leave the nest if anyone approaches. As during the incubation period, human intruders are vigorously attacked. The female feeds the chicks until they are at least 18 days old, but it is not known when they can feed themselves. At one nest doves were first brought when the young were about to leave the nest; this was the largest prey recorded up to that time, indicating that the female was hunting at that stage.

The nestling period at one nest was about 33 days. There are no details on the post-nestling period, but it is probably similar to that of the Red-breasted Sparrowhawk, whose breeding biology is much the same in most other aspects.

Information on breeding success is available from two study areas in the Transvaal. In 7 pair-years 4 young were reared, a replacement figure of 0,57 young per pair per year. More extensive results in another locality established that 28 young were reared in 32 pair-years, a productivity of 0,88 young per pair per year.

40 Little Sparrowhawk   /57.

Kleinsperwer

Accipiter minullus   PLATES 14 AND 16

DERIVATION
hawk : least — *accipiter* (L) : *minullus* (L)

IDENTIFICATION
Adult: This diminutive sparrowhawk, finely barred with brown on the underparts, has a ru-

fous wash down the sides and on the flanks. The upperparts are slate-grey or dove-grey, and the top of the tail is plain blackish with two distinct white 'eye' spots and a narrow white tip. The eyes are rich yellow, sometimes orange-yellow, the bill and gape black, the cere and legs yellow. In flight a broad white band on the upper tail coverts and the two 'eye' spots are diagnostic. From below the remiges are barred and there are three dark bars on the white undertail.

The most likely confusion is with the adult Little Banded Goshawk, which, however, has a cherry-red eye, no 'eye' spots on the tail and no white rump. Possible confusion with the Ovambo Sparrowhawk is discussed under that species. The much larger African Goshawk is superficially similar, particularly the male, and the most important distinction would be the white rump of the Little Sparrowhawk.

Juvenile: The underparts are buffy-white with pear-shaped dark brown blotches and some broad barring on the sides and flanks. The upperparts are brown with buff edges to the wing coverts. There are two 'eye' spots on the tail, but no white rump as in the adult. The eyes are pale grey and the legs and cere yellow. The only similar species is the juvenile African Goshawk, which also has pear-shaped markings below but is much larger. It differs in having a dark line down the centre of the throat (the Little Sparrowhawk has a plain white throat) and a white eyebrow. Also, it has no white spots on the tail.

Juveniles moult directly into adult plumage with no intermediate immature stage. Within the first month or two of its leaving the nest the eyes turn very pale yellow. One source states that adult plumage is rapidly acquired, within two months of leaving the nest. However, females in unchanged juvenile plumage have been found breeding when they must have been at least a year old, so the moult into adult plumage takes place at some stage thereafter, probably during the second year.

HABITAT

It occurs in a variety of woodland habitats, but not in thick forest, and it is found in drier thornveld where there are larger trees in the river valleys. Plantations of eucalypts and other exotic trees also provide a suitable habitat, especially for nesting.

STATUS AND DISTRIBUTION

This resident species occurs from the eastern Cape northwards to Mozambique and Zimbabwe and westwards to northern Botswana and northern Namibia. It is absent from the dry central and western regions. Extralimitally it is found northwards to Ethiopia on the east and Zaire on the west.

GENERAL HABITS

Because of its small size and habit of perching quietly within the canopy of a tree it is easily overlooked. It does not fly about or soar a great deal, and is usually glimpsed as it flies quickly from one tree to the next. Prey is captured in a quick dash from a tree, or sometimes from a perch on the ground, and birds and insects are caught in flight. It is an extremely agile and dashing little hawk able to manoeuvre through cover with great dexterity.

Prey consists mostly of small birds, very occasionally young chickens. Insects such as locusts and termites are also eaten, and lizards occasionally.

This species is noisy during the breeding season, largely silent during the rest of the year. The female makes a rapid high-pitched *kik-kik-kik-kik-kik* and the male a mellower *kew-kew-kew-kew-kew*. This call is used in courtship, as contact between the pair, and when intruders are attacked near the nest. When calling the female to accept food the male makes a slowly repeated *kiack . . . kiack . . . kiack* or a more rapid *wit . . . wit . . . kew-kew-kew-kew*.

BREEDING

For about six weeks before starting nest building the pair call a great deal, especially in the early morning. Display flights consist of flying about carrying nesting material with an exaggerated 'fluttering' flight. Mating takes place mostly in the early mornings. The male alights near the female perched on a branch and calls excitedly while fluffing out his feathers, especially on the white rump; he also droops his wings and raises his tail. The female responds by crouching with quivering wings, and copulation follows. This courtship behaviour takes place frequently until two weeks before the eggs are laid, and less often thereafter.

Nests are placed in the upper branches of trees, usually in a main fork, at 6–22 m above ground. The highest nest sites are often in eucalypts. Large sticks are used for the base of the

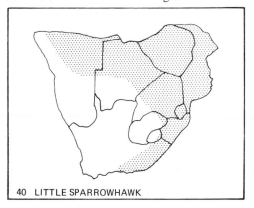

40   LITTLE SPARROWHAWK

nest, often bigger than those used by medium-sized sparrowhawks. On top of this coarse platform the cup is made with fine twigs and usually lined with a few green leaves. Some nests are substantially built, others flimsy and almost transparent. They measure 18–30 cm across and about 10–15 cm deep with a cup 7–9 cm across.

The nest is built by the female, occasionally assisted by the male. Sticks are broken off trees with the bill and then usually carried in the feet to the nest. In one case material was gathered within 20 m of the nest. Sticks appear to be placed rather haphazardly and some fall out of the fork. Sometimes a new nest is built each year close to a previous site, at other times the same nest or fork may be used at least three times in succession.

Little information exists on territory size but in two Transvaal study areas approximate densities of 5–6 pairs per 350 km² and 2 pairs per 270 km² were obtained. The sparrowhawks are aggressive at the nest and attack other raptors. Various birds such as Black Cuckoo, Red-billed Wood Hoopoe, Brown-hooded Kingfisher and a dove were driven off when they came within 40 m of one nest. A Boomslang in a tree adjacent to the nest was vigorously attacked by the male while the female remained incubating. The birds are most aggressive during the nest-building stage.

Eggs are laid mostly in October in southern Africa with occasional records for September, November and December. One to three eggs are laid, normally two, and only two clutches of three have been recorded. Eggs are invariably immaculate white, sometimes becoming nest-stained as incubation progresses. Descriptions of marked eggs have resulted from confusion with those of the Little Banded Goshawk (which also average larger). Measurements are: 34,8 × 28,1 (43); 32,6–37,8 × 26,9–31,6.

The interval between the laying of two eggs was 48 hours in one case. Incubation begins once the first egg is laid. At one nest the eggs were incubated almost the whole day after the fifth day. Both sexes incubated, the male for about 25 per cent of the time observed. The birds sat very steadily, rarely moving position. The longest spell by the male was three hours, that by the female six and a half hours. The female incubated at night, but once the male sat overnight. The share of incubation by the male was greatest after his early-morning and midday hunting spells when he brought prey for the female and relieved her at the nest. When not hunting, he was often on a favourite perch near the nest, where he would preen, rest and sleep. When not incubating, the female remained near

the nest and she never hunted for herself. All prey was brought for her by the male, who thoroughly plucked, decapitated and eviscerated birds before delivering them. He would always fly to the same branch and call her off the nest while he stood with one foot on the prey; she flew towards him and just as she reached the branch he would jump up and she snatched the prey from beneath him without alighting. The male then either landed on the same branch again or flew off.

Green leaves are brought by the female during the first third of the incubation period, always when returning to take over incubation from the male. However, he may also bring leaves at this stage as he has once been seen to do during the nestling period. Too few leaves are brought to be an effective lining.

Human intruders are fearlessly attacked by both birds if they climb to the nest, and this behaviour continues into the nestling period. At one nest a female only ceased incubating as the observer reached the nest; she then flew to a nearby branch and threatened him rather like an owl with feathers puffed out, wings spread and gape open. When the male arrived to attack she joined in vigorously, passing very close but not actually striking.

The incubation period was accurately obtained as 31–32 days in one case. At another nest it was established as not less than 28–29 days.

Where two young hatch, one may disappear unaccountably within the first few days. Once a smaller chick was found dead with peck marks on the head, suggesting attack by its stronger sibling. Although two young may be reared together, the possibility that Cainism occurs requires investigation.

The newly hatched chick is about 5 cm long and is covered in buffy down. The eyes are dark brown, the bill is black with a prominent egg-tooth, the gape pink, the cere pale yellow and the legs are pale orange. The first wing quills are visible on the sixth day and between then and the sixteenth day feathers grow rapidly until it is well covered except for down on the head and breast. Thereafter the main feather growth is that of the flight feathers. By the time it leaves the nest its gape is black like that of the adult.

During the first five days weight increases rapidly and co-ordination of limbs develops. Between 6 and 16 days it sits up, preens, stretches and stands for the first time. Between 17 and 20 days it performs vigorous wing exercises, adopts the adults' call and threatens intruders with raised and opened wings. It feeds

(1) The nest of a Little Spar-rowhawk; the clutch is probably incomplete.

(2) A female with her six-day-old nestling.

(3) This nestling is approxi-mately three weeks old.

itself properly for the first time just before it leaves the nest.

The female broods a great deal during the first half of the nestling period, occasionally assisted by the male until the young are nine days old. Once feathers develop she broods less, but still continues to do so, even attempting to cover a nestling ready to leave the nest. If young are exposed to direct sun she shades them. The male provides all the prey until near the end of the nestling period, when the female may also hunt. Prey is collected from the male in the same way as during the incubation period. Once a female passed pieces of food to a male perched on the edge of the nest and he fed them to the young, but there are no observations of a male feeding nestlings when by himself. All food is consumed after each delivery, the female eating what is left over when the young are small. She keeps the nest meticulously clean by removing food particles that catch in the nest sticks, picking any pieces off her toes before finally wiping her bill clean on a branch.

Two nestling periods were 25–26 days and 26–27 days. The young may jump onto branches near the nest before leaving. One nestling was able to fly prematurely at 21 days when the nest edge broke and it fell off. Young remain in the vicinity of the nest initially, but it is not known when they become independent.

41 Black Sparrowhawk /58.

Swartsperwer

Accipiter melanoleucus

PLATES 15 AND 16

DERIVATION
hawk : black : white — *accipiter* (L) : *melas* (G) : *leukos* (G)

IDENTIFICATION
Adult: The upperparts and head are black and the underparts and throat are white except for a 'waistcoat' of black which extends onto the lower breast and abdomen. There are 4–5 black bars on the tail, but they are only clearly visible on the pale silver-grey undertail. The eyes are wine red, but they may lighten to amber in older birds; the cere is lime-yellow, and the legs are yellow. In flight the underwing coverts are white, and the white remiges are traversed by 7–9 black bars. It is the only sparrowhawk that appears so predominantly white below. Both perched and in flight it should not be confused with any other species, and its large size also serves to identify it.

A rare melanistic form occurs which is wholly black except for a white throat. The tail lacks any barring. Cere and legs are yellow and the eyes red-brown. Possible confusion with the melanistic Ovambo Sparrowhawk is dealt with under that species. Melanistic Gabar Goshawks, apart from being much smaller with no white on throat, have red legs and cere, and show white barring on primaries and tail.

Juvenile and immature: Two juvenile forms occur, one rufous below, the other white. Both have the underparts streaked with brown; females are more heavily marked than males. The upperparts of both are dark brown with rufous edges to the wing coverts and scapulars. The eyes are grey-brown, the cere and legs yellow. White and rufous juveniles of either sex may be found in the same nest, and both develop into white-breasted adults. In the only known case where plumage was recorded, a melanistic adult developed from a rufous-breasted juvenile. Some juveniles occasionally have a tortoise-shell pattern on the upperparts and on top of the tail. In flight both forms are barred on the wings and tail, and the underwing coverts are either rufous or white depending on the colour of the underparts.

Rufous juveniles could possibly be confused with juvenile African Hawk Eagles, but the bare yellow legs, size, and different behaviour and flight would distinguish them. White-breasted juveniles might be confused with juvenile African Goshawks, but these have pear-shaped streaks below, a dark line down the centre of the throat, and a white eyebrow.

First moult into adult plumage commences gradually at the age of one year, with females starting a little ahead of males. By this stage the eye is a deep brown. At about fourteen months old some tail and wing feathers have moulted, dark feathers emerge on the upperparts and head, and some of the black 'waistcoat' feathers appear. During the next two months the process continues until the plumage is about three-quarters of the way to adulthood. By the age of eighteen months the bird resembles the adult except for some wing coverts remaining from juvenile plumage and fine 'whisker' streaks of black on the shafts of some breast feathers. The eyes are wine red at this stage. At the age of two years a new moult commences, and six months later all vestiges of immature plumage have disappeared, including the fine 'whisker' streaks on the breast. The eyes are slightly lighter wine red in colour and may lighten to amber by the time the adult is three years old.

HABITAT

This species is by no means confined to forests in southern Africa, indeed it is more frequently encountered in a variety of woodland habitats. It may occur in rather dry localities in riverine woodland where there are large trees. In many areas it is found in exotic plantations, especially eucalypts.

STATUS AND DISTRIBUTION

As far as is known, adults are resident. However, juveniles may disperse widely, and one ringed in Zimbabwe as a nestling was shot two years and three months later, 145 km away.

In the Transvaal, where this species has been intensively studied, it has been estimated that in recent times there has been an eightfold increase in the original population. This has resulted from the spread of exotic plantations into the treeless highveld, combined with a plentiful food supply in the form of doves and francolins in adjacent cultivated lands. The importance of exotic trees is illustrated by the fact that of 162 nest sites recorded in the Transvaal survey only 9 were in indigenous trees; the rest were in eucalypts (119), poplars (30) and pines (3). The Black Sparrowhawk is in no danger, except possibly from pesticides; its decrease would serve as a good indicator that pesticides are

reaching dangerous levels in the environment.

The distribution of this species is mainly eastern in southern Africa, extending from the south-west Cape (rarely) eastwards to Natal, Zululand, Mozambique, Swaziland, Transvaal and Zimbabwe. Its status in the Orange Free State is uncertain, but it probably occurs in the north. It also probably occurs in north-eastern Botswana as it has been found in adjacent areas of Zimbabwe. There are some records from northern Namibia. Extralimitally it extends northwards to Ethiopia across to west Africa.

GENERAL HABITS

Despite its large size, the Black Sparrowhawk is unobtrusive, especially outside the breeding season. It tends to remain in cover and rarely soars. Its flight is completely silent, and prey is captured in a swift dash, usually in flight; it can overtake a dove on the wing. Sometimes it will pursue quarry for a considerable distance over open country.

It preys mostly on birds ranging in size from a Little Bee-eater to an adult Crowned Guineafowl; one bird even arrived at a nest with the head and neck of an Egyptian Goose which it had presumably killed itself. Under conditions of falconry a bird weighing 0,7 kg caught a Crowned Guineafowl weighing 1,8 kg. Occasionally mammals are taken; rats, young hares, a Tree Squirrel and a young White-tailed Mongoose have been recorded. One shot juvenile had thrush's eggs and a small snake in its crop. Birds recorded as prey of this species, apart from those already mentioned, include Cattle Egrets (at a heronry), domestic chickens, francolins (ranging in size from Coqui to Swainson's), an Ovambo Sparrowhawk, a Little Banded Goshawk, an African Goshawk, a Wood Owl, various species of doves, a Green Pigeon, domestic pigeons, Crowned Plovers, a kingfisher, a Yellow-billed Hornbill, thrushes and a barbet. It also takes a variety of small birds but, as these are always thoroughly plucked away from the nest, identification is difficult. The only quantitative southern African prey study is from the Transvaal, where 292 items were collected from several nests, and birds comprised 98 per cent of the total. Doves and pigeons (67 per cent) and francolins (12 per cent) were the most important categories. In Kenya 145 prey items were analysed: doves and pigeons made up 80 per cent and francolins 13 per cent. The two prey studies clearly establish that the Black Sparrowhawk is a dove-and-pigeon specialist; in Kenya there was evidence that larger dove species were deliberately selected, Red-eyed Doves comprising 37 per cent

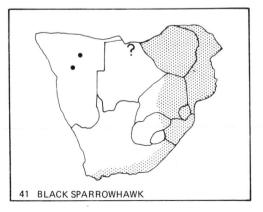

41 BLACK SPARROWHAWK

of the total. As textbooks labour the point that this species is a chicken thief, it is of note that chickens comprised only 3 per cent of the Transvaal prey sample.

Although noisy when breeding, this species is largely silent during the rest of the year. The female is deeper-voiced than the male. The contact call is a short, sharp, musical *kyip* by the male, answered by the female's deeper *chep*. When arriving near the nest with prey the male emits a series of *kyip* calls at about four-second intervals. The male and female may duet with an alternating series of *kyip-chep-kyip-chep* calls prior to egg-laying, presumably part of courtship. The female's begging call is a drawn-out, mewing *weeeee-uw* and that of the young when feathered is similar, a harsher more sibilant *schreeeee-uw,* which may be emitted persistently for long periods, especially after it has left the nest. In anxiety when disturbed at the nest, a loud, ringing *kow-kow-kow-kow-kow* is uttered and young can make this call from the age of three weeks if alarmed. During copulation a loud, trilling *trueeee-trueee-trueee* has been heard, probably made by the female.

BREEDING

No spectacular display flights are performed. One or both birds soar above tree level. A slow flight with exaggerated wing-beats is probably connected with courtship. The male brings prey for the female as part of courtship. Copulation takes place near the nest, the birds calling during the process. Mating has been observed during nest repair and the early part of the incubation period.

Nests are built in tall trees, usually in a fork in the main trunk. They have been recorded at heights of 7–36 m; 120 nests in the Transvaal averaged 15,6 m above ground. Various trees are used, but eucalypts are preferred where available. One nest was built in a euphorbia. Sticks 15–25 mm in diameter are used and nests measure 50–70 cm across (usually about 60 cm) and 40–75 cm deep. The cup is 20–25 cm across and thickly lined with green leaves, those of eucalypts being used where nests are in plantations of these trees. Nests as much as 90 cm across have been described, but these may originally have belonged to some other bird of prey, as the Black Sparrowhawk takes over disused nests. It has been known to use the nests of Wahlberg's Eagle, Long-crested Eagle, Gymnogene, Yellow-billed Kite and Bat Hawk. One pair bred on top of a disused Hamerkop's nest. One remarkable 'nest' was a mere depression in the leaves on the ground at the base of a poplar tree.

Both birds build or repair the nest, mainly in the early morning. At one nest the male was seen to do most of the building. The same nest may be used many years in succession, up to 10 years at least, and possibly 22 years in one case. Nests are even used again when they have been robbed the previous year. Alternate nests are never very far from a previous site.

In the Transvaal nesting densities are variable, depending on suitable habitat. The highest densities are 10 pairs per 650 km² and the lowest 1 pair per 650 km².

Eggs are laid from May to October in southern Africa but May records are rare. In the Transvaal there is a July/August peak (74 per cent of 89 records) and in Zimbabwe the peak is in September/October (84 per cent of 44 records). One to four eggs are laid, usually three, but clutches of two are not infrequent. Eggs are normally plain white, greenish-white when fresh, but they become heavily nest-stained by the time they hatch. Quite often eggs have faint red speckles and some underlying lilac spots, but these markings are always sparse. Measurements are: 56,3 × 43,9 (79); 52,0–61,1 × 40,1–47,8.

The laying interval in a clutch of two was at least 48 hours at one nest; incubation commenced with the laying of the first egg. No detailed observations have been made, but short watches at one nest established that the eggs were brooded most of the time and not left uncovered for more than three minutes. The female usually had a break in the early afternoon when the male incubated. The male has been observed to incubate at four other nests, once for nearly an hour, so this behaviour appears to be regular. On three occasions he has also been seen on a nest when it was too dark to see and was presumed to have brooded overnight. The bulk of incubation, however, is done by the female, the male often perching nearby when not hunting. He brings prey for the female, once a day during watches at one nest. Green leaves are brought to line the nest throughout the incubation period; only the female has been seen to bring them. When an observer approaches a nest, the female will often sneak away quietly and disappear into nearby trees. However, if the nest tree is climbed, both she and the male may attack vigorously, even striking from behind on occasions. Sometimes when an observer makes regular visits he may be attacked while still walking towards the nest. Large birds such as hornbills are chased from the vicinity of the nest. One accurate incubation period in Zimbabwe was 37–38 days; the same period was obtained at a nest in Kenya.

(1) The nest of a Black Sparrowhawk.

(2) Nestlings approximately two weeks old.

(3) These nestlings are close on 30 days old.

The newly hatched chick is covered in white down; the eyes are grey, the cere and legs flesh coloured. At two weeks old the cere and legs are pale yellow and the wing quills are just protruding through the down. At three weeks feathers are sprouting on wing coverts and scapulars and on the sides of the breast. Wing and tail feathers are emerging rapidly at this stage. By four weeks old the nestling appears to be half down and half feathers and a week later the last remaining down is on the head and breast; these areas are soon covered by feathers. By the end of the nestling period male and female young are easily distinguishable by their size and the thicker legs of females.

At an early age the chicks defecate clear of the nest, and droppings on the ground below are a good indication that a nest is occupied. First wing-flaps may be attempted at two weeks old. By the age of three weeks, young are able to stand and tear up prey for themselves. From this stage they spend much time preening and exercising their wings. They may threaten human intruders with slapping blows of the wings and when older they also strike out with their feet. They may still be fed by an adult at 31 days old although able to feed themselves competently.

When the young are small the female is almost constantly on the nest, and she is either on the nest or perched nearby for most of the nestling period. She first hunts when the young are nearly ready to leave. The male has been seen on a nest with small young, possibly brooding,

and he once fed 31-day-old nestlings, but his main function is to bring prey. When the female joins him in hunting at the end of the nestling period it is noticeable that larger items such as francolins are brought. Green lining is brought throughout the nestling period by the female, and the nest is kept clean by the removal of any inedible prey remains.

The nestling period varies from 40 to 47 days, but the young may leave at different times: in one nest the oldest of three young left at 40 days and the other two at 45 days. Before their first flight young move out to branches near the nest. They remain in the vicinity of the nest, where they are fed by their parents until they become independent between seven and eight weeks after leaving the nest.

Overall productivity in the Transvaal, inclusive of nest failures caused by human interference, was 1,4 young per pair per year (157 young reared in 109 pair-years). The same result was obtained from a limited sample in Kenya. Often one young in a brood fails to survive but at a nest in Zimbabwe four well feathered young would almost certainly have flown had the nest not been destroyed. Causes of breeding failure include robbery of nests by egg-collectors and unscrupulous 'falconers'; nests being blown down; trees being chopped down; adults or young being shot at the nest; and infertile eggs. There is conflicting evidence on the effect of pesticides, but they do not appear to pose a threat at present; further investigation is needed.

42 Little Banded Goshawk *159.*

Gebande Sperwer

Accipiter badius

PLATES 14 AND 16

DERIVATION

hawk : brown — *accipiter* (L) : *badius* (L)

Outside southern Africa the name Shikra is most often used for this species. It derives from the Hindi word *shikari*, a hunter.

IDENTIFICATION

Adult: The upperparts are blue-grey and the white underparts are finely barred with russet, including the throat. The cere and legs are yellow. It appears that the eyes of males are cherry-red, those of females orange; confirmation that this distinction is invariable is required. The

two central tail feathers are plain grey so that the closed tail appears unbarred above. Four black bars are visible when the tail is spread. In flight there is no white rump. The underwing coverts are finely barred with russet, the remiges have several narrow black bars, and four black bars are visible on the white undertail.

The distinctions between this species and the Little Sparrowhawk are described under that species. The Little Banded Goshawk also has a stockier build and more plump appearance, and its toes are shorter. Possible confusion with the Ovambo Sparrowhawk is discussed under that species. It could also be mistaken for a male African Goshawk, but the two species have different habitats and habits.

Juvenile and immature: The juvenile is brown above with buff edges to the wing coverts. The breast is covered in broad russet blotches; the rest of the underparts are broadly barred with russet. There is a black line down the centre of the white throat. The tail has five blackish bars, narrower than those of the adult. The cere, eyes and legs are yellow. In flight the underwing coverts are barred with russet, and the remiges are traversed with several narrow black bars. There is no white on the rump.

Confusion with the juvenile Little Sparrowhawk should not arise, because of the different patterns on the underparts, but the white 'eye' spots on the tail of the Little Sparrowhawk would be diagnostic. The juvenile Gabar Goshawk is superficially similar but is streaked not blotched on the breast. In flight it has a white rump.

An intermediate immature plumage is acquired at the first moult. The coloration of the plumage is darker than that of the juvenile, and the markings on the breast are more boldly defined as streaks rather than blotches. Birds may breed while in immature plumage. Adult plumage is acquired by the age of two years, although the eyes may still be yellow at this stage.

HABITAT

This common species is typical of savanna habitat in Africa. It often occurs along watercourses. In the Transvaal it is found in plantations of eucalypts during the breeding season. It is absent from treeless desert and thick forest.

STATUS AND DISTRIBUTION

Some populations in Africa and elsewhere in its wide range are migratory. In southern Africa it is apparently sedentary, although there is

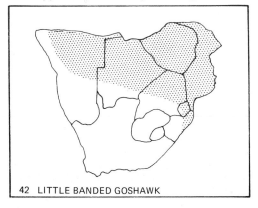

42   LITTLE BANDED GOSHAWK

some evidence of local movement, with an influx of birds to some areas in the winter months. This has been noted in Bulawayo, Zimbabwe, in the central Transvaal and in the Kruger National Park. These movements probably involve the dispersion of juveniles and immatures from their breeding areas; but further investigation is required.

It occurs widely in the north of southern Africa from Zululand across to northern Namibia. Extralimitally it is found northwards to the Sahara except for the forests of Zaire. It is widely distributed in southern Asia.

GENERAL HABITS

The Little Banded Goshawk perches within the canopy of a tree from where it hunts by dropping onto prey with a quick dash. Although capable of capturing birds in flight, it takes most of its prey on the ground. It hunts by flying from tree to tree and scanning the area before moving on. Less unobtrusive than most accipiters, it calls frequently, thus drawing attention to itself. It regularly drinks and bathes.

This species specialises in lizards, its staple diet. These are often seized when basking on the walls of buildings. Various types such as skinks and agamas are taken. In two nest studies in southern Africa Cape Rough-scaled Sand Lizards were most frequently caught; at one nest only males were brought, suggesting that their behaviour renders them more vulnerable to predation. Lizards made up 73 per cent of 91 prey items brought to a nest in the Transvaal. Insect food, including larvae, although difficult to assess quantitatively, probably ranks next in importance after lizards. Grasshoppers and termites are often eaten, the latter caught in flight and then taken to a perch to be eaten. Insects are an important part of the food of young recently out of the nest when they first hunt for themselves. Little Banded Goshawks may also be attracted to grass fires for the insects that are disturbed. Birds form a regular part of the diet and comprised 24 per cent of 91 items at the Transvaal nest mentioned above. Mostly small passerines are taken, some birds recorded being cisticolas, canaries, waxbills and weavers. Nests are also robbed of nestlings, in one instance a young Gorgeous Bush Shrike was taken and the incident was recorded by a bird photographer. Weaver nests are also sometimes raided for nestlings. Records of Little Swifts and a Palm Swift as prey must almost certainly imply predation while they were at their nests. Mammals make up a small part of the diet. These are usually small mammals such as mice, but small bats are also caught at dusk as they leave their roost. Frogs and snakes are very occasionally preyed on.

Various noisy calls are made. Frequent loud calling probably serves as territorial advertisement in a species that has a high nesting density and no regular territorial display flight. The main call of the male is a sharp repeated *ke-wick-kewick-kewick-kewick* used to make contact with the female, especially when he has prey for her. Both birds make this call when driving off other birds or mammals from near the nest. The female's main call is a plaintive repeated *kee-uu* used mainly as a soliciting call to the male. A rapidly repeated ringing *kee-kee-kee-kee* (or *tu-wi*) is made by both birds when attacking intruders near the nest, during chasing display flights and when soaring. During copulation the male utters a series of piping *wi-wi wi-wi-wi-wi* notes. Nestlings make a cheeping begging call but soon after leaving the nest they use the same soliciting call as the female.

BREEDING

Courtship consists of soaring in circles above the treetops, often to a considerable height. Undulating flights are also performed during which the wings are flapped rapidly in a fluttering manner. Chasing flights through the trees are another form of display. During all these activities the birds call noisily. The male also flies about near the perched female carrying nesting material, courtship behaviour similar to that of the Little Sparrowhawk. Feeding of the female by the male is a regular feature of courtship and is followed by copulation, often while she is still feeding. Either the male deposits prey on a branch for the female or she snatches it from him in flight. Mating takes place on regular perches near the nest during the nest-building and egg-laying period but ceases soon after the clutch is complete.

Nests are built in a main vertical fork or in a fork on a horizontal lateral branch. They are situated at heights of 5–18 m; those in eucalypts are usually high up, 13 nests in eucalypts in the Transvaal averaging 13 m above ground. Nests are flimsy structures made of small sticks about 5 mm in diameter with finer sticks and leaf petioles forming the cup. They measure 20–30 cm across, usually about 25 cm, and are 8–15 cm deep. The cup is lined with bark chips collected by the female during the egg-laying and early-incubation periods. She collects the bark by clinging to tree trunks and pulling it off with her bill. This species regularly uses numerous bark chips as a lining. One nest which was taken apart comprised 608 pieces of nest material, 174 of which were bark chips. There is one record

of an old nest of a Lizard Buzzard being taken over and lined before use; and two such records concerning the Little Sparrowhawk.

Both sexes build; at a nest in Nigeria the male did most of the construction. Before settling on a final site they may build several abortive nests. Sticks are broken off trees and carried in the bill. In addition to bark chips, twigs may be added to the nest during egg-laying and the first two weeks of the incubation period. At one nest the female added sticks when the nestlings were about two weeks old.

Although nests or nest sites are occasionally used two years in succession, the normal pattern is for a new nest to be built each year not far from a previous site. Nests tend to fall down before the following breeding season.

Nest densities may be high. In Nigeria 5 pairs occupied 6 km², an area of 1,2 km² per pair. In the Transvaal 7 nests ranged from 1,5 to 7,3 km apart, with an average of 4,7 km between nests. However, they were distributed according to the availability of suitable eucalypt plantations in the area. They bred in the same plantations as Little Sparrowhawks and Ovambo Sparrowhawks, but avoided those where Black Sparrowhawks nested. Other Little Banded Goshawks were not tolerated in the same plantation. After breeding they left the plantations.

Eggs are laid from September to November but the majority of laying records are for October. One to four eggs are laid, usually two or three; clutches of one and four eggs are rare. Eggs are dull white very variably marked with overlying red-brown spots and blotches with paler underlying red markings. Often the markings coalesce to form a cap at the large or small end, and eggs in the same nest may be quite differently marked. Some eggs are very lightly marked, others richly overlaid with red so that they resemble the eggs of a Gymnogene. Unmarked white eggs have not been recorded in southern Africa, thus eliminating any confusion with the white eggs of the Little Sparrowhawk. Measurements are: 37,0 × 29,6 (94); 33,2–43,2 × 27,4–34,2.

At one nest the two eggs were laid three days apart. Other less accurate observations suggest an interval of about two days between eggs. Incubation commences with the laying of the first egg. At a Transvaal nest with two eggs the first egg was incubated for 52 per cent of the time observed. This figure increased to 90 per cent once the clutch was complete. Most of the incubation was by the female (86 per cent) relieved for short spells (4 per cent) by the male once the clutch was complete, when he brought food for

(1) View of the nest site (arrowed) of a Little Banded Goshawk.

(2) A close-up of the nest which is lined with bark chips.

(3) A female with her nestlings of about 10 days old.

her. The longest spell by the male was 41 minutes with an average of 8 minutes. The female's longest spell was 161 minutes with an average of 40 minutes. Only the female was recorded brooding overnight. Food delivery by the male followed a typical pattern. On arrival at one of his favourite perches in the nest area he would alight and call to the female, holding the prey on the branch with one foot; the female would alight and take it from him. During daylong watches at the nest the male was observed to bring an average of seven food items a day. Most of the female's breaks from incubation were linked to prey delivery by the male. She never went far from the nest or attempted to hunt for herself, spending her time feeding, preening or perching inactively. In contrast the male spent over half of the daytime out of sight of the nest, presumably hunting. At dusk he flew off and did not roost anywhere near the nest. During incubation the female frequently changed her position and stood up to rearrange the eggs, which she would also do whenever she returned to the nest, unlike the male, who settled directly onto the eggs. Intruding birds and small mammals such as squirrels are chased away from the nest but humans are not normally attacked, although one female repeatedly struck anyone climbing to her nest.

When hatching is imminent the female is restless, frequently changing her position. At one nest she flew off and dropped a large piece of eggshell not long after the chick hatched. In the Transvaal an accurate incubation period of a few hours short of 30 days was obtained. In Nigeria a period of 28 days was established.

Newly hatched chicks are covered in pale buff-coloured down except for a whitish patch on the nape. The cere and legs are yellow, the bill is black, and the eyes are dark brown. At 10 days old the down is an off-white colour, the wing and tail quills just visible through the down. By 12 days first feathers break from the quills and by 14 days there is a V of feathers on the scapulars, and the wing and tail feathers are emerging rapidly. At about 16 days a bib of feathers appears on the upper breast. Before the age of four weeks nestlings are fully feathered and the brown eyes are changing to pale yellow.

Small chicks are weak, spending much of their time sleeping beneath the brooding female between meals. By the age of 10 days they can stand weakly to defecate; they spend most of the time preening or sleeping. The female still tears up prey and feeds them but they can swallow small lizards whole. It is not known when they first tear up prey for themselves. From the age of three weeks they perform wing exercises and jump onto branches near the nest.

When the chicks are small the female spends most of her time on the nest brooding, shading or feeding them. By the time they are 10 days old she spends more time off the nest but is always perched nearby. She still shades, broods and feeds them. However, when the nestlings are 14 days old, her time on the nest drops markedly to about 12 per cent during daytime. She still shades the young and feeds them but they are no longer brooded. She may attempt to capture prey at this stage but most of her time is spent perched in the vicinity of the nest.

There is one instance where a male brooded a day-old chick, but normally he does not visit the nest at all. His role is to provide food, a task he fulfils assiduously. During three day-long watches at a Transvaal nest the male brought an average of 8,7 prey items a day. During two short spells of observation totalling 280 minutes at a nest in Zimbabwe he brought 11 lizards, an average of one every 25 minutes, and the shortest time between consecutive captures was 5 minutes. These prey items were always handed over to the female away from the nest in the same way as during the incubation period. At one nest a 4-day-old chick was fed mainly lizards but by the age of 14 days mainly birds were brought, the larger items presumably meeting the increasing food requirements of the rapidly growing nestling. Birds are brought to the nest well plucked and quite often decapitated. Sometimes the female may cache excess prey on a favourite feeding perch, returning for it later and even retrieving it if it falls to the ground below.

A record of a nestling period of about 32 days was obtained in Nigeria, but young may flutter about in the nest tree before their first flight. Initially they return to the nest to be fed, but after two to three weeks out of the nest they can catch prey for themselves although still fed by the female. By the time they are four to five weeks out of the nest they are no longer dependent on their parents for food and catch many insects such as grasshoppers. Shortly after this they disperse from the nest area.

Breeding success in a Transvaal study was very similar to the situation in west Africa, where an average of one young per pair per year was obtained. Suspected causes of nest failure were a genet at one nest, and a Gymnogene at two other sites.

43 African Goshawk 160

Afrikaanse Sperwer
Accipiter tachiro

PLATES 15 AND 16

DERIVATION
hawk : tachiro — *accipiter* (L) : *tachiro* (L)

The name *tachiro* was given to this species by Le Vaillant and is probably a corruption of a Hottentot word. As it is a French creation, the *ch* should be pronounced as 'sh'.

IDENTIFICATION
Adult: The female is much larger than the male, sometimes almost twice his size. The barring on the white underparts extends onto the throat. Females are barred with brown, males more finely with rufous. The upperparts are dark slate or bluish-slate. The female has four dark bars on the tail; that of the male is indistinctly barred and has small white 'eye' spots on the upper surface. The eyes, cere and legs are yellow. In flight from below, the underwing coverts match the colour of the barring on the breast and there are five black bars on the remiges. The rump is plain, matching the rest of the upperparts. Possible confusion with Ovambo Sparrowhawk, Little Sparrowhawk and Little Banded Goshawk is dealt with under those species.

Juvenile and immature: The juvenile is brown above with buff edges to the wing coverts and scapulars. The white underparts are covered with brown pear-shaped blotches and some broad barring on the flanks. There is a black streak down the centre of the throat, and the eyebrow is white. The eyes are brown, the cere is greenish and the legs are yellow. The remiges and tail are barred and the rump is plain. Confusion with the juvenile Little Sparrowhawk and white-breasted juvenile Black Sparrowhawk is possible and is discussed under those species. A species that could easily be mistaken for the juvenile African Goshawk is the juvenile Cuckoo Hawk but it has short legs, wings that almost reach the tip of the tail, and a short occipital crest. In flight its outline would resemble that of a falcon rather than a sparrowhawk.

The juvenile blotching below is gradually replaced by barring, but no details are known of the period of transition to adult plumage.

HABITAT
This species is typical of forest in southern Africa although it is also found in plantations of exotic trees and thick riverine woodland.

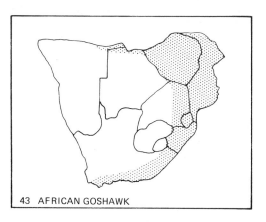

43 AFRICAN GOSHAWK

STATUS AND DISTRIBUTION
The African Goshawk is resident. Distribution extends from the south-west Cape along the eastern part of southern Africa to Mozambique, Zimbabwe, northern Botswana, the Caprivi Strip and northern Namibia. Extralimitally it extends northwards to Zaire on the west and Ethiopia on the east.

GENERAL HABITS
Because of its unobtrusive habits and forest environment, this species tends to be overlooked. However, its habit of flying high above the forest and calling in the early morning indicates its presence in an area. It hunts by stealth, flying from perch to perch where it can overlook open spaces and capture its prey in a quick dash from cover. It catches prey also by using cover to sneak up before a final surprise attack. Birds are caught in flight or on the ground.

Birds are its main prey, but small mammals are also quite often caught. As a rule it captures mainly smaller birds the size of bulbuls, but it is capable of killing a six-week-old chicken. Records of avian prey include a quail, doves, a trogon, mousebirds, a Didric Cuckoo, pipits, a shrike and weavers. Nestling birds are also taken. Mammalian prey records include forest squirrels, rats and mice. One bird chased a large bat but failed to catch it. A few reptiles such as lizards and chameleons are preyed on, and once an African Goshawk was found on the ground enmeshed by a Boomslang that it had presumably tried to capture. Other miscellaneous prey items are frogs, freshwater crabs, insects and earthworms. During nest observations in Kenya 36 birds, 15 mammals (mostly rats) and 5 reptiles were recorded.

The main call is a characteristic sharp *whit* . . . *whit* . . . *whit* repeated at two second intervals. It sounds like two rounded river stones being struck together with a glancing action. The call is made from a perch, usually high up a tall tree, or when flying at a considerable height so that the bird is often scarcely visible. The rather ventriloquial effect, especially when soaring, makes the bird difficult to locate. This call is used for contact between the pair and during territorial and courtship displays. The female also makes a drawn out *wheet-wheet* and a mewing call when soliciting the male for prey. The nestlings also make the latter call when begging for food.

BREEDING

Courtship consists of one or both birds flying about high above the trees while emitting the *whit* . . . *whit* call. After a few rapid wing-flaps the bird glides for a while, then flaps again. Slow, exaggerated wing-flaps are also used. Sometimes the soaring bird will plummet into the forest below.

Nests are built in tall trees, often along a watercourse, at about 9–20 m above the ground. They are placed in a main fork or on a lateral branch and are well concealed by surrounding foliage so that they are very difficult to detect from below. They also breed in plantations of exotics such as eucalypts or pines. One nest was built in a euphorbia. The main platform is constructed of substantial sticks with finer ones for the cup, which is copiously lined with green leaves that may cover the whole top of the nest. *Usnea* 'beard' lichens are also used for lining. Occasionally a nest is built on an existing structure, that of a Hadeda in one instance. Nests measure about 45–60 cm across and 45 cm deep with a cup 20 cm across, but sometimes nests are larger.

Both sexes build or repair the nest, for which sticks are either broken off trees or collected from the ground. Re-use of nests is variable. Sometimes new nests are built, usually not far from a previous site, at other times a nest may be used year after year, for eight consecutive years in one case. In Kenya the size of territory is not large and is estimated to be about 5 km^2. Soaring display flights, performed outside the breeding season, are a form of territorial advertisement in the same way that a Crowned Eagle displays above the forest.

Eggs are laid from September to November throughout southern Africa, with October the peak month. Two or three eggs are laid. They are plain white but become nest-stained by the end of the incubation period. They measure: 44,6 × 36,2 (33); 42,2–48,0 × 33,8–39,5.

Eggs are usually laid about two days apart, but in one instance two young hatched four days apart. The female incubates, fed by the male, and he has not been recorded to brood. She sits very tight until the nest is almost reached, but then is very wary about returning while anyone is in the vicinity. Green leaves are added to the nest throughout the incubation period. At a nest in Zimbabwe the eggs did not hatch in less than 35 days, probably very close to the actual incubation period. In Kenya the period was said to be 28–30 days, but this seems rather short.

The newly hatched chick is covered in white down. The eyes are dark brown and the cere and legs are coral red. At the age of two weeks the cere and legs are turning yellow and quills are breaking through the white down with feathers emerging from the wing quills. By three weeks feathers are breaking rapidly and at four weeks they cover the down except on the forehead and centre of the breast.

The chicks are first able to stand at about two weeks, and at 18 days old can feed themselves although the female also feeds them. Wing exercises are performed regularly from the age of three weeks and, before leaving, the young jump up onto branches near the nest.

During the early nestling period the female spends much of her time on the nest, but once the young start feathering she perches on guard in a nearby tree. The male provides most of the food, delivering it to the nest and departing immediately. Towards the end of the nestling period the female also hunts and brings prey. Fresh greenery is brought during the first three weeks of the nestling period. This species is not known to attack human intruders at the nest, tending to be rather wary. When on the nest with small young the female will crouch and puff out her feathers in threat if other raptors pass overhead.

Two nestling periods in southern Africa were not less than 32 and 35 days. The young remain near the nest for the first few days after flying, and roost on the nest or in the nest tree. They remain in the vicinity of the nest for about two months after their first flight before becoming independent.

There is no information on breeding success in southern Africa, but in 6 pair-years in Kenya 9 young were reared, or 1,5 young per pair per year.

44 Gabar Goshawk 161.

Witkruissperwer
Micronisus gabar

PLATES 14 AND 16

DERIVATION

small : sparrowhawk : gabar — *mikros* (G) : *Neisos* (G) : *gabar* (L)

Neisos was a legendary king of Megara in Greece, whose daughter Scylla proved her love for Poseidon by cutting off her father's purple hair, thus destroying his magical powers. He was transmuted into a sparrowhawk in compensation. Thus *nisus* is derived from Neisos and the European Sparrowhawk is known as *Accipiter nisus*.

The name *gabar* was given to this species by Francois Le Vaillant and is probably derived from a Hottentot word. The first syllable should be pronounced 'gar' as in garden.

IDENTIFICATION

Adult: Both grey and melanistic forms occur. The former are grey above and on the head and upper breast. The rest of the underparts are finely barred grey on white. The bill is black, the cere and legs are red, and the eyes are dark red-brown so that they appear wholly dark from a distance. In flight the underwing coverts are barred grey and white and the remiges are traversed by narrow black bars. The tail has four black bars and there is a broad band of white on the rump.

The most likely confusion is with the Lizard Buzzard, but this species is more stockily built and has a white throat with a black line down the centre. In flight both show a white rump, but the Lizard Buzzard has a single white bar on its tail a third of the way in from the tip. The plumage pattern of the Gabar Goshawk is similar to that of the Pale Chanting Goshawk and Dark Chanting Goshawk but both of these are very much larger, have very long legs, and their habits are different. Confusion with adult Ovambo Sparrowhawk, Little Banded Goshawk and Little Sparrowhawk ought not to arise as these species are all barred on the breast.

Melanistic birds are wholly black except for black and white barring on the primaries and faint white bars on the tail. There is no white rump. The eyes are dark red-brown and the cere and legs are red, the latter usually with black blotching. Distinctions between this species and melanistic Ovambo Sparrowhawks

and Black Sparrowhawks are discussed under those species.

Some books state that the melanistic form of the Gabar Goshawk occurs commonly, but the only analysis of the frequency of plumage types is from the Kruger National Park, where 14 birds out of 216 (6,5 per cent) were melanistic.

An albinistic individual has once been recorded in the Kruger National Park.

Juvenile and immature: Juveniles of the grey form are brown above with buff edges to the wing coverts. The underparts are washed pale buff with vertical red-brown streaking on the breast, and red-brown barring on the lower breast and abdomen. The eyes are grey on leaving the nest but soon turn pale yellow. The legs are yellow and the cere is dark grey. The underwing coverts are barred with red-brown and the remiges are narrowly barred with black. The tail is barred and the rump is white as in the adult. Confusion with the Little Banded Goshawk is possible and differences are described under that species.

Juveniles of the melanistic form develop directly into black plumage, the only difference being that the legs are yellow, not red as in the adult.

The juvenile plumage of the grey form is followed by an intermediate stage in which the underparts are white with more defined sepia-brown streaking on the breast and broader sepia-brown barring on the lower breast and abdomen. The eye is yellow. Details are required on the length of time taken to assume adult plumage.

HABITAT

This species occurs in savanna and is most frequently found in *Acacia* woodland, especially where there are taller trees.

STATUS AND DISTRIBUTION

Although it is apparently resident, seasonal fluctuations have been recorded in the Kruger National Park, where the numbers of birds increase from March to July. This increase is mainly the result of the dispersion of young birds after the breeding season.

Distribution extends throughout southern Africa in suitable habitat except for the extreme

(1) View of the nest site (arrowed) and habitat of a Gabar Goshawk.

(2) This nest has been completely covered with web by a colonial spider.

(3) A day-old nestling.

(4) First quills appear through the down at 9 days old.

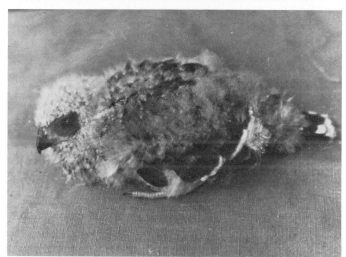

(5) By 17 days old feathers are emerging rapidly.

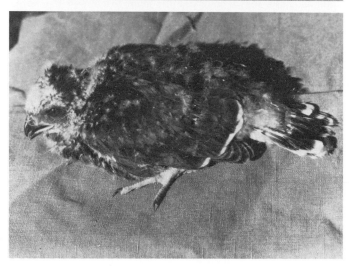

(6) The 21-day-old nestling is almost fully feathered.

south-west Cape. Extralimitally its range extends northwards to the Sahara and it also occurs in southern Arabia.

GENERAL HABITS

The Gabar Goshawk is usually seen perched within the canopy of a tree, or flying swiftly from one tree to the next, and it rarely soars. Two birds are often seen together outside the breeding season and paired birds probably remain together throughout the year. Three hunting methods are used: active pursuit, still-hunting and nest-robbing. Sometimes they may also hunt on foot, probably when prey has taken refuge in thick cover. Active pursuit involves prospecting flights, usually through trees, until prey is flushed and then pursued with great speed and agility. Considerable persistence may be shown, and in one case a small barbet was chased for one and a half minutes before it was eventually captured. In another incident a Striped Kingfisher was chased for a distance of 90 m before capture. Birds are normally taken in flight. When still-hunting the bird sits motionless within the canopy of a tree, watching the surrounding area, and then launches a surprise attack. Nest-robbing is a regular form of predation. In one incident which was photographed a five-day-old Laughing Dove was killed by being pecked on the neck before being removed. When robbing enclosed nests of weavers, waxbills and White-browed Sparrow-weavers, two techniques are used. Either a hole is pecked in the roof of the nest or, particularly in the case of suspended weavers' nests, the bird will hang upside down flapping and extract the nestling with its bill (in one instance it appeared as if the foot was used). The goshawk often watches a weaver colony before flying to a nest and probably uses the activities of the weavers and the calling of the young as a guide to occupied nests. Sometimes a large nestling flies off when the nest is inspected and it is then chased and caught. One immature Gabar Goshawk tried unsuccessfully to rob Sociable Weaver nests.

The main prey is birds, usually smaller species such as weavers, barbets, kingfishers, pipits and the smaller starlings. It also takes the chicks of francolins. However, it is capable of killing larger birds such as Cape Turtle Dove, White-browed Coucal and Crested Francolin. The francolin had recently been killed and weighed 238 g. The female goshawk responsible was trapped a short while later and weighed 207 g. This is the largest-known kill of this species in the wild, although a bird trained for falconry caught a Swainson's Francolin of approximately 450 g but was unable to kill it.

Small mammals such as mice are also occasionally caught. In one remarkable incident a Gabar Goshawk caught a bat almost as large as itself. Having difficulty in killing the bat, it flew to a small stream where the bat was held under water until it drowned.

A few reptiles such as lizards and small snakes have been recorded as prey. Once a bird was found on the ground entwined in the coils of a 75-cm snake which it may have attacked originally. Insects also form part of the diet, but it is difficult to assess their importance.

The call of this species is a rapidly repeated, high-pitched *kik-kik-kik-kik*, used when chasing other birds from near the nest, during courtship and as contact between male and female. It is also made by nestlings from the age of about 10 days.

BREEDING

At the onset of the breeding season the male calls a great deal from perches in his territory. Courtship takes the form of chasing flights through the trees, and the male also brings prey for the female.

Nests are placed in vertical forks in the upper branches of trees, especially acacias. They are usually 6–12 m above ground, although some nests are higher. Nests are small structures built with small sticks and they measure 25–30 cm across and about 15 cm deep with a shallow depression about 12 cm across. This depression is lined with finer twigs and spider nests. An interesting feature of nest construction is the deliberate incorporation in the early stages of nests of a colonial spider *Stegodyphus* sp. As the nesting cycle progresses the spiders cover with web the whole outside of the nest and sometimes even the surrounding branches. The function of this behaviour is probably to provide camouflage, although there may be other explanations. In Kenya there is a record of the nest of a Pale Chanting Goshawk being used, to which the Gabar Goshawks had made no additions so that no cobwebs were present.

There are few detailed observations on nest construction but at a nest in Kenya the female did most of the building. Nest construction takes about four to six weeks; at one nest it took a month from first construction until eggs were laid. New nests are built each year, never very far from a previous site. Sometimes a previous nest site may be used again after a lapse of years.

Little is known about the size of the nesting territory, but a pair in Zimbabwe occupied a copse of acacias about a hectare in extent year after year. Large birds such as Grey Loeries and birds of prey are chased away from the vicinity of the nest.

Eggs are laid from late August to November but most breeding records are for September and October. Two to four eggs are laid, usually three, and they are white with a bluish tinge when freshly laid. As incubation progresses they become nest-stained with yellowish marks. Measurements are: 39,8 × 31,0 (58); 37,2–43,8 × 28,0–32, 8.

Further observations are required on the laying interval between eggs and the commencement of incubation. At one nest eggs were laid two to three days apart and the chicks hatched at intervals, indicating that incubation commenced with the laying of the first egg. However, at another nest with two eggs the young hatched on the same day. Both sexes incubate but nothing is known of the extent of the male's share. On leaving the nest the sitting bird drops down steeply almost to ground level before swooping up into another tree. The same swooping approach is used when returning to the nest. The flight is silent. This species is not known to attack observers although it may fly past nearby. The incubation period is approximately 33–35 days but more accurate observations are required.

Newly hatched chicks of the grey form are covered in white down, those of the melanistic form in smoky-grey down. In the grey form the bill is black, cere and legs are orange-red and the eyes dark brown. The colour of the soft parts of newly hatched melanistic nestlings is not recorded. The account which follows deals with the grey form, but feather development of melanistic nestlings would be the same. First quills appear on the wings at the age of 7 days and the white down has changed to pale greyish. At 10 days old the down is darker greyish, the cere is turning grey and the legs are turning

yellow. First feathers are just appearing from the wing quills and on the scapulars. By 14 days old feathers are emerging rapidly from the wing and tail quills and to a lesser extent on the head, wing coverts and scapulars. The cere is grey and the legs are deeper yellow. At 17 days feathers are emerging rapidly from their quills and first feathers appear on the sides of the breast. Rapid feather growth takes place and by the age of 21 days the upperparts are completely feathered except for the forehead. The underparts are feathered except for a downy patch on the crop and down the centre of the abdomen. By the age of 28 days the body is fully feathered except for a small patch of down on the forehead.

It is not known when the young first stand, but they can stand well at the age of three weeks, by which stage they are performing vigorous wing exercises. They open their gapes in threat at intruders from the age of two weeks and even attempt to strike at them with their claws. Young may leave the nest to perch on branches nearby from the age of 26 days but they still return to the nest to be fed.

Parental behaviour during the nestling period has not been thoroughly studied, but the few observations that have been made indicate that behaviour is similar to that of other accipiters. The male's role is to supply the nestlings with food which the female collects from him near the nest. She remains on the nest for about the first two weeks, brooding, shading and feeding the chicks, but by 17 days she perches nearby and comes to the nest only to feed them. She still feeds them when they are three weeks old; it is not known at what stage they feed themselves.

The nestlings fly through the branches of the nest tree from about 30 days and may leave the nest tree at this stage, although they normally make their first long flight at about 35 days old. There are no observations on the post-nestling period or breeding success.

45 Pale Chanting Goshawk 162.

Bleek-singvalk
Melierax canorus

PLATES 15 AND 18

DERIVATION
song : hawk : melodious — *melos* (G) : *hierax* (G) : *canorus* (L)

The English name derives from *faucon chanteur* given to it by Francois Le Vaillant.

IDENTIFICATION
Adult: The upperparts, head and breast are grey with paler grey on the wing coverts. The rest of the underparts are finely barred grey and white. The bill is black, the cere and legs are

red, and the eyes are dark brown although they appear black at a distance. The long legs and upright stance also aid identification. In flight there are three black bars on the white outer-tail feathers and a broad white band on the rump. From above, the secondaries are white, contrasting with the black primaries. From below, the coverts are faintly barred with grey but the underwing pattern appears mainly white with dark tips. The pattern is similar to that of a male Pallid Harrier but the longer, thinner wings and the mode of flight immediately distinguish the harrier.

The most likely confusion is with the Dark Chanting Goshawk, although the distribution of the two species is largely mutually exclusive in southern Africa. However, there are areas where they overlap. They are more difficult to identify when perched but the paler wing coverts of the Pale Chanting Goshawk help to distinguish it from the uniformly darker grey Dark Chanting Goshawk. In flight the latter's rump is barred, not pure white, and it lacks white secondaries.

Juvenile and immature: The juvenile is brown above with pale buff edges to the wing coverts. Below it is white, heavily blotched with brown on the breast and barred with brown on the rest of the underparts. It appears mainly brown below. The bill is black, the cere dark orange or blackish, the legs are dull orange-yellow and the eyes pale yellow. In flight it has four bars on the tail and a broad white rump. The underwing coverts are mottled brown and white and the remiges are traversed above and below with narrow black bars.

The juvenile Dark Chanting Goshawk is darker brown and has a more distinct brown gorget. In flight it has narrow grey-brown barring on the white rump, a feature which immediately distinguishes it from the Pale Chanting Goshawk.

There are no observations on the transition from juvenile to adult plumage and this is an aspect which needs to be studied. The legs turn red before adult plumage is acquired.

HABITAT

This species is common and widely distributed in areas of low rainfall in southern Africa. It is a typical Karoo raptor and is also found in true desert. Where it occurs alongside the Dark Chanting Goshawk it inhabits more arid open scrub whereas the other is found in adjoining woodland.

STATUS AND DISTRIBUTION

It is resident throughout its range; statements

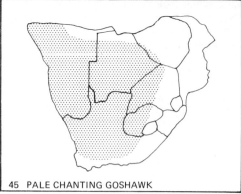

45 PALE CHANTING GOSHAWK

that some birds move northwards in southern Africa in winter require confirmation.

Distribution extends over much of southern Africa except for the south-west Cape and the moister eastern littoral regions. It is absent from Natal and Mozambique and most of Zimbabwe except in the south-west. In the Transvaal it is confined to the west and extreme north. Its range overlaps that of the Dark Chanting Goshawk in the northern Transvaal, northern Botswana and south-western Zimbabwe.

Extralimitally it extends into southern Angola. In east and north-east Africa the Pale Chanting Goshawk is regarded as a separate species *Melierax poliopterus* by some authorities because its range is widely separated from that of the southern population and it is smaller with differences in plumage. Others consider it merely a race *Melierax canorus poliopterus*.

GENERAL HABITS

Pale Chanting Goshawks are regularly seen in the same areas, pairs probably remaining together throughout the year. They always perch on a prominent vantage point such as a tree, fence post or telegraph pole, where they remain for long periods, even in the midday heat, before moving to another perch. Direct flight from one point to another is with rapid shallow wing-beats interspersed with glides. At other times they fly with slow elastic wing-beats like a harrier but they are also capable of flying very fast in pursuit of birds.

Hunting is done mainly from a perch, and prey is captured by gliding down slowly and catching it with the talons on the ground. Quite often they hunt on foot, running rapidly in pursuit of prey at times; mainly insects are caught by this means. Although generally considered a sluggish species, it is capable of capturing birds in flight. A Harlequin Quail was caught after a 100-m chase and in another incident a Crowned Plover was taken in flight. In the Kalahari Gemsbok National Park they have been observed on a number of occasions following foraging Honey Badgers for animals they may disturb. One case of piracy is recorded where a goshawk robbed a kestrel of a pipit. Conversely they are sometimes the victims of piratical attacks by Tawny Eagles.

There is no quantitative study of prey in southern Africa, but prey preferences are probably similar to those of Pale Chanting Goshawks in Kenya, where lizards are most often caught. Insects are next in frequency followed by birds and small mammals. In southern Africa carrion, particularly from road kills, is a regular source of food. In addition to lizards, snakes are also caught. Various insects are eaten but are not easily identified. Dung beetles, grasshoppers and harvester termites have been recorded. Various small birds are preyed on but larger kills such as Crested Francolin, Red-crested Korhaan and Spotted Eagle Owl are on record. A Rock Kestrel that stunned itself by flying into telegraph wires was quickly caught and killed by a nearby goshawk. Chickens round farm homesteads are sometimes eaten. Small mammals such as mice are caught; it is also capable of killing hares. Thus, while this species subsists mainly on smaller prey, it is capable of killing birds and mammals heavier than itself.

Except in the breeding season, this species is largely silent. Its name derives from its melodious chanting call, a loud piping *kleeu-kleeu-kleeu-klu-klu-klu* . . . which accelerates and becomes tremulous towards the end. It is made by both sexes either perched or in flight, throughout the breeding season, most frequently during display and nest building. This call is also made by nestlings from the age of seven weeks. Birds begin calling at first light, when, from a distance, the chanting could be mistaken for the call of a Fiery-necked Nightjar. Other calls recorded are: a musical *chee-chit, chee-chit* emitted by a bird flying with exaggerated shallow wing-beats, probably a courtship flight; a soft, unmelodious, squeaking *see-see-see-see* varying in pitch, made early in the breeding season; a low, rapid *ke-ke-ke-ke-ke* made by the female soliciting the male for prey and by nestlings; a chuckling *kja-kja-kja-kja-kja*, probably a variant of the previous call, used while arranging nest material; a vibrating wailing used as an alarm call and when chasing other birds of prey from the vicinity of the nest.

BREEDING

The account which follows is based to a large extent on breeding observations on the Pale Chanting Goshawk in Kenya. No study of breeding biology in southern Africa has been made.

During the early part of the breeding season the male and female call to each other for long periods in what may be termed a static form of courtship. They also call while soaring in circles, and undulating flights are occasionally performed. The male may carry a stick in his bill while flying around. A chasing flight, the male closely following the erratic weaving flight of the female, is another form of courtship, during which the male holds his tail fanned to show the black and white barring on the outer tail feathers. Copulation has been observed in the early stages of the breeding cycle as well as during the incubation period, and once in the early part of the nestling period.

Nests are usually placed beneath the canopy in a vertical fork, but some are situated on the tops of thorn trees, often hidden by creeper. They are 2,5–9 m above the ground, usually about 6–9 m. Nests are platforms made of pencil-thick sticks and are about 40 cm across but varying in depth from flat platforms to fairly bulky structures. The central depression is lined with miscellaneous items such as dung, rags, mud clods, grass, hair, pieces of skin and sheep's wool. In South Africa some nests are lined with a thick pad of wool. Cobwebs are not used in the construction of the nest.

Both sexes take an active part in building the nest. In one case many sticks were taken from buffalo weaver nests nearby. One nest took about a month to construct. Additions to the nest may be made during the incubation period and early part of the nestling period. Nests may be re-used or new ones constructed nearby.

In Kenya breeding pairs occupied areas of approximately 1,5–2,5 km². They were not aggresive towards conspecifics but other birds of prey near nests were driven away.

Eggs are laid from July to October in southern Africa but the number of breeding records is limited and the season may in fact be more extended. In Kenya two broods may be raised in a year but observations in our area are too scanty to know whether this occurs here too. One or two eggs are laid but confirmation of three-egg clutches is required. Eggs are white, greenish-white when very fresh. Measurements of southern African eggs are: 57,7 × 44,1 (15); 55,7–60,0 × 42,0–44,6.

In a clutch of two the eggs are laid a few days apart but there are no precise observations. Incubation is apparently mostly by the female, although a male was once seen to sit for ten minutes. When it is hot she may stand over the eggs shading them. When someone approaches, the female slips off the nest unobtrusively. The male brings food for the female, and avian prey is well plucked first. The incubation period is between 36 and 38 days.

When two eggs are laid, usually only one chick is reared. In Kenya the second egg or chick disappeared soon after the first chick hatched. Observations are required to establish whether sibling aggression occurs, but in Namibia there is a record of two young being reared together.

The newly hatched chick is covered in grey down above and white below with long hair-like plumes on the head and shorter ones on the back. The bill is black, the cere greyish and the legs are pale yellow. The eyes are brownish-grey changing to pale grey by about two weeks old and are yellowish by the time the nestling leaves the nest. The wing and tail quills are the first to emerge in the third week, followed by the scapulars. The feathers of the underparts emerge from four weeks on and form a distinct pattern of feathers on the upper breast with two lines of feathers extending from the shoulder to the abdomen. It is still downy on the crop, underwing coverts and on the head. At six weeks old it is fully feathered.

There are few details on parental care. Initially the female broods and tends the chick, and the male supplies prey. Quite early in the nestling period the female ceases brooding the chick and perches on guard near the nest, feeding it when prey is brought. Once the chick is about two weeks old she may also catch prey but she does not go far from the nest. By the end of the nestling period the male may take prey directly to the nest; once he fed a month-old nestling.

The young leave the nest between seven and eight weeks. During the first two weeks after the first flight they remain very close to the nest or even return to it. They are fed by their parents but they also catch insects for themselves in rather clumsy fashion. After two weeks the juveniles move farther afield but remain with their parents for at least another five weeks and probably longer.

There are no observations on breeding success. The breeding biology of this widespread and common southern African raptor is poorly known and further study would prove rewarding.

46 Dark Chanting Goshawk *163.*

Donker-singvalk
Melierax metabates

PLATES 15 AND 18

DERIVATION
song : hawk : changed — *melos* (G) : *hierax* (G) : *metabates* (G)

IDENTIFICATION
Adult: This species resembles the Pale Chanting Goshawk when perched but is uniformly darker grey on breast, head and upperparts and it does not have paler grey wing coverts. The colour of the soft parts of the two species is the same. In flight it may be distinguished by the fine grey barring on the white rump and by the plain grey secondaries. The tips of the wings are black but do not contrast with the rest of the wing as much as in the Pale Chanting Goshawk, which has a mainly pale wing.

Juvenile and immature: Although the pattern of the plumage is similar to that of the juvenile Pale Chanting Goshawk, it is darker with the gorget more clearly defined. The upperparts are grey-brown, the breast is brown with some white flecking and forms a distinct gorget whereas the rest of the underparts are distinctly barred brown and white. The bill is black, the cere greyish, the legs are dull orange and the eyes pale lemon-yellow. In flight the tail is broadly barred and the white rump has fine grey-brown barring, this latter feature being the most reliable distinction between it and the juvenile Pale Chanting Goshawk. The underwing coverts are mottled brown and white and the remiges are traversed by narrow black bars.

As with the Pale Chanting Goshawk, there is no information on the transition from juvenile to adult plumage.

HABITAT
This species inhabits a variety of woodland habitats in contrast to the Pale Chanting Goshawk, found in more open dry country. Where their distribution overlaps they tend to stay in different habitats (see under Pale Chanting Goshawk).

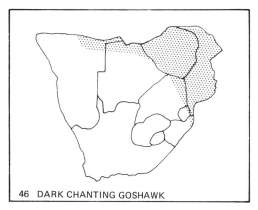

46 DARK CHANTING GOSHAWK

STATUS AND DISTRIBUTION

It is resident, occurring in northern Namibia, northern Botswana, Zimbabwe, northern and north-eastern Transvaal, eastern Swaziland, Zululand (rarely) and Mozambique. Extralimitally it is widely distributed northwards to the Sahara but not in the forested regions of Zaire or the dry north-east. It is also found in southern Arabia. An isolated race occurs in south-west Morocco.

GENERAL HABITS

The habits and hunting methods of this species are similar to those of the Pale Chanting Goshawk. However, as it lives in a less open environment, it does not forage on foot to the same extent. Although further observations are required, the prey preferences of the two species also appear to be similar. A number of random records indicate that lizards are its main prey and it also eats small snakes. It is capable of killing birds the size of a Natal Francolin or a Crowned Guineafowl. Small mammals such as mice and a Tree Squirrel have been recorded. Insects are also eaten. Like the Pale Chanting Goshawk it feeds also on carrion, a Spotted Eagle Owl killed by a car in one instance and in another a White-faced Owl which died when its wing caught on a barbed-wire fence.

The chanting call is similar to that of the Pale Chanting Goshawk but there are no detailed observations on other calls used during the breeding cycle. Like that species it is largely silent outside the breeding season. The downy nestling makes a drawn-out peeping begging call.

BREEDING

Courtship consists of prolonged calling from a perch, and soaring flights. Undulating and chasing flights have not been recorded, but as the breeding biology of the Dark Chanting Goshawk is little known they may occur.

The nest is a substantial platform of sticks placed in the main fork of a tree within the canopy about 5–9 m above ground. It measures about 35–60 cm across and the shallow central depression is lined with miscellaneous soft materials: dung, grass, spider nests, a sunbird's nest, a penduline tit's nest, fur and rags have been recorded. An interesting feature is that the outside of the nest may be festooned with cobwebs like that of the Gabar Goshawk, although the presence of web is not as invariable as in that species. The way they are covered indicates the activities of colonial spiders, but there are no direct observations to establish whether these nests are deliberately placed among the sticks in the early stages of construction, as is the case with the Gabar Goshawk. Both sexes build the nest but there are no observations on their share in this activity.

Eggs are laid from August to November but the majority of records are from Zimbabwe, where there is a laying peak in September and October. One or two eggs are laid, a single egg at least as often as two. The eggs are white, becoming nest-stained as incubation progresses. Measurements are: 52,5 × 41,6 (45); 47,0–57,8 × 39,0–45,5.

At one nest the second egg was laid about three days after the first, and incubation commenced with the laying of the first egg. As far as is known, only the female incubates and she slips off the nest secretively when an observer is still some distance away. The incubation period is not recorded but will probably be found to be similar to that of the Pale Chanting Goshawk (36–38 days).

Normally only one chick is reared. Obser-

View of the nest site (arrowed) of a Dark Chanting Goshawk.

(1) Nest of a Dark Chanting Goshawk with a newly hatched chick; an agama lizard lies on the nest behind the egg.

(2) At three weeks old the feathers are emerging rapidly; note the fine hair-like plumes on the head.

(3) By six weeks old the nestling is fully feathered.

vations are needed to establish whether any sibling aggression occurs where two chicks hatch. The newly hatched chick is covered in greyish down above and white down below. On the head and back there are fine hair-like plumes. The bill is blackish, the cere and legs are pale orange-red and the eyes are brown. At three weeks the cere is grey tinged orange at the base, the legs are pale orange and the eyes grey. Feathers are breaking rapidly from wing and tail quills and on the scapulars, wing coverts, throat and down the sides of the breast and ab-domen. By six weeks old the nestling is fully feathered and the cere is grey, the legs are dull orange and the eyes pale lemon-yellow.

There are no observations on parental care during the nestling period. At one nest the nestling moved out onto branches of the nest tree when 43 days old but returned to the nest periodically. It first flew from the nest tree when 50 days old. Nothing is known about the post-nestling period. The breeding biology of this species is poorly known and further information is needed.

---

47 European Marsh Harrier *164*

Europese Vleivalk

Circus aeruginosus

PLATES 17 AND 18

DERIVATION

hawk : rusty (coloured) — *kirkos* (G) : *aeruginosus* (L)

IDENTIFICATION

Adult: This large harrier is sexually dimorphic. Males are dull rufous below with indistinct streaking on the breast, and the head is pale greyish in contrast to the rest of the upperparts which are dark brown except for the blue-grey secondaries and tail. The eyes, cere and legs are yellow. In flight from below, the underwing coverts are rufous (almost white in old males), the remiges white with no barring, the wing tips black and the tail is grey. From above, the flight pattern is also diagnostic and the dark brown wing coverts and back contrast with the blue-grey remiges and tail. The primaries are black at the tips. The male cannot be mistaken for any other raptor in southern Africa.

The female is chocolate-brown with a creamy-white head and a mask of brown running through the eye. The 'shoulders' of the wings are also white. Many birds lack white on the throat; others are entirely uniform chocolate-brown. The soft parts are coloured as in the male. In flight both colour forms show no barring on the uniform brown wings and tail. White-headed and white-shouldered birds may possibly be confused with adult and juvenile African Marsh Harriers. They differ from the former in their dark brown, not rufous, coloration and in the absence of any barring on wings and tail. Juvenile African Marsh Harriers are also dark brown with some white on the head but they have a band of white on the chest and barring on remiges and tail. Uniform brown females might be confused with other plain brown raptors but their typical flight and hunting behaviour distinguish them as harriers and there is no other uniform dark brown harrier with which they could be confused in our area.

Juvenile and immature: Except for their dark brown eyes both male and female juveniles resemble adult females and can be either white on head and 'shoulders' or uniform brown. Little is known about progression to adult plumage but males start a gradual moult into adult plumage in their second year.

HABITAT

This species is found in marshy country or in adjacent open grassland. Its habitat requirements are very similar to those of the African Marsh Harrier, and the two species overlap in the summer months.

STATUS AND DISTRIBUTION

This Palearctic migrant is a scarce visitor to the north of our area from early October to February. Most records are from around Salisbury in Zimbabwe but it has also been recorded in Botswana, the Transvaal and Mozambique. The only specimen was collected at Potchefstroom in December 1869 by Thomas Ayres, but as this species is so distinct there is no reason to doubt sight records from observers of proven reliability. Most sightings in southern Africa have been of females or juveniles. The

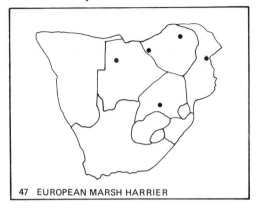

47   EUROPEAN MARSH HARRIER

European Marsh Harrier breeds from western Europe to about Lake Baikal in central Asia, and this population winters in Africa and India. Other races are widely distributed throughout the Old World including islands in the Pacific.

GENERAL HABITS

The European Marsh Harrier is usually seen hunting solitarily by quartering low over the grass or reeds and dropping down suddenly with a twist when quarry is sighted. Despite its solitary habits it has been recorded roosting communally with Pallid and Montagu's Harriers in Kenya. One bird hunting in the same area as an African Marsh Harrier was seen to fight with the resident species.

In Europe its prey consists of mammals, birds, amphibians, reptiles, insects and carrion. There are no records of prey in southern Africa but elsewhere in Africa its diet has included small Water Monitors (Leguaans), rodents, a bat roosting in reeds, birds' eggs, a Lesser Gallinule, young waterfowl, queleas and grasshoppers. In the Transvaal one struck a Cattle Egret but did not kill it. Being larger, this harrier probably takes bigger prey than the African Marsh Harrier.

48 African Marsh Harrier   165.

Afrikaanse Vleivalk

Circus ranivorus

PLATES 17 AND 18

DERIVATION

hawk : frog : eat — *kirkos* (G) : *rana* (L) : *vorare* (L)

IDENTIFICATION

Adult: The sexes are alike in plumage but the female is larger than the male. The upperparts are brown with prominent patches of white dappling on the 'shoulders' of the wings. The feathers of the face form a distinct disc outlined by white feathers. The breast is brown with white streaks and merges into plain rufous on the abdomen and thighs. The tail is brown above with bold black bars; on the underside it is dull silver-grey and the bars are indistinct. The eyes, cere and bare legs are yellow. In flight from below, the underwing coverts are buff with brown streaking and the white remiges are broadly barred with black. On the upper surface the boldly barred tail, plain rufous rump and white on the leading edges of the wings are characteristic. Possible confusion with females of the European Marsh Harrier, Montagu's Harrier and Pallid Harrier is discussed under these species.

Juvenile and immature: The juvenile is mainly chocolate-brown with some buff edges to the feathers of the upperparts, particularly on the 'shoulders' of the wings. There is a variable amount of white on the throat and nape and a distinct ragged band of white across the breast. The abdomen and flanks are dark rufous. In flight the tail is faintly barred with black and is dark brown above and greyish below. The underwing coverts are dark rufous and the remiges are grey with black barring. The eyes are dark brown and the cere and legs yellow. It could be confused with the female European Marsh Harrier; differences are dealt with in the text on that species. No details are known on the time taken to acquire full adult plumage.

HABITAT

This harrier is found in marshlands, including expanses of wet grassland. Although it occurs mainly in an aquatic habitat, it also ranges into dry surrounding country to hunt.

STATUS AND DISTRIBUTION

As fas as is known this species is resident, although in some localities it may be forced to move to other areas when grassfires destroy its habitat.

In some localities, for example the southwest Cape, it has become a rare species through

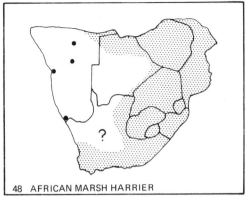

48 AFRICAN MARSH HARRIER

loss of its marshland habitat. There is no doubt that it requires urgent conservation attention in some regions.

Its distribution is mainly confined to the moist south and east of southern Africa and it is rare or absent in the dry central and western regions. Extralimitally it occurs northwards to Kenya.

GENERAL HABITS

The African Marsh Harrier is usually seen singly as it quarters at about 5–10 m above the ground. On seeing prey it checks suddenly and drops onto it. It also hunts with fast downwind rushes, using the lie of the land such as a stream bed to catch prey by surprise. Sometimes it catches fish in shallow water by snatching them from just below the surface. There are also records of its catching wounded birds shot by hunters. Low perches are used for resting but it appears to do all its hunting on the wing. It soars well, often to a considerable height, but does not hunt while soaring. During the breeding season the male and female each have their own roosting place or form. One observer suspected that several non-breeding birds were roosting communally in one patch of grass after fire removed the surrounding cover.

Prey consists mainly of rats, mice and birds. It also catches small reptiles, frogs, insects and occasionally fish. Carrion is also eaten. The largest prey caught is avian; there are reliable records of this species killing adult Red-billed Teal and Cape Teal. One Yellow-billed Duck was struck but not killed. Other avian prey records include Speckled Pigeon, Laughing Dove (11 at the plucking-post of one male), Black Crake, African Crake, Ruff, an adult and nestling Marsh Owl and various small passerines. Young birds are often caught and it also raids the nests of herons and egrets for small chicks or to eat their eggs. It is partial to eggs when available and will also visit deserted nests to eat

them. Reptiles and frogs are rarely caught; the only two records of the former are a 45 cm snake and a chameleon.

During courtship the male emits a soft *to woot* and the female a soft *chip*. A *kwerr* note and soft chuckling noises are also used. Before roosting the birds utter a very soft *chuck* note. A harsh chattering *yak-yak-yak* is used in alarm when the nest is inspected and a croaking noise is emitted during distraction behaviour. A sharp *pew* is emitted by the male just before a food-pass. Feathered nestlings make a soft whistling begging call.

BREEDING

Nuptial display consists of soaring to a great height during which the male dives down at the female who turns and presents her claws to him. Both sexes may perform 'skydancing' undulating flights, although the male quite often displays on his own. Soaring displays may sometimes involve neighbouring birds, perhaps as the result of mutual stimulation. One case of suspected polygamy has been recorded where two females were breeding simultaneously on one small vlei with apparently only a single male in attendance.

Nest sites are variable depending on habitat. They may be in dense reed beds or in fairly short grass, usually over or near water. In tall reeds the nest may be 1,2–1,5 m above the water, in shorter vegetation as low as about 40 cm. One pair in the south-west Cape bred in a wheatfield and another on a low bushy tree 3 m off the ground, an apparently unique site. The structure of nests depends on the site. In tall reeds a base of sticks or reeds is built and thickly lined with dry vegetable material. In grassland the nest may be mainly a pad of dry grasses with a few sticks as base material. It measures about 45–60 cm across, the depth depending on the situation. There is a central cup about 23 cm across in the thick pad of lining which covers the top of the nest.

At one nest the presumed female was seen to do all the building during a short watch. However, a male brought a stick to another nest during the incubation period and thus probably also assists with the initial construction. Several abortive nests may be built, as many as six in two weeks by one pair, before the final site is selected. Lining is added throughout the incubation period and sporadically during the nestling period.

Nests deteriorate rapidly after the breeding season and are only used once. However, in subsequent years nests are built in the same area.

(1) A female African Marsh Harrier shades her nestlings on a nest in dense reeds.

(2) Close-up of a nest.

(3) A nestling of about three weeks old; there are four infertile eggs in the nest.

There is little information on territory except that three pairs nested simultaneously at the points of a triangle each 3 km from the others. One nest was found 10 m from that of a Grass Owl which the harriers chased when it was flushed. Passing Marsh Owls may also be chased. Other African Marsh Harriers are driven away from the nest area.

South of the Limpopo eggs are laid mainly from June to November with a distinct September/October peak in the south-west Cape (65 per cent of 49 records for that area). In Zimbabwe eggs are laid from December to June. The eggs are rounded and white, some with a few red marks, and they become heavily nest-stained by the end of the incubation period. Three to six eggs are laid, usually three or four, a clutch of six being recorded on only two occasions. Measurements are: 46,6 × 37,1 (121); 41,0–54,5 × 32,4–40,3.

The intervals between the eggs of a clutch are not known accurately, although the young hatch about one to two days apart in most observations, and incubation thus presumably begins with the first egg. Most of the incubation is by the female, but a male was seen to brood for a short period at one nest. The female sits very tight, relying on the surrounding cover to conceal her, and she flushes at the last moment. She is fed by the male and leaves the nest to take food from him in an aerial food-pass. The incubation period at one nest was between 31 and 34 days and the indications were that it was probably close on 33 days.

Although the young hatch at intervals, there is no evidence of sibling aggression. However, the smallest chick of a brood may sometimes die, presumably from starvation. The newly hatched chick is covered in white down and has a black bill, dull yellow cere, dark brown eyes and pink legs. At 10 days old the down is buff-coloured and first feathers are appearing on the remiges. The legs are yellow. By 15 days brown feathers are breaking on the scapulars, the tail feathers are emerging and there is a dark patch of feathers on the ear coverts. From three weeks feathers appear rapidly and cover the body by the time it is a month old. The last remaining down is on the forehead.

The nestling shows threat towards intruders from about the age of 18 days. It can stand by the age of three weeks and tears up prey when 25 days old, although the female still continues to feed it. Vigorous wing exercises begin once it is a month old and it moves off the nest into surrounding vegetation before its first flight.

The female remains on the nest during the first week except to collect prey in the air from the male. She broods and shades the young much of the time, sometimes by spreading her wings like a parasol. It is not known when she first begins to leave the nest, but the young are left alone for periods of at least 30 minutes by the time they are 18 days old. The male, the main food-provider, passes prey to the female in flight or drops it on the nest once the young are about 25 days old. Very occasionally he alights briefly on the nest to deposit food. One male was seen to make a kill 6 km away and carry it back to the nest. Prey is normally brought decapitated and birds are first plucked. The nest is kept meticulously clean and the female removes anything not eaten. Humans near the nest are sometimes attacked by the female, who may even strike them. One female performed a distraction display by dropping heavily into the grass while emitting a croaking call. The behaviour was like that of a Marsh Owl but less vigorous.

The nestling period is between 38 and 41 days in a limited number of records; further observations are needed. The young may return to receive prey at the nest for at least two weeks after their first flight; there is no information on when they become independent. There are no details on breeding success, but in the dry winter months in the Transvaal, fires are a hazard to the breeding birds.

49 Montagu's Harrier *166.*

Blou-vleivalk

Circus pygargus

PLATES 17 AND 18

DERIVATION

hawk : rump : white — *kirkos* (G) : *puge* (G) : *argos* (G)

This species was named after Colonel G. Montagu (1751–1815).

IDENTIFICATION

Adult: This species is sexually dimorphic. The male is blue-grey on the upperparts and breast, and the rest of the underparts are white with some narrow chestnut streaks. There is a single black bar on the wing across the secondaries. The eyes, cere and legs are yellow. In flight from below, the wing appears mainly white with black primaries and a dark bar across the secondaries. The tail is pale and shows only faint barring. From above, the harrier appears almost entirely blue-grey except for black primaries and a dark bar on the secondaries. Superficially it resembles the Pallid Harrier from above but that species has only a wedge of black on the primaries and no bar on the secondaries.

The female is dark brown above and pale rufous below with darker brown streaking. The soft parts are coloured as in the male. In flight from below, the underwing coverts are pale rufous and the remiges and tail are barred. From above, the white band on the tail coverts and the four bold brown bars on the tail contrast with the rest of the uniform brown upperparts. The Pallid Harrier female is so similar that differentiation in the field is almost impossible. There are subtle differences in the head patterns of the two species, the Pallid Harrier having a more distinct collar of white behind the dark brown ear coverts, but this feature is not always constant and a very close view is required. Most experienced observers are agreed that the females of the two species cannot be distinguished with confidence. The females of both species have a superficial resemblance to the African Marsh Harrier but this species lacks the diagnostic band of white on the rump of the Palearctic migrants.

There is also a rare melanistic form of Montagu's Harrier, and both males and females occur in this plumage. They have not been recorded in southern Africa but if any did crop up they might be confused with the resident Black Harrier. The best way to distinguish them would be by the lack of a white band on the rump which is characteristic of the Black Harrier but absent in both male and female melanistic Montagu's Harriers.

Juvenile and immature: Juveniles resemble females except that they are warm rufous-brown below with no streaking. In flight from below they differ from females in having dark grey secondaries on which the transverse barring is only faintly discernible. They have dark brown eyes and yellow ceres and legs. Juvenile Pallid Harriers are very similar except for a more distinct whitish collar behind the dark brown ear coverts. The juveniles of the two species are very difficult to distinguish with certainty. At the first moult when about a year old the male becomes paler below, the upper parts and breast darken and the new tail feathers are grey. It is clearly recognisable as a male but

only when two years old does it acquire most of its adult plumage. Females become paler below and acquire brown streaking at their first moult.

HABITAT

It occurs where there is a mosaic of open grassland and marshy ground although it also hunts well away from water.

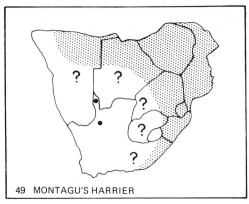

49   MONTAGU'S HARRIER

STATUS AND DISTRIBUTION

This Palearctic migrant occurs from October to April but there is one exceptionally early record in early September from Natal. Although formerly commonly recorded, this species has become scarce in southern Africa particularly in the last 20–30 years. This situation is linked to its decline in its Palearctic breeding range. It occurs mainly in the east of southern Africa and is absent from the more arid areas of the south and west where there is little suitable habitat. Its breeding range extends from western Europe to western Siberia and it winters in southern Asia, in north Africa along the Mediterranean and in the eastern half of Africa as far south as the eastern Cape.

GENERAL HABITS

The long, narrow wings and tail of Montagu's Harrier give it a graceful, buoyant flight as it flaps and glides at about 3–5 m above the ground. On seeing prey it drops onto it with a quick twist. It sometimes perches in trees or on fence posts but most of its hunting is done on the wing. It hunts until late in the evening before going to roost. Communal roosts in long grass are used, often in association with Pallid and European Marsh Harriers; about 160 birds were seen about 25 years ago in a mixed harrier group in Kenya. Such numbers are probably exceptional these days. In Zimbabwe six Montagu's Harriers were seen to roost together, although they were very sparsely distributed in the area. Birds come from far afield to a roost and the same spot may be used for several weeks at least.

In the Palearctic they prey on small mammals, birds, reptiles, amphibians and insects. In Africa the few available records indicate that much the same type of prey is taken. Insect prey includes grasshoppers and termites. One observer saw termites being caught in the most clumsy fashion. The bird took off from the ground, caught a termite in its claws, transferred it to its mouth, and then alighted before jumping up to catch the next one.

50 Pallid Harrier *167.*

Vaal-vleivalk
Circus macrourus

PLATES 17 AND 18

DERIVATION
hawk : big (i.e. long) : tail — *kirkos* (G) : *makros* (G) : *oura* (G)

IDENTIFICATION
Adult: This species is sexually dimorphic. The male is pale grey above and white below. The eyes, cere and legs are yellow. In flight it is uniform pale grey above and white below except for a wedge of black at the tip of each wing. One's impression is of a very pale harrier with some black on the wing tips. It may possibly be confused with a male Montagu's Harrier from above but there are distinct differences which are discussed under that species. The female closely resembles the female Montagu's Harrier and cannot be distinguished from it in the field (see text on that species).

Juvenile and immature: The juvenile closely resembles the juvenile Montagu's Harrier except for a more prominent collar of white behind the ear coverts. It is very difficult to distinguish in the field with certainty. At the age of a year the juvenile male commences its first moult, becomes paler below and acquires grey feathers above. It may be distinguished from the immature male Montagu's Harrier by the lack of any grey features on the breast. At the age of two years it resembles the adult male but still retains traces of juvenile coloration. The immature female gradually becomes paler below and acquires streaking.

HABITAT
Like Montagu's Harrier the Pallid Harrier is mainly a species of the open grassland and they quite often occur together. However, it also hunts amongst trees in light woodland and oc-

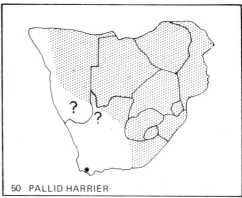

50 PALLID HARRIER

curs sporadically in much drier areas such as the Kalahari.

STATUS AND DISTRIBUTION
This species is a Palearctic migrant to southern Africa between October and April. Like Montagu's Harrier it was formerly commonly seen but is now scarce. It is more widely distributed than Montagu's Harrier and occurs farther west. There is a single record from near Cape Town in 1961. Its breeding range extends from Rumania eastwards to western Siberia. It winters in southern Asia and Africa. Extralimitally in Africa it is widely distributed and also occurs in the western regions, where Montagu's Harrier is absent.

GENERAL HABITS
The habits of the Pallid Harrier are very similar to those of Montagu's Harrier. Prey records in Africa include small mammals, small birds, lizards and many insects such as locusts, grasshoppers and beetles. It is attracted to grassfires.

51 Black Harrier 168.

Swart-vleivalk

Circus maurus

DERIVATION
hawk : black — *kirkos* (G) : *maurus* (G)

IDENTIFICATION
Adult: The black plumage of this harrier makes it unmistakable. Males and females are alike in colour but females are larger. When perched it appears almost entirely black except for grey secondaries and pale grey bands on the black tail. The eyes, cere and legs are rich yellow. In flight the broad band of white on the rump is the most diagnostic feature. The tail is boldly barred with black and white bands and the underwing coverts are black, contrasting with the silver-grey remiges which have a narrow black border along their hind edges. From above, the secondaries and inner primaries are grey. The only possible confusion that could arise is with the rare melanistic form of Montagu's Harrier which has yet to be recorded in southern Africa. Distinctions are discussed in the text on that species.
Juvenile and immature: The juvenile is dark brown above with buff edges to the wing coverts. The underparts are buff and the breast is covered with brown blotching. The eyes, cere and legs are yellow. The flight pattern is similar to that of the adult, but less clearly defined, and the underwing coverts are buff with black blotching. Little is recorded on the development of adult plumage, but an immature bird was black on the head and upper breast and from a distance was initially mistaken for a Black-breasted Snake Eagle until the diagnostic white rump was revealed.

HABITAT
This species is mainly a dry-country harrier and, although it may hunt on the fringes of wet areas, it is independent of marshland, unlike the African Marsh Harrier. It occurs in Karoo scrub, short grassveld, fynbos, renosterbos and in agricultural habitats, particularly wheat. In the south-west Cape and in Natal it is found in mountainous areas.

STATUS AND DISTRIBUTION
The status of the Black Harrier is the subject of many conflicting statements. At one time it was said to be nearing extinction and recently it

was thought to be increasing in numbers. It appears, however, that it was never in any danger of extinction, although a relatively scarce species, and that recent opinions of its increasing population are probably due to an increase in observers and observer awareness. Like the Booted Eagle it is easily overlooked, inhabiting many areas where there are few bird-watchers. During the last 100 years there has been no change in its range. At present it appears in no danger, unlike the African Marsh Harrier, which is declining seriously in some areas. However, the Black Harrier has the most restricted range of all harrier species and is therefore potentially vulnerable. Most of its natural habitat appears to be in no immediate danger, except on a local basis, and its ability to adapt to land used for agricultural crops such as wheat is in its favour.

The main distribution of this harrier is in the Cape Province but it also occurs regularly in Natal, Lesotho and the Orange Free State. In the Transvaal, Botswana and southern Namibia it is an occasional rare visitor. On present evidence it breeds only in the Cape Province south of 31° S. A single old record from Natal is for April, well outside the known breeding season, and is considered suspect. However, it may yet be found to breed in Natal and the Orange Free State.

Although there are records of this species in its breeding range throughout the year, it is seen less frequently during January to July, which is when it is most often seen (83 per cent

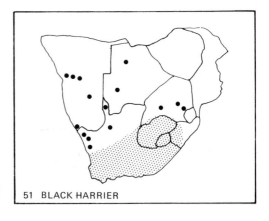

51 BLACK HARRIER

of all sightings) in its non-breeding range. It is clearly a partially migratory or nomadic species when not breeding. Occurrences in arid areas such as the Namib Desert have been linked with years of good rains but further investigation of this aspect is required.

GENERAL HABITS

Usually seen singly, it hunts in typical harrier fashion by quartering low over the ground. Its flight is silent. At times it makes persistent short stoops in the same spot, trying to flush prey from cover. Occasionally it hovers with spread tail and slowly flapping wings one to two metres above the ground. In one observation this method was used to hunt over small open patches amongst snow. Very occasionally it perches on the ground or a fence post to watch for prey. In one observation a bird used a power line as a vantage point while feeding on caterpillars in a vineyard. Birds may be captured in flight, in one case a domestic pigeon from a flock. This harrier has relatively shorter wings and a longer tail than the African Marsh Harrier, a structural difference that probably accounts for its greater agility. It may begin hunting before sunrise and also hunts after sunset when almost dark. In the only roosting observation a bird slept the night on a fence post in the middle of a vlei. Where water is readily available it likes to bath.

The prey of the Black Harrier is poorly known and further observations are required. The main categories so far recorded comprise birds up to about 350 g, small rodents, amphibians and insects. Occasionally it eats carrion and in one observation was seen feeding on dead young flamingoes. Avian prey consists of small birds and gamebird chicks but in one instance the eggs of a dove were eaten. Rodents caught are mostly rats and mice; species identified have been vlei rats and Striped Mice. Insect prey has included grasshoppers, beetles and caterpillars. Feeding may be opportunistic, for instance one bird returned in the early morning during three days to feed on caterpillars in the same vineyard.

There are two main calls, a mellow *pi-pi-pi-pi-pi . . .* used during courtship, as a contact call by the pair, and by the female soliciting the male when he has prey. A chattering *tjak-tjak-tjak-tjak-tjak . . .* is emitted in alarm when disturbed at the nest or when chasing intruding birds from the territory. A *kree-kree-kree* call similar to that of a Rock Kestrel is very occasionally used before a food-pass during courtship.

BREEDING

Undulating nuptial display flights are performed with calling at the top of each rise. High soaring is also used in display and also for territorial advertisement. The male brings prey for the female, who takes it from him in flight. Copulation often takes place, usually on the ground, as soon as she alights to feed. She crouches low and spreads her tail while the male mounts with flapping wings and a trampling action of his feet. Once mating is complete she feeds on the prey he has brought. Copulation is most frequent during the nest-building stage but may continue into the early part of the incubation period. One case of probable polygyny has been observed when two females bred successfully in the same vlei 200 m from each other and only one male was seen during short watches in the area.

Nests may be built in low reeds or sedge in or near marshy ground but also well away from water in such habitats as mountain fynbos or wheat fields. The Black Harrier is often independent of marshland for breeding purposes, unlike the African Marsh Harrier which rarely nests away from water. There is no record of a nest built in reeds standing in water of any depth, in contrast to the African Marsh Harrier. There is one record of a nest being built about 3 m off the ground in a leafy spider-gum tree but the nesting attempt was abandoned after a few sticks had been placed in position.

The nest is usually built on the ground but in a marshy situation may be placed in vegetation about 50 cm above the ground. It is always well concealed by surrounding vegetation. Some nests have a base of sticks lined with grass but most are a pad of dry grass or reeds, the amount of material used depending on their situation. They measure 35–45 cm across. An old record from the last century describes a lining of wool and hair and has not been verified since, but a recent description states that a nest contained 'rags and other rubbish'.

Both sexes build and add grass lining to the nest during the incubation and nestling periods. The female takes the major share in these activities. Nest material is usually carried in the bill but sometimes in the feet. A nest site is used only once but the same general area may be occupied over a period of years. A nest may be built within 20 m of a previous site or as far as 2,5 km away.

Information on territory is scanty but two occupied nests of two different pairs were about 2 km apart. A probable case of polygyny where two nests were 200 m apart has been mentioned. During the incubation and nestling

(1) A Black Harrier's nest is situated just in front of the figure.

(2) A close-up of the above nest.

(3) This nest was situated on the ground in mountain fynbos amongst bracken.

(4) Nestlings aged 8, 7 and 5 days.

(5) The same young 15, 14 and 12 days old.

(6) The nestlings at 22, 21 and 19 days old; feathers are emerging rapidly through the down.

periods at one nest the male vigorously drove off other birds of prey and White-necked Ravens which came within a radius of 500 m of the nest. These chases were persistent; once a pair of ravens were chased for 14 minutes and the harrier rose to a height of 300–400 m while driving them off. Mongooses and even small antelope near the nest may be dive-bombed but it has not been known to attack humans.

In 23 records where the month of egg-laying could be established (excluding the doubtful Natal April record), 2 are in July, 10 in August, 10 in September and 1 in November. The breeding season coincides with that of the African Marsh Harrier in the Cape Province. There is some evidence from Namaqualand that breeding may not take place in years of severe drought, but further investigation is required. Two to five eggs are laid, the usual clutch three or four. They are chalky-white in colour and become dirty white with yellowish nest-stains as incubation progresses. Occasionally eggs may be blotched with red; in one three-egg clutch one egg was plain white and two eggs well blotched. The plain egg was laid first. Eggs measure: 47,1 × 37,3 (20); 43,6–50,4 × 33,5–40,9.

At one nest the first two eggs were laid on consecutive days and the third and final egg two days after the second. Incubation began with the laying of the first egg. During 11 hours of observation on two days, only the female incubated, for 95,5 per cent of the time. Her only absences from the nest were to collect prey from the male several times a day in an aerial food-pass. Sometimes he had to make several low flights over the nest before she would leave to take the prey. She would eat it on a favourite perch and then collect nest material before returning to incubate. Sometimes the male made several trips with nesting material while she was feeding but he merely alighted briefly to deposit it. When not hunting or chasing off intruding birds, the male spent his time resting and preening on favourite perches about 50 m from the nest. Sometimes he flew low over the nest on an 'inspection' visit and the female would call to him in the same way as when he had food for her. The female sat very tight and only flushed when observers were nearly at the nest. The incubation period at this nest was 34 days and at another site the period was estimated to be close to this figure.

Newly hatched chicks are covered in white down beneath which the skin is pink. The dark brown eyes are open, the bill is black with a prominent egg-tooth, the gape is pink and the cere and legs are pale yellow. At a week old the down is tinged with buff and at two weeks old the thick second-down coat is buff-coloured. First feathers are just emerging on the remiges and scapulars. The cere and legs are rich yellow at this stage. At three weeks old feathers are breaking rapidly through the down on the upperparts and ear coverts but the heads and underparts of the chicks are still largely downy. The feather development of the smallest chick usually lags behind that of its older siblings. Subsequent feather development at the only nest studied could not be established because the chicks were eaten by a predator. However, most of the down would probably have been covered by feathers at the age of a month.

Initially the chicks are weak and lie prone most of the time. They defecate over the edge of the nest at an early age. By the age of two weeks they sit up on their haunches and threaten intruders with open gapes. At three weeks old they can stand and will turn on their backs and defend themselves with their claws if molested. Towards the end of the nestling period they will hide in vegetation surrounding the nest if disturbed.

Observations on parental attention are based on a single nest watched by the author at weekly intervals during the first three weeks of the nestling period until the young were eaten by a predator. Three day-long watches totalling 33 hours were made from a position 500 m from the nest. It was thus not possible to establish any details of behaviour on the nest itself. When the chicks were a week old the female was on the nest 98,8 per cent of the time. Her only absences from the nest were to collect prey from the male or to drop a piece of intestine after feeding the young. This latter behaviour was observed during all watches, and the nest was scrupulously clean whenever visited. The male brought prey on four occasions: twice the female took it from him in flight; once she received it at a favourite perch; and once he dropped briefly onto the nest to deliver it when she refused to leave the nest. When not hunting, the male rested and preened on a favourite perch or chased off intruding birds. However, much of his time was spent hunting out of view of the nest.

When the young were two weeks old the female was on the nest for 82 per cent of the time watched. Her absences ranged from 3 to 35 minutes. She hunted in the vicinity of the nest on a number of occasions and once caught prey 50 m away. She took grass back to the nest twelve times. The male continued his role as main food-provider and delivered prey seven times. The female took it from him five times in an aerial food-pass and twice he landed briefly to deposit it at the nest. Sometimes the female left the nest only three minutes after prey was brought, indicating that it had been distributed very rapidly to the chicks. The male's non-hunting activities were much the same as those during the previous watch.

Once the young were three weeks old the female's time on the nest dropped considerably to 38 per cent of the day. She spent her longest spell of nearly four hours on the nest in the afternoon, presumably shading the chicks. Otherwise her time was spent hunting (she caught nothing), 'loafing' on various perches near the nest or, for the first time, driving off intruding birds such as Steppe Buzzards. She took grass back to the nest only twice. All her time was spent within view of the nest. The male brought prey six times and she took it from him in the air each time, flying towards him or up from her perch if she was off the nest at the time. Throughout the nestling period prey was brought to the nest plucked and even rodents were partially plucked. The male sometimes used favourite plucking perches near the nest; at other times prey had presumably been plucked where caught.

At one nest the nestling period was between 36 and 41 days. The young apparently disperse quite soon from the immediate vicinity of the nest but may still be brought prey for about three weeks after leaving the nest.

At four nests in two seasons in Namaqualand 12 or 13 young flew successfully from 17 eggs. This record includes a suspected case of polygyny. In cases where the smallest chick disappears from a brood it is probable that it dies from starvation. On present evidence this species appears to be a successful breeder, but further observations are required.

52 Gymnogene 169.

Kaalwangvalk

Polyboroides typus

PLATES 13 AND 15

DERIVATION

Polyborus : like : typical — *polyborus* (G) : *eides* (G) : *typus* (L)

Polyborus is the genus of the Caracara, a strange hawk found in the New World, to which the Gymnogene was thought to be similar. *Polyborus* means having a wide diet.

IDENTIFICATION

Adult: The breast, head and upperparts are grey. Below the breast the underparts are finely barred black and white. The tail is black with a narrow white tip and a broad white bar across the middle. The feathers at the back of the head and neck are long and loose and give the impression of a mane. The bill and eyes are black and the cere, bare facial skin and legs are yellow. In excitement, particularly during courtship and when at the nest together, the birds flush pink or red on the bare skin of the face. In flight from below, the underwing coverts are finely barred black and white, and the rest of the underwing is grey except for a broad margin of black along the hind edge and on the primaries. As with the perched bird, the white tail bar is diagnostic.

The only possible confusion that may arise is with the chanting goshawks but they have red legs and ceres, no bare skin on the face and no tail bar. Their flight patterns and habits are also quite different from those of the Gymnogene.

Juvenile and immature: The juvenile is uniform dark brown with faint buff edges to the feathers of the upperparts. The tail is indistinctly barred with blackish. The bill is black, the cere greenish-yellow, the bare facial skin blackish, the legs are yellow and the eyes black. It is best identified by the small head, bare face and loose feathers at the back of the head. Its style of flight and habits are also important aids to identification.

The transition from juvenile to adult plumage is rather confusing. In some individuals grey feathers and barring replace the brown plumage directly while in others the head and breast become whitish with brown tips to the feathers. Further investigation of immature plumage is required but it has been established that it takes about two years to assume full adult plumage. Whatever their plumage, immatures can be identified by their appearance and habits rather than by coloration.

HABITAT

It occurs in a variety of forested and woodland habitats, especially along river valleys, and

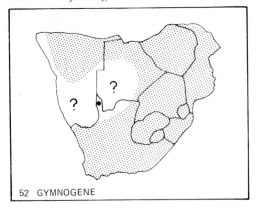

52 GYMNOGENE

in hilly or mountainous country. Although absent from more arid areas, it is widespread in the Karoo in wooded kloofs.

STATUS AND DISTRIBUTION

The Gymnogene is resident but wanders about locally outside the breeding season. It is widely distributed from the south-west Cape northwards and is only absent from the more arid regions of the west. Extralimitally it occurs northwards to the Sahara in suitable habitat. A closely related species is found in Madagascar.

GENERAL HABITS

This species is one of the most unusual and specialised of the birds of prey in southern Africa. It has a remarkable double-jointedness of the intertarsal or 'knee' joint and in a study of captive birds the forward flexion was 150° and the backward flexion 40°. It is also able to bend its leg sideways at this joint but to a much lesser extent. The effect of this adaptation is that the long leg can be inserted into holes in trees to extract nestlings of hole-nesting species such as woodpeckers, barbets and starlings, as well as small mammals and reptiles that live in holes. The small head is used to pry into crevices, and the bare facial skin is probably related to the habit of feeding on the husks of oil-palms where these are available. The Gymnogene has a lightweight body and long, broad wings and tail so that its flight is slow and buoyant, in keeping with its methodical searching habits, but it can also soar well. It has the ability to hang or even 'walk' upside down for quite long periods and it flaps its wings loosely while doing so. It also 'runs' up the trunks of trees with flapping wings searching in crevices and holes for prey. Although it normally forages in trees, it may also hunt on foot in open ground some distance from the nearest cover. The various adaptations of the Gymnogene enable it to fill an ecological

niche where it has little competition from other raptors.

The diet consists of birds' eggs and nestlings, small mammals including bats, frogs, fish (stranded in drying pools), lizards, small snakes, insects and oil-palm husks. There is also a record of a bird feeding on a piece of goat's meat hung up in a tree. The Gymnogene uses its agility to raid nests in inaccessible positions. It regularly raids the hanging nests of weavers, clinging upside down as it robs a nest of its contents. It also forages under the eaves of buildings, and preys on the nests of Little Swifts, swallows and House Sparrows. In one observation a bird perched on the gutter above a Little Swift colony, listened for a while, then flapped under the eave to hang from an occupied nest to extract the nestling. Listening probably plays a regular part in locating nestlings. Nest-robbing may be systematic and in one record a Red-winged Starling nestling was taken at 10h00 and the bird returned for the second one at 15h00. Hornbills are apparently safe from predation; a Gymnogene attempted unsuccessfully to break into the nest of a Grey Hornbill. There are several accounts of predation on heronries and Darter colonies, and both eggs and small chicks are eaten. The birds panic while the colony is being raided and make no attempt to return and defend their nests. At a Black-headed Heron colony the hawk arrived before dawn and spent much of the day there feeding on eggs. Its partiality for eggs includes hens' eggs. As a rule avian predation is mainly confined to colonial species such as weavers and White-browed Sparrow-weavers, or conspicuous nests like those of the Cape Sparrow, hole-nesting birds discovered in the course of foraging, and swifts and swallows nesting on buildings or on cliffs. Most of the prey of the Gymnogene is inactive or defenceless when caught. In a sample of 85 prey items reptiles and amphibians comprised

A Gymnogene robbing a weaver's nest.

41 per cent, birds (mainly nestlings) 33 per cent, small mammals 15 per cent and insects 11 per cent.

This species is mainly silent except during the breeding season. It emits a plaintive whistling *su-eeeee* or *su-eeeee-oo* which is used in varying intensities as contact between the pair, during courtship and mating, or in alarm. The male's voice is higher pitched than that of the female. A high-pitched *hweep-hweep-hweep* heard near the nest is probably a contact call. The feathered nestling solicits with a continuous series of rapid, querulous, whistling *pi-pi-pi-pi-pi* notes.

BREEDING

In nuptial display the male performs undulating flights either alone or in the presence of the soaring female. During upward flight the wingbeats are exaggerated and the wings almost touch below the body. Sometimes the male stalls, falls backwards a short way, then drops into his dive. When both birds are involved he dives down at the soaring female and she turns, extends her legs towards his and they touch claws briefly. The male may display up to 3 km from the nest and then return to it from a great height in a long, slanting flight during which he performs undulations. The male feeds the female as part of courtship, depositing prey on the nest for her or giving it to her directly. In one observed case of mating the male hopped rather sedately onto the back of the crouching female and then lowered himself onto her several times during about 15 seconds until the final attempt was successful. The faces of both birds flushed red during the process and when the male left shortly afterwards the female's face returned to its normal yellow colour after 30 seconds.

Nests are built within the canopy of a tree, or at the base of a tree or bush on a cliff ledge, or in a small cave in a cliff face. The height of nests is rather variable, depending on site, but they are usually at least 10 m above ground. Various trees are used, including eucalypts, Baobabs, euphorbias and in one case a Borassus palm. Sometimes the old nest of another species is taken over and added to, but usually they construct their own nest. It is built with thin sticks about a centimetre thick and measures about 60–70 cm across and 20–30 cm deep with a cup 20–30 cm across. The cup is copiously lined with green leaves.

Repair of an established nest takes about a month. Both birds build and the female may remain on the nest while the male makes several visits with material. When they are together on the nest their faces flush. They often perch near the nest. Nest sites are used for several years, up to nine years at one site, or they may move to an alternate site nearby. In a 76 km² study area in the Transvaal there were three or four breeding pairs, or one pair in 19–25 km². Individual pairs foraged up and down the valley in which they were nesting over an area of about 5–6 km².

Eggs are laid from September to November throughout southern Africa, mainly in September and October. One or two eggs are laid, the most beautifully marked of all raptors' eggs in southern Africa. The creamy ground colour is usually completely obscured by a red wash, overlaid with blotches of darker red that coalesce to cover the whole surface. Some eggs are only lightly marked and sometimes a well-marked and a poorly pigmented egg occur in the same clutch. Very heavily marked eggs are almost the colour of mahogany. The dark eggs are less conspicuous on their bed of leaves than those of many other raptors and there may be a certain survival value in their coloration. Measurements are: 55,8 × 44,0 (88); 51,0–63,0 × 40,6–47,3.

The interval between eggs where two are laid is not known. Both birds incubate, the male for about 10 per cent of the time and usually after delivering prey to the female. Their faces flush during these change-overs. She sits overnight. Both bring greenery to the nest and once a male brought prey in one foot and green leaves in his bill at the same time. When the male brings prey for the female he calls softly to her and she answers and leaves the nest to feed. She also leaves the nest to hunt for herself and does not appear to have much difficulty in finding food, which she may bring back to the nest. The birds are unobtrusive at the nest and either sit tightly or slip off quietly when disturbed, behaviour varying individually. The incubation period is 35 days.

When two chicks hatch, Cainism may occur, although not invariably, and at one nest chicks at least two weeks old were seen together. In one instance where details are available the chicks hatched about a day apart and there was little difference in their size. Despite this, the older nestling viciously attacked its sibling, pecking at its head and back in a typical Cain and Abel struggle. Cain was well fed when it made the attacks. Next day Abel was dead, almost certainly as the result of injuries rather than starvation. Other observers have also seen Cainism taking place.

There are very few details on nestling development. The newly hatched chick is covered with buff down and has long, fine downy

(1) A Gymnogene on its nest built on a bush growing from a cliff.

(2) A close-up of the beauti-fully marked eggs.

(3) A nestling of approximately three weeks old.

plumes on its head. The bare skin of the face is greenish-yellow, the legs are brownish and the eyes black. The second down is greyish above and white below and the legs gradually turn yellowish. By about three weeks old, feathers are emerging on the scapulars and wing coverts but not on the head. This pattern of feather development indicates no relationship to the snake eagles, to which the Gymnogene was thought to be allied. At the age of four weeks the nestling is well feathered but with down tufts still visible on the head.

The feathered nestling is unobtrusive on the nest and, if an observer approaches, it lies flat. This behaviour, together with the fact that it does not shoot its mutes clear of the nest, makes it difficult to be sure of the contents of a nest from below. It is normally inactive until near the end of the nestling period when it calls a great deal, performs wing exercises and climbs out onto branches round the nest.

Random observations totalling 70 hours at nests in Kenya have established the basic pattern of parental care. During the first two and a half weeks the female is on the nest for 60 per cent of the daylight hours. Initially the chick is closely brooded during the day and all night, but once it acquires its thicker second down it is brooded less often, although the female remains on the nest or perches nearby. The male may occasionally brood or shelter the nestling, for 30 minutes on one occasion, but his main role is to provide prey. He brings this to the nest and exchanges soft whistling calls with the female. If she is off the nest she comes back to receive it. As at other times when the pair are together, their faces flush. The male has not been seen to feed the young, and he usually departs soon after delivering prey, but on one occasion he remained on the nest with the female for half an hour. Quite often on leaving the nest, he perches in the vicinity. Small prey items are brought in the crop or in the bill; larger kills are carried in the feet. Once a female was seen to feed a nestling by regurgitation. After the first two and half weeks the female's time on the nest drops to about 20 per cent, but she continues to perch near the nest and only hunts actively once the nestling is well feathered. Both parents bring green sprays to the nest during the first half of the nestling period.

One observer in Zimbabwe established the nestling period as about 45 days but in Kenya it is said to be about 50–55 days, which seems rather long. Further observations are required. Post-nestling attachment to the nest appears to be brief and the young bird leaves the nest area within a week. It is not known how long it takes to become independent.

The only breeding success records available are from Kenya where in eight breeding attempts five young were reared, or 0,63 young per pair per year.

53 Osprey   *170-*

Visvalk

Pandion haliaetus

PLATES 10 AND 11

DERIVATION

Pandion : salt water : eagle — *Pandion* (G) : *hals* (G) : *aetos* (G)

Pandion was a legendary king of Athens, several of whose relatives were transformed into birds. It is presumed that he was changed into an Osprey, but no direct statement to this effect can be traced in the classical literature, so the story is probably of later, post-Renaissance origin.

IDENTIFICATION

Adult: The plumage is dark brown above and white below with an indistinct band of pale brown streaks across the upper breast. The most distinctive features are the white crown, loose shaggy crest on the nape, and the 'mask' of dark brown in which the large yellow owl-like eyes are set. The long wings reach the tip of the tail. The cere and bare legs are pale blue-grey. In flight the underwing coverts are white with distinctive dark patches at the carpal joints. The remiges and tail are narrowly barred with black.

The only species occupying a similar habitat with which confusion could arise is the juvenile African Fish Eagle. It is also white on the head but lacks a 'mask', has brown eyes, a short tail, dark blotching on the abdomen, and a quite different flight pattern. The fishing habits of the two species are also different.

Juvenile: The plumage of the juvenile is very

similar to that of the adult except for buff edges to the feathers of the upperparts. Adult plumage is assumed after about 18 months.

HABITAT

The Osprey is always found near water and fishes in lakes, dams, rivers, estuaries, lagoons and in the sea. Although likely to be found near any suitable expanse of water where there are fish, it is most frequently seen near the coast.

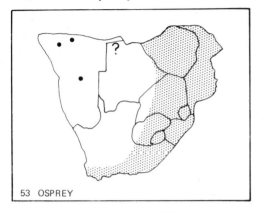

53 OSPREY

STATUS AND DISTRIBUTION

This Palearctic migrant is an uncommon visitor from October to March. However, immature birds may spend their first winter in Africa, and there are records for all months of the year in some localities in southern Africa. Two birds ringed in Finland and Sweden were recovered in Zimbabwe. Although this species is building up its numbers in Britain and Scandinavia, its decline in other areas of Europe has continued unabated since the 19th century and it is extinct in many places where it formerly occurred.

Its distribution is mainly in the eastern half of southern Africa but there are a few scattered records from Namibia. Extralimitally it has an almost cosmopolitan distribution.

GENERAL HABITS

The Osprey is normally seen solitarily on a prominent perch near water. It is well adapted for catching fish and has compact, slightly oily, water-resistant plumage. The large feet have long curved claws and there are short spines beneath the toes for holding its slippery prey. It hunts by flying above the water at a height of 20–30 m, although sometimes as high as 60–70 m, alternately flapping and gliding. When it sees a fish it may hover briefly or dive down immediately at an oblique angle. As it nears the water its wings are thrown back and it plunges in feet first to grasp its quarry. It often submerges completely but does not go deeper than a

metre. As it becomes airborne it gives a characteristic convulsive shake and flies off to a feeding perch, carrying the fish in both feet with the head pointing forward to minimise wind resistance. It may fly a considerable distance to a perch, probably to avoid piratical attacks from African Fish Eagles, and this gives the impression that the bird is flying to a nest (see under Breeding). It is capable of catching fish weighing about 3 kg. There are rare cases of its catching two fish in the same dive, one in each foot. Sometimes it takes fish from the surface of the water without submerging. In one observation from Namibia an Osprey was seen hunting from a pole 1,2 m above a shallow stretch of water. It merely jumped down, grabbed a catfish and hopped with it to the edge of the pan to eat it on a log. The Osprey is a very efficient hunter. Observers in California watched 639 foraging attempts, of which 82 per cent were found successful.

Although it is primarily a fish-eater, its diet in Europe includes small mammals, reptiles, amphibians, crustaceans and other invertebrates. Apart from the fact that it eats fish, little is recorded on its diet in southern Africa, and there are few details on which fish species it catches. In one case mullet were caught as a seine net was being pulled in. There is a record of one eating a freshly dead Reed Cormorant which it had probably killed itself. In Nigeria an Osprey caught a small mammal, probably a rat, 15 m from the shore of a lake well stocked with fish. It hunted in the same way as it would have done over water.

BREEDING

There is no properly authenticated case of breeding in southern Africa. It was said by the late Austin Roberts to have bred on the Berg River in the Cape in November. The description of the eggs does not match that of Osprey

An Osprey partially immersed as it catches a fish.

eggs but, although small, they fall within the size range of the species. Although a specimen was collected, it is probable that it was near a Yellow-billed Kite's nest of which it was mistakenly thought to be the owner. The colony of breeding Yellow-billed Kites near Hopefield on the Berg River was well known and was visited by a number of early ornithologists. Anyone finding a suspected Osprey's nest should take great care to authenticate it beyond all reasonable doubt. A suspected nest was seen on an inaccessible island of sheer rock on the Transkei coast. In Zimbabwe one bird flew off regularly, sometimes every 15 minutes, in the same direction carrying a fish.

However, such records are purely circumstantial. The Osprey may breed in southern Africa, as do certain other Palearctic migrants like the White Stork, but proof is so far lacking.

The nest is a bulky structure of sticks placed conspicuously on top of a rock, dead tree or similar situation. Two or three eggs are laid. They are elongated ovals, creamy in ground colour and richly overlaid with brown and red-brown blotches. Measurements from Europe are: 61,6 × 46,4 (100); 50,4–69,0 × 40,2–50,3. The two alleged 'Osprey' eggs from the Berg River measured 55,5 × 44,8 and 53,8 × 44,0 falling within the size range of the Yellow-billed Kite's eggs.

54 African Peregrine *171.*

Afrikaanse Swerfvalk
Falco peregrinus minor

PLATES 19 AND 20

DERIVATION

falcon : wanderer : smaller — *falco* (L) : *peregrinus* (L) : *minor* (L)

IDENTIFICATION

Adult: The sexes are alike in plumage but the male is about a third smaller than the female, hence the name tiercel used for the male by falconers. The upperparts are blue-grey and the head, neck and cheek patches are black. The underparts are creamy-buff, the unmarked throat and upper breast forming a gorget below which there is spotting and barring, the barring being concentrated mainly down the sides of the body. The large eyes are dark brown, appearing black from a distance, and the cere, orbital ring, legs and feet are rich yellow. The feet are very large, seeming almost out of proportion to the rest of the body. The build is stocky and the breast is very broad. When it is perched the wing tips reach the end of the tail.

In flight from below, the underwing coverts are finely barred with black and the remiges and tail are more broadly barred with blackish. The impression is of a powerful, compact falcon which appears mainly dark except for a white gorget.

The African Peregrine is most likely to be confused with the larger migrant Peregrine *Falco peregrinus calidus*, which is an uncommon visitor mainly to the eastern half of southern Africa as far south as Port Elizabeth. However,

the migrant Peregrine is often confused with the resident species so that the situation with regard to its distribution is unclear. The race *calidus* breeds in the tundra of the U.S.S.R. as far east as the Lena River (130° E). It migrates to southern Asia and Africa, occurring in southern Africa from about November to March. Apart from its larger size, which is only helpful to experienced observers, it is pure white, not buffy, on the underparts with much less barring and spot-

(a) An African Peregrine Falco peregrinus minor *and (b) a migrant Peregrine* Falco peregrinus calidus *to show difference in size and markings on the underparts.*

ting than the African Peregrine. A subtle difference is its narrower cheek patch which forms more of a distinct 'moustache' than that of the resident species. Both perched and in flight *calidus* appears whiter and less heavily marked on the underparts.

Confusion with the adult Lanner is possible, particularly at a distance, but this species is white or pinkish-white below without any markings. In flight it has pale underwing coverts and thus appears pale in contrast to the dark African Peregrine. The best single feature is the rufous 'barmitzvah cap' of the Lanner, which is quite distinct from the black 'hangman's hood' of the African Peregrine. There are also differences in shape, the Lanner being less stockily built with longer wings and tail.

Juvenile and immature: The upperparts of the juvenile are dark brown and the head pattern is like that of the adult. On the underparts it is very heavily streaked with dark brown, especially on the sides of the body. The eyes are dark brown and the cere, orbital ring, legs and feet are pale greenish-yellow. The underwing pattern is similar to that of the adult except that the barring on the underwing coverts is broader and more irregular.

The most likely confusion is with the juvenile Lanner, which is much less heavily streaked below and has a pale rufous crown. In flight it appears altogether paler than the juvenile African Peregrine.

Juveniles start to moult into adult plumage in their second year. The heavy streaking on the underparts gives way to barring on the sides of the body and a gradual moult continues until full adult plumage is attained. The time taken for the complete process varies individually.

HABITAT

Sheer cliffs, particularly in river gorges, are the main requirement of this falcon. It hunts in nearby open country but most of its time is spent near cliffs where it roosts and nests. The presence of water in its environment is a regular feature. Its habitat requirements are more specialised than those of the Lanner and account for its comparative rarity. African Peregrines, usually young and unmated birds, also occur in towns, but in Nairobi a pair nested on a building. No such nesting behaviour has been recorded in southern Africa. African Peregrines have been recorded hunting Speckled Pigeons on the island of St Croix near Port Elizabeth, a distance of 2,4 km from the mainland.

STATUS AND DISTRIBUTION

Adult African Peregrines are resident and may be found near their breeding cliffs through-out the year. Juveniles disperse once they become independent but nothing is known about the extent of their movements.

This magnificent falcon is rare in southern Africa, indeed throughout Africa. The only estimate of population in southern Africa is from the Transvaal where 10 breeding pairs were located in 286 300 km^2. On present evidence Lanners outnumber African Peregrines by some eleven to one in the Transvaal. Too little is known about former numbers to assess if there has been any decline in the population in southern Africa. However, pesticide residues have been found in eggs, and in Zimbabwe the aerial application of 'Dieldrin' to control termites in the lowveld irrigation schemes was thought to pose a serious threat to the local African Peregrine population. In view of the rarity of the species, the situation in some areas of southern Africa could well be serious. The sorry story of the decline of the Peregrine in other countries, in particular the U.S.A. and Britain, is too well known to require detailed repetition here. In both countries it approached the brink of extinction, indeed was extinct in the eastern U.S.A., as the result of the irresponsible use of persistent organochlorine pesticides which caused eggshell thinning, abnormal adult brooding behaviour and breeding failure. In the U.S.A. the Peregrine is now being bred in captivity and reintroduced into areas where it formerly occurred. The message with regard to southern African Peregrines is clear: unless responsibility in the use of pesticides is practised a similar serious decline could occur. Those pesticides that have been shown to have a serious effect on wildlife in other countries should be banned entirely.

The African Peregrine occurs widely in suitable habitat throughout southern Africa and extralimitally northwards to the Sahara. The Peregrine is probably the most cosmopolitan of all birds and some 17 races have been recognised, although the number varies according to different authorities. On present evidence only the migrant race *calidus* has been proved to reach southern Africa.

GENERAL HABITS

This falcon is able to capture prey with little difficulty and there are long periods of inactivity when it merely 'loafs' about on its favourite cliff. It bathes and drinks regularly, hence the importance of water in its habitat. Various hunting techniques are used and it either launches its attack from a high vantage point such as a cliff or circles up ('rings up' in falconer's parlance) to a considerable height. The attack commences with several rapid wing-beats to accelerate and then the wings are folded back so that it becomes a heart-shaped projectile as it hurtles towards its quarry. Usually the other bird is taken by surprise and the falcon strikes it behind the head with the hind talons, sometimes severing the neck, but the victim is also killed by impact. If it is not killed outright, then the falcon bites it on the back of the neck. Another method is to pursue its prey, usually in level flight, and grasp it with the talons, a technique referred to as 'binding to' by falconers. With species that remain in tight flocks like Red-billed Queleas it does not dive directly amongst them for fear of injury. Instead it swoops over them and selects a single quelea separated by the resultant panic. A technique of 'flush-hunting' has been observed in South Africa. After a short flight the falcon alights on the cliff, perches a short while, and then moves to another spot. Crevices are also inspected. Anything flushed is chased, but the method does not appear to be particularly successful. Once a bird is caught it is taken back to a favourite perch where it is plucked before being eaten.

Various estimates of the speed of a Peregrine's stoop have been made, varying from 160 to 410 km/h. Experiments using a type of air speedometer attached to the falcon have been attempted by falconers in Scotland. They arrived at speeds of approximately 70 km/h in cruising flight, 100 km/h in level chase and 135–145 km/h in a stoop. However, one authoritative textbook *The Birds of the Western Palearctic* states that a speed of at least 240 km/h is attained in a stoop. Whatever the case, the stoop of a Peregrine is one of the most spectacular sights in the world of birds. The African Peregrine has been seen to capture a swift with ease, but the element of surprise is important, and in level flight a Speckled Pigeon, if aware of the pursuing falcon, can outfly it.

Peregrines are specialist bird-killers and catch very little else. The African Peregrine is no exception and, except for termites, which few birds can resist, only avian prey has been recorded. Many species caught are those readily found in its cliff environment: Speckled Pigeons, African Black Swifts, Alpine Swifts and African Rock Martins. In towns the diet is Little Swifts and Speckled Pigeons, although the latter are largely replaced by Feral Pigeons, which are more easily caught. Other prey recorded includes Black Oystercatcher, migrant waders, doves, Green Pigeons, a small cuckoo, White-browed Coucal, Red-faced Mousebird, Lilac-breasted Roller, African Hoopoe, Black-headed Oriole, glossy starling, Red-winged Starling and sparrows. Most of the prey of the African Peregrine weighs between 25 g and 300 g. At three Transvaal eyries 21 prey items were recorded, of which pigeons and doves made up 46 per cent.

The calls of the African Peregrine are similar to those recorded for Peregrines elsewhere. Outside the breeding season the birds rarely call. During the breeding season they are often very noisy, especially during courtship, but at other times no calling may be heard for several hours. Most calls are made by both sexes and the female has a deeper voice. The loudest call is a raucous *kack-kack-kack* . . . which has a quacking quality and may rise to a crescendo. It is made by both birds in alarm when there are intruders near the nest and in territorial threat. Various wailing calls are used. The male emits a *klee-chip*, the female *klee-chuk,* in antagonistic situations such as territorial disputes, and when delivering prey to large young. Another wailing call is a high-pitched, querulous, whining *waaik* . . . *waaik* repeated slowly at intervals and used by the adults and large young. This call carries over a distance of at least a kilometre. It is used as a soliciting call by the female during copulation, and as a contact call, for example when changing over during incubation. A repeated creaking *wi-chew* call sounding like a rusty hinge is used by both sexes when changing over during incubation, as a greeting call when they are perched near each other, and especially during courtship. An unmated male uses this call to attract a female to his nest cliff. A chupping noise like the clucking of a domestic hen is used by the female when feeding small chicks. Various other whining and chittering calls are also uttered. Small chicks beg with a *chit-chit-chit,* later replaced by the *waaik* soliciting call. Nestlings hiss in defence if handled.

BREEDING

Peregrines remain mated for the duration of their lifetimes, but if a mate is lost it is soon replaced. The pair remain together during the year. The nuptial display of the African Peregrine has not been described but is doubtless similar to that of Peregrines in other parts of the world. At the onset of the breeding season various aerial displays are performed, either singly or by both birds together, to the accompaniment of much noisy calling. The displays are often spectacular and consist of high circling, undulating dives, looping the loop and figure-of-eight patterns. There is much aerial 'play' involved and the male chases the female, who will turn and present her talons to him. Sometimes they touch bills or 'kiss' in flight. Courtship feeding by the male is a regular feature; prey is passed to the female in flight or while she is perched, the male approaching her with a slow bowing ceremony while uttering chittering calls. An unmated male will attract a female by repeatedly flying to suitable nest spots on the cliff. Before laying, the female spends much time brooding in a nest scrape. Mating takes place frequently, several times an hour on occasions; an observer in Zimbabwe recorded copulation twelve times during the course of a day at one nest. The birds mate on a tree or rock perch near the nest, to the accompaniment of much calling.

Except for one nest on the wall of Kariba Dam, all nests in southern Africa have been recorded on inaccessible cliffs or sheer faces of old mine excavations or quarries. Nest sites often overlook water. Statements that it breeds in stick nests in trees require authentication, especially as this type of site is regularly used by Lanners. The African Peregrine is so closely linked to its cliff habitat that tree-nesting seems highly improbable. No nest is built and the eggs are laid in a scrape in the soil on a sheltered ledge or on the stick nest of some other cliff-nesting species such as a Black Stork, Black Eagle or White-necked Raven. High cliffs are preferred. In the Transvaal the average height of ten nest cliffs was 187 m; the height of the lowest cliff used was 140 m.

The same cliff is used for breeding year after year, although not necessarily the same nest spot. The African Peregrine is so sparsely distributed and so little studied in southern Africa

The eggs of an African Peregrine laid on the ledge of a sheer cliff (Photograph: Rob Jeffery).

that nothing is known about size of territory. It is doubtful whether a density of eight pairs in 3 100 km² as found in one area in Kenya could occur anywhere in our area, and it would be exceptional for two pairs to be only 3,2 km apart as found in Kenya. However, in the Victoria Falls gorges, Taita Falcons and African Peregrines breed within this distance of each other, although in different gorges. The nest area is vigorously defended against other birds of prey and White-necked Ravens flying past but Black Storks are ignored. The birds swoop at humans near the nest and in Kenya an observer was struck several times.

Eggs are laid from June to September in southern Africa, mostly in July and August, although further records are required to confirm this breeding peak. Clutches of three or four eggs, usually three, have been recorded. Elsewhere Peregrines lay between two and six eggs. Characteristically, the eggs do not touch each other in the nest. They are creamy or yellowish in ground colour with a heavy wash of reddish intermingled with small pepper spots. Eggs are variably marked, but normally most of the surface is handsomely covered with reddish. Measurements are: 51,1 × 40,7 (34); 48,0–56,1 × 39,1–42,0.

The eggs are laid at intervals of two to three days and incubation usually begins when the penultimate egg of the clutch is laid. Both sexes incubate. The only detailed nest observations of any kind on the African Peregrine were made in the Transvaal during the incubation period when a nest was watched for 61 hours from dawn to dusk on five days. The eggs were incubated for 98 per cent of the daytime by both birds and at night only by the female. The male did a third of the incubation during daytime and his average shift was 90 minutes with a range of 8 minutes to 254 minutes. The female's daytime shifts averaged 145 minutes with a range of 29 minutes to 243 minutes. The relieving bird flew in without calling and alighted beside its mate. Then the birds called to each other and a change-over usually took place. The male was often reluctant to cease incubating but after much mutual calling he always gave way to the female. However, on a number of occasions when he came to relieve the female, he was unable to dislodge her. During the five days of observation no particular pattern of shifts emerged except that the female always incubated at the end of the day. Next morning the male came to relieve her about half an hour before sunrise. The non-incubating bird would leave the vicinity of the nest for about two hours at a time when it would catch prey for itself. The sitting bird would not leave the nest to assist in chasing off intruding birds, and if its mate was absent then they would not be chased at all. On one occasion the female left the nest for almost an hour to catch and eat a passing pigeon. The male did not incubate in her absence. It remains to be established whether hunting by the female during incubation is normal for the African Peregrine. Observations in other countries have established that the male normally brings prey for her. The incubation period of Peregrines in Europe is 29–32 days and that of the African Peregrine will probably be found to fall within this range.

Because incubation only begins when the clutch is nearly complete, the difference in size of the chicks when they have all hatched is not great and no sibling aggression occurs. The chicks are covered in white down when they hatch and acquire a much thicker greyish second coat from the age of 10 days. First feathers emerge at about 18 days old and the cheek patch is prominent at this stage. Little is recorded on the co-ordination of the young except that they begin wing-flapping exercises and can first feed themselves at the age of three weeks.

The female broods the young closely for the first few days, rarely leaving the nest except to receive prey in an aerial food-pass from the male. Once the young are two weeks old, and have their thicker second coat of down, the female leaves them alone for long periods except when feeding them, although she still roosts on the nest at night. The male continues to provide all the prey, the female remaining on guard near the nest. Once the young can feed themselves at three weeks old she joins the male in hunting, although he still does the major share. The young may still be fed by the female after three weeks and the male may also feed them if he finds the female absent when he arrives with prey.

The nestling period is 35–42 days but the young are not strong on the wing when they leave the nest, although their skill increases rapidly. Their heavily streaked underparts act as an effective camouflage when they are perched on the cliff face. Post-nestling observations in Zimbabwe agree with those on Peregrines in Europe. The young falcons remain together near the nest initially, where they are fed, mostly by the male, for about three to five weeks. They snatch prey from the adult's talons in flight or catch it when it is dropped. They accompany their parents on hunting trips about six weeks after leaving the nest and can kill proficiently for themselves two weeks later, at which stage they become independent.

Nothing is known about breeding success in southern Africa. Apart from the few detailed observations on the incubation period, the breeding biology of the African Peregrine is poorly known. Much of what has been written here has been drawn from studies of Peregrines on other continents. While the breeding behaviour of the African Peregrine will doubtless be found basically similar, confirmation is required.

55 Lanner 172.

Edelvalk

Falco biarmicus

DERIVATION

falcon : two : armed — *falco* (L) : *bi* (L) : *armicus* (L)

The specific name *biarmicus* is probably a reference to the bill tip and the sharp notch behind it, hence 'two-armed'.

IDENTIFICATION

Adult: The female is larger than the male, and her underparts are pinkish or buffy, while those of the male are pure white; but confirmation that this colour distinction is constant is needed. The upperparts are blue-grey, with a diagnostic cap of rufous on the head. There is a prominent 'moustache' streak, the eyes are dark brown, and the cere, orbital ring, legs and feet are rich yellow. In flight from below, the underwing coverts match the colour of the body and the remiges and tail are barred. The impression is of a pale falcon with a long body and long wings and tail. Confusion with an adult African Peregrine is possible at a distance; distinctions are dealt with in the text on that species.

Juvenile and immature: The juvenile is brown above with buff edges to the feathers, and the pattern on the head is like that of the adult but paler rufous on the crown. The underparts are buffy with brown streaking. The eyes are brown, the cere and orbital ring pale greenish-white, and the legs and feet yellow. In flight from below it is dark brown on the underwing coverts with buff spotting. It has a buff tip to the tail, about 12–15 mm longer than that of the adult. It could be confused with a juvenile African Peregrine; differences are discussed in the text on that species.

Little is recorded on the transition to adult plumage except that moult of the contour feathers starts in the first year. The streaking on the underparts gradually disappears and the last vestige of juvenile plumage is some spotting on the underparts of birds which otherwise appear fully adult.

HABITAT

The Lanner occupies a wide spectrum of habitats from mountainous regions with high rainfall to deserts. It is most common in open country, usually avoiding thick woodland. Its habitat is far less specialised than that of the African Peregrine, in much drier country as a rule.

STATUS AND DISTRIBUTION

The Lanner is normally considered resident except for juvenile dispersion and local movements to areas of temporary prey abundance. However, there is some evidence of long-distance movement: an adult male ringed in the Kalahari Gemsbok National Park in March was recovered 2 087 km away in Malawi two months later. This suggests that some African populations may be migratory and further investigation of the nature and extent of these movements is required.

The Lanner is one of the commonest falcons in southern Africa, the breeding population in the Transvaal being roughly estimated at some 1 340 pairs. There is also evidence that it is extending its breeding range there by using crow nests on power pylons in flat treeless areas where there were previously no nest sites. On the debit side traces of organochlorine residues have been found in eggs. Although the situation does not seem serious at present, a careful watch should be maintained in case it deteriorates.

This falcon is found throughout southern Africa. Extralimitally it occurs throughout Africa and in Arabia, Iraq, Sinai, Asia Minor, Yugoslavia, Greece, southern Italy and Sicily.

GENERAL HABITS

It is normally seen singly or in pairs, but where there are flocks of queleas or swarming termites some 20 or more Lanners may be seen together. These aggregations are often made up of juveniles and immatures. It is not dependent on water like the African Peregrine and has been observed to sandbath. Inevitably accounts of the Lanner's killing abilities have suffered by comparison with those of the Peregrine, but it is capable of spectacular speeds and is an efficient killer much prized by falconers. While it does not match the speed of the Peregrine, the Lanner is more versatile in its hunting techniques. A stoop from a great height in the manner of a Peregrine is the method least often used; the Lanner usually catches prey in level chase and binds to it. A fast surprise approach low over the ground from behind cover is another effective technique. Prey is often snatched off the ground. Sometimes male and female hunt together and co-operate in making a kill. The Lanner is unusual in that it will also attack prey flying directly towards it. It may hunt at dusk and has been seen to catch and eat bats without alighting.

When preying on massed flocks of drinking Red-billed Queleas the falcon flies up and eats each one it catches on the wing. This prevents piracy by Tawny Eagles which are also in attendance at water-holes where queleas drink. Injured queleas are rarely retrieved when they fall into the water and are quickly caught by Tawny Eagles or, if they reach the edge, waiting Black-backed Jackals snatch them up. At one water-hole in Namibia some 15 Lanners, all juveniles or immatures, were watched for two hours as they preyed on drinking queleas. It was estimated that one in every three or four attempts was successful and that between 20 and 30 queleas were caught.

The Lanner also obtains food by piracy; in one observation a Black-shouldered Kite was robbed of a mouse it had just caught. In Durban it has been recorded to prey on nestling Feral Pigeons. It sometimes accompanies game-bird shoots to snatch flushed or wounded birds and also follows herdboys hunting quails with sticks and dogs. An early writer relates how the herdboys call to the falcons so that their presence makes the quails crouch until the last moment and then fly up within range of their throwing sticks. It is probably from some similar situation that falconry has its origins. The Lanner also eats carrion and comes down to offal put out for Lammergeyers in the Drakensberg.

Unlike the Peregrine, the Lanner is by no means a specialist bird-killer; its diet includes small mammals, reptiles and insects. Elsewhere in its range it is said to take guineafowl and 'bustards', but in southern Africa its prey is normally up to the size of a Speckled Pigeon. In one observation a Lanner was seen with a recently caught Yellow-billed Hornbill which it was unable to lift. It has been known to kill other small raptors such as a Lesser Kestrel. Red-billed Queleas are a favourite prey, especially for immature birds. It preys on poultry that is allowed to run free, especially round villages, and takes chicks up to the age of about six weeks. At one nest in Zimbabwe all 13 identified prey items were young chickens. In mountainous country Speckled Pigeons are favoured prey, and in towns it takes Feral Pigeons. Other avian prey recorded are: Grey Plover, Ruff, doves (frequently), Grey Hornbill, Little Swift, Black-headed Oriole, roosting European Swallows and Orange-throated Longclaw. These give an indication of the spectrum of avian prey but when flown by falconers Lanners regularly take larger birds such as francolins. Mice and bats, including fruit bats, have been recorded amongst mammalian prey. Insects such as locusts, grasshoppers, beetles and termites are eaten. Although lizards are included in its diet elsewhere in its range, they do not appear to have been recorded in southern Africa.

The Lanner is normally silent outside the breeding season. In Africa its calls have not been fully described and require further study. A harsh *kak-kak-kak*, less raucous than that of the Peregrine, is used with different intensities in alarm, as a contact call and by young soliciting the adults. A piercing *kirr-eee, kirr-eee, kirr-eee* . . ., which sometimes rises to a crescendo, is uttered if the bird is alarmed and with less intensity as a greeting call when the male is excited or approaches the nest with prey. It is not known whether the female also uses this call. When feeding nestlings she makes a soft clucking note. Adults and young hiss in threat. Small young make a cheeping begging call and a *kwurr, kwurr, kwurr* noise, like a nest of young sparrows, is uttered by hungry nestlings. In Europe the main soliciting call of the female and young is described as a plaintive *ueeh*, also used during courtship. In captivity the female made a whining note and the male a *chuk-chuk-chuk* call during copulation.

BREEDING

Nuptial display consists of spectacular aerobatics during which the male dives down at the female, who turns and presents her claws. The male feeds the female during courtship and may pass prey to her in flight. Copulation takes place on perches near the nest. In captivity a pair performed a bowing display before they mated and the male selected the nest site.

The Lanner breeds on cliffs by preference (68 per cent of 91 nest sites in the Transvaal) but also in the stick nests of other birds in trees or on power pylons. There is one record of a nest in a natural hollow in a tree where several branches converged. In contrast to the African Peregrine the Lanner may breed on low cliffs or koppies. It also nests on rock faces in old mine workings and quarries. There are several records of nesting on buildings in towns in southern Africa. No nest is made and the eggs are laid on bare earth or dassie droppings, or on the sticks or lining if the nest of another species is taken over. Cliff sites are either on a small ledge or in a niche, or in the stick nest of a cliff-nesting species such as a Black Stork, Black Eagle or White-necked Raven. In the case of a Black Eagle pair with an alternate nest the Lanner uses whichever site is not in use. Tree sites are usually in eagle or crow nests, and crows may be dispossessed when they are about to lay. Quite often nests are used which are in full sun for most of the day. In Zimbabwe a favourite tree site is in a Bateleur nest, possibly because they have usually reared their nestling by the time Lanners lay. However, at one Bateleur nest, a large nestling ready to fly was persistently dive-bombed by Lanners trying to take over the nest. Other eagle nests that have been used by Lanners are Wahlberg's Eagle, Martial Eagle and African Fish Eagle, but any suitable stick nest is likely to be utilised, a Black-necked Heron's nest in one case. The versatility of the Lanner in its choice of nest sites is a major factor in its success as a species, especially when compared with the specialised nest site requirements of the African Peregrine.

Nest sites may be used year after year if still suitable. In the Transvaal the average distance between nests was 3,1 km and 4,0 km in two study areas, but in another locality two pairs bred only 250 m apart. The Lanner is aggressive towards other large birds near the nest and there is a record of a Pied Crow being struck and killed when it passed too close to a nest. It may attack humans, but very rarely; once a small dog below a nest was vigorously attacked and put to flight.

The breeding season is clearly defined in southern Africa and eggs are laid mainly in July and August with very occasional records in September. Three to five eggs are laid. They are creamy in ground colour but this is usually obscured by a brick-red wash on which darker rust-red speckles and spots are superimposed. The eggs are handsomely but variably marked.

(1) The eggs of a Lanner laid on dassie droppings on a cliff ledge.

(2) A clutch of five eggs laid in a Bateleur's nest.

(3) A female feeds her downy nestlings approximately two weeks old.

Measurements are: 51,6 × 40,5 (70); 47,7–56,5 × 39,6–44,6.

The laying interval is usually two or three days and incubation starts when the clutch is nearly complete. Both sexes incubate, the female doing the greater share, but there are no detailed observations. The male feeds his mate near the nest and broods while she is away feeding. The incubation period is close on 32 days both in captivity and in the wild. A period of 35 days by one observer results from calculations being made from the time the first egg was laid.

The young all hatch within two or three days of each other and, except for the last to hatch, they are much the same size. No sibling aggression has been observed but sometimes the smallest chick disappears. The newly hatched chick is covered in white down and its flesh is pink. The legs are pale orange and the bill is pink with a prominent egg tooth. At 8 days old a thicker second coat of down begins to emerge and the eyes are brown, the bill is grey and the legs are dull yellow. By 11 days the second down coat forms a dense covering. First feathers appear through the down at 17 days and at three weeks old the feathers form a V-shape on the back and are emerging rapidly from the wing and tail quills. Thereafter feather growth is rapid, the underparts being covered by the age of four weeks. The nestling appears fully feathered by the age of five weeks except for wisps of down on the head and a shorter tail. The wing and tail feathers are fully grown by the age of seven weeks. Male and female nestlings may be distinguished by their size towards the end of the nestling period.

The development of the co-ordination of a nestling has been closely studied in captivity and agrees with less detailed observations in the wild. The day-old chick is weak and unable to lift its head. At three days it is able to sit up and its eyes open for the first time. It bites at any object that touches its bill and makes swallowing actions. By its fifth day it sits up confidently and makes preening actions for the first time. It can recognise food that is stationary whereas previously it was stimulated to gape by touch or movement. By the age of 10 days it clutches at objects with its feet and flaps its stubby wings while sitting up. A day later it shows its first threat reaction, raising its wings and hissing. From this stage onwards it regularly stretches and flaps its wings. It is first able to stand, though unsteadily, at the age of 19 days. From the age of three weeks bouts of preening are prolonged and it cocks its head to look at objects. It can pull prey to pieces for the first time at 26 days old. From this stage onwards wing-flapping exercises become frequent and vigorous and it treads the nest sticks with a mock killing action. In a tree site the young move out onto branches before their first flight and they jump back onto the nest and crouch if an intruder approaches.

The female broods the small young closely and the male provides prey. She fetches this from him at a favourite 'delivery' perch or sometimes in flight. Birds are brought already plucked and all chicks are fed until they are full. Once the chicks are 10 days old they are only occasionally brooded, by which stage they have acquired their thicker second coat of down. However, the male may brood and feed them if he finds the female absent from the nest. One female was twice seen to leave the nest during this early guarding stage and return after five minutes with small chickens from a nearby rural village. At one nest the female started to leave the young alone for short periods when they were 17 days old and by the time they were 26 days old she was away for as long as one and a half hours. However, on these occasions, the male was on guard near the nest.

Nestling periods of 38–47 days have been recorded but usually it is between 42 and 45 days. Males leave the nest sooner than females, in one case three days earlier. The young remain near the nest for the first week or two while they increase their flying skills. They chase each other about and make mock kills by snatching with their feet at grass tufts and similar objects as they fly past. First attempts at prey capture are unsuccessful. The young remain in the nest area for about a month and gradually increase their range. It is not known when they make their first kills or when they become independent.

There is little information on breeding success but broods of four young are sometimes raised. At a nest on a building in Salisbury, Zimbabwe, 10 young were reared in four consecutive breeding seasons, a replacement rate of 2,5 young per pair per year.

56 European Hobby

Europese Boomvalk
Falco subbuteo

PLATES 19 AND 20

DERIVATION
falcon : below : hawk — *falco* (L) : *sub* (L) : *buteo* (L)

The prefix *sub* means smaller in this context, i.e. smaller than a hawk.

IDENTIFICATION
Adult: The upperparts are slate coloured and there is a typical falcon 'cap' on the head and a 'moustache' streak below the eye. The throat is white and, except for the red thighs and under-tail coverts, the buff underparts are heavily streaked with black. The bill is gun-metal blue, the cere and legs are yellow and the eyes dark brown. When the bird is perched the long wings reach the tip of the tail.

In flight the long, thin wings give this species a swift-like silhouette. From below the heavily streaked underparts and underwing coverts give the impression of a dark falcon with contrasting white throat and red vent. The blackish remiges and tail have narrow buff bars.

Juvenile: It resembles the adult except for the lack of red on the thighs and vent and the dark brown upperparts with narrow buff edges to the wing coverts and scapulars. Because of the streaked underparts there is a superficial resemblance to juvenile Peregrines and Lanners in flight but the swift-like silhouette distinguishes it.

HABITAT
This species occurs in a wide variety of habitats except for desert and thickly forested areas. It is most often encountered in lightly wooded open country.

STATUS AND DISTRIBUTION
The European Hobby is a migrant from the Palearctic region, where it breeds. It arrives in late October and departs in March or early April. There is considerable local variation in the pattern of its occurrence, which is closely linked to rainfall. Sometimes it may not be recorded in an area for years.

In southern Africa it is found mainly north and east of a line from Port Elizabeth to Windhoek. It is rare in the southern part of its range, becoming progressively more common in the north. However, it occurs occasionally even in

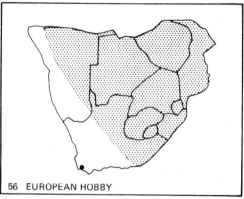

56 EUROPEAN HOBBY

the extreme south-west Cape. Extralimitally it has a very wide breeding distribution throughout the Palearctic region and all populations move southwards in the northern winter to southern China, northern India or Africa.

GENERAL HABITS
This graceful little falcon is most often seen on the wing hawking termites, its main food in Africa. Rapid wing-flaps are interspersed with glides as it circles back and forth, momentarily checking its fluent flight to pass a termite from foot to bill before sweeping on again. Its occurrence is linked to thunderstorms which cause termites to emerge. Often it hunts until it is al-

European Hobby feeding on termites in flight.

most too dark to see. Flocks of up to 100 birds occur, usually in association with other gregarious falcons. European Hobbies appear suddenly in an area and then disappear again as they follow the rain fronts. Insects such as grasshoppers and locusts are often eaten and European Hobbies are attracted to bush fires to catch insects which are flushed.

These falcons are very fast and can catch swifts and swallows in flight. European Swallows wintering in Africa are caught as they come to roost at dusk. A European Hobby was seen attempting to catch Little Swifts near their nesting colony and once the falcon had lost the element of surprise the swifts flew above it, rising higher and higher so that it was unable to gain height on them for a stoop. They may eat small birds in flight but usually they alight in a tree to pluck and dismember them. Bats are also preyed on at dusk. Very occasionally small mammals are caught on the ground but most of the prey of this species is taken on the wing.

57 African Hobby *174*

Afrikaanse Boomvalk
Falco cuvierii

PLATES 19 AND 20

DERIVATION
falcon : of Cuvier — *falco* (L) : *cuvierii* (L)

Baron Cuvier, a Frenchman, was a leading theoretical zoologist during the early part of last century.

IDENTIFICATION
Adult: The upperparts are slate-black and the underparts rufous finely streaked with black, but from a distance it appears plain rufous below. The bill is gun-metal blue, the cere and feet are yellow and the eyes dark brown. In flight the underwing coverts are rufous and the remiges and tail faintly barred with buff. The impression from below is of a mainly reddish falcon.

It could possibly be mistaken for a Taita Falcon, which is more heavily built and has the proportions of a Peregrine both perched and in flight whereas the African Hobby is altogether more slender. The bold rufous patches on the nape and the white throat of the Taita Falcon also distinguish it. The limited distribution of the Taita Falcon also eliminates confusion between the two species in most areas.

Juvenile: It closely resembles the adult except that the feathers of the upperparts are narrowly edged with rufous and the underparts are broadly streaked with black. When recently out of the nest the cere and bare skin round the eye are greenish-white but soon turn yellow. The rest of the soft parts are the same colour as the adult. Barring on the underside of the tail is more defined than in the adult. There is a superficial resemblance to the juvenile European Hobby but the rufous underparts clearly distinguish the African Hobby.

By the age of 15 months the rufous edges to the feathers of the upperparts have disappeared through wear, and the underparts are drab rufous. Adult plumage is acquired after the first moult but it is not known when this takes place.

HABITAT
This species is normally found in areas of higher rainfall where there is a mixture of open country and woodland. In east Africa it breeds in the middle of large towns such as Kampala.

STATUS AND DISTRIBUTION
Although it breeds and is presumably resident in the northern part of southern Africa (e.g. in Zimbabwe) its status elsewhere is uncertain. It is rare throughout its range in southern Africa but particularly in the south. Occasional birds recorded in the eastern Cape and Natal are probably vagrants. In east Africa it

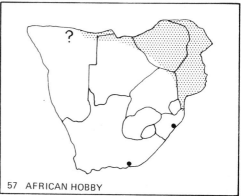

57 AFRICAN HOBBY

apparently makes local movements but it is not migratory.

This species occurs from the eastern Cape up the eastern part of the subcontinent to Mozambique and westwards to the Kruger National Park, Zimbabwe, northern Botswana and northern Namibia. Extralimitally its range extends to Ethiopia on the east and Ghana on the west.

GENERAL HABITS

The habits of this species are very similar to those of the European Hobby. It hunts on the wing, often when almost dark, and is partial to insects, particularly termites. However, African Hobbies are normally seen singly or in pairs in southern Africa, although in east Africa small flocks of about 20–30 birds may gather at a termite emergence. Records of other insect prey include beetles, cicadas, locusts and grasshoppers. Avian prey consists mainly of small birds such as weavers, waxbills and sparrows but on one occasion an unidentified species of dove was caught. This species matches the spectacular dexterity and speed of the European Hobby in pursuit of birds. Mammalian prey has not been recorded.

The call is a high-pitched shrieking *kik-kik-kik-kik* . . . used during courtship, as contact between the pair and when driving off intruders near the nest.

BREEDING

No courtship flights have been described but the male and female call noisily to each other at the commencement of the breeding season.

The disused nests of other birds of prey or crows are used for breeding and no nesting material is added. Nest sites have been recorded 9–30 m above ground but are usually about 18–24 m up. The size of the territory is not known but other birds of prey near the nest, even those as large as a Tawny Eagle, are vigorously attacked and driven away. They also fly close to human intruders climbing to the nest but do not strike them.

There are only three breeding records for southern Africa, all from Zimbabwe. One nest was found with eggs in September in a Wahlberg's Eagle nest, another was in a Yellow-billed Kite's nest and contained eggs in December, and a third in a Wahlberg's Eagle nest contained three young in December. The normal clutch is three eggs but a nest in Tanzania contained three chicks and a cracked addled egg, although the egg may possibly have belonged to a previous brood. Eggs are dull creamy-white in ground colour overlaid with fine speckles and blotches of dark red. Some eggs are washed with pale red-brown as well as being blotched and speckled. In some eggs the blotching may be concentrated in a cap at the small or large end. Markings are very variable and one egg of a clutch may be very lightly marked. Measurements of two Zimbabwean clutches are: 36,0 × 29,0, 37,5 × 31,0, 37,5 × 31,0 and 38,7 × 31,5, 40,3 × 31,0, 40,5 × 30,8. Measurements of eggs from Uganda are 39,2 × 31,1 (11); 38,2–40,3 × 30,7–32,0.

The incubation period is not known and there are no details on parental behaviour during this stage. The newly hatched chick is covered in dull white down with a greyish cere, and the bill is blackish at the tip. The legs are greenish-yellow. At the age of about two weeks the down is greyish and first wing and tail feathers appear through the down. No further details of feather development are known.

During the nestling period the male brings prey for the female, delivered at a perch near the nest or directly to her in flight. He does not visit the nest. At a Kenya nest the male brought only small birds, always well plucked. The length of the nestling period is unknown and there are no observations on the post-nestling period.

58 Sooty Falcon   *175.*

Woestynvalk

Falco concolor

PLATES 20 AND 21

DERIVATION
falcon : same colour — *falco* (L) : *concolor* (L)

IDENTIFICATION
Adult: The plumage is a uniform pale slate- grey except for black primaries and a small black 'moustache' streak below the eye. If a good view is obtained, thin black shaft streaks may be seen on the contour feathers. The cere, bare orbital skin and legs are yellow. The eyes

are dark brown. The feet are large for the size of the bird, and the toes attenuated. When it is perched the wing tips reach the end of the tail.

In flight the silhouette is like that of a European Hobby except that the wings appear even longer and more swift-like. The closed tail has a slightly pointed tip. There is no barring on the remiges and tail, and the black primaries are the only contrast to the uniform grey colour.

The Sooty Falcon can only be confused with the Grey Kestrel, which differs in being more stockily built with a large head and an almost parrot-like bill. When it is perched the wing tips of the Grey Kestrel are well short of the tip of the tail. In flight it has the broader wing of a kestrel and the tip of the tail is square, not pointed. From below the remiges and tail are faintly barred. Its flight is much heavier than that of the swift, graceful Sooty Falcon. As far as is known the range of the two species is mutually exclusive in southern Africa, but it is possible that they may overlap in Namibia as the Sooty Falcon has been recorded in the Kalahari.

A rare black form of the Sooty Falcon occurs but has not so far been recorded in southern Africa. Care should be exercised when identifying any that may be seen because of their similarity to the dark form of Eleonora's Falcon.

Juvenile: The upperparts are pale grey and the wing coverts and scapulars are edged with buff. The pale pinkish-buff underparts are diffusely streaked with dark grey. The head has a typical falcon 'cap' and well-defined 'moustache' streak, and the throat is plain pale buff. The soft parts are coloured as in the adult. In flight from below, the underwing coverts are mottled grey and buff and the remiges and tail are barred, the latter with a broad blackish terminal band.

Confusion with the juvenile European Hobby is possible but the juvenile Sooty Falcon is distinguishable by its greyer colour and indistinct streaking on the underparts.

HABITAT

In its breeding range this species inhabits desert regions but in southern Africa it is found mainly along the moist eastern littoral where there are large trees, often near water. However, it has also been recorded in the Kalahari.

STATUS AND DISTRIBUTION

This Palearctic migrant was first recorded in 1961 and has been seen regularly since. It must undoubtedly have been overlooked previously because of its crepuscular habits and probable misidentification. There are records in southern

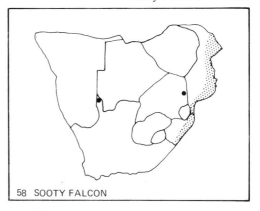

58 SOOTY FALCON

Africa from December to May, but most birds have been seen between January and March.

The main distribution of this species is along the eastern littoral from the Transkei through Natal and Zululand to Mozambique. However, it may be found to occur regularly over a much wider area as there are isolated records from the Kruger National Park and the Kalahari Gemsbok Park.

Extralimitally its breeding range extends from the eastern Sahara through the Sudan to the Nile and the Red Sea islands southwards to Somalia. It migrates via east Africa to Madagascar and south-eastern Africa. It is numerous in the non-breeding season in Madagascar, which is its main wintering area.

GENERAL HABITS

This interesting species breeds in desert regions on low cliffs, under rocks and on offshore islands. One site in the Libyan desert was under a cairn of sandstone slabs used to mark a camel caravan route in a place 'devoid of all vegetation, either living or dead, and its utter barrenness complete'. The temperature in the nest site which was shaded all day was 42 °C. The Sooty Falcon breeds late in the season (after the summer solstice) in order to feed on an abundance of migrating birds moving south when it has nestlings. This adaptation explains why this species arrives later than other migrant raptors in southern Africa.

Although it may hunt during the day, the Sooty Falcon is mainly crepuscular and rests in a shady tree, often a eucalypt, during the day. Sometimes several birds may roost together. It is a confiding species and may be found in built-up areas like Durban and Maputo, but it is easily overlooked. It hunts on the wing and is extremely fast and agile. In a downward stoop it may winnow its wings rapidly like a swift to accelerate in pursuit of prey. Its hunting behaviour is very like that of the European Hobby. Its prey consists of birds, bats and insects. During the breeding season it feeds on small migrant warblers and species up to the size of bee-eaters, orioles and hoopoes. In southern Africa it preys on small birds, including roosting European Swallows, as well as bats and termites. However, because of its crepuscular habits, information on its prey is limited and further information is needed.

59 Taita Falcon 176.

Taitavalk

Falco fasciinucha

PLATES 19 AND 20

DERIVATION
falcon : banded : nape — *falco* (L) : *fascia* (L) : *nucha* (L)
This falcon was first collected at Taita in Kenya

IDENTIFICATION
Adult: This handsome little falcon is stockily built and has the proportions of a Peregrine. The upperparts are slate with distinctive patches of rufous on the nape. There is a broad 'moustache' streak below the eye, the throat is white and the rest of the underparts are rufous with fine pencil streaks of black on the shafts of the feathers. The grey tail has fine black bars and the tip of the tail is buff. The bill is gunmetal blue darkening to black at the tip. The cere, bare orbital skin and legs are rich yellow and show up well even from a long way off. The eyes are dark brown.

In flight the rufous underwing coverts are barred with black and the remiges and tail are finely barred. From below, the impression is of a compactly built falcon with rufous underparts and a white throat. From above, the grey rump contrasts with the slate back.

The only possible confusion that may arise is with the African Hobby and differences are discussed under that species.

Juvenile: The juvenile closely resembles the adult bird but is browner above with narrow buff edges to the wing coverts and scapulars. It is paler rufous below and lacks the broad streaking characteristic of most juvenile falcons.

HABITAT
It is usually found in association with sheer cliffs such as those of the Zambezi escarpment. Outside the breeding season it wanders farther afield to hunt in surrounding woodland areas. Several birds were recorded using the huge Birchenough bridge in Zimbabwe as a look-out point in the early morning and late evening.

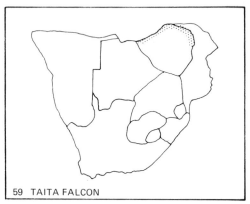

59 TAITA FALCON

This falcon often inhabits the same terrain as the Peregrine and competition with this larger species has been suggested as a possible reason for the rarity of the Taita Falcon. In the Victoria Falls area they occupy different gorges when nesting.

STATUS AND DISTRIBUTION
This species is resident. In southern Africa it has only been recorded in Zimbabwe and adjacent Mozambique. In Zimbabwe its distribution is restricted to the Zambezi escarpment and the eastern districts as far south as the Sabi river. It is not known to occur in the Matopos as stated in one textbook. Extralimitally its distribution is rather discontinuous and it occurs in Malawi, Tanzania, Kenya and southern Ethiopia.

GENERAL HABITS
The Taita Falcon often perches for long periods on cliffs or trees growing from them and may easily be overlooked in a short visit to an area. It flies with characteristic rapid, shallow wing-beats like a parrot, gaining height very quickly without gliding in between. In attack on prey it is capable of stupendous stoops and kills in flight like the Peregrine. Sometimes it stoops past its prey and swoops upwards to take it from below. It probably catches swifts as they show

alarm at its presence and take avoiding action by rising higher and higher to keep above it as it climbs.

Prey consists mainly of small birds up to the size of bulbuls but it is capable of taking much larger species. The following avian prey has been recorded: Black-eyed Bulbul (several records), a cisticola, Red-billed Queleas, African Rock Martin, White-collared Pratincole, Red-winged Starling and Purple-crested Loerie. Insects are also eaten and large butterflies and termites have been recorded. There are no records of mammalian prey; a captive adult refused to eat mice even when hungry although it ate birds readily.

There are two main calls, a squealing, quavering *kreee-kreee-kreee* uttered in short bursts. This is probably a soliciting call by the female as well as a contact between the pair. It is also made by small downy chicks begging for food. The other call is a typical loud falcon-like *kek-kek-kek* used in alarm and when chasing other birds from near the nest.

BREEDING

No spectacular nuptial displays have been observed but the male and female fly about calling a great deal. However, there are few observations on this stage of the breeding cycle. Copulation has been observed several times. The male flies directly onto the female's back, even while she is eating, and they call excitedly.

The few observed nests have all been situated on very high basalt cliffs in small erosion holes. Nest sites in the Victoria Falls gorges have been on cliffs about 140 m high and 35–42 m from the

top. One nest was in a hole 22 cm high, 45 cm wide and 30 cm deep. The eggs were laid in a shallow scrape in loose basalt rock particles at the very back of the hole. Another nest hole seen from a distance was estimated to be approximately twice the size of the one described. Nest sites appear to be chosen so that the eggs are in the shade for most of the day. Descriptions of stick nests built on cliffs by this species are erroneous.

In the Victoria Falls gorges the same sites have been occupied for up to eight years although an alternate site may occasionally be used. The straight-line distance between two nesting pairs was 5 km, and the actual distance along the cliffs in the twisting gorges was 12 km. The Taita Falcons are very aggressive towards other birds of prey near the nest and drive them off as soon as they appear.

The birds become active near their nests from about April onwards. The earliest records of eggs are for July but usually they are laid in August and September. Clutches of three and four eggs have been recorded. In one nest the four eggs are described as yellowish-buff in ground colour variably marked with small spots and blotches of yellowish-brown, one having a wash of this colour covering the top third of the egg while another had some small streaks of darker brown and a few faint underlying ashy marks. Two clutches in Zimbabwe measured: $45,2 \times 34,5$; $42,7 \times 34,1$; $42,5 \times 34,5$; $41,9 \times 34,7$ and $44,3 \times 34,7$; $42,2 \times 34,7$; $43,6 \times 34,7$.

At one nest short periods of observation established that both sexes incubate, the female sitting most of the time. The third and last laid

Habitat of the Taita Falcon below the Victoria Falls; a pair bred on the cliff in the foreground.

A clutch of three Taita Falcon eggs laid in a pothole in a sheer basalt cliff (Photograph: Rob Jeffery).

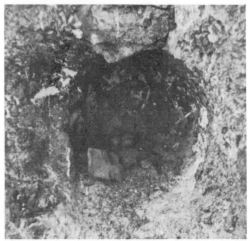

egg at this nest hatched in 26 days. The chicks hatched on successive days and egg-shells were removed from the nest.

Newly hatched chicks are covered in greyish-white down which appears a dirty grey colour by the age of 10 days. Initially the cere and legs are pale greyish but the legs begin to turn yellowish from the age of 10 days. The eyes are dark brown. There are no observations on feather development.

The chicks become active soon after hatching and crawl out from beneath the brooding female by the time they are three days old. By the age of 10 days the female has difficulty in brooding them and they shuffle about the nest chamber. There are no further details on the development of co-ordination of the nestlings.

Both sexes brood the chicks until they are at least 11 days old but there are no observations after this age. During a 13-hour watch at a nest with two chicks 10 and 11 days old the female was on the nest for 69 per cent of the time and the male for 10 per cent. For the remainder there was no adult on the nest although the female was often perched nearby. She left the nest for up to an hour and it was at these times that the male brooded the chicks. This behaviour is typical of parental attention during the early part of the nestling period. During the 13-hour watch prey was brought seven times by the male and twice by the female (in the late afternoon). Not all the male's prey was fresh and some was brought from his favourite plucking site where he cached excess prey in a larder. The habit of maintaining a larder is normal behaviour at this stage of the breeding cycle.

The length of the nestling period is unrecorded but in one case it was not less than about four weeks. At a nest in Malawi the adults and soliciting young were watched flying round together at least three weeks after they first left the nest. They never flew farther than 0,8 km from the nest site and returned to it at times. At this stage it appeared that the female was mainly responsible for feeding the young, and the male acted as a sentinel. Once when an intruding Peregrine flew by, an adult and the two young chased it away with much noisy calling.

60 Red-necked Falcon   *178.*

Rooinekvalk

Falco chicquera

PLATES 19 AND 20

DERIVATION
falcon : 'shikari' — *falco* (L) : *chicquera* (L)

As the name was given to this species by Daudin, a Frenchman, *chicquera* should be pronounced 'shikera', which is close to the Hindi *shikari*, meaning hunter. The Shikra (or Little Banded Goshawk) is of similar derivation.

IDENTIFICATION
Adult: This small, attractively marked species cannot be mistaken for any other falcon in southern Africa. It is chestnut on the head with a prominent darker red-brown 'moustache' streak. The rest of the upperparts are blue-grey with fine black bars throughout. The tail is grey with narrow black bars and there is a very broad black band near the tip which is white. The throat is white, below which is a broad band of pale rufous across the upper breast. The rest of the underparts are finely barred with black and white. The cere, bare orbital skin and legs are rich yellow. The eyes are dark brown. In flight the broad black band near the tip of the tail is diagnostic. The underwing coverts are barred with black and white and the remiges are faintly barred with black and grey.

Juvenile: On the head it is dark brown where the adult is chestnut and there are two small buff nape patches. The upperparts are darker grey than those of the adult with brown edges to the wing coverts and scapulars and some indistinct barring. The throat is white and the rest of the underparts are washed pale rufous with faint brown barring and thin 'pencil' streaks of brown on the shafts of the feathers. The soft parts are coloured like those of the adult. The flight pattern is like that of the adult and the broad band near the tip of the tail is diagnostic at all times. The juvenile moults directly into adult plumage but there are no observations on the duration of this transition.

HABITAT
Although closely associated with the distribution of Borassus palms in Africa, this species is found mainly in arid regions in southern Africa. In Botswana and Mozambique it is found where there are Borassus palms but it is not restricted

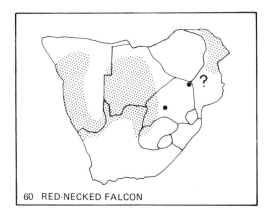

60 RED-NECKED FALCON

to these areas. It quite often hunts on open plains well away from trees. In the Namib desert it is found where there are thorn trees along dry watercourses.

STATUS AND DISTRIBUTION

As far as is known it is resident. Its distribution is mainly confined to the arid west. It occurs in the northern Cape, Namibia and Botswana. It is rare in the western Orange Free State and western Transvaal and there are occasional records from the northern Kruger National Park. It is widely distributed in northern Mozambique. There are no recent records from Natal and it has not been found in Zimbabwe, although it is to be expected as it occurs in adjacent areas. Extralimitally its distribution extends northwards to the Sahara in suitable habitat. It is also found in India south of the Himalayas.

GENERAL HABITS

The Red-necked Falcon is often found in pairs and in India the male and female are said to co-operate when hunting. It perches within the canopy of a tree or quite often in completely open areas on a low perch such as a log or clod of earth. It flies with rapid wing-beats and is very swift, catching most of its prey in flight. From a low perch it can launch an almost vertical attack on a bird flying overhead and has a remarkable rate of climb.

The main prey of this falcon is small birds, but it also catches insects, lizards, bats and small rodents. In one breeding study in southern Zambia 292 prey records were analysed; birds comprised 98 per cent of the total, with rodents and insects making up the balance. Most of the birds caught were small passerines, but some migratory waders, as well as plovers, doves, Collared Pratincoles, a Black Crake and an African Jacana were indentified. A total of 56 Collared Pratincoles, abundant on the flood-plain where the falcons nested, was recorded; this indicated that they were opportunistic feeders preying on the most abundant food source in their territories. In the Namib desert one female Red-necked Falcon killed five Common Quails in 24 hours. She was not breeding on the vulture's nest where they were found and had only partially eaten some of them. This behaviour suggests that food may be cached when abundant.

Outside the breeding season this falcon is rarely heard. One call is a shrill *ki-ki-ki-ki-ki*, but further details on calls and the context in which they are made are required.

BREEDING

No spectacular nuptial display flights have been described and the birds merely fly round near the nest site with much calling early in the breeding season.

Contrary to statements in some books, this species does not build its own nest. It takes over the old nest of some other bird of prey or crow and adds no lining. Sometimes it dispossesses a crow of its nest just before the crow lays. Eggs are also laid at the base of Borassus palm fronds where they join the main trunk. In desert regions nests may be as low as 4,5 m, those in palms as high as 24 m or more.

There is little information on size of territory except from the Kafue Flats in southern Zambia, where eight nests were found in fairly close proximity, the distance between adjacent sites ranging from 1,3 km to 3,2 km. The average territory size was 5,5 km². Such a high density would seem unlikely in the arid regions of southern Africa.

Eggs have been recorded from July to October in southern Africa but laying takes place mainly in August and September. Two to four eggs are laid, usually three. They are creamy in ground colour, rather chalky in texture and thickly overlaid with red-brown blotches, speckles and smears which usually cover the entire surface, although some eggs have bare areas with no markings. The amount of marking is variable and eggs tend to fade as incubation progresses. Frequently eggs are stained with excreta, which commonly fouls the nest in the incubation period. The measurements of southern African eggs, mostly from Namibia, are: 44,0 × 32,9 (29); 41,4–47,0 × 30,8–34,5.

Eggs are laid at intervals of one to three days and incubation begins once the clutch is complete. However, in a clutch of four, incubation may commence once the third egg is laid. Only the female has been observed to incubate, and the male brings food for her. Usually she leaves

(1) A Red-necked Falcon on a low perch in open treeless country; it launched an attack on a displaying pipit from this position.

(2) These eggs were laid in a derelict Lappet-faced Vulture's nest.

(3) An adult and nestlings about two weeks old in a Black Crow's nest (Photograph: Clem Haagner).

the nest to take prey from him, but occasionally he delivers it to the nest. When not hunting he may rest in the shade of the nest tree. Other birds of prey are attacked and driven off if they pass nearby. The incubation period is 32–34 days, averaging 33 days.

All young in a brood hatch within a period of one to two days. The newly hatched chicks are covered in creamy-white down; the cere and bare orbital skin are greenish-yellow and the legs flesh coloured. During the first two weeks the down darkens to greyish on the upperparts. The primary quills emerge at 14 days and by 17 days quills are sprouting rapidly on the upperparts. At 22 days the down has largely been replaced by feathers, and at 32 days the only remaining down is on the head. There are no observations on the development of co-ordination of the nestlings.

During the first five or six days the chicks are brooded constantly by the female; the male provides prey which she tears up for them. Once the young are five or six days old both parents hunt and bring prey to the nest.

The nestling period is 34–37 days and averages 36 days. The young are still with their parents for at least 24 days after leaving the nest, but it is not known when they become independent.

In a study in southern Zambia an average of 1,3 young per nest was reared, which was 44 per cent of all eggs laid. A lost clutch may be replaced; in one case a new clutch was completed within 19 days of the loss of the first.

61 Western Red-footed Falcon *(KESTREL)*

179.

Westelike Rooipootvalk

Falco vespertinus

PLATES 21 AND 22

DERIVATION

falcon : of the evening — *falco* (L) : *vespertinus* (L)

In this context *vespertinus* is used in the sense of 'western', i.e. where the sun is in the evening.

IDENTIFICATION

Adult: The male is identical to the Eastern Red-footed Falcon except that it has grey underwing coverts. It appears uniform slate-grey in flight except for the chestnut ventral feathers. Some individuals, possibly old birds, have a symmetrical pattern of silver-grey and black primary feathers. However, even these aberrant males cannot be mistaken for any other species.

Females differ markedly from those of the Eastern Red-footed Falcon. They are blue-grey above with transverse black barring but the head and nape are rufous-yellow and, except for the white throat and cheeks, this colour continues onto the underparts which have a few thin black pencil streaks not visible at a distance. There is a broad dark-brown 'moustache' streak below the eye. The soft parts are like those of the male except that they are paler orange-red. In flight from below, the underwing coverts are rufous-yellow and the remiges and tail are boldly barred black and white. The terminal band on the tail is broadest.

Juvenile and immature: The juvenile is brown on the upperparts with buff edges to the wing coverts and scapulars. The pattern on the head is like that of the female but the crown is pale brown and there is a narrow white collar on the nape. Except for the white throat the underparts are buff with brown streaking. The eyes are dark brown and the soft parts are orange-yellow. In flight from below, the underwing coverts are buff with some black streaking and the remiges and tail are barred black and white. There is a resemblance to the juvenile European Hobby but the barring of the flight feathers is bolder than in that species, the streaking on the underparts less pronounced and the underwing coverts are only lightly marked.

In males the juvenile plumage is replaced by darker slate-grey feathers on the upperparts and rufous-yellow below onto which the adult pattern is superimposed as it undergoes further moults. Female juveniles darken above and below so that they closely resemble the adult female except for the remnants of juvenile streaking on the underparts.

HABITAT

It is found in the same type of habitat as the Eastern Red-footed Falcon but being more western in its distribution it also occurs in drier regions.

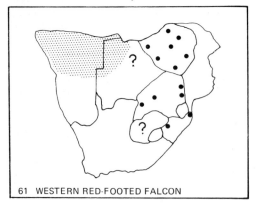

61 WESTERN RED-FOOTED FALCON

STATUS AND DISTRIBUTION

This migrant falcon is rare in southern Africa in comparison with the huge numbers of Eastern Red-footed Falcons whose distribution it overlaps in places. It arrives in November or December and leaves in March. Its distribution is mainly western and it is not uncommon in Namibia and Angola. In Botswana it is probably more common and widespread than present re-cords indicate. It also occurs in Zimbabwe, Transvaal, Orange Free State and the eastern Cape but is uncommon. There are only very occasional records from Natal.

The breeding distribution of this falcon extends from eastern Europe to Mongolia and does not overlap that of the Eastern Red-footed Falcon. The entire population winters in the southern part of Africa, passing south on a broad front in north Africa. The eastern populations first migrate westwards and pass north of the Caspian and Black Seas before meeting up with European birds moving south via the Balkans.

GENERAL HABITS

This falcon is similar in habits to the Eastern Red-footed Falcon with which it may roost, although completely outnumbered where their ranges overlap. This falcon winters entirely in Africa but has not been recorded in numbers commensurate with its breeding abundance. A possible explanation is that it occurs in regions that are little studied by ornithologists so that it has been largely overlooked.

62 Eastern Red-footed Falcon (KESTREL)

/80

Oostelike Rooipootvalk

Falco amurensis

PLATES 21 AND 22

DERIVATION

falcon : of the Amur — *falco* (L) : *amurensis* (L)

The Amur River is between Russia and China.

IDENTIFICATION

Adult: Males are dark slate-grey above and paler blue-grey below with chestnut on the lower abdomen, vent and thighs. The eyes are dark brown and the cere, orbital ring and legs orange-red. In flight the white underwing coverts contrast with the rest of the dark underparts, immediately distinguishing this species from the male Western Red-footed Falcon, the only species with which it can be confused.

Females are slate-grey above with indistinct blackish transverse barring which is more defined on the tail. There is a broad 'moustache' streak below the eye, and the throat is plain white. The rest of the white underparts are blotched and barred with blackish except for pale rufous on the lower abdomen, vent and thighs. The cere, orbital ring and legs are paler red than in the male. The eyes are dark brown. In flight the white underwing coverts are heavily blotched with black, and the black remiges conspicuously barred with white. The white undertail surface is broadly barred with black and there is a broader band near the tip. It resembles the European Hobby but that species is red on the vent and more heavily streaked with black on the underparts.

Juvenile and immature: The juvenile resembles the female but is dull grey-brown above with buff edges to the wing coverts and scapulars. The underparts appear more streaky below. The soft parts are orange-yellow. After the first juvenile plumage females become more blotched and barred below and in males the streaking on the underparts is gradually replaced by grey feathers

HABITAT

It is found in open grassland or lightly wooded country but requires tall trees such as a clump of eucalypts for roosting.

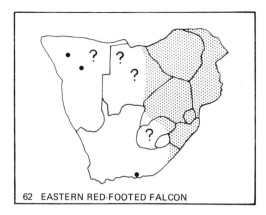

62   EASTERN RED-FOOTED FALCON

through Russia, but they have not been detected there either. The mystery of their return route remains to be solved.

STATUS AND DISTRIBUTION

This migrant falcon arrives in southern Africa in November or December and departs in March. Its distribution is mainly in the eastern half of southern Africa from Transkei northwards, although occasionally recorded farther south. In the west it is found in northern Botswana and northern Namibia, but is not plentiful in those areas where the Western Red-footed Falcon is more likely to occur.

This falcon breeds in eastern Siberia, Manchuria and northern China. Its migration pattern is interesting but incompletely known. On its way to Africa it flies from north-west India to east Africa, a distance of at least 3 000 km over the Indian Ocean. The birds are very fat in preparation for this epic journey and are said to be 'very good eating'. There is uncertainty about the path of their return journey to their breeding grounds. They pass through Kenya in April and may return to India by the same route. However, they have not been observed in India on the way back and it has been suggested that they pass north of the Himalayas

GENERAL HABITS

This falcon is gregarious at all times and may be encountered in small groups or large flocks. It often occurs alongside Lesser Kestrels, and the two species sometimes roost together. Less often it mixes with the Western Red-footed Falcon where the ranges of the two species overlap. It is best known for its communal roosting habits as roosts are quite frequently near human habitation in stands of eucalypts occupied year after year. Roosts of up to 5 000 birds are common; at one well-known roost near Salisbury in Zimbabwe an estimated 50 000–100 000 birds gathered. The falcons fly in when it is almost dark, gathering from over a wide area, and settle down with much shrill screaming which continues throughout the night. At a roost in Malawi the falcons shared the same clump of eucalypts as Pied Crows but the two species occupied different parts of it. The falcons fly from their roost before sunrise and disperse into the surrounding countryside to hunt. In Africa they are entirely insectivorous as far as is known, termites, grasshoppers and locusts being their main food. In one incident a group of about 150 falcons discovered a swarm of wild bees which they consumed in a short period. They are often seen resting on telegraph wires or fence posts, but hunting is done on the wing. They catch and eat termites in flight, one every three seconds on average, and snatch grasshoppers from the ground without alighting. They may hover when hunting prey on the ground but their graceful sweeping flight when catching termites is more reminiscent of a hobby than a kestrel.

63 Rock Kestrel   *181.*

Rooivalk

Falco tinnunculus

PLATES 21 AND 22

DERIVATION

falcon : little bell — *falco* (L) : *tinnunculus* (L)

This species has always been known as the Rock Kestrel in southern Africa, and this name has been retained in preference to Common Kestrel, applied to the nominate race in Europe.

IDENTIFICATION

Adult: Although the sexes are distinguishable, the difference is not nearly as marked as in the Common Kestrel in Europe. The male is mainly rufous with black spotting, except on the breast where there are fine black streaks. The head is blue-grey and the tail blue with a broad black terminal band and a white tip. When the tail is spread, narrow black barring is often visible on the outer tail feathers. It is not known whether this barring is individual variation or a remnant of immature plumage that later disappears. The bill is black, the eyes are dark brown and the cere, orbital ring and legs are yellow. In flight from below, the tail and underwing appear mainly silver-grey with black spotting on the underwing coverts and blackish barring on the remiges. From above, the blue rump and tail with its broad black terminal band are the most striking features. The male Rock Kestrel can be confused only with the male Lesser Kestrel; differences are discussed under that species.

The plumage of females is still uncertain. It appears that females closely resemble males except for narrow barring on the tail, including the central tail feathers. A captive breeding female had this plumage. Observations on wild pairs are needed to clarify the situation.

Juveniles and immature: The head of the juvenile is rufous with narrow black streaks, matching the rest of the upperparts. Its tail is rufous with narrow black bars and a broad terminal band; the tip of the tail is buff. Otherwise it resembles the adults. Confusion with the female Lesser Kestrel and juvenile Greater Kestrel is possible; the differences are discussed in the texts on those species. No observations have been recorded on the Rock Kestrel's transition to adult plumage.

HABITAT

This kestrel occurs mainly in mountainous terrain or adjacent areas. However, it is found also in open country far from mountains, as for example in Botswana or in the Namib Desert.

STATUS AND DISTRIBUTION

It is widespread and common. In mountainous country it is resident, but in the Transvaal there is evidence of winter immigration to the central and western highveld.

The Rock Kestrel occurs throughout southern Africa. Extralimitally it occurs northwards to Angola, southern Zaire and south-western Tanzania. Other races occur in Africa, Europe and Asia.

GENERAL HABITS

This attractive species is usually seen solitarily or in pairs, frequently perching on poles beside roads. It hunts from a perch or by hovering. Depending on the conditions, it hovers with rapidly winnowing wings or, on windy days, maintains its position on an updraught with little wing-flapping. After remaining in one spot for a while it sideslips downwind and takes up a new position. Prey is caught with a controlled parachute drop and then taken to a perch to eat.

There is little detailed information on the prey of the Rock Kestrel in southern Africa. Its prey consists of small rodents, occasional bats, small birds, lizards and arthropods such as spiders, locusts, grasshoppers and caterpillars. A bloated bont tick was brought to one nest.

It makes shrill high-pitched *kee-kee-kee* and *kik-kik-kik* calls when threatening Rock Kestrels and other intruders near the nest. A trilling *kreeee* is used during courtship, as a greeting call, in solicitation by the female and also for threat. It is from the tinkling quality of this call that the specific name *tinnunculus* is derived. Short, sharp *dzik* and *kit* notes are used in various contexts: when feeding chicks, inspecting a nest site, during display and mating, and when delivering prey or changing over at the nest. The chicks cheep initially and later beg with a *zirrr-zirrr* call.

BREEDING

Nuptial displays, to the accompaniment of much calling, consist of circling and chasing flights during which the male may dive at the female, who turns and presents her claws or jinks out of his way. He also swoops down on her while she is perched. He brings prey for her and may feed her for two months before the eggs are laid. Mating often takes place after prey delivery, usually on the nest or nearby. In the early stages the male flies to the nest to attract the female to it. They also perch together and nibble each other.

The most usual nest site is on cliff on a ledge

A Rock Kestrel peers out from its nest ledge on a sandstone cliff beside the sea.

or in a hollow. The old nest of a White-necked Raven is sometimes used and probably the stick nests of other cliff-nesting species. Old quarries and holes in road cuttings or dongas are also used for nesting. Where there are no cliffs, nests in trees are used, usually crow nests, but once an old Hamerkop's nest with no roof. Nest sites also include man-made structures such as church steeples, hangars and steel road bridges. Many years ago a pair bred on the City Hall in Cape Town. The eggs are laid on whatever surface there is in the nest and, apart from a slight scrape, no nest is made. Where stick nests are described as having been lined by the kestrel, the material would have belonged to the previous occupant.

There is no information on the territory of the Rock Kestrel except that it vigorously chases off other large birds or prey and White-necked Ravens.

Eggs are laid from August to November in southern Africa with a peak in September/October (89 per cent of 45 records). Three to five eggs are laid. They are creamy in ground colour but are heavily overlaid with dark red blotches and smears. Sometimes the ground colour is obscured by a reddish wash. The eggs are very variable, even in the same clutch, but are usually handsomely marked. Measurements are: 39,2 × 32,6 (67); 36,6–43,0 × 30,3–34,3.

At one nest the five eggs were laid at two-day intervals and incubation began once the clutch was complete. The incubating female is fed by the male, who may take over for short periods while she is off the nest feeding. The female sits very tight and may fly round aggressively once flushed. One incubation period of the Rock Kestrel was close on 30 days.

In one observation four eggs hatched on the same day and the fifth chick died in the shell. There is no sibling aggression but the smallest chick may sometimes die, probably from starvation. The newly hatched chick is covered in white down which thickens and becomes greyish above by the time it is a week old. Feathers emerge rapidly through the down from two weeks on, covering the body by the age of three weeks. There are few observations on the development of co-ordination except that the young can feed themselves at the age of 18 days. Once the young are about a month old they perch outside the nest.

At one nest the female remained on the nest almost continuously for the first nine days and the male brought prey. Birds were brought to the nest well plucked. After the first nine days the female began to leave the chicks alone in the nest and assisted the male in catching prey, although he still did the major share.

One nestling period of the Rock Kestrel was about 34 days. The young are fed near the nest by both parents and return to roost in it initially. The post-nestling period lasts about a month.

There is no information on breeding success. All aspects of the breeding biology of the Rock Kestrel require further study.

64 Greater Kestrel /8ᴅ.

Grootrooivalk

Falco rupicoloides

PLATES 21 AND 22

DERIVATION

falcon : *rupicolus* : like — *falco* (L) : *rupicolus* (L) : *eides* (G)

The Greater Kestrel was originally thought to be like the Rock Kestrel *Falco tinnunculus rupicolus*, hence *rupicoloides* or like *rupicolus*: rock : inhabitant — *rupis* (L) : *incola* (L).

IDENTIFICATION

Adult: This medium-sized kestrel is tawny-rufous in colour with black barring on the upperparts and sparse streaking on the underparts merging into barring on the flanks. The rump and tail are grey with black bars, the terminal bar of the white-tipped tail being broadest. The whitish eye is diagnostic, distinguishing this species from all other kestrels and falcons occuring in southern Africa. The cere, orbital ring and legs are yellow. In flight the entire underwing is silvery-white and the barred grey tail prevents confusion with the female Lesser Kestrel or juvenile Rock Kestrel. The sexes are similar in size and coloration.

Juvenile and immature: The juvenile differs from the adult in having streaks not bars on the flanks, a red-brown tail and rump which are more narrowly barred with black, a dark brown eye and a bluish-white cere and orbital ring. In flight it shows some brown streaking on the underwing coverts. When 3–4 months old the streaked flanks moult and become barred, the rump changes to grey and the cere and orbital skin turn yellow. At 10–11 months old the tail is moulted and becomes grey with bars like the adult. The eye changes to white when 18–36 months old. Young birds may breed when a year old but usually at the age of two years.

The juvenile could be confused with the female Lesser Kestrel but is more rufous in colour, especially on the underparts. The juvenile Rock Kestrel is also similar but has a pattern of spots, not streaks, on the underparts. The Greater Kestrel and Rock Kestrel are also usually found in different habitats.

HABITAT

The Greater Kestrel is essentially a species of the open country with short cover and is not found in wooded country or where the cover is more than about 50 cm in height. It occurs widely in semi-desert and desert conditions.

STATUS AND DISTRIBUTION

This species is resident in many areas but may be nomadic where annual conditions fluctuate and become unsuitable. It is widespread and common and appears in no danger at present, indeed it may have expanded its range in some areas (e.g. the Transvaal) where woodland has been cleared for agricultural purposes. It is distributed throughout southern Africa except where the habitat is unsuitable in the south-west Cape and in the wooded eastern areas. Extralimitally it occurs in southern Zambia and Angola. North of this its distribution is discontinuous and it is found in east Africa and in north-east Africa.

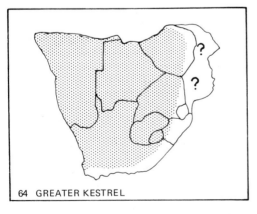

64 GREATER KESTREL

GENERAL HABITS

The Greater Kestrel is usually seen singly or in pairs. It hunts solitarily, mainly from a perch, and uses the highest available vantage point such as an electricity pylon. However, if high look-out points are not available, it perches low down on a termite mound, rock or similar situation. It usually remains on a perch for about fifteen minutes before moving off to a new spot. Prey is caught with a slow descent from a perch but if missed it may be briefly chased in flight or on foot. Hovering is also used for hunting, especially in windy conditions, and is usually at a height of 10–15 m. When hunting intensively it may hover as often as 100 times in succession and work an area for as long as an hour. Sometimes it makes long fast dashes over distances of up to 300 m to surprise avian prey or when sighting larger prey such as a rat or lizard. Very occasionally it is capable of even more dashing flights, stooping on birds or circling up with them as they gain height to snatch them in the air.

This species has the interesting habit of caching prey. This behaviour may occur at any time of the year, especially when prey is abundant, or during the incubation and early nestling period when the male provides an excess of prey which the female then caches. Cache spots are within or under tufts of grass, or under stones or clods; up to three items have been found cached at the same spot at one time. Males and females have their own cache spots.

Prey consists mainly of arthropods, especially grasshoppers, as well as termites, beetles, centipedes, scorpions, spiders and sunspiders (solifugids). Other larger prey is taken at any time, but particularly during the breeding season, and includes rodents up to the size of a vlei rat, lizards, small snakes and birds. Avian prey up to the size of a quail is caught, although usually smaller birds such as larks and finches.

There is no record of this species drinking or bathing but it may occasionally dust-bath.

Calling is heard mainly in the breeding season and it is largely silent at other times. In courtship and territorial display a shrill trilling *kwirrr* call is used. A double-noted *kweek-kweek* is made when threatening other intruding birds. When close to each other the birds exchange soft contact calls, the female a low *chuck,* and the male a higher-pitched *kwit.* On delivering prey to the nest the male alerts the female with a special chittering call.

BREEDING

First signs of breeding activity occur in about April, some four months before eggs are laid. The pair perch together at dawn in a promi-

View of a Greater Kestrel's nest site in a Black Crow's nest.

Eggs of a Greater Kestrel laid in a Pied Crow's nest (Photograph: Alan Kemp).

nent position, often near the previous year's nest site. Then the birds begin to soar together, sometimes dangling their legs, and the male performs 'flicker dives' — diving back and forth near his soaring mate and rocking from side to side to display his silvery-white underwings. The display is accompanied by the trilling *kwirrr* call. The female also occasionally performs 'flicker dives' but these are predominantly a male activity. Nearer the laying time the male starts to lead the female to the nest, swooping past her and flying ahead to alight with his wings held up. Copulation may start three months before laying, often after a visit to the nest. Courtship feeding occurs nearer the laying time, though it is not an invariable practice as the female may continue to hunt for herself.

The nest of another bird is used; there is no authentic evidence that this species ever makes additions to or builds a nest. There is one record of a site in a hole in a Baobab tree where the eggs were laid on wood chips on the floor of the hole. Crow nests are favoured; their nests are used whether built in trees, especially eucalypts, or on poles or pylons. They are usually situated from 2–20 m above ground. However, any suitable stick nest may be used, e.g. that of species such as Black-shouldered Kite and Secretary Bird. In one remarkable observation in east Africa a Greater Kestrel bred on an occupied Lappet-faced Vulture's nest and sat on eggs only 65 cm away from the incubating vulture. In another instance a Greater Kestrel bred in the same tree three metres from a nesting White-faced Owl.

The same nest may be used for several years until it falls apart, i.e. the frequency of moves is governed by how long a nest lasts. In a study area in the Transvaal territories were 600 hectares in extent, remaining this size each year. There was evidence that in the breeding season only part of the territory was utilised. Intraspecific encounters were infrequent and involved only the male on the boundary of his territory. Territorial advertisement, mostly by the male, is performed by 'flicker dives', perching prominently on a high vantage point and also possibly by high hovering or by soaring. Both sexes attack and drive off other species such as crows, buzzards, kites and herons, the female from near the nest and the male throughout his territory.

Over most of southern Africa eggs are laid from August to October with occasional November records. In Namibia laying may begin as early as July and there is a single record of eggs in March. Three to five eggs are laid, usually three, and a single clutch of seven eggs has been recorded. Eggs are creamy or pale buff in ground colour, very variably marked with speckles, spots, blotches and smears of dark red-brown. Some are well marked so that little of the ground colour is visible, others only lightly marked. Considerable variation may occur in the same clutch. Measurements are: 41,9 × 33,6 (119); 38,4–45,0 × 31,0–36,5.

Eggs are laid on successive days but in a clutch of four the last egg may be laid two days after the third. Incubation apparently starts once the clutch is nearing completion, as there is little difference in the size of the chicks after hatching. In one clutch of five, however, the young hatched on successive days, indicating that incubation began with the laying of the first egg. Most of the incubation is by the female, who is fed by the male. He brings larger prey such as lizards, birds and rodents and she leaves the nest to feed while he takes over incubation in her absence. He brings between four and six items to her daily. On two occasions the incubation period has been established as 32–33 days.

The newly hatched chicks are covered in white down tinged with brown. Their brown eyes are weakly open, and their ceres, bills and legs are pinkish and their gapes bright pink. At a week old the down is darkening to greyish and the feather tracts are visible on the upperparts. By two weeks old they are covered in a thick coat of dark grey down. The cere is grey, the bill horn coloured, the gape pale pink and the legs are yellowish. At three weeks old the feathers which have been concealed by the thick second-down coat are appearing, particularly on the wings and tail. At 25 days old the feathers have emerged rapidly and there is very little down visible. When the young leave the nest the last traces of down have disappeared. There are no observations on the development of co-ordination of the nestlings.

During the first week the female broods the chicks closely and the male brings prey. After this she spends an increasing amount of time off the nest although always in the vicinity, where she vigorously chases off intruding birds. Her calls attract the male, who joins in the chase. In the second half of the nestling period she hunts actively, delivering at least half the food requirements of the nestlings. In the course of one day's watch the female hovered 640 times and brought 110 grasshoppers to the nest while the male brought a few grasshoppers, four mice and a lizard.

The young leave the nest when just under five weeks old, often when they can do little more than flutter to the ground where they can easily be caught. Within three days they are strong on the wing and can fly considerable distances. From their first day they return to their nest tree or pylon at dusk to roost, scrabbling or fluttering up as best they can. The parents roost nearby and become very agitated at dusk, calling repeatedly and flying to the roost site to attract the young. They remain in the nest area for four to six weeks and attempt to capture prey for themselves when only a week out of the nest. The adults leave them more and more to fend for themselves after the first two weeks although they may still bring prey for them when they have been out of the nest a month.

In a Transvaal study area breeding success was rather variable, but on average two young were reared per pair, although four young were also regularly raised. Starvation was the main cause of nestling deaths; chicks three or four weeks old died, sometimes a whole brood. These losses were seemingly caused by delayed rains or other factors limiting food supply. Breeding takes place annually. A single brood is raised, although there is one record of two consecutive broods being reared in the same nest, presumably by the same pair. This occurred during a rodent population explosion.

Note: This account is based to a large extent on unpublished observations of Dr Alan Kemp.

65 Lesser Kestrel /83

Kleinrooivalk

Falco naumanni   PLATES 21 AND 22

DERIVATION

falcon : of Naumann — *falco* (L) : *naumanni* (L)

Naumann was a German zoologist who lived during the first half of the last century. This species used to be called Naumann's Kestrel.

IDENTIFICATION

Adult: Males of this slenderly built, graceful kestrel are handsomely coloured. The head is pale blue, contrasting with the unmarked pale chestnut-red back feathers. The secondaries are pale blue, the primaries black, and the tail is pale blue with a broad black terminal band and a white tip. On the creamy-buff underparts there are some small black spots but from a distance these are barely visible. The eyes are dark brown and the cere, orbital ring and legs are yellow. If a good view is obtained, the white claws are a diagnostic feature of this species. In flight the whole underwing is unmarked silvery-white. The only species with which confusion may arise is the adult Rock Kestrel which differs in being spotted on the upperparts with no blue secondaries. In flight the underwing coverts are spotted and the remiges barred. The gregarious habits of the Lesser Kestrel also distinguish it from the resident Rock Kestrel.

The female Lesser Kestrel is pale sandy-brown above with dark brown spotting. The tail is narrowly barred with black and has a broader terminal band. There is a slight 'moustache' streak below the eye, and the underparts are buff with narrow streaks of dark brown. The soft parts are of the same colour as the male. In flight the underwing coverts are buff with black spots and the pale greyish remiges and tail are faintly barred. The impression is of a pale kestrel. It could be confused with a juvenile Rock Kestrel but that species has spots not streaks below and is more rufous in colour. Female Lesser Kestrels are noticeably larger than males.

Juvenile and immature: Juveniles of both sexes resemble the female. Immature males are first recognisable by their pale blue heads and tail feathers as they gradually moult into adult plumage.

HABITAT

In southern Africa this species occurs in open country, especially in the 'sweet' grassland of the Highveld, and avoids well-wooded country. It is frequently found in or near towns and villages where there are clumps of eucalypts or other trees in which it can roost.

STATUS AND DISTRIBUTION

This Palearctic migrant arrives in October and departs in March or early April. It is abundant: in 1970 the South African population was estimated at 154 000 birds over an area of approximately 960 000 km². The population densities in the various provinces were: Orange Free State 74 000, Cape 45 000, Transvaal

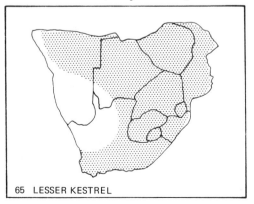

65 LESSER KESTREL

Lesser Kestrels roost in these eucalypts near a farmhouse and hunt in the surrounding open country.

30 000 and Natal interior 5 000. It is distributed from the south-west Cape northwards throughout southern Africa except in the arid west and is commonest in the highveld regions. In Zimbabwe it occurs in quite large flocks but the population density nowhere approaches that found in South Africa.

The Lesser Kestrel has a wide breeding distribution round the mediterranean eastwards through Asia Minor into southern Russia and China. Some birds migrate to India but Africa is the main wintering area. One ringed bird found at Queenstown, Cape, had come from the Dzambul region of Russia 8 785 km away.

GENERAL HABITS

These kestrels arrive at their traditional roosting sites in small groups initially but within a few days build up from a few hundred to thousands. One roost at Senekal in the Orange Free State was known to have been used for at least 28 years. Towns and villages are often used as roosting sites as they contain the only stands of large trees, usually eucalypts, in otherwise open treeless country. Although droppings foul the ground below roosts, the birds are rarely molested because they are recognised as beneficial to the farmer. Each evening the kestrels congregrate at their roost with much noisy high-pitched screaming and settle down for the night. However, in some towns that are well lighted, the birds may fly round after dark, probably feeding on nocturnal insects. In the early morning they disperse over a wide area into the surrounding countryside to hunt and are seen perched in scattered groups or flying about. Light and graceful on the wing, they hunt at a height of about 10–15 m. Most often they swing into the wind to hover briefly before

A flock of Lesser Kestrels hunting in open country.

sweeping off to turn into the wind again in a new position. Insects on the ground are taken in a graceful stoop, and termites are caught and eaten in flight. They are attracted to grass fires to catch insects disturbed. Prey in southern Africa is almost entirely insects but they have been recorded to catch finch-larks, and probably small rodents are sometimes taken. These kestrels are extremely useful in helping to control agricultural pests such as locusts but they sometimes suffer the effects of pesticides used to control these. Those in a position to do so would perform a valuable service by monitoring the size of roosts to see if there is any decline in the numbers of these kestrels.

---

66 Grey Kestrel *184.*

Grysvalk

Falco ardosiaceus

PLATES 20 AND 21

DERIVATION
falcon : slate-coloured — *falco* (L) : *ardosia* (L)

The Latin *ardosia* is a back formation from the French *ardoise*, slate.

IDENTIFICATION
Adult: This sturdily built kestrel has a relatively large head and bill. Its uniform slate-grey coloration prevents confusion with any other raptor except the Sooty Falcon, under which species differences are discussed. The eyes are dark brown, and the cere, prominent orbital ring and legs are yellow. In flight the underwing coverts are grey and the blackish remiges and tail are barred with pale grey. This barring is indistinct and does not show at at distance.

Juvenile: It closely resembles the adult and no differences are discernible in the field.

HABITAT
This species occurs in Hyphaene palm savanna and in a wide variety of other savanna woodland habitats.

STATUS AND DISTRIBUTION
As far as is known it is resident. It is seen either singly or in pairs and is nowhere common. In southern Africa it has a very restricted distribution in northern Namibia and occurs in Ovamboland west of Rundu. There are sight records from the northern Kalahari Gemsbok National Park near Union's End, which, however, is well beyond the known distribution of the species. The Sooty Falcon has recently been reported from this area, and 'Grey Kestrels' have probably been mistaken for this species. Extralimitally it is widely distributed northwards to the Sahara.

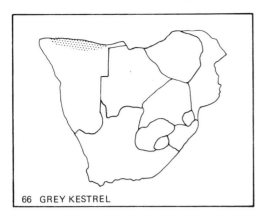

66 GREY KESTREL

GENERAL HABITS

The Grey Kestrel is normally seen on an exposed perch watching the ground below and it glides down diagonally to catch prey. Most of its hunting is from a perch although it also hovers over open ground like a Rock Kestrel. Insects are caught on the ground or in flight. It flies with fast, shallow wing-beats but at no great speed. However, it can fly rapidly at times, as when chasing bats.

The diet of this species consists of insects, lizards, frogs, worms and small mammals such as mice. In one incident a pair was seen trying to rob a Grey Hornbill of a lizard it was carrying. It has also been recorded eating the husks of oil-palms, pulling off the fruit with its bill and then holding it down with its feet while tearing off strips.

The call is described as a 'rattling whistle' rather like a squeaky bicycle. Another call is a chattering alarm note. The nestlings make a mewing call initially and then adopt the 'rattling whistle' of the adults when about to leave the nest.

BREEDING

The breeding biology of this species is poorly known and no nests have been found in southern Africa. Nest sites recorded extralimitally have been either inside a Hamerkop's nest or in a natural hole in a tree. Where a Hamerkop's nest is used the owners are sometimes dispossessed. In Angola a female was thought to be incubating eggs or brooding small young at the end of September. Another pair was seen at a nest in mid-August but the nest's contents, if any, were unknown. This slender evidence suggests that breeding in Namibia should be watched for from late July onwards.

Two to five eggs are laid. They are pinkish-buff in ground colour, mostly obscured with red-brown and some dark brown blotches, speckles and smears. Nine eggs measured in west Africa averaged 41,0 × 33,3. The incubation period is unknown. Downy young are undescribed and nothing is known of nestling development.

At the Angolan nest containing eggs or small young (probably the latter) the male delivered four lizards in four hours. On each occasion he called to the female, who left the Hamerkop's nest to take prey from him; after eating some she returned to the nest with it. The calling of the male to the female to receive prey nearby is probably the clearest indication of the whereabouts of a nest.

Observations at a nest in Tanzania indicated that the female assisted the male in hunting early in the nestling period. When the young were larger they came to the entrance of the Hamerkop's nest to receive prey. The nestling period lasted at least a month and the three young left the nest over a period of two days. They remained near the nest for a few days and then moved farther afield with their parents. It was not known when they became independent.

67 Dickinson's Kestrel /85.

Dickinsonse Valk
Falco dickinsoni

PLATES 21 AND 22

DERIVATION

falcon : of Dickinson — *falco* (L) : *dickinsoni* (L)

Dr John Dickinson was a medical missionary who travelled with Dr Livingstone's Shire River expedition in 1861. He died of blackwater fever in early 1863 at the ill-fated mission station at Mikorongo on the Shire.

IDENTIFICATION

Adult: This stockily built kestrel is recognisable by its pale grey head which contrasts with the rest of its slate-coloured upperparts. The tail is barred black and white with a broad terminal band. The underparts are uniform grey, darker than on the head. However, there is variation in coloration, some birds being paler grey below and on the head, others darker grey-brown. Paler birds occur mainly in southern Mozambique, the north-eastern Transvaal and Zimbabwe. The eyes are dark brown and the cere, orbital ring and legs are yellow. In flight it shows a distinctive white rump. The underwing coverts are grey and the remiges are narrowly barred black and white. The pale head, white rump and barring on the tail prevent any confusion with other grey-coloured kestrels and falcons.

Juvenile: It closely resembles the adult except for some fine white barring on the flanks. When recently out of the nest it has the cere and orbital ring very pale yellow. The juvenile is said to be browner below than adults, but because of the variation in adult coloration this distinction is probably not valid.

HABITAT

This species is usually found at low altitudes in a variety of woodland habitats. It frequently occurs where there are Hyphaene and Borassus palms but is by no means confined to such regions. Generally it likes a combination of woodland and open spaces, usually near water.

STATUS AND DISTRIBUTION

Although it is normally regarded as resident, there is evidence of local movements outside the breeding season. Further information is needed on the extent of these movements. Its distribution is confined to the northern part of southern Africa and it is found in Mozambique, north-eastern Transvaal (mainly in the Kruger National Park), Zimbabwe, northern Botswana, the Caprivi Strip and north-eastern Namibia. Extralimitally it occurs from Angola eastwards to Tanzania.

GENERAL IIABITS

Dickinson's Kestrel is usually seen perched prominently in a tree surveying the ground be-

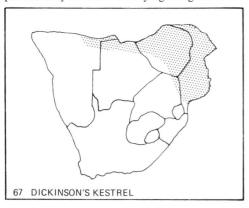

67 DICKINSON'S KESTREL

low. Prey is normally caught with a rather slow slanting glide but it is capable of bursts of speed and may dash from its perch to snatch a passing bird. One attempted to catch a Lilac-breasted Roller, which easily evaded it. In another incident the kestrel deliberately flushed a roosting Epauletted Fruit Bat and caught it in flight. At cane fires it flies above the smoke and stoops with closed wings at great speed to capture small birds such as warblers and cisticolas in flight. It regains height, turns into the wind and eats the bird while hovering. The kestrel may catch as many as four birds as well as other prey during a spell of hunting over a fire. Fires invariably attract this species; in some localities where cane fires are regular it can be seen waiting in the vicinity for the fires to be lit. As well as taking birds in flight it also catches insects, small rodents and other animals flushed out of cover by the flames. Another method of obtaining prey is to follow the plough for mice and locusts disturbed.

The prey of this species consists of small birds, bats, small rodents, lizards, chameleons, frogs, insects and the occasional small snake. Crab remains were found in one nest. The only quantitative prey analysis is from a nest in Zambia where 38 prey items were identified: 47 per cent insects, 32 per cent reptiles (mainly lizards), 13 per cent amphibians and 8 per cent mammals. These results indicate the importance of insects, mainly orthoptera, in the diet. The stomach of one dead bird contained 16 grasshoppers.

The main call is a high-pitched *keee-keee-keee* used as a contact call between the pair and when the birds are alarmed. A softer mewing trill *ki-ki-ki* is used by the female as a begging call when the male is near the nest with prey. The latter call brings large young onto the rim of the nest to receive prey whereas the *keee-keee-keee* causes them to drop back into hiding.

BREEDING

There are no observations on nuptial display.

Various nest sites are used. The most frequent is a hole in a tree, often a dead Hyphaene palm where these occur. The eggs are laid in the decayed hollow stump at the top where the crown has broken off or in a hole in the side of the main trunk. No nest is made; the eggs are laid on wood chips and other detritus lying in the hollow. On the Kafue Flats in Zambia, where more nests have been found than anywhere else, only Hyphaene palms were used although Borassus palms were also available. However, it breeds in Borassus palms elsewhere. Nest holes in the tops of palm stumps are always deep enough to hide the kestrel from view and vary from 20 to 75 cm in depth. On one occasion large young died when their nest hollow flooded. Natural holes in other trees such as Baobabs are also used for nesting. Another nest site, recorded a number of times in Zimbabwe, is inside a Hamerkop's nest. Generally an old nest is used but the kestrel may also dispossess the Hamerkops of a newly built nest. The height of nests varies from 7,5–18 m above ground. One unusual site in Zimbabwe was a hole in the girders of the huge Birchenough suspension bridge.

There is little information on territory. On the Kafue Flats pairs may breed close together and two occupied nests were only 275 m apart.

In Zimbabwe eggs are laid in September and October, as on the Kafue Flats in Zambia. There are too few records from other parts of southern Africa to indicate a breeding season but it will almost certainly be found to be similar to that in Zimbabwe. In the Kruger National Park young have been recorded in December. Clutches of one to four eggs are laid but a single egg has only once been recorded. Eggs are dull creamy-white in ground colour, usually almost entirely obscured by blotches, speckles and smears of reddish-brown and dark brown. They are very variable in their markings, even in the same clutch. Eggs measure: 39,3 × 31,4 (39); 35,8–42,1 × 29,7–33,8.

There are no observations on parental behaviour during the incubation period and it is not known how long eggs take to hatch. On the Kafue Flats the rate of egg failure was high: 11 out of 33 eggs failed to hatch, 9 were infertile and 2 contained small dead embryos.

Newly hatched chicks are covered in greyish-white down and the legs are a dull yellowish-flesh colour. At three weeks old the wing and tail feathers are growing rapidly and feathers are sprouting on the scapulars. Grey feathers are emerging on the sides of the face and on the flanks. The eyes are dark brown, the cere and orbital ring bluish-white and the legs lemon-yellow. By the time the young are a month old they are fully feathered with no traces of down.

There are no observations on the development of co-ordination of the young, except that at a month old they clamber up to perch on the nest rim, where they preen and stretch their wings.

Observations at a nest in Zambia established that the newly hatched chicks are tended by the female, who leaves the nest to collect prey brought by the male. However, she may also catch prey herself near the nest at this early stage. The sheltered nest presumably obviates the need for the young to be constantly brooded or shaded. By the time the young are a week old they are only brooded for about 25 per cent of the day. One of the adults, presumably the female, spends much of the time perched on the nest stump. When the young are three weeks old they are left unattended much of the time except for feeds. The longest time spent in the nest by the female at this stage was 16 minutes. Both parents feed the month-old nestlings, catching much of the prey in the vicinity of the nest. Larger prey items are brought decapitated. Food is merely passed to the young, and the adults spend only a few seconds on the rim of the nest. Prey may be delivered frequently; 20 items were brought in 8 hours on one day and 11 items in 14 hours on another day. Several small items such as insects may be delivered within a few minutes. Sometimes prey is cached on a favourite perch and collected later.

The length of the nestling period is unrecorded, but young appear fully feathered at 30 days old and spend much of their time on the nest rim, so it is probable that they make their first flight at about 35 days. Nothing is known about the post-nestling period.

68 Pygmy Falcon   *186.*

Dwergvalkie

Polihierax semitorquatus

PLATES 19 AND 22

DERIVATION
pale grey : falcon : half : collared — *polios* (G) : *hierax* (G) : *semi* (L) : *torquatus* (L)

IDENTIFICATION
Adult: This delightful diminutive raptor is more likely to be mistaken for a shrike than for a bird of prey. The male is grey above with a narrow white collar at the back of the neck and white below. The black remiges and tail have small white spots. The female resembles the male except for a patch of dark chestnut on her

back. Both have dark brown eyes and the cere, orbital ring and legs are red. In flight the spotted remiges and tail and white rump are diagnostic.

Juvenile: The plumage is similar to that of the adult except for a chestnut wash on the back and upper breast. The chestnut dorsal patch of the female is present at this stage, so the sexes may be differentiated. The young falcon may breed when a year old.

HABITAT

It occurs in arid or semi-arid acacia savanna, particularly where camel-thorn trees are found.

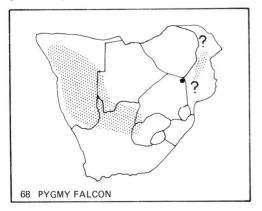

68 PYGMY FALCON

STATUS AND DISTRIBUTION

Although basically sedentary, Pygmy Falcons may make some minor local movements in winter. Distribution is confined mainly to the dry west of southern Africa; it is found in the northwest Cape, Namibia, the extreme west and south of Botswana and in the extreme west of the Orange Free State and the Transvaal where there is suitable habitat. Its western range thus exactly overlaps that of the Sociable Weaver and it breeds in the communal nests of this species. The range of the Pygmy Falcon is said to extend into southern Angola but confirmation of this is required.

There are reliable records from the northern Kruger National Park and the Gaza district of Mozambique. Unconfirmed sightings from Ndumu Game Reserve near the Mozambique border have been rejected, but the possibility that the species occurs there should not be entirely ruled out. These eastern Pygmy Falcons are probably off-shoots of the north-eastern population which occurs in east Africa, Somalia and the Sudan.

GENERAL HABITS

The head is often bobbed up and down before flying off or capturing prey and the tail is wagged up and down when excited. Both these actions remind one of a Pearl-spotted Owl, and the similarity is accentuated by the style of flight, which is undulating and consists of rapid wing-beats alternating with a dip in the flight path like a woodpecker. The Pygmy Falcon hunts from a perch and drops down to catch prey which is then carried back in one foot or the bill and eaten. It also attacks birds with a quick dash from a perch like a sparrowhawk. Termites are eaten on the ground or caught in flight and taken back to a perch to be eaten.

The diet consists mainly of insects, particularly beetles and grasshoppers, and lizards. In a study in the Kalahari the lizard most often caught was the Ocellated Sand Lizard but occasional agamas and skinks were also eaten. Lizards are most plentiful during the breeding season, when they are a major part of the diet. A few small rodents were recorded and even fewer birds. Although the falcon preys on Sociable Weavers, particularly nestlings when prospecting for a nest site, predation on its host species seems to be minimal. The weavers resent the presence of the falcons and will utter alarm notes whenever they are in sight. Pygmy Falcons have never been observed to drink, even after rain; it appears that all their water requirements are obtained from their prey.

Various calls have been described. A high-pitched *tsee-tsee*, a *twee-twee-twip* with the last syllable accented, and a *ki-kikik* with the accent on the first syllable. These three main calls are used with varying intensity for contact, greeting, soliciting and alarm. The female uses the first two calls at low intensity with a tail-wagging display and a submissive posture before mating and when the male has prey for her. The *tsee-tsee* call is emitted also by the chicks as a begging call. A soft purring *krrr-krrr-krrr* is made during copulation or during the tail-wagging display that precedes it. Fully feathered young adopt a threat posture when disturbed and utter a sharp, ringing *ki-ki-ki-ki-ki-ki*. The Pygmy Falcon is also said to mimic calls of the Sociable Weaver; a female was heard to emit a *chip-chip* very similar to the contact call of the weaver. This was just after being flushed from the nest and was accompanied by tail-wagging. Further detailed observations on possible mimicry and other aspects of calls are required.

BREEDING

The breeding biology of this species is still inadequately known owing to the difficulty of inspecting nests and the tendency of the parents to desert when they are disturbed. However, the basic breeding habits were estab-

The greeting display of a female Pygmy Falcon to her mate; she presents her chestnut back by adopting a submissive posture and at the same time wags her tail up and down (after Maclean 1970).

lished during the course of detailed research on the biology of the Sociable Weaver in the Kalahari Gemsbok National Park.

Pygmy Falcons remain together as a pair throughout the year. If a mate is lost, a new one is acquired from an adjacent territory, or the bird may pair up with one of its own offspring. The new mate adopts the original territory as its own.

Nuptial display takes the form of the tail-wagging ceremony and no aerial displays are described. The female plays the main part in this display. She perches near the male in a crouched submissive posture so as to show her chestnut back and white rump to maximum advantage and wags her tail up and down; the male may also wag his tail. In both sexes the black and white tail pattern is revealed. The ceremony is quite often triggered off by the male bringing prey as courtship feeding of the female. Copulation takes place on branches near the nest. When the male dismounts she remains in a submissive posture with her tail raised. After much head bobbing the male flies into the selected nest chamber, followed by the female.

In the western population of southern Africa Sociable Weaver nests are apparently used almost exclusively for breeding. It is also said to use the nests of Buffalo Weavers but these are absent from much of the range of the species in the west. However, in north-eastern Africa, the nests of White-headed Buffalo Weavers are almost always used. In the Kalahari a Pygmy Falcon was once found roosting in the nest of a White-browed Sparrow-Weaver, which was open at both ends, but confirmation that these nests are used for breeding is required. In southern Africa it is said to use the nest of 'star-

lings' with no mention of species, but the most likely host is the colonial Wattled Starling. Confirmation is required. Nothing is known of the breeding habits of Pygmy Falcons in the northern Kruger National Park and Mozambique.

Both occupied and unoccupied Sociable Weaver nest masses are used for breeding and roosting. Usually one chamber is used for breeding and another for roosting, but sometimes various chambers may be used, as many as ten in exceptional circumstances. In an occupied colony the Sociable Weavers may abandon their nest if so many chambers are used. As a rule only a single pair of Pygmy Falcons occupies a nest mass and they appear to be territorial. Ten breeding pairs in a study area in the Kalahari had a distance of about 800 m between pairs and only a quarter of the available colonies were occupied by the falcons. In view of this a record of two or possibly three pairs occupying a single nest mass in Namibia is remarkable.

The falcons quite often breed in a chamber used as a winter roost. One observer states that the nest entrance and chamber are enlarged but no mention is made of this in the Kalahari breeding study. Usually it is not possible to know which chamber is occupied by the falcons until the chicks hatch, when a rim of white droppings at the nest entrance indicates occupancy.

The breeding season extends from August to March but 25 nest records indicate a peak laying period in October and November (16 records). The rather extended breeding season may be due in part to the fact that two broods

White droppings round the entrance of this Sociable Weaver's nest indicate its occupancy by Pygmy Falcons.

are sometimes raised in a season. Two to four eggs are laid and there is some evidence to suggest that four eggs are laid if the rainfall was good at the end of summer the preceding season. The eggs are rounded, white and slightly coarse-grained. Measurements are: 28,0 × 22,5 (33); 26,1–29,8 × 21,3–23,7.

Eggs are laid at intervals of about two to three days and incubation may commence with the laying of the first or second egg. The male roosts with the female until the first egg is laid, then he moves to an adjacent chamber. Both sexes incubate, the female more than the male, and throughout the incubation period he brings prey for her, mostly lizards. He calls her from the nest to receive the food, which she eats before returning to the nest. If disturbed, the brooding bird flies out and perches nearby, where its alarm calls cause its mate to join it and both birds then call. When the bird remains in the nest it uses its bill and feet to attack the hand of the observer, but occasional birds remain quiescent while they are removed. When the eggs are almost hatching, the observer may be attacked and struck near the nest entrance. This aggressive behaviour continues into the nestling period. The incubation period is not accurately known but is more than 27 and less than 31 days.

The newly hatched nestling has bright pink skin covered in white down. Its eyes are closed at first but open within a few days. The first quills appear within a week, and by three weeks it is fully feathered except for some down on the head and a short tail. If disturbed in the nest large nestlings turn onto their backs and defend themselves with their feet.

There are few details on parental care in the nestling period. The male brings prey, usually a lizard, and calls the female from the nest to receive it. She apparently does little hunting until the chicks are fully feathered. At a nest presumed to contain young by the droppings at the entrance a male entered with a lizard while the female was off the nest. He remained within for 40 minutes before the female joined him and he most probably fed the chicks.

The young leave the nest between 27 and 40 days, usually at about 30 days. After their first flight they usually return to the original nest colony but do not always enter the correct chamber. They are fed by both parents and may remain with them for up to two months, by which time they can hunt for themselves. A second brood may be started two to six weeks after the young first fly and before they have left the territory.

Breeding success during the Kalahari study was influenced by human interference but 85 per cent of chicks that hatched flew successfully. Natural predation on eggs and nestlings appears to be minimal, although some chicks disappeared unaccountably soon after hatching, possibly through starvation, which occurred in one observed instance. In view of the high percentage of chicks that fly successfully, it is possible that Pygmy Falcons act as deterrents to snakes such as Cape Cobras and Boomslangs, which are known to prey on Sociable Weaver chicks. The situation requires further investigation, but it seems that the falcons may confer an advantage on their hosts.

69 Barn Owl 392

Nonnetjie-uil

Tyto alba   PLATE 24

DERIVATION
night owl : white — *tuto* (G) : *alba* (L)

IDENTIFICATION
Adult: The upperparts are a mixture of tawny-buff and grey overlaid with small white spots. The heart-shaped facial disc is white, accentuating the dark brown eyes, and the long bill is white. The underparts are white with small brown spots and there is a wash of pale tawny-buff across the upper breast. The long legs are tightly covered with white feathers. The wings and tail are barred with grey. When the owl is perched the long wings project beyond the tail and conceal it. In flight the underwing is white so that it appears ghostly white from below, an effect that has given rise to many superstitious beliefs about this owl.

The only species with which it can be confused is the Grass Owl, which differs in being very dark brown above so that the upperparts and white underside contrast sharply with each other. The habitats of the two species are markedly different and they rarely overlap to any extent.

Juvenile: When it leaves the nest it has very little down, unlike most other species of owls. It resembles the adult except that it is darker on the upperparts, and the underparts are washed with pale buff. Young birds of both sexes may breed when a year old.

HABITAT

This owl is often found in or near human habitation, even in the middle of towns, but also occurs in uninhabited areas. Its main requirement is some form of roosting and nesting site such as an old mine shaft, well or rocky outcrop in otherwise open country. It occurs in almost any habitat, including desert, but not in forest.

STATUS AND DISTRIBUTION

As far as is known, adults of this common and widely distributed species are resident, but young birds disperse from their breeding areas. One owl ringed as a nestling was recovered 50 km away two years later. Another was found about 10 km from its birthplace four years after it was ringed. This almost cosmopolitan species occurs throughout southern Africa.

GENERAL HABITS

The Barn Owl is well known to most people because of its association with buildings and its diet of rodents. A pair will use the same roost and nest site year in and year out if left undisturbed. However, because of their noisy calling and the smell from accumulated pellets, they are not always welcome in an attic. The best solution if the situation becomes intolerable is to block off all entry to the roof once the owls have reared their brood. A nest-box placed in a tree, water tower or similar situation nearby will usually be accepted so that the annoyance is removed without the loss of rodent control.

If disturbed at its roost during the day, the owl elongates its body, narrows its facial disc and closes its eyes to slits. It is almost entirely nocturnal in its habits, although said to hunt on dull days. In England it hunts well after sunrise and before sunset, but such behaviour has not been recorded in southern Africa. It would be dangerous for it to emerge in daylight as it is preyed on by eagles such as Wahlberg's Eagle, Tawny Eagle and African Hawk Eagle, presumably when flushed from a secure roost by some disturbance. At night it may be killed by the Giant Eagle Owl.

At dusk the owl emerges from its daytime roost to hunt, making its screeching call as it sets off. Several techniques are used, the most frequent being a flapping flight interspersed

A Barn Owl emerges from its roost to hunt.

with glides as it quarters the ground. Sometimes it hovers for short periods, scanning the ground carefully. On occasions it beats bushes with its wings to flush roosting birds. Another hunting method is 'perch-hopping'. The owl perches for a few minutes watching and listening and then moves off to another position. Experiments have revealed that it can catch prey in total darkness, by hearing alone, being accurate to one degree on both vertical and horizontal planes. As it pounces, the feet are spread wide side by side to give it a maximum killing area, and at the moment of impact it closes its eyes to protect them.

A Barn Owl usually regurgitates one pellet a day, in which the skulls of its prey are largely intact. Pellets accumulate in considerable quantities in the nest or below the roost, facilitating prey analysis. One researcher in the Transvaal established that an owl's daily consumption of vertebrate prey averaged 55 g with a range of 42–82 g. Daily consumption was highest in late autumn and winter. In an unpublished study the author calculated that during the incubation and nestling period the female and her brood of four young consumed approximately 34 kg of rats, mice and shrews. The same result was obtained from the second brood of five young.

There are many studies of the prey of this owl in southern Africa. The diet has been more comprehensively investigated than that of any other raptor species in our area. One extensive paper summarises some 13 500 remains of vertebrate prey from 28 localities in the Cape Province, Namibia, Transvaal and Natal. This study revealed that the owls are not selective, catching the most accessible prey within a certain size range. Rodents made up 75 per cent of the total, and most of the rodent species known in South Africa were recorded. In all areas except Namibia, rodents, shrews and birds accounted for 97 per cent of all vertebrate prey. In the Transvaal and Natal the Multimammate Mouse was the most important prey species. This mouse, as its name suggests, breeds at a prolific rate, and population explosions occur from time to time. In the dry western regions gerbils were the most frequent rodent prey. The size of rodent prey taken ranged from Pygmy Mice (10 g) to Angoni Vlei Rats (80 g). Studies in the Transvaal reveal that the diet of the Barn Owl there is subject to seasonal variation and only mammals are eaten during the winter months June to August, with birds and arthropods supplementing the mammalian diet during the rest of the year, mainly in the summer months. Seasonal variation in diet undoubtedly applies in other areas too.

The diet of the Barn Owl includes mammals, birds, arthropods, lizards and frogs. As already indicated, rodents and shrews are the most frequently recorded mammalian prey and rodents alone constitute an average of 80 per cent of all prey. Other mammals recorded are moles, bats, young hares and hedgehogs, the last two very rarely. Avian prey, consisting mainly of small passerines, may make up as much as 38 per cent of vertebrate prey. Species such as weavers, queleas and Red Bishops, which roost communally, account for about three-quarters of avian records. In one sample in coastal Namibia migrant Palearctic waders made up a quarter of the total vertebrate prey. Other avian prey records include francolin chicks, button-quails, a Black Crake, doves, colies, a Pied Barbet, woodpeckers, larks, swallows, bulbuls, robins, prinias, cisticolas, shrikes, starlings, white-eyes, sparrows, finches, waxbills and canaries. Arthropod remains are difficult to identify and quantify but in some arid areas they may form an important part of the diet. In a sample of 600 items in pellets from the Namib Desert, scorpions made up 57 per cent. Other arthropods recorded are sun spiders, beetles, crickets, mantids and termites. Lizards such as agamas, skinks and geckos have been recorded, mainly from arid western regions; these made up half the prey in the pellets of an owl in the Namib

Desert. Nocturnal geckos are most frequently recorded. Very few frogs are eaten, not more than three per cent of two samples in the Transvaal. The difference in the prey of the Barn Owl and that of the Grass Owl is not as marked as may be expected; such differences as there are may be attributed to their different habitats, the Grass Owl taking more vlei rats and the Barn Owl more Multimammate Mice, a reflection of their wet and dry environment respectively.

The calls of this owl are extremely difficult to describe. One researcher in Britain, with the aid of a tape recorder, has distinguished 17 'sound signals', including 2 non-vocal sounds. The full repertoire is too complex to describe in detail and what follows is an account of the main calls and sounds with interpretations of their functions. Perhaps the best-known call is a loud, drawn-out tremulous screech or scream — *schrrreeeee* — an eerie sound lasting about two seconds. It is made by both sexes, but with different tones, and serves as a territorial call, a display and contact call, and when driving off intruding birds, not necessarily other Barn Owls. The screech call is also delivered with a mellow, subdued purring intonation by both sexes as a 'come-over here' call during courtship. Sometimes screeching takes on a wailing quality during aerial courtship chasing flights. A drawn-out, high-pitched scream without tremulous intonation is uttered in flight in alarm. This call is used when human or other intruders are near the nest and the owl may attack and strike them. A very loud prolonged hissing note is used in defence to intimidate enemies, particularly when cornered, and it is often combined with bill-snapping. It is made also by nestlings once they start feathering and they weave their lowered heads from side to side in a noisy threat display. A snoring or wheezing noise, similar to the hiss, is emitted with less intensity and usually less volume. After the screech this is the sound most often heard and serves as a soliciting and contact call for the female and nestlings, becoming persistent once they are about two weeks old. It is also made by the female during copulation, the male responding with a repeated staccato squeaking. A soft chirruping or twittering is used by the male and female as a contact call when perched near each other and during mutual preening sessions. Before adopting the soliciting snoring call the small chicks make a series of chittering notes.

BREEDING

The pair bond is very strong; male and female roost together throughout the year, often side by side. They indulge in frequent bouts of mutual preening. The start of the breeding season is marked by increased screeching calls and much flying to and fro as well as aerial chases. Occasionally the male may hover momentarily in front of his perched mate and clap his wings softly. The female solicits the male with her snoring call and he feeds her, often well in excess of her requirements. They copulate frequently on or near the nest to the accompaniment of calling. Copulation takes place throughout the incubation period and during the early part of the nestling period, in one case when the oldest owlet was a month old. The nest site is selected by the male, who calls the female to join him at the selected spot. In one observation a wooden nest-box was used for the first time and contained no soft material. The male fed the female for about a month before laying, by which time a pad of pellets had collected and disintegrated, to serve as a bed for the eggs.

A wide variety of sites is used for nesting, and the following give an indication of the type of situation: inside roofs of houses, in farm outbuildings, in church steeples, in wells and mine shafts, in fissures in mine dumps, inside a Hamerkop's nest, in a hollow amongst the fronds of a palm, in holes in trees and amongst rocks on a hill. One nest was situated in the girders of an overhead factory crane in daily use. The feature of all nest sites is that they are enclosed in some way, thus relatively secure. There is one record of an unsuccessful attempt to breed in a hollow in the roof of a Sociable Weaver nest. As previously indicated, nest sites may be used year after year if the owls are undisturbed. Very little is known about size of territory in Africa but on a mine dump in Zimbabwe there were five nests within 100 m along one side and two others elsewhere on the same dump. This indicates a small territory and tolerance of neighbours where there are optimum nesting conditions.

Eggs have been recorded in all months of the year in southern Africa. In the winter rainfall region of the Cape Province the main laying period is from August to December, in spring and early summer. Elsewhere there is a distinct laying peak from February to May (60 per cent of 182 records). Three to twelve eggs have been recorded and larger clutches are always linked with years of rodent population explosions. The eggs are plain white with a matt surface and are oval in shape. Measurements are: $39,1 \times 31,3$ (116); $36,0–43,1 \times 28,9–34,5$.

Accurate observations on the laying interval in Zimbabwe established that eggs may be laid on consecutive days, although usually two or three days apart. Sometimes in the same clutch the interval varied between two and three days. In three observations eggs were laid during the night. When more than one brood is raised the first eggs of the second clutch may be laid while large young of the first brood are still in the nest. After the first egg is laid, the female seldom leaves the nest, usually once in the evening when she evacuates a large quantity of faeces. She flies round for a while to exercise, preens and then returns to incubate. As far as is known the male never broods and his role is to supply the female with food. Sometimes eggs disappear without trace and cracked eggs also disappear, probably eaten by the female as egg fragments have been found in pellets. The incubation period varies from 30 to 32 days. In one clutch of five in Zimbabwe the first egg hatched after 32 days, the second after 31 days, and the remaining three 30 days after they were laid.

The eggs hatch according to the intervals at which they are laid. The female hears the chick calling inside the egg 24 hours before it emerges and calls to it with a soft chattering note. Observations in captivity revealed that the female assisted the egg to hatch, and ate the shell fragments. Such behaviour would seem to be normal and has been observed in the closely related Grass Owl in the wild. No Cainism has been observed in the very early stages but sometimes partially eaten downy chicks are found in the nest. Possibly they are killed by their siblings, or die of starvation, and are then torn up by the female as food. There is one case on record in England of a 50-day-old nestling killed by its nest-mates aged 54 and 56 days old, but such behaviour must be exceptional. In years of abundant food as many as nine young, possibly more, may fly successfully from a single brood.

The newly hatched chick is a remarkable looking creature. It is pot-bellied with a large head, closed eyes and a long whitish bill. The pink body is sparsely covered with white down. There is little change during the first week but by nine days old the eyes are weakly open slits. At two weeks old the eyes are open and a thicker second coat of white down covers the body. By the age of three weeks the facial disc is distinct and first feathers are emerging from the wing quills. The month-old chick is still mainly downy but the facial disc is feathered and the wing and tail feathers begin to emerge rapidly from their quills. By the fifth week body feathers begin to emerge rapidly through the down and by seven weeks the owlet is fully feathered

(1) The nest of a Barn Owl at the bottom of a pit; the lack of pellets indicates that it is a new site.

(2) The mass of pellets at this nest site in a roof indicates that it has been used for many years.

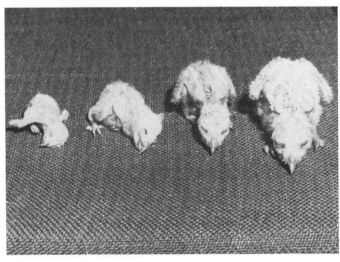

(3) Nestlings 1, 6, 8 and 11 days old.

(4) The same brood 12–22 days old.

(5) At 19–29 days old; feathers are emerging through the down of the older young. The smallest nestling is beginning to catch up in size.

(6) At 36–46 days old the nestlings are well feathered except for the youngest one.

except for some down on the abdomen.

The newly hatched chick is weak and unable to lift its head. It lies huddled against the other eggs or chicks. On its fifth day it emits its snoring begging call for the first time. By the time it is two weeks old it can lift its head up for long periods and shuffles about the nest. When three weeks old it can stand upright and swallow small prey whole. At five weeks old it swallows immediately any prey brought. It stretches and flaps its wings and may run and jump about if there is room around the nest site. It sways its head from side to side in threat when disturbed and rolls over onto its back and defends itself with its claws if attempts are made to handle it. By the time it is ready to leave the nest the nestling performs vigorous wing exercises and makes mock pounces onto prey if space in the nest permits. It spends much of its time at the entrance to the nest waving its head about excitedly and calling loudly in anticipation of the parent's arrival with prey. When the adult does arrive the wings are vibrated rather like those of a begging sparrow.

The female tends the small young closely, brooding them most of the time and feeding them on prey supplied by the male. She calls softly to the young, which do not gape until they feel the proffered food touch the bristles at the base of the bill. During the first two weeks the female eats the droppings of the chicks but after this time they back to the nest edge to defecate. When a nestling is two weeks old it has acquired its second coat of down and no longer requires brooding, and a week later it can feed itself. The female usually remains with the chicks during the day until the oldest is about a month old, when she leaves them alone in the nest. At this stage she begins to assist the male in hunting, although he still does the major share. She still feeds the smaller chicks and, rarely, the older nestlings may even feed their younger siblings. The survival of the smaller chicks is presumably linked to prey availability, and in good years there is often a superabundance of food. After the older young are fully feathered and stop growing, the small chicks rapidly catch up to their weight.

One pair in Zimbabwe was observed when there were seven feathered young in the nest, two of them almost ready to leave. It was a year of a population explosion of Multimammate Mice, and transect counts near the nest revealed that the area was teeming with them. Observations started at 18h00 and the first adult arrived with prey at 18h30, followed by its mate shortly afterwards. During 17 minutes feeding continued unabated and 24 rodents were delivered to the young, an average of 3,4 for each one. Although observations continued until 20h30 no further feeds were recorded and the young were presumably satiated. Rapid feeding rates were also observed on subsequent evenings. Prey was usually caught in the vicinity of the nest, and the adults were seen to catch mice and drop them without eating them. Such observations are probably exceptional and at another nest in a 'normal' year an observer recorded 7 prey items delivered in 4 hours. Whatever the availability of prey, most of it is caught shortly after sunset.

The young normally leave the nest when 50–55 days old. At a nest where there was a superabundant food supply (previously described) the oldest nestling left after about 45 days. The young owls return to the nest to roost for about a week after their first flight. They remain in the vicinity of the nest for about a month after their first flight and may be located by their noisy calling in the evening. They can catch prey by the end of their first month out of the nest and gradually disperse once they are no longer dependent on the adults for food.

Information on breeding success is rather patchy but in years of plentiful food supply it is not infrequent for broods of seven to nine young to be reared in southern Africa. At such times a second brood is often raised; at one nest during a rodent population explosion four consecutive broods of nine, seven, eight and eight young were reared in eleven months, a productivity of 32 young per annum for a single pair! In one study where high breeding success at several nests was noted in one year no breeding took place the following year. However, a high breeding output in good years usually results in a high mortality of juveniles from starvation when the rodent population explosion subsides.

70 Grass Owl *393*

Grasuil

Tyto capensis

PLATE 24

DERIVATION
night owl : Cape — *tuto* (G) : *capensis* (L)

IDENTIFICATION
Adult: The upperparts are dark brown and the prominent facial disc and underparts are white. There is a wash of tawny-buff across the upper breast. The eyes are dark brown, the long bill is white and the long legs are tightly covered with white feathers. The wings are long and project beyond the short tail. When the owl is flushed from long grass one's impression is of a two-tone owl almost blackish above and white below with a large head and prominent facial disc. It can be confused only with the Marsh Owl, which occupies the same habitat, and the Barn Owl, which is similar in appearance. Distinctions are discussed in the texts on these species.

Juvenile: On leaving the nest the juvenile has its upperparts feathered but its underparts still covered in thick buff down. The facial disc is buff coloured, not white as in the adult. Feathers emerging through the down cover the underparts by the age of two months and are tawny-buff in colour. The young resemble the adults except for the tawny-buff coloration of the face and underparts, which is retained for at least six months, at which stage the feathers of the lower breast and abdomen become paler. It is not known at what age the underparts become white, but probably not before the age of one year.

HABITAT
As its name indicates, this owl is found in grassland, usually in long grass and often in the vicinity of water.

STATUS AND DISTRIBUTION
The Grass Owl is resident but may make short local movements when its habitat is destroyed by grass fires. This species is nowhere common and is declining in numbers in some areas owing to loss of habitat. Its distribution extends from the south-west Cape (now rare) through eastern South Africa and northwards to Zimbabwe. One specimen apparently originates from the Caprivi Strip. There are old sight records from Damaraland in northern Na-

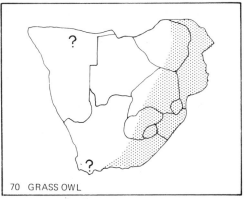

70 GRASS OWL

mibia, but its occurrence there requires confirmation. Extralimitally its range extends northwards to the Cameroons and Kenya with a single record from Ethiopia, where its status is uncertain. Outside Africa another race is found in southern and south-eastern Asia and south-eastwards to Australia.

GENERAL HABITS
The Grass Owl usually roosts in pairs in the long grass but post-breeding groups of several birds may be flushed within a small area. It uses regular roost sites where pellets accumulate, unlike the Marsh Owl which tends to have a succession of temporary roosts. The Grass Owl sits tight, but once disturbed it flies up with dangling legs and quickly drops back into cover again. This behaviour differs from that of the Marsh Owl, which usually flies round to inspect the intruder before hiding in the grass again. The Grass Owl hunts with quartering flight and drops suddenly onto its prey with long legs extended. It also hunts from a perch like the Barn Owl, but rarely because of the absence of suitable perches in its open habitat. Although mainly nocturnal, it also occasionally hunts during daylight.

The prey of the Grass Owl consists mainly of rodents and shrews ranging in weight from 100 g to 1,5 g, some birds and occasionally frogs and insects. It is less versatile than the Barn Owl in its spectrum of prey because of its more specialised habitat, but both may catch the same species. Comparative studies of the prey of the two owls show that usually the Grass Owl feeds

(1) Grass Owl habitat; a nest was situated just in front of the figure.

(2) The nest in long grass; a tunnel may be seen at the back of the nest.

(3) Nestlings four weeks old.

(4) A nestling at six weeks is still mainly downy, at which stage a Barn Owl would be well feathered.

(5) At seven weeks old the upperparts are feathered but the underparts are still mainly downy.

(6) By nine weeks old the young owl is fully feathered.

more on vlei rats, as may be expected because of its habitat. It catches birds less frequently than the Barn Owl; birds have never made up more than 10 per cent of prey samples. Identified avian prey includes a Black Crake, an Ethiopian Snipe, Laughing Doves, a Levaillant's Cisticola, a bishop, a weaver and a waxbill. Rather surprisingly frogs are very rarely recorded, suggesting that no particular effort is made to hunt them. Insect prey includes beetles, grasshoppers and termites but the numbers taken are difficult to assess quantitatively from pellets.

This owl rarely calls and is silent when flushed during the day. One call is a muted screech, similar to that of the Barn Owl but less strident. Both the female and young make a loud hiss 'like several angry Puffadders' when disturbed at the nest. It is an intimidating noise, probably effective in deterring predators. A snoring wheeze is made by nestlings when soliciting for food, and the female probably also uses this call when soliciting the male for prey. One observer describes a *kwark* call like that of the Marsh Owl, but mistaken identity is possible and confirmation is required. The calls of the Grass Owl are little known and further observations are needed.

BREEDING

Nothing is recorded on the nuptial behaviour of this species.

The nest is situated in a patch of rank grass, often beside a ditch or termite mound where the grass is tallest. It is a deep hollow or tunnel, and the nest itself is merely a flattened pad of grass. Usually there are 'compartments' nearby connected by tunnels, which distinguish the nest from that of a Marsh Owl which lacks them. Quite often the roost site is also used as a nest. Little is known about size of territory. In one vlei two Grass Owl nests were about 300 m apart. It may nest 20–50 m from a breeding Marsh Owl and there are two cases of nests only 3 m away from African Marsh Harrier nests – suggesting that it is tolerant of other species.

Eggs have been recorded from December to August but the peak laying time is from February to April (77 per cent of 56 records). This coincides with the period of maximum grass cover in late summer and autumn. Three to six eggs are laid; a clutch of six has been recorded once only. They are oval, white and matt in texture, becoming nest-stained as incubation progresses. Measurements are: 41,8 × 33,6 (44); 39,0–45,3 × 31,3–35,8. The eggs cannot be separated from those of the Marsh Owl by their size.

A Grass Owl flushed from its roost flies off with its legs dangling characteristically before dropping quickly into cover again.

Although further detailed observations are needed, it appears that eggs may be laid at intervals of about two days. The start of incubation varies, but several records indicate that the female may brood only when the clutch is nearing completion. In one case one of a clutch of four eggs hatched and the following day there were four young in the nest. At another nest eggs hatched on consecutive days. Sometimes the difference in size of the young indicates that incubation began soon after the first egg was laid. Usually, unlike the Barn Owl, it shows no great variation in the size of its young. Very little is known about parental behaviour in the incubation period except that the presumed female sits very tight and only flies off at the last moment. The incubation period is approximately 32 days, but accurate records are needed.

The chicks are covered in whitish down when they hatch but by the age of about 18 days they have a thick fluffy second coat of buff down and the facial disc becomes visible. This thick coat of down conceals the emergent feathers which only become clearly visible through the down, mainly on the wings, at the age of about six weeks. The facial disc is fully formed at this stage. A Barn Owl nestling of the same age is well feathered, and the retention of down by the Grass Owl, particularly on top of the head, serves as effective camouflage amongst the grass and undoubtedly has survival value. The seven-week-old Grass Owl is well feathered on the upperparts but the underparts are still entirely downy, becoming feathered some while after it leaves the nest.

There are no observations on the early co-ordination of the nestlings and it is not known when their eyes first open or when they first stand. However, this development will probably be found to be similar to that of the Barn Owl. At about a month old they can stand well, swallow prey whole and defend themselves by turning on their backs and using their claws to good effect. They back to the perimeter of the nest and defecate into the surrounding grass. From the age of five weeks they may wander off the nest into the surrounding grass and they hide in the nearby 'compartments' if disturbed. Wing-flapping exercises start at the age of six weeks and at seven weeks they can fly short distances.

When the eggs hatch the female broods the small chicks closely. At one nest she ate the eggshell soon after an egg hatched. She remains with the young for at least the first ten days, and by the time they are about a month old she no longer roosts with them in the nest. When the female ceases brooding she assists the male in bringing prey, but it is not known at what stage of the nestling period this takes place.

The nestlings first fly at the age of seven weeks although they wander off the nest two weeks before. They remain in a loose family group with their parents for at least a month after their first flight, probably for much longer, but there are no observations to indicate when they become independent. Nothing is known about breeding success. The breeding biology of this owl is very poorly known and further detailed observations are needed.

---

71 Wood Owl 394

Bosuil
Strix woodfordii   PLATE 23

DERIVATION
screech-owl : of Woodford — *strix* (L) : *woodfordii* (L)

This species was originally called Woodford's Owl after Colonel E.J.A. Woodford, who was Chief Inspector and Commissary-General of Musters, French Corps, from 1794 to 1817.

IDENTIFICATION
Adult: This medium-sized owl is warm red-brown above with white spotting on the wing coverts and scapulars. The tail is barred and protrudes beyond the wing tips. On the underparts it is barred russet and white. The facial disc is white, there are prominent white 'eye-brows' but no 'ear' tufts, and the eyes are dark brown. The bill and feet are yellow. There is no other owl with which this species can be confused in southern Africa.

Juvenile: The young leave the nest while they still have patches of down, particularly on the head. Initially their plumage appears paler than that of the adults, and the head is creamy. The plumage darkens gradually and at the age of three months they resemble the adults except that they are slightly paler on the head and the white facial markings are less pronounced. At the age of five months they are indistinguishable from adults.

HABITAT
This is a common forest species but is by no means restricted to this habitat. It also occurs in coastal bush, dense woodland, pine plantations and in wooded riverine strips.

STATUS AND DISTRIBUTION
It is resident and is the most likely species to be regularly encountered in forest. Its distribution extends from the south-west Cape to the eastern Cape and northwards to Zimbabwe. In the north of southern Africa it occurs westwards to northern Botswana, the Caprivi Strip and along the border of Namibia and Angola.

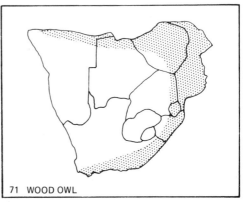
71 WOOD OWL

Extralimitally its range extends to Ethiopia and west Africa.

GENERAL HABITS

The Wood Owl is strictly nocturnal in its habits, and roosts in thick creeper or other dense foliage. As the white spots on the upperparts and the ventral barring blend well with the dappled light of its habitat, it is easily overlooked. The same roost is used year after year. The best indication of the presence of a pair is when they call at dusk. It is not particularly afraid of humans and will nest near houses. When discovered at its roost it will remain perched and watch the intruder, flying off only if provoked.

It catches prey by dropping onto it from a perch but it may sometimes catch insects such as moths and termites in flight. Its food is mainly insects but it also eats small rodents, frogs and birds. There is one record of a snake as prey. Insect prey includes beetles, weevils, grasshoppers, crickets, moths, caterpillars, mantises, cicadas and termites. Avian prey records are: Striped Kingfisher, Yellow-bellied Bulbul, Fiscal Shrike and a fully grown nestling Cape Turtle Dove. Very few pellets are found in nests or below roosts, possibly because of the insect diet, so an analysis of prey preferences is difficult. At one nest watched at night 21 items were brought, a small rodent, a frog and 19 insects. All prey was carried in the bill.

One early observer described this species as 'the owl with the lovely voice' and its call is one of the most characteristic night sounds wherever it occurs. Africans attach various meanings to the calls. The voice of the female is higher-pitched than the male, and they duet, but not on a regular basis or to a strict rhythm. They are most vocal for six weeks before laying, when they call from dusk to dawn. Two types of call are used to maintain contact and during courtship. The female emits a high-pitched *eee-yow*, answered by a low, gruff *hoo* from the male. Both also make a rapid *hoo-hoo, hu, hu, hu, hu, hu* call, the last five syllables delivered unevenly with a syncopated rhythm. Sometimes the female's *eee-yow* is answered by the full *hoo-hoo, hu, hu, hu, hu, hu* of the male. Soft *oop, oop, oop* and *hoo* calls, as well as bill-clacking, are made in alarm when the nest is inspected. The nestlings make a wheezing *shree, shree, shree* begging call repeated at short intervals. This call is maintained once they leave the nest and carries over a considerable distance.

BREEDING

No form of nuptial display has been described but the pair call a great deal to each other during the period before eggs are laid.

The usual nest site is a natural hole in a tree protected above, but some nests are in hollows open at the top. The hole varies in depth, and the floor of the nest may be 6–50 cm below the entrance. No lining is used and the eggs are laid on wood chips lying in the hole. Nests in holes have been recorded from 0,6 to 30 m above ground, but usually they are at a height of about 2–4 m. Sometimes eggs are laid on the ground at the base of a tree or under a log. Occasionally they breed in the nest of another raptor, for example in the nest of an African Goshawk at a height of 9 m, and in the probable nest of a Black Sparrowhawk 28 m up in a pine plantation. One pair made several attempts to breed in the funnel at the top of a drainpipe outside a farm outbuilding but failed each year because of disturbance. Eventually they moved to a dovecote in the farmhouse garden. The owls become very attached to a nest and will use it year after year. In one study it was thought that genets caused the birds to move to other nest sites. There are no observations on the size of territory in this species but regular calling is undoubtedly used for territorial advertisement.

Eggs are laid from July to October with a peak in September. One to three eggs are laid, usually two, and clutches of three are very rare. The eggs are rounded and white. Measurements are: 42,9 × 37,7 (11); 40,0–45,5 × 35,5–40,5. Further measurements are needed.

On three occasions the laying interval between two eggs was about 36 hours, but sometimes the period is longer, up to four days. Incubation commences when the first egg is laid. Apparently only the female incubates during the day, but it is not known whether the male does a share at night when the female leaves to hunt. The incubating bird sits tight, sometimes refusing to leave the nest when it is inspected. This species has not been known to attack observers at the nest, even after dark. The incubation period has been established as 31 days on three occasions.

The newly hatched chick has pink skin sparsely covered with white down which thickens within a few days. The bill is pale cream, the feet are pink and the eyes are closed. There is little change until it is 10 days old, when the eyes begin to open and the quills with feathers just emerging begin to push through the down. By 20 days old the chick is a mixture of feathers and down, with most of the feather growth on the wings and back; the tail has not yet emerged through the down.

(1) View of a Wood Owl's nest; the young have been placed at the nest entrance to indicate its position.

(2) A nestling about three weeks old.

(3) An adult alights at the nest with an insect carried in its bill.

The eyes are dark brown and the bill and feet are turning yellow. At 24 days old the wing feathers are almost fully grown and the tail feathers have emerged and are growing rapidly. When the chick is 30 days old the tail is almost fully grown and the last remaining down is on the head and underparts.

Little is recorded on the development of co-ordination of the nestlings. They are not aggressive when handled and after some initial bill-clacking remain docile. By the age of three weeks they can stand and come to the nest entrance to be fed. They remain quiescent during the day but at night stretch their wings out of the nest hole. The nest cavity remains remarkably clean; they defecate against the edges of the nest hollow but not out of the entrance.

The young are brooded by the presumed female when small and the duration of brooding behaviour varies. Sometimes the young are left alone in the nest by day when 10 days old, at other times the female stays in the nest until they are 23 days old. However, even when they are alone in the nest, she keeps watch from a perch nearby. On one occasion when chicks were about two weeks old a rudimentary distraction display was observed near a nest on the ground. A second bird, not the one flushed off the nest, called weakly and fluttered down from its perch. There are no observations on feeding behaviour when young are small but by the time they are 18 days old both parents are actively feeding them. Rapid visits are made to the nest from about 15 minutes after sunset. At one nest 10 visits were recorded between 18h25 and 18h50. Observations were discontinued at 21h45, by which time there had been 25 prey deliveries, mostly insects, in just under four hours.

The nestling period was 30, 35 and 37 days at three carefully observed nests, but the young emerge before they are able to fly properly. During their first three weeks out of the nest they remain near the nest, where they are fed by the adults. The young of one pair observed then moved farther afield and took up residence with the adults at their roosting thicket. They gradually become less dependent on their parents, learn to hunt for themselves and eventually move away. However, a family group may remain together for up to four months after the young have left the nest. On one occasion an observer placed two recently fledged orphaned Wood Owls with two just out of another nest. No aggression was shown towards them by their foster parents, and all four young were reared together.

Observations were made on two pairs in Zimbabwe: in a total of 13 pair-years 17 young flew successfully, a replacement rate of 1,3 young per pair per year. In three years eggs disappeared or were found broken and once a three-week-old nestling disappeared. Genets were thought to be possible predators as they were often found sleeping in holes in trees similar to those used by Wood Owls for nesting.

72 Marsh Owl   *395*

Vlei-uil

Asio capensis   PLATE 23

DERIVATION
horned owl : Cape — *asio* (L) : *capensis* (L)

IDENTIFICATION

Adult: The main feature of this dull-brown owl is its pale-brown facial disc surrounded by a black rim. Its large dark-brown eyes give it a rather startled expression. There are two small tufts on the forehead between the eyes, but these are seldom raised and are not a good feature for identification. In flight the wings appear long for an owl and there are diagnostic pale-buff patches near the wing tips. The only species regularly found in the same habitat is the Grass Owl, which is easily distinguishable by its two-tone coloration: dark brown above and white below with a prominent white facial disc. It has a large head, making it appear top-heavy. Its habits are different, it rarely calls when flushed, and it hunts only very occasionally during daylight.

Juvenile: The young bird resembles the adult once fully feathered but it is downy on the head and underparts when it leaves the nest. It takes approximately ten weeks before the last down on the underparts is replaced by feathers. A captive juvenile commenced its first moult when eight months old, and during the next two months it moulted its primaries and secondaries symmetrically and grew a new tail. A second

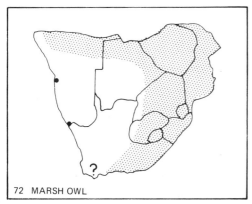

72 MARSH OWL

moult began at the age of twenty months, and wing feathers were moulted over a period of five months. However, the tail feathers were all dropped at the same time and then regrown.

HABITAT

This species is found in grassland, often near water, and frequently in the same habitat as the Grass Owl and African Marsh Harrier. It occurs in isolated pockets of habitat in otherwise unsuitable terrain, as for example in river deltas in the Namib desert.

STATUS AND DISTRIBUTION

Although stated to be resident, this species is undoubtedly nomadic to a certain extent, especially when its habitat is destroyed by grass fires. It often occurs in considerable numbers locally, sometimes concentrated into a small marshy area if the surrounding country has been burnt. As many as 30–40 birds may be found in about two hectares.

Its distribution is mainly in the eastern half of southern Africa from the south-west Cape to Zimbabwe, but in the north it extends westwards into northern Botswana and northern Namibia. Isolated pockets of distribution are found in western Namibia. Extralimitally it occurs northwards to Ethiopia and in Madagascar. In west Africa its distribution is rather patchy and there is an isolated population in Morocco.

GENERAL HABITS

This is the only owl in southern Africa that is gregarious; 25 birds or more may be seen flying round in the evening performing aerobatics prior to hunting. Even when not occurring in large numbers several birds may be flushed within a small area, presumably a post-breeding family group. Hollows in the grass are used as roosts, but they are not frequented consistently for long periods like those of the Grass Owl,

and do not contain many pellets.

The Marsh Owl hunts from a perch or on the wing, mostly in quartering flight with buoyant, steady wing-beats from one to three metres above the grass. Occasionally it also hovers for short periods. Prey is caught with a quick pounce. The hunting behaviour is very similar to that of harriers and it may hunt over the same ground as the African Marsh Harrier during the day. It frequently hunts about two hours after sunrise and before sunset, and on dull days may be seen flying about at other times too. It is quite often seen perched beside roads, probably waiting for rodents to cross. There is a record of a Marsh Owl flying out over the sea at dusk and foraging low over the water, but to what purpose is not known, and it disappeared from view out to sea.

Prey consists mostly of small rodents and birds as well as many insects such as beetles and grasshoppers. Occasional frogs and lizards are also eaten. In one large sample of pellets, in addition to many insects 280 vertebrate remains were analysed. These comprised 236 Multimammate Mice, 11 vlei rats, 10 shrews, 4 Striped Mice, 4 unidentified rodents and 15 small birds. Another small pellet sample contained 17 birds and 4 rodents. Avian prey consists mainly of small passerines, but terns and doves have been recorded, and the largest item was a Dabchick found on a nest. Marsh Owls frequently cache prey when there is an excess.

A hunting Marsh Owl to show the pale patches near the wing tips.

The main call is a harsh, croaking *quark* uttered singly or in rapid succession and used during courtship or in alarm near the nest when disturbed. An extraordinary squealing noise is made during a distraction display (see under Breeding). The bill is snapped when alarmed. Another call is a snoring *kor*, but it is not known in what context this is made. Small young have a chittering begging call, replaced by a wheezing *too-eeee* noise when they are older. The wheezing call is ventriloquial and carries far.

BREEDING

Nuptial display takes the form of the pair flying around in wide circles at dusk and on moonlit nights with slow, deliberate wing-beats. Sometimes the wings are clapped. Aerial chases also occur and sometimes the male and female fly towards each other and touch feet briefly. Displays are accompained by the noisy croaking call.

The nest is a deep hollow in long grass, sparsely lined with a thin pad of dry grass. The surrounding grass may be bent over to form a canopy concealing the nest. It is often situated near water where the cover is tallest but it may also be some distance from the nearest marshy area. The nest is not connected by a series of tunnels to surrounding compartments like that of the Grass Owl. In Nigeria at least four pairs inhabited a swampy area of about twelve hectares and the occupants of a territory would drive away intruding Marsh Owls. However, if a pair were disturbed by an observer, they would tolerate the intrusion of several neighbouring owls as they all flew round to inspect the danger. Little is recorded on size of territory in southern Africa but nests of Marsh Owls have occasionally been found about 75 m apart. A Marsh Owl with chicks chased off an African Marsh Harrier, Yellow-billed Duck and a Blacksmith Plover when they came near the nest. Very occasionally human intruders are attacked at the nest.

The breeding season is very extended in southern Africa and eggs are laid mainly from February to September with very occasional records in October, November and December. However, March and April are the peak months (66 per cent of 111 records), and this ties in with the time of maximum grass cover over most of the range of this owl. In our area two to five eggs, usually three, are laid. In Nigeria a clutch of six eggs has been recorded. Eggs are rounded and white. Measurements are: 40,0 × 34,1 (55); 37,9–43,0 × 32,4–36,0.

The eggs are laid at intervals of about two or three days, to judge by the hatching of the chicks. At one nest with four eggs two eggs hatched together so that incubation probably began with the second egg. The third egg hatched about two days later and the fourth egg three days after the third. Little is recorded of incubation behaviour except that the owl sits tight and returns to the nest soon after disturbance. It is not known if both sexes incubate but the presumed male is usually flushed from a roost not far from the nest during the day. In the latter part of the incubation period and continuing throughout the nestling period a remarkable distraction display is performed by one of the birds, sometimes both, during the day and at night if observers are near the nest. On being flushed from the nest the owl flies round uttering its croaking call and then suddenly plummets into the grass as if shot. It flops about feigning injury and emits a loud squealing call. After a while it flies up and repeats the performance. Sometimes the owl moves away from the observer and drags its wings in the same way as a plover performing the broken-wing distraction display. The incubation period has been recorded on one occasion as 27–28 days.

The newly hatched chick has pink skin, covered with buff-coloured down. The bill is black with a prominent white egg-tooth, and the feet are pink. The eyes are closed. At a week old the down is a dirty white colour and quills are beginning to emerge. The feet are grey and the eyes are open to slits. By 10 days old the dark brown eyes are fully open and the facial disc is clearly defined. Feathers are emerging on the back and on the wings but the chick still appears downy. The nestling leaves the nest when about 18 days old, still mainly downy. At the age of 30 days the back and wings are well feathered but the head and underparts are still downy. By the time it is 50 days old, only the forehead and underparts are downy. It is fully feathered by 70 days old.

Initially the chick is weak and helpless but by 10 days it is able to stand and shows resentment when observers are at the nest. In addition to its begging call it also performs a tap-dance with its feet in anticipation of a meal. It defecates into the grass round the perimeter of the nest so the nest itself remains completely clean. From the age of two weeks the nestling defends itself with its claws when handled.

Very little is known of parental attention. Eggshells disappear soon after eggs hatch and are presumably removed or eaten. When the young are small the female remains on the nest and tears up prey brought by the male. She distributes it equally to her brood and even the

(1) A Marsh Owl's nest.

(2) These nestlings range in age from seven to two days.

(3) A young owl eight weeks old.

smallest chick shows a steady increase in weight. At one nest in Zimbabwe the female roosted with the young until they left the nest at 18 days old, but in Nigeria the female roosted nearby once all the eggs had hatched and the oldest nestling was about 10 days old. Further observations are needed.

The nestlings normally leave the nest when about 18 days old, sometimes as early as 14 days, well before they can fly, and spread out into the surrounding grass where they establish temporary roosts. This dispersal of the brood has survival value but it makes observations on the post-nestling period difficult, as the young are not easy to locate. They are fed by the adults until they are at least five or six weeks old, at which stage they can fly weakly. It is likely that they remain with their parents much longer, as presumed family groups of several birds may be regularly flushed in a small area.

73 African Scops Owl *396*

Kleinooruiltjie

Otus senegalensis   PLATE 23

DERIVATION
horned owl : of Senegal — *otus* (L) : *senegalensis* (L)

IDENTIFICATION
Adult: This small owl is about the size of a Laughing Dove but has a short tail which does not project beyond the wing tips. It occurs in two colour forms, brown and grey, both of which are extremely cryptic, an effect enhanced by the 'ear' tufts and the pattern of streaking on the underparts. The grey form is illustrated. The eyes are lemon-yellow. The only species with which it can be confused is the White-faced Owl, which is much larger and has a white face, that of the Scops Owl being grey.

Juvenile: It resembles the adult.

HABITAT
It is found in dry woodlands and is absent from forest and desert areas.

STATUS AND DISTRIBUTION
This species is widely distributed and common in suitable habitat. Although apparently resident in most areas, there is some evidence that birds from south of the Limpopo may move north into Zimbabwe in winter. Further investigation is required. It occurs from the eastern Cape northwards but is absent from the Karoo and dry west. Extralimitally it is found northwards to the Sahara. There is a very similar Eurasian Scops Owl, considered by some authorities to be conspecific with the African species.

GENERAL HABITS
During the day it roosts motionless right against the trunk of a tree, or on a broken vertical branch, where its cryptic coloration makes it almost impossible to see. If it detects danger, it closes its eyes to slits, elongates its body and raises its 'ear' tufts, all of which make it look like a piece of a dead branch. As dusk approaches it begins to call, a ventriloquial *prrrup* that sounds more like an insect than a bird. The call is repeated at short intervals, the male and female answering each other. It hunts by dropping onto its prey from a perch, and its diet appears to consist mainly, if not exclusively, of arthropods. Recorded items are mantids, cockroaches, crickets and scorpions. Pellets contain a considerable amount of fibrous plant material which may be ingested intentionally as a binding for the insect remains.

BREEDING
The breeding biology is very little known and the only study in Africa was cut short by a Tree Monitor (Leguaan) which robbed the nest.

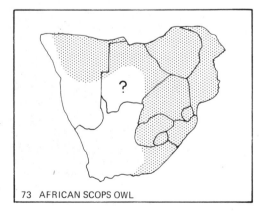

73 AFRICAN SCOPS OWL

A roosting African Scops Owl blends perfectly with the trunk of the tree (Photograph: Alan Weaving).

An African Scops Owl on the edge of its nest hole (Photograph: Alan Weaving).

The eggs are laid in a natural hole in a tree, and nests have been recorded 1,2–9 m above ground. The depth of the vertical nest holes in two records was 30 cm and they had no protection from rain.

The few available breeding records indicate that eggs are laid from September to November. Two or three eggs are laid, usually three. They are rounded and white. The measurements of two clutches are: 30,0 × 25,0 and 29,5 × 25,5; 30,5 × 27,0, 30,8 × 27,0 and 31,1 × 26,8.

One nest was observed when it was thought to contain eggs, but the presumed female sat so tight that it was not possible to be certain. The male roosted in a coppice 120 m away and began calling at sunset before moving off to hunt. After a while he came to the nest, paused on the rim and then entered to feed the female. No calling was heard when he arrived at the nest. On occasions the female came up onto the edge of the nest, where the male fed her. Apart from these few brief observations nothing is known about the breeding biology of this species.

74 White-faced Owl 397.

Witwanguil

Otus leucotis

PLATE 23

DERIVATION
horned owl : white : eared — *otus* (L) : *leukos* (G) : *otos* (G)

IDENTIFICATION
Adult: This medium-sized owl has prominent 'ear' tufts and a short tail which does not project beyond the wing tips. It is dove-grey above with a bar of white spots along the edge of the scapulars. The face is white, accentuated by a black rim, and the eyes are orange. The underparts are greyish-white with narrow dark brown streaks. It can only be confused with the much smaller Scops Owl; differences are discussed under that species.

Juvenile: It resembles the adult but the eyes are yellow initially and the feathers on the face are greyish.

HABITAT
It occurs in a variety of woodland habitats but is commonest in acacia thornveld.

STATUS AND DISTRIBUTION
This resident owl is not uncommon in suitable habitat but is easily overlooked. Its distribution extends northwards of a line from Durban across to the Orange River. Extralimitally its range extends northwards to the Sahara.

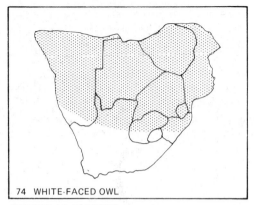

74 WHITE-FACED OWL

GENERAL HABITS

During the day the White-faced Owl roosts in trees but does not conceal itself as effectively as the African Scops Owl. Sometimes it perches on thin branches where easily seen. If alarmed, it elongates its body, raises its long 'ear' tufts and closes its eyes to slits. First calling may be heard in the late afternoon and it begins hunting as it becomes dark. It returns to its favourite roost just before sunrise. Prey is caught by pouncing onto it from a perch. Its diet consists mainly of rats and mice, some insects and spiders, and the occasional bird. In one prey study, pellets contained 85 per cent rodents, 10 per cent arthropods and 5 per cent birds. Mammalian prey records include vlei rats, gerbils, shrews, various species of mice and a Tree Squirrel, the largest item ever recorded. Birds up to the size of a Laughing Dove are caught. Arthropods such as grasshoppers, hawk moths and sun spiders are eaten.

The main territorial and contact call is a rapidly repeated bubbling hoot drawn out at the end: *wh-ho-ho-ho-ho-ho-ho-ooo*. In alarm when disturbed at the nest it utters an extraordinary snarling call, exactly like two fighting tomcats. At the nest the female emits a soft chirruping noise when the male brings her prey. Small downy young make a soft chittering, begging call.

BREEDING

Display consists of calling with the bubbling hoot, during which the male may walk along the branch on which the female is perched, bobbing his head up and down. He also chases after her when she flies off.

There are two types of nest site. Most often the old nest of another bird is taken over, also natural hollows where several branches converge. The following nests have been used, some of which were so flimsy that eggs could be seen through the sticks from below: Black-

shouldered Kite, Lizard Buzzard, Gabar Goshawk, Little Banded Goshawk, 'heron', Grey Loerie, Pied Crow, Black Crow, Scaly-feathered Finch, Cape Sparrow and Wattled Starling. In the case of the last three species the eggs were laid in a flattened place on top of the nests. Some observers suggest that this species builds its own flimsy nest, but no direct evidence has been produced. This misconception has probably arisen because they often breed on an old Grey Loerie's nest, an insubstantial structure, which may have been thought to have been built by the owls.

The breeding season extends from June to November; there is a record of a nest with eggs in February in Namibia. However, the peak laying months are August to October. Two or three eggs are laid which are rounded and white. Measurements are: 38,8 × 32,3 (53); 37,0–41,4 × 30,4–33,3.

Incubation commences with the laying of the first egg. The female incubates during the day. At dusk the male calls to her and she leaves the nest, presumably to receive prey. He then comes to the nest to incubate. During the night the male broods for about half an hour at a time, the female for three hours. Both male and female turn the eggs at night, but the female does not turn them during the day. She sits very tight in the daytime, flattening herself on the nest if observers approach, and sometimes she can be caught on the nest. She defends herself with her claws and at night may fly down and strike an observer. This defensive behaviour continues into the nestling period. The incubation period on two occasions was 30 days.

The newly hatched chick is covered in greyish-white down. The eyes are closed; they open weakly when it is about four days old. At about 16 days feathers have largely replaced the down and by 23 days the nestling is almost fully feathered.

Initially the chicks are weak and helpless, but at a week old they are more active and able to sit up. When two weeks old they move about the nest a great deal and at three weeks old start wing exercises. Before their first flight they move out onto branches near the nest.

The small chicks are almost continually brooded by the female, the male providing food. She tears up prey for the chicks initially and the male does not feed them. The young may still be brooded when two weeks old but they are active and she has difficulty in covering them. By the age of three weeks they are left alone on the nest for long periods; but more detailed observations on the decrease of parental attention are needed.

These White-faced Owl's eggs are laid in a Little Banded Goshawk's nest.

This White-faced Owl's nest is in a hollow where several branches converged; the adult is with a nestling about five days old.

At one nest the young bird was perched several metres from the nest when 33 days old and two days later it could not be located. Young remain with their parents for at least two weeks after leaving the nest; further post-nestling observations are required.

At a nest studied in Zimbabwe for six consecutive years two or three young were reared each year, three young on two occasions. In the six years a total of 14 young were reared, a replacement rate of 2,3 young per pair per year.

75 Pearl-spotted Owl 398

Dwerguiltjie

Glaucidium perlatum

PLATE 23

DERIVATION
very small owl : wearing pearls — *glaukidion* (G) : *perlatus* (L)

IDENTIFICATION
Adult: This delightful diminutive owl is brown above with small white spots, those on the long tail being distributed in rows. There is a bar of large white spots on the edge of the scapulars. Below, it is white with broad brown streaking. At the back of the head is a remarkable 'false face' formed by two patches of dark feathers surrounded by white. There are no 'ear' tufts on the rounded elfin head, and the large yellow eyes are surrounded by white feathers. The bill and large feet are dull yellow.

The only other small owl with which it can be confused is the superficially similar Barred Owl, but this species is barred not spotted above, has a much larger 'puffball' head, and a gorget of transverse barring on the breast, below which

A Pearl-spotted Owl showing the 'false face' on the back of the head.

the white underparts are boldly spotted. The calls of the two species are also quite different.

When it moults, all the tail feathers are dropped at the same time, so that the observer may be confronted with a small tailless owl. However, the other characteristic features of plumage would confirm identification.

Juvenile: The juvenile leaves the nest resembling the adult but has a short tail and no spotting on the head and back.

HABITAT

It occurs in bushveld, particularly acacia woodland.

STATUS AND DISTRIBUTION

This common resident is widely distributed from the Orange River northwards. It is absent from Natal except in northern Zululand. Extra-limitally it is found northwards to the Sahara but not in the forested regions of the Congo basin.

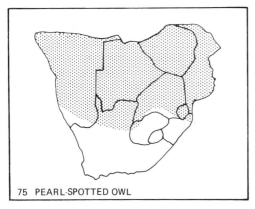

75 PEARL-SPOTTED OWL

GENERAL HABITS

The Pearl-spotted Owl flies about and hunts freely during daylight, making no great effort to conceal itself, so that it is often mobbed by small birds. It has a fast, dipping, woodpecker-like flight which is not silent like that of most other owls. When perched it has a characteristic habit of wagging its tail up and down or flicking it from side to side, particularly in excitement or when alarmed, and it also bobs its head up and down like a falcon. In threat it extends itself to full height, raises the feathers on the back of its head and glares directly at the object of its concern. It baths in shallow water during daylight and also 'showers' with spread wings and tail when it rains. A captive bird, slightly injured when first received, played possum when handled. It would lie on its back with eyes closed and allow itself to be rolled about. However, if picked up and thrown into the air, it flew normally.

Most of its hunting is from a perch and it merely drops down to catch prey, but it can also swoop down from a vantage point and catch bats in flight as they come to drink. A Masked Weaver was snatched as it was building its nest. The relatively large feet and claws enable this owl to kill prey as large as itself on occasions, a Laughing Dove or Cape Turtle Dove in one observation. Although direct evidence is lacking, it may rob the nests of hole-nesting species such as barbets or woodpeckers, possibly when prospecting for a nest site itself. This behaviour has been recorded in the closely related Pygmy Owl in North America. A Pearl-spotted Owl was seen to enter the chambers of a Sociable Weaver's nest but it did not emerge with anything. There is one record of piracy in which the owl repeatedly robbed a wood hoopoe as it approached its nest with food. Prey consists of insects, small mammals, birds, amphibians, lizards and an occasional small snake. Insects appear to be its staple food; caterpillars, beetles, grasshoppers and termites have been recorded. Rats, mice and small insectivorous bats are recorded items of mammalian prey. Avian prey consists mainly of small passerines but it can also kill a dove its own size.

The main call of this owl is remarkably loud and penetrating for its size and may be heard both day and night. It consists of a clear whistling *tiu-tiu-tiu-tiu* . . . beginning quietly and rising to a crescendo, at which point a second bird may join in antiphonally. When heard for the first time it is hard to believe that the volume can continue to increase as the call progresses. This crescendo call is heard less often from October to January during the breeding season than at other times of the year. The male and female exchange soft *too-woop* and *tee-weep* contact calls, the higher-pitched *tee-weep* being made by the female. In alarm when a nest is inspected, soft *peee-ooo* or *peep peep* notes may be made, sometimes followed by the crescendo whistle. During the early part of the breeding season a ventriloquial *peep* call is made at about 30-second intervals for long periods, usually by the female, but also by both birds perched in separate trees.

BREEDING

For about a month before laying, the female emits her monotonous *peep* soliciting call almost continuously near the nest. The male feeds her regularly and they mate frequently. No special nuptial displays have been described.

The usual breeding site is the nest hole of one of the larger barbets or woodpeckers, occasion-

This Pearl-spotted Owl is about to enter its nest hole which originally belonged to a barbet.

ally natural holes. They will also use artificial nest-boxes if provided. There is some evidence that nests may be lined with green leaves, unusual behaviour for an owl; but further corroboration is required. The height of nest holes does not appear to be of importance and they have been found from 1,2 m to 10 m above the ground. The same nest may be used for several consecutive years, or a number of different holes may be used within a small area. One nest hole used for several years had to be abandoned when wild bees moved in. The territory does not appear to be large, and occupied nests have been found 200 m apart in one instance and 500 m in another. The nest is vigorously protected against other hole-nesting species such as hornbills, barbets and rollers, which disturb the owls when prospecting for nest sites. Other species such as thrushes and shrikes that come near the nest are also chased off. Human observers are not attacked but a bird disturbed from a nest may perch nearby, call and wag its tail about.

Eggs are laid from August to October, mostly during September and October. Two to four eggs are laid, usually three. They are rounded and white. Measurements are: 31,0 × 25,8 (25); 28,0–33,8 × 24,0–27,2.

Little is known about the intervals between eggs except that in one clutch of three the third egg was laid between 31 and 55 hours after the second. Incubation may commence on completion of the clutch or earlier, as in one nest two chicks were about two days older than the third. One observation of a male brooding two small chicks and an unhatched egg for 50 minutes indicates that the sexes may share incubation, but

in what proportion is not known. Although there is no direct evidence at present, it is probable that the male feeds the incubating female, as with another closely related species. The brooding bird sits very tight and usually cannot be induced to leave the nest even by loud banging on the tree. If an inspection light and mirror are used to inspect the nest, the owl lies flat, face down, and remains motionless, looking very much like debris at the bottom of the hole; such behaviour probably has survival value in the event of predators' looking into the nest. The incubating bird leaves the nest for short periods both during the day and at night. One accurate incubation period was 29 days, another not less than 28 days. Eggshells are either removed or eaten, as there is no sign of them after eggs hatch.

The newly hatched chick is tiny; one weighed 7 g. Its pink skin is covered in white down, the bill is greyish and the eyes are closed. By the age of 10 days it is covered with thicker greyish-white down, there are black bristles at the base of the bill, and the eyes are still closed. At 13 days the eyes are open, the down is grey and first feather tracts are just visible. At 17 days brown feathers are rapidly replacing the down, and the head is fully feathered shortly afterwards, although there is still a fair amount of grey down on the rest of the body. By the age of 21 days the nestling is fully covered with feathers, and the bill is pale greyish-yellow. Because of the difficulties involved in inspecting nests, little is known of the behaviour of the young. When feathered they lie flat with their faces downwards like the adult if the nest is inspected.

The female stays in the nest when the chicks are small and the male may also brood them as mentioned earlier under incubation behaviour. His main role is to supply food, which he brings during the day and at night. The female puts her head out of the nest entrance from time to time and makes her soliciting *peep* call. She also leaves the nest for short periods during day and night. When not hunting, the male perches in the vicinity, spending his time resting or chasing other birds from near the nest when necessary. During a spell of night observation lasting 40 minutes an observer recorded a frog, a toad and 23 Harvester Termites being brought to two 26-day-old young. It is not known at what stage nestlings are first left unattended in the nest; further observations on parental attention are needed.

Before their first flight the young take turns at peering out from the nest entrance. At one nest the nestling period was close on 31 days, at another not less than 27 days. The young do not return to the nest once they have left; in one instance they established themselves 200 m away, where they remained for several days. Nothing further is known of the post-nestling period.

Information on breeding success is scant.

Breeding takes place each year. In one locality two pairs reared between 13 and 17 young in four consecutive seasons. It appears that not all chicks that hatch survive. Sometimes eggs disappear unaccountably from a clutch. A pair raise only one brood in a season.

76 Barred Owl *399.*

Gebande Uiltjie

Glaucidium capense

PLATE 23

DERIVATION
very small owl : Cape — *glaukidion* (G) : *capensis* (L)

IDENTIFICATION
Adult: The upperparts are brown with fine white barring on the head, narrow fawn barring on the back and tail, and a conspicuous V of white feathers on the mantle. It has no 'false face' on the back of the head like the Pearl-spotted Owl. There is a gorget of brown and white bars on the breast, below which the white underparts are boldly blotched with brown except for some broad barring on the flanks. The eyes are rich yellow, the bill greenish-yellow and the feet dull yellow. Birds in the eastern Cape are very dark brown above with rufous barring and a pattern of small chevron marks instead of barring on the head (see also Status and Distribution).

This species can be confused only with the Pearl-spotted Owl; distinctions are discussed under that species. The much larger 'puffball' head of the Barred Owl, which also lacks 'ear' tufts, is a particularly useful feature, especially in poor light where details of plumage cannot be seen. Like the Pearl-spotted Owl, this species also moults all its tail feathers at the same time so that it is tailless for a while.

Juvenile: It resembles the adult on leaving the nest, except for a short tail and some down on the head and abdomen where the blotching is indistinct. At the age of 50 days its tail reaches full length, and the pattern of blotching on the underparts is distinct.

HABITAT
It inhabits woodland, including acacia, particularly where there are larger trees along rivers. It overlaps the Pearl-spotted Owl, but tends to occur in denser woodland.

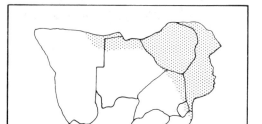

76 BARRED OWL

STATUS AND DISTRIBUTION
This resident species, quite common in suitable localities, can easily be overlooked. It was first described in 1834 from two specimens obtained in the eastern Cape, where the plumage is very much darker than that of birds found farther north. It was not recorded in that area again until a bird was found dead at Kenton-on-Sea in 1980! Its status and distribution in this area are understandably poorly known. In the north its distribution extends from northern Zululand northwards to Zimbabwe, northern Botswana and northern Namibia. Extralimitally its range extends from Angola across to east Africa but it is absent from the Congo basin.

GENERAL HABITS
As far as they are known, the Barred Owl's habits appear to be similar to those of the Pearl-spotted Owl. It also moves about freely during daylight and has the same fast dipping flight, but it rarely wags its tail. Prey is caught by dropping onto it from a perch. It is probable that it is more nocturnal in its hunting habits than the Pearl-spotted Owl; but more observations are needed. Little is known of its diet but it appears

(1) A Barred Owl emerging from its nest, a natural hole in a tree.

(2) A nestling about three weeks old.

(3) The young owl at about five weeks old.

that insects are most frequently eaten. Other prey recorded includes lizards, a frog and a bird. Further information is required.

The main call is a repeated *krrooo, krrooo, krrooo . . .* quite like a high-pitched Cape Turtle Dove. It is a rather mournful sound with none of the volume or vivacity of the Pearl-spotted Owl's crescendo call; it also calls during day and night. It sometimes utters a soft, mellow *twoo, twoo, twoo . . .* call, and at the nest a soft *twoop*. The nestling makes a rapidly repeated, wheezing *chip-chip-chip* begging call. A captive juvenile attempted adult vocalisations when two months old but the full *krrooo, krrooo, krrooo* was only achieved when it was seven months old.

BREEDING

Nothing has been recorded on courtship behaviour.

The nest site is a natural hole in a tree. According to the few available records eggs are laid on wood chips at the bottom of the hollow 15–30 cm below the entrance. The Barred Owl has not been found breeding in woodpecker and barbet nests, perhaps because it is larger than the Pearl-spotted Owl and cannot get through the entrance holes. In the few instances where nest heights have been recorded they have been 5–6 m above ground.

From nine breeding records it appears that eggs are laid in September and October. The usual clutch is three eggs, which are rounded and white. Nests have been found with two young but whether these represented the full original clutch is not known. One clutch measured $30,0 \times 26,0$; $32,0 \times 28,0$; and $33,0 \times 27,0$; and the range in another clutch of three was $32,0–34,0 \times 27,3–27,5$.

In one instance it was established that incubation commenced before the completion of the clutch. The incubating bird sits very tight and one was lifted bodily off its eggs. The incubation period is unknown but will probably be found to be close to that of the Pearl-spotted Owl.

The newly hatched nestling is undescribed but is almost certainly covered in white down, as older nestlings have whitish down. One chick estimated to be three weeks old was well feathered except for a downy head and posterior. Its eyes were yellow, the bill greyish-yellow and the feet dull yellow. At this age it does wing-flapping exercises.

Only one nest has been observed. The presumed female stayed in the nest with the single chick throughout the day until it was about 16 days old. No food was brought to the nest during the day but the birds may have been inhibited from doing so because people were camping near the nest tree. Overnight observations when the nestling was 18–20 days old established that most of the food was brought between 20h00 and 21h30 with only random visits during the rest of the night and no increase in feeding activity at dawn. Both birds fed the nestling, mostly on insects, but the presumed female also remained in the nest with the chick for long periods during the night.

A captive nestling made its first short flight at an estimated age of 33 days. A few observations on the post-nestling period in Tanzania established that the young hopped from branch to branch when just out of the nest and could fly to nearby trees two days later. They were left unattended during the day but the adults came to feed them at dusk. This behaviour would seem to confirm that this species is more nocturnal in its hunting behaviour than the Pearl-spotted Owl.

77 Cape Eagle Owl 400.
Kaapse Ooruil
Bubo capensis   PLATE 24

DERIVATION

horned owl : Cape — *bubo* (L) : *capensis* (L)

The large race of the Cape Eagle Owl found in Zimbabwe northwards to Kenya is *Bubo capensis mackinderi*, often called Mackinder's Eagle Owl, after Sir Halford Mackinder, who made the first ascent of Mount Kenya. For convenience when distinguishing the two races in the text, the names Cape Eagle Owl and Mack-

inder's Eagle Owl will be used for South African and Zimbabwean populations respectively.

IDENTIFICATION

Adult: There is no consistent difference in the coloration of the sexes but the female is larger than the male. The upperparts are dark brown with an intermingling of tawny blotching, particularly on the neck. There are prominent 'ear'

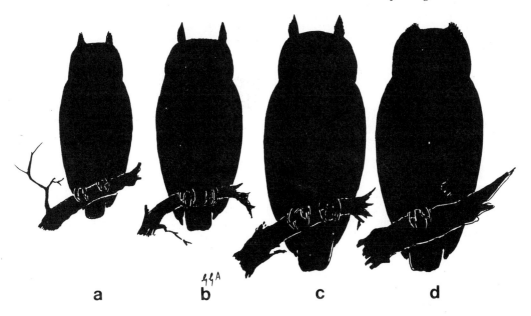

The relative sizes of eagle owls: (a) Spotted Eagle Owl, (b) Cape Eagle Owl, (c) Mackinder's Eagle Owl, (d) Giant Eagle Owl.

tufts, the eyes are orange and there is a patch of white on the throat that is especially conspicuous when it calls. On the breast there are two patches of dark brown blotching to give the effect of 'breast-plates'. Below this the rest of the underparts are broadly barred with a mixture of dark brown, tawny and white. The feathers on the legs and very large feet are creamy-white.

Confusion with the Giant Eagle is unlikely; the main differences are mentioned in the text on that species. The most similar species is the Spotted Eagle Owl, which lacks the 'breast-plates', is finely barred on the underparts and has small feet. The pale colour of the grey form distinguishes it from the tawny-coloured Cape Eagle Owl. However, the rufous form of the Spotted Eagle Owl can easily be mistaken for a Cape Eagle Owl and also has orange eyes. It can be safely identified only by the fine barring on the underparts and by its small feet if a good view is obtained. In South Africa Cape Eagle Owls and Spotted Eagle Owls are not easily separated by size, but in Zimbabwe Mackinder's Eagle Owl, which does not differ in coloration from the Cape Eagle Owl, is very large, almost the size of a Giant Eagle Owl.

Juvenile: It resembles the adult when it leaves the nest except that it is still downy on the head, has barred feathers on the back, lacks 'ear' tufts and has pale orange eyes. By the time it is about five months old it is not readily distinguishable from its parents.

HABITAT

This species occurs in rocky or mountainous terrain, often with thick woodland in a river valley nearby, and in the south-west Cape it inhabits mountain fynbos right down to sea level. In Zimbabwe Mackinder's Eagle Owl is found mostly in areas of bare granite outcrops with associated woodland. One Cape Eagle Owl was photographed on the ledge of a building in the middle of Johannesburg where it was conspicuous. Such behaviour is most unusual and it may have been a hand-reared bird.

STATUS AND DISTRIBUTION

The Cape Eagle Owl is resident but may wander about locally outside the breeding season. Because of its habitat and unobtrusive habits it is very easily overlooked and is probably more common and widely distributed than is known at present. Unlike the Spotted Eagle Owl, it is not often killed on roads by traffic at night. Mackinder's Eagle Owl was recorded in Zimbabwe only in 1967, since which time it has been found to be widely distributed and not uncommon in areas of suitable habitat. The Cape Eagle Owl is confined to South Africa, occurring mainly from the south-west Cape up the eastern side of the country to the eastern Transvaal. It is probably more widely distributed in the Karoo than is known at present and it has been found to occur as far west as the Calvinia

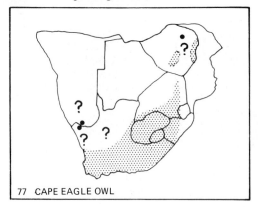

77   CAPE EAGLE OWL

district. There is a single record from near Vioolsdrift on the Orange River so it may occur throughout the north-west Cape. There is a single record from southern Namibia just over the Orange River. In time it will probably be found in other parts of Namibia. Mackinder's Eagle Owl occurs in Zimbabwe and adjacent montane Mozambique. Extralimitally its distribution is rather discontinuous (although it may have been overlooked in intervening areas) and it occurs in Malawi, Tanzania and Kenya. Another race, intermediate in size between the Cape Eagle Owl and Mackinder's Eagle Owl, is found in Ethiopia.

GENERAL HABITS

During the day the Cape Eagle Owl roosts in a secluded shady spot on the ground behind cover, sometimes in a small cave or on a ledge, less often in trees. It sits very tight, relying on its cryptic coloration, and only flies off at the last moment. Thus it is very easily overlooked. If flushed, it may perch in the open, where it is vigorously mobbed by other birds, including White-necked Ravens which often occur in the same habitat. At dusk it flies from its roost to perch at various strategic look-out points from which it hunts by observing the movements of its quarry, which it catches with a swift, silent swoop.

One of the main requirements of this owl is an abundance of large prey of one type. In Kenya mole-rats were found to be the main prey in one area. In a study in the Matopos hills in Zimbabwe 925 prey items were collected from several sites and analysed by weight. Mammals accounted for 99 per cent of the total weight, the small balance consisting of a few birds, scorpions, insects and lizards. Greater Red Rock Hares made up 63 per cent of the total weight of mammalian prey, with dassies and Scrub Hares being the next weightiest items

(23 per cent). The same prey pattern was established in less extensive studies in another locality in Zimbabwe and at Cradock in South Africa. In all three studies red rock hares were the most important prey and only young dassies were caught, the adults presumably being too strong to overpower.

In the following summary of prey recorded it will be noted that there is a close association between some of the prey species and the rocky or montane environment of this owl. Analysis of prey is facilitated by ossuaries which accumulate at the sheltered nest sites, and a good indication of the diet of a pair may be obtained from these bone collections. The pellets of this species are much larger than those of the Spotted Eagle Owl and contain larger bones, for example the leg bones of Greater Red Rock Hares. The following mammalian prey have been recorded: red rock hares, Rock Dassie, Yellow-spotted Rock Dassie, Scrub Hare, Springhare, Hedgehog, genet, Civet, mongooses, Tree Squirrel, golden mole, cane rats, vlei rats, rats, mice, shrews and rock elephant shrews. Avian prey recorded are: Hamerkop, Bald Ibis (nestlings), Lanner, Rock Kestrel, Crowned Guineafowl, francolins, a plover, Speckled Pigeon, Cape Turtle Dove, Mottled Swift, Barn Owl, Cape Robin, Red-winged Starling and domestic chickens. Other prey recorded are: small lizards, scorpions, spiders, sun spiders, grasshoppers, beetles and freshwater crabs.

The call is a double- or triple-noted hoot, *hu-hooooo* or *hooooo-hu* and *hu-hooooo-hu*, used as a territorial or contact call and also in alarm. A rather similar call is a short mellow *coo-cook* or *coo-coo-cook*, rather like that of the Speckled Pigeon, used in nuptial display, in greeting between the pair and occasionally in alarm. At one nest a pair exchanged a rapid explosive series of 20–30 of these hoots when the male came to the nest with prey. The hooting calls differ in quality and rhythm from the calls of the Spotted Eagle Owl, which regularly duets. It remains to be established whether the Cape Eagle Owl also duets. Very occasionally the hooting call is made during the day. A sharp *wak-wak*, as well as bill-clacking and hissing, is used in alarm. The female solicits the male with a wheezing *shreeer* repeated at intervals of a few seconds; this call is used also by the nestlings once they abandon their infantile chittering. It is ventriloquial, carrying over a considerable distance. When feeding the nestlings the female emits a soft, growling *gruk, gruk* and behaves rather like a clucking broody hen while tending them.

BREEDING

Little is known of nuptial display, which appears to be mainly vocal. Before breeding, the male and female roost near each other during the day. At dusk they perch together and exchange hoots, the female remaining bolt upright and the male facing her and bowing with each hoot. Their white throats puff out and act as conspicuous visual signals in the darkness.

Nest sites may be at ground level or on a ledge or in a cave with a drop below. All nests are well concealed by surrounding rocks, grass or bushes in sheltered situations, often on a hill slope above a wooded river valley, not necessarily in association with water, and in Zimbabwe most streams are dry in winter when the owls breed. The nest is a shallow unlined scrape in the soil, in and around which pellets and bone fragments accumulate as the breeding season progresses. According to some textbooks this species breeds in old stick nests of raptors or crows, but authentication of these records is lacking and they have almost certainly arisen from misidentified Spotted Eagle Owls using such sites. In Kenya nests have been found on low tree stumps, and in one case in a hollow in the fork of a tree 15 m above ground, but no such sites have been recorded in southern Africa.

A nest site, although not necessarily the same nest scrape, may be occupied for many years. The first nest in Zimbabwe was found in a cave a year after the species was first recorded in the country, and eight years later the original observer returned to confirm the record and found the owls breeding in the same cave. However, alternate sites some distance away are used, particularly after a nest has been robbed by a predator. In a study in the Matopos eight breeding pairs of Mackinder's Owls were located in 620 km², a density of one pair per 77,5 km², although not all pairs may have been located and only about a tenth of the area contained suitable habitat. The closest nests were 2,25 km apart and the farthest 10,5 km. In a Kenya study nest territories were approximately 2 km². Nothing is known about population density in South Africa, where the Cape Eagle Owl has been little studied.

In Zimbabwe eggs are laid in late May, June or July (nine records). The few authentic South African records indicate a similar breeding season except that in the south-west Cape eggs may also be laid in August. Normally two eggs are laid, sometimes three, and there is one record of a single egg. Eggs are rounded and white. Measurements of Mackinder's Eagle Owl eggs in Zimbabwe are: 57,8 × 46,5 (19); 55,0–60,7 × 44,0–48,4. They are appreciably larger than those of the Spotted Eagle Owl. Measurements of Cape Eagle Owl eggs in South Africa are: 53,1 × 44,6 (9); 52,0–54,5 × 42,2–46,8. Eggs cannot be distinguished from those of the Spotted Eagle Owl by size alone so careful identification of the incubating adult is essential.

The following breeding details are based mainly on studies of Mackinder's Eagle Owls in Zimbabwe and Kenya. There is very little published information on the breeding of the Cape Eagle Owl in South Africa, but the basic breeding biologies of the two races will doubtless be found to be very similar.

The female makes a nest scrape and then sits in it as if brooding for some days before laying. In Zimbabwe eggs were laid at least two days apart in one instance, four days apart in another. In Kenya two eggs were laid on consecutive days in one nest. Incubation commences with the laying of the first egg. Only the female incubates during the day and it is not known if the male relieves her at night. She sits very tight, relying on her camouflage, and only flies off when an observer is almost at the nest. Once the coast is clear she returns quickly. At one site no prey remains or pellets were found on the nest during the incubation period, indicating that the female probably leaves the nest to feed. In Zimbabwe one incubation period was close on 34 days and in Kenya approximately 36 days.

Even where two chicks hatch four days apart the smaller gains weight steadily and there is no evidence of sibling aggression. In Kenya three young have been reared successfully together but there is no record of this in southern Africa. The skin of the newly hatched chick is pink covered in off-white down; the eyes are closed and the bill and feet are greyish. At the age of one week the down is thicker and greyer, first quills are just discernible on the back and along the hind edge of the wings, and the eyes are still closed. By the age of two weeks the eyes are open and are pale yellow. Quills are sprouting rapidly but feathers are not yet emerging. At four weeks old the chick is thickly covered in greyish down through which feathers are rapidly emerging to give a pattern of black transverse barring above and below. The wing feathers are breaking from their quills, and tail feathers are just emerging. The throat is conspicuously white and the feet appear almost too large for the body. The eyes are deeper yellow, the cere is grey and the bill black. At the age of seven weeks the nestling is well feathered, the last remaining downy areas being on the underparts, head and upper back. The wing and tail feath-

(1) View of the habitat and nest site (arrowed) of Mac-kinder's Eagle Owl in the Matopos, Zimbabwe.

(2) A close-up of the above nest.

(3) Nestling Mackinder's Eagle Owls 8 and 4 days old.

(4) The nestlings 19 and 15 days old; a young Red Rock Hare and a young dassie lie on the nest.

(5) The nestlings at 34 and 30 days old.

(6) The nestlings at 55 and 51 days old; note the large feet.

ers are well grown but have not emerged fully from their quills. The eyes are pale orange.

The newly hatched chick is weak, is unable to raise its head and is largely inactive except for weak chittering, begging calls. By the time it is two weeks old the chick has developed its co-ordination and can stand and walk about the nest scrape shakily. It backs to the edge of the nest to defecate like a diurnal raptor but the droppings merely fall on the perimeter of the nest. When handled it hisses and claps its bill and at three weeks old it may spread its wings in threat, although it is usually rather confiding and docile like most owl nestlings. At the age of six weeks, possibly even earlier, it wanders off the nest into surrounding cover if the nest site permits this.

The small chicks are almost continuously brooded by the female, even at night, except when they are fed. The male supplies prey and there is usually more food on the nest than the female and her young can consume. A large item like a Greater Red Rock Hare weighing as much as 2 kg can last several nights, so prey is not always brought each night. The excess food attracts scavengers like White-necked Ravens, and probably carnivorous mammals, against which the female has to protect her nestlings. The young are still brooded during the day when about three weeks old but at night the female stands near them and does not brood. She also leaves the nest at night for short periods. One nest was watched overnight at at this stage and contained a young Greater Red Rock Hare and two small dassies when observations began in the late afternoon. During the night the female fed the two young for 10–15 minutes on six occasions, twice shortly after sunset and four times during the four hours before dawn. The male did not visit the nest with prey that night. In two studies in Zimbabwe the average daily intake of food during the nestling period for the female and young was calculated at 650–670 g. In the early stages this results in an excess of prey, but when the nestlings begin feathering most of the food brought is consumed in a short while. By the time the young are a month old the female no longer roosts with them by day although she perches where she can keep a watch on the nest. The owls have not been known to attack humans at the nest. In Kenya an injury-feigning distraction display has been recorded.

The duration of the nestling period is difficult to establish, as the young wander off the nest when about six weeks old. At one site in a cave on a cliff the young left when about 60–70 days old and a captive nestling could only fly competently when about 70 days old. In South Africa a young Cape Eagle Owl was first able to fly between 70 and 77 days. The young wander some distance from the nest and hide in thick cover during the day, emerging at dusk to be fed by the adults and sometimes returning to the nest for a meal. They are very difficult to locate by day because of their cryptic coloration; the best method of finding them is to listen for their characteristic *shreeer* soliciting call at dusk. They remain with the adults for about two to three months after leaving the nest, then they disperse and become independent. However, further observations on the post-nestling period are required.

Even if one allows for the difficulty in locating alternate nest sites when the owls move away, it appears that annual breeding is by no means regular. In the Matopos apparent non-breeding years have resulted in low reproductive success; in 26 pair-years 10 owlets were raised, a figure of 0,38 young per pair per year. The ground nest site is vulnerable to predation and it is thought that not only White-necked Ravens but also other predators and scavengers, particularly nocturnal mammals such as genets, may be responsible for the disappearance of nestlings. Further observations are needed, as well as breeding success studies from other localities.

78 Spotted Eagle Owl 401

Gevlekte Ooruil
Bubo africanus

PLATE 24

DERIVATION
horned owl : African — *bubo* (L) : *africanus* (L)

IDENTIFICATION
Adult: This medium-sized owl is the smallest of the three southern African eagle owls. The sexes are alike in colour and cannot usually be distinguished by size in the field. Both grey and rufous colour forms occur but the former is far commoner. The grey form is ash-grey above with some white spots, and whitish below with fine grey barring and a variable amount of blotching on the breast. The 'ear' tufts are prominent and there is a distinct facial disc bracketed with black. The bill is black, the eyes are yellow and the feathers of the legs and feet are white. The rufous form has a similar pattern of markings, and orange eyes. The Spotted Eagle Owl, especially the rufous form, can be confused with the Cape Eagle Owl; differences are discussed in the text on that species.
Juvenile: The young owl leaves the nest while it is still downy on the head and underparts, and only the facial disc, back, wings and tail are feathered. It has a pattern of black barring on the upperparts, also visible on the emergent feathers beneath the downy areas. The 'ears' at this stage show as downy bumps. The eyes are yellow. By the age of about three months it is fully feathered, resembling the adult except for shorter 'ear' tufts.

HABITAT
This species, occurring in a wide variety of habitats, is commonest in rocky areas. It is found in desert but not in evergreen forest or open flat grassland. In southern Africa it has adapted to urban conditions and breeds on buildings.

STATUS AND DISTRIBUTION
The Spotted Eagle Owl is a common resident species. Road counts in the south-western Cape revealed a density of 0,6–1,8 birds per 16 km, the higher figure being recorded in an area where there was a population explosion of gerbils at the time. In Zimbabwe 10 birds were seen in 80 km during a single night's count. An observer in Namibia counted 26 dead Spotted Eagle Owls along a 200 km stretch of road. It is difficult to assess to what extent the considerable mortality on roads affects overall numbers but there is no evidence to indicate a population decline. Tests on a small sample of birds for organochlorine residues revealed only small amounts. This species occurs throughout southern Africa. Extralimitally it is found northwards to the Sahara and in southern Arabia.

GENERAL HABITS
During the day the Spotted Eagle Owl roosts on the ground or in a tree, relying on its cryptic coloration to avoid detection. If an intruder approaches, the eyes are closed to slits and the 'ears' raised to maximum height. The pair will be found roosting near each other and they are very sedentary in their habits. At dusk the owls emerge to hunt and may regularly be seen at the same spots along a road, either standing in the road or perched on poles alongside it. Prey is normally taken by pouncing onto it from a perch but insects are sometimes caught on foot. In the Kalahari this owl was seen in the company of a Pale Chanting Goshawk in broad daylight as they followed a foraging Honey Badger for anything it might disturb. In another unusual observation a fruit bat was caught in flight.
The prey of the Spotted Eagle Owl consists mainly of arthropods, small mammals and birds. It also feeds occasionally on amphibians, reptiles and fish. Carrion in the form of road kills is also probably eaten but confirmation is required. The late G. J. Broekhuysen made an analysis of 1 076 prey records derived from his own observations, from the literature and from unpublished sources. The total number of species identified was 62. Arthropods, mostly insects, comprised 67 per cent of the 1 076 items, mammals 17 per cent and birds 14,5 per cent. The small balance was made up of reptiles, amphibians and fish. Although arthropods made up the greatest number of items analysed, mammals and birds accounted for a greater weight of food.
Arthropod prey includes a wide variety of insects such as locusts, grasshoppers, crickets, beetles and termites. Other items are scorpions, spiders, millipedes and, rarely, fresh-water

crabs. Mammalian prey consists mainly of rats, mice, shrews, moles and mole-rats. Species such as gerbils, subject to population explosions, are regularly taken and in one study in the Namib Desert made up 93 per cent of the prey recorded. Occasionally larger mammals such as a Night Ape or young hares are caught. Avian prey includes a variety of small species but birds as large as a Lanner, Crested Francolin, Redwing Francolin, Speckled Pigeon, Feral Pigeon and Double-banded Sandgrouse have been recorded. In one case a Yellow-billed Hornbill disturbed at night by the observer was caught and killed. One was seen with a Rufous-cheeked Nightjar, which may have been a road casualty. Doves are quite often preyed on; one pair living near the coast regularly caught roosting Common and Arctic Terns. Reptilian prey records are of small snakes, lizards and geckos. In the Namib Desert geckos comprised seven per cent of one prey sample. Fish are very rarely recorded. In summary, the Spotted Eagle Owl feeds mostly on insects, small mammals and small birds, the last two categories being the main prey items when breeding. However, as some of the larger mammalian and avian prey records indicate, it can at times kill large prey for its size.

The main call is hooting, used by both sexes for contact and during courtship. The male hoots *hoo-hoo*, the second *hoo* lower than the first. The female uses a triple hoot *hoo-hoohoo*, the middle *hoo* higher than the first and last, which are on the same pitch. The hooting calls are often used in duet, the male starting and the female following immediately so that it sounds like a single call. Detailed observations during the breeding cycle established that both sexes may call throughout the night; the male's peak calling times were at dusk and dawn, and those of the female between 01h00 and 02h00 and at dawn. There was no correlation between peak calling times and prey delivery. In alarm both sexes emit a wailing *kee-ow* hoot and also click their bills. During distraction displays a chittering call is used. At the nest the female utters a growling *paroo* on seeing the male approach, probably a soliciting call. A soft purring note and broody *kapok-kapok-kapok* sounds are used by the female when 'talking' to her nestlings. Newly hatched chicks emit soft *chirr* and *tjelep* begging calls, later succeeded by a characteristic ventriloquial wheezing *churrr*, 'midway between a severe dose of nasal catarrh and a concrete mixer'. It carries far. Sometimes it is used with a sleepy intonation as a greeting call to the parents when the nestling is fully fed. In annoyance when handled,

nestlings chitter and click their bills. Both young and adults hiss in threat. Juveniles make their first attempts at hooting when about four or five months old.

BREEDING

The pair remain together for their lifetimes but a mate is soon replaced if lost. In one observation the female disappeared when there were young in the nest and a short while later the male acquired a new mate. Courtship consists of the male and female calling to each other in duet but no accompanying displays have been observed. The male feeds the female during the courtship period. Mating takes place on the ground or on the branch of a tree, in observed instances at dusk and dawn.

Various nest sites are used. An analysis of 359 records established that 61 per cent were ground sites, 26 per cent in trees and 11 per cent on buildings. The remaining sites were in miscellaneous situations such as on stacks of hay or on a pile of maize bags. No nest is made and the eggs are laid on the available surface of the chosen site. 'Ground' nests are amongst rocky outcrops, on the ledge of an old quarry or small cliff, in an eroded donga and various similar situations. Sometimes the nest of a White-necked Raven on a cliff is used. Nests on buildings may be considered as a deviation from a cliff site. These nests have been on ledges of buildings, in the top of a gutter downpipe, between the sloping roof and a wall, and quite often in ornamental window boxes. Tree nests are usually in a hole or in a hollow where several branches converge, or on the nest of some other bird or prey, Hamerkop, crow or Sociable Weaver. One nest was on the drey of a Grey Squirrel, another on an accumulation of pine needles caught on the thickened part of a branch. In some sites such as window boxes, providing no cover, the female may be exposed to full sun for most of the day.

The same site may be used year after year. In one instance a nest on a small cliff face in a suburban garden was being used 40 years after it was first found. It was not known if it had been occupied all this time but the observer had lived in the house as an adult for 15 years during which the owls bred every year. A move to a new site is never very far, the owls are conservative and reluctant to move unless their nest site is no longer suitable or they are seriously disturbed. Very little is recorded about size of territory but in Zimbabwe three breeding pairs were located in an area of 5,8 km^2.

The main laying season is from August to October throughout southern Africa (90 per cent of 257 records). The remaining 10 per cent of records are for May, June, July, November and December. Two to four eggs are laid; in 297 clutch records 68 per cent were for two eggs, 29 per cent for three eggs and 3 per cent for four eggs. There is some evidence that larger clutches are laid in years of plentiful food supply. In Zimbabwe during a year of a rodent population explosion, all three nests found in an area of 5,8 km^2 contained four eggs. Eggs are rounded and white. Measurements are: 49,1 × 41,1 (80); 47,1–54,2 × 39,1–44,4.

The eggs are usually laid at intervals of two or three days, incubation beginning after the first egg is laid. At one nest where accurate observations were made, three days elapsed between the first and second eggs, and four days between the second and third eggs. At another nest three chicks hatched at daily intervals, suggesting that eggs were laid a day apart. Further observations on the laying interval are needed. In one instance an egg was laid between 08h00 and 14h00. Incubation behaviour during 105 hours of observation divided equally between day and night established that the female brooded all day and left the nest three times each night for short periods varying from 6 to 28 minutes, averaging 12 minutes. Most of her breaks off the nest (83 per cent) were between 18h00 and 20h00. Her absences from the nest during night observations were just under 5 per cent of the time. The male took no share in incubation, visiting the nest on five occasions at night, only once with prey, and usually he called to the female, who left the nest to receive prey from him which she ate away from the nest. While brooding, the female sits very tight,

A Spotted Eagle Owl on its nest on a quarry face to show its excellent camouflage.

relying on her cryptic coloration for concealment. She moves very little, occasionally changing her position and tucking the eggs in beneath her before settling again. As may be expected, she changes her position and moves about more often at night. Some females nesting on buildings become so used to people that they refuse to leave the nest and have to be lifted up for the contents of the nest to be inspected. The incubation period lasts between 30 and 32 days; the chick takes two days to emerge, from the first sign of pipping of the eggshell.

Although the young hatch at intervals, sibling aggression by older chicks has not been recorded. The newly hatched chick is covered in white down and its eyes are closed. At seven days old the eyes begin to open gradually and are grey coloured. By the age of two weeks the chick has a thicker second coat of greyish down, and first feathers are emerging through the down on the wing coverts, the scapulars and along the hind edges of the wings. The eyes are dull yellow at this stage. When the nestling leaves the nest at the age of six weeks its wing feathers are almost fully grown but the tail is only half its final length. The facial disc is fully formed with black 'brackets', and the eyes are yellow like the adult's. The head and underparts are mainly downy, although a pattern of transverse barring similar to that on the feathered upperparts is visible beneath the down.

Initially the chicks are weak, and lie in a huddle unable to lift their heads. After two days they respond to any noise near them by stretching up their necks. For the first two weeks they spend much of their time sleeping in a prone position. By 17 days old they sit up well and can stand at the age of three weeks. Once they can stand they become far more active, stretching and flapping their wings, preening, nibbling their toes and scratching their heads. If the nest is not enclosed they walk backwards to defecate over the edge of the nest. The time of their first threat behaviour towards intruders is somewhat variable, usually at about 25 days old. From the age of a month they clamber about the nest and peer over the edge if it is an enclosed situation such as a hole in a tree. A few days before they are due to leave they may wander off the nest and fall to the ground if the nest is in an elevated position. Towards the end of the nestling period, if the nest site permits, the young owls pounce on objects in or near the nest and make mock kills.

The female broods the small chicks almost continuously both day and night during the first few days. Eggshell fragments found in pellets indicate that at least some of the shells are eat-

(1) A Spotted Eagle Owl (arrowed) on its nest in the window-box of an occupied house.

(2) These eggs are in a Black Crow's nest.

(3) A nest in a niche in a river bank.

(4) A 16-day-old nestling.

(5) The nestling at 30 days old; the nest is a hollow in an oak tree.

(6) The 44-day-old nestling just after it left the nest.

en when the eggs hatch. The male provides prey, which the female tears up for the chicks. She stimulates them to beg by touching their bills with hers and closes her eyes as the food is passed. Prey is normally brought decapitated. During nine nights of observation the average was four deliveries a night. Once the young are two weeks old the female no longer broods them at night, spending about a quarter of the night-time with them. The male continues to provide prey, which is either brought to the nest or fetched from him by the female. She may also hunt at this stage but whether she catches prey herself or receives it from the male is uncertain. However, as prey deliveries increase after the first two weeks, she probably also hunts actively. The male does not tear up prey for the young but may feed small items such as insects directly to them. He spends very little time on the nest, only 18 minutes during 117 hours of night-time observation during the nestling period. The time at which the female leaves the young alone on the nest by day varies, probably related to the type of nest site. She may leave them as early as 11 days or only after five weeks, but she remains on guard nearby where she can see the nest. Once the young are three weeks old her time on the nest at night drops to about 3 per cent. The young are able to swallow smaller rodents whole at this stage so only large ones still need to be torn up.

During the nestling period the adults may be very bold in attacking intruders at the nest; there are a number of reports of observers being struck and severely clawed. More confiding birds nesting on buildings sometimes remain on the nest, spreading their wings in threat if the observer approaches too close. Sometimes a distraction display is performed in which the owl moves awkwardly along the ground, dragging its wings to feign injury.

Although the young may leave the nest earlier, especially at sites on the ground, they usually remain in the nest for close on six weeks. The young owls cannot fly properly when they leave the nest and remain nearby for some weeks. They are fed for at least five weeks after leaving and probably longer. One juvenile was thought to have made its first kill when seven weeks out of the nest, at which stage it was flying competently. As the young owls become independent, they disperse, about four months after leaving the nest; two ringed juveniles were found 11 km and 17 km away from their nests at this stage.

There is little information on breeding success. Occasionally two consecutive broods may be reared, the female laying her second clutch while young from the previous brood are still in the area. At three nests in Zimbabwe each with four eggs a 92-per-cent nestling success was recorded, owing to the rodent plague in the area.

Note: The information for this account has been drawn largely from the unpublished book 'It's an Owl's Life' by the late Professor G. J. Broekhuysen.

79 Giant Eagle Owl 402 .

Reuse-ooruil

Bubo lacteus   PLATE 24

DERIVATION
horned owl : milky — *bubo* (L) : *lacteus* (L)

This species was originally called the Milky Eagle Owl because of its pale colour, hence *lacteus*. It is also called Verreaux's Eagle Owl in some books but the name Giant Eagle Owl is most often used in southern Africa.

IDENTIFICATION
Adult: This owl, the largest in Africa, can usually be identified by its size alone. Females are larger than males. It is pale sepia-grey above and finely barred grey and white below. The dark brown eyes are set in a white face bracketed with black; the pink eyelids are diagnostic. The 'ear' tufts are relatively short compared with other eagle owls and are not often raised except when it is inquisitive or annoyed. The large bill is pale blue-grey, with heavy black bristles at its base. The feet are huge. It could possibly be confused with the Spotted Eagle Owl and Cape Eagle Owl, particularly the large northern race of the latter, but these owls have yellow or orange eyes and more prominent 'ear' tufts and lack pink eyelids.

Juvenile: The young bird leaves the nest when it is still partially downy. It differs from the adult in being finely barred grey and white on the upperparts and it has no 'ear' tufts apart from slight downy 'bumps'. The young owl is al-

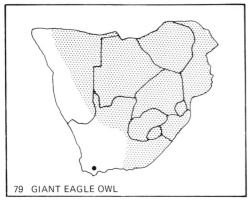

79 GIANT EAGLE OWL

together paler than its parents, but by the age of five months is darker above and has developed 'ear' tufts, so that it is no longer readily distinguishable as a juvenile. From a pair and their offspring observed over several years it appears that the young owl may breed once it is three years old.

HABITAT

It inhabits savanna woodland, especially acacia, and is often found in riverine strips where there are large trees. Not found in forest, it occurs mainly in drier habitats.

STATUS AND DISTRIBUTION

This sedentary species may be found in the same small area year after year. It is nowhere plentiful but is regularly encountered in suitable habitat. It is widely distributed except for the arid western regions and south-western Cape, but there is a single recent record from Bredasdorp. It is rare in the eastern Cape and Natal. Extralimitally it is found northwards to Ethiopia and west Africa but not in the forested Congo basin.

GENERAL HABITS

During the day the male and female are usually found roosting near each other within the canopy of large trees; quite often a young bird from a previous brood is also in the vicinity. They are reluctant to fly off, relying on their cryptic coloration to avoid detection. Despite its somnolent appearance this owl remains alert during the day; there are several records of kills during daylight, even at midday, presumably when opportunity arose. If flushed during the day, the owl is mobbed by a variety of birds, including diurnal raptors, which recognise it as a potential enemy.

At dusk it sets off to hunt in earnest. With a silent, flapping flight, effortless and buoyant for so large a bird, it glides up to an elevated van-

tage point from which it surveys the area. It swoops down upon its prey, catching some of its victims in trees, particularly roosting birds such as guineafowl. It is also capable of a vertical somersault to catch a passing beetle in the air, remarkable dexterity for its size. It also hunts on foot, either in shallow water for amphibians and fish, or on the ground for insects. In game reserves in east Africa where water-holes are floodlit it may be seen feeding on scarab beetles and other insects right amongst large ungulates such as buffaloes. On one occasion an owl puffed up its feathers and threatened a rhinoceros that came too close. It also sits in roads occasionally and may be killed by traffic.

Even allowing for its size and powerful feet, this owl is capable of killing remarkably large prey such as a Vervet Monkey or a roosting Secretary Bird. Once it was shot while attacking a roosting Peacock, whose frantic cries brought its owner to the rescue. At the other end of the scale it feeds on birds as small as white-eyes and on insects. It may aptly be described as an omnivorous nocturnal butcher, regularly including other species of owls in its diet. Occasionally it also eats carrion such as hares and snakes killed on roads at night. One observer ran over a Springhare and found the owl feeding on it when he returned by the same route later that night.

The following recorded items of prey illustrate that it feeds on almost anything that it can catch or overpower. Hedgehogs are the most favoured mammalian prey where their distribution overlaps that of the owl, their most serious enemy. The skin of the hedgehog is usually discarded, neatly peeled off, but sometimes pieces of skin with spines attached are recovered from pellets, indicating that the owl can ingest the spines without harm. Mammals ranging in size from a Vervet Monkey to a shrew are caught. The following is a not too detailed list to indicate the range taken: a Warthog piglet, hares, Springhares, genets, mongooses, Suricates, dassies, galagos, Ground Squirrels, fruit bats, cane rats, gerbils, rats and mice. There is one record of this owl feeding on a Common Duiker, thought to be a road casualty. As already indicated, it catches birds ranging in size from a Secretary Bird to white-eyes. Avian prey records are: African Black Duck, Yellow-billed Duck, nestlings of eagles, vultures and other raptors, an adult Gymnogene, domestic chickens, guineafowl, francolins, quails, a young Crowned Crane, korhaans, dikkops, sandgrouse, doves, pigeons, Senegal Coucal, Barn Owls, Grass Owl, Marsh Owl, Spotted Eagle Owls, rollers, Yellow-billed Hornbills, Pied

Crows, tits, bulbuls, shrikes, sunbirds and weavers. Birds are usually plucked before they are eaten. Other prey includes frogs, toads, snakes (including venomous species), small lizards, monitor lizards (leguaans), fish such as barbel, scorpions, sun spiders, beetles, moths and termites. A quantitative prey analysis of 59 items in Kenya comprised 56 per cent mammals, 27 per cent amphibians, 15 per cent birds and a snake. There are no published prey analyses in our area but various random samples indicate that mammals are most often taken, then birds.

The calls of this owl, particularly its hooting, have been the subject of many varying descriptions. There are two main calls, a deep, resonant hooting and a whistling note. A deep double hoot *oop-oop*, very like the booming call of the Ground Hornbill, is most often heard. It is used as a contact call between the pair, as territorial advertisement, and also in alarm. In nuptial display the pair sit close together, jerking their bodies up and down and slightly flicking their folded wings to the accompaniment of short grunting hoots. One bird, probably the male, calls *uh-uhu-uh-uh*, to be answered with a deeper *uh-uh* by its mate. The duet may continue for some time, for at least 15 minutes on one occasion, until the birds became aware of the observer's presence. A plaintive, whistling *pseeeeee-eee-eew* is uttered by the female, and by the nestling once it has abandoned its infantile chittering. Used as a soliciting call, it also serves as a contact between the female and her youngster. Although of no great volume, it is ventriloquial in quality, carrying over a considerable distance. One female and her large nestling called to each other every 10–15 seconds over a distance of 800 m during the course of a whole afternoon. It is not known whether the male also makes this call. A weird resonant *ooo-aaa-au* is made during alarm and distraction behaviour near the nest. A low *whok* as well as bill clacking are used in alarm. Young, and occasionally the female, may hiss when disturbed at the nest.

BREEDING

No nuptial behaviour other than that already mentioned in the section on calls has been described.

The Giant Eagle Owl lays its eggs on top of the nest of another species or in a hollow in a tree. It adds no lining nor other material to the nest. One nest site was on top of a large orchid growing out from the stem of a palm 4,5 m above ground. In east Africa it has been known to lay in debris on the flat roof of a high building, and in a large petrol drum placed in a tree

as a beehive. Usually it takes over nests not in use, but it may also dispossess the rightful owner by 'squatting' in the nest and resisting all attempts to dislodge it. In one instance a Hamerkop was deprived of its half-completed nest in this manner. Sometimes Wahlberg's Eagles returning from migration to breed have had to build a new nest on finding a large owl nestling in their previous year's nest.

The nests of the following species have been used for breeding (as this owl will undoubtedly make use of any suitable stick platform, these serve merely as examples of sites): Hamerkop (in one instance the owl was nesting on top and an Egyptian Goose was incubating eleven eggs inside), Secretary Bird, White-backed Vulture, Lappet-faced Vulture, White-headed Vulture, Hooded Vulture, Yellow-billed Kite, Tawny Eagle, Wahlberg's Eagle, African Hawk Eagle, Martial Eagle, Crowned Eagle, Bateleur, Fish Eagle, Pied Crow, Buffalo Weaver and Sociable Weaver. Heights of nests vary from 6 to 25 m above ground. The same nest may be used each year; if it falls down, the owls will move to the nearest suitable site. Nothing is recorded of size of territory for this species.

Eggs are laid in the cool, dry season from June to August with occasional records for April and May. One or two eggs are laid, usually two; reports of three eggs require confirmation. They are rounded and white, sometimes with small nodules on the surface. Quite often one egg is markedly smaller than the other; one such clutch measured 65,0 × 54,0 and 58,5 × 51,0. Measurements are: 62,6 × 51,4 (30); 58,0–65,9 × 48,0–54,0.

Nothing is recorded of the laying interval in a clutch of two, except that the second chick may hatch 'some while' after the first. As far as is known, only the female incubates during the day, the male roosting in the vicinity. He brings prey for her at night but whether he incubates is not known. Although nest sites are often exposed to full sun throughout the day, the female appears to suffer no discomfort. She sits very tight and cannot be dislodged by banging on the tree or shouting. The incubation period has not been accurately obtained but is approximately 32–34 days; confirmation is required.

It is very rare for two young to be reared together; there are no such records in southern Africa. Although further detailed observations are required, it appears that the smaller chick is dominated by its sibling and dies from starvation at an early stage. It may also be attacked by the stronger chick; but further information on the nature and extent of this behaviour is needed. Little is known of the development of the nestling. When first hatched it is covered with whitish down; this thickens and is greyish by the age of three weeks, by when barred feathers are emerging. The eyelids are pale pink but the black 'brackets' on the side of the face are not yet visible. At the age of six weeks the nestling is finely barred above and below, and the black 'brackets' on the face are clearly defined. It is still very downy, particularly on the head, and is not fully feathered by the time it leaves the nest at about two months old.

There is no information on nestling behaviour in the early stages nor on when the eyes open nor on when it can first stand. At three weeks old it makes the *pseeeeee-eee-eew* begging call as well as its chittering noise. By the age of seven weeks it may snap its bill at an observer but it usually lies prone in the nest with eyes half closed. During the day it is largely inactive although it sometimes stands up. After dark it becomes active, walking about the nest, preening and performing vigorous wing-flapping. Its behaviour at night is very like that of a diurnal raptor at the end of the nestling period. When the parent arrives it calls excitedly, bobbing its head about in ludicrous fashion. It also sometimes performs a hunger 'dance', swaying about and transferring its weight from one foot to the other.

Like so many aspects of the breeding biology, information on parental attention during the nestling period is sketchy. The female remains with the chick until it is at least three weeks old and broods it during the day; also at night but not continuously. The male brings prey to the nest at night during this period and roosts nearby during the day. It is not known when the nestling is first left alone, but the female is no longer with it by the time it is seven weeks old although she roosts nearby. Both adults hunt at night at this stage, and the female may still tear up prey for the nestling. There is usually a favourite 'plucking' perch not far from the nest, where birds are plucked and hedgehogs 'peeled'. If this perch can be found it provides valuable information on the diet of a pair. During the nestling period and continuing into the post-nestling period remarkable distraction displays may be performed, both day and night and by either sex. The adult flies low over the ground with drooping wings, or alights and drags its wings, or flops about, all to the accompaniment of bill-clacking and calling. It is an effective display of injury-feigning; in one instance it successfully lured dogs away from a young bird recently out of the nest and hiding on the ground. The owl may also alight on a branch and limply flap its wings about like the flags of a semaphore signaller. Sometimes it hangs ludicrously upside down from a branch and when approached will drop off and crash into the undergrowth. Despite its size, this owl rarely attacks humans, but there is a case on record where someone handling a young bird on the ground at night was severely clawed when both adults swooped down.

The nestling period is difficult to establish, as the young owl leaves the nest before it can fly properly and its departure may be precipitated by attacks from other birds of prey. However, it appears that it leaves when about two months old, although unable to fly properly for about another month. It remains near the nest, to which it may occasionally return to roost, and is fed by the adults. It is remarkably inactive, making little effort to fly even when able to do so. When discovered on the ground it may feign death, lying prone with its head on one side and its eyes closed. If watched from a distance, it will be seen to open its eyes cautiously and return to life. However, in its death-shamming state, it can be picked up and will remain moribund. If thrown into the air, it will fly off normally. Similar remarkable behaviour is recorded of the Pearl-spotted Owl.

The juvenile remains with its parents until the following breeding season, although it is capable of killing for itself when about five months old. It may still be fed by the male even when he is supplying prey for the female and a nestling. In Kenya the late Joy Adamson provided a wild pair and their offspring with mole-rats and chicken heads and they became very confiding. At one stage the adults and three young from successive broods were seen together in perfect amity. One of the young owls even helped by bringing food for a chick in the nest. The situation in Kenya was probably exceptional, but it appears from other observations that young from a previous brood are not driven off. Despite the fact that the juvenile remains with its parents until the following nesting season, annual breeding appears to be normal. Apart from the Kenya record of three young reared in successive years there is no information on breeding success. Many aspects of the breeding biology of this fascinating owl remain to be investigated.

(1) The eggs of a Giant Eagle Owl laid in the nest of a Wahlberg's Eagle.

(2) A fully grown nestling in a Bateleur's nest; it lies prone to try and avoid detection.

(3) The head of a Giant Eagle Owl is just visible as it broods its eggs on top of a Buffalo Weaver's nest.

(4) A nestling on top of a Hamerkop's nest.

(5) An adult has just delivered a hedgehog to its nestling of about three weeks old. Note the huge feet.

(6) A nestling approximately seven weeks old exercises its wings.

80 Pel's Fishing Owl *4o3*.

Visuil

Scotopelia peli

PLATE 24

DERIVATION
night : dove : Pel's — *skotos* (G) : *peleia* (G) : *peli* (L)

H. S. Pel was a Dutch government official on the Gold Coast from 1840–50. The unusual use of *peleia* for an owl may be a pun based on the conversion of Pel's name into the generic name.

IDENTIFICATION
Adult: The sexes are alike in colour but the female is larger than the male, a difference that is only apparent if they are seen together. This large owl is tawny-rufous in colour above and paler tawny below. The upperparts are narrowly barred with black, the underparts rather variably marked with small spots and streaks as well as some barring on the abdomen. There are no 'ear' tufts on the large shaggy head and there is no distinct facial disc. The large eyes are dark brown, the bill is horn coloured, the bare legs and claws are whitish. The legs are normally concealed by a 'skirt' of feathers when the owl is roosting. Because of its large size and distinctive colouring it cannot be confused with any other southern African owl.

Juvenile: The young owl leaves the nest while still mainly covered in pale buffy down except for pale tawny-rufous feathering on the scapulars, wings and tail. The feathers are barred with black like the adult. Feathers emerge very gradually and replace the down. At the age of 10 months the juvenile is similar to the adult but slightly paler. At 15 months old it is indistinguishable from the adult.

HABITAT
This owl is found in forest beside large rivers, estuaries, or swamps. It occurs mainly along low-lying river systems, particularly those that dry up into a series of pools in the winter months. Large trees for nesting and roosting are an essential requirement of its habitat.

STATUS AND DISTRIBUTION
This resident owl is common in suitable habitat such as the Okavango delta. In the eastern Cape, on the edge of its range, it is rare, but there is no direct evidence that its numbers have declined. In Natal it is also rare, except in

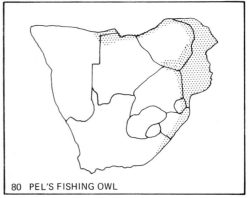

80 PEL'S FISHING OWL

northern Zululand. Its distribution extends from Transkei northwards to Mozambique and Zimbabwe, thence westwards to the Okavango river in northern Botswana and north-eastern Namibia. Extralimitally its range extends northwards to the Sahara.

GENERAL HABITS
Pel's Fishing Owl is entirely nocturnal. During the day it roosts in a shady spot in a large tree, usually between six and eighteen metres above ground. Because of its unobtrusive habits it is easily overlooked. The male and female roost in the same or adjacent trees and may change their roost depending on the cover provided during a particular season. If disturbed during the day, the owl flies off reluctantly with much noisy wing-flapping and may perch in full sunlight on top of a tree. Any African Fish Eagle in the vicinity will vigorously attack the owl and even strike it.

As darkness falls the owls leave their roost and the pair may hunt together. Fish are caught from a perch between one and two metres above the water or sometimes from a sandbank. From vantage points overlooking still or shallow water, the owl swoops down like an African Fish Eagle to take fish from the surface of the water. At the moment of impact with the water the eyes are closed. The long curved claws and spicules on the underside of the feet are adaptations for holding slippery fish. The rudimentary facial disc and noisy flight indicate that hearing is not important in locating prey. At first light the owls return to their roosts.

The prey of this owl is made up almost entirely of fish, but frogs, crabs and freshwater mussels have also been recorded. It is said also to eat birds, but a captive adult caught in the wild refused to eat them even when very hungry. A captive juvenile ate large insects, caterpillars and mice, but these are unlikely to be eaten in the wild. Pellets of fish scales and bones are cast up but soon disintegrate once dry. An observer in the Okavango delta area examined approximately 100 pellets, all with fish remains except one with crab remains. Species from nine genera were recorded *(Clarias, Synodontis, Hepsetus, Seranochromis, Tilapia, Guathonemus, Hydrocynus, Schilbe* and *Petrocephalus)* but the most commonly taken fish were catfish (barbel) *Clarias* sp., squeakers *Synodontis* sp. and African Pike *Hepsetus odoe.* It was found that the owls preferred the heads of fish except for those of catfish and squeakers. Sometimes only the head was eaten and the fleshy body discarded. Most of the fish recorded ranged in weight from 100 to 250 g. The largest fish found in a nest weighed 500 g; the heaviest recorded was 2 kg.

This owl is unusual in that it calls mainly between midnight and dawn, particularly in the last few hours before dawn. The main call is a deep sonorous hoot *hooommmmm-hut*, sometimes preceded and often followed by a low grunt. The hoot is audible over a considerable distance, up to 3 km away on a still night. The call is often made in duet, the male in a higher pitched voice than the female. When it is calling, the throat is puffed out noticeably. Hooting is heard throughout the year, most often on moonlight nights and at the onset of the breeding season. Protracted vocal duets are performed in nuptial display, lasting 10–15 minutes. They may be repeated several times during the night. The duet begins with a series of low grunts *uh-uh-uhu* from the male, gradually working up to a peak, followed by a tenor *hoommm* which is answered by the female's deeper and more sonorous hoot and further grunting. The hooting call is made by the pair for contact throughout the year and for courtship.

Another call is a high-pitched, penetrating trill emitted with the bill wide open. Sometimes the trill is followed by a screaming sound. It is used during distraction display and also, apparently, as a contact by a bird calling its mate off the nest.

The small chick makes a soft cheeping call. At about five weeks old it makes a variety of soft hooting sounds but the main soliciting call is an eerie, wailing *miew*, which has been somewhat fancifully described as sounding like 'a cry of a lost soul falling into a bottomless pit'. The juvenile continues to use this call when it leaves the nest and it carries over a distance of at least a kilometre. In alarm the bill is clicked.

BREEDING

Nuptial display consists of duetting. The birds perch near each other on some conspicuous perch such as a dead tree or stump projecting above the water. No jerking movements of the body like those of courting Giant Eagle Owls seem to be performed.

The nest site is in the fork of a large tree trunk or in a hole or in a hollow where a trunk has broken off. The nest hollow is about 30–40 cm in diameter. No nest is made, the eggs being laid on wood chips and other debris lying in the hollow. Accounts of stick nests or the top of a Hamerkop's nest being used for breeding require confirmation, especially as in two of the three records a clutch of four is given. A favourite tree is the ebony tree *Diospyros mespiliformis*; in the Okavango delta eleven of the twelve sites found were in this tree, the remaining one in an African Mangosteen *Garcinia livingstonei.* Other trees used for nesting have been a Baobab, an *Acacia albida* and figs. Nests are situated 3–12 m above ground, usually higher than 6 m, and often near water, although sometimes as much as 200 m away.

Limited evidence during two breeding seasons in Botswana indicates that the same nest is generally used again. However, in two territories alternate sites 250 m and 300 m away were used. Population density varies according to conditions. In Ethiopia a pair was located every 6–7 km along a stretch of river. In the Okavango delta, where optimum conditions are found, the territory may be 1 km². In the Usutu fig forest in Ndumu Game Reserve, Zululand, three pairs were located along a 4,8 km stretch of river.

In a study in the Okavango delta sixteen breeding records were obtained, four in February, seven in March, three in April and one each in January and June. The highest water level in the area is in March, the lowest in December. Further evidence that eggs are laid when the water level is highest was obtained on the flood plain 160 km south of the study area. Two nests were found in June, when the flood waters had percolated through the swamp to reach their highest level. Young are reared as water levels are dropping and fish presumably are more easily caught. In Zimbabwe the few available records indicate that eggs are laid in about April. A 1930 Zululand record is of a nest

A juvenile Pel's Fishing Owl recently out of the nest; its head and underparts are still entirely downy.

found with an egg in December, but three subsequent records indicate that eggs are laid in March or April. One or two eggs are laid, usually two, and they are rounded and white. The measurements of eggs from the Okavango delta are: 62,5 × 52,1 (10); 59,8–65,1 × 51,0–53,5. A single egg from Zululand measured 59,0 × 49,2.

The interval between the laying of two eggs is not known but is not in excess of five days. Little is known about adult behaviour during the incubation period except that the female sits tight during daylight and is assumed to do most of the incubating. Whether the male relieves her at night is not known. The incubation period is not less than 33 days or more than 38 days, probably near 33 days.

No case is known of two nestlings being reared together. In the Okavango delta study four out of thirteen eggs were known to be addled and in other instances the second egg (or chick?) disappeared soon after the first hatched. Detailed observations are required, but it is probable that where a second chick hatches it cannot compete with its older sibling, a situation similar to that found in the breeding cycle of the Giant Eagle Owl. The newly

hatched chick is covered in white down. Its eyes are closed, beginning to open when it is 7 days old. At 17 days a thicker coat of buffy down begins to appear and covers the chick entirely a week later, when feathers emerge from the quills on the scapulars and wings. These feathers and those on the tail are the only ones to have emerged fully by the time the nestling leaves the nest, otherwise it appears mainly downy.

Observations on parental care are scanty. The female broods the small chick closely and flushes reluctantly. One nest was watched during the night, when the chick was about two weeks old. Fish were brought three times between 21h00 and 05h00. They were torn up and fed to the chick, whether by both sexes is not known. At several nests the female performed a distraction display. The owl perched on a branch with outspread wings and walked drunkenly up and down while making a trilling call. After some minutes it would drop to the ground and crash through the undergrowth, where it would flop about until approached too closely. At one nest regularly visited the female attacked the observer from behind and struck him with both feet. At other nests the owls swooped down but did not actually strike.

The nestling period is 68–70 days. The juvenile remains with its parents for at least four months after leaving the nest and may be heard calling in their territory seven months after leaving. A captive juvenile had not made its first kill after four months out of the nest, despite the availability of a shallow pool well stocked with fish.

In the Okavango delta study the indications are that 11 young were raised in 20 pair-years, a replacement rate of 0,55 young per pair per year. Nesting was recorded in consecutive seasons following the successful rearing of a nestling but at other times no breeding occurred. Eggs or chicks sometimes disappeared unaccountably; on one occasion monkeys had been seen in the nest tree below which a freshly broken egg was found.

The breeding biology of this owl is fairly well known through the efforts of a single observer in Botswana but further study would prove rewarding.

References

GENERAL REFERENCES

Many of the following references were consulted for a number of species and are listed here to avoid frequent repetition under the specific references. Also included are a number of books recommended for further reading, which cover various general aspects of raptor biology; most of these are readily identifiable by their titles, for example *Birds of Prey — Their Biology and Ecology* or *Owls — Their Natural and Unnatural History*.

Boshoff, A. F. 1979. Variation in the Afrikaans vernacular for some eagles in the Cape Province. *Bokmakierie* 31: 22–23.

Boshoff, A. F. & Vernon, C. J. 1980. The distribution and status of some eagles in the Cape Province. *Annals of the Cape Provincial Museums (Natural History)* 13(9): 107–132.

Brown, L. 1955. *Eagles*. London: Michael Joseph.

Brown, L. 1970. *African Birds of Prey*. London: Collins.

Brown, L. 1970. *Eagles*. London: Arthur Barker.

Brown, L. 1976. *Eagles of the World*. Newton Abbot: David & Charles.

Brown, L. 1976. *British Birds of Prey*. London: Collins.

Brown, L. 1976. *Birds of Prey — Their Biology and Ecology*. Feltham: Hamlyn.

Brown, L. & Amadon, D. 1968. *Eagles, Hawks and Falcons of the World*. Feltham: Country Life.

Brown, L. H., Gargett, V. & Steyn, P. 1977. Breeding success in some African eagles related to theories about sibling aggression and its effects. *Ostrich* 48: 65–71.

Burton, J. A. (ed.). 1973. *Owls of the World*. Weert: Peter Lowe.

Chapin, J. P. 1932. *The Birds of the Belgian Congo*. Part 1. New York: American Museum of Natural History.

Chapin, J. P. 1939. *The Birds of the Belgian Congo*. Part 2. New York: American Museum of Natural History.

Clancey, P. A. 1964. *The Birds of Natal and Zululand*. Edinburgh and London: Oliver & Boyd.

Clancey, P. A. 1971. *A Handlist of the Birds of Southern Mozambique*. Lourenço Marques: Instituto de Investigacao Cientifica de Mozambique.

Clancey, P. A. (ed.) 1980. *S.A.O.S. Checklist of Southern African Birds*. Pretoria: Southern African Ornithological Society.

Cramp, S. & Simmons, K. E. L. (eds.) 1980. *The Birds of the Western Palearctic*. Vol. 2. Oxford: Oxford University Press.

Cyrus, D. & Robson, N. 1980. *Bird Atlas of Natal*. Pietermaritzburg: University of Natal Press.

Grossman, M. L. & Hamlet, J. 1965. *Birds of Prey of the World*. London: Cassell.

Layard, E. L. & Sharpe, R. D. 1884. *The Birds of South Africa*. London: Bernard Quaritch.

McLachlan, G. R. & Liversidge, R. 1978. *Roberts Birds of South Africa*. Cape Town: John Voelcker Bird Book Fund.

Newman, K. 1971. *Birdlife in Southern Africa*. Johannesburg: Purnell.

Newton, I. 1979. *Population Ecology of Raptors*. Berkhamsted: Poyser.

Porter, R. F., Willis, I., Christensen, S. & Nielsen, B. P. 1974. *Flight Identification of European Raptors*. Berkhamsted: Poyser.

Prout-Jones, D. V. 1974. *An Introduction to the Birds of Prey of South Africa*. Cape Town: Purnell.

Smeenk, C. 1974. Comparative-ecological studies of some east African birds of prey. *Ardea* 62: 1–97.

Smithers, R. H. N. 1964. *A Check List of the Birds of the Bechuanaland Protectorate and the Caprivi Strip*. Cambridge: Trustees of the National Museums of Southern Rhodesia.

Snow, D. W. (ed.) 1978. *An Atlas of Speciation in African Non-passerine Birds*. London: Trustees of the British Museum (Natural History).

Sparks, J. & Soper, T. 1970. *Owls — Their Natural and Unnatural History*. Newton Abbot: David & Charles.

Stark, A. & Sclater, W. L. 1903. *The Birds of South Africa*. London: Porter.

Steyn, P. 1973. *Eagle Days*. Johannesburg: Purnell.

Tarboton, W. 1978. A survey of birds of prey in the Transvaal. First progress report (cyclostyled): Transvaal Provincial Administration Nature Conservation Division.

Thomson, A. L. 1964. *A New Dictionary of Birds*. London & Edinburgh: Nelson.

Wynne, O. E. 1969. *Bibliographical Key — Names of Birds of the World*. Privately published by Col. O. E. Wynne.

SPECIES REFERENCES

Figures in brackets indicate the number of citations contained in a paper. References may thus be accumulated on a 'snowball' basis as explained in the introduction.

1. Secretary Bird *Sagittarius serpentarius*
Brooke, R. K. 1958. Incubation and nestling periods revealed by Rhodesian nest record cards. *Ostrich* 29: 133–136.

Brooke, R. K. & Hodgson, C. J. 1971. Winter food of the Secretarybird as revealed by pellets. *Bull. Brit. Orn. Club* 91: 121–125. (11 references.)

Brown, L. H. 1955. Supplementary notes on the biology of the large birds of prey of Embu district, Kenya Colony. *Ibis* 97: 38–48.

Finch-Davies, C. G. 1920. Notes on South African Accipitres. *Ibis* (11)2: 412.

Fry, C. H. 1977. Etymology of 'Secretary Bird'. *Ibis* 119: 550.

Karmali, J. & Karmali, J. 1968. A study of the Secretary Bird. *Bokmakierie* 20: 63–65.

Kemp, M. I. & Kemp, A. C. 1978. *Bucorvus* and *Sagittarius*: two modes of terrestrial predation. *Proc. Symp. African Predatory Birds* pp. 13–16. Pretoria: Northern Transvaal Ornithological Society.

Steyn, P. 1961. Observations on the Secretary Bird. *African Wild Life* 15: 191–198.

Wolff, S. W. 1978. Secretary Bird swallowing egg. *Bokmakierie* 30: inside back cover.

2. Palm-nut Vulture *Gypohierax angolensis*

Austen, W. M. 1953. Palm-nut Vultures *Gypohierax angolensis* in Raphia Palms at Mtunzini, Zululand. *Ostrich* 24: 98–102.

Brooke, R. K. & Jeffery, R. D. 1972. Observations on the biology of *Gypohierax angolensis* in western Angola. *Bull. Brit. Orn. Club* 92: 15–21. (27 references.)

Brooke, R. K. & Cooper, K. H. 1978. The Palmnut Vulture: South Africa's rarest breeding bird? *African Wildlife* 32: 28–29.

Donnelly, B. G. & Irwin, M. P. S. 1972. The food of *Gypohierax angolensis*. *Bull. Brit. Orn. Club* 92: 22.

Feely, J. M. 1971. Palm-nut Vulture *Gypohierax angolensis* near Ladysmith. *Natal Bird Club News Sheet* 194: 3.

Moreau, R. E. 1933. A note on the distribution of the Vulturine Fish-Eagle *Gypohierax angolensis* Gmel. *Journal of Animal Ecology* 2: 179–183. (7 references.)

Pakenham, R. H. W. 1939. Field notes on the birds of Zanzibar and Pemba. *Ibis* (14)3: 526–530.

Serle, W. 1954. A second contribution to the ornithology of the British Cameroons. *Ibis* 96: 50.

Thomson, A. L. & Moreau, R. E. 1957. Feeding habits of the Palm-nut Vulture *Gypohierax*. *Ibis* 99: 608–613. (14 references.)

3. Lammergeyer *Gypaetus barbatus*

Barnes, B., Morrison, D., Pearse, R. & Symons, G. 1962. Lord of the African skies. *Journal Mountain Club of South Africa* 64: 32–36.

Berthold, P. 1968. Letter to the editor. *Bokmakierie* 20: 102.

Berthold, P. 1969. Letter to the editor. *Bokmakierie* 21: 24–25.

Boshoff, A. F., Brooke, R. K. & Crowe, T. M. 1978. Computerized distribution mapping scheme for vertebrates in southern Africa, illustrated by a range decrease in the Bearded Vulture *Gypaetus barbatus* (Linn.). (16 references.)

Boswell, J. 1970. Age of acquiring adult plumage in *Gypaetus barbatus*. *Bull. Brit. Orn. Club* 90: 120.

Brown, L. H. 1977. The status, population structure and breeding dates of the African Lammergeier. *Raptor Research* 11: 49–58. (33 references.)

Clancey, P. A. 1966. The Lammergeyer in South Africa. *Bokmakierie* 18: 60.

Clancey, P. A. 1968. Letter to the editor. *Bokmakierie* 20: 102–103.

Dodswort, P. T. L. 1912. Letter to the editor. *Ibis* (9)6: 208–210.

Hiraldo, F., Delibes, M. & Calderon, J. 1979. El Quebrantahuesos *Gypaetus barbatus* (L.). Sistematica, Taxonomia, Biologia, Distribucion y Proteccion. Instituto Nacional para la Conservacion de la Naturaleza. Monografias No. 22. (English summary only.) (287 references.)

Huxley, J. & Nicholson, E. M. 1963. Lammergeyer *Gypaetus barbatus* breaking bones. *Ibis* 105: 106–107.

Jilbert, J. 1976. Letter to the editor. *Bokmakierie* 28: 76.

Newman, K. B. 1969. Some notes on the feeding habits of the Lammergeyer *Gypaetus barbatus*. *Bokmakierie* 21: 84–87.

North, M. E. 1948. The Lammergeyer in Kenya Colony. *Ibis* 90: 138–141. (5 references.)

Penzhorn, B. L. 1969. Golden Gate se Lammergeiers. *African Wild Life* 23: 289–298. (13 references.)

Porter, R. N. 1970. Letter to the editor. *Bokmakierie* 22: 24.

Rudebeck, G. 1956. Observations on the Bearded Vulture *(Gypaetus barbatus)* in South Africa, with notes on behaviour and field characters. *South African Animal Life* Vol. 4: 406–415. Stockholm: Almqvist & Wiksell. (33 references.)

Siegfried, W. R. & Frost, P. G. H. 1973. Body temperature of the Lammergeier *Gypaetus barbatus* (Aves: Accipitridae). *Bonn. Zool. Beitr.* 24: 387–393. (8 references.)

Steyn, P. 1970. Letter to the editor. *Bokmakierie* 22: 23–24.

Sycholt, A. 1979. Kingdom of the Lammergeyer. *Family Radio & TV* (October): 54–59.

Symons, G. 1969. Threat to Lammergeyer *Gypaetus barbatus*. *Natal Bird Club News Sheet* 175: 2.

Symons, G. 1979. Some notes from the Estcourt area. *Albatross* 257: 4.

4. Egyptian Vulture *Neophron percnopterus*

Anonymous. 1978. Versatile Egyptian Vulture. *Israel Land and Nature* 4: 81.

Brooke, R. 1978. The Egyptian Vulture and other rare birds. *Bokmakierie* 30: 92–93.

Brooke, R. K. 1979. Tool using by the Egyptian Vulture to the detriment of the Ostrich. *Ostrich* 50: 119–120. (12 references.)

Brooke, R. K. 1979. Predation on Ostrich eggs by tool-using crows and Egyptian Vultures. *Ostrich* 50: 257–258.

Clinning, C. F. 1980. Sight records of the Egyptian Vulture from South West Africa/Namibia. *Madoqua* 12: 63–64.

F.R.S. 1860. South African ornithology. *Cape*

Monthly Magazine 8: 212.

Lawick-Goodall, J. 1968. Tool-using bird: the Egyptian Vulture. *National Geographic* 133: 630–641.

Mundy, P. J. 1978. The Egyptian Vulture *(Neophron percnopterus)* in southern Africa. *Biological Conservation* 14: 307–315. (39 references.)

North, M. E. W. 1947. Breeding of the Egyptian Vulture in Kenya Colony. *Ibis* 89: 662–663.

Patten, G. 1979. Egyptian Vulture. *Witwatersrand Bird Club News* 107: 16.

Skead, C. J. 1971. Use of tools by the Egyptian Vulture. *Ostrich* 42: 226.

5. Hooded Vulture *Necrosyrtes monachus*

Fraser, W. 1980. Hooded Vulture in the Okavango. *Witwatersrand Bird Club News* 110: 5–6.

Howells, W. W. 1978. Stranded fish as a food source for large birds. *Honeyguide* 96: 18.

Mundy, P. J. 1974. Hooded Vultures perching on animals. *Ostrich* 45: 31.

Mundy, P. J. 1980. The comparative biology of southern African vultures. Unpublished D.Phil. thesis, University of Zimbabwe. (215 references.) This thesis is to be published in book form in 1982.

6. Cape Vulture *Gyps coprotheres*

Boshoff, A. F. & Vernon, C. J. 1980. The past and present distribution and status of the Cape Vulture in the Cape Province. *Ostrich* 51: 230–250. (54 references.)

O'Connor, T. 1980. The status of the Cape Vulture in the Orange Free State Province of South Africa. *Vulture News* 3: 3–6. (7 references.)

Mundy, P. J. 1980. (Consult this reference under Hooded Vulture.)

7. White-backed Vulture *Gyps africanus*

Mundy, P. J. 1980. (Consult this reference under Hooded Vulture.)

8. Lappet-faced Vulture *Torgos tracheliotus*

Anthony, A. J. 1976. The breeding biology of the Lappet-faced Vulture *Torgos tracheliotus* (Forster) in the Gonarezhou National Park, Rhodesia. Certificate in field ecology thesis, University of Rhodesia. (28 references.)

Clinning, C. 1980. Vulture study in South West Africa. *Vulture News* 3: 7–10. (5 references.)

Mundy, P. J. 1980. (Consult this reference under Hooded Vulture.)

Vernon, C. J. 1979. Notes on birds of prey in Zimbabwe Rhodesia. *Honeyguide* 99: 28.

9. White-headed Vulture *Trigonoceps occipitalis*

Howells, W. W. 1978. Stranded fish as a food source for large birds. *Honeyguide* 96: 18.

Mundy, P. J. 1980. (Consult this reference under Hooded Vulture.)

Plaskett, G. 1972. Tawny Eagle/vulture behaviour. *Witwatersrand Bird Club News Sheet* 80: 11.

10. Black Kite *Milvus migrans migrans*

Brooke, R. K. 1974. The migratory Black Kite *Milvus migrans migrans* (Aves: Accipitridae) of the Palaearctic in southern Africa. *Durban Museum Novitates* 10: 54–66. (27 references.)

11. Yellow-billed Kite *Milvus migrans parasitus*

Andrews, W. E. 1978. Yellow-billed Kites taking frogs from water. *Honeyguide* 93: 42.

Beesley, J. H. 1956. South African Kite fishing. *Bull. Brit. Orn. Club* 76: 108.

Bell-Cross, G. 1974. Observations on fish-eating birds in Central Africa. *Honeyguide* 77: 29–30.

Benson, C. W. 1971. Some collecting experiences. *Honeyguide* 66: 35.

Desai, J. H. & Malhotra, A. K. 1979. Breeding biology of the Pariah Kite *Milvus migrans* at Delhi Zoological Park. *Ibis* 121: 320–325. (7 references.)

Jensen, R. A. C. 1972. The Steppe Eagle *Aquila nipalensis* and other termite-eating raptors in South West Africa. *Madoqua* 1: 73–76.

Jonsson, G. N. 1945. Weaver nests destroyed by Egyptian Kite. *Ostrich* 16: 238.

Macdonald, M. A. 1980. Breeding of the Black Kite in southern Ghana. *Ostrich* 51: 118–120.

Marchant, S. 1953. Notes on the birds of south-eastern Nigeria. *Ibis* 95: 40.

Meyburg, B.-U. 1967. Beobachtungen zur Brutbiologie des Schwarzen Milans *(Milvus migrans)*. *Vogelwelt* 88: 70–85.

Meyburg, B.-U. 1971. On the question of the incubation period of the Black Kite *Milvus migrans*. *Ibis* 113: 530. (6 references.)

Morphew, J. 1970. Yellow-billed Kite fishing. *Natal Bird Club News Sheet* 179: 2.

Schütte, G. W. 1968. Fish Eagles and kites. *Lammergeyer* 8: 51.

Scogings, P. 1980. Some observations on Yellow-billed Kites. *Albatross* 258: 3.

Tree, A. J. 1963. Yellow-billed Kites *Milvus migrans* fishing. *Ostrich* 34: 179.

Van Someren, V. G. L. 1956. Days with birds. *Fieldiana: Zoology* Vol. 38. Chicago Natural History Museum.

12. Black-shouldered Kite *Elanus caeruleus*

Bell, C. 1978. Observations on a breeding pair of Black-shouldered Kites. *Honeyguide* 95: 26–27.

Broekhuysen, M. & Broekhuysen, G. 1974. Black-shouldered Kite builds on telephone pole. *Bokmakierie* 26: 36.

Brooke, R. K. 1965. Roosting of the Black-shouldered Kite *Elanus caeruleus* (Desfontaines). *Ostrich* 36: 43.

Collar, N. J. 1978. Nesting of Black-shouldered Kites in Portugal. *British Birds* 71: 398–412. (21 references.)

Forbes-Watson, A. D. 1977. Maximum carrying potential of Black-shouldered Kite *Elanus caeruleus*. *Scopus* 1: 44.

Kriek, S. 1970. Vrou leer Blouvalkie se geheime ken. *Huisgenoot* Vol. 42 No. 2508: 12–14.

Madden, S. T. 1977. Notes on two nests of the Black-shouldered Kite. *Ostrich* 48: 115–116.

Malherbe, A. P. 1963. Notes on birds of prey and some others at Boshoek, north of Rustenburg during a rodent plague. *Ostrich* 34: 95–96.

Mendelsohn, J. (in press). The timing of breeding in Blackshouldered Kites in southern Africa. *Proceedings 5th P.A.O.C.* (19 references.)

Siegfried, W. R. 1965. On the food of the Black-shouldered Kite *Elanus caeruleus* (Desf.). *Ostrich* 36: 224.

Silbernagl, P. 1979. Behaviour: Black-shouldered Kite. *Promerops* 137: 3.

Skead, D. M. 1967. Additions and annotations to the list of birds of Weenen County, Natal. *Ostrich* 38: 33.

Skead, D. M. 1974. Roadside counts of the Black-shouldered Kite in the central Transvaal. *Ostrich* 45: 5–8. (9 references.)

Steyn, P. 1963. The 'Wagtail' Kite. *Bokmakierie* 15: 9.

Steyn, P. 1971. The crepuscular hunting habits of the Blackshouldered Kite. *Ostrich* 42: 158. (4 references.)

Steyn, P. 1971. Moments with a Black-shouldered Kite. *African Wildlife* 26: 98–99.

Tarboton, W. R. 1977. Food consumption and pellet production in the Black-shouldered Kite *Elanus caeruleus*. *Zoologica Africana* 12: 252–255. (5 references.)

Tarboton, W. R. 1978. Hunting and energy budget of the Black-shouldered Kite. *Condor* 80: 88–91. (13 references.)

Van der Merwe, F. J. 1975. Waarnemings oor die Blouvalk. *Bokmakierie* 27: 56–59. (5 references.)

Van der Merwe, F. & Heunis, F. 1980. Nest building in the Blackshouldered Kite. *Ostrich* 51: 113–114.

Van Someren, V. G. L. 1956. Days with birds. Fieldiana: Zoology Vol. 38. Chicago Natural History Museum.

Whitelaw, D. 1979. Behaviour: Black-shouldered Kite. *Promerops* 140: 7.

13. Cuckoo Hawk *Aviceda cuculoides*

Brown, L. H. & Bursell, G. 1968. A first breeding record of the Cuckoo Falcon in Kenya. *Journal East African Natural History Society* 27: 48–51.

Finch-Davies, C. G. 1920. Notes on South African Accipitres. *Ibis* 11(2): 617–619.

Jeffery, R. D. 1977. Three nests of the Cuckoo Falcon in Rhodesia. *Honeyguide* 90: 33–34.

Madge, S. G. 1971. Cuckoo Falcon's nest near Livingstone. *Bull. Zambian Orn. Soc.* 3: 22–23.

Sheppard, P. A. 1910. Field-notes on some little-known birds, including two new species, from observations made during the nesting-season of 1909 near Beira. *Journal South African Orn. Union* 6: 39–40.

Snell, M. L. 1963. Cuckoo-Hawk. *Honeyguide* 42: 13–14.

Vernon, C. J. 1979. Two unusual Rhodesian birds of prey. *Honeyguide* 97: 35.

Weaving, A. 1977. Observations on a breeding pair of Cuckoo Falcons. *Honeyguide* 90: 28–31.

14. Bat Hawk *Macheiramphus alcinus*

Beesley, J. S. S. 1976. Bat Hawk *Macheiramphus alcinus*. *Ostrich* 47: 216.

Black, H. L., Howard, G. & Stjernstedt, R. 1979. Observations on the feeding behavior of the Bat Hawk *(Macheiramphus alcinus)*. *Biotropica* 11: 18–21. (16 references.)

Colebrook-Robjent, J. F. R. 1971. Breeding of the Bat Hawk *Macheiramphus alcinus* in Zambia. *Bull. Brit. Orn. Club* 91: 151.

Heigham, J. B. 1974. Bat Hawks in Lagos and Benin City. *Bull. Nigerian Orn. Soc.* 10: 51–53.

Milstein, P. le S., Olwagan, C. D. & Stein, D. J. 1975. Field identification of the Bat Hawk. *Bokmakierie* 27: 12–14. (5 references.)

Pooley, A. G. 1967. Some miscellaneous ornithological observations from the Ndumu Game Reserve. *Ostrich* 38: 31–32.

Thomson, W. R. 1975. Notes on the Bathawk in Rhodesia. *Bokmakierie* 27: 52–53.

15. Honey Buzzard *Pernis apivorus*

Blom-Bjorner, S. 1945. Occasional notes. *Journal East African Natural History Society* 18: 159.

Brooke, R. K. & Irwin, M. P. S. 1969. The status of the Honey Buzzard in Rhodesia. *Ostrich* 40: 135. (7 references.)

Kieser, J. A. 1976. More notes on Benfontein's avifauna. *Bee-eater* 27: 7.

Tree, A. J. 1973. Honey Buzzard *Pernis apivorus*. *Ostrich* 44: 127.

Woodall, P. F. 1971. Further notes on the status of the Honey Buzzard in Rhodesia. *Ostrich* 42: 301.

16. Black Eagle *Aquila verreauxii*

Bowen, P. 1970. Some observations of the Cape Vulture. *African Wild Life* 24: 125–128.

Brown, L. H. 1974. A record of two young reared by Verreaux's Eagle. *Ostrich* 45: 146–147.

Brown, L. H., Gargett, V. & Steyn, P. 1977. Breeding success in some African eagles related to theories about sibling aggression and its effects. *Ostrich* 48: 65–71. (29 references.)

Dick, J. A. & Fenton, M. B. 1979. Tool-using by a Black Eagle? *Bokmakierie* 31: 17.

Gargett, V. 1965–1979. Black Eagle Survey: Rhodes Matopos National Park. Annual Reports of the Matabeleland Branch of the Rhodesian Ornithological Society.

Gargett, V. 1970. Black Eagle Survey, Rhodes Matopos National Park: a population study 1964–1968. *Ostrich* suppl. 8: 397–414. (7 references.)

Gargett, V. 1971. Some observations on Black Eagles in the Matopos, Rhodesia. *Ostrich* suppl. 9: 91–124. (22 references.)

Gargett, V. 1972. Observations at a Black Eagle nest in the Matopos, Rhodesia. *Ostrich* 43: 77–108. (11 references.)

Gargett, V. 1975. The spacing of Black Eagles in the Matopos, Rhodesia. *Ostrich* 46: 1–44. (80 references.)

Gargett, V. 1977. A Black Eagle lays her second egg. *Bokmakierie* 28: 83–84.

Gargett, V. 1977. A 13-year population study of the Black Eagles in the Matopos, Rhodesia, 1964–1976. *Ostrich* 48: 17–27. (18 references.)

Gargett, V. 1978. Black Eagles in protected and unprotected habitats. *Proc. Symp. African Predatory*

Birds, pp. 96–102. Pretoria: Northern Transvaal Ornithological Society. (7 references.)

Gargett, V. 1978. Sibling aggression in the Black Eagle in the Matopos, Rhodesia. *Ostrich* 49: 57–63. (21 references.)

Gillard, L. 1976. Black Eagle *Aquila verreauxi*. *Witwatersrand Bird Club News Sheet* 93: 10.

Jackson, G. 1969. Black Eagle *Aquila verreauxi*. *Natal Bird Club Newsletter* 177: 1.

McCrea, R. 1977. Black Eagle: prolonged use of nest sites. *Honeyguide* 91: 38.

Mouritz, L. B. 1915. Notes on the ornithology of the Matopo district, Southern Rhodesia. *Ibis* (10)3: 203.

Oatley, T. B. & Pinnell, N. R. 1968. The birds of Winterskloof, Natal. *South African Avifauna Series* 58: 6.

Pearson, T. B. 1962. Foods and feeding. *Lammergeyer* 2: 63.

Pitman, C. R. S. 1960. An unusual case of predation by *Aquila verreauxi*. *Bull. Brit. Orn. Club* 80: 67.

Pringle, V. L. 1959. Stanley Cranes vs. Black Eagle. *African Wild Life* 13: 169–170.

Rowe, E. G. 1947. The breeding biology of *Aquila verreauxi* Lesson. *Ibis* 89: 387–410 & 576–606. (18 references.)

Scotcher, J. S. B. 1973. Piracy by Black Eagle. *Natal Bird Club News Sheet* 218: 2–3.

Siegfried, W. R. 1963. A preliminary report on Black and Martial Eagles in the Laingsburg and Philipstown divisions. *Cape Prov. Dept. Conservation — Investigational Report* No. 5: 1–15.

Siegfried, W. R. 1968. Breeding season, clutch size and brood sizes in Verreaux's Eagle. *Ostrich* 39: 139–145. (32 references.)

Skead, D. M. 1967. Additions and annotations to the list of birds of Weenen County, Natal. *Ostrich* 38: 33.

Tarboton, W. 1980. Breeding: big nests. *Witwatersrand Bird Club News* 111: 14–16.

Taylor, D. C. 1968. Black Eagle. *Lammergeyer* 8: 52.

Vernon, C. J. 1965. The Black Eagle Survey in the Matopos, Rhodesia. *Arnoldia* 2(6): 1–9. (13 references.)

Visser, J. 1963. The Black Eagles of Zuurhoek, Jansenville. *African Wild Life* 17: 191–194.

Wyatt, J. K. 1966. Verreaux Eagle: letter to the editor. *Black Lechwe* 5: 31–32.

17. Tawny Eagle *Aquila rapax*

Anonymous. 1975. Notes from the parks. *Wild Rhodesia* 6: 40.

Barbour, D. 1975. Do eagles use moonlight to hunt? *Honeyguide* 82: 37.

Boshoff, A. F., Rous, R. C. & Vernon, C. J. 1981. Prey of the Tawny Eagle in the Colesberg district, Cape Province. *Ostrich* 52: 187–188.

Harris, G. & Wurts, G. 1973. Bateleur kill. *Witwatersrand Bird Club News Sheet* 84: 7.

Howells, W. W. 1978. Stranded fish as a food source for large birds of prey. *Honeyguide* 96: 18.

Kemp, M. I. & Kemp, A. C. 1978. *Bucorvus* and *Sagittarius*: two modes of terrestrial predation. *Proc. Symp. African Predatory Birds* pp. 13–16. Pretoria:

Northern Transvaal Ornithological Society.

Milstein, P. le S. 1975. The biology of Barberspan, with special reference to the avifauna. *Ostrich* suppl. 10: 38.

Plaskett, G. 1972. Tawny Eagle/vulture behaviour. *Witwatersrand Bird Club News Sheet* 80: 11.

Saunders, C. 1975. Odd observations in 1975. *Hartebeest* 7: 23.

Snelling, J. C. 1970. Some information obtained from marking large raptors in the Kruger National Park, Republic of South Africa. *Ostrich* suppl. 8: 415–427.

Steyn, P. 1973. Observations on the Tawny Eagle. *Ostrich* 44: 1–22. (51 references.)

Steyn, P. 1980. Further observations on the Tawny Eagle. *Ostrich* 51: 54–55.

Vernon, C. J. 1979. Prey remains from seven Tawny Eagle nests. *Honeyguide* 100: 22–24.

18. Steppe Eagle *Aquila nipalensis*

Brooke, R. K., Grobler, J. H., Irwin, M. P. S. & Steyn, P. 1972. A study of the migratory eagles *Aquila nipalensis* and *A. pomarina* (Aves: Accipitridae) in southern Africa, with comparative notes on other large raptors. *Occ. Pap. Nat. Mus. Rhod.* B5 (2): 61–114. (98 references.)

Jankowitz, M. 1976. Tawny or Steppe Eagle? *Bokmakierie* 28: 64–65.

Jensen, R. A. C. 1972. The Steppe Eagle *Aquila nipalensis* and other termite-eating raptors in South West Africa. *Madoqua* 1: 73–76.

19. Lesser Spotted Eagle *Aquila pomarina*

Brooke, R. K. *et al.* 1972. (Consult this reference under Steppe Eagle.)

Editor. 1974. Local News. *Safring News* 3: 3–4.

Meyburg, B.-U. 1973. Studies of less familiar birds: Lesser Spotted Eagle. *British Birds* 66: 439–447.

20. Wahlberg's Eagle *Aquila wahlbergi*

Anthony, A. J. 1979. Patagial tagging of Wahlberg's Eagle. *Safring News* 8: 28. (6 references.)

Brown, L. H. 1978. A note on the movements of Wahlberg's Eagle *Aquila wahlbergi* in Kenya. *Bokmakierie* 30: 107.

Cackett, K. 1969. More observations on pale phase Wahlberg's Eagles. *Honeyguide* 57: 24–25.

Cannell, I. 1970. Eagle striking observer. *Honeyguide* 61: 37.

Gargett, V. 1968. Two Wahlberg's Eagle chicks — a one in forty-eight chance. *Honeyguide* 56: 24.

Goodman, P. S. 1968. Wahlberg's Eagle. *Flauna* 1: 11–12. Cyclostyled: Hilton College, Natal.

Jarvis, M. J. F. & Crichton, J. 1978. Notes on Long-crested Eagles in Rhodesia. *Proc. Symp. African Predatory Birds*, pp. 17–24. Pretoria: Northern Transvaal Ornithological Society.

Kemp, A. & Mendelsohn, J. 1975. What colour is Wahlberg's Eagle? *Bokmakierie* 27: 72–74.

Lees, S. G. 1968. Notes on the nesting of Wahlberg's Eagle. *Ostrich* 39: 192–193.

Newman, K. 1970. Letters to the editor. *Honeyguide* 63: 38.

Steyn, P. 1962. Observations on Wahlberg's Eagle.

Bokmakierie 14: 7–14. (6 references.)

Steyn, P. 1980. Observations on the prey and breeding success of Wahlberg's Eagle. *Ostrich* 51: 56–59. (11 references.)

Tarboton, W. 1977. Nesting, territoriality and food habits of Wahlberg's Eagle. *Bokmakierie* 29: 46–50. (8 references.)

Tuer, V. 1973. Notes on the African Hawk Eagle and Wahlberg's Eagle in the Matopos. *Honeyguide* 75: 19–21.

21. Booted Eagle *Hieraaetus pennatus*

Brooke, R. K., Martin, R., Martin, J. & Martin, E. 1980. Booted Eagle, *Hieraaetus pennatus*, as a breeding species in South Africa. *Le Gerfaut* 70: 297–304. (33 references.)

Donnelly, B. G. 1966. The range of the Booted Eagle, *Aquila pennata* (Gmelin), in southern Africa with a note on field identification. *Annals Cape Prov. Museums* 5: 109–115. (28 references.)

Steyn, P. & Grobler, J. H. 1981. Breeding biology of the Booted Eagle in South Africa. *Ostrich* 52: 108–118. (20 references.)

22. African Hawk Eagle *Hieraaetus spilogaster*

Kinahan, J. 1975. Effect of weather on nestling weight of an African Hawk Eagle. *Ostrich* 46: 181–183.

Louette, M. 1975. Fruit-bat as prey of the African Hawk-Eagle. *Bull. Brit. Orn. Club* 95: 172–173.

Meyburg, B.-U. 1974. Sibling aggression and mortality among nestling eagles. *Ibis* 116: 225–226.

Steyn, P. 1975. Observations on the African Hawk-Eagle. *Ostrich* 46: 87–105. (39 references.)

23. Ayres' Eagle *Hieraaetus ayresii*

Brown, L. H. 1953. Attack by a shrike on the eaglet of *Hieraaetus ayresi*. *Ibis* 95: 145–146.

Brown, L. H. 1955. Supplementary notes on the biology of the large birds of prey of Embu district, Kenya Colony. *Ibis* 97: 58–64.

Brown, L. H. 1966. Observations on some Kenya eagles. *Ibis* 108: 539–544.

Brown, L. H. 1974. Is poor breeding success a reason for the rarity of Ayres' Hawk-Eagle? *Ostrich* 45: 145–146.

Brown, L. H. & Davey, P. R. A. 1978. Natural longevity, as determined by plumage variation, in Ayres' Eagle *Hieraaetus dubius*. *Bokmakierie* 30: 27–31.

Finch-Davies, C. G. 1919. Some notes on *Hieraaetus ayresi* Gurney Sen. (*Lophotriorchis lucani* Sharpe et auctorum). *Ibis* (11)1: 167–179. (12 references.)

Lendrum, A. L. 1975. Observations on Ayres' Hawk Eagle. *Honeyguide* 81: 41–43.

Lendrum, A. L. 1975. Further notes on Ayres' Hawk Eagle in Bulawayo. *Honeyguide* 83: 40–41.

Lockwood, G. 1979. Ayres' Hawk Eagle in Parkhurst. *Witwatersrand Bird Club News* 105: 5.

Phillips, R. 1978. The nesting of Ayres' Hawk-Eagle *Hieraaetus dubius* in the south-eastern lowveld. *Honeyguide* 94: 27–30.

24. Long-crested Eagle *Lophaetus occipitalis*

Hall, D. 1979. Records of Longcrested Eagles rearing two young. *Ostrich* 50: 187.

Hall, D. 1979. Food of the Longcrested Eagle. *Ostrich* 50: 256–257.

Hall, D. G. 1979. Observations at three Longcrested Eagle nests in the Nelspruit district. *Bokmakierie* 31: 65–72.

Jarvis, M. J. F. & Crichton, J. 1978. Notes on Longcrested Eagles in Rhodesia. *Proc. Symp. African Predatory Birds*, pp. 17–24. Pretoria: Northern Transvaal Ornithological Society. (22 references.)

Sclater, W. L. & Moreau, R. E. 1932. Taxonomic and field notes on some birds of north-eastern Tanganyika Territory. *Ibis* (13)2: 500–501.

Steyn, P. 1978. Observations on the Long-crested Eagle. *Bokmakierie* 30: 3–10. (12 references.)

Wakeford, R. 1979. Raptor observations. *Albatross* 256: 4

25. Martial Eagle *Polemaetus bellicosus*

Boshoff, A. F. & Palmer, N. G. 1980. Macro-analysis of prey remains from Martial Eagle nests in the Cape Province. *Ostrich* 51: 7–13. (26 references.)

Brooke, R. K., Cannell, I. C. & Jeffery, R. D. 1971. New distributional records of raptors in western Angola. *Bull. Brit. Orn. Club* 91: 165–166.

Brown, L. H. 1952. On the biology of the large birds of prey of Embu district, Kenya Colony. *Ibis* 94: 613–620.

Curry-Lindahl, K. 1971. Prey of the Martial Eagle. *Africana* 4 (5).

Dean, W. R. J. 1975. Martial Eagles nesting on high tension pylons. *Ostrich* 115: 116–117.

Denyer, L. C. 1960. Aggressive Martial Eagle. *Lammergeyer* 1: 43–44.

James, H. W. 1925. Birds observed in the Somerset East district, Cape Province, Union of South Africa. *Ibis* (12)1: 626.

Kemp, A. & Kemp, M. 1974. Don't forget the big birds. *African Wildlife* 28: 12–13.

Knight, C. W. R. 1937. *Knight in Africa*. London: Country Life.

Maclean, G. L. 1973. The Sociable Weaver, Part 4: Predators, parasites and symbionts. *Ostrich* 44: 250.

Pooley, A. C. 1970. Powerful eagle. *Lammergeyer* 11: 82.

Siegfried, W. R. 1963. A preliminary report on Black and Martial Eagles in the Laingsburg and Philipstown divisions. *Cape Prov. Dept. Conservation — Investigational Report* No. 5: 1–15.

Steyn, P. 1970. Prey of the Martial Eagle. *African Wild Life* 24: 172.

Steyn, P. 1980. Notes on the prey and breeding success of the Martial Eagle. *Ostrich* 51: 115–116.

Tarboton, W. 1976. Martial Eagles: an unusual breeding episode. *Bokmakierie* 28: 29–32. (7 references.)

Thorn, D. & Peacock, J. 1962. Martial Eagle. *Honeyguide* 39: 27.

26. Crowned Eagle *Stephanoaetus coronatus*

Brown, L. H. 1953. On the biology of the large birds

of prey of the Embu district, Kenya Colony. *Ibis* 95: 74–84.

Brown, L. H. 1955. Supplementary notes on the biology of the large birds of prey of Embu district, Kenya Colony. *Ibis* 97: 184–188.

Brown, L. H. 1966. Observations on some Kenya eagles. *Ibis* 108: 531–572. (11 references.)

Brown, L. H. 1971. The relationship of the Crowned Eagle *Stephanoaetus coronatus* and some of its prey animals. *Ibis* 113: 240–243.

Brown, L. H. 1972. Natural longevity in wild Crowned Eagles *Stephanoaetus coronatus*. *Ibis* 114: 263–271.

Clark, J. V. 1970. Observations on the Crowned Eagle *Polemaetus coronatus*. *Lammergeyer* 12: 74–77.

Daneel, A. B. C. 1979. Prey size and hunting methods of the Crowned Eagle. *Ostrich* 50: 120–121.

Editor. 1970. Field outing to Kilgobbin forest, Dargle. *Natal Bird Club News Sheet* 188: 1.

Fannin, A. & Webb, D. 1975. Notes on the breeding of the Crowned Eagle. *Honeyguide* 82: 36.

Harwood, J. 1971. Crowned Eagle. *Bokmakierie* 23: 82–84.

Jarvis, M. J. F., Currie, M. H. & Palmer, N. G. 1980. Food of Crowned Eagles in the Cape Province, South Africa. *Ostrich* 51: 215–218. (17 references.)

Kemp, A. C. 1969. An unusual nesting site of the Crowned Eagle. *Ostrich* 40: 23.

Pringle, V. L. 1977. Herons have their problems. *Eastern Cape Naturalist* 60: 29.

Snelling, J. C. & Barbour, D. Y. 1969. Crowned Eagle. *Bokmakierie* 21: 67–69.

Steyn, P. 1964. The Crowned Eagle at home. *African Wild Life* 18: 95–101.

Stjernstedt, B. 1975. Eagle attack. *Black Lechwe* 12: 18–22.

Tuer, V. & Tuer, J. 1974. Crowned Eagles of the Matopos. *Honeyguide* 80: 32–41. (7 references.)

Webb, D. 1975. Notes on the breeding of the Crowned Eagle: an addendum. *Honeyguide* 84: 45.

27. Brown Snake Eagle *Circaetus cinereus*

Steyn, P. 1964. Observations on the Brown Snake-Eagle *Circaetus cinereus*. *Ostrich* 35: 22–31. (11 references.)

Steyn, P. 1972. Further observations on the Brown Snake Eagle. *Ostrich* 43: 149–164. (30 references.)

Steyn, P. 1975. Supplementary notes on the breeding of the Brown Snake Eagle. *Ostrich* 46: 118.

28. Black-breasted Snake Eagle *Circaetus pectoralis*

Barbour, D. Y. 1974. Adaptability of the Black-breasted Snake Eagle. *Honeyguide* 80: 51–52.

Child, G. 1964. *Circaetus pectoralis* Smith feeding on fish. *Ostrich* 35: 122.

Davies, C. G. 1910. A second contribution to the ornithology of eastern Pondoland. *Journal South African Orn. Union* 6: 10.

Editor. 1960. *Rhodesian Orn. Soc. Bulletin* 32: 2–3.

Lorber, P. 1971. Roosting of Black-breasted Snake-Eagles. *Honeyguide* 67: 32.

Naylor, R. T. 1974. A large roost of Black-breasted Snake Eagles. *Bull. Zambian Orn. Soc.* 6: 24.

Osborne, T. O. 1975. A Black-breasted Snake Eagle roost at Blue Lagoon National Park. *Bull. Zambian Orn. Soc.* 7: 29.

Pooley, A. G. 1967. Some miscellaneous ornithological observations from the Ndumu Game Reserve. *Ostrich* 38: 31.

Stevenson, R. H. R. 1953. Congregation of Black-breasted Harrier Eagles. *Bokmakierie* 5: 48.

Steyn, P. 1966. Observations on the Black-breasted Snake Eagle *Circaetus pectoralis* A. Smith. *Ostrich* suppl. 6: 141–154. (12 references.)

Steyn, P. 1971. Distinguishing the Martial and Black-breasted Snake Eagle. *Bokmakierie* 23: 35.

Woods, P. 1975. Black-breasted Snake-Eagle: communal roost. *Honeyguide* 83: 47–48.

29. Southern Banded Snake Eagle *Circaetus fasciolatus*

Brooke, R. K. 1971. Breeding and breeding season notes on the birds of Mzimbiti and adjacent low-lying areas of Mozambique. *Annals Natal Museum* 21: 55–69.

Brown, L. H. 1969. A first breeding record for the Southern Banded Snake Eagle *Circaetus fasciolatus* in Kenya. *Ibis* 111: 390–391.

Christian, R. J. B. 1965. On the eggs of the Southern Banded Harrier-Eagle *(Circaetus fasciolatus)* and Red-necked Buzzard *(Buteo auguralis)*. *Oologists' Record* 39: 15–17.

Daneel, A. B. 1965. On the eggs of the Southern Banded Harrier-Eagle *(Circaetus fasciolatus)*. *Oologists' Record* 39: 14–15.

Daneel, A. B. 1966. On the range of the Southern Banded Harrier Eagle. *Oologists' Record* 40: 73–75.

Kreuger, R. 1970. First finding of the egg of *Circaetus fasciolatus*. *Ibis* 112: 117–118.

Roberts, A. 1948. *The Birds of South Africa*. London: Witherby.

Zimmerman, D. A. & Mumford, R. E. 1965. First specimens of three species from Kenya. *Auk* 82: 282–283.

Zimmerman, D. A. 1970. An earlier nesting record of *Circaetus fasciolatus* in Kenya. *Ibis* 112: 264.

30. Banded Snake Eagle *Circaetus cinerascens*

Benson, C. W. & Benson, F. M. 1977. *The Birds of Malawi*. Limbe: Mountford Press. (10 references.)

Chapin, J. P. 1932. *The Birds of the Belgian Congo*. Part 1. New York: American Museum of Natural History.

Madge, S. G. 1972. Western Banded Snake-Eagle breeding near Ndola. *Bull. Zambian Orn. Soc.* 4: 25–26.

31. Bateleur *Terathopius ecaudatus*

Brown, L. H. 1955. Supplementary notes on the biology of the large birds of prey of Embu district, Kenya Colony. *Ibis* 97: 191–202.

Steyn, P. 1965. Some observations on the Bateleur *Terathopius ecaudatus* (Daudin). *Ostrich* 35: 203–213. (14 references.)

Steyn, P. 1980. Breeding and food of the Bateleur in Zimbabwe (Rhodesia). *Ostrich* 51: 168–178. (38 references.)

Vernon, C. J. 1979. Counts of Bateleurs in Rhodesia, mainly made in 1971. *Honeyguide* 100: 50–54.

32. African Fish Eagle *Haliaaetus vocifer*

Brown, L. 1980. *The African Fish Eagle*. Cape Town: Purnell. (26 references.)

Colebrook-Robjent, J. F. R. 1974. African Fish Eagle rearing three young. *Ostrich* 45: 144–145.

Craib, C. 1978. Fish Eagles in the southern Transvaal. *Witwatersrand Bird Club News* 102: 3.

Cyrus, D. 1977. Visit to Botswana. *Albatross* 243: 3.

Fannin, J. & Agar, B. 1972. Observations from Mozambique. *Natal Bird Club News Sheet* 209: 1.

Fraser, W. 1971. Birds at Lake Ngami, Botswana. *Ostrich* 42: 129.

Gillard, L. 1974. Fish Eagle *Haliaaetus vocifer* robbing other species of prey. *Witwatersrand Bird Club News Sheet* 87: 23.

Hutton, A. L. S. 1978. Letters. *African Wildlife* 32: 50.

Jarvis, M. J. F., Bourn, H. & Currie, M. H. 1980. Some observations of Fish Eagle twins. *Bokmakierie* 32: 84–85.

Milstein, P. le S. 1975. The biology of Barberspan, with special reference to the avifauna. *Ostrich* suppl. 10: 38.

Newman, K. 1980. Notes from Malawi. *Bokmakierie* 32: 122.

Prout-Jones, D. V. & Milstein, P. le S. 1980. Field-sexing of the Fish Eagle. *Bokmakierie* 32: 78–84. (16 references.)

Schütte, G. W. 1969. Unusual prey. *Lammergeyer* 10: 102.

Steyn, D. J. & Milstein, P. le S. 1975. Raptors eating eggs. *Bokmakierie* 27: 47.

Taylor, R. D. & Fynn, K. J. 1978. Fish Eagles on Lake Kariba. *Rhodesia Science News* 12: 52–53.

Tree, A. J. 1973. Birds on Lake McIlwaine. *Honeyguide* 76: 32–35.

Uys, C. J. 1980. Fish Eagle takes coot on the wing. *Promerops* 145: 8.

33. Steppe Buzzard *Buteo buteo*

Broekhuysen, G. J. & Siegfried, W. R. 1970. Age and moult in the Steppe Buzzard in southern Africa. *Ostrich* suppl. 8: 223–237. (9 references.)

Newman, K. B. 1977. Observations on raptor migration. *Bokmakierie* 29: 75–79.

Newman, K. B. 1978. 1978 raptor and stork migration report for the Transvaal. *Bokmakierie* 30: 61–64.

Schmitt, M. B., Baur, S. & Von Maltitz, F. 1980. Observations on the Steppe Buzzard in the Transvaal. *Ostrich* 51: 151–159. (13 references.)

Siegfried, W. R. 1968. Steppe Buzzards feeding on caterpillars in vineyards. *Ostrich* 39: 155.

Siegfried, W. R. & Frost, P. G. H. 1971. Indeterminate *Buteo* breeding in the south-western Cape. *Ostrich* 42: 73–74. (10 references.)

34. Mountain Buzzard *Buteo tachardus*

Barbour, D. Y. 1965. *Buteo buteo* breeding near George. *Ostrich* 36: 96.

Brooke, R. K. 1974. *Buteo tachardus* Andrew Smith

1830. *Bull. Brit. Orn. Club* 94: 59–62. (15 references.)

Courtenay-Latimer, M. 1941. Breeding of the Mountain Buzzard. *Ostrich* 22: 20–23.

Martin, R., Martin, J. & Martin, E. 1979. Mountain Buzzards breeding in the CBC area. *Promerops* 137: 3.

Siegfried, W. R. 1968. The Mountain Buzzard. *Bokmakierie* 20: 58–59.

Thomson, R. C. 1977. Mountain Buzzard display. *Witwatersrand Bird Club News Sheet* 96: 5.

35. Jackal Buzzard *Buteo rufofuscus*

Boddam-Whetham, D. 1981. Jackal Buzzard. *Diaz Diary* 90: 8.

Charlton, D. O. 1972. Mating of Jackal Buzzards *Buteo rufofuscus*. *Natal Bird Club News Sheet* 206: 2.

Frost, P. G. H. 1967. Jackal Buzzard *Buteo rufofuscus* hovering. *Ostrich* 38: 204.

Johnson, P. 1970. Jackal Buzzard. *Witwatersrand Bird Club News Sheet* 72: 1.

Norgarb, C. & Lasbrey, J. 1953. Jackal Buzzards. *Ostrich* 24: 33–36.

Rowsell, P. 1975. Jackal Buzzard's nest. *Natal Bird Club News Sheet* 230: 4.

Steyn, P. 1980. Jackal/Augur Buzzard. *Promerops* 144: 6.

Symons, R. E. 1926. Bird life in the Drakensberge: notes on the habits of the Jackal Buzzard *(Buteo jackal)*. *S. Afr. Journal of Nat. Hist.* 6: 25–27.

Trauseld, W. R. 1971. A risky meal. *Lammergeyer* 13: 56.

36. Augur Buzzard *Buteo augur*

Brooke, R. K. 1975. The taxonomic relationship of *Buteo rufofuscus* and *B. augur*. *Bull. Brit. Orn. Club* 95: 152–154. (6 references.)

Lendrum, A. L. 1977. Two interesting raptor sightings in the Bulawayo-Essexvale area. *Honeyguide* 90: 45.

Lendrum, A. L. 1979. The Augur Buzzard in the Matopos, Rhodesia. *Ostrich* 50: 203–214. (17 references.)

Snell, M. L. 1978. Revised list of birds seen above 2 100 m at Inyanga. *Honeyguide* 94: 10.

Steyn, P. 1963. Hours with the Augur Buzzard. *African Wildlife* 17: 99–102.

Weaving, A. J. S. 1972. Augur Buzzards at the nest. *Bokmakierie* 24: 27–30.

37. Lizard Buzzard *Kaupifalco monogrammicus*

Brooke, R. K. 1971. Breeding and breeding season notes on the birds of Mzimbiti and adjacent lowlying Mozambique. *Annals Natal Museum* 21: 58.

Chittenden, H. N. 1979. The incubation, nestling and post-nestling periods of the Lizard Buzzard. *Ostrich* 50: 186–187.

Hall, D. 1978. Recovery of ringed Lizard Buzzard. *Witwatersrand Bird Club News* 101: 14.

Scott-Donelan, A. D. 1972. Stalemate. *African Wild Life* 26: 95.

38. Red-breasted Sparrowhawk *Accipiter rufiventris*
Boddam-Whetham, A. D. 1968. Red-breasted Sparrowhawk *Accipiter rufiventris* in O.F.S. *Ostrich* 39: 35.

Grobler, J. H. 1981. Notes on the Red-breasted Sparrowhawk in the Mountain Zebra National Park. *Ostrich* 52: 124–125.

Vincent, J. 1962. Foods and feeding: Red-breasted Sparrow Hawk *Accipiter rufiventris*. *Lammergeyer* 2: 64–65.

Winterbottom, J. M. 1958. European Sparrowhawk, *Accipiter nisus*, in South Africa. *Ostrich* 29: 129–130.

39. Ovambo Sparrowhawk *Accipiter ovampensis*
Brown, L. H. 1970. Recent new breeding records for Kenya. *Bull. Brit. Orn. Club* 90: 2–3.

Kemp, A. C. & Kemp, M. I. 1975. Observations on the breeding biology of the Ovambo Sparrowhawk, *Accipiter ovampensis*, Gurney (Aves: Accipitridae). *Annals Transvaal Museum* 29: 186–190.

Krienke, W. 1932. Notes on *Accipiter ovampensis*, the Ovambo Sparrowhawk. *Ostrich* 3: 112–114.

40. Little Sparrowhawk *Accipiter minullus*
Colebrook-Robjent, J. F. R. & Steyn, P. 1975. On the nest and eggs of the Little Sparrowhawk *Accipiter minullus*. *Bull. Brit. Orn. Club* 95: 142–147. (12 references.)

Liversidge, R. 1962. The breeding biology of the Little Sparrowhawk *Accipiter minullus*. *Ibis* 104: 399–406. (14 references.)

Steyn, P. 1972. The Little Sparrowhawk at home. *Bokmakierie* 24: 13–16.

41. Black Sparrowhawk *Accipiter melanoleucus*
Brown, L. H. & Brown, B. E. 1979. The behaviour of the Black Sparrowhawk *Accipiter melanoleucus*. *Ardea* 67: 77–95. (36 references.)

Dean, W. R. 1968. Unusual nest of a Black Goshawk. *Ostrich* 39: 264.

Hart, J. 1977. Observations on the breeding of the Black Sparrowhawk *Accipiter melanoleucus* in Zaire. *Ostrich* 48: 45–46.

Hartley, R. 1976. Some notes on the plumage of Black Sparrowhawks. *Bokmakierie* 28: 61–63.

Malherbe, E. 1970. Observations on the breeding of the Black Goshawk. *Witwatersrand Bird Club News Sheet* 69: 2–8.

Pitman, C. R. S. 1935. The eggs of *Accipiter melanoleucus* — the Black Sparrowhawk. *Oologists' Record* 15: 38–45.

Pringle, V. L. 1971. The Black Sparrowhawk *Accipiter melanoleucus*. *Bee-eater* suppl. 1: 2–3.

Tarboton, W., Lewis, M. & Kemp, A. 1978. The status of the Black Sparrowhawk in the Transvaal. *Bokmakierie* 30: 56–59. (7 references.)

Vernon, C. J. 1967. Some observations from the journals of K. W. Greenhow. *Ostrich* 38: 48–49.

42. Little Banded Goshawk *Accipiter badius*
Colebrook-Robjent, J. F. R. & Steyn, P. 1975. On the nest and eggs of the Little Sparrowhawk *Accipiter minullus*. *Bull. Brit. Orn. Club* 95: 142–147. (12 references.)

Parnell, G. W. 1963. Gymnogene and Little Banded Goshawk. *Honeyguide* 42: 8.

Smeenk, C. & Smeenk-Enserink, N. 1977. Observations on the Shikra *Accipiter badius* in Nigeria. *Ardea* 65: 148–164. (46 references.)

Steyn, P. & Barbour, D. Y. 1973. Observations at a Little Banded Goshawk's nest. *Ostrich* 44: 140–141.

Tarboton, W. R. 1978. Breeding of the Little Banded Goshawk. *Ostrich* 49: 132–143. (12 references.)

Vernon, C. J. 1966. The birds of Hillside, Bulawayo. *Ostrich* 37: 223.

43. African Goshawk *Accipiter tachiro*
Gargett, V. 1968. African Goshawk nest in the Matopos. *Honeyguide* 54: 26–28.

Hare, H. L. 1945. Goshawk and Boomslang. *Ostrich* 16: 75–76.

Lawes, M. 1979. Raptor observations. *Albatross* 256: 4.

Meyer, E. 1970. Diet records. *Natal Bird Club News Sheet* 185: 2.

Van Someren, V. G. L. 1956. Days with birds. *Fieldiana: Zoology* Vol. 38. Chicago Natural History Museum.

44. Gabar Goshawk *Micronisus gabar*
Batchelor, A. L. 1980. Attempted nest predation by immature Gabar Goshawk. *Ostrich* 51: 190.

Kemp, A. C. & Snelling, J. C. 1973. Ecology of the Gabar Goshawk in southern Africa. *Ostrich* 44: 154–162. (23 references.)

Kemp, A. C. & Kemp, M. I. 1976. Nesting cycle of the Gabar Goshawk. *Ostrich* 47: 127–129.

Martin, J. & Martin, E. 1974. Gabar Goshawk *Micronisus gabar*. *Ostrich* 45: 134.

McGrew, W. C. 1980. Gabar Goshawk drowns its prey. *Ostrich* 51: 53.

Smeenk, C. & Smeenk-Enserink, N. 1975. Observations on the Pale Chanting Goshawk *Melierax poliopterus*, with comparative notes on the Gabar Goshawk *Micronisus gabar*. *Ardea* 63: 93–115. (32 references.)

Van Someren, V. G. L. 1956. Days with birds. *Fieldiana: Zoology* Vol. 38. Chicago Natural History Museum.

45. Pale Chanting Goshawk *Melierax canorus*
Clancey, P. A. 1960. Miscellaneous taxonomic notes on African birds. *Durban Museum Novitates* 6: 14–18.

Guy, R. D. 1971. Goshawks, Ratels and wild honey. *African Wild Life* 25: 53.

Smeenk, C. & Smeenk-Enserink, N. 1975. Observations on the Pale Chanting Goshawk *Melierax poliopterus*, with comparative notes on the Gabar Goshawk *Micronisus gabar*. *Ardea* 63: 93–115. (32 references.)

Steyn, P. 1973. Courtship flight of the Chanting Goshawk. *Ostrich* 44: 85.

Wyndham, C. 1937. Nesting habits of the Chanting Goshawk *Melierax canorus*. *Ostrich* 8: 45–46.

46. Dark Chanting Goshawk *Melierax metabates*

Babich, K. 1979. Diet: Dark Chanting Goshawk. *Witwatersrand Bird Club News* 107: 17.

Bradford, H. J. 1966. On some snakes and birds. *Honeyguide* 48: 24.

47. European Marsh Harrier *Circus aeruginosus*

Ayres, T. 1871. Additional notes on birds of the territory of the Transvaal Republic. *Ibis* (3)1: 147–148.

Hopcraft, C. 1977. Observations at Marievale. *Witwatersrand Bird Club News Sheet* 96: 6.

Meinertzhagen, R. 1956. Roost of wintering harriers. *Ibis* 98: 535.

Steyn, P. 1974. Some records from Wankie National Park. *Honeyguide* 78: 24–27.

Tree, A. J. 1973. Birds on Lake McIlwaine. *Honeyguide* 76: 32–35.

48. African Marsh Harrier *Circus ranivorus*

Benson, C. W. 1971. Some collecting experiences. *Honeyguide* 66: 35.

Cooper, J. 1970. African Marsh Harrier. *Honeyguide* 64: 28.

Malherbe, E. 1970. Observations on the breeding of the African Marsh Harrier. *Witwatersrand Bird Club News Sheet* 70: 1–8.

Milstein, P. le S. 1975. The biology of Barberspan, with special reference to the avifauna. *Ostrich* suppl. 10: 39.

Nichol, W. 1963. Observations on the nesting of the S.A. Marsh Harrier. *Bokmakierie* 14: 32–34.

Nixon, R. D. 1969. In brief: unusual prey of the Marsh Harrier. *Bokmakierie* 21: 71.

Roberts, E. L. 1978. African Marsh Harrier. *Cape Bird Club Newsletter* 132: 4.

Steyn, D. & Milstein, P. le S. 1975. Raptors eating eggs. *Bokmakierie* 27: 47.

Tomlinson, D. N. S. 1974. Studies of the Purple Heron, Part 1: heronry structure, nesting habits and reproductive success. *Ostrich* 45: 180.

Tree, A. J. 1963. Yellow-billed Kite *Milvus migrans* fishing. *Ostrich* 34: 179.

Whitelaw, D. A. 1976. Behaviour. *Cape Bird Club Newsletter* 123: 9.

49. Montagu's Harrier *Circus pygargus*

Harwin, R. M. 1962. Letters to the editor. *Honeyguide* 62: 38.

Parnell, G. 1971. Letters to the editor. *Honeyguide* 65: 44.

50. Pallid Harrier *Circus macrourus*

Allan, D. 1978. Notes on the Pallid Harrier. *Bokmakierie* 30: 79–80.

Hornby, H. E. 1970. Letters to the editor. *Honeyguide* 63: 33.

Martin, J., Martin, E. & Martin, R. 1963. Pallid Harrier *Circus macrourus* at Vergelegen, Somerset West. *Ostrich* 34: 47–48.

Mouritz, L. B. 1915. Notes on the ornithology of the Matopo district, Southern Rhodesia. *Ibis* (10)3: 199.

Symonds, E. 1887. Notes on a collection of birds from Kroonstad, in the Orange Free State. *Ibis* (5)5: 325.

51. Black Harrier *Circus maurus*

Van der Merwe, F. 1981. Review of the status and biology of the Black Harrier *Circus maurus*. *Ostrich* 52: 193–207. (112 references.)

52. Gymnogene *Polyboroides typus*

Astley Maberly, C. T. 1934. On the foraging method of the Banded Gymnogene. *Ostrich* 5: 73–74.

Bayer, F. 1933. 'Stunting' of the Banded Gymnogene. *Ostrich* 4: 38.

Brown, L. 1972. The breeding behaviour of the African Harrier Hawk *Polyboroides typus* in Kenya. *Ostrich* 43: 169–175. (10 references.)

Burton, P. J. K. 1978. The intertarsal joint of the Harrier-Hawks *Polyboroides* spp. and the Crane Hawk *Geranospiza caerulescens*. *Ibis* 120: 171–177. (9 references.)

Colebrook-Robjent, J. F. R. 1974. Some comments on the African Harrier Hawk. *Ostrich* 45: 147. (4 references.)

Cooper, J. E. 1980. Additional observations on the intertarsal joint of the African Harrier-Hawk *Polyboroides typus*. *Ibis* 122: 94–98. (3 references.)

Dean, W. R. S. 1969. On the food of the Gymnogene. *Ostrich* 40: 22.

Forbes-Watson, A. D. 1977. African Harrier-Hawk *Polyboroides typus* feeding on carrion. *Scopus* 1: 22.

Grabant, C. 1963. Gymnogene robs Darters. *Honeyguide* 41: 5.

Howells, W. W. 1978. Stranded fish as a food source for large birds. *Honeyguide* 96: 18.

Langham, K. 1976. Mating behaviour of Gymnogene. *Honeyguide* 87: 28.

Lendrum, A. L. 1974. Gymnogene and White-browed Sparrow-weaver. *Honeyguide* 78: 45–46.

Marshall, B. 1972. Gymnogene feeding on Darter eggs. *Honeyguide* 72: 34.

Pillans, O. 1967. Unusual behaviour of a Gymnogene. *Honeyguide* 50: 23.

Pringle, V. L. 1977. Herons have their problems. *Eastern Cape Naturalist* 60: 29.

Symons, G. 1973. Observations on the Banded Gymnogene *Polyboroides typus*. *Natal Bird Club News Sheet* 213: 3–4.

Thurow, T. L. 1979. Ecology and behaviour of the Gymnogene *(Polyboroides typus)*. M.S. thesis, Brigham Young University. Abstract only consulted as published in *Raptor Research* 14: 96.

Tree, A. J. 1977. Gymnogene preying on Little Swift colony. *Honeyguide* 90: 41.

53. Osprey *Pandion haliaetus*

Braine, S. G. & Braine, J. 1970. Osprey fishing in shallow water. *Ostrich* 41: 263.

Harwin, R. M. 1973. Letter to the editor. *Honeyguide* 76: 43–44.

O'Sharkey, E. J. 1974. Letter to the editor. *Honeyguide* 77: 46.

Österlöf, S. 1977. Migration, wintering areas and site tenacity of the European Osprey *Pandion h. haliaetus*(L). *Ornis Scandinavica* 8: 61–78.

Skinner, N. J. 1964. Unusual behaviour of an Osprey. *Bull. Nigerian Orn. Soc.* 1: 15.

Thorpe, C. & Boddam-Whetham, A. D. 1977. Unusual diet for Osprey *Pandion haliaetus*. *Ostrich* 48: 47.

Tree, A. J. 1975. Letter to the editor. *Honeyguide* 84: 46.

Ueoka, L. & Koplin, J. R. 1973. Foraging behaviour of Ospreys in northwestern California. *Raptor Research* 7: 32–38. (7 references.)

54. African Peregrine *Falco peregrinus minor*

Campbell, T. 1953. Records of the African Peregrine *Falco peregrinus perconfusus* Collins and Hartert. *Ostrich* 24: 52.

Condy, J. B. 1973. Peregrine Falcons in Rhodesia. *Honeyguide* 75: 11–14.

Ellenberger, P. M. 1949. Peregrine Falcon *Falco peregrinus perconfusus*. *Ostrich* 20: 40.

Hallamore, C. 1972. Observations on the African Peregrine by a falconer. *Honeyguide* 69: 13–16.

Hickey, J. J. 1969. *Peregrine Falcon Populations*. Madison: University of Wisconsin Press.

Peakall, D. B. & Kiff, L. F. 1979. Eggshell thinning and DDE residue levels among Peregrine Falcons *Falco peregrinus*: a global perspective. *Ibis* 121: 200–204. (15 references.)

Randall, R. & Randall, B. 1978. Peregrine Falcon on St Croix. *Bee-eater* 29: 18.

Ross, G. J. B. & Black, R. A. R. 1972. Comments on the South African races of *Falco peregrinus*. *Ostrich* 43: 135–136. (9 references.)

Tarboton, W. 1979. A Peregrine strikes. *Witwatersrand Bird Club News* 105: 7–9.

Tarboton, W. R. (Unpublished script.) Behaviour of the African Peregrine during incubation.

Thomson, W. R. 1978. Falcon research: a plea for information. *Honeyguide* 96: 44–45.

Young, S. 1976. The winged thunderbolt. *Bokmakierie* 28: 53.

55. Lanner *Falco biarmicus*

Barbour, D. Y. 1971. Notes on the breeding of the Lanner. *Bokmakierie* 23: 2–5.

Craib, C. 1977. Notes on the Lanner in the southern Transvaal. *Witwatersrand Bird Club News Sheet* 97: 5–6.

Dalling, J. 1975. Lanners in central Salisbury: the first four years. *Honeyguide* 84: 23–26. (4 references.)

Davies, C. G. 1911. Notes on the birds of the district of Matatiele, East Griqualand. *Journal South African Orn. Union* 8: 37–38.

Ebbutt, D. 1964. Lanner Falcon attacking Pied Crow. *Bull. Nigerian Orn. Soc.* 1: 12–13.

Kellow-Webb, E. G. E. & Dingley, G. 1972. Lanner Falcon's nest in central Salisbury. *Rhodesia Science News* 6: 358–359.

Kemp, A. C. 1972. The use of man-made structures for nesting sites by Lanner Falcons. *Ostrich* 43: 65–66.

Kemp, A. C. 1975. The development of a Lanner Falcon chick, *Falco biarmicus* Temminck (Aves: Falconidae). *Annals of the Transvaal Museum* 29: 191–196.

Macartney, P. 1973. Lanners 1973. *Wild Rhodesia* 2: 27–29.

Nichols, G. & Campbell, H. 1978. Lanners in Durban. *Albatross* 251: 4.

Peakall, D. B. & Kemp, A. C. 1976. Organochlorine residue levels in herons and raptors in the Transvaal. *Ostrich* 47: 139–141.

Reynolds, J. F. 1974. Piracy by a Lanner. *British Birds* 67: 25–26.

Sinclair, J. C. & Walters, B. 1976. Lanner Falcons breeding in Durban City. *Bokmakierie* 28: 51–52.

Snelling, J. C. 1973. Lanner Falcons breed in captivity: U.S.A. *Bokmakierie* 25: 27–33 & 50–55. (12 references.)

Steyn, P. 1980. Breeding and food of the Bateleur in Zimbabwe (Rhodesia). *Ostrich* 51: 168–178.

Tree, A. J. 1963. Grey Hornbill *Tockus nasutus* as prey of the Lanner Falcon *Falco biarmicus*. *Ostrich* 34: 179.

Vernon, C. J. 1980. A Lanner in a heron's nest. *Bee-eater* 31: 30.

56. European Hobby *Falco subbuteo*

Chittenden, H. 1979. Large flock of European Hobbies. *Albatross* 254: 1.

Cruikshank, R. A. 1980. European Hobby in the southwestern Cape. *Ostrich* 51: 127.

57. African Hobby *Falco curvierii*

Brooke, R. K. 1969. The African Hobby, *Falco curvierii*, at Livingstone. *Puku* 5: 219.

Brooke, R. K. & Howells, W. W. 1971. Falcons at Birchenough bridge, Rhodesia. *Ostrich* 42: 142–143. (7 references.)

Pitman, C. R. S. 1966. A further note on the breeding of the African Hobby *Falco curvieri* Smith. *Ostrich* 37: 6–7.

Steyn, P. 1965. A note on the breeding of the African Hobby *Falco curvieri* Smith. *Ostrich* 36: 29–31. (6 references.)

Tree, A. J. 1973. African Hobby Falcon. *Ostrich* 44: 128.

58. Sooty Falcon *Falco concolor*

Booth, B. D. McD. 1961. Breeding of the Sooty Falcon in the Libyan desert. *Ibis* 103a: 129–130.

Clancey, P. A. 1969. The Sooty Falcon as a South African bird. *Bokmakierie* 21: 50–51.

Clancey, P. A. 1969. *Falco concolor* Temminck in South Africa. *Bull. Brit. Orn. Club* 89: 10–11.

Moreau, R. E. 1969. The Sooty Falcon *Falco concolor* Temminck. *Bull. Brit. Orn. Club* 89: 62–67. (28 references.)

59. Taita Falcon *Falco fasciinucha*

Benson, C. W. & Smithers, R. H. N. 1958. The Teita Falcon *Falco fasciinucha* at the Victoria Falls. *Ostrich* 29: 57–58.

Brooke, R. K. & Howells, W. W. 1971. Falcons at Birchenough bridge, Rhodesia. *Ostrich* 42: 142–143.

Colebrook-Robjent, J. F. R. 1977. The eggs of the Teita Falcon *Falco fasciinucha*. *Bull. Brit. Orn. Club* 97: 44–46. (4 references.)

Dowsett, R. J. 1983. Breeding and other observations on the Teita Falcon *Falco fasciinucha*. *Ibis* 125: 362–366 (16 references.)

Holliday, C. S. 1965. A note on the Teita Falcon. *Puku* 3: 71–73.

Hunter, N. D., Douglas, M. G., Stead, D. E., Taylor, V. A., Adler, J. R. & Carter, A. T. 1979. A breeding record and some observations of the Taita Falcon *Falco fasciinucha* in Malawi. *Ibis* 121: 93–94. (7 references.)

Madge, S. G. 1971. Some notes on the Taita Falcon *Falco fasciinucha*. *Bull. Zambian Orn. Soc.* 3: 49–50.

Woodall, P. F. 1971. Bird notes from northern Sengwa gorge, Rhodesia. *Ostrich* 42: 148–149. (6 references.)

60. Red-necked Falcon *Falco chicquera*

Colebrook-Robjent, J. F. R. & Osborne, T. O. 1974. High density breeding of the Red-necked Falcon *Falco chicquera* in Zambia. *Bull. Brit. Orn. Club* 94: 172–176. (9 references.)

Fry, C. H. 1964. Red-necked Falcon *Falco chicquera* hunting bats. *Bull. Nigerian Orn. Soc.* 1: 19.

Maclean, G. L. 1958. A nest of the Rufous-necked Falcon *(Tinnunculus ruficollis)* in the Namib. *Ostrich* 29: 88–89.

Malherbe, A. P. 1963. Notes on the birds of prey and some others at Boshoek, north of Rustenburg during a rodent plague. *Ostrich* 34: 95–96.

Osborne, T. O. 1981. Ecology of the Red-necked Falcon *Falco chicquera* in Zambia. *Ibis* 123: 289–297. (15 references.)

Robinson, E. R. & Stuart, C. T. 1975. Bird feeding records from South West Africa. *Ostrich* 46: 190.

61. Western Red-footed Falcon *Falco vespertinus*

Moreau, R. E. 1972. *The Palaearctic–African Bird Migration Systems*. London: Academic Press.

62. Eastern Red-footed Falcon *Falco amurensis*

Benson, C. W. 1951. A roosting site of the Eastern Red-footed Falcon. *Falco amurensis*. *Ibis* 93: 466–467.

Mendelsohn, J. M. 1979. A note on hunting in Lesser and Eastern Redfooted Kestrels. *Ostrich* 50: 121–122.

Michell, C. S. 1962. Eastern Red-footed Kestrels. *Honeyguide* 37: 6–7.

Tree, A. J. 1966. The occurrence of *Falco amurensis* in the Albany district of the eastern Cape. *Ostrich* 37: 196.

63. Rock Kestrel *Falco tinnunculus*

Bowker, F. 1919. The South African Kestrel *(Cerchneis rupicola*, or Kranz Hawk*)*. *Cape Times:* 24 October.

Crass, R. C. 1944. The birds of Sulenkama, Qumbu district, Cape Province. *Ostrich* 15: 12.

Siegfried, W. R. 1965. Rock Kestrel and road casualties. *Ostrich* 36: 146.

Tree, A. J. 1975. In 'New distributional data'. *Ostrich* 39: 271.

64. Greater Kestrel *Falco rupicoloides*

Broekhuysen, G. J. & MacLeod, J. G. R. 1962.

Greater Kestrel *Falco rupicoloides* record near Cape Flats. *Ostrich* 33: 26.

Dean, W. R., Steyn, D. & van Reenen, A. 1968. On a second brood by a Greater Kestrel *(Falco rupicoloides* A. Smith*)* in the north-eastern Transvaal. *Oologists' Record* 52: 54.

Hunt, C. 1978. Observations on the Greater Kestrel. *Bokmakierie* 30: 35.

Kemp, A. C. 1978. Territory maintenance and use by breeding Greater Kestrels. *Proc. Symp. African Predatory Birds* pp. 71–76. Pretoria: Northern Transvaal Ornithological Society. (3 references.)

Malherbe, A. P. 1963. Notes on the birds of prey and some others at Boshoek, north of Rustenburg during a rodent plague. *Ostrich* 34: 95–96.

Pitman, C. R. S. 1965. A communal nest of the Lappet-faced Vulture *Torgos tracheliotus* (Forster) and East African Greater Kestrel *Falco rupicoloides arthuri* (Gurney). *Bull. Brit. Orn. Club* 85: 93–95.

65. Lesser Kestrel *Falco naumanni*

Kolbe, F. F. 1972. The Lesser Kestrels of Senekal, Orange Free State. *Bokmakierie* 24: 18–21.

Mendelsohn, J. M. 1979. A note on hunting in Lesser and Eastern Redfooted Kestrels. *Ostrich* 50: 121–122.

Preston, J. 1976. Lesser Kestrel *Falco naumanni*. *Bokmakierie* 28: 68–69.

Siegfried, W. R. & Skead, D. M. 1971. Status of the Lesser Kestrel in South Africa. *Ostrich* 42: 1–4. (9 references.)

66. Grey Kestrel *Falco ardosiaceus*

Dean, W. R. J. 1974. Breeding and distributional notes on some Angolan birds. *Durban Museum Novitates* 10: 112.

Loosmore, E. 1963. Grey Kestrel in Tanganyika. *Journal East African Natural History Society* 24: 67–70.

Serle, W. 1939. Field observations on some northern Nigerian birds. *Ibis* (14)3: 659–660.

Serle, W. 1943. Further field observations on northern Nigerian birds. *Ibis* 85: 281–282.

Sinclair, J. C. & Dean, W. R. J. 1974. Grey Kestrel *Falco ardosiaceus*. *Ostrich* 45: 134.

Wells, D. R. 1965. Grey Kestrel eating oil-palm nut fibre. *Bull. Nigerian Orn. Soc.* 2: 110.

67. Dickinson's Kestrel *Falco dickinsoni*

Benson, C. W. 1952. Notes from Nyasaland. *Ostrich* 23: 145.

Brooke, R. K. 1972. Rhodesian habitat of Dickinson's Kestrel. *Honeyguide* 70: 29.

Brooke, R. K. & Howells, W. W. 1971. Falcons at Birchenough bridge, Rhodesia. *Ostrich* 42: 142–143. (7 references.)

Clancey, P. A. 1968. Variation in *Falco dickinsoni* P. L. Sclater, 1864. *Bull. Brit. Orn. Club* 88: 120–122.

Colebrook-Robjent, J. F. R. 1976. Dickinson's Kestrel nests close together. *Ostrich* 47: 143–144.

Colebrook-Robjent, J. F. R. & Tanner, I. C. 1978. Observations at a Dickinson's Kestrel nest. *Proc.*

Symp. African Predatory Birds pp. 62–70. Pretoria: Northern Transvaal Ornithological Society.

Cook, G. 1971. Nest record of a Dickinson's Kestrel. *Honeyguide* 68: 33–34.

Edwards, E. A. 1972. Distribution records from the Selous and Hartley districts. *Honeyguide* 71: 23.

Hanmer, J. A. 1978. Dickinson's Kestrels hawking birds at cane fires. *Bokmakierie* 30: 78.

Talbot, J. N. 1976. On the Dichwe lemon forest and its avifauna. *Honeyguide* 88: 30.

Vernon, C. J. 1979. Notes on birds of prey in Zimbabwe Rhodesia. *Honeyguide* 99: 29.

68. Pygmy Falcon *Polihierax semitorquatus*
Daneel, A. B. 1966. In search of the Pygmy Falcon. *Oologists' Record* 40: 42–50.

Maclean, G. L. 1970. The Pygmy Falcon *Polihierax semitorquatus*. *Koedoe* 13: 1–21. (29 references.)

69. Barn Owl *Tyto alba*
Bunn, D. S. 1972. Regular daylight hunting by Barn Owls. *British Birds* 65: 26–30.

Bunn, D. S. 1974. The voice of the Barn Owl. *British Birds* 67: 493–501.

Bunn, D. S. & Warburton, A. B. 1977. Observations on breeding Barn Owls. *British Birds* 70: 246–256. (6 references.)

Coetzee, C. G. 1963. The prey of owls in the Kruger National Park as indicated by owl pellets collected during 1960–61. *Koedoe* 6: 115–125. (9 references.)

Davis, D. H. S. 1959. The Barn Owl's contribution to ecology and palaeoecology. *Ostrich* suppl. 3: 144–153. (22 references.)

Dean, W. R. J. 1973. Analysis of a collection of Barn Owl *Tyto alba* pellets from Warmbaths, Transvaal. *Zoologica Africana* 8: 75–81. (9 references.)

Dean, W. R. J. 1975. *Tyto alba* prey in South West Africa and the northern Cape. *Zoologica Africana* 10: 217–219. (3 references.)

De Graaff, G. 1960. 'n Ontleding van uilklonte van die Nonnetjiesuil. *Ostrich* 31: 1–5. (9 references.)

Grindley, J., Siegfried, W. R. & Vernon, C. J. 1973. Diet of the Barn Owl in the Cape Province. *Ostrich* 44: 266–267.

Kirk, H. D. 1956. Barn Owl family life. *African Wild Life* 10: 289–292.

Kolbe, F. F. 1946. The case for the Barn Owl. *African Wild Life* 1: 69–73.

Maclean, G. L. 1973. The Sociable Weaver, Part 4: predators, parasites and symbionts. *Ostrich* 44: 250.

Nel, J. A. J. & Nolte, H. 1965. Notes on the prey of owls in the Kalahari Gemsbok National Park, with special reference to small mammals. *Koedoe* 8: 75–81. (10 references.)

Payne, R. S. 1962. How the Barn Owl locates prey by hearing. *Living Bird* 1: 151–159.

Perry, G. S. 1980. An unusual Barn Owl nesting site. *Honeyguide* 101: 17–19.

Skead, C. J. 1963. Contents of pellets of Barn Owl *Tyto alba* at a rural roost. *Ostrich* 34: 171–172.

Stuart, C. T. 1975. A short note on the diet of *Tyto alba* at Sandwich Harbour, Namib Desert Park, South West Africa. *Madoqua* Series 2, 4(74–80): 103.

Vernon, C. J. 1972. An analysis of owl pellets collected in southern Africa. *Ostrich* 43: 109–124. (29 references.)

Vernon, C. J. 1980. Prey of the Barn Owl from the Lundi River. *Honeyguide* 101: 10–13.

Warburton, T. 1972. Barn Owl in focus. *World of Birds* 1: 23–29. (11 references.)

Wilson, V. J. 1970. Notes on the breeding and feeding habits of a pair of Barn Owls, *Tyto alba* (Scopoli), in Rhodesia. *Arnoldia (Rhodesia)* 4(34): 1–8. (7 references.)

70. Grass Owl *Tyto capensis*
Bamberger, L. 1973. Letter to the editor. *Honeyguide* 74: 38.

Boddam-Whetham, A. D. 1969. Behaviour of young Grass Owls. *African Wild Life* 23: 70–72.

Craib, C. L. 1974. Grass Owls *Tyto capensis* and Marsh Owls *Asio capensis* occupying adjacent territories. *Witwatersrand Bird Club News Sheet* 86: 12.

Davidson, I. H. & Biggs, H. C. 1974. Grass Owl chicks: weight recordings. *Ostrich* 45: 31.

Earlé, R. A. 1978. Observations at a nest of a Grass Owl. *Ostrich* 49: 90–91.

Ellis, G. 1973. Behaviour of a nesting owl. *Witwatersrand Bird Club News Sheet* 84: 12.

Horner, R. F. 1971. Observations on breeding of Grass Owl *Tyto capensis*. *Natal Bird Club News Sheet* 197: 1–2.

Lees, S. G. & Wood, A. D. 1978. Grass Owl eating eggshell. *Honeyguide* 94: 22–25.

Lockwood, G. 1978. Interesting prey items for Grass Owl. *Witwatersrand Bird Club News* 103: 7.

Masterson, A. 1973. Marsh Owls and Grass Owls. *Honeyguide* 73: 17–19.

Tucker, J. J. 1974. Letter to the editor. *Honeyguide* 79: 46–47.

Vernon, C. J. 1972. An analysis of owl pellets collected in southern Africa. *Ostrich* 43: 109–124. (29 references.)

Vernon, C. J. 1980. Prey of six species of owls at Zimbabwe Ruins: 1970–1975. *Honeyguide* 101: 26–28.

71. Wood Owl *Strix woodfordii*
Allan, D. & Ballantyne, D. 1980. Wood Owl breeding in raptor nest. *Witwatersrand Bird Club News* 109: 17.

Harvey, J. F. 1977. The return of the Wood Owls. *Bokmakierie* 29: 54–55.

Scott, J. 1980. Further notes on the Wood Owl. *Honeyguide* 103/104: 4–8.

Steyn, P. & Scott, J. 1973. Notes on the breeding biology of the Wood Owl. *Ostrich* 44: 118–125. (40 references.)

72. Marsh Owl *Asio capensis*
Craib, C. L. 1974. Grass Owls *Tyto capensis* and Marsh Owls *Asio capensis* occupying adjacent territories. *Witwatersrand Bird Club News Sheet* 86: 13.

Dean, W. R. J. 1969. Distraction display by the Marsh Owl. *Ostrich* 40: 23–24.

Dixon, J. E. W. 1970. Miscellaneous notes on South West African birds. *Madoqua* 2: 45–47.

Hustler, K. 1978. The crepuscular habits of the Marsh Owl. *Witwatersrand Bird Club News* 106: 4–5.

Masterson, A. 1973. Marsh Owls and Grass Owls. *Honeyguide* 73: 17–19.

Smith, V. W. & Killick-Kendrick, R. 1964. Notes on the breeding of the Marsh Owl *Asio capensis* in northern Nigeria. *Ibis* 106: 119–123. (6 references.)

Vernon, C. J. 1971. Owl foods and other notes from a trip to South West Africa. *Ostrich* 42: 153.

73. African Scops Owl *Otus senegalensis*
Weaving, A. J. S. 1970. Observations on the breeding behaviour of the Scops Owl. *Bokmakierie* 22: 58–61.

74. White-faced Owl *Otus leucotis*
Cyrus, D., White, D., Espie, I. & Bruzas, C. 1976. White-faced Owlet in Pietermaritzburg. *Albatross* 242: 2.

Malherbe, A. P. 1963. Notes on the birds of prey and some others at Boshoek, north of Rustenburg during a rodent plague. *Ostrich* 34: 95.

Van der Weyden, W. J. 1973. Geographical variation in the territorial song of the White-faced Owl *Otus leucotis*. *Ibis* 115: 129–131. (8 references.)

Worden, C. J. & Hall, J. 1978. Observations on the White-faced Owl *Otus leucotis* at Cleveland Dam, Salisbury. *Honeyguide* 94: 31–37.

75. Pearl-spotted Owl *Glaucidium perlatum*
Steyn, P. 1979. Observations on Pearl-spotted and Barred Owls. *Bokmakierie* 31: 50–60. (39 references.)

76. Barred Owl *Glaucidium capense*
Steyn, P. 1979. Observations on Pearl-spotted and Barred Owls. *Bokmakierie* 31: 50–60. (39 references.)

77. Cape Eagle Owl *Bubo capensis*
Benson, C. W. & Irwin, M. P. S. 1967. The distribution and systematics of *Bubo capensis* Smith (Aves). *Arnoldia (Rhodesia)* 3(19): 1–19. (44 references.)

Brooke, R. K. 1973. Notes on the distribution and food of the Cape Eagle-Owl in Rhodesia. *Ostrich* 48: 137–139. (16 references.)

Clinning, C. F. 1980. The occurrence of the Cape Eagle Owl in South West Africa. *Madoqua* 11: 351–352.

Gargett, V. & Grobler, J. H. 1976. Prey of the Cape Eagle Owl *Bubo capensis mackinderi* Sharpe 1899, in the Matopos, Rhodesia. *Arnoldia (Rhodesia)* 8(7): 1–7. (16 references.)

Gargett, V. 1978. Mackinder's Eagle Owl in the Matopos, Rhodesia. *Proc. Symp. African Predatory Birds*, pp. 46–61. (21 references.)

Grobler, J. H. 1980. The Cape Eagle Owl and Spotted Eagle Owl in the Mountain Zebra National Park. *Bokmakierie* 32: 94–98. (10 references.)

Martin, R. & Pepler, D. 1977. Notes on the Cape Eagle Owl. *Bokmakierie* 29: 68–69. (5 references.)

Mathews, N. J. C. & Scott, L. B. 1980. A new distributional record for the Cape Eagle Owl. *Bokmakierie* 32: 99–100.

Sessions, P. H. B. 1972. Observations on Mackinder's Eagle Owl *Bubo capensis mackinderi* Sharpe on a Kenya farm. *Journal East African Natural History Society* 138: 1–20. (28 references.)

Steyn, P. & Tredgold, D. 1977. Observations on the Cape Eagle Owl. *Bokmakierie* 29: 31–42. (10 references.)

78. Spotted Eagle Owl *Bubo africanus*
Bannister, A. B. 1970. Letters. *Bokmakierie* 22(2): back cover.

Benson, C. W. 1962. The food of the Spotted Eagle-Owl *Bubo africanus*. *Ostrich* 33(4): 35.

Berry, G. 1971. Spotted Eagle Owls in Houghton. *Witwatersrand Bird Club News Sheet* 73: 20.

Beven, G. 1946. Some notes and records of South African birds. *Ostrich* 17: 66.

Brain, C. K. 1959. Owl's prey. *Bokmakierie* 11: 14.

Brown, L. 1979. *Encounters with nature.* Oxford: Oxford University Press.

Butchart, D. 1980. Parental care in the Spotted Eagle Owl. *Witwatersrand Bird Club News* 110: 17.

Carnegie, A. J. M. 1961. The stomach contents of a Spotted Eagle-Owl *(Bubo africanus)*. *Ostrich* 32: 97.

Dixon, J. E. W. 1968. Prey of large raptors. *Ostrich* 39: 202.

Grobler, J. H. 1980. The Cape Eagle Owl and Spotted Eagle Owl in the Mountain Zebra National Park. *Bokmakierie* 32: 94–98. (10 references.)

Heathcote, R. C. & Rowe Rowe, F. T. 1958. Observations of a Spotted Eagle Owl's nest. *Bokmakierie* 10: 8–10.

Lendrum, A. & Lendrum, J. 1975. Unusually large clutch size of the Spotted Eagle Owl *(Bubo africanus)*. *Honeyguide* 82: 48.

Mitchell, B. L. 1964. Owl prey. *Puku* 2: 129.

Murray, C. d'C. 1951. An unusual item in the diet of *Bubo africanus*. *Ostrich* 22: 121.

Neethling, J. H. 1973. Letters. *Bokmakierie* 25: 108.

Nel, J. A. J. 1969. The prey of owls in the Namib Desert. 1: The Spotted Eagle Owl at Sossus Vlei. *Scientific Papers Namib Desert Research Station* IV(37–53): 55–58.

Robbins, B. 1972. Spotted Eagle Owl: predation. *Lammergeyer* 15: 76.

Siegfried, W. R. 1965. On the food habits of the Spotted Eagle Owl. *Ostrich* 36: 146.

Siegfried, W. R. 1966. Relative abundance of raptorial birds in the south-western Cape. *Ostrich* 37: 42–44. (2 references.)

Steyn, P. 1963. Birds — many and various. *African Wild Life* 17: 293–299.

Tarboton, W. 1975. Spotted Eagle-Owl *Bubo africanus* fledging period. *Witwatersrand Bird Club News Sheet* 88: 7–8.

Welbourne, R. G. 1973. Prey of the Spotted Eagle Owl. *Witwatersrand Bird Club News Sheet* 83: 17–18. (11 references.)

79. Giant Eagle Owl *Bubo lacteus*
Brown, L. H. 1965. Observations on Verreaux's Eagle Owl *Bubo lacteus* (Temminck). *Journal East*

African Natural History Society 25: 101–107.

Daneel, A. 1979. Death-shamming by a Giant Eagle Owl nestling. *Honeyguide* 98: 19.

Dunning, J. 1973. Do hawks form part of an owl's diet? *Witwatersrand Bird Club News Sheet* 83: 16–17.

Gillard, L. 1979. Giant Eagle Owl. *Witwatersrand Bird Club News* 104: 5–6.

Ginn, P. J. 1970. Giant Eagle Owl *Bubo lacteus*. *Honeyguide* 64: 27.

Newman, K. 1970. Giant Eagle Owl. *Witwatersrand Bird Club News Sheet* 71: 16.

Pitman, C. R. S. & Adamson, J. 1978. Notes on the ecology and ethology of the Giant Eagle Owl *Bubo lacteus*. *Honeyguide* 95: 3–23 & 96: 26–43. (75 references.)

Thomson, R. 1977. Giant Eagle Owl. *Witwatersrand Bird Club News Sheet* 99: 8.

Vernon, C. J. 1980. The Giant Eagle Owl and the guineafowl. *Bee-eater* 31: 18–19. (4 references.)

Vincent, A. W. 1946. On the breeding habits of some African birds. *Ibis* 88: 315.

80. Pel's Fishing Owl *Scotopelia peli*

Benson, C. W. & Pitman, C. R. S. 1959. Further breeding records from Northern Rhodesia. *Bull. Brit. Orn. Club* 79: 20.

Benson, C. W. & Pitman, C. R. S. 1961. Further breeding records from Northern Rhodesia. *Bull. Brit. Orn. Club* 81: 161.

Brown, L. H. 1976. Observations on Pel's Fishing Owl *Scotopelia peli*. *Bull. Brit. Orn. Club* 96: 49–53. (8 references.)

Gurney, J. H. 1859. Note on Pel's Owl *(Scotopelia peli)*. *Ibis* (1)1: 445–447.

Liversedge, T. N. 1980. A study of Pel's Fishing Owl *Scotopelia peli* Bonaparte 1850 in the 'Pan Handle' region of the Okavango Delta, Botswana. *Proceedings 4th Pan-African Ornithological Congress* 291–299.

Pooley, A. G. 1967. Some miscellaneous ornithological observations from the Ndumu Game Reserve. *Ostrich* 38: 32.

Thomson, R. W. 1972. Pel's Fishing Owl. *Honeyguide* 71: 27–28.

Index